THIRD EDITION

EUROPEAN HISTORY IN A WORLD PERSPECTIVE

Early Modern Times

Cartography by Norman Adams.

Cover design by Daniel Thaxton.

Published simultaneously in Canada.

Printed in the United States of America.

International Standard Book Number: 0-669-85555-3

Library of Congress Catalog Card Number: 74-11706.

EUROPEAN HISTORY IN A WORLD PERSPECTIVE

Early Modern Times

VOLUME II

Shepard B. Clough
Columbia University

David L. Hicks
New York University

David J. Brandenburg
American University

Peter Gay
Yale University

D. C. HEATH AND COMPANY
Lexington, Massachusetts Toronto London

Preface to the Third Edition

The great success of the first and second editions of this work has encouraged the authors and the publisher to present this third edition. The text has found enthusiastic users literally around the world and has elicited from them a demand that our story include the happenings of the last few years. Indeed, we realize that textbooks must be renewed frequently to bring the record up to date, to include new findings of scholarship, and to introduce the best of the new pedagogical devices.

This new edition has been thoroughly revised, and much of it has been rewritten to obtain greater fluency and clarity. The bibliographies have been simplified and reduced in bulk to indicate more precisely where students may best go for additional reading. Each part now contains an illustrated section on the major contributions received from the past. Charts and tables have been used to assist the student in fixing events in their complex relationships in time. All the maps have been revised and replotted in two colors for greater clarity, and many new maps have been added. A great effort has been made to introduce illustrated material that will add to the comprehension of styles, techniques, personalities, and physical conditions. Lastly, sections have been added on the history of Africa and the East, for the effects of these regions on the western world have been so great and their history so neglected by Europeans and Americans that we believe our readers should have this material at their disposal.

The Third Edition is available in two bindings—a two-volume paperbound edition: *Ancient Times to 1715* and *1715 to the Present;* and a three-volume paperbound edition: *Ancient and Medieval Times, Early Modern Times,* and *Modern Times.*

The authors who have collaborated in the writing of *European History in a World Perspective* are specialists in their respective fields with broad experience not only in research and writing, but also in teaching. It seems appropriate to list here all the authors even though they may not have contributed to this particular volume. The division of writing is as follows: Nina G. Garsoian, Professor of Armenian Studies and Byzantine History and Chairman of the Department of Middle East Languages and Cultures, Columbia University: Parts I–IV and Chapter 3 in Part V; David L. Hicks, Associate Professor of History, New York University: Part V, Chapters 1–2 and 4–5 and Parts VI–VIII; David J. Brandenburg, Professor of History, The American University: Part IX, Chapters 1–4, Part X, Chapters 1–3, Part XI, Chapter 1 and Chapters 3 and 4, and Part XII. Peter Gay, Professor of History, Yale University: Part IX, Chapter 5, Part X, Chapter 4, Part XI, Chapter 2; Shepard B. Clough, Professor Emeritus of European History,

Columbia University: the Introduction on "The Nature of History" and portions of Chapter I, Part XI; Otto Pflanze, Professor of History, University of Minnesota: Part XIII and Chapter 5 of Part XIV; Stanley G. Payne, Professor of History, University of Wisconsin, Madison: Part XIV, Chapters 1–4, Part XV, Chapter I, and Parts XVI and XVIII; Robert E. Frykenberg, Professor of History and South Asian Studies, University of Wisconsin, Madison: Chapters 2–4 of Part XV and Chapters 1–3 of Part XVII; G. Wesley Johnson, Associate Professor of History, University of California, Santa Barbara: Chapter 5 in Part XV and Chapter 4 in Part XVII. Professor Brandenburg wishes to state that Millicent H. Brandenburg is, in fact, co-author with him and that she did most of the picture research and caption writing for his sections of this edition.

Any endeavor like this one involves a great number of persons to whom thanks for their generous help are due. The authors are particularly grateful to the late Garrett Mattingly, Miriam Haskett, Albert Mott, Robert Shipkey, Josef L. Altholz, Theophanis G. Stavrou, Hans Rogger, and Eugen Weber. For their help in preparing the Third Edition the authors would particularly like to thank Linda C. Rose, Robert J. Scally, Thalia Cosmos, Carl G. Anthon, O.B. Hardison and the helpful staff at the Folger Shakespeare Library, Ira N. Klein, James A. Malloy, Jr., Renate Shaw and her colleagues in Prints and Photographs at the Library of Congress, and Kathleen Wilson.

CONTENTS

Introduction

The Nature of History

At the beginning of every scientific investigation and, indeed, at the beginning of every attempt to increase our knowledge and understanding, it is essential to state as precisely as possible what the object of the investigation is, what steps will be taken in the process of analysis and synthesis, and what methods will be employed in furthering the undertaking. Such a statement is particularly necessary in the study of history, for this subject is used to encompass so much and so wide a variety of concepts that the uninitiated frequently become confused and then lost in its labyrinthian twists and turns.

The Study of History In essence, history is the total recorded past of humankind on this earth—the totality of human experience. Inasmuch as all aspects of this great experience are not of equal importance either to an understanding of how the world of the present got the way it is, or in comprehending how men lived in the past, or in learning how changes were made that got us from primitive society to the present complex societies, the historian has to make selections from the total record for special study. These selections, based upon the major categories of man's behavior in society, provide the historian with his orienting themes. Thus the historian endeavors to explain how man has provided for his material wants at various times in the past and how our present economic system came into being (economic history); he tries to describe how men have organized their social relationships for continuing the society, for procreation, for training the youth, and for establishing rules of conduct (social history); he makes an effort to analyze the way people in society create a government to bring together all members for collective action, to effect compliance with common rules, and to determine policies to be followed (political history); and he aspires to ascertain what the basic values of the society are—what people strive for, be it a place in the hereafter or some goal on this earth, and by what means they hope to achieve their ends, whether through the intercession of a divine being or beings or reliance on their own resources (intellectual history).

This division of man's activities through time for study provides one essential means for making sense out of the vast record of the past, but it is obvious that all mankind in all parts of the world cannot be treated at once. Consequently, the historian selects segments of mankind for study. On the largest scale, mankind is divided into *cultures* or *civilizations*, each with distinctive ways of making a living, of organizing socially, of governing, of thinking, of creating esthetic works, and of establishing basic values. Thus historians and other social scientists recognize such cultures as the Greek, the ancient Egyptian, western European, the Eskimo, the Chinese, and the Russian Communist. Parts of these cultures may, in turn, be set apart for study in order to get further understanding of some particular phase of life, such as the city of recent times, the philosophy of the Greeks, or the art of the Egyptians. And, by the same token, the historian may legitimately study relations among cultures or their parts and how one culture has been influenced by others. Indeed, in recent times one of the great developments in the world has been the way in which nearly every culture has attempted to take on some aspects of western European civilization, especially the economic.

Once the historian has selected his segment of human society for study, he then has to make a decision regarding the time-span over which he intends to trace and analyze behavior. Indeed, the historian must not only select periods for study, but he must also divide his period into sections of time for purposes of clarity and effect, much as the dramatist separates his play into acts and scenes. To some extent such divisions will be determined by major changes in development, but sometimes they may be arbitrary and mere literary conveniences. Thus, the student, as well as the historian himself, should never forget that changes in the stream of human experience are seldom so abrupt as represented in history books and that always some parts of former ways of doing things and formerly held values continue to be held by some members of a society when other ways and values have been adopted by a majority.

Finally, the historian needs some criterion for deciding what are the important things he should isolate for study and what are the unimportant and the insignificant, which he may ignore. Obviously the Battle of Waterloo was more important in the Napoleonic period than the head cold of Josephine in 1799; the invention of the steam engine was more important than the curling iron; and World War II was more important than the Spanish-American War. To handle this problem of what is important the historian should, although he not always does, select for study those subjects (things and men) that have affected *most* men *most* profoundly for the *most* time. The historian should observe the rule of the *three mosts*—he should eschew the ephemeral.

The Character of European Culture In the economic phase of man's activity, western Europe developed a system of production based upon the use of composite mechanisms, which stretch all the way from the fulcrum and lever and the bow and arrow down to the most complex computing machines and giant metal presses of the present, and upon intricate processes that reach from the use of friction to create fire to, let us say, the catalytic method of refining petroleum. This system of production has made increasing use of inorganic materials, which were stored over millions of years in the earth's crust and which were infinitely more abundant than organic materials produced in relatively short periods of time. Furthermore, the processes of production have been moved by power or energy largely from inorganic resources and sometimes transformed by power mechanisms, like the waterwheel, the steam engine, the internal combustion engine, the electrical dynamo, and the atomic pile. Western man has had at his disposal power sources never equalled in any previous culture. Then, too, man was able to conquer space by rapid means of transportation and thereby bring large quantities of materials together from very distant parts for the use of men in the West. Lastly, western man has made enormous improvements in strains of growing things and in the breeds of animals, as well as in soil fertility, so that what he grew yielded many times more per acre and per unit of human input than that obtained by his ancestors of ancient times.

The great productive systems of the present depend in large part upon the ability of individuals to specialize in some aspect of economic activity—in what economists usually refer to as the division of labor. Individuals nowadays seldom endeavor to be economically self-sufficient in the sense of themselves's producing everything they may need for consumption; they rely, instead, upon the exchange of goods and services with others. This reliance upon the market has been made possible, in part, by cheap and rapid transportation and by communication of information about goods and their supplies, and also, in part, by the institution of money, which is a medium of exchange, a measure of value, and a store of wealth. Indeed, money is one of the most important inventions of man, ranking with fire and the wheel, because of its role in establishing a division of labor.

On the social side of European culture the great characteristic of our present day is the enormous complexity of groupings compared with the rather simple family and tribal organizations among primitive peoples. Peoples now fall into groups determined by their families, fortunes, professions, religions, political affiliations, education, and even physical characteristics. Human relations are regulated in large part by the standards set by the groups to which people belong and relations become anarchic when individuals are torn from their groups by some disturbance like war. Nevertheless, within European culture a basic ethic persists—an ethic which comes from the Christian-Jewish tradition—based upon the Golden Rule of doing unto others as you would have others do unto you, and upon the Ten Commandments. In time this ethic became written into law codes and the laws came to be more nearly the same for all groups in society. In the past, the family was a central institution for regulating procreation, for educating the youth in the fundamentals of the culture, and in caring for the aged and the infirm. More recently, as the task of training has come to be more technical and as relations among men have become more impersonal, because of the division of labor, the schools have taken on more of the training task and state organizations have assumed many of the responsibilities for the aged and the infirm (the welfare state).

Other important characteristics of present-day social existence pertain primarily to the increase in population, the lengthening life span of man, and to ever-greater concentrations of population in cities and their suburbs. In the last three and a half centuries, the population of Europe has grown sevenfold, which has been made possible, in part, by access to the resources of overseas areas. The average length of life of individuals, technically called "expectation of life at birth," has gone up from the twenty-five or thirty years that it was from Roman times to the middle of the eighteenth century to nearly seventy years in the majority of European countries. This has meant that more people can make use of technical training over long periods, and put that training to greater use, but it also means that a larger percentage of the population lives beyond the productive ages and becomes dependent upon society.

Today, in the more economically advanced countries of Europe, some 65 percent of the population lives in cities of 2,500 or over, whereas at the end of the eighteenth century, only some 15 percent of the population lived in such agglomerations. This means that the lives of more and more people are regulated by city customs and values. Among such values are a desire for a higher standard of living, which has led to the curtailment of size of families, a demand for more man-made works of art and spectator entertainment, and a drive for more popular participation in the affairs of government.

In the political realm of human activity, the trend in European history has been toward the establishment of larger states, to endow these states with a sovereignty that implied no other power existed over them, to extend their functions until they invaded every phase of life, and to have these states coterminous with "nationalities," or subcultures of western culture, to which individuals came to attach great emotional loyalties. Many of the traditional histories of Europe have, indeed, concentrated their attention primarily on these issues and upon relations among states, which is an indication of how important they loom in the public life of European peoples. In the present work, emphasis will be placed upon them, but always with the end in view of making clear the long and arduous process by which our present-day political system came into being. Furthermore, an effort will be made to show what social groupings controlled political organizations, which ones wanted change, and how those in power used the machinery of the state for advancing the policies they favored. Lastly, considerable attention will be given to the tensions that arose among states in the process of state-building and to the strife that developed among national states—a strife that in the twentieth century seriously threatened the very continuation of European culture and greatly lessened the position of Europe in the world.

In intellectual life, the outstanding achievement of western culture has been the development of science, for it has permitted man to extend his control dramatically over the physical universe. The basic principle of scientific thought has been the ascertainment of the various factors, including their quality and their magnitudes, and the manner and timing in which they came together, which were necessary to produce event "x" and which invariably did produce event "x". The more accurate and precise the data resulting from the application of this principle were and the more thoroughly the explanation for event "x" could be established through repetitive experimentation or observed experience, the more "scientific" the knowledge was considered to be.

Even though in some fields of activity, as in the social sciences, it is recognized that the investigator cannot control all the forces at work, is largely an observer, and cannot know even all of the factors involved, as for example the functioning of Napoleon's endocrine glands during the Battle of Waterloo or what Brutus had for breakfast before he turned sourly against Julius Caesar, the theory of knowledge employed in the name of science in all fields is essentially the same. How this epistemology, or theory of knowledge, came into being over millennia of time will be a recurring theme in the pages ahead. So, too, will be the uses to which scientific knowledge has been put in conquering the physical world. It has made possible the practical elimination of famine; it has freed man from many of the scourges of pestilence and disease; and it has given him so much confidence in himself and his methods that he believes he can accomplish almost any physical task he may set for himself. Western man has from this confidence developed a firm conviction in "progress" toward a more ample fulfillment of his goals. This confidence has, in turn, led to a great optimism regarding the future, albeit that this optimism is mitigated from time to time by man's realization that he has not been able yet to control relations among men according to the culture's values.

On the esthetic side of man's life, the West has tended to glorify the arts. By his oft-repeated use of the expression—"the finer things of life"—western man indicates how highly he esteems works of art. Moreover, in spite of the fact that he places the appreciation of esthetic productions high in his scale of values, he rates creativity in the arts above passive enjoyment. In fact, he invariably places the activist above the passivist in all efforts in conformity with the culture's values.

About the respective merits of the various arts and of the multitudes of artistic styles western men differ very widely. Esthetic judgment seems to be a highly individualistic thing and esthetes have been at a loss to establish an objective measure for determining excellence. This is embarrassing for the historian, who has to rely so heavily upon specialists for forming his own conclusions. He knows, to be sure, that men learned in the arts do set standards that establish some criteria for judging craftsmanship and accomplishment. In the final analysis he is forced to acknowledge that he must accept as esthetically great what most competent judges have most consistently and most universally considered great.

Finally, students of history should have before them one other major consideration—that is, a general conception of the goals of our culture, for it is in terms of these goals that judgments about various historical trends or events are made; and contrary to what is often contended, historians are forever making judgments, and in the opinion of many quite properly so. Be that as it may, however, the values that the West attaches to achievements in various categories of human existence constitute our present-day conception of levels of civilization. These levels are determined, so far as those in western European culture are concerned, by the degree to which men establish control over their physical universe, are able to regulate human relations among all mankind according to the Golden Rule, and succeed in producing generally recognized masterpieces in architecture, painting, literature, sculpture, music, philosophy, and science. The more a people realizes both qualitatively and quantitatively these tenets of civilization without exception, the more civilized it is. And conversely, the less it realizes them, the less civilized it is.

Some Problems in Historical Study: Evidence, Causation, and Change The historian, much like the lawyer, proceeds to describe human behavior through time by collecting evidence. Sometimes this evidence is scanty, as in the case of population statistics when no censuses were taken. In such instances, the historian has to rely upon subsidiary data like baptismal and death records, or he has to infer size by the walls of cities, the height of buildings, and the number of persons using dwelling units. At other times, evidence may be overwhelming, as for example, the records of World War II. In such cases, selection and condensation are necessary and the historian has to guard against falsifying the story, by choosing what is most representative and what is the most relevant to the immediate issue he is investigating.

Both in the amassing of evidence, as well as in the selection of segments of history for study, in the subsequent analysis of why events took place, and in passing judgment as to the desirability of certain behavior, the historian is confronted with the danger of being influenced by his personal likes and dislikes, or his own subjective set of values. The Parisian writing about the Franco-Prussian War of 1870 may produce a very different account of the war than the German; the anti-Catholic may regard the seizure of the Papal States in the nineteenth century in another manner from the members of the Vatican; and the social reformer may look upon the industrial revolution in quite another way from the economist interested in economic growth. The historian acts, like all the rest of us, on the basis of the set of values he has acquired in his maturing, and what he writes is related to these values. This is the problem of relativity. Its dangers can be minimized by keeping judgments about the desirability of an event or of a development relevant to the values of the culture rather than to the values of the individual and by making whatever values are brought into play clearly explicit.

Once the historian has managed to keep his own prejudices and hopes from coloring his work (or makes clear what his prejudices and hopes are), and has amassed evidence regarding the character of events, he is then concerned with an explanation of how and why these events took place. Here he comes face to face with the knotty question of causation. What were the causes of the event—the war, the invention, the style of art, or the way of thought. In trying to ascertain the "causes" for any event, a temptation exists to seek a simple explanation, a single cause. In fact, some historians have tried to explain all of the past on the basis of geography, or of climate, or of economic forces, or of patterns of thought, or of the action of a supernatural power. Unfortunately, monocausal explanations are *ipso facto* inadequate for explaining what is very complex.

The task of the historian is, then, to establish what are the multiple and necessary factors involved in any development or in the background of any event. This is not an easy affair, for so many and such varied kinds of forces come into play that the historian has to exercise his own judgment and has to have very broad competences. He has to know something of psychology, something of economics, and something about sociology, politics, law, art, philosophy, and the physical sciences. And in addition, he must know the languages of the area he is treating, and the techniques for measuring quantities of evidence (statistics), and he must be able to present his materials and his conclusions in effective speech or writing. His task is, indeed, formidable, but not impossible, especially if he has begun early enough in his life to acquire proper training. At all events, the historian finds immense satisfaction in trying to understand human behavior so that man may adopt those policies that will help establish more readily than would otherwise be the case the kind of a world that is in conformity with the basic values of his culture. And there is a great sense of achievement in attempting to provide a synthesis of the various aspects of human activity that go to explain the world in which we live.

In the process of attempting to explain how humans have developed the kinds of cultures that exist today or have existed at various times in the past, the historian inevitably becomes involved in the phenomena of *change*. This is a subject of such great importance in historical study that a few words about it here may prove useful to the student, for the historian, *perforce,* is primarily concerned with periods of change rather than with periods in which things remain static.

Change is always the result of something new being introduced into a given situation—a platitude that has been raised to what might seem to some a great height of erudition by an elaborate theory of innovation. Contrary to what many observers have said, change may come from any one of the aspects of human existence. It may be initiated by an increase in population, or, for that matter, by a decrease. It may come about from the invention of a new machine, like the steam engine. It may be started by a new pattern of thought, like that of science or Christianity. It may get its original impetus from the appearance of a great leader, like Alexander the Great or Napoleon. It may begin with an alteration in climate, like a long period of drought or flood. Or it may result from a change in the alignment of groups in society and a consequent shift in the locus of power, as in the French Revolution. It may come from within a society (autonomous change), or it may come from without the society (adaptive change). In any case, change is always impending, if for no other reason than that the actors on the stage of life are always being renewed. The more gradual change is, the more easily societies seem to be able to adjust to it.

The facility with which change is effected in any society depends in large part upon the range of opportunities for alternative decisions open to the members of the society in question. The greater the range, the more extensive change may be; and the less the range, the less the change to be expected.

The extent of the range of opportunities for alternative decisions will depend upon the degree of rigidity in the case under analysis. If a society's culture, institutions, groups, ideologies, and leadership are rigidly fixed in traditional patterns, change will occur more slowly and with greater travail than in a society characterized by flexibility in values and institutions and by mobility of people up and down the social scale.

Rigidity will depend to a considerable degree on the extent to which a proposed change affects favorably the status of those segments of society that possess influence, authority, and power. This proposition represents a drastic modification of the traditional belief that underprivileged classes are the breeding ground of change. It seems clear that the upper groups of society are responsible for a large measure of change, especially that which does not at once threaten their positions, for they have the means of initiating new undertakings and their positions of power give them some immunity from social sanctions when breaking with tradition.

Secondly, rigidity will depend on the extent to which there is a fear of change in society and conversely will be weakened when *progress,* which implies change, is glorified. Thirdly, rigidity is increased if a society has little surplus energy or resources for experimentation—if it lives from hand to mouth and can run no risks. And fourthly, rigidities in society depend in part on physical environment and in part on the biological characteristics of members of the group. Thus, change in desert cultures has been less than in the rich valleys of navigable rivers; and it has been less among bodily weak and inactive peoples, like the Pygmies, than among the physically strong and active like the western Europeans.

Finally, attention should be drawn to the fact that change will vary in rate, size, and direction according to the nature of the innovation, the nature of the environment in which it is introduced, and the leadership that is given it. It will almost certainly affect some phase of life more rapidly than others, so that some phases will seem to be *leading* in the process of change while others will be *lagging.* Among those who favor change, criticism will be directed toward the *lags;* and among the reactionaries who oppose change, criticism will be directed toward the *leads.* Rate of change will depend in large part upon the urgency with which the society feels a need for what is new and upon its ability to adopt it. And the magnitude and direction of change will likewise be determined primarily by social need, awareness of that need, and ability to do something about it.

In the vast panorama of the past, change as effected by people is of fundamental importance. Only by understanding it in relation to goals toward which society should strive can they form public and private policies that will give them more nearly the kind of world they want. The study of the past has a very practical side—it is at the bottom of most human decisions, whether it be the purchase of an automobile or the defense of one's religious belief. From this it should follow that the better the understanding of the past, the better will be everyday decisions.

FURTHER READING

A great many introductions to the study of history exist for the use of students. See especially Homer C. Hockett, *The Critical Method in Historical Research and Writing* (1955); Jacques Barzun and Henry F. Graff, *The Modern Researcher* (1970); and Marc Bloch, *The Historian's Craft* (1953).

The study of history involves a number of philosophical problems, particularly those having to do with a theory of knowledge (epistemology), the selection of issues for study, the choosing of data relevant to these issues, and the personal preferences and prejudices of the historian. These matters are discussed in W. H. Walsh, *An Introduction to Philosophy of History* (1964); Herbert Butterfield, *Man on His Past: The Study of the History of Historical Scholarship* (1955); Pieter Geyl, *Use and Abuse of History* (1970); and Ernst Cassirer, *The Problem of Knowledge: Philosophy, Science, and History since Hegel* (1950). Excerpts from many of the recent writers on the philosophy of history are to be found in Hans Meyerhoff, *The Philosophy of History of Our Time* (1959). Also, Ronald H. Nash, ed., *Ideas of History,* 2 vols. (1969).

For an understanding of the philosophy of history represented in the present work, see *Theory and Practice in Historical Study,* Bulletin 54 of the Social Science Research Council (1946) and *The Social Sciences in Historical Study,* Bulletin 64 of the Social Science Research Council (1954).

Various historians of the relatively recent past, their methods, and their points of view have been discussed by G. P. Gooch, *History and Historians of the Nineteenth Century* (1959); Bernadotte Schmitt, *Some Historians of Modern Europe* (1942); Trygue Tholfsen, *Historical Thinking, An Introduction* (1967); Felix Gilbert and Stephen R. Graubard, eds., *Historical Studies Today* (1972); and Samuel William Halperin, ed., *Essays in Modern European Historiography* (1972). Different interpretations of certain periods and different types of history are found in collections of passages from well-known historians. Shepard B. Clough, Peter Gay, and Charles K. Warner, *The European Past,* 2 vols. (1970); Fritz Stern, *The Varieties of History* (1972); and in the series *Problems in European Civilization,* edited by Ralph W. Greenlaw and Dwight E. Lee.

Every student of history should have a good English dictionary and an encyclopedia, at least of desk size, *The Columbia Encyclopedia* (3rd ed., 1963), or *Le Petit Larousse.* He should also have a guide to names, dates, and events, such as William L. Langer, ed., *An Encyclopedia of World History* (1972); and an historical atlas, such as William R. Shepherd, *Historical Atlas* (1964), or Edward W. Fox, *Atlas of European History* (1957).

PART VI THE CLOSE OF THE MIDDLE AGES

The light of the thirteenth century dimmed in the fourteenth and early fifteenth. In every way, the medieval civilization of northern Europe was in decay. Economic progress slowed, political life was disrupted by war and domestic strife, and the authority and influence of the Church began to decline. This century and a half was a period of economic depression with important social consequences. It was also a period in which the feudal monarchies reached the inherent limits of their growth. There arose a new kind of "feudalism," which only a new kind of monarchy could suppress. The Empire of the Hohenstaufen disintegrated into separate, virtually autonomous political entities, while the imperial crown devolved into a mere symbol of vanished powers. The ascendancy of the Church over the lives of Christians gave way before the advance of secular forms of social and political organization. Overblown and complacent, the Church closed its eyes to the need for self-examination and internal reform, even though faced with revolt from within and heresy from without. Church and Empire, the two great universal institutions of medieval civilization, would never recover what they lost. Europe would arrange itself along new social and political lines. These lines begin to be visible at the close of the Middle Ages. Thus, in the midst of decay we can discern growth, as one phase of European civilization was transformed into another. By the middle of the fifteenth century, modern history had begun.

SOUTH ROSE WINDOW, NOTRE DAME, PARIS. (Alinari-Scala)

LEGACY OF THE PAST

(Above) *The Recording and Accounting of Tax Receipts from the Cover of the Tax Accounts Record for the Year 1474, Siena.* (Benvenuto de Giovanni del Guasta, Siena, 1436–1518, Alinari.)

(Opposite page) *The Privileges of Citizenship.* Sienese citizens come before the city officials to pay their annual taxes. (Guasta, Alinari.)

The late Middle Ages saw the breakdown of authority, the ravages of war and disease, economic decline, social and spiritual unrest, and revolution: the lot of fourteenth- and fifteenth-century man was a hard one. Perhaps because of its gloom historians have studied the late Middle Ages less fully than other periods. But the history of bad times always has much to tell us, ourselves the victims of war and revolution and bewildering changes in society, economy, and government.

Specific examples of our heritage from the late Middle Ages are numerous: the English Parliament, still shaping itself then but recognizeable and in being for good; the professional standing army, permanent, maintained by national governments; a system of regular taxation which, though cruelly discriminatory almost everywhere, established for the future that every man must contribute to his nation's support. But above all, the spirit of the late Middle ages was closely akin to ours. It, as is ours, was a deeply troubled time, and the spirit was one of frustration and cynical resignation, of sad nostalgia for a better past and a deep fear for a more terrible future.

HI PRAEFVRVNT ÆRAR
IO·KT·IAN·MCCCCLXVII
ANDREAS·D·XPHORI
CAPACIVS·CAM
NICOLAVS·BAPISTAE
VENTVRINVS
THOMMAS·VRBA
NI·IOANNELVS
DINVS·BERTOCCI·MARTVS
ALOISIVS·OLDOBRANDI
CERETANVS MATHEV
S PINOCII·SCRIP·SATO

HI VERO·KT·IVLII·M·CCCCLXVIII
ANDREAS CAPACIVS
MANNVS·BARTHOLOMAEI·VITEL
LONVS·S·IACOBVS·PETRI·HV
MIDVS·KATHERINVS·NANN
IS·NERII·NICOLAVS·PIC
COLMINI·PICCOLMINEVS
MATHEVS·PINOCII·SCRIP
SARDVINVS·LEONAR
DI·ARDVINVS·TAB·

MAJOR EVENTS, 1260-1474*

1250–

Siete Partidas, Castilian law code, written 1250's

Rudolf of Habsburg elected first Habsburg emperor (1273)

1275–

Boniface VIII elected pope (1294)
Boniface VIII issues bull *Clericis Laicos* against Philip the Fair (1296)

1300–

Boniface VIII issues bull *Unam Sanctam* (1302)
French defeated by Flemish at Courtrai (1302)
Beginning of Avignonese papacy (1309)

1325–

Marsiglio of Padua completes *Defensor Pacis* (1326)
Philip VI, the first Valois, becomes king of France (1328)
Beginning of Hundred Years' War (1337)
Jan van Artevelde becomes Flemish leader (1337)

English defeat French at Crécy (1346)
Black Death (1348–49)

1350–

English, under "Black Prince," defeat French at Poitiers (1356)
Emperor Charles IV promulgates the Golden Bull (1357)
Étienne Marcel and Third Estate of France issue "Great Ordinance" (1357)
Revolt of the *Jacquerie* in France (1358)

* *For 1260–1305 see also Major Events, Part V.*

Treaty of Brétigny between England and France (1360)
Formal organization of the Hanseatic League (1367)

1375–

Beginning of the Great Schism (1378)
Revolt of the *Ciompi* in Florence (1378)

Peasants' Revolt in England (1381)

Death of John Wyclif, founder of Lollardy (1384)
Treaty of Aljubarrota brings House of Avis to Portuguese throne (1385)

Richard II deposed; Henry IV, Bolingbroke, becomes king of England (1399)

1400–

Council of Pisa elects third pope, John XXIII (1408)

Council of Constance meets, ends Great Schism (1414–18)
Jan Hus burned at the stake (1415)
English, under Henry V, defeat French at Agincourt (1415)
Martin V elected pope and Renaissance papacy begins (1417)

Henry VI of England proclaimed king of France (1422)
Charles VII inherits French throne, is called "King of Bourges" (1422)

1425–

Pope Eugenius IV breaks with Council of Basle, begins struggle to defeat Conciliarism (1430's)

Treaty of Arras between France and Burgundy (1435)
End of Hussite Wars in Bohemia (1436)
Pragmatic Sanction of Bourges confirms rights of Gallican Church (1438)
Council of Ferrara-Florence meets under papal auspices (1439)

End of Council of Basle: Conciliarism defeated (1449)

1450–

Pius II declares Conciliarism heretical (1460)
Catalans revolt against king of Aragon (1460's)

Death of Henry IV; succession war begins in Castile (1474)

1475–

1 Political Developments

From the second quarter of the fourteenth to the third quarter of the fifteenth centuries, England and France were at war. Though actual fighting was sporadic, both great feudal monarchies remained on a war footing all of the time and war was the chief influence in political life. The immediate cause was a claim to the French throne put forward by Edward III of England (1327–1377) on the death of the last Capetian, Charles IV, in 1328. Philip V had left no sons; the nearest French heir was his cousin, Philip of Valois, who was a nephew of Philip the Fair. Edward III, on the other hand, was Philip the Fair's grandson. A pretty feudal problem! Philip of Valois declared himself King Philip VI of France (1328–1350). Edward III refused to recognize him, insisting on his own claim, and war broke out in 1337. Of course, the war's real causes were more complex and less noble.

THE OPENING OF THE HUNDRED YEARS' WAR

Ever since the Angevins had mounted the English throne, bringing with them vast fiefs in France, the crowns of France and England had been at loggerheads. The goal of every French king was to drive the "foreigner" out, and by 1328 they had been quite successful. At Edward III's accession, only a small stretch of land along the Gascon coast remained to the English, a last beachhead of the old Angevin empire, and the French were trying to push them off of that. At stake besides family pride were the wealth of the rich vinyards around Bordeaux and the trade of Bordeaux itself. To lose Gascony would badly hurt English merchants and shipowners, would deprive the English crown of a lucrative source of tax revenue, and would compel English gentlemen to buy their "claret" wines at considerably higher prices.

More important than Gascony was Flanders. The count of Flanders was a vassal of the king of France, but the cloth manufacturers in such rich Flemish towns as Ghent and Bruges bought most of their wool in England and sold most of their finished cloth there. The trade was vital to English sheep raisers and wool merchants and to the king, whose taxes on both exported wool and imported woolen cloth brought him far more revenue than the taxes on Bordeaux wine. The wealth deriving from Flemish industry also attracted the kings of France. In their role as overlords, they sought control of it, using as their excuse and opportunity the endemic civil disorder in the towns. The kings allied themselves with the town patriciates, whose exclusive governments were challenged by the guildsmen. The guildsmen, chiefly weavers and fullers whose fortunes were wholly dependent on cloth manufacturing, turned for support to the kings of England. From the time of Philip the Fair, the two crowns played out their rivalry in Flanders. It was in answer to pleas from his Flemish friends that Edward III declared war on Philip VI in 1337.

Methods of Warfare Used by the King of France in the Fifteenth Century. At the rear stand mounted knights, flags flying. In the left foreground infantry take aim with crossbows. In the center, three cannon are ready to batter down the walls of a besieged city. (Courtesy of the Trustees of the British Museum.)

War was not unwelcome in those days to the men who could fight it. To a king it brought glory and the sure respect of his adventurous and usually restless nobles, while it kept the nobles conveniently occupied. For the nobles themselves, war was the very reason for their existence. The first decisive victory was by the English fleet off Sluys in 1340. This, together with the capture of the port of Calais in 1347, gave England a dominance of the Channel which it would hold for many decades. On land, two great battles, both won by England, took place—at Crécy in 1346 and Poitiers in 1356—before the Treaty of Brétigny was signed in 1360. At Poitiers, King John II of France (1350–1364), his son, and a number of his knights were captured and carried off to England, where they were held—in luxury—for high ransoms. The treaty released them but left over a third of France in nominal possession of England.

Crécy and Poitiers proved the superiority of English over French armies. Both had large contingents of men-at-arms—mounted, armored knights—whose fighting technique consisted of charging in a loose body, lances lowered, and flailing about with hand weapons when they met the charging enemy. But the English had a far more effective infantry. It was armed with pike and longbow, the latter particularly deadly. Although not as consistently accurate as the crossbow (weapon of the less numerous French infantry), it could be shot much more rapidly. A skilled bowman could shoot an arrow every three or four seconds, each capable of penetrating chain mail at medium range and dropping a horse at much longer distance. Many bowmen shooting together could loose a continual storm of arrows and turn a mounted charge into a shambles, easy prey to English horsemen held in reserve.

FRANCE AND ENGLAND DURING THE HUNDRED YEARS' WAR

Poitiers ended the first phase of the war. Already the war's effects were profound, contributing substantially to the economic ills from which both countries suffered and hastening the decline of royal power. In England, there was evidence that the monarchy had overextended itself before the war began; in France, the fact became clear with the accession of John II. As we have seen in earlier chapters, feudal monarchy was limited monarchy. Kings governed, indeed were expected to govern, with strength and wisdom but within the accepted circumscription of law and custom. They were supposed to dispense justice clearly and fairly, pay their own expenses, and take the council of their "natural" advisors, the vassals-in-chief of the realm. Most of the time, things went fairly well, as during the reign of Louis IX, though even Louis, his piety notwithstanding, was inclined to assert his prerogatives more firmly than conservatives liked. Kings with the loftier view of royal authority being purveyed by Roman lawyers—kings such as Edward I and Philip the Fair—provoked widespread anger and discontent. The day when a king could act "at his pleasure" and contrary to traditional practice had not yet arrived. He simply did not command sufficient money or men. In an emergency, he was forced to appeal to his subjects and each appeal, however readily and humbly granted, sapped his power and prestige. Furthermore, his subjects soon found that they could use his appeals as bargaining points to gain concessions of their own. The situation for royalty was particularly dangerous if the king were stupid or weak and his subjects self-seeking and powerful.

King John II of France. Called "the Good" for no other reason than his chivalric qualities, John was captured at Poitiers with his son Philip and several lieutenants and taken to England and held for high ransom. The Frenchmen made a great hit with the English ladies and both sides were happy when the ransom was paid and they went home. (The Louvre.)

France and England suffered from feeble kings during most of the fourteenth and fifteenth centuries. In France, the first three successors to Philip the Fair were his sons who were short-lived and, except for Philip V (1316–1322), were inconsequential.[1] Their reigns were uneventful as they coasted along on their father's reputation. But none produced an heir, thus ending the direct Capetian line and bringing Philip VI, the first Valois, to the throne in 1328. Philip VI escaped the consequences of his own foolishness and the ignominy of the English victories. Instead, the work of repair and recovery fell to his equally incapable son, John II. Fortunately for the kingdom, John spent a good part of his reign a prisoner in England, while rule was in the hands of the clever and tough-minded Dauphin. The Dauphin's problems were serious ones. The peasants rose in revolt and the Third

[1]Besides Philip V, they were Louis X (1314–1316) and Charles IV (1322–1328).

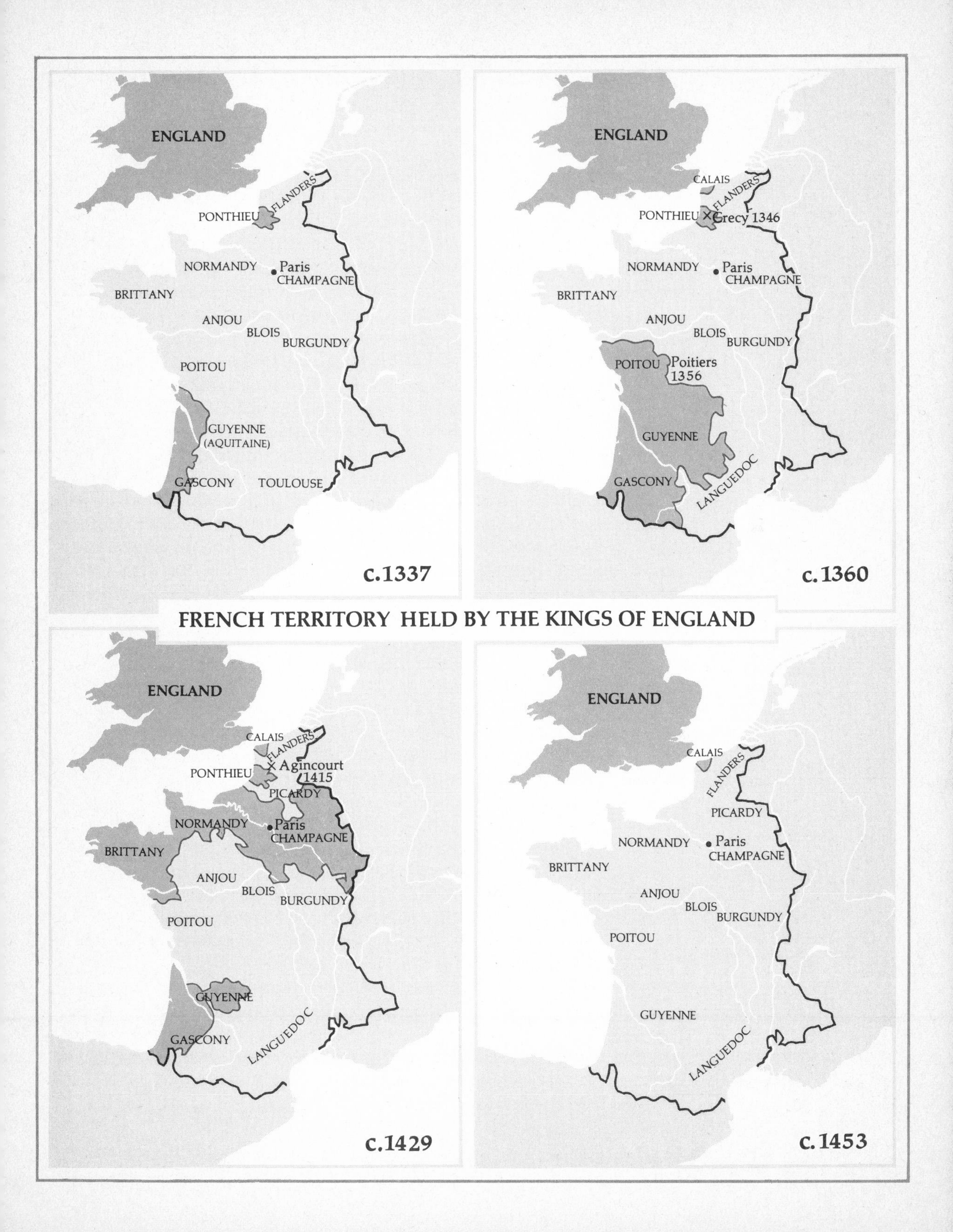

FRENCH TERRITORY HELD BY THE KINGS OF ENGLAND
ENGLAND
FLANDERS
PONTHIEU
NORMANDY
Paris
CHAMPAGNE
BRITTANY
ANJOU
BLOIS
BURGUNDY
POITOU
GUYENNE
(AQUITAINE)
GASCONY
TOULOUSE
c.1337
ENGLAND
CALAIS
FLANDERS
PONTHIEU
Crecy 1346
NORMANDY
Paris
CHAMPAGNE
BRITTANY
ANJOU
BLOIS
BURGUNDY
POITOU
Poitiers
1356
GUYENNE
GASCONY
LANGUEDOC
c.1360
ENGLAND
CALAIS
FLANDERS
PONTHIEU
Agincourt
1415
PICARDY
NORMANDY
Paris
CHAMPAGNE
BRITTANY
ANJOU
BLOIS
BURGUNDY
POITOU
GUYENNE
GASCONY
LANGUEDOC
c.1429
ENGLAND
CALAIS
FLANDERS
PICARDY
NORMANDY
Paris
CHAMPAGNE
BRITTANY
ANJOU
BLOIS
BURGUNDY
POITOU
GUYENNE
LANGUEDOC
c.1453

Estate, headed by Etienne Marcel, provost of the merchants and artisans of Paris, led the Estates General to challenge the crown's financial powers. In 1357, the audacious Estates, called following the defeat at Poitiers, refused the royal request for war taxes except on condition that its members collect them and supervise their expenditure. Marcel and his followers went even further, drawing up a "Great Ordinance" embodying radical ideas that would have turned France into a species of constitutional monarchy if introduced. But the Dauphin proved adequate to the crisis. He won over the First and Second Estates whose clerical and noble members had little sympathy for middle-class radicalism, and in the process blocked the assembly's best opportunity to become a "parliament" in the English sense. Unlike the English Parliament, the Estates General remained divided, prey to class jealousy, a tool of the crown.

After the Dauphin had become king as Charles V (1364–1380), he continued to force the royal prerogative on a now-compliant Estates General. Indeed, in every way he proved himself the strongest and most capable French monarch since Philip the Fair. Under his guidance, France recovered from Poitiers and slowly but surely won back much of the territory that had been lost. To support the necessary military effort, Charles got the Estates General to agree to regular taxation: a *taille,* or tax on non-noble property; a *gabelle,* or salt tax; and an *aide,* or sales tax on merchandise and wine. In theory, these were emergency taxes to prosecute the war; in fact, they remained permanent throughout Charles' reign. They permitted him to maintain a standing army, which he used sparingly but effectively. And he was blessed with good generals. The English were on the run and the foundations of a new, stronger French monarchy were laid by the close of the reign. But the king had a conscience, and on his deathbed he ordered discontinuance of the property tax, his principal source of revenue.

In England, Edward III's long reign also witnessed a reaction against royal authority, provoked largely by the high cost of the war. But Edward had neither the foresight nor the will to act in the manner of his French contemporary. In his efforts to raise money, Edward was obliged time and again to call the Parliament whose constitutional role was thereby greatly clarified and regularized over the years. The "Commons" in particular made gains. Quietly, peacefully, and in strict accordance with law, the middle-class country gentry and townsmen established precedents out of which would evolve their undisputed right to approve taxation and pass on legislation. Unlike the French Third Estate, which only represented the towns of France, the Commons represented both rural and urban interests and worked in harmony with the "Lords" of the nobility and high clergy.

However, Parliament was not yet the great representative body it would become, for it was not yet independent of the king on the one hand and the great barons on the other. During the tempestuous reign of Richard II (1377–1399), both the crown and its baronial opposition used the Parliament as a tool of their policies. This in itself is significant, however, for it meant that the Parliament enjoyed considerable prestige and was not something to be scoffed at, as was the Estates General.

"New" Feudalism The most immediate threat to royal authority in the late fourteenth and fifteenth centuries was the high nobility, for the middle-class commoners, despite their aggregate wealth, were not truly influential in government. In England and France, the high nobility had been immensely strengthened by the kings' practice of bestowing large chunks of the royal domain on younger sons. The kings, of course, did not view their realms as unified "states" but as their personal properties, to be united or divided at their pleasure. In France, this "appanage" system created a group of practically autonomous territories within the realm, each headed by a rich and powerful magnate of the royal blood whose natural inclination was to oppose monarchial centralization. The last and ultimately the most dangerous instance of the system occurred in 1361, when John II gave the duchy of Burgundy to his son Philip, who immediately set to work building a state that would soon rival France itself. In England, Edward III followed a similar practice, marrying off his younger sons to rich heiresses and awarding them large fiefs. Thus evolved what is usually termed "new" or "bastard" feudalism to distinguish it from the true feudalism of an earlier time. None of the great royal magnates on either side of the channel sought to do away with monarchy or even to make themselves independent of it. Rather, they used their wealth and the swarms of armed retainers they gathered around themselves to dominate the crown to further their private ends. Of course, pride and self-interest drove them into quarreling, making French and English politics for nearly a century a story of brutal and unreasoning factionalism.

Richard II was the first to suffer. Placated by favors in Edward III's day, the barons sought further privileges during the new king's minority. On coming of age, Richard tried to turn the tables on them. He was a thorough-going monarchist, with even a touch of the tyrant about him, but his methods were clumsy and inadequate. In 1399, a faction of barons headed by Henry Bolingbroke, the duke of Lancaster, deposed him and Lancaster set himself up as Henry IV (1399–1413). His act was wholly illegitimate, a fact that dogged the Lancastrians thereafter. Henry never managed to satisfy his ambitious baronial allies and most of his short reign was given over to suppressing rebellion. Parliament, which had validated Henry's claim to the throne, made the best of his indebtedness, gaining more power than ever before. Henry was succeeded by his soldier son, Henry V (1413–1422), the "Prince Hal" to Shakespeare's Falstaff, who immediately renewed the war in France. At home, opposition to the Lancasters began to crystalize around the house of York whose heir called himself the rightful king.

In France, factional strife among the high nobility broke out during the long and tragic reign of Charles VI (1380–1422). Charles, like Richard II of England, ascended the throne as a minor, and from the age of twenty-four was a madman, "the plaything of every kind of intrigue, a poor puppet whose name served to satisfy the most insatiable appetites." His first attack of insanity came in 1392, and thereafter his lapses into insanity were frequent. Government fell into the stronger and bolder hands of his uncles and cousins, first the duke of Burgundy and then the party led by the duke of Orléans, the Armagnacs. Neither side possessed a grain of public responsibility. An imaginative, though under the circumstances impractical, plan of governmental reform drawn up by the burgesses of Paris, heirs of Etienne Marcel, was adopted by the Burgundians but annulled by the Armagnacs. The French crown, for the next generation, would be solely a means to enhance the nobles' power and fill their pocketbooks.

The situation in France made Henry V's military task an easier one. He was a spirited and intelligent king who loved war and also saw it as a way to occupy his restless barons. In 1415, he landed in Normandy with a sizeable army, which was soon decimated by dysentery, and was forced

The Battle of Agincourt, 1415. This highly stylized interpretation shows Henry V of England (Shakespeare's Prince Hal) confronting the French host. As at Crécy and Poitiers, the English longbow won Agincourt, but the artist preferred to depict the knights in full armor (much more elaborate than the chain mail of an earlier day), and a roughhewn infantry hacking at their enemy with swords and pikes. (Leiden University Library.)

to face the French in a much weakened condition. But the hard lessons of Crécy and Poitiers had still not been learned by the French nobility. At Agincourt, English bowmen once more defeated French mounted knights with terrible losses, perhaps 4,500 French to about 100 English. The Armagnac faction was wiped out and power fell once more to the Burgundians. A treaty was signed in 1420 at Troyes, giving Henry V everything he wanted.

He married the king's daughter and was named heir to the French throne. Both Henry and the mad Charles VI died in 1422, and the crowns of both France and England passed to Henry's infant son, Henry VI of England (1422–1461). The duke of Burgundy became England's ally, while the rightful Dauphin, Charles, to whom most of France south of the Loire remained loyal, fled to the town of Bourges in Touraine. Charles' enemies derisively called him "king of Bourges," and it was only with great perseverance that Joan of Arc persuaded him to accept the crown, at Rheims, as king of France in 1429.

GERMANY IN THE LATER MIDDLE AGES

By the death of the great Emperor Frederick II in 1250, it had been determined that Germany would pass to the princes. The following years simply confirmed this. The Hohenstaufen dynasty sank into insignificance. The papacy invited Charles of Anjou, brother of King Louis IX of France, to invade Sicily, which he did successfully in 1266. Northern Italy, which Frederick had failed to reconquer, became for practical purposes independent of imperial authority. Germany, which Frederick had permitted to continue full speed down the road to political anarchy, was virtually independent of imperial authority too. With the crown's resources and power gone, Frederick's successors had only their personal wealth and the authority they wielded in their own domains to set against the combined strength of the princes. The situation for Empire was hopeless. The princes, who zealously guarded their right of imperial election, time and again chose as emperors men whose resources were small and who would not pose a threat to them.

In 1273, after an "Interregnum" of almost twenty years, during which they proceeded to confirm their autonomy, the electors chose Rudolf of Habsburg (1273–1291). Rudolf was a minor count, who they thought would make a safe emperor. Rudolf fooled them by working strenuously to recoup the declining imperial fortunes and managed to make his own house the most powerful in the Empire. By arranging the marriage of his son Albert to the heiress of Austria, Rudolf inaugurated the brilliantly successful marriage policy that made the Habsburgs the greatest of European dynasties and gave meaning to the phrase: *Bella gerant allii, tu, felix Austria, nube* ("Others make war, you, happy Austria, marry"). Albert I of Habsburg (1298–1305) also tried to revive imperial pretensions, as did Henry VII of Luxemburg (1308–1313). Henry went to Italy, hoping to recapture the authority and prestige enjoyed there by the Hohenstaufen three generations before, but he failed. Germany itself was prey to centrifugal forces too powerful to counteract. Later emperors, Ludwig the Bavarian (1314–1347), for example, accepted the inevitable and turned their whole attention to using the imperial crown to feather their own nests.

The Golden Bull The failure of the German emperors was recognized and written into legal form by Emperor Charles IV (1347–1378). Charles, once and for all, settled the question of whether the Holy Roman Empire was

to be a monarchy or a loose confederation of princes in favor of the latter. Charles was a statesman, the most able emperor since Frederick II, but he was also a realist. He believed that if power lay with the princes, they should bear some constitutional responsibility for all of Germany; even a confederation could maintain internal order and present some sort of a united front to the outside world. The Golden Bull, which he promulgated in 1356, regularized electoral machinery and established a kind of central authority. The emperor was to be chosen by a majority vote of seven lay and ecclesiastical electors: the king of Bohemia, the Count Palatine of the Rhine, the Margrave of Brandenburg, the duke of Saxony, and the archbishops of Mainz, Cologne, and Trier. The Bull also tried to establish a semi-permanent

Emperor Charles IV and his Son Wenceslaus at a Banquet Given by King Charles V of France in the 1370's. The banquet crowned a huge celebration in honor of the emperor's visit to Paris. Although emperors had little real authority at home in Germany by this time, their prestige remained unparalleled among the princes of Christendom. (Bibliothèque Nationale, Paris.)

concert or committee of electors to supervise German affairs but nothing came of it. A *Reichstag,* or Diet, was called occasionally, in which the electors met as a first "estate," the lesser princes as a second, and urban representatives as a third; but its function was largely ceremonial. It could not raise money or maintain an army, or for that matter keep the public peace. The emperor was virtually powerless and the Diet was determined that he remain that way.

The Golden Bull gave strong impetus to the evolution of princely power in Germany. Although far slower and never so complete, the political tendency in each of the large and small principalities was similar to that in the great monarchies. The rulers sought to augment their authority in

CHRISTIAN RECONQUEST OF SPAIN

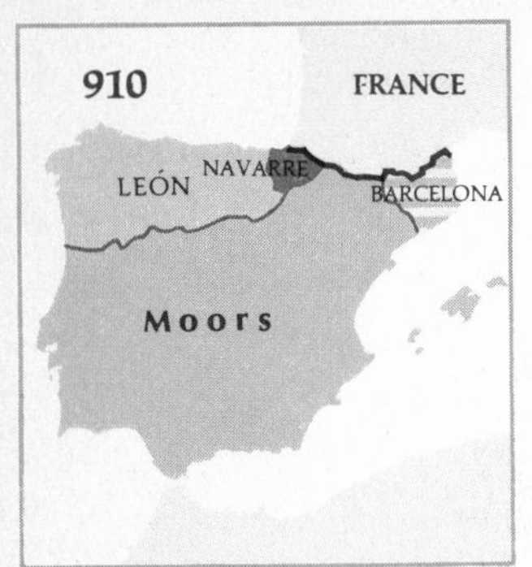

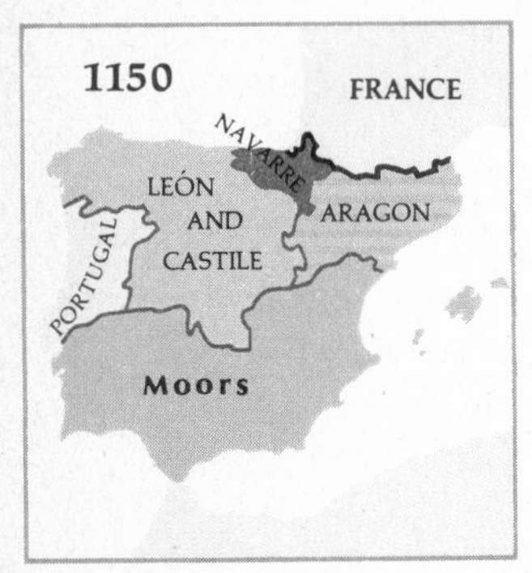

their own territories, to suppress the remnants of feudalism, to introduce centralized financial and judicial institutions, and so on. Like the kings of England and France, they were continually in need of money and were obliged to appeal to their subjects. Thus, representative bodies of estates called *Landtage* appeared. Indeed, in most of the states they gained considerable influence. At the same time, free cities developed. Self-governing, and owing only nominal allegiance to the emperor, these cities grew fat on trade and industry. By the close of the fifteenth century there were more than two hundred separate political entities in Germany. It is not surprising, therefore, that disorder, crime and even petty war were continuous. The breakdown of imperial authority had brought chaos in its wake.

The Habsburgs This was the political condition of Germany when the Habsburgs finally won *de facto* control of the imperial crown in the fifteenth century. From Albert V (1438–1439) in a line only momentarily broken in the mid-1700's up to the Napoleonic wars, scions of this house were elected emperor. Albert V was insignificant and harmless. Frederick III (1440–1493) was perhaps the weakest of all the late medieval emperors, a man who made his monogram A. E. I. O. U. (*Austria est imperare orbi universo,* "Austria has imperial sway over the world") a joke. But he was lucky, for the hereditary lands he frittered away were consolidated again under his son, Maximilian, whom he arranged to marry to the daughter and sole heiress of Charles, duke of Burgundy. Thus, when Maximilian I became emperor in 1493, he joined the Austrian lands with the Netherlands.

Maximilian was also a dynast to whom the Empire was merely a stepping-stone to personal and family greatness and more specifically a source of money. He used the unsettled European situation as an excuse to bargain with the Diet, although with little profit. A charming man and a dreamer, he was known to contemporaries as *Massimiliano pochi denari* ("Maximilian always broke"). After assuring himself that the cause of monarchy was indeed hopeless in Germany, he acquiesced without heart to several constitutional innovations that might have strengthened the confederation and brought a measure of internal peace had not his and the princes' lack of interest and cooperation robbed them of their effectiveness. Maximilian's only real successes were dynastic. He joined his house with the recently united houses of Aragon and Castile by arranging the marriage of his son Philip to Joanna, daughter of Ferdinand and Isabella, and with the house of Hungary by arranging the marriage of his daughter Mary to the king of Hungary's son. The child of the marriage of Philip and Joanna was the great Emperor Charles V, heir to half the world.

THE IBERIAN KINGDOMS

We have not as yet looked at the Iberian kingdoms in the Middle Ages. Their history during that period was confused and chaotic, but unified by the central event of medieval Iberian life: the *Reconquista,* the centuries-long series of wars by which Christian crusaders freed the peninsula from the Moors. The wars, begun before Charlemagne when only the far north was in Christian hands, did not end until 1492, when Granada in the far south was taken. The Iberian kingdoms of Leon, Castile, Navarre, Aragon, and Portugal, and the counties of Barcelona (usually called Catalonia), and Valencia were established in the wake of the slow Muslim retreat. The Reconquest gave birth to Portugal and Spain; it was the greatest and most successful of the crusades engaged in by the European peoples.

The Moorish occupation and Reconquest gave a unique quality to Iberian history and were decisive in shaping the character of the Spanish and Portuguese. The languages with their numerous Arabic words, the music with its distinctive Near Eastern harmonies, the architecture with its minarets and oddly pointed arches; these are only three of the obvious legacies of Islamic culture. More important was the long crusade itself, its effect on political institutions, on social patterns, and on cultural and religious ideals. All were forged in war—religious war—and all reflected their origins.

Iberian institutions and society resembled those of France and England, but also differed in important ways. There were kings and counts, royal courts using Roman law, representative assemblies, and so on. But there was, for example, no feudalism of the true northern European sort outside of Navarre, where French influence was strong. Rather, the Iberian kings were military leaders, the nobles their lieutenants, not their vassals, bound by a simple oath of loyalty easily abrogated, not by a reciprocal contract. In theory, all reconquered land belonged to the king who gave it, together with certain rights attached to it, into the custody of his lieutenants as a reward for services and in return for their promise to pacify it, encourage Christians to settle on it, and convert its Muslim inhabitants. These pieces of land were vast, and the nobles—called *grandees*—who held them were tremendously rich and powerful. Their wealth, their special privileges (they paid no direct taxes, for example), the fortresses and castles they occupied, and the large private armies they commanded often made them for practical purposes independent of the crown. The grandees were the chief obstacle in the way of increased royal authority in the late Middle Ages and early modern times.

The Iberian kings, particularly the kings of Castile and Leon (which were united in the thirteenth century and thereafter usually called simply Castile) and Portugal, preferred to assert their authority and derive their resources from the many towns they founded or recaptured in former Muslim territory. Christian colonists had been settled in these towns which, unlike their northern counterparts, were really frontier outposts, their inhabitants pioneers in a hostile land. Each town had been granted extremely liberal privileges of self-government by a charter called a *fuero.* But the kings had been generally successful even during times of weakest monarchy in maintaining some judicial and tax authority, and when they needed money they turned to the towns. The earliest "third estate" in Europe, called together in the late twelfth century as a representative assembly with clergy and nobility, was made up of Iberian townsmen, and its chief business was royal finances.

Levels of Lawmaking. Medieval and late medieval men revered the law and held the application of justice as the first duty of government. Here in this fifteenth century representation laws are seen being made, broken, and the guilty punished. (The Pierpont Morgan Library.)

There were several of these *Cortes,* as they were called. In the kingdom of Castile, it was the creature of the crown. Although a few occasions of recalcitrance can be cited, most of the time it assented humbly to the king's requests for money. Indeed, it became so amenable to royal pressure that nobles and ecclesiastics, who paid no direct taxes, stopped attending its meetings by the end of the fifteenth century. The *Cortes* of Castile, like the Estates General of France, was also a useful device for sounding out public opinion and winning support for royal policy. In Portugal, the *Cortes* showed a freer spirit; it was generally tight-fisted and played a more conspicuous role in policy making. And, in the so-called "Crown" of Aragon, comprising the kingdom of Aragon with Catalonia and Valencia, each with a *Cortes,* stubborn opposition was the rule. The Catalonian assembly, dominated by the middle-class businessmen of the city of Barcelona, was particularly sensitive to the slightest royal threat to its ancient rights. But those of Aragon and Valencia were hardly more cooperative. The king could bend none of them to his will. Doubtless the independence of these Aragonese *Cortes* and the subservience of the Castilian—and therefore the much superior financial position of the Castilian king—goes far to explain why Castile in time developed the strongest of the Iberian monarchies and dominated the peninsula.

Castile and Aragon The rise of Spain under Castile's leadership will be examined in a later chapter. In the fourteenth century, the Castilian monarchy was still weak and beset by war against neighboring Christian kingdoms and Moors and by rebellions of powerful and ambitious grandees. Only occasionally did Castile bring forth an effective king. Alfonso X, "the Wise" (1252–1282), issued one of the great law codes of the Middle Ages in the *Siete Partidas* (1254). Founded chiefly on Roman law, this code was an attempt to institute a common law for all of Castile. But it was ahead of its time and was not adopted for a hundred years and then not in its entirety. Ironically, Alfonso X himself was deposed by his own nobility in a manner contrary to his law code.

Alfonso XI (1312–1349) was less visionary, more concerned with power than justice. He understood that his financial strength depended on his controlling the Castilian towns. Therefore, he sent into most of them a new official, the *corregidor,* to supervise royal justice and tax collection. He also introduced a sales tax, the *alcabala,* which struck townspeople most heavily. At the same time, he overawed his nobility by his military prowess. But, though a great success while alive, the royal authority he wielded was very personal and did not survive him. For a century and a quarter after his death, Castile was prey to rivalries among pretenders to the throne and civil wars brought on by over-mighty nobles seeking to control the throne themselves. Not until the reign of the great Isabella at the end of the fifteenth century did internal peace and order return.

The Crown of Aragon, its strength and prestige derived largely from its association with Catalonia, pretended to a role in European politics during the years that Castile, in turmoil, turned in on itself. In 1412, a serious succession problem was solved by the Compromise of Caspe, the three *Cortes* settling on the Castilian claimant who became Ferdinand I (1412–1416). Ferdinand's sons, Alfonso V (1416–1458), and John II (1458–1479), spent much of their time pursuing the Mediterranean policy of Catalonia, protecting and extending the "empire" brought together by the Catalans under the leadership of the merchants of Barcelona. To Majorca, the Balearics, Sardinia, and Sicily, Corsica and the kingdom of Naples were added by mid-century. Alfonso was so taken up with the glory of his conquests that he moved his court to Naples, leaving his brother John as regent to deal with problems at home.

And problems there were, most pressing an incipient revolt in Catalonia. The great prosperity founded on commerce enjoyed by Barcelona in the Middle Ages had waned by 1450. Depression combined with social conflict affecting all classes from peasants to nobles brought open revolution in the early 1460s. John II, newly crowned, won out after ten years of confusing and destructive fighting. But the Catalonian economy was in ruin. The Crown, so dependent on Catalonian prosperity, was never so poor or weak, and the Crown's Mediterranean commitments remained. John's solution was to put all his considerable energy and intelligence into arranging the marriage of his son Ferdinand to the princess of Castile. The marriage of

Ferdinand and Isabella united Spain. Aragon was the junior partner, but Ferdinand gained the resources to carry on his father's policies.

FURTHER READING

Best on this period now is D. Hay, *Europe in the Fourteenth and Fifteenth Centuries* (1966). Two other recent general works on the late Middle Ages are W. K. Ferguson, *Europe in Transition, 1300–1520* (1962); and S. Harrison Thomson, *Europe in Renaissance and Reformation* (1963). An older survey, still a useful interpretation though somewhat dated, is E. Cheyney, * *Dawn of a New Era, 1205–1453* (1936), which contains an extensive, revised bibliography. See also J. Hale, et al., eds., *Europe in the Late Middle Ages* (1965); and M. Aston, * *The Prospect of Europe: The Fifteenth Century* (1968), which tries hard to be contemporary in its emphasis on social and cultural history.

The best survey of France in the fourteenth and fifteenth centuries is contained in É. Perroy, * *The Hundred Years' War* (1951), which also includes much on England as well as an excellent detailed treatment of the war itself. P. S. Lewis, ed., * *The Recovery of France in the Fifteenth Century* (1972), does not fulfill the promise of its title, but is useful on certain special subjects.

For England, the *Oxford* series includes M. McKisack, *The Fourteenth Century, 1307–99* (1959), and E. F. Jacob, *The Fifteenth Century, 1399–1485* (1961). A. R. Myers, * *England in the Later Middle Ages* (rev. ed., 1956), is readable and good. G. M. Trevelyan, * *England in the Age of Wycliff* (4th ed., 1909), is a classic work by a great modern historian.

For Germany, the most easily available work, which is a bit sketchy on this period, is G. Barraclough, * *The Origins of Modern Germany* (1949). F. L. Carsten, *Princes and Parliaments in Germany* (1959), is more specialized but good; and G. Strauss, *Manifestations of Discontent in Germany on the Eve of the Reformation* (1971), a collection of contemporary sources, is better than any secondary work extant in clarifying the German problem of the fifteenth century.

There is little good in English on the Iberian peninsula in the late Middle Ages, but W. C. Atkinson, * *A History of Spain and Portugal* (1960), provides a short survey. Traditional, but all there is in English, is H. V. Livermore, *A History of Portugal* (1947).

*Books available in paperback edition are marked with an asterisk.

2 The Church

The Roman Church, with the papacy at its head, also fell on hard times after the middle of the thirteenth century. Although it continued to wield immense financial and judicial power throughout Christendom, it slowly lost its political and, more crucial by far, its moral influence. It ceased to command the affection, the respect, and the unquestioned obedience it had had in the days of Innocent III. The Church had become secularized. In the two centuries since Pope Gregory VII had won its independence and bestowed on it the mission of unifying and pacifying feudal Europe, it had grown into a community of tens of thousands, its headquarters at Rome filled with a veritable army of bureaucrats, its papal court large, lavish, and immensely expensive. Spirituality had inevitably given way to worldliness. Participation in secular affairs had become the pope's chief task. The business of religion had become more important than religion itself and among most churchmen, defense and perpetuation of the institution more vital than the care of men's souls. The long struggle with the Hohenstaufen and the more recent but equally sharp battles with other secular rulers sapped the Church's prestige by emphasizing its worldliness. And these battles were only beginning. The rise of the secular states challenged the pope's claim to universal dominion. Every ruler, whether king, duke, despot, or free-city council, sought to divest himself of foreign authorities, of which the Church was the strongest. Furthermore, this new force, the secular state, was unifying the people of Europe in a different way, at the same time demanding their undivided loyalty and allegiance. The Church could not halt this inexorable tide; it could only be hurt by it.

BONIFACE VIII AND PHILIP THE FAIR

The struggle broke into the open during the papacy of Boniface VIII (1294–1303). Boniface was a tough and ambitious man, wholly convinced of his own righteousness and the righteousness of the traditional papal position. He claimed all the authority to manage the affairs of Christendom that Innocent III had claimed, and more. He ran headlong into King Philip the Fair of France. The issue was a significant one: in principle, whether a secular ruler was master of his own house; in practice whether Philip had the right to tax and judge all his subjects, both clerical and lay. The king had no doubts in the matter. In 1296, he ordered the French clergy to support him with money in his war against England. Complaints reached the pope, who issued the bull *Clericis Laicos* forbidding such taxation without papal sanction, under pain of excommunication. Philip's stubborn resistance caused Boniface to back down for a time. But the fight resumed shortly, this time over Philip's claim to civil jurisdiction over a French bishop who had incurred his enmity. It seemed a trivial issue, but it was one on which Boniface chose to take his stand. He reiterated the points made in *Clericis Laicos,* and in a harangue opening the Jubilee Year 1300, he made even more extravagant claims for papal supremacy. A pamphlet war broke out, one side denying the pope's right to secular power absolutely, the other confirming it in strongest terms. King Philip IV took more direct action. With the support of the Estates General and armed with the ideas of a Roman lawyer named William of Nogaret, he had drawn up a list of charges against Boniface accusing the old man of heresy, sorcery, murder, and sexual perversion, and declaring his election illegal. Nogaret then set off in the summer of 1303 to apprehend the culprit for trial. The lawyer with a few hundred soldiers found Boniface in his summer home at Anagni in early September. Seated fully robed on his throne, the pope was an impressive figure and Nogaret gave up his plan of capture. Indeed, the aroused citizenry of Anagni rioted until the invaders fled the city. But the shock and humiliation were too much for Boniface who died soon afterwards. His successor, Benedict XI (1303–1304), sensed the winds of change and let Philip have his way. The papacy was never again the same.

At the height of the battle of words in 1302, Boniface VIII issued the bull *Unam Sanctam,* setting out his claim of papal supremacy in uncompromising terms. In it, he propounded the doctrine of the "two swords":

We are told by the words of the Gospel that in [Christ's] fold there are two swords, a spiritual, namely, and a temporal. For when the apostles said, "Behold here there are two swords . . . the Lord did not reply that this was too much, but enough. . . . Both swords, the spiritual and the temporal . . . are in the power of the Church; the one, indeed, to be wielded for the Church, the other by the Church; the one by the hand of the priest, the other by the hands of kings and knights, but at the will and the sufferance of the priest. One sword, moreover, ought to be under the other, and the temporal authority subjected to the spiritual. . . .[1]

The pamphleteers employed by Philip the Fair were clever, but not up to an adequate answer. Within two decades, however, several answers had been found, of which the most effective was the *Defensor pacis,* "Defender of the Peace," by the Italian, Marsiglio of Padua, published in 1326 for Emperor Ludwig of Bavaria. Ludwig was at odds with Pope John XXII over

[1]This is the translation from E. F. Henderson, *Select Historical Documents of the Middle Ages* (London: George Ball, 1896).

the pope's claim to decide a disputed imperial election. Marsiglio was a theologian and Roman lawyer, a brilliant controversialist willing to attack the papal claims head on.

Marsiglio's aim was to prove unequivocally that political units of whatever kind were wholly independent of the pope in matters both spiritual and temporal. ". . . The efficient power to establish or elect the ruler belongs to the legislator or the whole body of citizens, just as does the power to make laws," he wrote.[2] He denied that the pope possessed any special authority as bishop of Rome, arguing that he and all bishops were equally successors of the apostles. Therefore,

It is the sentence of judgement . . . of the legislator, or the ruler by his authority . . . that must approve or disapprove candidates for ecclesiastical orders, and appoint them to a major or minor post or headship, and remove them therefore or prohibit them to exercise it, or even, if out of malice they refuse to exercise their office, compel them to do so. . . .

He even went so far as to insist that, not the pope but a "general council composed of all Christians or of the weightier part of them, or to those persons who have been granted such authority by the whole body of Christian believers" should run the Church and decide "doubtful questions" of doctrine.

The *Defensor Pacis* was extreme for its time and for this reason and because it was condemned by the Church was not immediately influential. It was used later in the century, however, to help justify Conciliar theories (see below) and thereafter by numerous rebels and patriots at ideological war with the Holy See. Most notable of these was Martin Luther, whose appeal to Germany to accept his religious reformation was founded on Marsiglio's anti-papal arguments.

THE AVIGNONESE PAPACY AND THE GREAT SCHISM

On the death of Benedict XI, the bishop of Bordeaux, probably with the connivance of Philip the Fair, was elected Clement V (1305–1313) and took up his residence in 1309 at Avignon, a city in Provence. For close to seventy years, the popes remained at Avignon, which became a papal possession, while Rome fell prey to banditry and economic decay. In the minds of the Avignonese popes the "Babylonian Captivity" (as the Florentine poet Petrarch bitterly labeled it) was temporary. Each intended to return to the city of St. Peter but each was a Frenchman with a certain loyalty—though by no means subservience—to the kings of France, who naturally enough found the situation to their advantage. Furthermore, even before the popes took up residence at Avignon the Papal States in Italy showed signs of incipient anarchy. The Roman nobility, among the most irresponsible in

[2]This and the following quotations are the translation of A. Genvirth, *Marsilius of Padua: the Defender of Peace,* Vol. II (New York: Columbia University Press, 1956).

The Palace of the Popes, Avignon. This magnificent structure suggests much about the wealth and worldly values of the Avignonese papacy. (Giraudon.)

Europe, were concerned not at all with order but only with expanding their country estates; the ambitious rulers of Milan and Naples made use of every opportunity to gain territory at the pope's expense; the communes and principalities subject to Rome pressed always for greater autonomy. Only a forceful pope, resident at Rome, could preserve some sort of authority within the Papal States. Absence provoked anarchy and anarchy kept the pope away from Rome.

Certainly the papacy, as distinct from the Church at large, suffered few privations from the long sojourn at Avignon. Indeed, this period was one of the most glorious in papal history, if glory be measured in administrative excellence and fiscal efficiency. The Avignonese popes were on the whole hard-working and imaginative administrators. One can point particularly to John XXII (1316–1334) and Benedict XII (1334–1342). They and their successors were primarily interested in buttressing and extending papal authority over the Church itself rather than in carrying on the essentially secular struggle of Boniface VIII. Part of their effort was directed at assuring themselves large and regular revenues. Expenses were huge for the new papal palace at Avignon, for the magnificent papal court, for the cardinals, curia, and papal armies (used for self-protection and in unsuccessful attempts to pacify the distant Papal States). From a typical medieval institution with its wealth in land, the papacy came to depend chiefly on money revenues. These ranged from Peter's Pence, a small but traditional levy on England and several other kingdoms, to "services" and "annates," the most important of all. "Services" were taxes, usually one-third the annual income, from benefices for which the pope had "provided" incumbants. The practice of "reserving" archbishoprics, bishoprics, and abbacies for papal "provision" was vastly extended during the period of the Avignonese papacy. "Annates," or first fruits, were the entire first year's income from certain of the "reserved" benefices. Other important sources of revenue were "voluntary gifts"—extraordinary levies on the clergy and hardly voluntary—indulgences for good works, and fees paid for papal dispensation from such canonical prohibitions as marriage between relatives closer than third cousins.

The necessity for this money grubbing, at least from the pope's point of view, was lost on most contemporaries, and criticism of papal avariciousness was widespread. Mammon seemed to have captured the See of St. Peter. "Whenever I entered the chambers of the ecclesiastics of the papal court, I found brokers and clergy reckoning the money which lay in heaps before them," wrote a Spanish official. "No poor man can approach the pope. He will call and no one will answer because he has no money in his purse to pay."

Equal in importance to revenues for the Avignonese popes—though revenues were certainly a factor in efforts to achieve it—was re-establishment of their right of appointment to and supervision of high ecclesiastical positions. Traditionally, in the Middle Ages, as we have seen, princes and other powerful men controlled the appointment of prelates, and often popes had little real say in the matter. Moreover, once appointed, the prelates were virtually independent of papal authority. Beginning with Innocent III in the early thirteenth century, papal theory held that all ecclesiastical offices were at the disposal of the pope by virtue of his *plenitudo potestatis,* his unlimited power. By the practice of "reservation" described above, the successors of Innocent III and especially the Avignonese popes increased and broadened their jurisdictional authority to include most of the benefices in Europe. Indeed, never before or since was papal authority within the Church so great. But its time was short; popes could not win against the power and ambition of secular rulers. The transformation from the late medieval to the Renaissance papacy came quickly and the new was significantly different from the old.

The Great Schism The Great Schism had much to do with the speed of this transformation. Begun in 1378, the Great Schism lasted until 1417. In 1377, Gregory XI (1370–1378), under heavy pressure from Italians in particular, moved back to Rome. The city had gone to seed, its economy, dependent on the papal presence, ruined, and its society, prey to bloody feuding among the great families, in utter disorder. When Gregory died in early 1378, fear of the Roman mob caused the cardinals to elect an Italian as Urban VI (1378–1389), apparently against their better judgement. Their hesitancy was justified, for Urban proved himself little short of a madman, violent, insulting, jealous of the cardinals, neglectful of curial business. In August a rump session of French cardinals declared Urban's election to have taken place under duress. They proceeded to elect a Frenchman, who took the name Clement VII (1378–1394). Clement took up residence at Avignon. Thus began a forty-year period in which scandalized Europeans watched as two

St. Catherine of Siena. This fresco by her disciple Andrea Vanni was painted in the early fifteenth century in the Sienese style. Catherine, like most women of her time, could barely read or write, but she possessed immense character and inward strength. By the sheer force of her spirituality she convinced Pope Gregory XI to return to Rome in 1378 from his Babylonian captivity at Avignon. (Church of S. Dominic, Siena/Alinari-Scala.)

popes, each convinced of his own legitimacy, each claiming the spiritual powers of St. Peter, each administering the Church, collecting taxes and naming prelates, villified each other in the most terrible terms. Europe took sides, France and its friends supporting Avignon, the rest, notably England, supporting Rome. A council of cardinals meeting at Pisa in 1409 to find a solution ended by electing a third pope! From 1409 to 1415 there were three popes. Christendom was in spiritual chaos. Spiritual loyalty gave way to purely political considerations, for no one could be sure who was the true pope. And the European, whatever else he may have been, was still a religious man. Hence, he felt a deep resentment and fear. Who could say whether a bishop had been rightfully consecrated, and more important, whether a priest the bishop had ordained was a true priest, capable of performing his sacramental duties? Some said that no soul entered heaven during the entire period of the Great Schism.

LATE MEDIEVAL RELIGION AND CONCILIARISM

Reactions to the Babylonian Captivity and the Great Schism were bitter and various. Governments opposed the growing centralization of Church administration during the Avignonese papacy. The money conscious begrudged papal taxation. Ecclesiastical politicians resented papal interference in local Church affairs, in defiance of the traditions of local election. The pious everywhere were disturbed by papal worldliness and corruption and horrified by the spectacle of a two-headed Church. Of the secular governments, England acted most strongly. A number of laws, known collectively as the Statutes of Provisors and Praemunire, were issued in the second half of the fourteenth century seeking to limit papal administrative and judicial authority in England. Elsewhere, there were similar though less forceful efforts. The thinking that motivated them was to give impetus to the development of the so-called "national" churches, the "English Church," the "Spanish Church," the "Gallican (French) Church," and so on. These churches were considered by their leaders as members of the Universal Church, whose head was the bishop of Rome, but as possessing a large degree of administrative independence. Thus, the Gallican Church asserted a claim to elect a hierarchy, collect taxes, and in other ways manage ecclesiastical affairs in France with only nominal reference to papal supremacy. In general, secular government and princes favored this development, for it simplified their job of unifying and centralizing the state.

Spiritual life among the masses of people was shaped in part by the situation in which the papacy found itself. The sanctity and dedication of prelates and parish priests probably reached a nadir around 1400. Although the Avignonese popes had made some attempt to reform the secular and regular clergy, the results were minimal. Bishops, often absentee, left diocesan business to underlings, themselves often corrupt; priests were frequently illiterate and immoral; monks and friars lazy and mercenary. In 1429, a provincial synod at Paris enacted forty-one canons, among them:

> *2. Clergy are forbidden to gossip or laugh in church, or to play foolish or unbecoming games on holidays, at any rate during divine service.*

7. The sacred vessels and appointments will be kept clean; dancing, profane songs, games and markets will not be held in sacred precincts.

8. Bishops will not ordain any clerk not of good life, who does not know the Epistles and Gospels, who cannot read and sufficiently understand the rest of the service. Some who wish to have the sub-diaconate are unaware that this involves continence: they must be told in advance. No one will be inducted into the cure of souls without previous examination, with particular reference to the administration of the sacraments and his own morals.

11. The officers of episcopal courts extort money and perpetrate every kind of irregularity; bishops will reform their courts. . . .

14. Abbots and monks will not dwell outside their monasteries. They will follow exactly the old rules for costume. In particular, they are forbidden to wear short tunics, long cloaks, silver belts, etc.

22. Blasphemy and perjury among the clergy should be punished twice as severely as among laymen.

23. Concubinage is so common among the clergy that it has given rise to the view that simple fornication is not a mortal sin. No bishop shall tolerate any clerk living in concubinage, still less will he allow his connivance to be purchased.[3]

The late Middle Ages was also a time of economic decline and social disruption. The relative stability of an earlier day gave way to rapid, and what was for many Europeans traumatic, change. The nature of this change is described in the next chapter. Combined with the unhappy condition of the Church, it drove many people into a more individualistic spirituality, personalized mysticism at best, ignorant superstition at worst. Around the Virgin Mary a cult was created; the saints were venerated with more ardor than ever before. Great preachers such as San Bernardino da Siena, who flayed their listeners with dire threats of hellfire, were immensely popular. Less orthodox but equally commonplace was the virtual worship of relics, usually bogus, and images of Christ, the Virgin, and the saints. The sale of indulgences also increased as the doctrine of Purgatory gained acceptance. Even less wholesome was the wider incidence of witchcraft and black magic; the first papal bull condemning these practices was issued in the fifteenth century.

(Opposite page) *San Bernardino of Siena Preaching before the Church of St. Francis in his Native Town.* Bernardino was one of Italy's most popular preachers in the early fifteenth century, drawing hundreds of listeners to his earthy, but deeply spiritual, sermons. He thundered against vanity, sexual license, and bad government in a way that made sense to city people with urban problems. (Duomo, Siena/Anderson-Scala.)

But this was more or less orthodox and the Church could accommodate it. More serious were the several heresies that flourished. The most typical of these were more than anti-papal; they were anti-institutional, stressing the idea of a more simple Church, stripped of material wealth and political power and reunified by a recrudescence of individual piety. The more radical envisaged a Church patterned on that of the Apostles. The Spiritual Franciscans, strict observants of St. Francis' rule, were declared heretics by Pope John XXII for teaching that neither priest nor pope had the right to own

[3]Reprinted in Denys Hay, *Europe in the Fourteenth and Fifteenth Centuries* (New York: Holt, Rinehart & Winston, 1966), pp. 304–305.

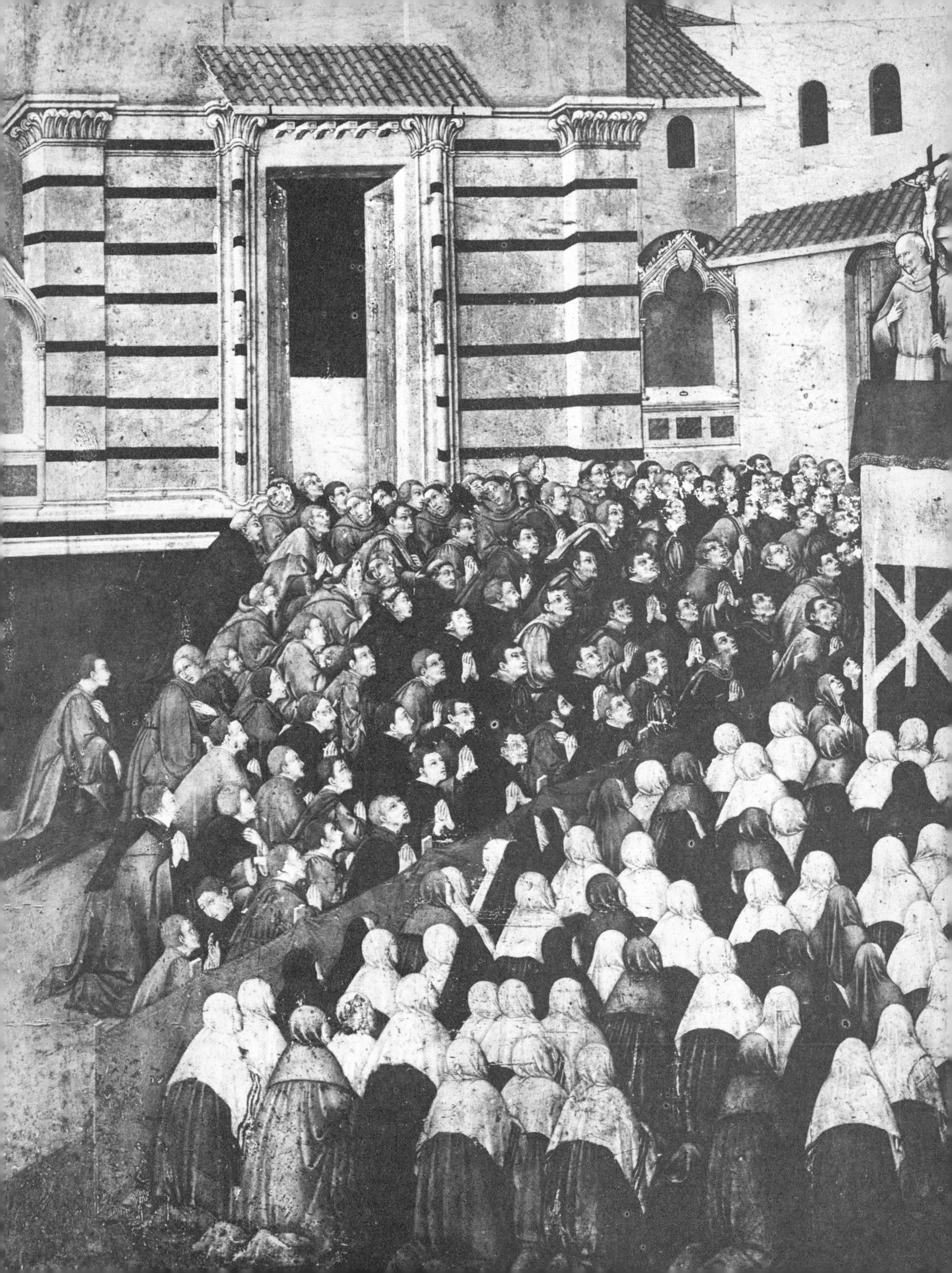

property. The most famous and influential of the Spirituals was the theologian William of Occam (1280–1342), whose brilliant tracts against Thomistic theology on the one hand and papal authority on the other were used by such disparate figures as Emperor Ludwig of Bavaria in the fourteenth century and Martin Luther in the sixteenth. Marsiglio of Padua also came under the influence of the Spirituals.

Jan Hus. The Bohemian religious reformer was burned at the stake in 1415 by the good fathers of the Council of Constance. Although not very radical, his condemnation was the simplest way for the Council to root out heresy. (Lutherhalle, Wittenburg.)

Lollards and Hussites The Spirituals were mystics, adherents to Augustinian rather than Thomistic theology, but their doctrines were for the most part orthodox. John Wyclif (1320–1384), an Englishman, and Jan Hus (1369–1415), a Bohemian Czech, taught heretical doctrines and criticized the Church as an institution. Wyclif was a scholar, a master at Oxford, where the ideas of William of Occam survived. Argumentative and bold, he attacked the temporal claims of the papacy while asserting that the Bible was the sole source of spiritual authority. In many ways he prefigured the men of the Protestant Reformation in advocating salvation by faith alone and in denying the real presence of Christ in the bread and wine of the Mass. But he was a rebel born before his time. The Wyclifites, or "Lollards" as they were called, became fairly numerous, especially among the lower classes. The Church, however, supported by the crown, was able to suppress them.

The Hussites were more successful; indeed, under their banner the first successful revolt from Rome was accomplished. Jan Hus, a master at the University of Prague, had drawn some of his doctrines from Wyclif. Around him sprang up a religious movement that permeated the Czech population of Bohemia and took on a strong patriotic coloring when the German element at the university and among the population opposed it. Riots broke out in 1410 and both sides took up arms. Hus was summoned before the Council of Constance to answer charges of heresy, condemned, and burned despite a guarantee of safety. But the Czechs fought on, and the "Hussite Wars" continued for several decades. Both popes and emperors failed to quell the determined revolutionaries. In 1436, the Hussites, whose radicals were already losing out to those with views closer to the old Church, were granted religious concessions, chiefly the right to receive both bread and wine at communion. The Hussite Church, as it emerged from the conflict, was far more Roman in its beliefs and practices than Hus himself had been.

Conciliarism and the "Renaissance Papacy" Within the Church itself, the Great Schism provoked another kind of rebellion, momentarily far more dangerous to the papacy than either secular legislation or heresy. This was "Conciliarism," the theory that the Universal Church, the body of the faithful as represented by their bishops assembled in "Council," held spiritual and temporal authority above the pope and cardinals. The theory's origins may be traced to the doctrines of the twelfth and thirteenth century canonists and were doubtless influenced to some extent by the evolution of the parliamentary idea in secular governments. But Conciliarism came to the fore only with the Schism, for which it seemed to provide an answer. By the very nature of their claim, neither of the rival popes could give way to the other voluntarily or submit to arbitration by authorities they considered their inferiors. The advocates of Conciliarism, however, held that the papal claim was false and that a Council was the pope's superior. Therefore, they said, the Council could depose one or both rivals and elect a true pope, healing the rupture in Christendom. At the same time, a Council could effectively extirpate heresy and reform ecclesiastical abuses. The more radical Conciliarists went even further, striking at the very heart of the papal doctrine of spiritual autocracy by advocating the right of Councils to help rule the Church. If carried out, this concept would have transformed the Church government into a constitutional monarchy.

The Conciliar Movement—and it had come to be that by the beginning of the fifteenth century—gained the support of most princes and many churchmen. The abortive council called by the Conciliarists at Pisa in 1409 was followed by another, which met at Constance in what is now Switzerland from 1414 to 1418. The Council of Constance was successful in its major aim: it healed the Schism. The council fathers deposed the Avignonese pope and the successor to the pope elected at Pisa, and convinced the Roman pope to resign. In 1417, they elected Cardinal Oddo Colonna, member of a great Roman family, as Martin V (1417–1431). The fathers also declared themselves bound to extirpate heresy and "to reform the Church in head and members." The first was symbolically accomplished by the burning of Jan Hus in 1415. Accomplishment of the second, so important to the future health of the Church and all Christendom, was stalled from the first by political considerations and wrangling among the fathers themselves. Everyone gave lip service to the need for reform, but few were willing to surrender their own vested interests. Some action was taken before the election of Martin V, but it was on relatively minor matters. After his election, Martin was able to keep the fathers divided, getting them to agree to leave additional measures to him. He, of course, was fearful that truly substantive reform would limit his own power and prerogatives.

The Council of Constance adjourned in 1418 with plans having been made for periodic future councils. Indeed, the decrees *Sacrosancta* (1415), which declared a council superior to the pope, and *Frequens* (1417), which established regular council meetings, were a kind of constitution for a new sort of Church, one to be ruled chiefly by council. Councils met first at Pavia (transferred to Siena) in 1424 and then at Basle in Switzerland from 1431 to 1449. Both clung tightly to a rigid Conciliarist position, and an open break with the pope took place in the 1430's when the fathers began systematically to strip away the sources of papal income. If they had been successful, these actions would have left the pope entirely dependent on the council for money. But Eugenius IV (1431–1447) fought back with spirit and imagination. He declared Basle dissolved and called a council of his own: this Council of Ferrara-Florence (1438–1439) briefly reunited the Roman with the Eastern Orthodox Church and brought Eugenius great prestige. He also won the support of most of Europe's secular rulers by giving up many of the papal judicial and financial rights that the rulers believed to conflict with their own. In return they promised to recognize his spiritual headship of the Church. The fathers at Basle countered by "deposing" Eugenius and electing an anti-pope, Felix V, but they had no real hope of winning. After 1449, Conciliarism, although a living idea until the mid-sixteenth century, was no longer a movement threatening the papacy. By the bull *Execrabilis* (1460), Pius II (1458–1464) forbade anyone to appeal from a pope to a council under pain of anathema.

Thus the popes of the fifteenth century re-established the old papal autocracy. But it was a different autocracy from before, for many of the sources of its strength had gone to pay for victory over Conciliarism. The deals made with secular rulers had given to the "national" churches, whose existence we have noted, most of the wealth and authority exercised previously by the pope himself. The Gallican Church, for example, by the Pragmatic Sanction of Bourges (1438) abolished the practices of reservation

The Renaissance Pope Pius II Crowned by the Virgin Mary. Siena, his native town, and of which Mary was patron and protector, is below. In the upper corners are the imperial eagle (as Aneaus Silvius Piccolomini, Pius was ambassador to the emperor) and the coats of arms of Siena. (State Archives, Siena/Alinari-Scala.)

and provision, thus eliminating services and annates, and declared its intention to elect prelates to the benefices of France. Substantially the same rights were successfully claimed by other national churches, including those of Spain and England. The result was seriously to limit the pope's administrative authority and, above all, to cause his income to plummet disastrously. The total annual income of the papacy in the fifteenth century was only a fraction of what it had been in the Avignon period, and almost half of it came from the pope's own Papal States. Hence it is not surprising that to protect and bring order to the Papal States was uppermost in the minds of these "Renaissance popes." To do so, they were forced to play the role of Italian princes, to maintain armies and practice diplomacy, a role hardly calculated to enhance their already fuzzy spiritual image. Although most Renaissance popes had a penchant for politics and pleasure, their worldliness was in large part the result of circumstances they could not control.

FURTHER READING

Most of the general works cited for the previous chapter have sections on the Church in this period. The classic study of the papacy, old but still invaluable for its detail, is L. von Pastor, *History of the Popes,* vols. I–VII (1905–1953). M. Creighton, *A History of the Papacy,* vols. I–IV (1887–1894), though fair, does not compare. A. C. Flick, *The Decline of the Medieval Church,* 2 vols. (1930), must be read with a critical eye. For students with French, the best studies are E. Delaruelle, et al., *L'eglise au Temps du Grand Schism et de la crise conciliaire* (1962–1964); and R. Aubenas, *L'eglise de la Renaissance, 1449–1517* (1951). On special subjects, T. Boase, *Boniface VIII* (1933), and W. Ullman, *The Origins of The Great Schism* (1948), are worth noting; as are B. Tierney, *Foundations of the Conciliar Theory* (1955); and the introductory essays in J. H. Mundy and D. M. Woody, *The Council of Constance* (1961). The standard work on Conciliarism after Constance is the monumental H. Jedin, *The Council of Trent,* vol. I (1957). The best recent study of the Avignonese papacy is G. Mollat, * *The Popes of Avignon, 1305–1378* (1963). Two late medieval heresies are treated in D. L. Muzzy, *The Spiritual Franciscans* (1907); and K. B. McFarlane, *John Wycliffe and the Beginning of English Nonconformity* (1952). On the Hussite wars, see H. Kaminsky, *A History of the Hussite Revolution* (1967). Views of the struggle between the papacy and France in the early fourteenth century are contained in C. T. Wood, ed., * *Philip the Fair and Boniface VIII* (1967). Perhaps the clearest insight into the Renaissance papacy remains *The Commentaries of Pius II* (ed. and trans. by F. A. Cragg and L. C. Gable, 1936–1957), which has been abridged as * *Memoirs of a Renaissance Pope* (1962).

*Books available in paperback edition are marked with an asterisk.

3 Economic and Social Developments

In most of northern Europe, the late Middle Ages was a time of economic and social as well as political crisis. The fourteenth and early fifteenth centuries were in bleak contrast to the prosperous centuries that went before. Population shrank, trade and manufacturing languished, and food was in short supply. Famine in the decades after 1300 was common, and to famine were added the ravage of war, disease, and social revolution. Europeans, who greeted the new century with optimism, were thrown into confusion, even despair, as their art, literature, and religious practices attest.

THE FALL IN POPULATION

After 1250 or so, the population of Europe stopped growing and in some areas began to decline. By the early fourteenth century, the decline was general. The number of people had simply outrun the quantity of food available. This is largely to be explained in terms of technological insufficiency; Europe, for the time, was over-urbanized. Given the primitive agricultural methods and the inadequate systems of transport—and given the fact that townspeople consumed food but had no hand in producing it—the land under cultivation could not supply Europe's needs.

The population decline was sharply accelerated by natural disasters, by the destruction of war, which caused sudden food shortages and famine, and by disease. Famine had always been a threat in a time of poor food storage and distribution, but it seems to have been more severe and more general in the early fourteenth century—probably because there were more people, particularly more townspeople, to starve. War, too, took on a more destructive character. Armies were composed mostly of mercenaries, soldiers who fought for money. Mercenaries, whether noble knights or peasants, cared little for noncombatants or for the land on which they fought. Looting and burning followed wherever they went.

Burying Victims of the Black Death at Tournai in the Netherlands. (Bibliothèque Royale, Brussels.)

Nature capped man's work by loosing the bubonic plague, the fearsome Black Death, for which there was neither warning nor remedy, on an unsuspecting Europe. Infected rats, bearing fleas and lice, which transmitted the disease to humans, are believed to have been carried from China in ships.

They reached Italy in late 1347 and within months had spread throughout the Italian peninsula, into Switzerland, Germany, and eastern Europe. The plague arrived in France early the following year, then moved on to Spain and England. For two years it raged, destroying between 35 and 65 percent of the urban and somewhat less of the rural population. Probably, famine and general undernourishment made more people susceptible and the death toll higher. The Black Death did not stop after one attack, but became endemic in Europe, breaking out time after time in the fourteenth and later centuries.

The fall in population seems to have been the major cause of economic decline. Commerce and industry contracted. The home market was smaller than before and this at a time when many foreign markets were lost because of changing political conditions in the Near East. Workers were fewer and wages higher; goods cost more, but profits were less. The rural economy was also affected, but in ways that our meager research can only let us guess at. Fewer mouths in town and countryside meant less consumption of agricultural products and lower prices. Where famine conditions had prevailed before the Black Death, now there were surpluses in many parts of Europe. But surpluses were only temporary. Rural workers, already in short supply, moved to the towns where wages were high. Lords were obliged to let some of their lands go fallow and give in to the demands for lower rents and better forms of tenure put forward by the remaining peasants. Manufactured goods rose in value while land values declined and agricultural income shrank. Many lords were impoverished and entire manors were abandoned. This contributed to the breakdown of the manorial system already underway.

The effects on the European spirit of depopulation and depression were many and extremely complex. Doubtless the Black Death killed off many of the best Europeans, those who did not flee but stayed behind to tend to their affairs or to care for the sick and dying. Certainly, the generation after 1348 seems to have been overburdened with second- and third-rate men. But the loss was only temporary. If the men of the 1360's and '70s were a lesser breed than their fathers, their sons were not. Their sons were merely different. From the great to the small, the following generation was changed—often subtly—in its attitudes and its aims. In broad terms, the change might be summed up as a loss of optimism. Having been confronted with death or stories of death, men of the post-plague generation were fatalistic about life, less ambitious and materialistic, less certain of this world and the next. The new mood is clearly stated in the literature and art, and is evident in the workings of society itself.

Not all classes of the population suffered equally from the Black Death or from its economic consequences. Hardest hit by the disease were the poor people of the towns, living in crowded hovels, often hungry. Most fortunate were the rich, both nobles and townspeople: they were better fed, better housed, usually able to escape the worst in their country houses. The mortality rates in rural areas are difficult to judge, but they are generally believed to have been lower than in the towns. If any class improved its economic position, it was the peasantry. The lords were in no position to resist peasants' demands for greater freedom. Workers in towns used the labor shortage to press for higher wages. The lower class in both town and country savored the benefits gained and wanted more; insurrections, not of the wholly oppressed but of those one step from oppression, brought on Europe's first age of revolution. To some degree, the character of the other classes also changed. Many noblemen and merchants died, to be replaced by new men, less steeped in tradition, less wedded to the ideas and methods of the past. The new nobility was perhaps less responsible than the old, as the political life of France and England suggests. The new businessmen were less adventurous, less willing to take risks for big profits, but they were more flexible, more willing to find profits in new places and by means of new techniques.

BREAKDOWN OF THE MANORIAL SYSTEM

By the beginning of the fourteenth century, the traditional pattern of medieval agriculture was giving way and the pattern of the future was being established. The manor before 1300 had ceased to be isolated, as it came more and more under the influence of an urban, money economy. The rise of towns; the expansion of trade; the improvements in communications; the introduction of new commodities in quantity; and, most of all, the greater amount of coin in circulation contributed to the uprooting of manorial self-sufficiency. The lord found the merchant's wares tempting. He sampled them, liked them, and came to depend on them. His taste developed and broadened, and what had before been rare luxuries became necessities, whether exotic spices from the Far East, elaborate armor from Milan, or fine wool cloth from Flanders. To acquire the cash he needed to buy, the lord began to sell the produce of his manor. The towns were a large and lucrative market. A few lords became capitalist farmers in areas where a single crop such as grain, fruit, or wine did particularly well. But most of them travelled an easier road. In effect, they abandoned active farming altogether, dividing up their demesne lands among free tenants who paid annual rents and commuting the dues of serfs who worked land held in tenure to money payments. For these lords, the manor became simply a source of money income.

This development had important economic and social consequences. The lord ceased to be the prince of a petty state, becoming instead a *rentier*, a modern "landlord." He no longer had personal ties to his peasants and often did not reside on his manor. As a *rentier*, he was prey to inflation, a condition that prevailed virtually throughout the late Middle Ages and early modern times. The arrangements he made with his tenants and former serfs stipulated fixed rents, and sums that may have been fully adequate at first shrunk as the years advanced. Lords with smaller holdings edged toward impoverishment, a movement hardly impeded by their extravagance and poor financial practices. These lords were often forced to sell out, usually to the rising men of the middle class, eager to better their social status by

From the Duc de Berry's Tres Riches Heures. Shearing sheep and cutting hay were some of the peasants' July labors. (Musée Condé/Giraudon.)

acquiring noble land. Other lords tried to supplement their income by entering the personal service of a greater lord or the king as mercenary soldiers or administrators. Thus, the social character of Europe's nobility was transformed.

The effects were no less important for Europe's peasants, who completed their slow climb to freedom. This process had begun, as we have seen, on the lands opened up by colonizers such as the Cistercian monks. Prospective settlers on these lands were usually offered free leases as an inducement, and many of them grabbed at the opportunity to escape servile status. Also, many serfs bought their freedom from lords in need of cash. The serfs paid a lump sum or regular installments in money or kind, signing a contract as free tenants or even leaving the manor to take up occupations in town. The effect over a period of time was to confuse what had formerly been a fairly clear relationship between the peasants and the land. For practical purposes, the tenants "owned" the land they held under contract and could even acquire more. Furthermore, they came to resent the rents they paid and sought to evade them, for they had come to think of themselves as owners. On the whole, time worked to their advantage. Their quasi-ownership became traditional, however strenuously the lord opposed it. Then, too, the inflation that ruined lords with small properties helped the peasants, for rents were established inalterably by contract. The depression did not arrest these general trends significantly. Instead, it stimulated them by further weakening the economic position of the lords. The progress of emancipation of the European peasantry was fastest in England, where all but a trace of serfdom disappeared by the end of the fifteenth century, and

A Medieval Windmill. To work efficiently, a mill's sails have to face squarely into the wind. In this case, the whole mill was simply turned by hand by means of the long "tailpole" shown here stretching from the mill to the ground. (Courtesy, Trustees of the British Museum.)

somewhat slower, though equally steady, in France, Germany, and the Iberian peninsula.

The breakdown of the manorial economy and its replacement by an economy based on money undermined the feudal system. Feudalism did not provide for payments in coin, whether for military services or for agricultural produce and physical labor. Money depersonalized what was an essentially personal, one may say patriarchal, relationship. The process inevitably created profound social tensions. The traditional security of both lords and peasants, founded on their self-sufficiency and mutual dependence, was destroyed. Now each man fended for himself. Thus occurred what appears superficially to be a paradox: the peasants, with their financial positions improved, revolted. Royalty everywhere benefited, for it was the king who inherited the responsibilities and the loyalties given up by the feudal lords.

COMMERCE MATURES

Throughout the thirteenth and into the fourteenth centuries, commerce and industry continued to prosper and the towns to grow. The area of most striking development was still Italy. There, in Venice, Florence, Genoa, Siena, Milan, and other cities, as will be seen in later chapters, an ideal geographic position combined with favorable political and social conditions to produce a glittering urban middle-class civilization. In northern Europe, the development was slower and less spectacular and the imprint of urbanism on society less marked, but it was noteworthy nevertheless. The towns of Flanders retained their leadership in the manufacture and sale of woolen cloth. England, by the reign of Edward I, was the principal supplier of raw wool for the Flemish drapers; and the English crown was deriving considerable tax revenue from the wool trade. The wine trade of Bordeaux, the last important French port in English hands, was also lucrative. French trade did not compare with Flemish or English, although Philip V made some effort to improve it. Its center remained the northeast, the area close to and under the influence of Flanders. But the most significant commercial growth in the century or so before depression hit was in the towns of Germany, and even during the depression, Germany seems to have suffered less than the older commercial areas of Europe.

The German Leagues The German towns had begun to trade in the eleventh and twelfth centuries, but their greatest period was the thirteenth and early fourteenth, for commerce, like agriculture, expanded to the east, beating against the frontiers and opening new areas to urban life. The earliest towns to flourish were in the valley of the Rhine, a natural trade route. Cologne led the way; Mainz, Frankfurt, Strassburg, and Basle were rivals. Later, the towns closer to the heart of modern Germany rose to prominence, Hamburg and Bremen on the North Sea, Lubeck on the Baltic, and Frankfurt on the Oder River. Still later came Königsberg and Danzig in far-off Prussia. Some of these towns joined together in leagues for mutual protection and advantage in the thirteenth and fourteenth century. They were able to do so because, like the towns of Italy, they were virtually independent of high authority.

The greatest of the leagues was the Hanseatic League, begun in the 1260's, formally organized in 1367, and not dissolved for some 250 years. At its height, this League comprised almost eighty towns scattered across northern Germany from the Rhine to beyond the Vistula. Besides Cologne, Hamburg, Bremen, Lubeck, and Danzig, these included such towns as Hanover, Dortmund, and Magdeburg. The League was, in effect, an alliance or loose confederation whose purpose was to secure trade monopolies, hunt out new areas of exploitation (it even founded new towns), and see that each member town benefited proportionately from the lucrative northern trade. It even had a species of government and carried on military campaigns. In the years of economic decline, the Hanseatic towns were not unaffected but their League did much to cushion the shock.

The Merchants of Bruges The focal point of all European trade was first Bruges, later Antwerp in the Low Countries. There the northern and southern routes met and merchants gathered from everywhere to do business. Bruges replaced the Champagne fairs as the chief meeting place of merchants during the first half of the fourteenth century. The fairs declined for several reasons. Champagne was now in the hands of the French crown, which was not nearly so interested in supporting them as the count had been. Furthermore, France and England were engaged in the ruinous Hundred Years' War, and the Champagne area was the scene of sporadic fighting. Most important, however, the fairs had been rendered obsolete by new trade routes and new methods of transportation. With the introduction of the sea-going galley by Venice around 1300, goods in large quantity could be carried by way of the Mediterranean, Atlantic, and English Channel to and from Italy and Flanders and England. The old overland passage through Champagne lost its former preeminence; though other transalpine routes continued to be used. At Bruges, the merchants founded *fondachi*, "countinghouses," and received many privileges from local authorities. Bruges was a "free" port with few restrictions to hamper business activities. Indeed, it was a foreigners' town, where Italians, Germans, French, Aragonese, Catalonians, and English bought, sold, and exchanged their wares on equal terms with the native Flemish.

The merchants who congregated at Bruges were a far cry from the dusty peddlers who travelled the roads of Europe with packs on their backs and settled the *faubourgs* in an earlier day. Nor were they like the traders who first visited the Champagne fairs. Rather, the new merchant was a capitalist entrepreneur who managed his affairs from his countinghouse. Most of his transactions were done on paper with bills of exchange (promissory notes) and letters of credit. Enterprises were usually undertaken by groups of such men, each man becoming a shareholder in an association resembling our modern stock company. This permitted large-scale ventures with small individual investment and limited risk and is evidence of rising overhead and of the evolution of more sophisticated business practices. It may also be evidence of a more cautious—and more inventive—outlook in the business community, perhaps prompted by the incipient depression. Certainly the day of the daring individual, the gambler who took great chances for great profits, was passing. The merchants of Bruges were of medium wealth, apparently satisfied to remain that way.

Market Scene in a Fifteenth-Century Town. A jeweler, fishmonger, and potter display their wares on a busy day at the market.

Nevertheless, they were clearly motivated by a desire for gain. This was contrary to Christian principle, which had always emphasized the doctrine of the "just price," that nothing should be sold for more than its worth. Worth was determined by adding to the cost of production a sum to provide the workman a living wage. It did not include a percentage for a "middle man," and certainly none for pure profit. Usury, lending money at interest, was strictly prohibited. Commerce and banking, even on a mediocre scale, were simply not valid pursuits for good Christians. In changed social circumstances, the older ethic was bound to change. The great thirteenth century scholastics Thomas Aquinas and Duns Scotus argued that a businessman deserved a fair return for the risks he took, and other writers went further. They even found certain cases where interest taking might not be sinful, though the question of usury remained a sticky one well into early modern times. Merchants themselves, however, were imbued from childhood with a more rigorous, old-fashioned view, and many of them sought to salve their consciences in their later years with good works and philanthropy.

INDUSTRY AND THE CRAFT GUILDS

In the late Middle Ages, the merchant's profession was not confined only to buying and selling. In a few areas, notably Italy and Flanders, where the cloth industry was highly developed, merchant-industrialists manufactured the goods they sold. They bought the raw wool and the materials needed to finish it, parcelled them out to workers at home or gathered together in a factory building, and marketed the finished product. Cloth making was particularly well suited to this development because it was made up of many separate processes: weaving, dying, fulling, shearing, and so on. Workers specialized in each process and could be hired on a time or piece-rate basis. One such entrepreneur was Jean Boine Broke, a "draper" (*drapier*) of Douai in Flanders during the second half of the thirteenth century. Boine Broke operated a large establishment with salaried labor and also used the "putting out" system. He was a man of wealth and political power, an influential member of the guild merchant of Douai and a town concilman several times. He was the prototype of our modern captain of industry. There were others like him, especially in the city of Florence, but they constituted a relatively minor part of European industry.

The Craft Guilds Most industry was of the handicraft type, the artisans organized into craft guilds. This period was the great age of the craft guilds, of their proliferation and their social and economic influence. We have already discussed the organization of the guild merchant and noted that the craft guild sprang from it as local manufacturing prospered under the influence of expanding commerce. The guild merchant as it matured tended to become aristocratic and exclusive, its membership restricted to the great merchants engaged in long-distance trade. Usually, too, the guild merchant dominated the town government, setting political and economic policies fashioned in its own interest. The craft guilds were organized in response to this situation. They were composed of the small businessmen, the artisans and storekeepers catering to the local market. Their purpose was to secure the most favorable economic conditions for their members: monopoly of sales, and the right to fix prices and regulate entrance requirements and working conditions. They naturally came into conflict with the merchant governors, who as consumers and employers of labor preferred that the local market remain competitive. On the other hand, the town's lord, the count, the duke, or king, encouraged the formation of craft guilds to balance the political strength of the guild merchant. Usually the conflict resolved itself in compromise. The craft guilds received the privileges they wanted, and the town authorities insisted they maintain fair prices and adequate standards of quality. Paris saw the proliferation of over one hundred such guilds and the Flemish towns almost as many; the influence of the kings of France and the counts of Flanders is evident here. In England, the crown permitted guilds everywhere and regulated them strictly in the public interest.

The craft guild from its origins was an association of masters. Each master was a full member with the right to take part in determining guild policy. He was also a skilled artisan who had proven his abilities by years of training and perhaps the production of a "masterpiece." He might be a baker, a shoemaker, a saddler, or a goldsmith or armorer. Usually the nature of his craft determined his social standing; a butcher, for example, was several rungs below a shoemaker, who was himself the social inferior of a physician. The guilds, however, were not like modern trade unions; rather, they were associations of independent businessmen, each of whom labored for himself with the help of one or more apprentices and perhaps a journeyman or two. Apprentices were young men, often the master's sons or nephews, entrusted to his care and instruction. They probably lived in his house as members of his family. They came to him at a very tender age, ten or twelve, and were put to work at simple tasks. It was excellent preparation and produced artisans of great skill. Journeymen (from the French *journée,* meaning "day") were salaried workers, former apprentices awaiting entrance to full guild membership.

Conditions in the workshops of the artisans were generally good. Often the artisans lived where they worked, in rooms behind the workshop and store. The latter fronted on the street, and was perhaps equipped with a large opening, covered by a wooden awning which could be raised in good weather. A shelf might be attached on which wares could be displayed. Hours, because artificial light was lacking, would be from sunup to sunset, six days a week. Prices, as we have said, were established by the guilds in collaboration with municipal authorities, as were the standards of quality. Failure to comply resulted in a fine or even expulsion from guild membership. Therefore, there was small opportunity for a craft guildsman to become rich. Instead, he had security of job and status. Moreover, he was a contributer to the common good, a functional being like a knight, a priest, or a peasant. In this respect, the craftsman much more than the merchant fulfilled the medieval social ideal.

In the early days of the craft guild, entrance to the masters' ranks was fairly simple, for there was a need for workers to satisfy the continually increasing demand for goods. Most young apprentices could hope to attain full guild membership at a reasonably early age. By the fourteenth century, however, the demand for goods had begun to fall off. At the same time the movement of peasants from the country filled the towns with potential workers. The mid-century depression turned the gradual stagnation of the market into a precipitate decline. These things confused and frightened the masters, for it upset their carefully regulated industry. They drew their guild membership about themselves like a protective cloak. Admission to guild membership was made more difficult. The apprenticeship period was lengthened and requirements made more rigorous. Entrance fees were introduced and in some cases made prohibitive, and standards for the masterpiece were made impossibly exacting. The masters sought refuge in corporatism, in group resistance. Naturally enough, their actions raised the ire of nonguildsmen, whether merchants, churchmen, or lowly journeymen, and there were voices raised to disband the guilds. The helpless journeymen increased in numbers even as their hopes for relief dimmed; indeed in some of the more highly industrialized towns a true proletariat of wage workers appeared. The journeymen organized associations of their own, hoping to attain in concert what they could not attain individually. We find a few examples of journeymen going on strike. But the merchants and artisans buried their own differences in the face of such danger. Everywhere, journeymen's associations and striking were declared illegal.

SOCIAL UNREST AND REVOLUTION

The ingredients of conflict were at hand. And, beginning at the end of the thirteenth century, insurrections occurred sporadically in Europe as the lower classes of country and town rose up to challenge their betters. Some of these insurrections were simply mindless outbursts of anger and resentment. Others had organization, leadership, ideas, and clear aims. A few succeeded in laying waste a rural area or in controlling an urban government, but only briefly. The forces of royalty, nobility, and patriciate were too strong in the long run. It was not yet the time for social equality and democracy. Each insurrection had its own immediate causes, a bad harvest, a rise in unemployment, a sudden heavy tax levy. But all originated in the profound social, economic, and political changes that were taking place in the fourteenth century. These changes created tension, fear, insecurity, and in some cases real physical hardships among the uncomprehending masses of people. They also improved the lot of some and made them want more. Rebellion was, on the one hand, a way to fight back, a way to restore the good old days when manorial life was safe and secure and town life held promise. On the other hand, rebellion was a means to secure gains won and perhaps add to them. We can only examine very briefly a few of the most typical insurrections, the *Jacquerie* of 1358 in France, the Peasants' Revolt of 1381 in England, and the urban uprisings in Flanders in the late thirteenth and fourteenth centuries.

The *Jacquerie* The *Jacquerie* (a term probably derived from *jacque,* the peasant's jerkin) was an expression of a peasantry outraged and frustrated by the destruction of war. It took place in the neighborhood of Paris where French and English armies had devastated the land and where bands of unemployed mercenaries called *écorcheurs* had continued to burn and rob even after the fighting had ended. Many local landlords had made league with the marauders, and the wrath of the peasants was directed against these. The peasants, badly armed and badly led, roved through the countryside, setting fire to manor houses and murdering their occupants, often with horrible brutality. This was as far as their planning went, however, and they were put down with ease by the crown. Some 20,000 peasants were massacred.

The Peasants' Revolt The English Peasants' Revolt was much more rational in its motivation. It was the culmination of many years of unrest among peasants and town workers, traceable to efforts by the king and Parliament to institute a series of poll taxes to help pay for the war with France, and, under pressure of the landlords, to protect and restore the landlords' privileges. The Black Death, as we have seen, left fewer workers with higher wages in its wake. Government legislation, the Statute of Laborers, tried to turn back the clock by prescribing wages and working conditions at a pre-plague level. This, together with extremely unpopular taxes, was too

This illustration from Froissart's *Chronicles* shows the rebel Wat Tyler struck down by the lord mayor of London during the English Peasants' Revolt of 1381. The artist reflects well Froissart's firm belief in the monarch's duty to preserve law and order even at the expense of social justice. Most Englishmen, of all classes, believed the same thing in 1381. (Courtesy of the Trustees of the British Museum.)

much for the peasants and workers, who resisted. They saw an opportunity to bargain with their lord, to take advantage of his economic difficulties to achieve greater freedom and even perhaps become property owners themselves. From fairly reasonable demands, elimination of the remaining banalities, for example, they turned to an attack on the entire social system. Many of the malcontents were true social revolutionaries, who asked:

Whanne Adam dalfe and Eve span;
Who was thanne a gentilman?

Riots and mob action broke out in various parts of England in the summer of 1381, the spark apparently the third and highest poll tax introduced the year before. Leaders like Wat Tyler appeared. The lower classes of London lent their support, and a frightened king granted concessions in a charter of liberty. But reaction was swift, as all propertied groups joined together. The charter was repudiated, and soldiers and the courts finished the work of suppression and punishment.

Urban Revolutions Urban revolution in these years generally took two forms. One set shopkeepers and artisans, the craft guildsmen, against merchant patricians for the prize of town government. The other set wage workers against the property-owning classes, also for a share in government. The second is well illustrated by the *Ciompi* revolt of poor wool carders who achieved a moment of victory and political power in Florence at the end of the 1370's. The uprising in 1382 of journeymen in the cloth and metal trades at Rouen was bloody and unsuccessful. Rebellions by craft guildsmen occurred in many places, notably in Italy, where a number of guild constitutions were introduced. In Paris, in 1382, the men of lesser guilds, led by the butchers, rose against the patrician governors in protest against a sales tax. Barricades were thrown up, foreshadowing many later Parisian revolts and the city was taken over for a short time.

In the towns of Flanders where industrial progress was far advanced, the guildsmen began to contend for political rights in the first part of the thirteenth century and continued to do so for more than two hundred years. After 1300, the issue broadened to include the king of France. The guildsmen aligned themselves with the Count of Flanders, the patrician governors with the king, who had annexed the county. In 1302, the proud cavalry of Philip the Fair was soundly beaten at Courtrai by a motley army of artisans and shopkeepers. The patricians' power was broken and the victorious guildsmen received a share in the government. In later Flemish revolutions, the figure of Jan van Artevelde of Ghent looms large. Virtual dictator of the Flemish towns from 1337 to 1345, his seizure of power is more properly attributable to industrial troubles arising from the Hundred Years' War, specifically a threatened English embargo on export of raw wool, than to the ambitions of the craft guildsmen.

ECONOMIC REVIVAL

The depression of the late Middle Ages lasted perhaps a century. Revival was probably underway by the mid-fifteenth century in some places and the improved political situation of the next two generations accelerated it. It seems clear, however, that where economic progress had gone furthest prior to the decline, revival was slowest. In Italy, Flanders, and the Hanseatic towns, a mature commerce and industry adjusted to change only with difficulty and on the whole without complete success. Italy was victim of forces beyond its control: northern economic expansion, the advance of the Turks in the Near East, and new trade routes. The old textile towns of Flanders suffered from their own short-sightedness. The protectionism with which their businessmen surrounded themselves stifled new growth, and Flemish industry moved to freer towns and into the countryside where cheaper labor, fewer legal restrictions, and waterpower to run machines were available. The north German Hansa towns expanded their trading areas very little after their formal confederation in 1367. Rather, they were content to preserve what they already had. Symptomatic of Flemish and Hanseatic stagnation was the eclipse of Bruges as a commercial and financial center. A part of the reason for Bruges' decline was doubtless the silting up of the mouth of the Wien River which caused the town to lose its value as a port. But equally important was the economic condition of Flanders as a whole and the decline of the Hansa whose members stuck by Bruges to the end. As Bruges went down, Antwerp in neighboring Brabant came up. Antwerp's golden age would arrive with the discovery of new routes to the Far East when the town on the Scheldt would become Europe's spice market.

General economic growth was greatest, then, in those places which had been less well developed in the thirteenth and early fourteenth centuries, chiefly England, Holland, and southern Germany. English growth was aided by the policies of the crown. On the lookout for sources of income, the crown encouraged business, while regulating it carefully and taxing it. England's principle trade had always been in raw wool, but it was carried on by independent merchants. In the mid-fourteenth century, the crown awarded a monopoly of export to the so-called "Company of the Staple," which all wool merchants joined. Its seat was at Calais, the English port on the French channel coast through which all wool exports passed. There, wool was graded, taxed, and shipped to manufacturers on the continent. Meanwhile, a native textile industry was making great strides, particularly in rural areas, as English manufacturers took advantage of the social and political troubles in the Flemish cities. This industry was in the hands of entrepreneurs who "put out" the raw wool to be worked up by individuals or established factories. These last were located beside streams, for English inventors had developed a means of fulling by waterpower. By the end of the fifteenth century, England was transformed from primarily an exporter of raw wool to an exporter of finished cloth.

Holland, or more exactly the maritime provinces of the northern Netherlands, then lands of the duke of Burgundy, also began its rise to commercial eminence in these years. Beginning in local and short-distance commerce, the Dutch expanded their activities eastward, becoming serious rivals of the Hanseatic League by 1500. Their primary aim was to secure the carrying trade from the Baltic area to western Europe. They were remarkably successful, becoming within a few generations the virtual monopolists in this field. Hence they were ready to duplicate their feat when Portugal went into the spice business. They became the chief carriers of Portuguese spices from Lisbon to the Antwerp market. The Dutch were also merchants, particularly of the herring caught by their fishermen, salted in a secret way and famous throughout Europe. Finally, the textile industry began to grow in Holland about the same time as in England and for essentially the same reasons. The town of Leiden turned into one of the chief clothmaking towns of Europe.

The Fuggers The most striking development occurred in the towns of southern Germany, especially Augsburg and Nürnberg, where trade and manufacturing prospered and where the first great banking houses of northern Europe made their appearance at the close of the fifteenth century. The decisive influence in the rise of such bankers as the Welsers, Hochstetters, Imholts, and Fuggers was the discovery of silver in the Tyrol and Hungary. This, on top of profits from regular mercantile activities, provided huge surpluses to lend. The Fuggers were greatest of all. Beginning in the textile trade, they became bankers to popes and kings, building up a capital of over five million gold gulden before their financial alliance with Spain proved their undoing. Jacob the Rich (1459–1525) was the business genius who contributed most to the Fuggers' success by first entering into the political affairs of the Habsburgs. Jacob provided the money to buy votes for the election of Charles V as Holy Roman Emperor in 1519 and to pay for Charles' later ventures. In 1560, Charles' son Philip II of Spain owed the Fuggers four million gold gulden. Spain's frequent bankruptcies eventually brought about the firm's decline. The Fuggers, however, for all their wealth, were not so advanced in their business practices as their Italian counterparts. The bank remained throughout its lifetime a closely held

Jacob Fugger and his Bookkeeper. As the inscriptions on the cabinet show, Fugger's banking business was European-wide. But from the first, he was deeply involved with the king of Spain and the house of Habsburg. As they rose and fell, so too did the Fugger bank. (Bettmann Archive.)

family enterprise, dominated by a single family member. Moreover, the Fuggers were not typical of northern businessmen, most of whom operated on a far smaller and less spectacular scale.

FURTHER READING

The best general introduction, though somewhat rarified, is H. A. Miskiman, * *The Economy of Early Renaissance Europe, 1300–1460* (1969). D. Hay, *Europe in the Fourteenth and Fifteenth Centuries* (1966), is a good survey, although the sections on the European economy tend to confuse rather than clarify; Hay's social analyses are good. W. K. Ferguson, *Europe in Transition, 1300–1520* (1962), is thorough on economic matters but also does not attack satisfactorily the problem of the late medieval depression. Indeed, the character, extent, and length of the depression are far from settled; see the essays by M. M. Postan and R. Lopez in the *Cambridge Economic History,* Vol. II (1952); Vol. III (1963) is devoted to "Economic Organization and Policies"; and Vol. I, "The Agrarian Life of the Middle Ages," (1966), is most useful for background. All contain bibliographies. The English economy has been most thoroughly studied; see, for example, E. E. Power and M. M. Postan, eds., *Studies in English Trade in the Fifteenth Century* (1941); E. M. Carus-Wilson, *Medieval Merchant Adventurers* (1954); and S. Thrupp, *The Merchant Class of Medieval London, 1300–1500* (1948). On other places, the following have value: J. Streider, *Jacob Fugger the Rich* (1932); R. de Roover, *Money, Banking, and Credit in Medieval Bruges* (1948); P. Dollinger, *The German Hansa* (1970); G. Luzzatto, *An Economic History of Italy* (1961); and H. S. Lucas, *The Low Countries and the Hundred Years War* (1929). An aspect of the fifteenth-century French economy is treated in A. B. Kerr, *Jacques Coeur* (1928). Recent and good on the Black Death, is P. Siegler, * *The Black Death* (1969), which deals mostly in England; and the collections of interpretations, W. M. Bowski, ed., *The Black Death* (1971). Social questions are the subjects of P. Lindsay and R. Grove, *The Peasants' Revolt, 1381* (1950); and D. Nicholas, * *Town and Countryside: Social, Economic and Political Tensions in Fourteenth Century Flanders* (1971).

*Books available in paperback edition are marked with an asterisk.

PART VII

As the Middle Ages drew to a troubled close in northern Europe, the dawn of the Renaissance broke over Italy. "Renaissance" means rebirth, and it refers specifically to the intellectual and artistic flowering that began in Italy in the fourteenth century and eventually spread across the Alps. We may employ the term, however, in a more general sense to describe the entire process of change that transformed medieval into modern Europe. Using it this way, "Renaissance" applies first to a new view of the world. Renaissance man was heir of medieval man, but more secular, more concerned with everyday problems of politics and business than with questions of salvation and the relationship of the soul to God, more attracted to the beauties of nature than the piety of saints. The people of the Renaissance were closer in spirit to ourselves.

The term "Renaissance" may be applied in the second place to the political, economic, and social conditions of early modern times. The weakness and turmoil that characterized late medieval monarchies did not last. They revived toward the end of the fifteenth century under the guidance of strong kings and took a course that would lead to absolutism. The vague political unity of Europe under Church and Empire—the "Christian Commonwealth"—split into separate territorial aggregates called "states." These states, autonomous, omnicompetent, amoral, power hungry, became the means to order society, the sources of law, and the recipients of personal loyalty. Their internal development and their rivalries are dominant features of modern European history. So too is the story of the expansion of the European states. From the start, Europe was too small to contain them and they began to extend their interests across the seas. The European, curious, ingenious, energetic, confident of his inherent superiority, carried his civilization, for good or ill, around the globe. He discovered new lands, populated them, and gained fabulous wealth for himself and his state. The commoners of Europe were ultimately the chief beneficiaries of the ideas, institutions, technology, and wealth created by king and empire builder. Although the balance was not turned in their favor, the middle class made notable progress, particularly as businessmen and government servants. And the lower class continued its slow climb toward freedom.

EMBLEM OF FLORENCE BY LUCA DELLA ROBBIA. (Alinari-Scala.)

THE RENAISSANCE

LEGACY OF THE PAST

View of Florence. (Alinari-Scala.)

Both Voltaire in the eighteenth century and Jacob Burckhardt in the nineteenth believed that their "modern" world began in the Italy of the Renaissance. Their belief was founded on what twentieth-century historians would judge faulty premises, but it was right. The Italian Renaissance produced the capitalist entrepreneur and the proletarian, the artist as hero and the humble teacher as "educator," the intellectual as pundit and adviser to princes, the woman as sex symbol. The cultivated man of the Italian Renaissance—the *uomo universale*—was the model for European chancellors, prime ministers, civil servants, and dilettantes until a generation ago. The peculiar ideas of the humanists about the family; the roles and responsibilities of women and children; about business and profit joined to paternalism; about government, and how it should apply justice equally to all; about religion, and how God should be treated with pious respect but with moderate emotion or sentiment: all these ideas are with us still. We are, indeed, children of the Italian Renaissance.

We must not, however, overlook the most obvious of our legacies. Renaissance Italy was the first truly urbanized society in European history. The problems of city life, whether discovering a source of pure water or the best way to keep the rich and the poor from each others' throats, are the major problems that beset us today, when the West is almost wholly urbanized.

MAJOR EVENTS, 1300-1525*

1300– Venetian galleys begin trade with northern Europe (c. 1300)

Dante completes the *Divine Comedy* (1321)

1325–

Death of Giotto (1336)

Petrarch crowned poet laureate at Rome (1341)

Collapse of Bardi and Peruzzi, two greatest Florentine banking houses (1344)

Black Death (1348–49)

1350– Boccaccio completes the *Decameron* (1353)

1375–

Pope returns to Rome from Avignon (1377)

Ciompi establish short-lived democratic regime at Florence (1378–82)

Medici bank founded at Florence (1397)

1400– Chaucer completes *Canterbury Tales* (c. 1400)

Gian Galeazzo Visconti dies; his Milanese empire crumbles (1402)

Donatello completes *David*, first nude statue since antiquity (1408)

Council of Constance meets (1414–18)

English, under Henry V, defeat French at Agincourt (1415)

Portuguese take Ceuta, beginning expansion of Europe (1415)

**For 1300–1474 see also Major Events, Part VI.*

	Martin V becomes pope, ending Great Schism, beginning Renaissance papacy (1417)
	Henry the Navigator founds school for exploration at Sagres (1419)
1425–	Masaccio paints *Tribute Money* (c. 1427)
	Charles VII crowned king of France with help of Joan of Arc (1429)
	Brunelleschi designs Pazzi Chapel (c. 1430)
	Joan of Arc burned at the stake (1431)
	Cosimo de' Medici gains power in Florence (1434)
	Lorenzo Valla writes the *Donation of Constantine* (1440)
1450–	Francesco Sforza becomes duke of Milan (1450)
	End of Hundred Years' War (1453)
	Peace of Lodi establishes balance of power among Italian states (1454)
	Beginning of War of Roses between Lancaster and York (1455)
	Lorenzo de' Medici, "the Magnificent," assumes control of Florence (1469)
	Edward IV of York defeats Lancastrian forces at Tewksbury (1471)
1475–	
	Charles the Rash of Burgundy killed (1477)
	Isabella makes good her claim to Castilian throne (1479)
	Spanish Inquisition established (1481)
	Henry Tudor defeats Richard III at Bosworth Field, becomes Henry VII, first Tudor king of England (1485)
	Bartholomew Diaz rounds Cape of Good Hope (1485)
	Columbus discovers New World (1492)
	Castilians take Granada, ending *Reconquista* (1492)
	Death of Lorenzo de' Medici (1492)
	French, under Charles VIII, invade Italy (1494)
	Death of Pico della Mirandola (1494)
	Vasco da Gama sets sail for India (1498)
1500–	
	Spanish take kingdom of Naples, beginning two-hundred-year domination of Italy (1504)
	Johann Reuchlin publishes first Hebrew grammar (1506)
	Erasmus publishes *Praise of Folly* (1509)
	The Medici return to Florence, ending "Florentine Republic" (1512)
	Michelangelo completes painting of Sistine Chapel (1512)
	Machiavelli writes *The Prince* (1513)
	Portuguese empire established as Albuquerque takes Ormuz (1515)
	Francis I invades Italy; indecisive battle with Spanish at Marignano (1515)
	More publishes *Utopia* (1516)
	Cortez completes conquest of Mexico (1522)
	Magellan begins voyage around the world (1522)
1525–	
	Castiglione publishes *The Courtier* (1528)

1 Italy in the Renaissance

Contemporaries, naturally enough, were not aware of our broad definition of the Renaissance. Rather, their definition was a more limited one. But define the Renaissance they did, for they were well aware of the contrast between their world and the world of the Middle Ages. They ascribed the contrast to their own discovery of Roman and Greek culture. The "revival of antiquity" after a thousand years of neglect was for them the outstanding characteristic of their "age of gold"; and they looked with scorn on medieval ignorance and barbarism. This narrow vision of the Renaissance as simply the rediscovery of classic learning persisted for centuries, finding its clearest statement in the writings of Voltaire, Edward Gibbon, and other classic-minded historians of the eighteenth-century Enlightenment. The Romantics of the nineteenth century were more sympathetic to medieval civilization but retained and even emphasized the vivid contrast between the Middle Ages and the Renaissance. Jacob Burckhardt, whose great essay *The Civilization of the Renaissance in Italy* was published in 1860, declared: "My starting point had to be a vision. . . , the first mighty surging of a new age." But Burckhardt refused to limit his conception to the revival of antiquity alone. Rather, he saw a fresh and original spirit in every aspect of Renaissance life: a new kind of state, "the outcome of reflection and calculation"; a new kind of society, freed from the moral standards of the past; a new kind of individual, self-conscious and many-sided, a "universal man"; and crowning it all, a new culture, influenced by classic forms, but uniquely shaped by "the discovery of the world and of man." To Burckhardt, this new civilization was wholly an Italian phenomenon, fruit of the union of Greek and Roman culture with the "genius of the Italian people." But even Burckhardt realized that the dividing line between "medieval" and "modern" was not easily defined, and that Italian genius alone could not explain the revolution in art and ideas that was the Italian Renaissance. But he was describing a civilization and was not much interested in its causes. Later historians, inspired by his great synthesis, have tried to complete his work. In the last two generations, they have concentrated on studies of Italy itself, its economy, society, and political structure.

ITALY'S UNIQUE CHARACTER

Italy above all was the land of the Renaissance. There it was born and reached maturity before spreading to the rest of Europe. Indeed, at the very moment when the medieval monarchies beyond the Alps were disintegrating in war and domestic strife, Italy was evolving the unique political, economic, and social environment in which the new civilization could thrive. This evolution took place in the city-states of the center and north, and its causes are complex. First among them is the fact that the city-states were politically independent. Although still nominally owing allegiance to the emperor after the fall of the Hohenstaufen in the mid-thirteenth century, they were for all practical purposes free of imperial authority. The pope, at Avignon after 1309, exercised no more than a weak moral influence over them. Furthermore, feudalism had disappeared almost everywhere north of Rome, and the field was cleared of the third great barrier to complete urban autonomy. Hence, each city-state was left to determine its own political destinies, to establish whatever kind of government its citizens wished, and to compete for territory with its equally free neighbors.

The second major cause was economic. The lifeblood of these city-states was business—commerce, industry, and banking. The fortunate geographic position of Italy, jutting out as it does in the center of the Mediterranean Sea, made it a natural way station in the trade between western Europe and the Near East. Italians were the greatest merchants in that trade and accumulated fortunes of unprecedented size. They also invested heavily in export industries and banking. As their wealth grew, so too did their cities. This flourishing business activity, more than any other single factor, accounts for the remarkable development of the Italian city-states.

We shall have more to say later about Italian political and economic conditions in the fourteenth and fifteenth centuries. It is enough now to note that the combination of independence and early-day capitalism gave rise by 1300 to a vigorous urban society, dominated by middle-class citizens whose political aims coincided with their mercantile interests. In most places, governments were republican, though controlled by men whose wealth was founded on trade. Other groups, the city-dwelling petty nobility, the professional men, the shopkeepers, and artisans, were usually denied a significant political role. At this time, the political power of the great merchants was virtually unchallenged. And their society was the image of themselves. Although still medieval in many ways, in essential respects the society was new. The rigid class structure of the past had been broken, as status through birth or through membership in a closed corporation gave way to status through personal achievement. Religion, though still practiced as before, was no longer a primary concern. Wealth and political power were the goals sought and the criteria of success.

The men of this society looked at the world around them, not as priests or knights but as middle-class laymen. Most of them acquired an education of sorts as a tool of their daily work, and many gained the money and leisure time necessary to develop intellectual and esthetic tastes. Seeing themselves as outside the traditional medieval hierarchy, as alien to it in a sense, they tended to reject the cultural values of the past and adopt values that reflected their own ideals and personalities. Materialistic, individualistic, imbued with a love of life and the world around him, this "new" man invaded the cultural preserves of Europe, so long dominated by clergy and nobility. In his hands, Renaissance civilization took shape.

ITALIAN RENAISSANCE ECONOMY

From the very beginning of the so-called "Commercial Revolution" in the tenth and eleventh centuries, merchants from Venice, Genoa, Pisa, and elsewhere in Italy monopolized the trade between western Europe and the Near East. Favored by geography, by the peculiar Italian political situation, and by few religious scruples, Italians became the great middlemen of their age. At a time when trade north of the Alps was still largely of the local or short-distance variety, they established themselves in Constantinople and in Muslim cities. Rare goods were their special interests. Spices, silks, cottons, and sugar from as far away as India and China were obtained from Byzantine and Muslim merchants in exchange for gold and silver or woolen cloth, metals, and other western products. Carried up the rivers by boat and over the primitive roads by pack animal or cart, the luxuries of the East found willing purchasers at the fairs and in the market places of Europe. The Italians grew rich from huge profits in this trade, and as they did so they expanded their operations. They became "capitalists" in the modern sense of the term, directing their international commercial ventures from

Venice in 1338. Although fanciful, this view shows very well the architectural styles, the lagoon and canals, and the central role played by overseas commerce. That the Venetians themselves are larger than life is perhaps natural: they were the most self-assured of all Italians in the period of their greatness. (The Mansell Collection.)

a home office through branches and agents. A new type of ocean-worthy ship, the Venetian galley, was introduced around 1300, making possible transport of goods to Flanders, England, and other northern areas by way of the Atlantic. Meanwhile, improved business techniques were being developed to limit risk, facilitate exchange, and simplify accounting and management procedures. These included various forms of partnership, arrangements by which a number of people invested in a single enterprise, bills of exchange and checks, double-entry bookkeeping, and even a kind of marine insurance. If, as one historian has recently written, Italian businessmen were two centuries ahead of their northern counterparts in commercial and financial methods,[1] the reason was the unparalleled breadth and vigor of Italian economic activity.

Manufacturing Commercial development was accompanied from the first by the growth of manufacturing. New wealth and new markets created an increased demand for all sorts of goods. Tailors, shoemakers, hatmakers, and other skilled craftsmen, as well as tradesmen such as butchers, grocers, bakers, and spice dealers, became prosperous selling only in the local market. But sizeable expansion took place mainly in industries that lent themselves to production on a large scale for the export trade or were connected with overseas commerce in some way. Notable examples were clothmaking and finishing; shipbuilding; and, in the late fifteenth century, printing.

These industries were not of the medieval guild type, but were organized along quite modern, "capitalistic," lines. The manufacturer was in fact an entrepreneur, usually a great merchant who wanted a profitable outlet for his surplus commercial capital. He owned the means of production, supplied tools and raw materials, paid wages, and sold the finished products for his own gain. His labor force was divided in a modern way, too, each worker being assigned to a special phase of the operation. But there was one essential difference between these early "factories" and today's: tasks were mostly performed by hand with hand tools rather than by power-driven machines. Venice and Genoa were shipbuilding cities, Venice later a printing center. Preeminent for clothmaking and finishing was Florence. There, two great guilds, the *Arte di lana* and the *Arte della Calimala,* not craft guilds but associations of merchant-industrialists, controlled virtually all production and employed (in the 1330's) almost one third of the city's entire population. It is important to remember, however, that this "capitalist" industry was the exception rather than the rule. Most manufacturing in Italy, as elsewhere in Europe, was done by individual craftsmen. Nor did the cities of Italy enjoy an industrial supremacy in Europe as they did a commercial and, as we shall see, a banking supremacy. Almost from the beginning, northern cities, especially those of Flanders, were important competitors.

[1] R. Lopez, "The Trade of Medieval Europe: the South," *Cambridge Economic History of Europe*, II (Cambridge: Cambridge University Press, 1952), p. 291.

Page from a Renaissance Arithmetic Text by Filippo Calandri. This page shows a practical lesson—such texts were not intended to teach theory—in changing the coins called *soldi* for *dinari*, a simple money transaction. (The Metropolitan Museum of Art, Rogers Fund.)

Banking The development of banking in Italy was also closely allied to the expansion of trade. Like large-scale industry, lending was a natural outlet for surplus commercial capital. But more than industry and even more than trade, Italians dominated European banking from the thirteenth century until the rise of the German houses in the sixteenth century. Indeed, the greatest Italian fortunes were made in this way. The first Italian bankers of note were from Siena. The acquisition of silver mines in the twelfth century, together with profits from commerce, provided them with funds for money lending and changing. Within a short time, however, the Florentine merchant-industrialists had preempted the field, first the Bardi and Peruzzi families, then in the later fourteenth and fifteenth centuries, the Medici, the Pitti, the Strozzi, and others. In the early days, great nobles and ecclesiastical princes were the chief borrowers; eventually the feudal monarchs and the pope himself got heavily in debt and paid huge rates of interest. Thus bankers became deeply involved in papal and secular politics. The Bardi and Peruzzi houses collapsed in the early 1340's in the wake of King Edward III's bankruptcy. Although, as we have noted, the Church in her canon law had strict rules against "usurious" financial practices, the changed times demanded usury and the rules were overlooked, explained away, or cleverly circumvented.

Economic Decline The phenomenal economic prosperity of the Italian city-states was once thought to have continued uninterrupted from the eleventh until at least the end of the fifteenth century. In recent years, however, some historians have become convinced that Italy, even more than northern Europe, experienced economic decline beginning early in the fourteenth century and continuing well into the fifteenth. The historians who hold this view find the causes to be roughly similar to those already discussed for the northern European depression. But in Italy's more mature urban economy, they say, the effects were intensified. Political and social unrest was more disruptive. Wealth was concentrated in fewer hands, and the gulf between rich and poor grew wider. The spirit of business adventure gave way to conservatism; safe investment in land was preferred to gambling for high stakes. Rich men, possessors of inherited wealth, tended to withdraw from direct involvement in business activities, buying country villas, building fine town houses, and patronizing artists and men of letters instead.

Other historians, on the basis of significant though limited evidence, suggest that this view of the depression and its effects is highly exaggerated. They note, for example, that Florence recovered with remarkable speed from the banking troubles of the 1340's and from the Black Death. The city's economy was again sound by about 1360. Although hardly a serious rival of Florence, Siena too regained its previous economic position within a decade or two after the Black Death struck. Thus, the historical problem remains unsolved, the focus of considerable controversy. Students, therefore, might best avoid concluding that Renaissance culture was somehow tied closely to economic depression.

ITALIAN RENAISSANCE POLITICS

The period from about 1250 to 1500 in Italian political history has often been called the "Age of Despots." During those years, many republican city-states succumbed to dictatorship, and the dictator or despot became Italy's most distinctive political feature. Much has been made of this fact by Burckhardt and his followers in their search for hero-figures exemplifying "individualism," but we must not let it obscure the existence of several city-states of the first rank that retained their republican constitutions along with the idea of liberty (*libertas*) they embodied. Of the five great states that dominated Italy in the fifteenth century, Venice and Florence were republics; Naples was a kingdom on the northern European style; and the Papal States were a unique elective monarchy. Only Milan was a despotism. Moreover, while Ferrara, Mantua, Urbino, Rimini, and a number of smaller states were ruled by a single man, Siena, Genoa, Lucca, and several others held fast to their medieval traditions. This survival of republicanism is an important key to understanding Renaissance civilization, for, though the despot patronized painters, sculptors, and writers liberally and with taste and discrimination, he was usually obliged to import them from a republic in whose free atmosphere they were born and reared.

Dictatorship came to the medieval republics as the solution to domestic political chaos. In the course of the thirteenth century, most governments had fallen under the control of merchant oligarchies. With growing economic prosperity, other groups such as shopkeepers, professional men, artisans, even wage earners, sought to gain their share in government, and factional strife ensued. In a few places, notably Venice and Florence, the merchant oligarchs were able to hold off or make peace with their rivals with relative ease. In a few others, Siena being the leading example, a coalition of factions produced accord. But elsewhere, the contenders felt compelled to settle their quarrel by calling in an impartial peacemaker, a strong man on whom they conferred absolute authority for life. He was sometimes a military figure, for the people's desperate decision to exchange political rights for domestic harmony was often made under the threat of foreign war. Sometimes he was head of one of the great local families and a leader of one of the factions. In the late thirteenth and early fourteenth centuries, many such men won power.

The dictator was not a king in the northern European sense at all. He had no heritage of royal blood and commanded no feudal loyalty. The institutions by which he ruled were not those of monarchy. To the citizens who selected him, he was a necessary evil, a last resort to be taken when all other measures had failed. Hence, the very foundation of his rule was extra-legal. Once in office, however, he sought to establish himself more firmly in several ways: by modifying the old republican machinery of government along more centralized lines; by earning—or buying—an imperial or papal title; by creating a colorful nobility of his friends and a brilliant court; by commissioning public works to bring employment to the poor and honor and prestige to himself and his city; by achieving fame in war and diplomacy; and so on. His aim was to make himself indispensable

to his fellow citizens. But even if he were successful enough to pass his office on to his heirs, the dictator remained essentially temporary and insecure. An outstanding few, such as the Visconti of Milan and the Este of Ferrara, managed to construct a kind of monarchy for themselves, but most lived in fear, constantly prey to assassins' knives and rivals' ambitions. The character, aims, and methods of this sort of Renaissance "despot" were set down for all time by Niccolò Machiavelli in *The Prince.*

Republican institutions also underwent changes in the fourteenth and fifteenth centuries. Under the leadership of the ruling groups, the old institutions were adapted to fit the new needs of the territorial state. Traditionally, an elaborate system of elected councils and magistratures made and carried out the laws. This process was designed to frustrate potential dictators and assure representation to assorted medieval guilds and corporations, but it was slow and cumbersome. To achieve greater administrative speed and efficiency, executive authority was frequently centralized in a smaller, more workable body such as the *Dieci* (Ten) in Venice or the *Balía* in Siena. The councils and magistratures continued to exist as reminders of the past but played a less important role than before in the decision-making process. This arrangement preserved the spirit and tradition of republicanism, while providing most of the practical advantages of dictatorship. At the same time bureaus or commissions, staffed with "experts"—virtually civil servants—carried on the day-to-day business of government. It was in this republican institutional context that the Medici arose in Florence. They, too, preserved the spirit of republicanism, for they were not dictators of the more familiar type but simply leaders of the strongest political party. They bear a striking resemblance to the "bosses" of American big-city politics.

RENAISSANCE WARFARE AND DIPLOMACY

Whether dictatorship or republic, the states of Renaissance Italy were bent on territorial expansion and aggrandizement or on devising a defense against their avaricious neighbors. Hence each was continually preoccupied with war and war's peacetime equivalent, diplomacy, both of which under the pressures of necessity were developed to high arts. The mercenary army became the mainstay of warfare. These *condottieri,* as they were called, were captained by soldier-businessmen who sold their services to the highest bidder with little or no thought of loyalty or patriotism. The citizens of the republics, whose medieval forebears had defended themselves valiantly as militiamen, were now only too happy to leave the fighting to others, while the dictators would rather hire foreign troops than risk arming their own subjects. Besides, mercenaries were far better soldiers than were the citizens. At the hands of inventive mercenary generals, an entire new method of waging war evolved. Since fighting was their business, the *condottieri* shied away from decisive encounters that might decimate their men and threaten

The Condottiere Guidoccio da Foligno, by Simone Martini. The town on the left is under siege, the "town" on the right is not a town at all but an elaborate, moveable siege wagon. The banners are of the republic of Siena, for Guidoccio was in the pay of the Sienese. (Palazzo Communale, Siena/Alinari-Scala.)

their means of livelihood. War became a chess game of maneuver and siege with few, relatively bloodless, battles. Furthermore, since most mercenary armies consisted of cavalry (it could move more easily from place to place), infantry engagements were rare. This kind of warfare was harshly criticized by Machiavelli, who ascribed Italy's military failures after the French invasion of 1494 to it. In fact, however, the *condottieri* for the most part fought with tactical skill and bravery. Their weakness lay in their small numbers and in their lack of heavy infantry, good light artillery, and adequate methods of fortifications.

Diplomacy evolved even further than warfare in these years. Indeed, Renaissance Italy was the birthplace of modern diplomatic machinery and techniques. As the great states extended their borders, gobbling up smaller states and contending with each other for territory, war became endemic in Italy. Each state had to know what the others were doing and thinking and what alliances were being made and unmade. Especially after the Peace of Lodi brought a kind of primitive balance of power situation to the peninsula in 1454, accurate information and ready communication among the powers were indispensable. Negotiation and argument replaced open war. The battles were no longer fought by soldiers but by diplomats whose oratorical skill and capacity for intrigue made them more admired than successful generals. Under these circumstances, new diplomatic tools were invented, the most important of them being a new kind of diplomatic officer, the resident ambassador. Replacing the "herald" or "orator," who was sent from one state to another to accomplish a single task or mission, the resident ambassador was assigned to a foreign post permanently. He represented his government on all occasions and kept it regularly informed of important affairs. Almost unknown outside Italy before 1500, these new diplomatic officers were destined to become the chief instruments of European international relations.

THE PAPAL STATES AND THE KINGDOM OF NAPLES

By the middle of the fifteenth century, the political outlines of Renaissance Italy were complete. Three large states, the duchy of Milan and the republics of Venice and Florence, dominated the north and north-central parts of the peninsula. Numerous smaller states, among them the duchies of Ferrara and Modena under the Este, the marquisate of Mantua, and the republics of Siena, Lucca, and Genoa, had managed to survive but exerted slight influence in political affairs. The central and southern parts of the peninsula were covered by the Papal States and the kingdom of Naples.

Renaissance Italy's most chaotic political conditions prevailed in the States of the Church. Nominally under the direct sovereignty of the pope, in practice these states went their own way with little interference from their overlord. The "Babylonian Captivity," the Great Schism, and the fact that the papacy was an elective monarchy with frequently shifting political aims, provided sufficient opportunity in the fourteenth century for local landed magnates and petty dictators to assert their own rival authority. The worldly popes of the fifteenth century paid closer attention to their temporal do-

Caesar Borgia by an Unknown Artist. Caesar, who had a flair for the dramatic, often wore sombre clothes, set off in a spectacular way. After his face had become ravaged by syphillis, he liked to appear by candle light, all in black, wearing a beautifully-wrought golden mask. (The Uffizi/ Alinari-Scala.)

mains, from which all but a small part of their revenues now derived, and succeeded in exerting some centralizing influence, but not until the conquests of Caesar Borgia, ambitious son of Pope Alexander VI (1492–1503), and of the warrior Pope Julius II (1503–1513) did anything like true pacification and unification take place. Despite this tenuous hold on their own domains, the popes of the fifteenth century were little different from secular monarchs. They lived in luxury and splendor, maintained brilliant courts and patronized art and literature, sent out ambassadors and made alliances, waged wars and plotted assassinations, and used their spiritual position for purely political ends. Their wealth, still great though much less than it had been before, served for the most part to further their own and their relatives' ambitions. Naturally enough, they neglected their religious duties, and by the early sixteenth century the cries of reform-minded critics were echoing throughout Christendom.

The kingdom of Naples was of little importance in the cultural life of the Renaissance, though its influence in peninsular affairs was considerable. Prey to constant rivalry for the crown between the heirs of Charles of Anjou and the house of Aragon, the kingdom was also torn by periodic uprisings of a powerful and undisciplined landed nobility. The accession of the Aragonese candidate in 1435 brought a certain measure of internal peace for several decades although the Anjou claim remained alive, providing Charles VIII of France with an excuse for his invasion of Italy in 1494.

THE DUCHY OF MILAN

The duchy of Milan was Renaissance Italy's most successful dictatorship. The principal city of the Lombard plain in the Middle Ages, under the leadership of the Visconti and Sforza dukes, Milan grew to become a large territorial state whose expansionist ambitions kept Italian political life in a turmoil throughout the fourteenth and early fifteenth centuries. The greatest of the Visconti was Giangaleazzo (1378–1402), who inherited a sizeable dominion and a tradition of family rule dating back to 1277. An ambitious and unscrupulous man, Giangaleazzo bought the title "duke" from the emperor to add to his title "imperial vicar" and dedicated his life to extending Milanese power. He was remarkably successful; by the date of his untimely death he had conquered outright or brought under indirect control every state in northern and central Italy except Venice and Florence.

Many saw Giangaleazzo as a new Caesar, destined to unite Italy under a strong monarchy. But on his death his empire collapsed, and his sons were hard put to salvage even the old state of Milan from the ruins. His younger son, Filippo Maria, died without legal heirs in 1447, having spent most of his life struggling with the new problem of Italy's balance of power. After a brief revival of republicanism, Francesco Sforza (1450–1466), a famous *condottiere* and husband of Filippo Maria's illegitimate daughter, won the duchy by force of arms. A rough, unlettered man of illegitimate birth, Francesco was a wise and prudent ruler who brought peace, prosperity, and the culture of the Renaissance to Milan. His most colorful successor was his younger son Lodovico, called "Il Moro" (1479–1500).

Lodovico, though of austere habits himself, subsidized the greatest writers and artists of the day, including Leonardo da Vinci, and made his court one of the most magnificent in Europe. Meanwhile, he spent his time devising complicated international intrigues and gaining the reputation as Italy's wiliest diplomat. It was he who invited the French into Italy in 1494, thus opening the way to the Swiss, the Austrians, the Spanish, and other foreigners whose hunger for the spoils of conquest made the peninsula a helpless battleground for the next sixty-five years. Victim of his own devious diplomacy, Lodovico was driven out of Milan by the French in 1500. Fought over for a generation, Milan finally became a province of the king of Spain.

Francesco Sforza by Bonifacio Bembo. (Alinari-Scala.)

THE REPUBLIC OF VENICE

Venice had enjoyed unequaled material prosperity and political stability among the Italian states since the late thirteenth century. This great city, with its canals and lagoons, its palaces and churches, remains today one of the great monuments to western civilization. Venice was wedded to the sea, as the Venetians themselves recognized in their annual symbolic "marriage" ceremony. Centuries of profitable international trade had created and developed a rich and vigorous upper-middle class whose members had contrived a unique system of government to preserve and promote their political aims. By 1300, they had closed their ranks to all Venetians but themselves and their descendants, thus establishing an hereditary oligarchy of about 2 percent of the population that endured for the unprecedented span of five hundred years. Ultimate authority rested with the Great Council of all the oligarchs, and executive powers were delegated to the *doge* and his advisors. In time, however, the *doge* became a figurehead, as the Senate (a smaller body elected by the Great Council) and the Ten (a secret magistrature charged with hunting down traitors) assumed his functions. Unlike other Italian states, where domestic strife was endemic, there was neither great rivalry among the rulers of Venice nor particular dissatisfaction among the unfranchised lower class. Factionalism was simply not a problem for the Most Serene Republic. For this reason, the Venetian constitution became the object of much admiration and study among Italian and European political theorists.

The oligarchs tied government policy tightly to their own commercial interests. Before 1400, Venice took little part in the affairs of Italy, concentrating instead on keeping the sea lanes safe for its shipping and on building a small colonial empire along the Dalmatian coast and among the Greek islands of the Adriatic. But in the early fifteenth century, Venetian statesmen concluded, after much wrangling, that a mainland state was necessary for self-protection and profit. They pursued a policy of territorial aggrandizement with tenacity and singlemindedness even after the Milanese peril was gone, and Venice became Italy's most aggressive state in the following century. By 1454, its armies had carved out a territory, larger than Milan's, which included such ancient independent cities as Vicenza, Padua, and Verona. Venice ruled this subject area in its own interests, giving its people no voice in Venetian affairs. At the time of the French invasion, Venice was Italy's strongest state and one of the ranking states of Europe.

THE REPUBLIC OF FLORENCE

For all Venice's size, power, and wealth, it produced only a fraction of the intellectual and artistic genius of its sister republic, Florence. Dante, Giotto, Petrarch, Boccaccio, Brunelleschi, Donatello, Masaccio, Botticelli, Machiavelli, Michelangelo: all were Florentines. This city of fewer than one hundred thousand souls was the source and the inspiration of most of what we call Italian Renaissance civilization. What is the reason? No adequate answer has yet been given, but part of it must be found in the vital atmosphere of Florentine urban republican society. This society was not closed once and for all as was that of Venice. Rather, it was constantly changing in response to the constantly changing political and economic life of the city.

From the middle of the thirteenth century, Florentine political life was plagued by factionalism. Although the upper-middle-class merchant-industrialists and bankers, representatives of seven major guilds, managed to hold a major share of power through most of the fourteenth and early fifteenth centuries, they were challenged time and again by the nobles, the lesser guildsmen, salaried workers, and, most effectively, by "new men" who equalled them in wealth but not in social status or political influence. These years were notable for political unrest, including several revolutions; two short-lived dictatorships; and in 1378, the brief, extremely democratic regime of the *Ciompi,* the woolworkers. The unrest was closely related to the growing pains Florence experienced in transforming itself from a medieval commune to a territorial state. The government of the commune was hardly more than a conglomeration of corporate groups with diverse and oftentimes conflicting interests. The government of the territorial state was more impersonal, more responsive to the individual Florentine. Its people were *citizens,* equal before the law; Florence was a *state* in other words, very much like a modern state. This transformation came about because the huge costs of war demanded that not just the richest corporations but every Florentine share the financial burden of his homeland. Besides citizen responsibility, war and the financing of war demanded efficient and honest administration, and again the old, haphazard ways of the communal government did not suffice. Specifically, citizens were asked to invest in what today we would call government bonds, the debt was funded, financial and other administrative procedures were improved, and the territory around the city, the *contado*, united more closely (chiefly for tax purposes) with the central government. At the same time, Florentine ideas about what constituted a "good" government and a "good"

Lorenzo de' Medici, il Magnifico (center), *and Friends.* Lorenzo was a man of parts. Although a bad business man, he was a knowledgeable patron of the arts, an excellent poet, and an extraordinary diplomat. He was also a bit of a playboy, who loved to watch the joust, a sport in which he and his friends acted the part of cavaliers. (Chiesa di S. Trinita, Florence/ Alinari-Scala.)

citizen changed from medieval to recognizably modern. These ideas are among those basic to the Renaissance.

Following the fall of the *Ciompi* in 1380, the major guildsmen returned and established a government more restricted in membership than the one that ruled before 1378. Out of a struggle for control of this government Cosimo de' Medici, a leading banker, emerged in 1434. Cosimo and his heirs brought relative civic peace to Florence. They exiled their enemies, broadened the base of rule by giving a number of new men the vote and by championing the cause of the poor, and deftly used the old republican constitution to maintain themselves. But they assumed no title or other mark of legal status to set them apart. During their sixty years of uninterrupted rule, the Medici remained private citizens, directing both their vast commercial and banking interests and the affairs of Florence from their palace. They rarely held public office themselves and were careful to uphold at least the outward forms of medieval republicanism. Cosimo (1434–1464) and his son Piero (1464–1469) assured that a majority of offices were filled by their friends by the simple expedient of eliminating the names of their enemies from consideration. Piero's son, the great Lorenzo the Magnificent (1469–1492), introduced a new governing council with a permanent membership of one hundred men of the Medici party and heard cries of "tyrant!" from the outraged Florentines. Necessarily, the informality of Medici rule limited the family's authority somewhat, but it conformed to the spirit and tradition of republicanism so dear to every citizen. Indeed, none was more aware than Lorenzo himself that a more formalized despotism was undesirable and impossible to establish.

Lorenzo was the most famous of the Medici and a talented poet in his own right. Although his personal preferences ran to mosaics and medallions, he had the good sense and good taste to subsidize Italy's finest painters, sculptors, and men of letters to celebrate Florence and the name of Medici. The city on the Arno was Europe's center of culture during his lifetime, a place of unsurpassed pleasure and beauty. In business and domestic affairs, he was careless and extravagant but in foreign affairs his skill and foresight were outstanding. A brilliant diplomat, he built on the prestige and friendships of his grandfather Cosimo and made Florence, if not the most powerful, at least the most influential state in Italy. Using the balance-of-power situation that existed in the peninsula after 1454, Lorenzo kept Italy in a condition of relative peace for twenty years. Of his influence, Machiavelli wrote in his *History of Florence:* ". . . As soon as Lorenzo de' Medici was dead, there sprung up those fatal seeds, which soon accomplished the downfall of Italy, and which, none knowing how to destroy, will perpetuate her ruin." In 1494, two years after Lorenzo's death, his weak and incompetent son Piero was forced into exile by the French, and most Florentines were glad to see him go. For the next eighteen years, the citizens strove to find a purer republicanism than the Medici brand, first under the guidance and inspiration of the fanatically austere Dominican monk, Girolamo Savonarola (1452–1498), and then by means of a popular but hesitant government

Girolamo Savonarola. The impassioned Dominican's prophecies and political ideas gained a large following among the little people of Florence (known as *"Piagnoni"* or "Crybabies"), who delighted in his admonition to burn the "vanities." Great bonfires of cheap jewelery, mirrors, cosmetics, pornographic pictures and books lit up the Florentine skies, until Girolamo himself was burned in 1498. (Museo di S. Marco, Florence/Alinari-Scala.)

headed by Piero Soderini. The Medici heirs returned behind Spanish pikes in 1512, pale shadows of their great forebears. Ousted again from 1527 to 1530 they once more secured Spanish help to return. A few years later they established themselves as dukes of Tuscany. So ended the Republic of Florence.

ITALY AND EUROPE

When the northern Europeans marched over the Alps in 1494, they found the Italian state system and the Italian states different from anything they had known before. Unlike their own monarchies, steeped in feudal and religious tradition, these states were wholly sovereign and secular, fixed in no hierarchy and bound by no code of morality, but wholly self-conscious and power hungry. In other words, these were *modern* states, made by people and for people, the first to appear on the European scene since the fall of

Rome. We have examined some aspects of this modernity: the connection between economic ends and political means, the displacement of an ordered society by a society founded on individual achievement, and the development of such institutions as the resident ambassador and the dictatorship. But one must be wary not to go too far. For Italy of the Renaissance, while it gives us a glimpse in microcosm of Europe of a later day, reminds us of medieval Europe as well. The Italian states were transitional, as was the culture they nurtured. We shall be safe to confine ourselves to the conclusion of Jacob Burckhardt, who wrote in the Introduction to *The Civilization of the Renaissance in Italy:* in the states of Renaissance Italy ". . . for the first time we detect the modern political spirit of Europe . . . the state as a work of art."

FURTHER READING

For the medieval background, best is D. Waley, * *The Italian City Republics* (1969); but the only good new book in English covering Italy during the Renaissance is D. Hay, * *Europe in the Fourteenth and Fifteenth Centuries* (1966). There has been a plethora of monographs, however, most of which Hay cites in his footnotes. The relevant sections of W. K. Ferguson, *Europe in Transition, 1300–1520* (1962), and the same author's * *The Renaissance* (1940), are as useful as any introductions one may find. Lewis W. Spitz, * *The Renaissance and Reformation Movements,* vol. I (1972), is disappointingly traditional, but covers the ground and is up-to-date. An excellent survey of recent scholarship, connecting culture to political and social conditions, is D. Hay, * *The Italian Renaissance* (1961). See also the more conventional J. H. Plumb, * *The Italian Renaissance* (1965); this book contains a good bibliography. Naturally, no student of the Renaissance should leave unread the classic essay of J. Burckhardt, * *The Civilization of the Renaissance in Italy* (1860). It is one of the great works of nineteenth-century historiography, and its first chapter, "The State as a Work of Art," lays the groundwork for all future Italian political history of the Renaissance. In the Burckhardt tradition, and in itself a classic, is J. A. Symonds, * *The Renaissance in Italy,* 7 vols. (1875–1886); for politics, one should note particularly volume one, "The Age of the Despots." A highly interpretive essay, which tries to establish the relationship between culture and the economy and society, is A. von Martin, * *Sociology of the Renaissance* (1932).

Of the numerous books on more specialized subjects, one may note C. M. Ady, * *Lorenzo de' Medici and Renaissance Italy* (1955), traditional and unimaginative in its interpretation, but useful for the beginner; F. Schevill, * *The Medici* (1949), a popular account; I. Origo, *The Merchant of Prato* (1957), a charming personal study of a late medieval businessman; R. de Roover, *The Rise and Decline of the Medici Bank* (1963), an important economic study;

*Books available in paperback edition are marked with an asterisk.

and G. Mattingly, * *Renaissance Diplomacy* (1955), a brilliant account of the origins of modern diplomatic practices.

A bit trendy, but containing some interesting articles is L. Martines, ed., *Violence and Civil Disorder in Italian Cities 1200–1500* (1972). F. Schevill, * *History of Florence* (1936), is the best general account of an Italian Renaissance state in English. On Florence in the fourteenth century, compare Gene A. Brucker, *Florentine Politics and Society, 1343–1378* (1962), with M. Becker, *Medieval Florence in Transition,* I and II (1967–1968). Far and away the best on the fifteenth century is G. Brucker, * *Renaissance Florence* (1969). Also in English are: C. M. Ady, *The Bentivoglio of Bologna* (1937); D. Muir, *A History of Milan under the Sforza* (1924); the excellent J. K. Hyde, *Padua in the Age of Dante* (1965); D. Herlihy, *Medieval and Renaissance Pistoia* (1967); and J. Larner, *The Lords of the Romagna* (1965).

2 The Culture of the Italian Renaissance

Jacob Burckhardt, in *The Civilization of the Renaissance in Italy,* attributed the difference between Renaissance culture and its predecessors to something he called the "Italian genius." This in turn he attributed largely to Italian "political circumstances," specifically the freedom of the Italian city-state from higher authority and the absence there of a strong feudality. These conditions determined that each city-state would be peopled by commoners who decided their own political destinies. In the preceding chapter, we concluded that great weight must also be given to Italy's mercantile economy. Commerce and industry created a group of wealthy middle-class laymen. Political circumstances and a mercantile economy joined to create a unique *urban* environment. Renaissance culture was distinctly urban in character, its participants city people leading an active life of business and government, mingling, exchanging ideas, competing for profits and prestige. Still another important influence on the character of Renaissance culture was Italy's heritage from the classical world. All Europeans were part of this heritage, of course, but Italians were part of it in a special way. They believed themselves the only true legatees of their great Roman forebears and with good reason. They lived closest to the center of the old Empire and they possessed Roman towns, Roman law, and the city of Rome itself. They were conscious of this fact throughout their history, but in the Renaissance it pervaded the intellectual scene.

THE CIVIC CULTURE OF FLORENCE

Although one may cite a few precedents elsewhere, Renaissance culture began and developed in its most original way in Florence. The contributions of Rome, Milan, Venice, and other Italian states came later and were for the most part elaborations of ideas and art forms already in use by the Florentines. The question that arises is: Why Florence? And the answer lies in the nature of Florentine society and in the intellectual needs and cultural values of the Florentines.

Florentine upper-class society of the fourteenth century was many sided. Most immediately striking was its secular and nonaristocratic character.

Clerical and feudal patterns, dominant in northern Europe, were virtually nonexistent there. Instead of a rigid hierarchy based on birth or function, people were ranged in various social levels chiefly on the basis of wealth and political influence. Furthermore, Florentine society was dynamic; there was mobility among social groupings so that individuals had the opportunity for personal success. The surest roads to success were business and politics. The city was mercantile and republican; all of Florence was dedicated to the pursuit of material things, and citizens took an active, continuing part in government. Hence, the Florentines developed character traits different from those typical of medieval man. They tended to be materialistic, ambitious, practical, competitive, individualistic, middle class—in many ways like men of today. Their gaze was on the world about them; they measured a man's status by things they could see and touch. They enjoyed luxury and liked to display their affluence by building and furnishing fine houses, by endowing churches, by patronizing artists and writers.

But Florentines were more complex than this description would suggest. Most of them had at least a basic knowledge of letters and arithmetic as necessary tools of their daily lives, and they saw to it that their children had the same. There were numerous secondary schools where fundamentals of Latin grammar, rhetoric and allied subjects were taught. Higher education was confined almost wholly to law and medicine. As a recent commentator has observed: "the main bent of Italian learning was towards the concrete, the practical problems of government and administration, rather than towards the metaphysical or the theological."[1] Ideas were not foreign to the Florentine but they were ideas of the market place and the council chamber, not of the cloister and the court. This sort of education nourished an intense patriotism, founded above all on the Florentine republican constitution. Citizens believed their constitution to be the embodiment of *libertas,* the bulwark of civic freedom. In the course of the fourteenth century, this ideal became more than merely a matter of political persuasion; it became an article of faith, a dogma of a kind of secular religion, which it was the duty of every Florentine to preserve at all costs.

Florentines were more conventional in their religious views. Religion and the dictates of the Church were of great importance to them. Although they were probably anticlerical, distrustful of churchmen who meddled in politics, they were sincerely pious, conforming with diligence to the Church's spiritual requirements. Theological speculation was of little interest, although some were troubled by the strictures in canon law forbidding the common business practice of usury and by such clear Biblical warnings as "Love not the things of this world." These seemed to apply to another society but they were difficult to explain away. An individual Florentine might salve his conscience by setting aside a portion of his profits for charity, "for the account of Messer God," or by specifying in his will that his debtors be given back the interest they had paid him.

[1]D. Hay, *The Italian Renaissance* (Cambridge: The Cambridge University Press, 1961), p. 70.

From this description, we may gather some idea of the Florentine system of values. But, until the middle of the fourteenth century, the Florentines had no body of thought or culture peculiarly their own in which these values could be expressed. Indeed, the most popular ethical code was that of the Franciscans, which condemned profit making and the active life of politics, while lauding poverty and contemplation. Hence, conditions were right for the creation of new forms and ideas that better reflected the reality of Florentine society.

FOURTEENTH-CENTURY LITERATURE

The names of three Florentines, Dante, Boccaccio, and Petrarch, stand out for all time in the literature of the late Middle Ages and early Renaissance. Each, in a distinct way, was a product of both cultures. Though great in their own right, they were also transitional figures. Dante Alighieri (1265–1321) was medieval in his thought and in his view of mankind and the world. His social and religious ideal was the universal Church, his political ideal the universal Empire. He was imbued with the theology, metaphysics, and natural science of the scholastics. His Latin was the vigorous Latin of the Church. At the same time, he lived the life of a typical Florentine. The son of a good family and a man of substance, his persistence in pressing his political beliefs led to his expulsion from the city. He remained in exile for the last twenty years of his life, but never forgot his *patria,* "the fairest and most renowned daughter of Rome," and all of his writings give evidence of his passion for politics. Furthermore, his best work is not in Latin but Florentine which, because of his enormous literary stature, became "Italian."

The influence of the old and the new is evident in Dante's work. As a youth, he wrote lovely sonnets and *canzoni* in the vernacular, many of them to Beatrice Portinari, an older woman with whom he fancied himself in love. He used northern poetic forms, the songs of the troubadours and the lyrics of Provence, as well as the chivalric theme of idealized womanhood, but in a more natural, human way. His *De Monarchia,* composed in exile, defends imperial power against papal claims to temporal sovereignty with traditional arguments in traditional Latin style. His autobiographical work, *Vita Nuova,* is written in fine Italian verse and prose. But he will be forever remembered for the *Divine Comedy,* an epic poem of overpowering sweep and grandeur. This is Dante's great contribution to Western civilization. It tells a complex and fantastic story of a journey through Hell, Purgatory, and Paradise. Each place is peopled with figures from life. Most were the author's contemporaries, twenty-two of them Florentines. Often Dante's political prejudices show through, as when he assigns Boniface VIII to Hell, though the pope is still alive. Thus, the work has many elements we may characterize as "Renaissance." But it is essentially medieval, an allegory meant to represent (Dante told his patron) "mankind as by its merits or demerits it exposes itself to the rewards or punishments of justice."

Boccaccio and Petrarch were less medieval in their intellectual outlook than Dante, but neither may be categorized as wholly "Renaissance men." Giovanni Boccaccio (1313–1375) was a typical Florentine of his day, at home

This fourteenth-century portrait of Dante is in the pre-Renaissance style, but evokes very well the brooding sensitivity of this remarkable man. (Biblioteca Riccardiana/ Alinari-Scala.)

in the secular atmosphere of the city on the Arno. His father was a partner in the great Bardi banking firm and young Giovanni was trained as a bookkeeper. He found this dull, turned to law, and finally to writing and scholarship. Dante was his idol, and two years before his death Boccaccio accepted a municipal post as lecturer on the *Divine Comedy.* Although he was also a classical scholar who wrote a few polished Latin verses and a treatise on classical mythology, Boccaccio's fame rests on his poetry and prose in the vernacular. His masterpiece, *The Decameron,* had an influence on Italian prose style as profound as the effect of the *Divine Comedy* on Italian poetry. This is a book of tales, mostly traditional, ostensibly told by ten young men and women over a period of ten days while living in refuge from the plague of 1348 in Fiesole, outside Florence. The tales are funny, lusty, frequently profound in their understanding of human folly. They are meant to amuse, but also to delineate character and no one, neither patricians nor nobles nor priests, escaped Boccaccio's barbed wit. In its own time and since, *The Decameron* has been condemned as sacrilegious and pornographic. It is neither, but merely a true picture of Florentine society as Boccaccio observed it.

Boccaccio never seemed troubled by the conflict between the medieval ideals expressed by Dante and the Renaissance ideals portrayed in his own great book. But for his more famous and influential friend, Francesco Petrarca, usually called Petrarch (1304–1374), this was the central problem. Indeed, Petrarch was truly torn between the past and the present, between

Christianity and pagan classicism. This conflict appears in his life, some of which he spent at the papal court at Avignon and some of which he spent at the courts of the Italian dictators. On the one hand he was a "European," foreshadowing Erasmus in his wide acquaintance with important personages in every western country and in his prestige among them. On the other hand, he was a natural recluse who loved nothing better than to exile himself to his farmhouse at Vaucluse, near Avignon, and study in the manner of a monk.

Also in his works of imaginative literature, Petrarch was a man of two minds. Throughout his life, he wrote sweet and graceful sonnets and love lyrics in the vernacular tradition. Their style may be traced to northern European models but their content was drawn from Petrarch's own secular world. They are subtle, naturalistic, full of human emotion—and were very popular. Largely on their account, Petrarch was crowned "poet laureate" at Rome in 1341. But to the author himself, his vernacular poetry was *juvenilia,* shallow and old-fashioned. He took more pride in his Latin works, the mediocre poem *Africa* and the letters and treatises. For these he is studied by Renaissance scholars; for his beautiful verses in Italian, he ranks high in Italian literature.

HUMANISM AND THE HUMANISTS

The word "humanism," though it has been used in various ways in modern times, may be defined as an intellectual movement that stressed the study of the classics and the imitation of classic modes of thought and expression. In point of fact, the word "humanism" is an invention of the nineteenth century. Renaissance men spoke only of "humanists," teachers and scholars of the *studia humanitatis,* the "humanities." The *studia humanitatis* were the group of scholarly disciplines including grammar, rhetoric (speaking and writing), history, poetry, and moral philosophy, but excluding theology, metaphysics, logic, the natural sciences, law, and medicine. By definition then, humanism was limited to those subjects that treat of man and his life on earth; its subject matter was not concerned with the nature of God, the universe, or the hereafter, except indirectly as man's ethical principles affect his salvation. These facts must be kept in mind, for too often humanism is taken to be the only significant intellectual movement of the fourteenth and fifteenth centuries. In reality, scholasticism, with its theological emphasis, continued to be a dominant force in the universities of the north, while in Italy for the first time the philosophy of Aristotle became an important field of study at such centers of learning as the University of Padua.

Petrarch Petrarch is usually credited with founding humanism in the middle of the fourteenth century. Although he had a few lesser predecessors, this is in a large sense true. He was the first to read and appreciate the Latin classics, principally Cicero, for their own sake and to see the relevance of the classic ideal to his own society. (Though hungry to read Homer in the original, he learned no Greek.) He worshipped his ancient idols with a fervid, often blind, passion, emulating their style and using them as authorities in

Although Petrarch was not the first Italian literary man to recall and revere the classic Roman tradition, because of his immense prestige and the wide dissemination of his writings, he may be said to have been the father of humanism and the Italian Renaissance. (Bibliothèque Nationale, Paris.)

commenting on the world around him. In the process he became an expert Latinist, giving to the language a verve and flexibility unknown since Cicero's day. He was also the first to possess a true sense of history, to see the ancient world as existing at a specific time in the past. Indeed, it was he who coined the term "Dark Ages," to describe the period between the decline of Rome and his own day. Since he was a literary figure of wide repute, his interests took hold; and the classics, and expressing the classic ideal through historical and other forms of writing, gained popularity. But in an important sense, Petrarch was only a precursor of humanism. He was not wholly committed to the Ciceronean ideal of the *vita activa*, the active life—or rather he misread Cicero, believing him to have taught a doctrine more in harmony with the medieval tradition of contemplative spirituality. Petrarch himself, as we have noted, preferred the aesthetic life, condemning those who participate in government and business.

Florentine Civic Humanism What Petrarch began was left to succeeding generations to complete. Boccaccio brought Petrarch's humanism to Florence (Petrarch himself, though a Florentine, rarely lived in his native city) where it gained immediate popularity, for it fitted well into Florentine society. These were ideas that a Florentine could understand. In Florence, too, humanism matured under the direct influence of unique Florentine conditions. Earlier we noted the urban, middle-class character of Florentine life and the transformation of the Florentine government into that of a modern state. Between about 1380 and 1440, Florence was threatened several times by Milanese and Neapolitan imperialism. Under these influences, Florentines came to see themselves as Italy's unique defenders of republicanism and *libertas*—the two were opposite sides of a single coin. Their patriotism was strengthened and their attitude toward their city's traditions and toward their own role as citizens was transformed. Humanists such as Coluccio Salutati (1331–1406) and Leonardo Bruni (1369–1444), both chancellors of the republic, reexamined Florentine history, finding preserved there the ideals of civic freedom and citizen responsibility inherited from republican Rome. Julius Caesar, founder of the Empire, was declared a tyrant, Brutus a patriot and hero. Cicero was recognized as advocating the active life, of teaching that men must participate in government in order to preserve their liberty. Republicanism was identified with virtue and intelligence. Bruni quoted Tacitus as saying that "after the republic had been subjected to the power of one man, those brilliant minds vanished." This judgment was something new.

Very soon, other classical authors were discovered to be sympathetic to mercantile pursuits and to the accumulation of wealth; this too was new. Aristotle and Martial believed that a man could be rich as well as virtuous. Money provided a means to help the less fortunate and leisure time to cultivate the mind. Men with money could build great buildings and patronize the arts. By the time of Leon Battista Alberti (1404–1472), the life of luxury was the good life; the only question was whether most of a man's wealth should be in cash or land. Thus the activities of the Florentines in politics and business were conveniently justified.

The Development of Humanism Humanism, with its new interest in antiquity, found ready acceptance in most of the cities of central and northern Italy during the fifteenth century, for its intellectual appeal was broad. It matured further, added new and varied characteristics, becoming a highly complex movement and one difficult to define precisely. However, its outlines may be observed in the humanism of Petrarch as developed by the Florentines around 1400. In the first place, humanists were concerned primarily with practical questions of ethics: How shall a man conduct himself in order to be virtuous, understanding "virtue" to mean moral virtue. They wrote theoretical treatises, as well as handbooks, on such subjects as wisdom, happiness, love, the family, the education of the young, the qualities that make a good prince, the problems of nobility, and the ideals of a courtier—princes, nobles, and courtiers being of the Italian rather than the northern European type. They were not concerned about religious issues per se, and almost none were anti- or even non-Christian. Descriptive as well as didactic works, particularly works of history, gained great popularity among the Italian upper classes. Princes, high government officials, rich merchants, and bankers tried to live as the humanists prescribed, striving to gain distinction in various fields of activity and adopting the label "*uomo universale,*" ("universal man") if successful.

The humanists sought the answers to their questions in the classics. The ancient writers became "authorities," and were revered and venerated in much the same way as the Bible, Aristotle, and the early Church Fathers had been by medieval philosophers. The favorite source was Cicero, though all were valued highly. Indeed, it seems to have been their antiquity rather than the profundity of their thought that was the source of their prestige. The humanist preoccupation with classic sources led to the discovery of many long-forgotten manuscripts. In the course of the Renaissance, most of Plato and Neoplatonic writings were brought to light, as well as such authors as Epictetus, Marcus Aurelius, Lucretius, Pliny, Xenophon, Plutarch, and Lucian. Poggio Bracciolini (1380–1459), who worked forty years for the papacy before becoming chancellor of Florence, was particularly adept at tracking down old manuscripts, travelling over all of Europe in his quest. Manuscript collecting became a mark of esteem for those who could afford it. Frederick of Montefeltro, duke of Urbino in the third quarter of the fifteenth century, kept thirty to forty copyists busy and invested more than 30,000 florins to fill his classical library. The industry of men such as Poggio and Frederick, though it often reached ludicrous proportions, made possible the recovery by 1450 or thereabouts of almost all surviving ancient manuscripts.

The humanists also favored the intellectual disciplines and modes of expression of their classic teachers. The declamatory essay, the dialogue, the letter, poetry, and history were used to instruct and edify. History was held in especially high esteem as a guide to the conduct of government and war, and for the first time since antiquity, scholars studied the past with reasonable accuracy and objectivity. Subject matter was secular and primary sources were consulted. This new approach may be seen in the treatment of Caesar: his statue was clothed now in a toga, the knight's armor it had worn in the Middle Ages discarded along with the medieval conception of history.

The Revival of Ancient Languages Whatever the mode of expression, the way one said something was as important as what one said, and the humanists vied with each other to perfect a correct classic style. To do so required a close study of the ancient texts. This, in turn, required learning virtually a new Latin syntax and vocabulary. Medieval Latin, however useful it may have been to the theologians and lawyers, was deemed inadequate for the new ways of thought. "For many centuries," wrote the humanist Lorenzo Valla (1405–1457), "not only has no one spoken in the Latin manner, but no one who has read Latin has understood it." Furthermore, the manuscripts were often bad copies, full of errors, so they had to be corrected before they could be understood. It followed that the humanists, in the course of deciphering the texts, developed the rudiments of a new intellectual discipline, critical philology. First they carefully examined the text itself to determine its authenticity, grammatical structure, style, and so on; then they interpreted the text's meaning. The most famous of the critics was Valla, who skillfully and objectively dissected many documents, including several dating from the early Christian era. He proved the "Donation of Constantine," by which the fourth-century emperor had supposedly bequeathed temporal power to the papacy, to be false. In comparing the Greek texts, he found certain of Jerome's translations in the Vulgate inaccurate. This was the first rumble of thunder to come when northern humanists, who were more interested in the Christian than the pagan classics, applied the critical method to Biblical and Patristic sources with even more telling results.

Valla worked from the Greek texts of the Bible. In his day, many humanists knew this second great classical language. Indeed, the most fruitful humanistic studies after the middle of the fifteenth century were the recovery of Greek manuscripts and their translation into Latin. The revival of Greek began at the turn of the fourteenth century and gathered momentum thereafter. Although Petrarch had wanted to read Homer in the original, had tried to learn Greek, and had urged his contemporaries to do likewise, few obeyed him. The first flush of enthusiasm for things Roman blinded the early humanists to the glories of Greek civilization. Succeeding generations were more flexible, though Latin always remained the favorite for reasons of taste as well as convenience. The Church council held at Florence in the late 1430's, which the Greeks were invited to attend, and the conquest of Constantinople by the Turks in 1453, which drove many Greeks into exile, gave a strong impetus to Greek studies by furnishing many more competent teachers with knowledge of sources. By 1450, Pope Nicholas

V (1447–1455) was directing a large-scale project at the Vatican aimed at translating the known Greek texts into Latin. Venice was another important center for such work. At the Venetian Academy a group of scholars made translations and the pioneer printer Aldus Manutius published them.

The revival of Greek opened up wholly new vistas to the humanists. Most important was a fresh interest in Plato. During the course of the fifteenth century the remainder of Plato's writings were recovered and translated into Latin, most of them by Marsilio Ficino (1433–1499) at Florence. Ficino founded and headed the Platonic "Academy" (really only a group of scholars and artists) with the financial backing of Cosimo de' Medici. There, he evolved a school of Neoplatonic philosophy, the only school of philosophy to come out of the Renaissance, which tried to reconcile Plato, his Hellenic commentators, and other ancient thinkers with mature Christian theology. This Neoplatonism was not very original but it was appealing, with its emphasis on ideal truth and beauty, on the dignity of man and on his divine nature and creativity, and in its religious orientation and rejection of materialism. This last suggests correctly that the Florentines had by this time lost some of the civic and mercantile spirit that had distinguished earlier humanism, for Ficino's philosophy was very popular. Few laymen understood its full ramifications but in simplified form it had great influence on literature and art for the next century, particularly the concept of "Platonic," or intellectual love. Lorenzo the Magnificent, Angelo Poliziano (1454–1494), and Michelangelo wrote "Neoplatonic" poems and Botticelli drew on "Neoplatonic" themes in his most famous paintings.

Niccolo Machiavelli. The first political theorist of modern Europe to see clearly beyond his own time, Machiavelli took contemporary Italian experience—the day-to-day problems of city-states in conflict—and created a political theory about the State for all time. (The Uffizi/Alinari-Scala.)

Following Greek, Hebrew was revived, and Pico della Mirandola (1463–1494), Ficino's celebrated pupil, was the most important single figure in its revival. Pico, during his short life, was brash and brilliant. Before he was twenty he conceived the idea of bringing all the world's knowledge together in a single great compendium. He read Latin, Greek, Hebrew, and Arabic sources with fantastic energy and virtuosity, compressing everything into nine hundred propositions, which he offered to debate with any scholar. He was fascinated by the Cabala and Jewish mysticism, and tried to fit them into a Christian context. His achievements were transitory, except for his *Oration on the Dignity of Man,* extolling philosophy and justifying man's central place in the universe. His influence, however, was profound upon such important northern humanists as Johann Reuchlin, his pupil and the greatest Hebraist of his day, and John Colet of England. Like Greek, Hebrew became a formidable tool of the northern humanists in their reading of Christian sources.

Machiavelli and Courtly Literature The popularity of Ficino's Neoplatonism suggests that Florentine values had changed in significant ways by the late fifteenth century. Although still secular in their point of view, the Florentines had lost some of their enthusiasm for the materialistic and hotly patriotic ideals of the early humanists, preferring something more subtle, more transcendental, less obviously mundane. This change corresponded with and can be traced to an aristocratic tendency in Florentine society as the upper class *ottimati* entrenched themselves in government, as they consolidated the wealth they had possessed now for generations, investing in rural property and secure urban enterprises, and as the Medici family more and more assumed the air of a princely dynasty. The old devotion to liberty and the psychological need to justify their worldly life waned.

But rebels remained, in whom republicanism was so deeply ingrained that nothing could shake it, and they carried on the tradition of Salutati and Bruni. The most famous was Niccolò Machiavelli (1469–1527). Machiavelli was the son of a good but poor Florentine family that had been in the thick of Florentine politics for generations. He received an adequate though not outstanding education, learning Latin and reading the Roman classics but neglecting Greek entirely. He always preferred to write in Italian and his prose style became a model for later writers. In 1498 he entered government employ in a secondary post which demanded hard work and carried little prestige but which provided excellent administrative and diplomatic experience. The so-called "Florentine Republic" survived until 1512, and Machiavelli served it as a civil functionary and junior ambassador in several European capitals, at the court of Cesare Borgia and as a military expert. He reorganized the Florentine militia (he despised mercenary troops) and won back rebellious Pisa, but lost ignominiously to the Spaniards in 1512. He then went into exile, emerging several times to accept minor government jobs and ending his life more or less in disgrace. He began to write in exile, producing poetry, plays (*Mandragola* is a comic masterpiece), biography, *The Art of War*, a *History of Florence*, *Discourses on Livy*, and most famous of all, *The Prince.*

Machiavelli's opinions on politics and government have been hotly debated for centuries and the problems they raise are still unresolved. In *The Prince,* he seems to advocate tyranny as the only sure antidote to man's natural egoism and contentiousness. Domestic peace is to be sought at all costs, even to the exclusion of liberty. In practice, any action by a dictator is "good" so long as it serves the state, and the state is amoral, selfish, power-hungry, with no higher end than its own preservation. But it is only by means of a strong and ordered state that man's dangerous natural qualities can be curbed. This recognition of the state as a sovereign entity, set apart from such ideal conceptions as the "Christian Republic," was one of Machiavelli's greatest contributions to modern thought. In the *Discourses,* on the other hand, and less clearly in the *History of Florence,* his old-fashioned republicanism and love of liberty appear. Only in a republic, he asserts, can man's highest intellectual and spiritual aspirations be attained. Indeed, he gives to patriotism almost religious qualities. A dictator may be necessary to put degenerate republics on the right track again, but only as an expedient and only temporarily.

The *Discourses* seem to contradict *The Prince,* creating the riddle of Machiavelli's thought. Some scholars have suggested that *The Prince* may be a bitter travesty on contemporary Italy, an expression of an idealistic man's disillusionment with the failure of republican institutions even in his beloved Florence. Others have seen it as a realistic appraisal of man and politics. A recent scholar has suggested that *The Prince* is a sincere but youthful effort, the product of a half-educated mind. The *Discourses*, on the other hand, written some years later, reflect Machiavelli's mature views gained through intimate contact with the old Florentine civic humanist tradition as preserved by a group of republican intellectuals.[2]

This trend toward aristocratic ways of thought appeared earlier and was more marked in the dictatorships for obvious reasons. While the primitive humanism of Petrarch was accepted and elaborated on, Florentine humanism and its identification of liberty and middle-class business with culture was never welcome. At the same moment that Salutati and Bruni were extolling the virtues of freedom, the humanist Giovanni Conversini, writing for the Paduan dictator, could say: "Where the multitude rules, there is no respect for accomplishment that does not yield a profit; . . . everybody has as much contempt of poets as he is ignorant of them and will rather keep dogs than maintain scholars or teachers." And inevitably, as the despotisms assumed monarchical characteristics, they drew closer to the culture of northern Europe, adopting courtly modes of behavior and fostering pseudo-chivalric ideals. The humanism that emanated from the despotic courts justified the rule of a single man and glorified the prince.

But as in the case of the Florentines, the dictators and their people remained essentially secular, sophisticated, and urban, interested above all in the affairs of man and this world. *The Courtier*, published in 1528 by Baldassare Castiglione (1478–1529), is a good measure of the Renaissance character of the Italian courts. This is a book of rules for the gentleman and lady of the new style. It consists of a series of conversations, among men and women at the court of Urbino, in which qualities of mind and body and standards of behavior are debated at length. To a casual eye, the ideal courtier is the image of the medieval knight, but a closer examination reveals his modernity. High birth is an asset, but personal accomplishments and manners are more important. Athletic talent is a requisite, especially a good game of tennis, together with a "passable" knowledge of the humanities. In love, the courtier should be discreet, in war courageous. He should know music and chess. But these qualities of the *uomo universale* are not enough for the courtier to achieve true nobility; he must also dedicate his life to serving his prince. For the humanist ideal of public service was not confined to republics. It was present, in a different form, in the princely courts as well.

THE FINE ARTS

Down the centuries, the fine arts have seemed to laymen and scholars alike to express most clearly and fully the Renaissance ideals of the individual, of nature, of classic form, and of beauty for its own sake. Giorgio Vasari

[2]H. Baron, "Machiavelli: the Republican Citizen and the Author of the Prince," *English Historical Review* (April 1961).

The Chess Players by Girolamo da Cremona. By the third quarter of the fifteenth century, Italian patricians had fallen into a way of life not much different from that of the northern aristocrats. Games were typical diversions. But such writers as Castiglione stressed more serious activities: the "noble" man must serve his prince and his state. (Metropolitan Museum of Art, Griggs Bequest.)

(1511–1574), in his *Lives of the Most Eminent Painters, Sculptors, and Architects,* coined the term "rebirth" to describe the art of his day, and later scholars and critics followed his lead. They emphasized the "revival of antiquity" as the source of Renaissance art, emphasizing the contrast with the art of the preceding "age of faith," which they labeled "Gothic" (itself a term of derision), formless, unnatural, aesthetic, and for the most part ugly and badly executed. They dismissed Gothic art as religious, its sole aim to arouse spiritual emotion in the beholder. Renaissance art they praised as rational, human, even pagan.

In fact, the contrasts are not so easily defined. Gothic art, the art of northern Europe, laid great stress on man and nature. It was grounded in realism; indeed exact representation of minute detail was a criterion of excellence. Gothic artists used classic models and, particularly in the fourteenth and fifteenth centuries, secular subject matter. Furthermore, Renaissance art was strongly religious in content, reflecting the taste of the artists and their patrons. Why this confusion in the minds of scholars and critics? One reason is their failure to understand and appreciate Gothic art and to distinguish carefully between it and Byzantine art, which was dominant in Italy before 1300. Another is their failure to observe the influence of the Gothic style on Italian art in the fourteenth century. Recent scholarship has corrected these deficiencies, but it still remains true that the art of the Renaissance was different from any that had gone before.

The Supremacy of Florence As with humanism, we can trace Renaissance art to Florence at the turn of the fourteenth century, where three great figures introduced a revolutionary style: Masaccio (1401–1429) in painting, Donatello (1386–1466) in sculpture, and Brunelleschi (1377–1446) in architecture. Prior to this time, the arts in Florence, as well as elsewhere in Italy, were under the influence first of Byzantine then of Gothic styles. The great Florentine painter Giotto (1276–1336) foreshadowed the future in much the same way as his contemporary Dante. Giotto's paintings were the first to incorporate linear perspective, to be three-dimensional, and to have (as the famous critic Bernard Berenson said) "tactile value." His people and settings are recognizable. But he was a primitive compared to his fifteenth-century successors. His technique was undeveloped and his materials, tempera and fresco, did not lend themselves to subtle workmanship. After Giotto, there was retrogression in Florentine painting, a resurgence of the Byzantine tradition, and acceptance of northern Gothic. A recent commentator has suggested this was partly due to social dislocation and unrest following the Black Death of 1348, which for a generation or so stimulated a more conservative religiosity.[3]

The new style was introduced at the same moment that Salutati and Bruni were defining civic humanism—not by coincidence, for the new ideals of Republican Rome, of the *vita activa* as practiced by Cicero, found their way into art. Artists began to emulate classic rules of taste and technique, particularly in building and sculpturing. They recognized, as the Greeks and Romans had, the nobility of the human body and its beauty. They concentrated on achieving symmetry and harmony of composition, developing the science of optics and the study of anatomy. Donatello's *St. George* and *David* embody what the artists learned, as does Masaccio's *Adam and Eve.* Brunelleschi's Pazzi Chapel is a model of classic design. Subject matter was still religious for the most part, but the fusion of classicism and Christianity inevitably worked to the latter's detriment.

The Expulsion of Adam and Eve from the Garden by Massacio. Massacio died at twenty-seven but not before he had mastered the technique of "atmospheric perspective"—blending and subordinating the background so that the figures in the foreground are separated and stand out in space. As we can see by the anguish of Adam and Eve, Massacio painted living human beings with emotions. (Chiesa del Carmine, Florence/Alinari-Scala.)

The Florentines accepted the new style, though somewhat more slowly than they had accepted civic humanism. Like civic humanism, it portrayed graphically their new ideal of man and the world. To patronize artists became the fashion; the public had money and taste; and, besides, such humanists as Alberti lauded the virtue of investment in culture. The status of artists improved enormously. From anonymous craftsmen they became famous and respected individuals, friends of popes and princes, rich in their own right. As the Florentine style spread over Italy, artists and patrons appeared at Venice, Rome, Milan, and at the princely courts. The style matured and became more flamboyant while the subject matter became more secular. By the first years of the sixteenth century, the heights were scaled and Renaissance art began its decline.

The number and quality of the artists in the century after the originators we have discussed above was truly amazing. In the direct Florentine tradition

[3]M. Meiss, *Painting in Florence and Siena After the Black Death* (Princeton: Princeton University Press, 1951).

Pazzi Chapel by Brunelleschi. The architect deliberately copied the Roman style. One can picture Brunelleschi, with Donatello (sculptor) and Massaccio (painter) sitting over a bottle of Tuscan wine and listening to the vision of Roman republicanism as expounded by the historian Lorenzo Bruni, then going forth to capture it in stone or paint. (Alinari-Scala.)

was Piero della Francesca (1416–1492), who studied Masaccio's frescoes in the Brancacci Chapel and learned perspective from Brunelleschi. Piero retained the classic style of his teachers, his paintings illustrating the emotional effect of pure form without sentiment or shallow romanticism. His sense of composition was outstanding, and he was one of the few landscape painters of ability in fifteenth-century Italy. Piero's greatest work is the *Legend of the Holy Cross* at Arezzo. Andrea Mantegna (1431–1506), who worked mostly at Padua, was another who preserved in his painting a deep reverence for Roman antiquity. Indeed, of all Italian painters he was most strongly influenced by classicism. His greatness, however, lies in his mastery of perspective, as seen clearly in his *Agony in the Garden.*

Other painters of the fifteenth century, however, turned from pure classicism to a more romantic style. Of these, the most successful was Sandro Botticelli (1444–1510) whose lyrical, melancholy style ties him more closely to the Gothic North than to his native Florence. His themes were drawn from both pagan and Christian sources, and he was particularly influenced by the Neoplatonism of Marsilio Ficino. But all his paintings are infused with a purity of spirit that blunts their often voluptuous beauty. His *Birth of Venus* depicts a girl as virginal as his madonnas; indeed, in point of fact he used the same model, Simonetta Vespucci, toast of Laurentian Florence, for them all.

Raphael, da Vinci, and Michelangelo But these men and their contemporaries were only the prelude to the High Renaissance of Raphael, da Vinci, and Michelangelo. Leonardo da Vinci (1452–1519) was the closest the

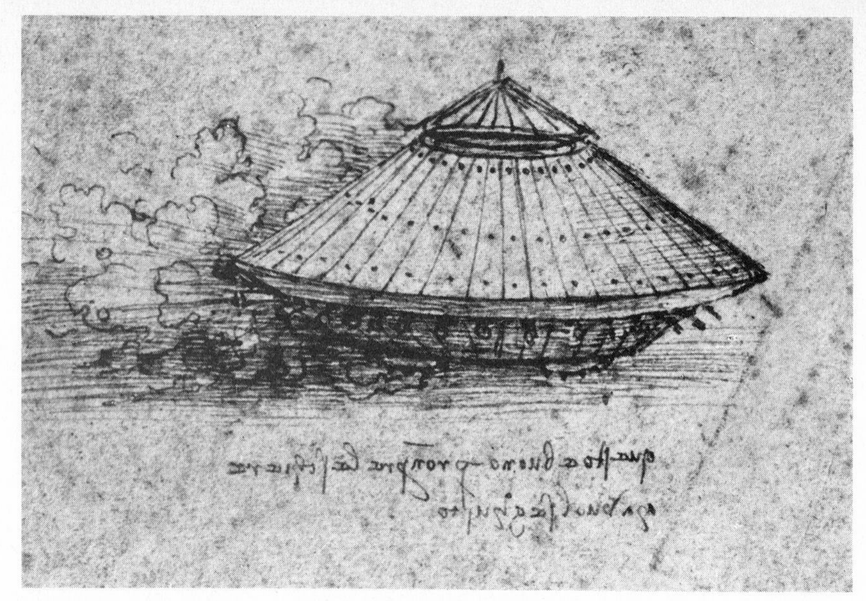

Leonardo da Vinci's Design for a Tank. Offering his services to Ludovico Sforza of Milan, Leonardo wrote, "I can make sound, indestructible armoured vehicles. If these reach the enemy with their cannon they can compel the largest forces to retreat." (Anderson, Rome.)

Renaissance came to a universal genius, painter, sculptor, musician, and scientist and inventor. Although he painted relatively little, each of his paintings is a masterpiece. The *Mona Lisa* is a remarkably effective attempt to convey the soul of a human being through a portrait. The *Madonna of the Rocks* is the archetype of the new naturalistic religious style. *The Last Supper,* however, is da Vinci's greatest painting. Though in bad condition today, we can still see that its composition and its delineation of character are masterly, and that the technique of blending light into shadow, called chiaroscuro, fulfills the hope of Masaccio almost a century earlier.

In contrast to da Vinci, Raphael (1483–1520) produced many paintings in his brief and brilliant career, nearly all of them models of the intellectual and technical achievements of the Renaissance. Indeed, in a real sense, Raphael's painting sums up Renaissance art. Born in Umbria, he visited Florence in his youth, coming under the influence of da Vinci and Michelangelo. At the behest of Popes Julius II and Leo X, he did his major work in Rome, which by 1500 had become the cultural center of Italy and Europe. Though not possessed of the original genius of the two great Florentine artists, he was nevertheless gifted with an unerring sense of design and balance, with faultless good taste, and most of all with the ability to make the best use of what others had devised. He never ceased to learn, but he never plagiarized; his talent brought something unique to each of his paintings. His many madonnas are perfect jewels but his masterpiece is the *School of Athens.* This is the ultimate statement of Renaissance classicism and the finest group painting of the age. The complex, closely knit design achieves unity effortlessly through the compositional skill of the master.

Michelangelo Buonarotti (1475–1564) was quite a different type from either da Vinci or Raphael, a dynamic genius, driven to create. He painted

Young Lady with a Unicorn by Raphael. Raphael painted religious and secular subjects alike with warmth and humanity. The unicorn symbolized feminine purity and chastity. (Gabinetto Fotografico Nazionale.)

little, regarding the art as secondary to sculpture, and he always painted with a sculptor's eyes. Still his magnificent frescoes covering the walls and ceiling (more than 600 square yards of surface) of the Vatican's Sistine Chapel, completed in 1512, are perhaps the greatest single achievement of the Renaissance. Lying flat on his back on a high scaffold, quarrelling almost daily with Pope Julius II who demanded greater speed, worrying that his color sense did not match his sense of form, the artist rendered his symbolic masterpiece. The subject is immense—the Creation, the expulsion of Adam and Eve, and the Flood on one level, Christ's Passion on the other. Today, the colors have faded and the walls have cracked, but visitors will stand

The Creation of Adam by Michelangelo. A detail from the massive frescoes commissioned by Pope Julius II covering the ceiling of the Sistine Chapel. God awakens Adam to life by a touch. (Alinari-Scala.)

or sit or lie for hours to contemplate and absorb this great work of religious imagery.

But Michelangelo was first of all a sculptor, the best the Western world has known. His *David, Moses,* and *Pietà,* his figures on the Medici tombs, reveal a grandiose conception and a faultless technique. A man of deep religious conviction, influenced by both conventional Christianity and Neoplatonism, Michelangelo was able to infuse his marble figures with a spirituality that strikes us forceably even today. To complete his mastery of the arts, Michelangelo finished the plans for St. Peter's Cathedral in Rome after the death of Bramante, the first architect.

Michelangelo, like Raphael, was drawn to Rome. Besides that city and Florence, Venice had become a center of the painting art by the early years of the sixteenth century. Giovanni Bellini (1430–1516) was the master who gave Venetian painting its characteristic style: design expressed through color, often opulent, sometimes riotous, always striking to the eye. The Florentine classic discipline gave way at Venice to freer composition, the Florentine austerity to sensuous languor. Giorgione (1477–1510) carried the style forward, the concept of free composition in such semi-landscapes as *Fête Champêtre,* the idea of sensuous languor in literally hundreds of canvasses. *Fête Champêtre* has no central mass, no pyramidal symmetry as have the typical Florentine paintings. Rather, the figures are at the sides and the observer's eye is allowed to penetrate to the distant landscape in the center. In Titian (1477–1576) the Venetian style reached fulfillment and oil painting its highest development. This prodigious worker painted every kind of

(Opposite page)
Michelangelo's David. Michelangelo used the biblical David to glorify the human body. Completed in 1504, the statue of the proud youth, confident of victory, was placed in the central square of Florence as a symbol to the Florentines. (Alinari-Scala.)

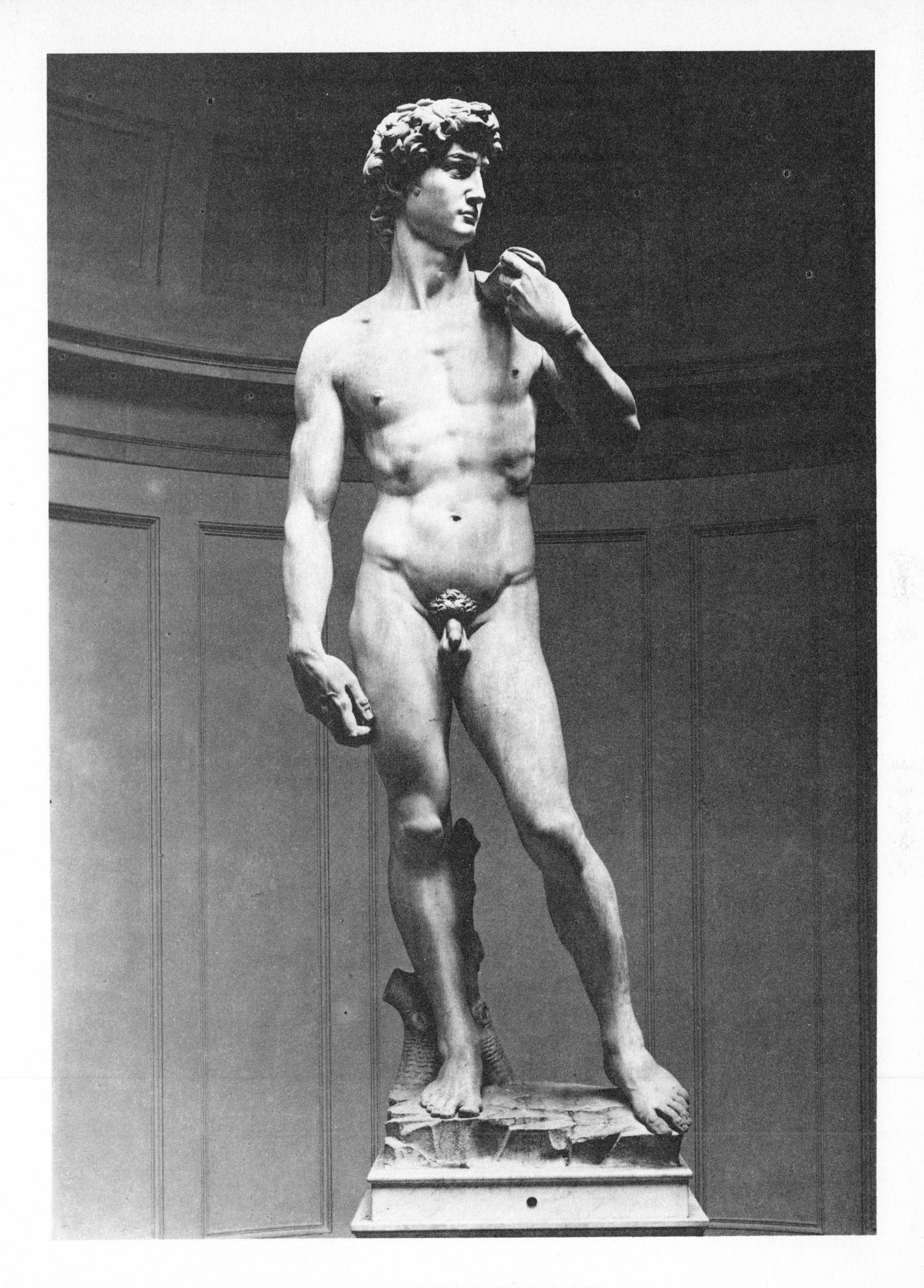

subject from small portraits to sumptuous, even erotic, nudes from altarpieces to pagan mythologies. It is impossible to pick his best or even his most representative work, but the *Assumption* and *Bacchus and Ariadne* are typical of his middle years.

FURTHER READING

A number of works cited for the previous chapter, particularly those by Burckhardt, Symonds and Hay, include much on Italian humanism. The most important recent study of humanism's origins is H. Baron, * *The Crisis of the Early Italian Renaissance* (rev. ed., 1966). The best short summary is P. O. Kristeller, * *Renaissance Thought I & II* (1955, 1965); but see also the brilliant E. Garin, * *Italian Humanism* (1965), and the controversial G. Toffanin, *History of Humanism* (1954). A valuable discussion of pre-Petrarchian humanism is contained in R. Weiss, *The Dawn of Humanism in Italy* (1947). Selections from leading humanists, together with critical introductions, are to be found in E. Cassirer, et al., * *The Renaissance Philosophy of Man* (1948).

Important studies by a great historian of ideas are to be found in P. O. Kristeller, *Eight Philosophers of the Italian Renaissance* (1964). G. Holmes, *The Florentine Enlightenment* (1969), is a bit pretentious but useful. On Machiavelli, the literature is enormous. Outstanding for its perceptiveness is the interpretation of F. Chabod, * *Machiavelli and the Renaissance* (1958). Other interpretations, along with a bibliography, are contained in the collection by D. L. Jenson, * *Machiavelli: Cynic, Patriot, or Political Scientist?* (1960). A good short biography is J. R. Hale, * *Machiavelli and Renaissance Italy* (1961). F. Gilbert, *Machiavelli and Guicciardini* (1965), is a fine study of the two great Renaissance historians. R. Ridolfi, *The Life of Niccolo Machiavelli* (1963), is standard. On other writers in the vernacular, see J. H. Whitfield, * *A Short History of Italian Literature* (1960).

A classic interpretation of Renaissance painting is B. Berenson, * *Italian Painters of the Renaissance* (1952). A. Hauser,* *A Social History of Art*, 2 vols. (1951), a provocative if somewhat narrow attempt to discover the environmental bases of art, includes several chapters on the Renaissance. F. Antal, *Florentine Painting and Its Social Background* (1948), is a Marxist interpretation. E. Panovsky, * *Studies in Iconology* (1939), is a brilliant analysis of certain aspects of Renaissance art. The best recent work on architecture is R. Wittkower, *Architectural Principles in the Age of Humanism* (rev. ed., 1962), but see also Peter Murray, *The Architecture of the Italian Renaissance* (1963); and J. White, * *Art and Architecture in Italy 1250–1400* (1966) for a good background. A brilliant recent study of certain social aspects of architecture is R. A. Goldthwaite, "The Florentine Palace as Domestic Architecture," *The American Historical Review*, vol. 77 (Oct. 1972). Sculpture is treated in J. Pope-Hennessy, *Italian Renaissance Sculpture* (1958). On Renaissance music see G. Reese, *Music of the Renaissance* (rev. ed., 1959).

*Books available in paperback edition are marked with an asterisk.

3 The Culture of the Northern Renaissance

The culture of northern Europe in the fourteenth and fifteenth centuries is too often set against that of the Italian Renaissance—to the North's disadvantage. It is pointed out that theology and philosophy continued to dominate northern universities; that urban styles of life and thought were but a weak echo of the aristocratic styles of life and thought to be found at the northern courts; that religion for almost everyone had degenerated into superstition and near-heresy. The Renaissance is seen as creative and new, northern culture as sterile and backward. Obviously, there is some truth to this view. But on the whole, it is quite unfair for, though northern culture was in a broad sense traditional in this period, it was also vital and innovative in a number of important ways.

THE WANING OF THE MIDDLE AGES

Northern culture remained essentially medieval in the century and a half between 1350 and 1500, but the conditions out of which that culture sprang were changing. Classic feudalism was long gone, victim of a money economy and the growing power of kings. Wars were now fought by mercenaries, and the romance of courtly love and knightly combat was to be read of in books or played out on the tournament fields. At the courts of France, England, and Burgundy the tradition of service to a lord began to be transformed into an ethic of service to the state. Townspeople, if they delighted in emulating the nobility—living "nobly," marrying their daughters to noble sons, buying titled land—were nevertheless imbued with patriotism and civic pride for their cities. Urban histories and panagyrics to urban life were numerous, particularly in the busy mercantile cities of the Netherlands and Germany. Although late medieval piety was notable for its exaggerated veneration of saints and relics and its excesses of self-mortification and penance, it was also characterized by intense and original forms of individual spirituality, foreshadowing the mysticism of the Protestant and Catholic Reformations. The compulsion to create great theological systems in the manner of Thomas Aquinas had given way to nitpicking analysis, but analysis that could be applied with profit to scientific questions. And, if the ideals of the Italian Renaissance made little headway in the North before 1500, after that date they were combined with native ideals to produce a unique "Christian humanism."

The Universities and Late Medieval Science There is no doubt that much that was thought and written in European universities of the late fourteenth and fifteenth centuries was inconsequential. The teachings of William of Occam, which among his intellectual heirs came to be called the "*via moderna,*" emphasized critical analysis of specific theological and philosophical questions and discouraged bold and sweeping syntheses. Since a mind the equal of Occam's was rare, most of his followers buried themselves in trivia, in petty argument over unimportant details. But out of the universities, too, came the Conciliar Theory, a brilliant solution to the problem of the Great Schism, and the theories that laid the intellectual groundwork of the scientific revolution of the sixteenth and seventeenth centuries.

Nicole Oresme of the University of Paris, and his Armillary Sphere. Oresme was one of a number of late medieval scientists who questioned the traditional Aristotelian scientific views. Though their contrary arguments were often also wrong, their skepticism became an important element in the thought and method of scientists who came after them. (Bibliothèque Nationale, Paris.)

Particularly important advances were made in the development of the modern scientific method and in physics. In both fields, Aristotle's thought was pervasive throughout the entire period, but scientists ("natural philosophers") came to regard it with less blind worship and with more critical insight. At the universities of Paris and Padua, they debated various methods for explaining natural phenomena, and finally arrived at one (discarded by Aristotle as "circular reasoning") which in essence is what scientists use as their method today: isolate and describe a natural phenomenon; invent a hypothesis to explain it; test the hypothesis through observation and experiment; and modify it if necessary, to end up with a general theory that explains *all* such phenomena. This method was not perfected before the seventeenth century, but in elementary form was applied earlier to a range of natural phenomena, including several having to do with motion. Aristotle believed an object moved because it was seeking its "natural" place in the universe (a falling stone was seeking its "home" in the center of earth) or because it was continously being moved (as a horse pulling a cart). But why did a stone accelerate when dropped from a window? Why did an arrow remain in flight when it left the bowstring? Aristotle's answers were unsatisfactory to such thoughtful men as Jean Buridan (d. 1358) of the University of Paris. Buridan concluded that a mover (say a bowstring) must impress some special motive power on the object moved (an arrow), which continues after the two have separated. This *impetus,* as he called it, is not overcome until superior forces, gravity and air resistance, interfere and bring the arrow to the ground. In freely falling bodies, *impetus* added to natural gravity causes acceleration. These were not the correct answers, of course, for not until the seventeenth century was the idea of *inertia* fully elaborated. But they were significant because they indicated that men asking scientific questions had begun to break the intellectual ties that bound them to Aristotle.

The Court of Burgundy Life for the European nobility at the various courts was different only in degree during the late fourteenth and fifteenth cen-

This fourteenth-century French carving on the lid of a small ivory casket depicts a joust. Long after such exercises had become archaic in actual warfare, they remained popular games. (Walters Art Gallery, Baltimore.)

Fifteenth-century Belgian Parade Shield. Chivalry and courtly love had become romantic fantasy by this time, something hardly to be considered expressions of reality. (Courtesy of the Trustees of the British Museum.)

turies. Whether kings, dukes, or lesser men were at their heads, the courts had become the places where nobles sought opportunity and prestige, curried the favor of "bigger" men, and showed off splendid entourages. The tradition that would lead straight to Louis XIV and Versailles was well underway. Precedence and manners were ends in themselves, and everywhere the ideals of knighthood, of chivalry, and of courtly love persisted—indeed, were nurtured and elaborated—though they bore little relation to the real world. A nobleman's favorite occupation was jousting in honor of his lady-love, in heavy armor and with elaborate ceremony. The heroic past, for the most part highly romanticized legend, became the model for the present. The *Roman de la Rose* and *Tristan and Isolde,* though dating from long before, were immensely popular; and about 1470, the Englishman Thomas Mallory composed the *Morte d'Arthur,* immortalizing the knights of the Round Table, Sir Launcelot, Guinevere, and the rest.

No court in Europe compared with that of Burgundy. The dukes' title derived from the duchy of Burgundy bordering east-central France, but their wealth and power came from the Netherlands, over most of which they also ruled. For most of the fifteenth century, these "Great Dukes of the West," as the Turkish sultan called them, outshone all the kings of Europe in their display and in their devotion to traditional noble ideals. Their banquets were magnificent and costly, one of them featuring a huge pastry, which when brought to the table and opened was found to contain twelve musicians who began to play. Their tournaments and jousts were unrivalled in their pageantry. In 1430, the greatest of the Burgundian dukes, Philip the Good (1419–1467), founded the Order of the Golden Fleece, ostensibly to promote a crusade against the infidel, but in fact to glorify himself and his nobles. It became the most prestigious of all knightly orders, though it had no real military function at all. In the dukes' hands, tradition became ritual, stylized, governed rigidly by protocol, made to survive long after its reasons for being were gone. But the dukes were not stupid, and there were reasons for all this. They were not kings, and this great disadvantage they tried to overcome by the splendor of their courts. Philip in particular succeeded very well at this, and at the same time won the respect and loyalty of his nobles. To the old traditions was added a new and more vital one, an ethic of devotion and service to the duke. It was an ethic that had not yet found its way to the courts of England, France, or Spain.

The "Devotio Moderna" Southern Germany was prepared somewhat earlier than the rest of Europe for the reception of Italian ideas. Court culture in Germany was insignificant; the cultural and intellectual centers were the towns. Nominally, the emperor was sovereign over the greatest of these towns, but for practical purposes, they were independent, their citizens self-governing. In the late Middle Ages, the towns prospered through trade and industry, and many of the citizens grew rich. An urban patrician class arose which resembled that of Florence and other Italian republics. Indeed, the relationship between these German townsmen and the Italians was even

Detail from the Court of Duke John the Fearless of Burgundy. What men and women wore in the fifteenth century was an infallible guide to their position in society and very often to their occupation. (Versailles/Alinari-Scala.)

closer, for travel across the Alps was a regular thing, and Italian humanists had begun to leave an imprint as early as the middle of the century. Probably the most influential Italian was Aeneas Sylvius Piccolomini (1405–1464) who served in a number of capacities in Germany, among them as diplomat for the Emperor Frederick III, before becoming Pope Pius II. One of the first outstanding non-Italian humanists in all of Europe was the Fresian Rudolf

Agricola (1444–1485). Agricola studied for some years in Italy, then visited various parts of Germany and the Netherlands, ending his days at Heidelberg. His interest in classical studies spread to other German universities. But his ideas, and humanist ideas in general, were only lesser rivals of the late medieval tradition. Their deep and pervasive influence came only when they merged with Christian ideas early in the sixteenth century.

For Germany was a religious land, the scene of several powerful movements of mystical piety in the fourteenth and fifteenth centuries. As we shall see in our study of the Reformation, these movements were partly a reaction to the growing materialism of the Church, which many simple people found insufficient to their spiritual needs, and partly a defense against the uncertainties of a changing world. Master Eckhart (1260–1327) and his disciple, Johan Tauler (1300–1361), were early figures. Tauler was a preacher of wide repute who taught a common-sense piety stressing personal goodness and brotherly love. The most important movement, however, in terms of its influence on European thought, was the *devotio moderna.* This was a form of simple, personal worship that sought in love and faith a closer union with God. Its founder was Gerard Groote (1340–1384), a lay preacher and advocate of clerical reform. Its great book was *The Imitation of Christ* by Thomas à Kempis (1380–1471), a spiritual guide surpassed in its popularity over the centuries only by the Bible. The book's character, and the character of the movement, may be seen in the following passage:

He who follows Me, says Christ our Saviour, walks not in darkness, for he will have the light of life. These are the words of our Lord Jesus Christ, and by them we are admonished to follow His teachings and His manner of living, if we would be truly enlightened and delivered from all blindness of heart.

Let all the study of our heart be from now on to have our meditation fixed wholly on the life of Christ, for His holy teachings are of more virtue and strength than the words of all the angels and saints. And he who through grace has the inner eye of his soul opened to the true beholding of the Gospels of Christ will find in them hidden manna.[1]

The teachers of the "new devotion" were the "Brethren of the Common Life." They were laymen, sworn to clerical vows but members of no regular order, whose aim was to cleanse and revitalize the Church by reforming its communicants. They concentrated especially on the instruction of young people. They began their work in Holland at the turn of the fourteenth century, and in the course of the next hundred years founded schools throughout the northern Netherlands and down the Rhine into Germany and Switzerland. They taught a highly individualistic doctrine, short on

[1]From the edition edited by Harold C. Gardiner, S. J., published by Image Books (New York: Doubleday, 1955), p. 31.

formal theology and on those popular religious practices, such as the purchase of indulgences, that went under the name of "good works" and long on Bible reading and faith. They inculcated in their students a deep respect for right conduct and good Latin, though they were not themselves particularly sympathetic to the pagan classics and humanist moral philosophy. Their teaching pervaded the areas into which it went, becoming in many places the predominant religious expression. It is not at all surprising that some of their pupils, who included Erasmus of Rotterdam and Martin Luther, found in the education they absorbed at schools of the Brethren the spiritual inspiration with which to transform Italian into northern humanism.

NORTHERN HUMANISM

Italian culture, as we have noted, was not wholly foreign to northern Europe at the turn of the fifteenth century. Scholars and men of affairs had made individual contacts for generations. A few humanists (Poggio and Petrarch are two examples) had lived in the northern lands, and northerners had studied in Italy and worked at the Vatican and elsewhere. The printed book, invented about the middle of the fifteenth century, was also a means of disseminating humanist ideas, although it was not nearly so important prior to 1500 as it was in the next two or three decades. The Italians were not especially eager to see their writings in print; they considered themselves to be communicating with an intellectual elite who could afford hand copies, not with the "masses." But the Aldine press was active in Venice before 1490, and the northern presses began to print classics and humanist books in quantity as soon as the ideas of the Renaissance became popular. Indeed printing was the chief cause of the Renaissance gaining such wide and rapid popularity, and the northern humanists were the first Europeans to write for a mass audience.

The Italian Influence After about 1490, the flow of the new learning to the north became heavier and more continuous. Doubtless the Italian wars, which began in 1494 after lengthy diplomatic preparation, were a most important stimulant, for they focused all eyes on Italy and increased traffic across the Alps a thousand-fold. It became fashionable for monarchs and great lords to employ Italian clerks and administrators who were trained in the classic school. Such men brought with them their skill in Latin as well as their knowledge of Italian political methods and their concept of the state as developed in Renaissance Italy. Other Italians left their homeland to become tutors and teachers in the schools and households of the North where they established the humanist program of classic studies. This program emphasized human conduct in this world rather than preparation for the next. Henry VIII received this sort of education, as did Francis I of France and his brilliant sister, Marguerite of Angoulême. At the Spanish court, Ferdinand and Isabella saw that all their children were taught in the humanist manner. This does not mean, of course, that European royalty and nobility abandoned religious training or instruction in such chivalric pastimes as jousting, riding, and hunting. Rather, humanism was grafted on to the traditional educational programs. But in the long run, it secularized them and subverted much of their medieval ideal.

As in education, so too in other areas of northern culture: the humanism of Italy was adapted to new social and intellectual needs. "The essential condition for the North's comprehension of Italian innovations was that these should be in a form which would be intelligible to a society that was in the main princely and aristocratic."[2] This requirement virtually eliminated the pure civic humanism of Florentine's Salutati and Bruni and its tradition as kept alive by the Machiavelli of the *Discourses.* This humanism was too urban and middle-class, too anti-monarchical in spirit. More attractive was the mature humanism of the Italian courts so well expressed by Baldassare Castiglione in *The Courtier.* Castiglione's ideas could be readily made to fit the court culture of the North and could reinvigorate it and give it new direction. Northerners also found attractive the philological and historical techniques developed by Lorenzo Valla and the Florentine historians. Valla had shown that the Latin and Greek languages could be used as powerful scholarly weapons; with Machiavelli and his contemporaries a new method of history had reached maturity, a history which distinguished between past and present, which relied on sources, and which saw politics as man's most important secular activity. For the new monarchs of the North, this offered an excellent means to personal glorification. Finally, to the more spiritual-minded northerner, the Neoplatonism of Ficino and the Florentine Academy offered a more exciting and more immediate Christianity than dry scholasticism. In its mysticism and its rejection of rationalism, Neoplatonism had a kinship with such northern religious movements as the *devotio moderna.*

The first important evidence of Italian influence on the northern lay mind was in the field of history. Polydore Vergil (1470–1555), actually a native of Italy, wrote a propagandistic *History of England* for the Tudors. In Spain, two Italian scholars, Lucio Marineo Siculo (1446–1533) and Pietro Martire d'Anghiera (1459–1526), wrote several humanist histories under royal patronage, one a history of Spain, another an account of King Ferdinand's life, and a third a history of the discovery of the New World. Germany was a particularly fruitful area for humanist historiography, partly because of a strong feeling of patriotism and partly because of a sense of inferiority toward things Italian. In 1500, Conrad Celtis (1459–1508) published Tacitus' *Germania* and part of a projected work covering German history, geography, society, and politics, called *Germania Illustrata.* Jacob Wimpfeling (1450–1528) also wrote several works of German history. France lagged behind Germany in rewriting its history, perhaps because its best humanists were oriented toward spiritual matters.

The Christian Humanists If the ultimate effect of humanism on the secular northern mind was great, its effect on religious thought was, in the short run, even greater. Immediately attracted to it were many scholars whose

[2]D. Hay, *The Italian Renaissance* (Cambridge: Cambridge University Press, 1961), p. 188.

interests were primarily spiritual, who for one reason or another were dissatisfied with the Church as an institution and with scholastic theology. These men, the Christian humanists, discovered in Italian humanism the bases for a new society, modeled on pagan and Christian antiquity, which they considered relevant to sixteenth-century man. From the Italians they took over an admiration for Greek and Roman classics, which they believed compatible with orthodox Christianity, and a sense of the past, with which they studied not Greece and Rome but the early Christian church. The Christian humanists read the Bible and patristic literature more intensively than did their mentors, and even the pagan authors were always carefully placed in a Christian context. Like the Italians, they hunted down old manuscripts and published editions of the ancient works, using a hard-won knowledge of classic Latin, Greek, and Hebrew and the literary techniques of critical philology. Naturally enough, their studies confirmed their disgust with a corrupt Church—to which the early Church presented a bright contrast—and sharpened their dislike of complex theology. Their ideal was the simple, pure faith of the Apostles, although in practice the large majority were orthodox. While several flirted with heresy—and passionate souls such as Martin Luther and Huldreich Zwingli carried their belief to its logical end in Protestantism—most Christian humanists objected only to the superstructure of Catholicism, the popular superstitions, the gaudy practices and ceremonies, and the waste and materialism of the huge, complex Church bureaucracy.

The simple faith of the Christian humanists was the keystone of their new society. Their vision of this society was curiously archaic in some ways and far ahead of their time in others. They believed in the unity of Christendom under the headship of pope and emperor. They ignored or were unaware of the rise of the early national states. Within Christendom, they believed humanist culture would prevail; an aristocracy of intellectuals would direct it; governments would be ruled by pious, philosopher kings; war would be unknown. Religious practice would be according to their ideal but no one would be punished for a dissenting opinion. Wise, kind, optimistic, and wholly impractical in its day, was the perfect world of the Christian humanists. Its achievement would come through education, writing, and teaching. Even more than the Italians, these humanists strove to communicate their ideas, confident that man was reasonable and good and master of his fate, that ignorance was the great enemy, and that society could be transformed if everyone saw the light.

Three early Christian humanists of distinction and influence were the German, Johann Reuchlin (1455–1522), the Frenchman, Jacques Lefèvre d'Étaples, and the Englishman John Colet. We have already noted Reuchlin's skill as a Hebraist and his debt to Pico della Mirandola. More than any other individual, Reuchlin brought the new learning to the attention of his fellow Germans. After studying in Florence in the 1490's he returned to Germany convinced of the usefulness of the Hebrew language in understanding the Old Testament. To this end he published a Hebrew grammar

St. Jerome in his Study by Albrecht Dürer. (Metropolitan Museum of Art, Fletcher Fund.)

in 1506, another in 1518, and in 1517 a work on the Cabala. In so doing he aroused the ire of the Dominican scholastics of the University of Cologne and of a converted Jew named Pfefferkorn who wanted Hebrew books banned. A controversy ensued which split intellectual Germany into advocates of humanism versus advocates of scholasticism—to Reuchlin's sympathizers, progressives versus reactionaries. Soon it took on social and political connotations. Humanism was identified with German patriotism and with anti-papalism, and the consequences for the German Reformation were extremely important. The humanist side produced a wonderfully effective satire, *The Letters of Obscure Men.* Probably written by the young scholar-knight Ulrich von Hutten, this purported to be a collection of letters from

Reuchlin's opponents. The letters were brilliant concoctions which demonstrated the scholastics' pettifogging ignorance and bad Latin.

Jacques Lefèvre d'Étaples (1455–1536) also studied in Italy, where he was much impressed by the Neoplationism of the Florentine Academy and by the nonscholastic approach to Aristotle taught at the University of Padua. Previously, he had earned a doctorate at the University of Paris so that by his mid-thirties he had become familiar with all phases of European philosophical thought. But his interests were theological, and his important work resulted from his critical study of the New Testament and the Church Fathers. "We must affirm nothing of God except what the Scriptures tell us," he wrote in his translation of the early Greek Christian John of Damascus. His Psalter of 1508 and his *Commentary* on the Pauline Epistles of 1512 established him as the leading Biblical scholar of his day. In both works he set down parallel texts of Greek, the Vulgate, and his own Latin translations from the Greek, a method of critical philology that was humanist inspired. In 1522 and 1523, his *Commentary* on the Gospels and a Latin translation of the New Testament appeared, both the fruit of humanist labors.

Lefèvre's theology influenced his contemporaries more than his scholarship. From Paul and Augustine he derived a doctrine of salvation through faith alone that anticipated but was less rigid than the doctrine taught later by Luther and the Protestants. While Lefèvre denied that "good works" (participation in the sacraments, prayers for the dead, pilgrimages, charitable acts, and so on) were equal to faith as a means to gain God's saving grace, he insisted that man because he possesses free will can prepare himself to receive grace through reason and good conduct. This view was in conformity with that of his fellow Christian humanists. They refused to believe that human nature was inherently corrupt, that man's will was not free, or that God was wholly inscrutable in His selection of men for salvation. These were pivotal points of disagreement with most Protestants. Lefèvre also adhered to the common Christian humanist view that the Church was rife with abuses, and he took part in movements for reform through example and education. Despite his essentially orthodox thought, he was cited for heresy by the University of Paris and forced to recant. He did so humbly, again like a typical Christian humanist, few of whom were tough-minded or hot-blooded or self-righteous enough to be religious revolutionaries. Ironically, however, his opinions were one of the chief inspirations of early French Protestantism.

John Colet (1467–1519) was a teacher and preacher rather than a scholar or theologian, and his lasting fame rests on his work as dean of St. Paul's Cathedral and founder of St. Paul's School in London. Colet, like Lefèvre, studied at the Florentine Academy after having received a solid scholastic education in England. He developed an enthusiasm for Neoplatonism and became convinced of the humanist view that the thought of the ancients must be gleaned directly from ancient sources. He preached and taught in the new manner. In his lectures on Paul's letters, he tried to discover what Paul was trying to say, what his words meant in their historical context.

He was primarily a moralist; dogmatic intricacy, that is, "glossing the text" and other scholastic practices, he ignored. But Colet never wholly escaped his youthful medieval training, remaining throughout his life a precursor rather than a true exemplar of mature Christian humanism. He knew little or no Greek, accepted the Vulgate uncritically, and saw no benefit in reading the pagan classics. Indeed, he condemned secular Italian humanism. But he was a decisive influence on two men whose lives and work represented Christian humanism's fulfillment, Sir Thomas More and Desiderius Erasmus.

Sir Thomas More Sir Thomas More (1478–1535) was truly a universal man, an embodiment of the Ciceronean *vita activa.* He was a lawyer; a statesman; a theologian; a humanist poet and prose writer; a husband and father; and at the end, a martyr to his religious and political beliefs. Even more remarkable is the fact that he did all these things well and with modesty and charm. He had the advantage of the best education England had to offer:

Sir Thomas More (second from left) and his Family by Hans Holbein. Styles of dress are well illustrated (compare with the court of Burgundy a century earlier), as is the bookish character of the household. It was not at all unusual for both men and women of More's class to read and write Latin quite adequately. (National Gallery, London.)

St. Anthony's School, Oxford, the Inns of Court for law, and the company of learned and influential men in the household of Cardinal Morton where he lived as a page. He quickly demonstrated his brilliance in law and was taken by Henry VIII into government service, where he rose steadily in position and favor. He was knighted, became Speaker (the voice of the crown) in the House of Commons, Chancellor of the duchy of Lancaster, and finally in 1529 Lord Chancellor, the highest judicial and administrative post in the realm.

More wrote many things, but his most famous and important work is *Utopia,* a humanist's picture, partly serious and partly satirical, of the ideal society. He brought to it the scholar's knowledge of history and philosophy, and the active man's instinct for practical affairs. It is fundamentally a plea for a world founded on reason. In *Utopia,* men live "by the laws of nature" which they discover for themselves through their reasoning power—a good Ciceronian idea. They satisfy their political and economic needs by governing themselves and by holding their income and property in common. They practice a quasi-Christianity free of ignorance and superstition. The secret of their success is self-control: they curb their pride and their egoism, letting wisdom rule their actions. They are tolerant, peace loving, healthy, and happy. More was too much a realist to expect to find *Utopia* in actuality: ". . . I must confess," he wrote at the end of the book, "that there are many things in the Utopian Commonwealth that I wish rather than expect to see followed among our citizens." He was giving his readers a lesson in moral philosophy. Although more clever and imaginative than such lessons as given by most humanists, it was clearly in the Renaissance tradition. His influence on later social reform was immense and long lasting and his imitators down the years have been legion.

More's life ended with his arrest and imprisonment for treason in 1535. He would not accept the separation of the English Church from Rome and refused to swear allegiance to King Henry as the Church's Supreme Head. His reasons were only in small part theological—the new church was like the old one except in the matter of headship—so much as historical and political. The center of Latin Christendom had always been Rome, and the pope had always been head of the Latin Church. To deny these things was to contribute to the dissolution of the Christian union, something More in good conscience could not do.

Desiderius Erasmus Desiderius Erasmus of Rotterdam (1469?–1536) was the greatest of More's fellow humanists, an intellectual giant to his contemporaries and a man whose thought embodied all the strengths and weaknesses of the Christian humanist movement. Erasmus was born in Holland, the illegitimate son of a priest (a fact of which he was deeply ashamed). His early education was in the schools for the Brethren of the Common Life, where he learned the rudiments of Latin and probably absorbed something of the simple, personal, reformist faith of the *devotio moderna.* A monastic career offered the best opportunity for a boy of his background, though it provided little intellectual stimulus. He became a priest in 1492, but left the monastery to further his education at the University of Paris and to pursue the life of a wandering scholar. While still in his twenties, he became infatuated with the pagan classics, convincing himself that they did not conflict with Christianity. He also learned to despise scholasticism. His future was not set, however, until he met and talked with John Colet at Oxford in 1499. Colet taught him the value of studying the Christian classics as the means of bringing order out of the theological, moral, and organizational chaos into which the Church had fallen. Erasmus was deeply impressed and began immediately to learn Greek so he might read the New

Testament and the Greek Fathers in the original. He also worked at the techniques of critical philology developed by Lorenzo Valla, going so far as to publish Valla's *Annotations* on the New Testament in 1506. His aim was to clarify and elucidate the texts so that their meaning would be indisputable.

The fruit of his labors was a Greek edition of the New Testament, the first of its kind, and editions of the Fathers, including all of Jerome's letters. The New Testament was impressive and influential. It proved the Vulgate to be in error at several important points, and it demonstrated for all of Europe the usefulness of critical philology. These were two lessons learned

Erasmus of Rotterdam by Quentin Matsys. (Galleria Corsini, Rome/ Alinari-Scala.)

quickly by Martin Luther who formulated his Protestant doctrines in part through reading this New Testament—not at all what Erasmus had in mind!

Erasmus preferred to be known as a scholar, but in fact he was more often a popular moralist and occasionally a literary hack. Not a profound or original thinker, he was nevertheless clever, witty, and a fine Latin stylist. Furthermore, he was a man whose income was derived solely from books and patrons' favors. He wrote to sell, directly for the press, the first European writer to do so. For these reasons, his books are of varying type and quality. The *Adages*, published first in 1500 and many times thereafter, is a collection of quotations from the Latin classics, a handbook for preachers, teachers, and those who want to appear learned. The *Manual of a Christian Knight* is a guide to good conduct and proper spiritual practices for the uneducated layman. It reveals Erasmus' own anti-dogmatic religious views. *The Praise of Folly* is his most famous book, a beautifully contrived and executed satire on human behavior, at once biting and understanding. "Without me," says Folly, "the world cannot exist for a moment. For is not all that is done among mortals full of folly; is it not performed by fools for fools?"

No society, no cohabitation can be pleasant or lasting without folly; so much so that a people could not stand its prince, nor the master his man, nor the maid her mistress, nor the tutor his pupil, nor the friend his friend, nor the wife her husband for a moment longer, if they did not now and then err together, now flatter each other, now sensibly conniving at things, now smear themselves with some honey of folly.

Folly is everywhere, but most in evidence in the Church, where simple Christianity has been overwhelmed by dogma, display, and self-interest. The *Colloquies* pursue the same theme in a series of dialogues, again notable for their common sense and knowledge of human nature.

In his scholarship and popular writing, Erasmus developed a program of Church reform. It involved turning the religious clock back to the days of the Apostles when men believed and practiced the "philosophy of Christ." Not being a theologian, he was vague as to doctrinal details; indeed, he was not much interested in them, believing that tolerance and brotherly love would iron out any differences. His program was an important part of both the Protestant and Catholic Reformations, but he refused to commit himself wholly to either side. He hated unpleasant controversy between extremist positions; he hated the Protestant theology that seemed to rob men of dignity by denying them free will; he hated the growing bigotry of the Catholics. And most of all, like More, he hated to see Christian unity split asunder.

THE FINE ARTS

The fifteenth and early sixteenth centuries witnessed the flowering of late Gothic art and music in the Burgundian Netherlands and Germany. At the hands of such masters as Jan van Eyck, Rogier van der Weyden, Hans Memling, Albrecht Dürer, and others, the medieval promise of vivid, inspiring, naturalistic painting was fulfilled. At the same time, the tradition of medieval sculpture, begun in the cathedral-building period, was developed, though less spectacularly, by artists such as Claus Sluter. The work of these men owed almost nothing to the new style taking shape in Italy. Indeed, the flow of ideas and techniques was rather in the opposite direction and the similarities with Italian art were matched by important differences. In general, painting and sculpture in the north were realistic in the extreme—an exhausting attention to exact representation was one of northern painting's distinguishing features. Furthermore, the artists' point of view was humane and naturalistic and their subject matter often secular; portrait painting, for example, was probably more popular in the Netherlands than in Italy, and landscapes formed the background in many paintings. These are evidences of further evolution of Gothic naturalism, which we have observed in the sculpture of the cathedrals. Religious subjects were still favored, but man and his world found an increasingly important place. This is well illustrated by the preoccupation of the Flemish painters in depicting material things such as furs, jewels, fabrics, and furniture in exact detail. By so doing, the painters showed off their technique and at the same time pleased their wealthy, luxury-loving patrons.

The most striking difference between northern and Italian art of the fourteenth and fifteenth centuries is the former's lack of classic influence. The Italians, from Masaccio and Donatello forward, were consciously imitating antiquity. They studied perspective and anatomy in a quasi-scientific way. The northerners, on the other hand, remained true to their empirical method; if they reproduced human figures and landscapes with marvelous accuracy, it was because they were keen observers, intent on capturing life as it was. Ignorance of antiquity kept northern art tied more closely to traditional themes and essentially unsophisticated in its approach to them.

The Emergence of Painting A significant advance in northern art in the later Middle Ages came with the emergence of painting. High Gothic was distinguished by great sculpture; painting was a secondary medium at best, though excellent work was done in manuscript illumination. In the fourteenth century, the illuminated book gained greater popularity, particularly in France and the Netherlands where it served as a form of conspicuous consumption for the nobility and rich burghers. Patrons multiplied and so did painters. Technique improved, too, as an examination of the many "Books of Hours" reveals. These personal devotional manuals were in great favor. Panel painting also came into its own in the fourteenth century, overtaking all of the plastic arts in the next years. The most important reason was a steadily growing demand by lay patrons for *objets d'art* to decorate their lavish homes, although the invention of oil painting and its increasing use around 1400 also had an influence.

The "Flemish School" The first northern painter of note and a founder of the so-called "Flemish School" was Jan van Eyck (1380–1441). Van Eyck's work is marked by the typical Flemish passion for minute detail, which in lesser hands made every larger painting a group of book illuminations, but which in van Eyck's hands provides the means to realism as effective as that used by the Renaissance Italians. But his paintings, however realistic, lack the life, the sense of spatial organization, and the profundity that distinguish those of the Italian masters. For comparison, one might choose his full-length portrait of the merchant Arnolfini and his wife or the *Adoration of the Lamb,* a highly naturalistic work.

Wedding Portrait of Giovanni Arnolfini and Wife by Jan van Eyck. Modern in technique, van Eyck still saw symbolism in all he painted—the dog represented faithfulness; the fruit, the lost paradise of Eden; the mirror and crystal beads, purity; the single lighted candle, Christ as the light of the world.

Jan van Eyck shares with his brother Hubert, with the Master of Flémalle, and with Rogier van der Weyden the right to be called founder of the Flemish School. The Master of Flémalle, once thought to be legendary, is now known to have executed a part of the Ghent altarpiece. Van der Weyden 1400–1464) was the most sensitive and perhaps the most talented of the Flemish painters. His masterpiece, the *Descent from the Cross,* combines the best of the newer representational and the emotion-charged medieval styles. He had many followers and his great example tended to prolong the late Gothic tradition in the face of a growing Italian influence.

The outstanding Flemish painters of the second half of the fifteenth century were Hugo van der Goes (1440–1482) and Hans Memling (1430–1494). Van der Goes filled his pictures with drama and tension, products

St. Luke Making a Portrait of the Virgin by Roger van der Weyden (Roger of the Meadow.) The most influential of the Flemish painters, van der Weyden impressed his contemporaries by his meticulous attention to detail. (Museum of Fine Arts, Boston.)

of a half-mad mind but gripping nonetheless. Memling was a sharp contrast, a brilliant and deliberate technician who lacked originality. He concentrated on portrait painting and made a great success of it. A third painter, Gerard David (1460–1532), was not quite the equal of the other two. He is known best for his landscapes and for seeing the Flemish School to an anticlimactic end.

Both Hieronymus Bosch (1450–1516) and Pieter Brueghel (1525–1569) were heirs of that school but both were so original, both indeed so unique, as to make their heritage only a part of their undoubted genius. Bosch created a world of his own, a fantasy world crowded with men and monsters out of his incredible dreams. Most of his dreams have a strong religious content, twisted by his personal demons. One of his less horror-filled paintings but nonetheless symbolic is *The Garden of Earthly Delight.* Brueghel was quite a different sort of painter: earthy, direct, full of life. His colorful and humorous peasant scenes fix sixteenth-century rural life before our eyes for all time. For paintings by Bosch and Brueghel see Part IX, Chapter 3.

German Painting In Germany, late Gothic art reached its highest development later than in the Netherlands in the work of Albrecht Dürer (1471–1528) and Matthias Grünewald (1480–1530). Dürer was something of a universal man, who painted, drew, sketched, made wood cuts, and dabbled in science. A Nürnberger by birth, he travelled over Germany and visited Italy where he came in contact with the techniques of the Renaissance. These he made good use of, but he always retained late Gothic qualities in his art. His engravings are particularly good and his portraits outstanding, especially his *Self-Portrait.* Grünewald, who came from Frankfurt, was more intense, more brooding, and more given to symbolism. His style is almost purely German in its derivation. His *Crucifixion* is terrible in its tragedy, somehow summing up the religious emotionalism of the Middle Ages in a style that is new. His colors are brilliant, even garish, giving to the scene a primitive vividness unmatched in either Italy or the Netherlands.

Other Arts Northern European sculpture did not keep pace with painting in the fourteenth and fifteenth centuries. The High Gothic style of the cathedral period gave way to uninspired affectation in most places. In the Netherlands, however, and in the duchy of Burgundy, which felt Flemish influence strongly, a more vital and less artificial style evolved in the hands of such men as Claus Sluter (13??–1406). Sluter was clearly in the tradition of Gothic naturalism, but his was naturalism of a simple, unsophisticated kind. He worked on the portal of Chartreuse of Champmol and on the tomb of the Duke of Burgundy, Philip the Bold, at Dijon, the Burgundian capital. But his masterpiece is the *Well of Moses,* a group sculpture of Moses, David and four prophets.

As in painting and sculpture, Flemings dominated northern music throughout the fifteenth century. Indeed, they dominated European music as a whole, since for the most part Italian Renaissance music was undistinguished. They built on medieval polyphonic foundations as developed particularly in England and Italy and made use of a vigorous native musical tradition and liberal support from such patrons as the Church and the Duke of Burgundy. In the hands of such composers as Guillaume Dufay (1400–1474), Johannes Ockeghem (1420–1495), and Josquin des Prez (1450–1521), medieval polyphony underwent considerable refinement in both the method of its composition and its presentation. By the end of the fifteenth century, composers of this advanced school conceived and wrote down all the parts of a musical piece simultaneously instead of one after the other. The result was better balance and a closer integration of harmony. By the same time, the choir had replaced individual voices as the chief instrument of performance. Thus the composer was permitted greater freedom and range in his work. The compositions performed were still predominantly religious, although the *chanson* was popular at the noble courts and in the houses of the wealthy.

FURTHER READING

In every way a worthy companion to Burckhardt's essay on the Italian Renaissance is the brilliant assessment of French and Burgundian culture in the fifteenth century, J. Huizinga, * *The Waning of the Middle Ages* (1924). A good brief summary of the pre-Renaissance culture in the North is Hans Baron's contribution to G. R. Potter, ed., *The New Cambridge Modern History,* vol. I. There is little in English on the universities of the fifteenth century, but histories of science necessarily contain some information. Of these, the standard work is A. C. Crombie, * *Medieval and Early Modern Science,* vol. II (1963); but see also M. Boas, *The Scientific Renaissance, 1450–1630* (1962). Best on Burgundy in English are the excellent studies of R. Vaughn, *Philip the Bold* (1962), *John the Fearless* (1966), and *Philip the Good* (1968).

F. Seebohm, *The Oxford Reformers* (2nd rev. ed., 1869) remains standard, though its assessment of Colet's importance is exaggerated. M. M. Phillips, * *Erasmus and the Northern Renaissance* (1949) is a well-balanced introduction. A. Hyma, *The Christian Renaissance* (1924), while obstinate in its rejection of Italian influences in the North, is a good study of the *devotio moderna.* W. E. Campbell, *Erasmus, Tyndale, and More* (1949), is useful, and H. O. Taylor, **Thought and Expression in the Sixteenth Century,* 2 vols. (1920), is still valuable. The best biography of More is R. W. Chambers, *Thomas More* (1935). On Utopia, see J. H. Hexter, * *More's Utopia* (1952), a brilliant analysis. Of the many biographies of Erasmus, J. Huizinga, * *Erasmus and the Reformation* (1924), is readable and on the whole fair-minded.

On humanism in various parts of Europe, two excellent works are D. Bush, *The Renaissance and English Humanism* (1939), and L. W. Spitz, *The Religious Renaissance of the German Humanists* (1963).

On France, A. Denieal-Cormier, *A Time of Glory: The Renaissance in France, 1488–1559* (1968) is good. And on Spain, M. Bataillon, *Érasme et l'Espagne* (1937) remains a classic.

Now standard is E. Panofsky, *Early Netherlandish Painting,* 2 vols. (1953). A shorter introduction is M. J. Friedländer, *Early Netherlandish Painting from van Eyck to Brueghel* (1956). Broader coverage is provided by O. Bensch, *The Art of the Renaissance in Northern Europe* (1945).

*Books available in paperback edition are marked with an asterisk.

4 Renaissance Monarchy

The kingdoms north of the Alps reached their political nadir in the second quarter of the fifteenth century. Everywhere centrifugal forces were disrupting the work of the great feudal monarchs of the twelfth and thirteenth centuries. Decades of civil and foreign war, a succession of weak and minor kings, and concerted efforts by such rival powers as great nobles, towns, and the "national" churches to assert their independence had robbed the crowns of much they had gained. In France, Charles VII, Joan of Arc's hesitant Dauphin, was "king of Bourges," while half of his realm, including Paris and the whole northeast, was still held by the English and Burgundians, and large parts of it were ravished by marching armies. In England, the gentle and incompetent Henry VI, subject of two of Shakespeare's worst plays, was the helpless victim of rivalry between great families, soon to break out in the violent War of the Roses. The Iberian Peninsula, apparently divided irreparably into several realms fighting among themselves, could boast of no single strong state or monarch. Only the duchy of Burgundy, a haphazard collection of feudal territories stretching from the North Sea to Switzerland and having unity only in the person of the duke, could make a pretense of power and determination. Yet a half century later, Burgundy's life had been cut short, its dukes were extinct and its lands absorbed by the Austrian Habsburgs. And meanwhile, France, England, and united Spain had gained new life under the strong, purposeful hands of a most remarkable collection of monarchs.

THE GROWTH OF MONARCHY

Many factors were involved in this astonishing recovery. For one thing, the feebleness of the great monarchies was more apparent than real. Each of them had, or would soon have, a firm economic base in agriculture and in resurgent trade and industry. With a few years of peace, the countryside would flower again. Peace would also help the towns. The urban economy was on the upswing by the middle of the fifteenth century: population was increasing, trade was expanding once more and would accelerate rapidly under the impetus of Portuguese and Spanish overseas expansion, and industry, stimulated by technological improvements in mining, artillery making, printing, shipbuilding, and the like, was advancing beyond the limits set by the craft guilds. Thus, each government possessed good potential sources of revenue, an available supply of money being the measure of royal power in that day.

Furthermore, the economic revival worked to the detriment of those elements in society which opposed centralized government and the enhancement of royal power. In the most general terms, the dissolution of the manorial system, the development of a money economy, and the growing interdependence of town and country, what we may call the tendency toward economic unification of the European states, undermined the economic and hence the social and political foundations of feudalism. Whether noblemen suffered, as in France, or took advantage of the new situation, as in England, matters less than the fact that their position of privileged independence was everywhere weakened. At the same time, the middle classes, always more amenable to the accretion of royal power, gained strength. From this we must not conclude that the nobles disappeared from the kings' councils, or indeed from the king's favor, to be replaced by merchants. In point of fact, the latter were merely tolerated because they had money and administrative skill. The former remained the single most powerful political force everywhere in Europe outside of Italy and Switzerland, owners of most of the landed property, natural military leaders, and a social elite. But theirs was a political force which might harass and delay but could never again reverse the forward surge of monarchy.

Monarchy was too deeply rooted. In England, France, and the Iberian kingdoms, a royal tradition extended back hundreds of years, and no subject, not even the most conservative baron, could deny it. This was the great treasure the feudal kings bequeathed to their heirs. The feudal kings had founded their authority on the feudal system, and in trying to extend it beyond its natural limits had provoked a reaction against it. But the tradition endured. Furthermore, and this may seem a paradox, the long period of war and rebellion, or virtual anarchy, had enhanced the tradition. The psychological tenor of the mid-fifteenth century was favorable to the revival of strong central government. The masses of people of every class and station wanted peace and security which the rule of the great nobility had failed to provide. Thus a strong king who would assert his traditional rights would be readily accepted. Furthermore, the institution of kingship was still in the process of definition. A strong king who was also an imaginative one could make more of monarchy than had his medieval predecessors. And Roman law was prepared to justify all his actions in the name of ancient precedent. Significantly, the term "majesty" was introduced about this time to describe the unique attributes of kingship. For at this time, first in Italy and then in the north, we see developing the idea of the modern state, sovereign, all-powerful, omnicompetent, amoral, with the king as its natural head set apart from any archaic notion of a feudal hierarchy. The idea gained strength with the decline of the Church and Empire, whose claims to universal spiritual and secular dominion were directly contrary to the concept of a sovereign state.

The monarchs who appeared around the middle of the fifteenth century made use of tradition, of favorable economic, social, and political conditions, and of novel political ideas. They also took advantage of whatever opportunity offered, though they did not act according to a rational plan, and they were blessed by singularly good fortune, particularly in their marriages. The problems they attacked were old ones: to assure a reliable and sufficient income (a proper king could not be down-at-the-heel), to provide a loyal, permanent armed force (a king's business was to keep peace at home and make war abroad), and to extend the royal judicial and administrative authority throughout the realm and over all subjects (a king was bound by natural and divine law, but he was their interpreter and dispenser). Some of the solutions were traditional; others were new; together, their effect was to create a kind of monarchy significantly different from any that had gone before.

THE FRENCH MONARCHY

The ordeal of the Hundred Years' War was not yet ended when recovery began for the French monarchy. The people had already set to work making fallow fields bloom and ruined cities rise again and Charles VII had begun to gather together the scattered pieces of his realm. As she has proven many times since, the "sweet land" of France has remarkable powers of recuperation. Her population was huge for that day, perhaps fourteen million by 1500, as compared to three or four million for England and seven or eight million for Spain. Her agricultural resources were unsurpassed in an age when real wealth still sprang from the soil. And her geography, her water and mountain boundaries, her excellent river communications, her lack of natural barriers to unity, and her sheer size inspired in the people a sense of national identity and contributed to the crown's efforts to consolidate the realm and establish a centralized government. To France's inherent strength the campaign of Joan of Arc brought a dramatic outpouring of patriotic fervor which found a symbol in the semi-religious figure of the king and manifested itself in a virtual holy war to drive out the English invaders. The French people wanted an end to political chaos and wanted the restoration of monarchy. After 1435, the year of Burgundy's withdrawal from her alliance with England, France and the French crown were on the upgrade. The initial work of restoration fell to Charles VII (1422–1461).

Charles VII Charles VII deserves to be called the "Well Served." A weak and apathetic man, unsure of his right to the crown (he feared he was of illigitimate birth), given to consulting soothsayers, Charles was swept along by the forces around him and by councillors with more determination and inventiveness than he. But he listened well and was able, during his reign, to rehabilitate the crown's prestige, launch the counterattack against the English, and repair the framework of royal authority that had broken down under the impact of war and resurgent feudalism. Under the inspired leadership of the peasant girl Joan of Arc, the demoralized French renewed the Hundred Years' War against their English and Burgundian foes. First

Charles VII of France by Jean Foucquet. A "most victorious king," according to the legend on the painting, Charles reigned during the last three decades of the Hundred Years' War and, though Joan of Arc got him crowned, it was his own skill and good sense that won the war and brought new strength and prestige to the French monarchy. (The Louvre.)

Joan persuaded Charles to be crowned at Rheims (1429), a necessity if he were to possess the unique qualities of kingship. Then, with a few troops, she attacked Orléans and drove out the English garrison. Captured by the Burgundians, she was given over to the English who tried and condemned her for heresy. She was burned at the stake in 1431, the victim more of politics than of religious zeal. But her spirit had done its work. In 1435, Burgundy made a separate peace with Charles, and the next year Charles won back Paris; no longer could he be derided as "king of Bourges." In the next years, the crown raised money, reorganized and re-equipped its army, and slowly won back all of France from the English with the exception of the port of Calais. The Hundred Years' War finally ended in 1453.

It was the need to prosecute the war that provided the excuse for Charles and his advisors to strengthen the royal authority. In 1439, the Estates General authorized Charles to raise a royal army and pay for it out of the *taille,* the property tax on non-noble land. Charles V had been given the same authority two generations earlier but he relinquished it. His grandson did not, but continued to collect the *taille* year after year without consulting the Estates. The representative body was divested of its most important function and its principal source of power: control of the purse. It met several times between 1561 and 1614, and last of all in 1789, always during periods of weakened monarchy. But its role was insignificant in government. Provincial estates retained greater nominal authority; they continued to vote taxes, but usually supplied the king with what he wanted. To the *taille,* Charles added the *aides,* a sales tax, and the *gabelle,* a salt tax. With the revenue collected he created a standing army of twelve thousand cavalry called *gens d'ordonnance* and initiated development of artillery. He also encouraged the formation of a kind of citizen militia of archers in the towns, but the people were apathetic, and lack of good infantry became the French army's chief weakness.

Meanwhile, Charles revived and extended royal justice by establishing high courts in the principal cities of the realm. These provincial *parlements* were modeled on the *Parlement* of Paris, whose functions they performed in their own areas. Charles also used the Pragmatic Sanction of Bourges, a virtual declaration of independence from Rome issued by the French clergy in 1438, to strengthen his hold over the Gallican Church. In theory, this declaration reasserted the clergy's right to elect their own bishops without papal interference, but in practice it meant that through careful management of episcopal elections many posts would go to the king's nominees. Thus, it assured that in most circumstances the Gallican Church would remain the crown's ally.

Charles found another ally in the lower nobility and the middle class, and favored these groups at the expense of the high nobility, whose irresponsibility he wisely distrusted. The famous merchant-industrialist and banker, Jacques Coeur, became his chief fiscal agent, personal financial adviser, and source of ready loans. Under the influence of Coeur and other businessmen, the crown assisted commerce and industry through subsidization, grants of monopolies, and tax immunities, and by inaugurating a kind of early-day mercantilism. Charles, and particularly Louis XI (1461–1483), taxed the burghers heavily but protected their towns and employed them and the lower nobility in the royal administration. The high nobility was eased out of the king's councils where possible. However, they retained their privileges of tax immunity and superior social position as compensation, and they were assigned to top army commands and encouraged to pay homage as courtiers to the kings. The French monarchs felt neither the need nor the inclination to destroy the high nobility but wanted simply to tame it.

Louis XI Charles also began reconsolidation of the French realm and assertion of French prestige and power in Europe, but most of this work was left to his successors. Louis XI, who came to the throne in 1461, was

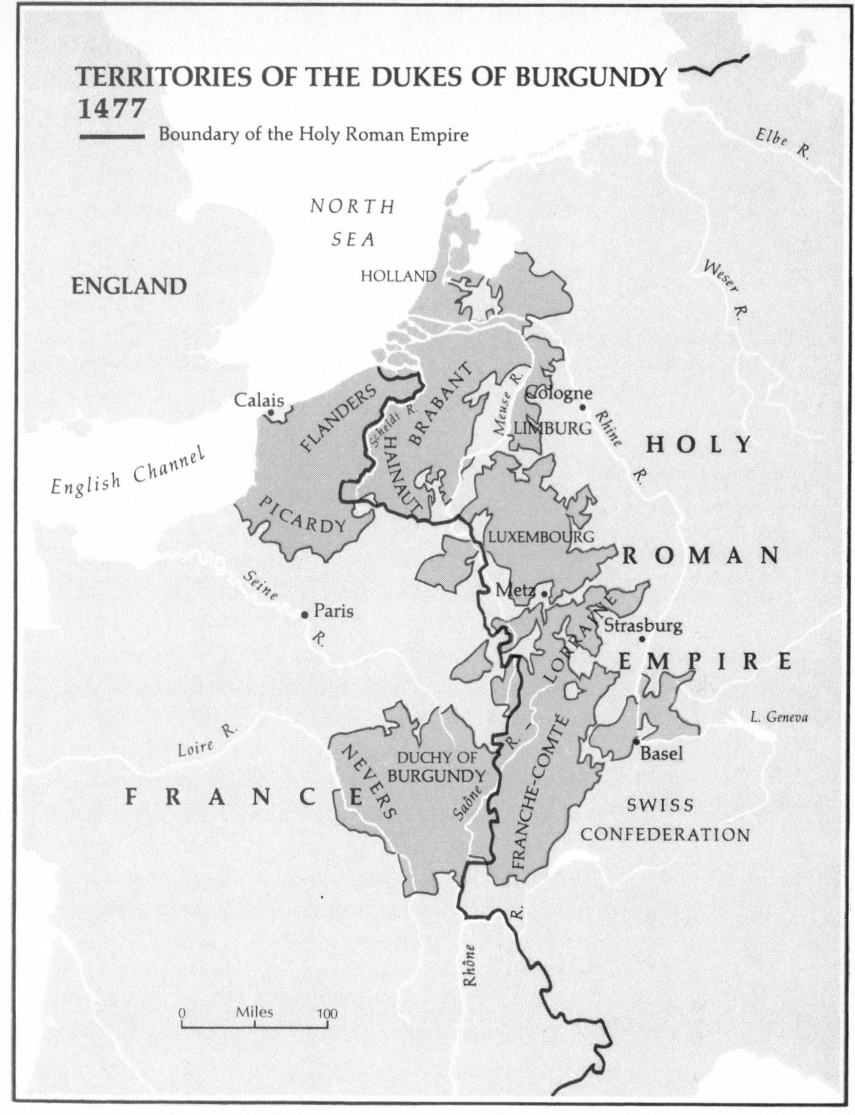

as much unlike his father as a son could be. Small and physically weak, his spindly legs supporting a round body and a large, ugly head, Louis was obliged to depend on cunning and ruthlessness. Fittingly, he quickly gained the nickname "Spider." He defeated his enemies, both domestic and foreign, by a combination of skill and luck which inspired admiration in his contemporaries. Louis' most famous victory was over Charles, Duke of Burgundy (1467–1477). Charles' odd, conglomerate state included the Low Countries, Luxembourg, parts of Lorraine, Franche Comté, and the duchy of Burgundy, all joined solely by fealty to the duke himself—but possessing resources and leadership to make it a worthy foe of France. Indeed, in the 1460's, Burgundy had greater wealth and prestige than its larger but still war-weary

Sketch for an Equestrian Statue of the Emperor Maximilian I. The equestrian statue was classical in origin and had become popular during the Italian Renaissance. Maximilian, whose imperial ambitions exceeded his ability to gain them, was not much of a soldier himself, though he certainly looks like one here.

neighbor, and the Burgundian duke, the handsome and chivalrous scion of a younger branch of the Valois, outshone his misshapen and ill-tempered cousin. But Charles was not called *le Téméraire* (the Rash) without reason. His ambition to fashion a truly unified "middle kingdom" between France and Germany and trade his ducal crown for the crown of a king was carried forward with foolish haste. Louis waited and subsidized Charles' Swiss enemies who defeated and killed the duke at Nancy in 1477. Since he left no son, his lands were partitioned. Most of them went to his daughter Mary, whose marriage to Maximilian of Habsburg was the first step in bringing together the Spanish, Burgundian, and Austrian inheritance into the worldwide empire of Emperor Charles V. But Louis made good his claim to the duchy of Burgundy, appanage of the French crown, and assured himself that no "kingdom of Burgundy" would arise on his border.

Louis used fortuitous deaths to win back several other appanages alienated in the past. As in the case of the Burgundian inheritance, lands in fief to the crown returned to the crown in the absence of direct male heirs. Louis managed to outlive most of the junior branches of his family and thereby regained Anjou, Maine, Provence, and Guienne. Louis' son, Charles VIII (1483–1498), acquired the duchy of Brittany by marriage to the Duchess Anne, and Charles' cousin and successor, Louis XII (1498–1515), brought with him the great Orléans inheritance and made sure of Brittany by divorcing his wife and marrying Anne himself. Thus in the space of fifty years, France was remade.

Feudal Reaction The great vassals did not submit willingly, and the entire period was one of frequent rebellion. The height of feudal reaction came during the minority of Charles VIII in the 1480's. The regent, Charles' elder sister, Anne de Beaujeu, was a wise and prudent woman, but could prevent neither a civil war, the *Guerre des Folles* (the "Fools War" as it was aptly named), nor a meeting of the Estates General in 1484. However, royal authority was by now too firmly intrenched to be upset by the nobility. Indeed, Charles VIII could not have set out on his invasion of Italy in 1494 had it been otherwise. The reigns of both Charles VIII and Louis XII were largely taken up with war in Italy. Domestic problems, of such great concern to their predecessors, were relegated to the background. France was strong and united, the people loyal and obedient, and the crown respected. It was the envy of Europe. As the Emperor Maximilian commented, "The Emperor is a king of kings; the king of Spain a king of men; and the king of France a king of beasts."

THE ENGLISH MONARCHY

Restoration of the English monarchy began with the defeat of the Lancastrian forces at Tewksbury in 1471 and the firm establishment of Edward IV, first of the Yorkist kings, on the throne. England had passed through a costly and humiliating war abroad and a debilitating political crisis at home. The English domains in France, excepting only Calais, were lost for good in 1453 and with them the venerable English dream of continental empire. England became an island politically and psychologically as well as geographically and her insularity was to have a decisive influence on her future history. While the English did not turn their backs on Europe, they ceased to concentrate their energies there, preferring instead to create a strong and prosperous state within the confines of their island and to dabble in continental politics only when they saw advantage in it. The English kings, first Edward IV and then the Tudors, found isolation and insularity a natural ally in their struggle to revive the authority of the crown.

The Wars of the Roses The kings' first problem was to secure the crown itself and to guarantee the line of succession. The hopeless feeblemindedness of Henry VI (1422–1461), last of the Lancastrian kings, created a vacuum at the center of power that was filled by the barons of the realm, the king's cousins and the great nobles. The barons ran the government entirely in their own interests through the Great Council, but they maintained an uneasy peace among themselves until the war with France was over. Then, in 1455, incipient rivalry between the royal family and its Lancastrian supporters, who were governing for poor Henry, and a faction pledged to Richard, Duke of York, burst into open conflict. For the next thirty years, the barons engaged in sporadic and bloody fighting, killing each other off and demonstrating time and again their irresponsibility, their disregard for law and order, and their utter incapacity to rule. The Wars of the Roses, romantically named for the red rose of Lancaster and the white rose of York, were neither as intense nor as disruptive as historians once believed. The average Englishman was hardly touched at all, and daily life, trade, and farming went on pretty much without interruption. But the wars left a deep and lasting impression on Englishmen, a fear of incipient political anarchy and a profound desire for strong public authority to assure domestic peace. The people were eager to help the crown to restore itself.

Edward IV and Richard III Richard of York was dead in 1460, but his youthful son Edward made good his father's claim to the throne in 1461. A decade of further strife ended in victory for the Yorkist cause, and during the remaining years of his life, Edward IV (1461–1483) labored to put the royal house in order. He reasserted the crown's prerogatives which the barons had usurped, revived the royal courts, began to rebuild the royal administration, and made himself financially independent of the Parliament. He had intelligence and the good will of the people, but he was handicapped by an overfondness for dissolute living which sapped his determination and his health and which may have caused his death at the age of forty. Unfortunately for the House of York, the new king, Edward V (1483), was a minor and his uncle, Richard, Duke of Gloucester, was ambitious and unscrupulous. Richard seized power, made Parliament declare Edward V illegitimate while making himself king, and shut the deposed boy and his younger brother in the Tower of London. Whether Richard III (1483–1485), the "Crookback Dick" of dark legend, then ordered the "little princes"

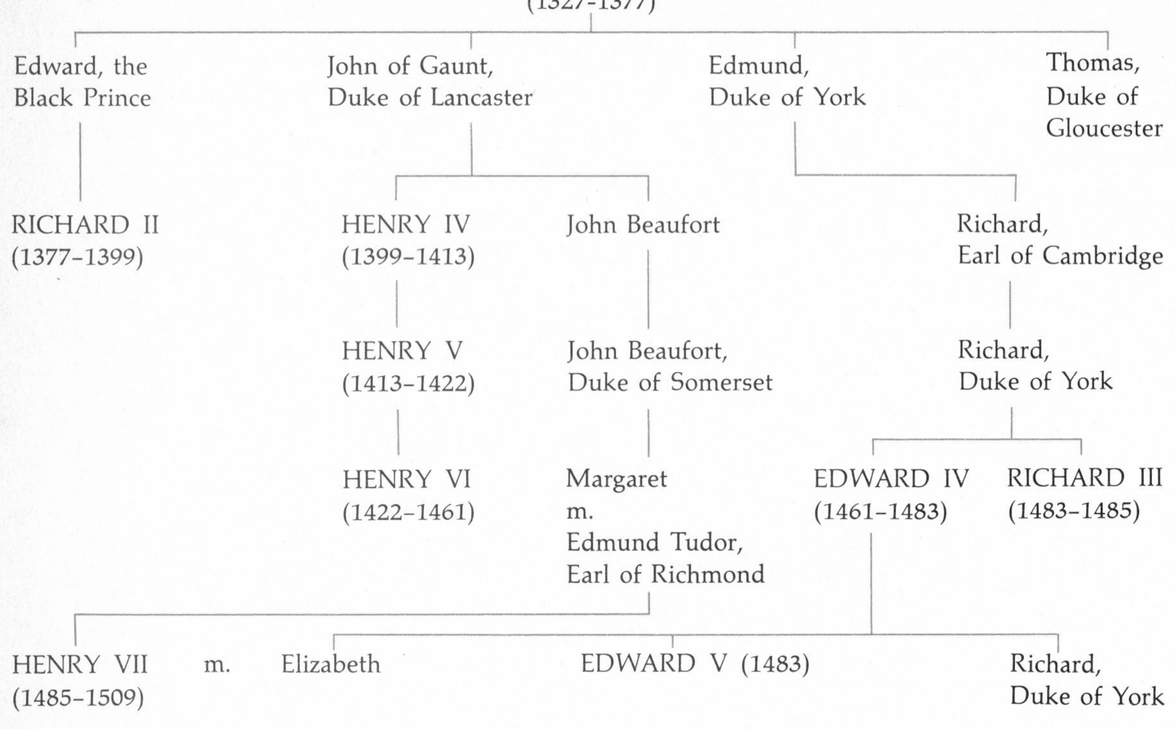

murdered has never been proved and is doubted by many historians. But many contemporaries were convinced he knew of their fate. His unpopularity, his insecure hold on the crown, and his inability to harness the royal resources revived Lancastrian hopes in the person of Henry Tudor, Earl of Richmond. Henry gathered an army in France and invaded England in the summer of 1485. He met and defeated the royal forces at Bosworth Field in August. Richard was killed in the battle. Thus was born by conquest the long and illustrious dynasty of Tudors (1485–1603).

Henry VII Henry VII (1485–1509) must be counted one of England's greatest monarchs. He built his monarchy upon the foundation laid by Edward IV, but unlike Edward he brought to the task hardheaded wisdom, strength of purpose, and a clear idea of what he wanted the finished structure to be. Though his subjects did not love him—how could this austere, parsimonious, clerk-like figure inspire love?—they respected him and for the most part supported his work. But he had to start slowly, for his hereditary right to the crown was even more questionable than his predecessor's. Descended from a bastard branch of the Lancaster family that had been specifically excluded from succession, Henry's first and most critical problem was to insure his position. He quickly gained Parliamentary sanction and married the sister of Edward V, then spent the next fifteen years ruthlessly putting down plots and rebellions, and turning back invasions.

The Tomb of Henry VII and his Wife Elizabeth of York in Westminster Abbey, London. Such elaborate tombs were common for the rich and powerful, and by the Tudors' time the influence of Italian sculptors is clear. Lesser men and women still made do with simpler representations, etched and hammered in brass. (National Monuments Record.)

The Scots, the French, and the emperor lent aid to Yorkist pretenders and to the adventurers Perkin Warbeck and Lambert Simnel, posing as pretenders. But by the turn of the century, the major domestic opposition was crushed and careful diplomacy had won over most foreign enemies. In 1501, Henry carried off the foreign policy coup of his career by arranging a marriage of the Prince of Wales with Princess Catherine of Aragon, daughter of Ferdinand and Isabella of Spain. The prince soon died but the alliance was saved by Catherine's marriage to his brother, the future Henry VIII. Henry VII was not a seeker after glory through war; his diplomatic activities were aimed primarily at making friends for the House of Tudor.

From the beginning of his reign, Henry took measures to destroy the private power of the barons. He ordered illegal castles and fortresses torn down and outlawed "livery" and "maintenance," the practices which permitted the high nobility to keep or "maintain" bodies of armed retainers wearing the insignia, or "livery," of their patrons. He also enforced the peace of the realm by means of the Court of Star Chamber. This court, so named because of the star-ceilinged hall where it met, was actually only a part of the Great Council and an old institution. Henry broadened its authority to include cases against recalcitrant noblemen, which local courts, often under the thumbs of the law-breakers themselves, were unable or unwilling to try fairly. In these somewhat high-handed endeavors, he was given the full support of the urban middle class and the gentry, the non-noble country squires, who preferred order in the state to archaic feudal privilege and who hated and feared the barons.

It was men from these groups that Henry utilized as councillors and administrators. Commoners trained in the law were given posts in the government, and minor noblemen and untitled gentry replaced the barons. They were hard-working and loyal, dependent entirely on Henry's favor. Henry installed no royal agents in the countryside but relied on the services of local officials, particularly the justices of the peace, whose obedience was assured through respect rather than force. Most of these officials were also recruited with care from the local gentry. Nor did Henry create a standing army on the French model. He continued to rely on knights and yeomen of the kind so successful through most of the Hundred Years' War.

The reign of Henry VII brought prosperity to the kingdom and wealth to the crown. Henry encouraged commerce and industry and viewed the rise of the middle class with approval. Business boomed, and England was started on the road to economic greatness. But his own income was derived largely from other sources. He regained much of the royal domain—and its revenues—that had previously passed out of the crown's hands and confiscated the estates of his adversaries. He took full advantage of his feudal responsibilities, collecting a tidy sum from his vassals for homage, wardship, and marriage. His common subjects paid "tunnage and poundage," duties on goods shipped from overseas. Henry was the most tight-fisted of English kings; not only did he insist on frugality and careful expenditure, but he checked the household ledgers himself, approving each column of figures with a big "H." On Henry's death in 1509, the crown had a full treasury, but with it a tradition of stuffy austerity that had little appeal for bluff, lusty Henry VIII. That handsome and fun-loving young man managed to spend his father's savings in a few years and was in debt for the rest of his long reign.

Henry's healthy financial condition explains why he rarely called Parliament into session after his first few years. He did not need grants of money and he feared that the Commons would insist on exercising its traditional right to supervise his spending. But Parliament did not die out as did its equivalent in France, the Estates General. It was still the place where a king less provident than Henry would have to go to ask for money, and under the pressure of events of the next few decades, notably the Reformation, it was to become far more influential. Parliament's day had only just begun. The first Tudor brought peace, unity, considerable centralization, and solvency to England, but it was still a second-rate power compared to France and united Spain.

THE SPANISH MONARCHY

As we noted earlier, there was little natural historical unity about the Iberian Peninsula in the mid-fifteenth century. Divided into a dozen distinct regions by mountains and plateaus, Spain's river communications were poor and its climate highly diversified. Its peoples were further compartmentalized by customs and language—Portuguese, Galician, Catalan, Valencian, Basque, and Castilian were spoken—and by economic interests and political traditions. While the peasants and poor landed nobility of Castile were struggling to scrape a living from the rough, unfertile soil of their plateau, Portuguese seamen were bringing home gold, ivory, and guinea pepper from equatorial Africa, and the merchants of Barcelona were trading with Italian cities and the Muslim East. Politically, there was deep-rooted separatism, founded on the patterns set by geography and hardened by centuries of tradition. The kingdoms of Castile, Aragon (which included semi-autonomous Catalonia and Valencia), Navarre, and Portugal each pursued their own interests, usually quite divergent and often conflicting. Castile and Aragon, the two whose union would be achieved by the marriage of Isabella and Ferdinand, had long traveled opposite political paths, divided by history and by the most formidable mountain range on the peninsula. To a contemporary observer it would have seemed most improbable that Aragon would gain any measure of greatness in European politics and that Castile and Portugal would combine to establish a world empire across the seas.

Castile The kings and people of Castile were forged and tempered by five hundred years of crusading. Hard-bitten, warlike, rigidly orthodox in religion, and independent in spirit, they had slowly pushed back the Moors until only a tiny territory around the southern city of Granada remained to be won. The bulwarks of Castilian society were the petty noble knight and the peasant. The economy was almost wholly agricultural and pastoral, dominated by sheep herding and by the great association of sheep raisers, the *Mesta.* The monarchy, always limited in its freedom of action by a rich and virtually independent great nobility, reached bottom under Henry IV (1454–1474). Henry's reign saw a powerful aristocratic reaction, complicated by an involved dispute over establishing an heir to the throne. Henry was not called "the Impotent" for his political ineptitudes alone, and the daughter he insisted to be his own was commonly regarded as the child of an adulterous relationship between the queen and a courtier named Beltran de la Cueva. Eventually, two parties formed, one Henry's own, which supported "La Beltraneja," as the girl was nicknamed, and one a party of discontented nobility and high churchmen, which supported first Henry's half-brother and then his half-sister, Isabella. Isabella was thought tractable to a revival of aristocracy. Using intelligence and taking advantage of luck, Isabella made good her claim between 1474 and 1479.

Aragon Aragon was less rural in its economic character, had a less influential nobility, but possessed a strong representative tradition embodied in several *Cortes,* one for each of the country's constituent parts. There, nobility and townsmen clung together in defense of "liberty and privilege" against royal encroachment. Aragon was oriented toward the Mediterranean. Its coastal cities, above all Barcelona, were important in overseas commerce and its political fortunes were closely bound up with Italy. Sicily was Aragonese, and an illegitimate branch of the Aragonese house had reigned in Naples since the 1430's. Like Castile, Aragon passed through troubled times in the mid-fifteenth century. A long and unresolved struggle with France over the small kingdom of Navarre, straddling the Pyrenees, and a rebellion in Catalonia had sapped the monarchy's energies. John II (1458–1479), a far more able king than Henry IV in Castile, fought determinedly, however, and was able to pass his crown on to his son Ferdinand. John's great plan to join Aragon and Castile by a marriage between Ferdinand and Isabella was opposed by France, Portugal, and dissident groups within both kingdoms, but by perseverance on the part of the two principals, it bore fruit in 1469.

Ferdinand and Isabella Isabella became Queen of Castile in 1474 and Ferdinand King of Aragon in 1479. Each was only "consort" to the other, their crowns and realms remaining separate, united only in the persons of the monarchs. Under the circumstances, neither of the "Catholic Kings," as they were called, seemed to have the resources to bring real strength to the union. Moreover, they had quite distinct personalities and interests. Isabella was a daughter of the crusades, fanatically devoted to the Church and bent on completing the conquest of Granada. That done, she directed her energies to assuring orthodoxy in Spain and imperial success overseas. Ferdinand, on the other hand, was a man of the Renaissance, calculating, unscrupulous, cynical, a supreme diplomat, and a master of political intrigue. Machiavelli said of him in *The Prince:* ". . . from being a weak king he [became] for fame and glory the first king in Christendom, and if you regard his actions you will find them all very great and some of them extraordinary." Ferdinand was thoroughly European in his political outlook. He saw the great enemy as France and the chief battleground as Italy. Still, however disparate their aims, Isabella and Ferdinand were united in their determination to create a strong monarchy by suppressing rival political authorities while concentrating the machinery of government in their own hands.

An old and well-established tradition of monarchy worked for Isabella and Ferdinand in both Aragon and Castile. In Aragon, however, they could not break down the equally old and well-established tradition of local independence. They let the Aragonese run their own affairs to a large degree, requesting, though not always receiving, taxes of the *Cortes* and treating local privilege gently. In Castile, circumstances were more favorable. Aristocratic power (despite attempts to strengthen it) was not firmly based in law. Feudalism of the variety found in France had never existed there. There were a number of great landed magnates to compete with the crown, but no princes of the blood to demand their ancient rights, and no serfdom by means of which the lesser nobles (the *hidalgos*) could control the peasantry. Hence, the nobility could be controlled to a large degree by reasserting the crown's traditional rights. With the support of most Castilians, who preferred strong royal authority to aristocratic anarchy, the nobles were put in their place with relative ease by Ferdinand and Isabella.

The Madonna and Child, Flanked by St. Thomas Aquinas and St. Dominic, with the "Catholic Kings" and their Family at Worship. (The Prado, Madrid.)

They revived the old leagues of town militia, called *hermandades,* creating the *Santa Hermandad* in 1476. In this way, they got themselves an army to fight for Isabella's claim to the throne and then against the Moors of Granada, and a kind of rural police force to defend against brigandage and banditry. At the same time, Ferdinand leashed the three great crusading orders of knighthood, potential pockets of anti-royal reaction, by making himself head of each, and Isabella directed that baronial castles and strong places be leveled. Meanwhile, she and Ferdinand turned to the towns, traditional source of royal power in Castile. They reestablished the *corregidor* as the crown's overseer of town government and through him reasserted the crown's judicial and financial prerogatives. Finally, they called on the pliable Castilian *Cortes,* composed now only of townsmen, to win support for their policies and money to pay for them.

The Catholic Kings thus with relative ease solved their money problems. The *Cortes* voted regular *servicios,* and these were the crown's principal source of revenue. New taxes were also introduced and old ones revived, notably the *alcabala,* a levy on sales transactions. The Spanish Church paid a third of its tithes to the crown. Ferdinand's headship of the three knightly orders brought the crown significant financial as well as political returns, for the orders controlled huge landed estates. And, in exchange for its support, the crown shared in the profits of the Mesta. By the second quarter of the sixteenth century, gold and silver from the New World began to flow into Spain, and the crown collected its *quinto,* a fifth. By this time, too, the Low Countries, fruit of a dynastic marriage alliance with the Habsburgs, and Italy were supplying huge tax revenues. Wealth stimulated the hunger for glory and power, and Spain began her long journey down the golden road to greatness and ultimate decay.

Ferdinand also created a professional standing army using as its nucleus the *Santa Hermandad,* and his generals developed it into Europe's finest army during the wars in Italy. Especially effective was the Spanish infantry, whose tactics were modeled on those of the Swiss and German *Landsknechte.* Their chief weapon was the pike; and closely ranked, rigidly disciplined formations of Spanish pikemen advancing slowly to the beat of drums became the most frightening sight on Europe's battlefields.

Finally, Ferdinand and Isabella bent Spanish Catholicism to the service of the crown. They obtained from the papacy the right to dispense ecclesiastical offices at their own discretion. By appointing men of loyalty, character, and piety, like Cardinal Francisco Ximenes de Cisneros, they cleansed the Spanish Church of corruption and incompetence and made it a potent force for monarchy. In 1481, Ferdinand and Isabella established the Inquisition to root out Jewish and Muslim converts, "new Christians," who were suspected of practicing their old faiths in secret. At about the same time, they gave new life to the *Reconquista,* the crusade against the Moors. Begun centuries before, this long war had made little progress for nearly a century and a half. The old Moorish kingdom of Granada had degenerated into a weak and peaceful fief of the Castilian crown, its subjects hardworking farmers and artisans. But Isabella could not rest until it was conquered. Outfitted in white armor, bearing the red cross of Castile, she personally led her army to victory in 1492. At the same time, the work of Christianization began. Jews, middle-class businessmen for the most part, were made to choose between conversion or exile; the Muslims too, though promised religious freedom, were soon given the same choice. The inquisitors saw that the converts were sincere, but many chose exile.

Thus, the Inquisition and the *Reconquista* became the chief instruments in the creation of religious uniformity, which in time was transformed into fanaticism and into a unique Spanish patriotism. From a melange of peoples with a variety of faiths, the Spanish became the most solidly Christian of all Europeans. But unity of the faith was achieved by badly weakening the economy, for Jews and Muslims comprised an important commercial and industrial group. Their loss could not be made good by the "old Christians" who, in the words of the contemporary historian Francesco Guicciardini of Florence, thought business "dishonorable because all of them have the pretentions of nobility."

THE INVASION OF ITALY

Modern European international politics began on that autumn day in 1494 when King Charles VIII of France led his army over the Alps in quest of the throne of Naples. The invasion of Italy set off the first great power struggle among the states of Europe as we know them today. It was a power struggle that kept Europe aflame for the next sixty-five years and established the broad patterns of war and diplomacy for the more distant future. It also spelled the end of the medieval ideal of a universal republic embracing all Christians. Henceforth, European international politics would be predicated on the existence of sovereign states, without morals or responsibility in satisfying their craving for power. The situation that had prevailed among the states of Italy for several generations now prevailed among the greater states of the north and ironically Italy would be its chief victim.

This is not to say there were no precedents for invasion. For centuries, northern European princes, most notably the emperors themselves, had made the trek down the peninsula to assert a claim, to extort money from weak city-states, or to be crowned by the pope. But they all returned home, and doubtless this was in the mind of Duke Lodovico Sforza of Milan when he extended his invitation to the French. But he failed to comprehend the changing times, the energies that had been generated in the reawakened monarchies, newly unified under strong kings who were eager to seek honor in war. He did not realize the lure of the rich Italian cities to these money-hungry kings. Nor, finally, did he appreciate the weakness of the states of Italy compared to the states of the north. But his action was inspired by fear, not careful calculation. He had usurped the Milanese throne from his nephew; and his nephew's father-in-law, King Alfonso of Naples, was threatening to restore it to its rightful heir. Venice, Florence, and the papacy stood aside, refusing to come to his aid and Lodovico turned desperately to France.

Charles VIII welcomed the chance. France was ready and its young king, physically weak and mentally unstable, had always dreamed of fighting a war when he reached manhood. War, after all, was the business of kings. He had the old Angevin claim to Naples, inherited in 1480, as an excuse, a good army of brave and bellicose nobility, growing restless in peaceful France, and the prospect of little opposition among the jealous, disunited states of Italy. Moreover, the conquest of Naples appeared to his simple mind as a possible first step to greater glory, a new crusade against the Turks. Charles' councillors and cronies encouraged him, some for selfish reasons, such as the refugees from Italy who looked for a chance to upset the governments that had exiled them, others for reasons of state, such as those who saw huge profits in the sale of French "friendship" to weak Italian governments. Thus, for a variety of reasons, many of which would appear ephemeral, illogical, or downright stupid to a statesman of today, Charles accepted Lodovico's invitation. Amid chivalric pomp and splendor, the king set out on the journey that would change Italian and European politics forever.

Victory was easy. Charles and his troops reached their destination without serious resistance, putting the king of Naples to hasty flight. But the Italian and European powers had become aroused at this sudden expansion of French power. A "Holy League" was formed in 1495, including Milan (Lodovico had had second thoughts), Venice, the papacy, the Emperor Maximilian, and the Catholic Kings of Spain. The French were isolated and, when Spanish troops appeared, had no alternative but to withdraw from Italy, taking home little more to show for their efforts than hundreds of cases of syphilis, known thereafter as the "Italian" or "Neapolitan" sickness from the place of its presumed origin.

Nevertheless Louis XII, within months of his coronation in 1499, was once again in Italy, prosecuting the claim derived from his Visconti grandmother to the duchy of Milan. He quickly unseated Lodovico, who returned briefly in 1500 but was captured and cast into a French prison. He proclaimed the Sforzas upstarts and himself duke and prepared to attack Naples, nemesis of his predecessor. His success was hardly more substantial than Charles'. Ferdinand of Aragon, who had already made clear his determination to maintain Spanish hegemony in the southern kingdom, lulled Louis into a false sense of security by agreeing to divide the spoils, then turned on his partner and declared war. By 1504, Gonsalvo de Córdoba and his tough Spanish soldiers had defeated the French. Naples passed wholly and for two centuries to Spain.

The northern Europeans were clearly in Italy to stay. Spain was in the south, France, for the time being, in the north, with Emperor Maximilian and soon Henry VIII of England and the Swiss meddling in peninsular affairs when the opportunity offered. The golden days (as nostalgic contemporaries saw them) of Italian isolation were over; the "Italian system" of independent states, balanced one against the other, was destroyed. With Milan and Naples under foreign yoke, the next victim was Venice. The "League of

The Genoese, Asking Grace from Louis XII of France. This is 1499 and the second French invasion of Italy. Others followed, for the lure of Italy, its wealth, its culture, drew Frenchmen, Germans, and Spaniards into war and destruction for the next three generations. (Bibliothèque Nationale, Paris.)

Cambrai," a cynical alliance of most Italian and European states, combined against Venice in 1508. She escaped with her sovereignty but lost much of her territory. In 1511, the same powers, minus France but joined by Venice, were brought together by the warlike Pope Julius II in a new "Holy League" aimed at driving the French out of Milan. The great French captain Gaston de Foix led his army to early successes, among them the famous battle of Ravenna in which he lost his life. However, the weight of superior numbers soon told and the French retreated across the Alps once more. One might have thought they had learned their lesson, but almost the first act of Francis I on becoming king in 1515 was to equip a new army and march south. He won a great victory at Marignano and again seized Milan. The Italian Wars had only just begun.

FURTHER READING

There are no really thorough and up-to-date surveys of the later fifteenth- and early sixteenth-century monarchies. D. Hay, *Europe in the Fourteenth and Fifteenth Centuries* (1966) provides background but no more; so do J. Hale, et al., *Europe in the Late Middle Ages* (1965), a collection of articles; and D. Waley, *Later Medieval Europe* (1964), an English-style textbook. M. P. Gilmore, * *The World of Humanism, 1453–1519* (1952), is adequate and includes an excellent bibliography. G. Potter, ed., *The New Cambridge Modern History,* Vol. I, is best on cultural history, worst on social and economic history; some chapters on political history are better than others, but none is truly outstanding. A brilliant analysis from the standpoint of international relations is G. Mattingly, * *Renaissance Diplomacy* (1955).

For France see the long-needed J. H. Shennan, *Government and Society in France, 1461–1661* (1969). For particular subjects, see P. S. Lewis, ed., * *The Recovery of France* (1971); and J. R. Major, *Representative Institutions in Renaissance France* (1960).

An excellent introduction to England are the two Penguin volumes, A. R. Myers, * *England in the Late Middle Ages* (1952), which goes to 1536; and S. T. Bindoff, * *Tudor England* (1950). J. H. Elliot, * *Imperial Spain, 1469–1716* (1964), covers the reign of Ferdinand and Isabella in detail; J. Lynch, *Spain Under the Habsburgs,* vol. I (1964), begins in 1516 but has a good discussion of the heritage of the Catholic Kings—both books have good bibliographies. H. Holborn, *A History of Germany,* vol. I, *The Reformation* (1959), provides a useful summary of the fifteenth-century background.

*Books available in paperback edition are marked with an asterisk.

5 The First Empires

Modern western scientific, technological, and economic achievements are unique and serve to distinguish our civilization from all others. Equally striking is the manner in which the West expanded from its base on a small peninsula of the great Eurasian land mass across the broad oceans to the farthest parts of the globe. For good or ill, the entire world since the fifteenth century has been westernized at least in some degree. Indeed, until the twentieth century, much of the world was dominated politically and economically by the nations of Europe. Even now, in a day when most direct European control has been thrown off, the non-European peoples retain many important European ideas, skills, and aims.

This fact does not presume the superiority of western civilization. At the time expansion began, the West was relatively weak. Famine, war, plague, social unrest, political and religious dissent; all of these things were present in the Europe of 1400. China, on the other hand, was strong. Between 1403 and 1430, the Chinese emperors sent seven great maritime expeditions many thousands of miles south and west into the Indian Ocean, the Persian Gulf, the Red Sea, and along the east coast of Africa. Each of the fleets is said to have carried over 27,000 men, or about as many as Philip II of Spain, the most powerful ruler in Christendom, could put together with almost infinite pains a century and a half later to man his one-shot Armada which sailed a few hundred miles to its defeat. The Chinese fleets seem to have returned safely to their ports on the coast of the China Sea.

Therein lies a significant fact: the Chinese made their seven voyages; they saw the world of the Spice Islands (which they knew well enough already), India, Persia, Arabia, and Africa; they made their diplomatic contacts; and they collected tribute from the barbarian principalities along the shores of the Bay of Bengal, the Indian Ocean, the Persian Gulf, and the Red Sea. Then they went home to stay. They felt no compulsion to conquer or to dominate the areas as they probably could have done with ease. South Asia and Africa seemed to have nothing to offer them; their world at home was complete. The Europeans, for a variety of reasons, believed otherwise.

MEANS AND MOTIVES FOR EXPANSION

The first European empires could not have been possible had Europe not been prepared. By the early fifteenth century, Portugal, and by the late fifteenth century, Spain, possessed the incentive and the material resources to initiate and carry through the immense enterprise of global expansion. After the 1380's, Portugal was favored by prudent, farsighted, and long-lived kings of the native house of Avis, who were willing to indulge the speculations and experiments of Prince Henry the Navigator. Ferdinand and Isabella by the 1490's had come to see the advantages of empire. Under purposeful monarchs, the two Iberian kingdoms had attained relative internal peace and stability, fairly strong central government, and considerable prosperity. The chief domestic problems were on their way to solution and monarchs and subjects alike could direct their energies outward. Under similar conditions, France turned to international war. So did Spain and to a lesser extent Portugal, but both also turned to overseas expansion.

Technical Superiority of the Portuguese The Portuguese were first. A maritime people, whose interest in European affairs was never great, their eyes were turned naturally to the sea, and they had a long tradition of trade with North Africa. They were also a crusading people, hard-bitten fighters who had won back their land from the Moors. Most of them were farmers and fishermen, industrious but poor. The backbone of the population was the minor noble class, the *fidalgos,* trained for fighting and adventure. There were no serfs and few great nobles; there was an artisan class and a few influential merchants. Altogether, the Portuguese numbered only a million to a million and a half. How then did they build their empire?

One of the Earliest Surviving Brass Astrolabes, Dating from about 1200. At sea, astrolabes gave a rough estimate of latitude; estimates of longitude could not be made until the chronometer was invented in the eighteenth century. (Courtesy of the Trustees of the British Museum.)

Technological preparation was a decisive factor. Three branches of technology were involved; geography and astronomy and their application to navigation; ship design and sailing skill; and fire arms and naval gunnery. Up to that time, the most influential geographical and astronomical treatises were Ptolemy's *Geography* and *Astronomy* (usually called by its Arabic name, *Almagest*) and the *Imago Mundi,* written by a theologian of Paris, Pierre d'Ailly, in 1410. The *Imago Mundi* was a potpourri of fact and fiction from ancient and medieval sources; the *Almagest* was an ancient text, inaccurate on many important points. But interest in them reflected Renaissance man's love of classic learning even when belied by observable fact. Most maps were beautifully drawn but fanciful. Sailors, therefore, depended largely on practical sailing experience embodied in crude charts, or *portolani,* on a few simple navigational instruments, and on information gained from other sailors. Much sailing was done within sight of the coast or by dead reckoning. However, during the course of the fifteenth century remarkable strides were made. Hydrographers drew quite adequate charts of coastlines and harbors including estimated latitudes and noting winds and currents. Navigators learned to plot a rough position by the North Star and by shooting the sun with an "astrolabe" or quadrant, and contrived a sophisticated compass marked with thirty-two points. Longitude was still unknown, as was a reliable method of gauging speed. But by 1500, feats of navigation were performed that would have been impossible a hundred years earlier.

Progress in ship design was equally great. The European ship of 1400 was small, clumsy, and slow. It was broad of beam and square-rigged, and was adequate only for short trips within sight of land if the wind was right. Lack of maneuverability made exploration of coastlines difficult. The Portuguese, borrowing from the Arabs, developed a modified "lateen caravel." This design had a slimmer hull, a deeper keel, a sternpost rudder, and one or more triangular "lateen" sails hoisted obliquely to the masts, giving the ship far better handling qualities and permitting it to sail closer to the wind. Further development produced a ship called the *caravella redonda,* which combined the advantages of both square and lateen rigging, that is, it could run, reach, or tack with almost equal facility. It also had a tiller attached to a rudder, further improving its steering characteristics. All later sailing ships were simply improvements on the *caravella redonda.*

New navigational techniques and better ships would have meant nothing had not the Portuguese been able to sweep their opposition from the seas. Portuguese naval gunnery was superior to that of the Muslim fleets in the Mediterranean, indeed to that of any European power in the fifteenth century. Muslim ships carried shipboard artillery, but it was of an inferior sort, and their tactics were rudimentary and ineffective. The ships of Portugal, on the other hand, had well-made guns that were products of a better technology—and their crews knew how to fight with them. In the early days, only a few pieces were mounted at bow and stern. But soon cannon were mounted along the gunwales, trained to fire broadside. Naval warfare was revolutionized. The Portuguese, with many fewer ships at sea, defeated the combined Egyptian, Turkish, and Indian navies and ruled the eastern seas.

Motives for Expansion Given these means, the Europeans could begin their overseas expansion. What were the motives that sent them on their way? One of them was the lure of the unknown. Europe at that time was small and circumscribed. Renaissance men had a vague notion of what lay beyond their world from ancient tales and from the accounts of a few Franciscan missionaries and such redoubtable travelers as Marco Polo. They knew that the earth was round, that it nurtured races and cultures far different from their own. They had heard stories of lost continents in the Atlantic and of utopian kingdoms such as that of Prester John. And they wanted to see for themselves. Some, of which Prince Henry the Navigator is a good example, possessed a true spirit of scientific inquiry. One of his chief aims in sponsoring voyages of discovery was simply to advance human knowledge. Others were simply curious to see strange lands and meet strange people.

Another motive was religious zeal. The crusading tradition of holy war against the infidel was still very much alive in fifteenth-century Europe, particularly in the Iberian Peninsula. Portugal owed its existence to a long crusade; in Castile the battle was still going on. Prince Henry was involved with this tradition. A deeply pious man and a good soldier, he and his brothers won their spurs crusading at Ceuta in 1415, and he died shortly after returning from a campaign against the Muslims in 1460. He knew that the power of the Turks in the eastern Mediterranean made a frontal attack impracticable but he considered they might be successfully outflanked or taken in the rear if troops and supplies could be moved around Africa by sea. His plan envisioned a meeting and alliance with the legendary Prester John whose kingdom was thought to lie somewhere in Africa or Asia and who was reputed to be rich, powerful, and Christian. Henry also hoped to convert vast numbers of heathens.

To curiosity and religious zeal was added the desire for profit. Although probably exaggerated by some historians, economic motives must certainly be numbered among the reasons for overseas expansion in the fifteenth century and they became increasingly important as time passed and the wealth of empire was revealed. We must keep in mind that Renaissance monarchs did not sponsor and help finance voyages of discovery, any more than they fought wars, solely to line the pockets of their subjects. Continually beset by money worries, they veiwed empire building as simply another means of filling the royal treasury, for a full treasury gave them freedom of action at home and the wherewithal to pursue their dynastic ambitions abroad. Hence, the acquisition of gold and silver was their rosiest dream, and indeed both Portuguese and Spaniards found new sources of bullion, the latter in such volume as to affect the course of European political and economic history. But the rulers were also interested in commerce from which they could derive revenues directly and which they could tax. The quest for new lands and new trade routes was pressed forward with these considerations firmly in mind.

For centuries, as we have seen in an earlier chapter, Italians, primarily Venetians, had supplied Europe with products of the Orient: Chinese silks, Indian cotton cloth, precious stones, rhubarb (valued as a medicine), and above all, spices. The spices were pepper from India and the East Indian islands (the west coast of Africa yielded an inferior substitute called "Guinea pepper"), cinnamon from Ceylon, nutmeg and mace from the East Indies, ginger from China, and cloves from the Molucca island group. Rare and costly because the quantities available were small, they were nevertheless in great demand. The Church used spices for incense; rich laymen used them to preserve and flavor food. They were also used in embalming. It is not true that strong seasoning was needed to cover the taste of tainted meat, for some fresh meat was available to most people most of the time. Rather, the use of spices was a measure of status and wealth, and the people of that day simply liked a highly aromatic and pungent cuisine. The profits from Oriental trade were huge. A merchant might lose five cargoes and yet show an overall profit on a sixth. The Italians, who monopolized the western end of this trade, dealt in the Levant with Muslims who had purchased the goods in the Indian market (probably from Chinese merchants) and had transported them across the Indian Ocean, up the Red Sea or Persian Gulf, and overland to such Mediterranean ports as Alexandria. The goal of Portuguese and Spanish explorers was to bypass this ancient route, to find a new route directly to the Orient by sea. The Portuguese chose to sail east around Africa, the Spanish to sail west into the unknown Atlantic.

This was their original economic goal. As the explorations progressed and as footholds were gained in India and the "Spice Islands" (the East Indies) and in America, broader economic horizons opened up. The Portuguese learned to cultivate sugar in the Cape Verde Islands and in Brazil and to trade in ivory and slaves (gang labor was ideal in the sugar fields). The Spanish discovered that sugar grew well in the Caribbean islands and that parts of South America were good places to raise cattle and horses. At the beginning of the sixteenth century, the Portuguese, followed closely by the French and English, began fishing in the teeming waters off Newfoundland, the famous "Grand Banks." At about the same time, the first colonial settlements were founded and the flow of immigrants from the Old World to the New began.

THE VOYAGES OF DISCOVERY

Preparations for Portuguese expansion began in 1419, the year Prince Henry established a center for study of navigation and seamanship at the village of Sagres on the southwestern tip of Portugal, overlooking the Atlantic. There he brought together academicians and men of practical experience: astronomers and geographers, cartographers, instrument makers and shipbuilders, travelers and sailors, men of various nations particularly Italians, Jews, and Arabs. With their knowledge and the crown's money, a systematic program of discovery and exploration was launched. Henry pursued the task with single-minded devotion throughout his life. His inspirational leadership, his genius for organization and planning, his unflagging confidence, and his skill in justifying his expenditures to the king were indispensable ingredients of his ultimate success. Indeed, there would have been no Portuguese expansion, and thus no Portuguese empire, without Prince Henry. And he never took a voyage himself.

Early Explorations Progress was slow at first, for many psychological as well as technical obstacles had to be overcome. In 1434, Gil Eannes passed Cape Bojador at about 25 degrees North, proving false the legends of burning tropical sun and boiling seas. After that the pace quickened. By 1442, Cape Blanco, just south of the Tropic of Cancer, was reached and a bit of gold dust and the first few Negroes were taken home to Portugal. Six years later, a trading station, or "factory," was built on Arguim Island in Cape Blanco Bay and commercial activity began. Meanwhile, the first Portuguese settlements were founded in the Azores and Madeiras off the coast of northwest Africa, and after their discovery in the 1440's, in the Cape Verde Islands farther south. In time, the Azores developed a flourishing fishing industry, the Madeiras gained fame for their sweet wines, and the Cape Verdes became an area of large-scale sugar production. Prince Henry's dream had begun to pay dividends at his death in 1460.

Progress slowed again after 1460 until John II came to the throne in 1481. For most of the years between, responsibility for further expansion rested with a private merchant of Lisbon named Fernando Gomes. By arrangement with the crown (Alfonso V perferred fighting wars to directing voyages of discovery and exploration), Gomes agreed to explore one hundred leagues (300 miles) of African coastline and pay a certain sum each year in return for exclusive rights to trade. This kind of contract became common in later years, particularly in France and England. John II, however, let it expire in 1484. An able and ruthless monarch who ordered all foreigners caught trading clandestinely along the Guinea coast thrown to the sharks, John wanted fast results and large profits. He was more interested in commerce than Prince Henry had been and his efforts were pointed toward that goal. In 1482, a trading station was established on the West African Coast at Elmina, which became chief entrepôt for the trade in gold dust, ivory, slaves, and Guinea pepper. After about 1481, some 170,000 ducats in gold were delivered to Lisbon annually. By the mid-1480's, Diogo Cam reached the mouth of the Congo River, and in 1488 Bartholomew Diaz discovered the Cape of Good Hope. Nine years later Vasco da Gama (1460–1524) sailed for India.

Vasco da Gama Gama's voyage was one of mankind's epic adventures. It is fitting that Portugal's greatest work of art, and one of European literature's great epic poems, *The Lusiads* (1572) by Luis de Camoens, should celebrate it in proper Virgilian style. But like previous voyages, it was the result of King John's meticulous planning based on thorough study of all available sources of information. This staff work is one of the distinctive features of Portuguese empire building and goes far toward explaining how a state so small and so poor could accomplish a feat so large. Preparation for the voyage took almost a decade; part of that time was apparently spent in feverish waiting to see if Columbus had reached India by sailing west in 1492. Unfortunately, the Portuguese policy of secrecy has kept us from knowing all the details but we can be sure that nothing was overlooked. Diaz' records, particularly of winds and currents, were analyzed along with a valuable report from Pedro da Covilham, an agent whom John had sent to India by the Mediterranean-Red Sea route to look for Prester John and to investigate sailing conditions and the workings of the spice trade.

The decision to go forward was made in 1495, and Gama with his tiny fleet, four ships loaded with trinkets and cloth, set sail in July 1497. They sailed roughly south, striking just short of the Cape—three months at sea and 4,500 miles, unbelievable navigation for that day. Landing again on the coast of East Africa, they fought a skirmish with the natives, picked up a skilled Arab pilot, and sailed on to Calicut on the Malabar Coast in May 1498. After considerable bickering with the local Hindu ruler and with Muslim merchants intent on preserving their commercial monopoly, Gama returned to Lisbon the following year. Manuel II, king since 1495, immediately declared himself "Lord of the Conquest, Navigation, and Commerce of Arabia, Persia, and India," a fantastic title it took only fifteen years to make good.

Christopher Columbus and Spanish Exploration Meanwhile, the Spanish explorations had begun. A sea captain from Genoa named Christopher

Columbus (1451–1506), an experienced navigator and veteran of several voyages of exploration under the Portuguese flag, was able to convince Ferdinand and Isabella that the shortest route to the Orient lay westward. This notion, to which Columbus clung stubbornly until the end of his life, was not without foundation in tradition. Such sources as the *Imago Mundi,* Marco Polo's writings, and the *Almagest* were doubtless known to him. He tinkered with their often wild inaccuracies and came up with an even wilder inaccuracy of his own: that the distance from Europe to Zipangu (Japan) was only three thousand miles. He first approached John II of Portugal, but after council with learned geographers John rebuffed him. The Spanish sovereigns were less well informed. Eager to compete with their small Iberian neighbor, they agreed to outfit three ships, a slim enough contribution considering the possible benefits. The voyage was well conceived and almost perfectly executed. The *Niña,* the *Pinta,* and the *Santa Maria,* their sails ablaze with the red crusading crosses of Castile, got underway in August 1492 and reached their assumed destination on schedule, further bolstering Columbus' belief in his geographical fancies. Their first landfall was actually the island of San Salvador in the West Indies. After several short exploratory cruises, on one of which the *Santa Maria* was wrecked, he made once more for Spain, bearing a few pieces of native gold jewelry and some Indians in full costume.

Columbus was welcomed by Ferdinand and Isabella who believed his claims (the Portuguese were doubtful), and in 1493 set off on another expedition in command of seventeen ships to establish a base on Hispaniola, now known as Haiti, for continuing on to Japan and India. He had no better luck the second time. In all, he made four voyages, sighting Trinidad and other Caribbean islands, and exploring the mouth of the Orinoco and the coast of Central America. But he never reached the Orient. He died in 1506, rich but disillusioned, still refusing to face the momentous fact that he had discovered a new world.

Other Explorations Other states and other explorers followed quickly on the heels of Columbus. In 1497 and 1498, the Cabots discovered Newfoundland, Nova Scotia, and New England, under commission of King Henry VII of England. In 1500, Corte-Real, searching for a "Northwest Passage," a waterway through Canada to the Pacific, followed the English to Newfoundland, and his fellow Portuguese, Pedro Cabral, sighted the coast of Brazil. Beginning in 1497, Amerigo Vespucci (1451–1512), a Florentine and a representative of the Medici bank in Spain, made a series of voyages roughly along Columbus' routes, surveying much of the coast of Central America and northern South America. His descriptions were exact enough to confirm that Columbus had hit upon a previously unknown continent and his writings became so popular that his fame outstripped the discoverer's. On a map drawn by a German cartographer in 1507, Vespucci's name, latinized with the usual feminine ending into "America," was applied to the unknown continent. Inland exploration began shortly after the turn of the century. Ponce de Leon discovered Florida in 1512, Balboa, the Pacific

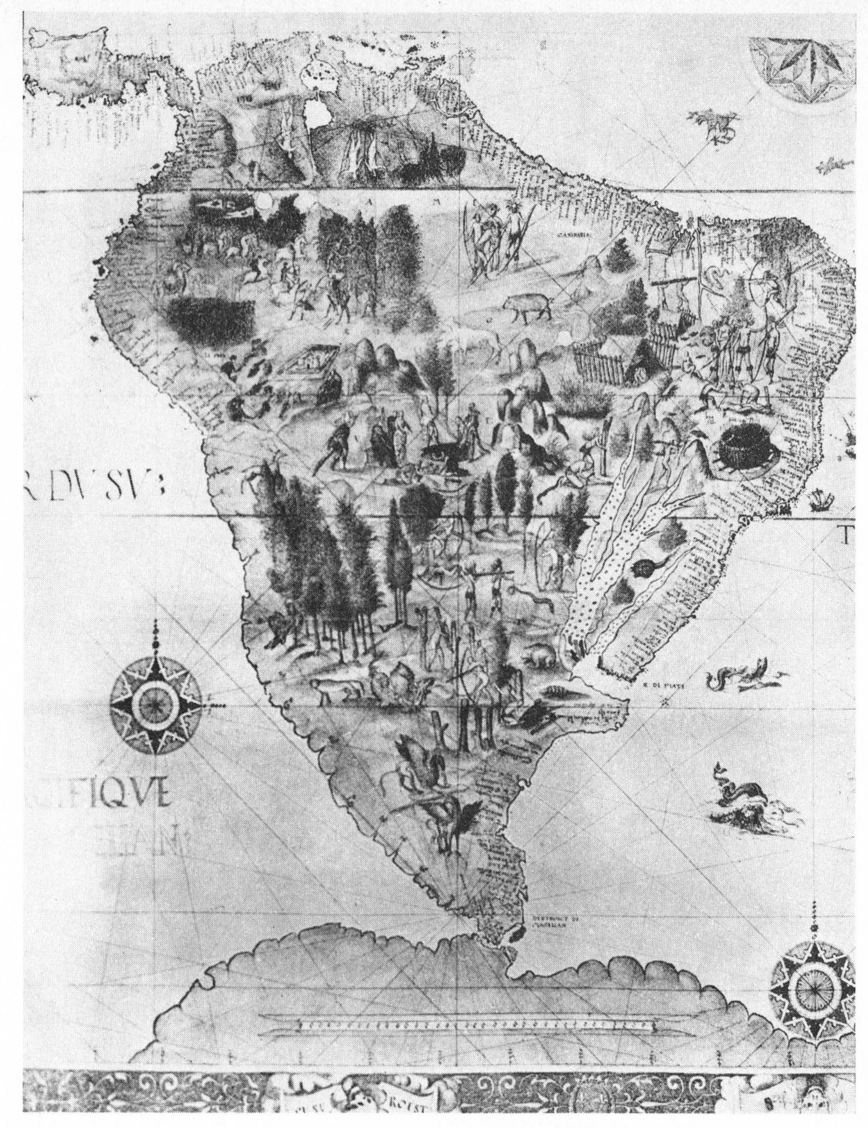

A surprisingly accurate map of South America, part of a map of the world drawn about 1550 for the king of France. As with most such maps, this one is embellished with fantastic men and animals, including cannibals cooking, winged mammals, and the inevitable sea monsters. (Schoenfeld Collection, Three Lions.)

Ocean in 1517. By 1522, Cortés and his *conquistadores* had won Mexico and Magellan had begun his voyage around the world.

Line of Demarkation Meanwhile, the Portuguese and Spanish areas of discovery and exploration were being defined by papal decree and treaty. Appeal to the pope was normal in that day. As the nominal head of Christendom, he traditionally distributed non-Christian lands to the secular monarchs who promised in return to pacify and convert the heathens and infidels. Formal agreements between states were obviously more binding. Beginning in the 1450's, the Holy See issued a series of bulls giving the

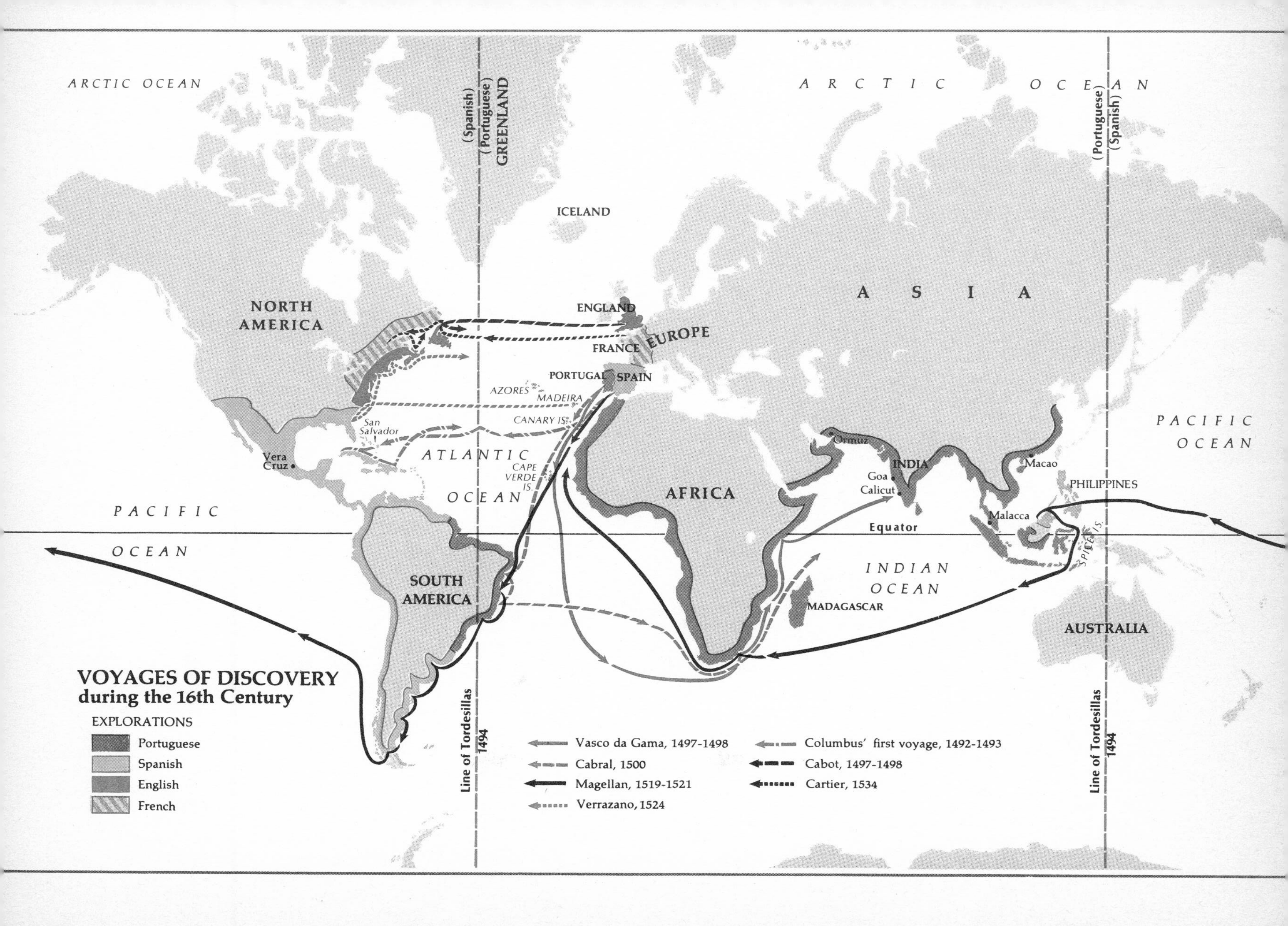
VOYAGES OF DISCOVERY
during the 16th Century
EXPLORATIONS
Portuguese
Spanish
English
French
Vasco da Gama, 1497-1498
Cabral, 1500
Magellan, 1519-1521
Verrazano, 1524
Columbus' first voyage, 1492-1493
Cabot, 1497-1498
Cartier, 1534
ARCTIC OCEAN
(Spanish)
(Portuguese)
GREENLAND
ICELAND
NORTH AMERICA
ENGLAND
FRANCE
EUROPE
PORTUGAL
SPAIN
AZORES
MADEIRA
CANARY IS.
San Salvador
Vera Cruz
ATLANTIC
OCEAN
CAPE VERDE IS.
PACIFIC
OCEAN
SOUTH AMERICA
AFRICA
A S I A
Ormuz
INDIA
Goa
Calicut
Macao
PHILIPPINES
Malacca
Equator
SPICE IS.
INDIAN OCEAN
MADAGASCAR
AUSTRALIA
PACIFIC OCEAN
(Portuguese)
(Spanish)
Line of Tordesillas 1494
Line of Tordesillas 1494

Portuguese exclusive rights to conquer and rule all regions inhabited by infidels "as far as the Indies." But the discoveries of Columbus complicated matters, for the Spanish Pope Alexander VI was quick to grant Spain dominion over the New World. By bulls issued in 1493, a line of demarkation was established one hundred leagues west of the Azores, running north and south around the entire globe. Lands west of the line were Spanish, lands east of the line Portuguese. The Portuguese were unsatisfied, however, and through direct negotiations with Spain, culminating in the Treaty of Tordesillas of 1494, they had the line moved 270 leagues (700 miles) farther west. Thereby, Portugal gained Brazil. (Some historians have suggested, though there is no proof, that the Portuguese crown was already aware of Brazil's existence at the time the treaty was made.) The presumptuous Europeans had divided the world in half. Neither the papal decrees nor the secular treaties were observed by the other states of Europe.

THE PORTUGUESE EMPIRE

By 1515, the Portuguese eastern empire was established. Careful planning and organization by a handful of resourceful and tough-minded men made possible such breathtaking speed. By the time Gama returned from Calicut in the summer of 1499, the main strategic points along the route to India were marked on the map and a detailed scheme, incorporating lessons learned in Africa, was evolved for exploitation of Oriental commerce. Force would be used ruthlessly. With the help of superior European technology including ships and guns, rivals would be eliminated. For the Portuguese sought not competition but monopoly. Naval dominance would be buttressed by the capture and fortification of port cities between East Africa and the trading areas. Factories would be established at suitable locations along the Malabar Coast and the Malay archipelago and among the East Indian islands, while commercial privileges would be obtained by whatever method was most effective—diplomacy, bribes, threats, or conquest. Administration would be simple and direct, assuring close control by the crown. The aim, combining Portugal's old crusading heritage with her newer love of money, was summed up in Gama's reported answer to the ruler of Calicut. When asked why he had come, he said it was to find "Christians and spices."

This eastern empire was not a land empire, an empire of settlement, but a maritime empire, one dedicated solely to exploitation and profits through trade. The Portuguese were not colonizers. There were few enough of them in their own land as it was, and indeed the nature of their subject areas—wild and tropical Africa, civilized and populous India—discouraged emigration. Further, except for a steady and sincere though not particularly successful missionary effort by friars and Jesuits, they left the natives to themselves so long as business was not interrupted. There was considerable intermarriage, since very few women left Portugal, and natives were introduced into menial jobs and the lower ranks of the bureaucracy. But on the whole, these first Europeans overseas were content to remain interlopers, holding their empire by strength alone, strangers in a strange land. Their cultural influence on the natives was slight; this came later with the Dutch,

Vasco da Gama in his Old Age. A minor nobleman and therefore a soldier by trade, he commanded ships because sailors were of a lower class and unfit to command. But he was an exception: he fought as well at sea as on land, and his title, "Admiral of India," was earned by his skill, not his social position. (Museu Nacional de Arte Antiga, Lisbon.)

the French, and above all the English whose colonial policies were built on the precedents laid down by the Portuguese.

Naked power was asserted first by Gama himself on his second voyage to India in 1502. In retaliation for the murders of some traders left the previous year by Cabral, he bombarded Calicut and decisively defeated a larger Arab fleet off the Malabar Coast. Portuguese commerce was now centered at Cochin and Cananor farther south but it was limited in extent and it was competitive, not at all in accord with Portuguese plans. Hence in 1505, Dom Francesco de Almeida, the first viceroy, led a well-manned expedition into the Indian Ocean to break the old Arab trade monopoly. Systematically, Almeida attacked commercial cities from East Africa to India, driving out the Arab merchants, exacting tribute from the Arab rulers, and constructing forts and installing garrisons. It was a crusade, passionate and vicious. Almeida concentrated also on preparing bases for merchant shipping and naval war. In 1507, Socotra, at the entrance to the Red Sea, was captured, cutting the Arab trade route to Alexandria. In the next two years, he trounced the Turkish, Egyptian, and Indian Gujerati navies in the great sea battles of Chaul and Diu. Better guns, greater firepower, more maneuverable ships—these were the secrets of Portuguese success.

Almeida was replaced as viceroy in 1509 by Affonso de Albuquerque, the first of the great soldier-statesmen of Europe's expansion. Albuquerque carried the Portuguese plan forward with brilliance. By foresight and daring strategy, he secured his predecessor's gains and extended Portuguese influence beyond India to Malaya, the East Indies, and north to the mainland of China. His first act was to seize the Indian port city of Goa which he transformed into Portugal's chief naval base and commercial entrepôt in the East. In 1512, he captured Malacca on the Malay Peninsula about where Singapore is today. This large mercantile city became the advanced post for trade with Java, Siam, Pegu, Ceylon, and the Moluccas. A year later he sent a ship to Canton and in due course established a trading station at nearby Macao. Macao is still a Portuguese colony. Meanwhile, Albuquerque finished Almeida's work in the Indian Ocean. He failed to take Aden on the Persian Gulf but Ormuz, occupied in 1515, was an adequate substitute. Now Portugal had convenient bases at every point on the route from Lisbon to the East and her navy ruled the sea.

Spices, of which pepper was by far the most important, and other oriental luxury products began to flow into the European market in quantities never before known. Early each year, the Portuguese dispatched a fleet to India. Riding the prevailing westerlies down the African coast and the southwest monsoons across the Indian Ocean, it made Goa in September. There it loaded its precious cargo, bought for the most part with silver and gold (the highly cultivated Orientals turned up their noses at almost everything European except horses, which they prized), and set sail once again in January on the northeast monsoons. Besides spices, the ships carried the same products that had enriched the Venetians for so long: rare metals and gems, silks, and drugs. The fleet reached Lisbon in July after a trip of eighteen to twenty months. Once home, the cargo was delivered to the warehouses of the government's *Casa da India,* the India House, where royal agents took out the crown's share, as much as 60 percent, and issued expensive merchant's licenses to sell the rest. In the beginning, profits were enormous, but they fell off steeply as supply approached demand. After about 1505, the crown fixed prices and imposed restrictions on sales in an effort to create artificial scarcity. The spice trade became a state monopoly and the entire financial structure of the government became dependent on it.

Indeed, Portugal's destiny was soon tied inextricably to her empire. For a while, she seemed destined for glory. The ruling house grew rich and began to live in great luxury. Much was spent on abortive crusades. A few favored merchants also made fortunes. But the glory was temporary and the wealth an illusion. Indeed, the most consistent profits for the Portuguese themselves derived from their carrying trade among ports in the Far East. King Manuel II and his successors spent more than they made, borrowing from German and Italian bankers on future cargoes. Since neither the kings nor the merchants had sufficient capital, these same bankers also supplied the funds to outfit the Indies fleets. Other non-Portuguese, Dutch and Flemish for the most part, transported the spices in their own ships from Lisbon to Antwerp, which became the center of distribution for all Europe; thus, much of the profit went into the pockets of foreigners. Never did Portugal possess a monopoly of the European spice trade: the Venetians, dealing as they always had with Arab middlemen and offering high-quality merchandise, were earning more than ever by the second quarter of the sixteenth century. The crown faced insoluble problems even to compete effectively. This, together with the restrictive commercial policies of the crown, limited the development in Lisbon and other cities of a large, urban middle class, broadly based on a thriving capitalist economy as in Venice. Nor did the spice trade stimulate the growth of associated activities such as shipbuilding, since most Portuguese ships were purchased abroad. Portugal and the Portuguese remained very much the same as before, a society of peasants, country gentry, and local tradesmen and artisans. Even Portuguese culture was almost wholly untouched: no palaces, no art, no outstanding works of literature except the epic poem of Camoens. In the words of the contemporary author of *O Soldado Pratico,* the glory and the wealth of empire was like smoke, unsubstantial and quickly blown away.

THE SPANISH EMPIRE

From the outset, Spain's empire was different from Portugal's, largely because America was different from West Africa and the Orient and invited a different sort of imperial policy. It began as an empire of plunder and settlement and remained so throughout its three-hundred year history. The discoverers and explorers were accompanied by soldiers, missionaries, and administrators and were followed closely by everyday folk whose aim was to build a new life for themselves in a new land. It was soon realized that profits, to individuals as well as to the crown, accrued from mining and agriculture, not from commerce. These facts may be observed as early as 1493 when Columbus sailed west from Spain for the second time. His fleet was not fitted out for war and trade in the Portuguese manner but for exploration and colonization. Its principal cargo was fifteen hundred men of various skills and professions, volunteers attracted by promises of fortune and adventure, bent on establishing a settlement on the island of Hispaniola. This first European outpost in the New World was a failure but it set a pattern for all the rest.

The earliest settlements everywhere were unstable and unprofitable. Most of the settlers were undisciplined men, men without jobs, veterans of European wars against the Moors and the French who much preferred to rob Indians and hunt gold than live peaceably by farming or stock raising. Moreover, the crown had not yet contrived a body of colonial institutions or laid down a detailed and consistent colonial policy. The institutions and policy that appeared were fundamentally Castilian, derived from the peculiar historic tradition of that austere kingdom adapted to New World conditions. For example, semi-independent towns, so characteristic of Castile, were the political building blocks of Spanish America while treatment of the conquered Indians owed much to experience gained with the conquered Moors of Granada and the occupation of the Canary Islands in the 1480's. But for the first few years, the settlers had to shift for themselves. Nor was Columbus himself much help. As the first viceroy he was entirely out of his element, unable to lead men on land and a wretched administrator. His replacement sent him home in irons. Despite these handicaps, by the time Charles I, later emperor Charles V, ascended the united thrones of Spain in 1516, permanent colonies were planted on Hispaniola, Jamaica, Cuba, and other Caribbean Islands, and at one or two places in Central America. Meanwhile, a good part of the coastline from Florida around the Gulf of Mexico and south to northern South America was explored and mapped and the great work of winning the Indian kingdoms of Mexico, Central America, and Peru got underway.

Hernando Cortés. With his victories in Mexico—New Spain—Cortés cemented Spanish power in the New World and produced the first substantial treasure for the Spanish crown. (Radio Times Hulton.)

The Conquistadores This conquest, really a series of conquests, extended Spanish dominion throughout the accessible parts of Central and South America. It made possible a large and rapid increase in colonization and brought many new souls into the Christian fold but its chief purpose as far as the *conquistadores* themselves were concerned was self-aggrandizement. Most of these men were Castilian knights, spiritual heirs of the crusade, who combined greed and bravura with a deep devotion to their faith and their king. A few thousand of them, ill-equipped by European military standards, overwhelmed a relatively primitive but courageous, warlike, and much more numerous people in hardly more than three decades. Here was a feat of empire building to rival the Portuguese, yet no easier to explain. Better weapons, including horses and a few firearms, tighter discipline and more tactical flexibility, greater physical strength and stamina, the wisdom and good luck to exploit their enemies' superstitious fears and to make allies of their enemies' enemies; all of these factors must be taken into account. But equally important and perhaps decisive was the Spaniards' unquenchable confidence born of religious and patriotic fervor and, as part of this, their awareness of their own cultural superiority. To the *conquistador,* an Indian was a heathen and a savage, little better than an animal; the idea that one might be defeated by him in battle was inconceivable.

Hernando Cortés was probably the greatest, certainly the most admirable, of the *conquistadores.* In 1519, he sailed from Cuba with six hundred men to invade Mexico, announcing: "I come, not to cultivate the soil like a laborer, but to find gold." He vowed to present King Charles with "more provinces than his ancestors gave him cities!" His first acts on landing were to burn his fleet (he would win or die) and to found a town which he named *Vera Cruz*, "True Cross." To the Indians he offered peace in return for allegiance to Spain and Christianity. By 1521, after three years of story-book exploits against the Aztecs, he had fulfilled his vow: Mexico was conquered. The work of Cortés was carried forward in the 1520's and 1530's by men no less determined or fearless than himself, though more brutal and self-seeking. Among them were Cortés' own lieutenants, who subdued the Mayas of Central America, remorselessly obliterating a barbaric but remarkable civilization. Another *conquistador*, the notorious Francisco Pizarro, was an unprincipled adventurer who attacked the Inca kingdom of Peru with an army smaller than that of Cortés. He found the Incas an easy match but the government he set up soon fell prey to discord among the victors themselves, and Pizarro and many of his followers died in civil war. However, he was able to dispatch parties to explore north and south in areas that are now Ecuador and Chile. Further conquest and exploration completed Spain's New World empire by mid-century.

Incan Gold Ear Ornament in the Form of a Warrior, ca. 1400. (Museum of the American Indian, Heye Foundation, New York.)

Machu Picchu. Situated high in the Peruvian Andes, this citadel was abandoned by the Incas after the Spanish conquest. It was "lost" and not rediscovered until 1911. (Pan American.)

Church and State On the heels of the *conquistadores* came missionaries and administrators. Towns were built including Mexico City on the site of the ruined Aztec capital and settlers moved in. Indian civilization was quickly and effectively replaced by the civilization of Spain. The Indians themselves, accepted as free men with souls and descendants of Adam and Eve after a prolonged political and theological discussion led by the Dominican Bartolomé de las Casas, were systematically converted and made subjects of the Spanish king. Most of them were also put to work for the conquerors and settlers who were given grants of land, rights of tribute (*repartimiento*) and labor (*encomienda*) over specified native villages in return for guarantees of missionary work and protection. The Indians were thus relegated to a social and economic position much like the free peasants of Europe under the domination of a Spanish "aristocracy." Many native customs and laws were respected, however, and chiefs were often placed in minor administrative jobs. Moreover, the Indians had recourse to local Spanish courts where they could sue for redress of grievances. This colonial policy, as noted earlier, was founded on the tradition and experience of the Spanish at home, and in theory it was enlightened, just, and humane, though often in practice it was none of these. The so-called "Black Legend" of Spanish ignorance and cruelty is in some ways exaggerated, but it is impossible to explain away the many millions of Indians who died of disease (measles above all), overwork, and general ill treatment in the early years of Spanish occupation.

For governmental purposes, Spain divided her empire into "kingdoms," the two largest being New Spain (roughly Mexico) and New Castile (roughly Peru). These kingdoms were considered to be appendages of the crown of Castile, in effect personal possessions of the monarch. First Isabella alone, then Charles I, Philip II, and their successors after the Spanish crowns were united in a single person, governed through a Council of the Indies in Spain and viceroys in America. The viceroys were assisted and advised (often they were defied and even overruled) by a number of *audiencias,* technically courts of appeal but actually cabinet councils staffed by professional lawyers and located in principal cities. The "old conquerors" such as Cortés played a minor role in government or no role at all: the crown, in the midst of eliminating noble power and privilege at home, was determined that no independent nobility would arise overseas. The leading characteristic of the colonial government—and it became more noticeable as time wore on—was a blind loyalty to royal authority and an inordinate respect for the forms of law, which stifled initiative, lowered efficiency, and slowed the administrative process to a snail's pace.

Spain was slower than Portugal to receive dividends from empire. Spanish hopes of finding a convenient western passage to the commercial wealth of the Orient remained high until Magellan's voyage proved them futile. Agriculture and cattle-ranching, which soon became, along with mining, the colonists' chief occupations, produced little revenue for the mother country. Nor did the New World yield significant quantities of gold and silver until the rich Indian kingdoms were conquered and new mines were discovered in the second quarter of the sixteenth century. From the beginning, however, a trickle of bullion and precious stones reached Spanish shores; and after 1504, the crown claimed one-fifth for itself. Collection of the *quinto*, as the royal share was called, was in the hands of agents of the *Casa de Contratación*, the royal House of Trade—modeled on the Portuguese *Casa da India*—which was located in the port city of Seville. Trade with America was not a royal monopoly but a monopoly of the merchant guild of Seville. The crown, while burdening traders with all sorts of regulations and licensing requirements, was really interested only in the *quinto*. Though it amounted to only a fraction of the royal income, it had disproportionate political, economic, and social effects on Spain and on Europe. These we shall examine in later chapters.

FURTHER READING

Now the standard work in English on the earlier expansion of Europe is J. H. Parry, * *The Age of Reconnaissance, 1415–1650* (1963), which is particularly good on technology and organization for empire. An excellent introduction is the same author's * *The Establishment of the European Hegemony, 1415–1715* (1961). Stimulating is D. L. Jensen, ed., * *The Expansion of Europe: Motives, Methods, and Theory* (1967).

On exploration in general see B. Penrose, * *Travel and Discovery in the Renaissance* (1955); P. Sykes, * *A History of Exploration* (3rd rev. ed., 1950); and J. B. Brebner, * *The Explorers of North America* (1933). S. E. Morison's, *The European Discovery of America* (1972), is good. A unique collection of sources—diaries, journals and the like—is contained in translation in the many volumes issued by the *Hakluyt Society* since the mid-nineteenth century. A good study of certain aspects of technology is C. Cipolla, *Guns, Sails, and Empire* (1965).

On Portugal, see, above all, D. R. Boxer, *The Portuguese Seaborne Empire* (1969), which contains an admirable bibliography. Also interesting are E. Prestage, *The Portuguese Pioneers* (1933); E. Sanceau, *Henry the Navigator* (n.d.); and H. Hart, *Sea-Road to the Indies* (1950). The latter is concerned chiefly with Vasco da Gama. Standard now for Spain is J. H. Parry, *The Spanish Seaborne Empire* (1966). S. E. Morison, * *Admiral of the Ocean Sea*, is the best biography of Columbus; F. J. Pohl, *Amerigo Vespucci, Pilot Major* (1944) is also good. *The Journal of Christopher Columbus* has been translated and edited by C. Jane and L. A. Vigneras (1960). A great historian's classic works are W. H. Prescott, * *History of the Conquest of Mexico* (1843), and * *History of the Conquest of Peru* (1847), published in various editions, including paperback. Recent and excellent on the institutions implanted in America is Charles Gibson, * *Spain in the New World* (1966).

*Books available in paperback edition are marked with an asterisk.

PART VIII

The religious revolution of the sixteenth century, which we call the Reformation, followed close on the Renaissance and completed western Europe's passage from the Middle Ages to modern times. In 1500, the Roman Catholic Church was the last great stronghold of medievalism. No one had yet challenged its claim to universal dominion. It stood splendid in its Renaissance trappings—rich, proud, complacent. But the great days of Innocent III were passed; the sixteenth century was not the thirteenth. The resurgence of the territorial state, the revitalization of economic life and the progress of capitalism, the breakdown of feudal society, the emergence of new ideas, and a new appreciation of man's role in the universe: all these forces that were transforming medieval into modern Europe worked in some measure to sap the power and influence of the Church. Furthermore, as an institution the Church no longer commanded the loyalty and respect of an earlier day, for too often and in too many ways it had compromised the Christian ideal. Doubtless it had been obliged to do so in order to survive. In surviving, however, the Church had been infected with secularism: moral decay, love of material things, indifference to the spiritual needs of the faithful. Hence, its hold over the minds of men had been seriously weakened and it went into battle against Protestantism without its most powerful weapon.

"THE CREATION OF THE WORLD," DETAIL OF WOODCUT FROM 1534 BIBLE OF MARTIN LUTHER. (New York Public Library)

THE REFORMATION

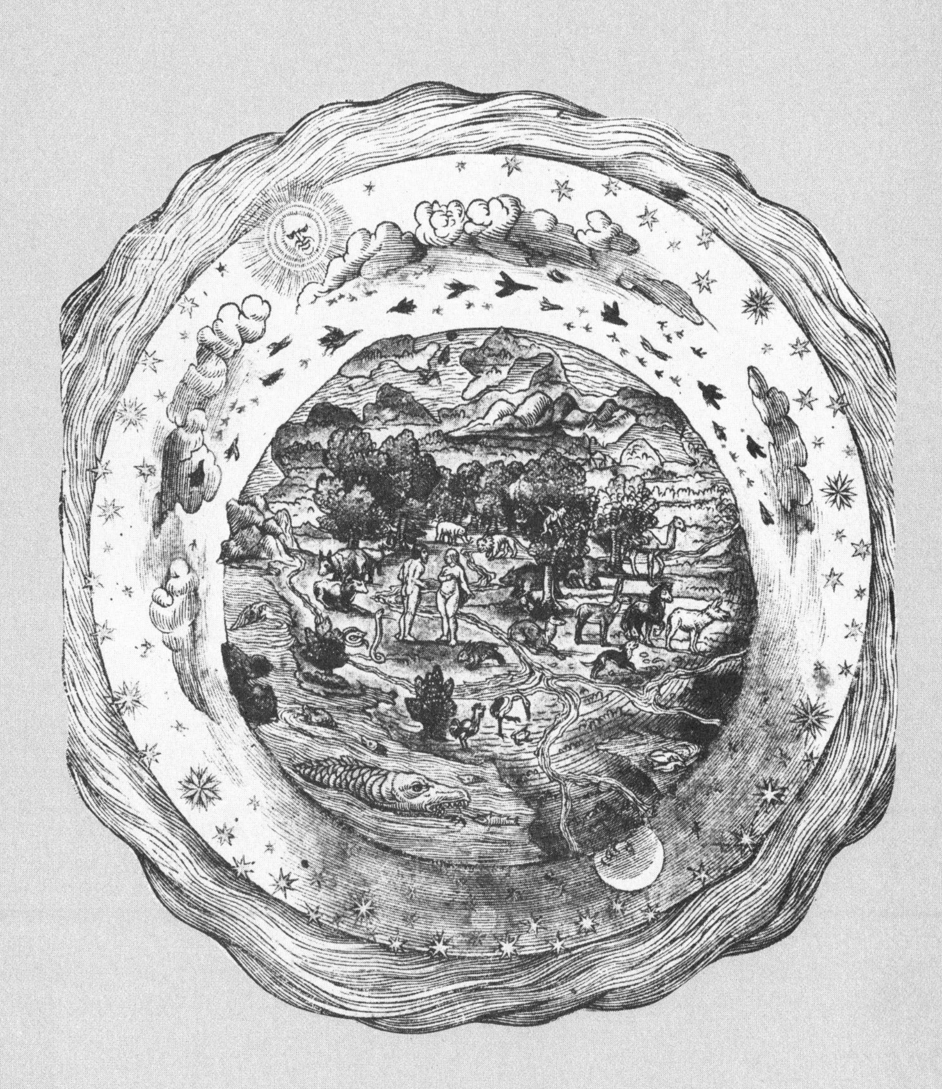

LEGACY OF THE PAST

(Opposite page)
Luther and his Friends by Lucas Cranach the Elder. To the fore is Elector John Frederick of Saxony. Over his right shoulder are Luther and the Swiss reformer Oecolampadius, and over his left Zwingli and Melanchthon. (The Toledo Museum.)

Lutherans and Presbyterians, Baptists and Episcopalians, Unitarians and Mennonites—these and all the other Protestant Churches come straight from the Reformation. So too does the modern Catholic Church, changed almost not at all from the close of the Council of Trent in the 1560's to the opening of Vatican II in the 1960's. During the first half of the sixteenth century, after a millenium of unity, "the seamless robe of Christ" was rent, and the old Christian church was fragmented. To most people of the time, convinced of their own righteousness, the Reformation was the work of either God or the Devil, and toleration of dissent was unthinkable. But a few disagreed, insisting that everyone could decide his own religious beliefs and responsibilities for himself. They are the originators of our modern idea of "freedom of conscience."

Also stemming from the first half of the sixteenth century is the modern idea of "international law," the body of regulations that governs the conduct of states and their relationships among one another. The France of Francis I, the England of Henry VIII, the Spain of Charles V were not really "states" in today's sense. Rather they were loosely organized territorial aggregates, united in a personal way by heads of great royal families. But they acted like modern states: kings taxed, kept order, dispensed justice, raised armies, and fought wars. War became a way of life in Europe, and for most of the rest of European history was more common than peace. Out of almost continual conflict came in this period the first hesitant suggestions by men of good will that states, like individuals, must be subject to the rule of law.

MAJOR EVENTS, 1505-1565*

1500–

Luther enters Augustinian monastery at Erfurt (1505)

Council of Pisa meets with support of Louis XII (1511)
Fifth Lateran Council meets at direction of papacy (1512)
Leo X elected pope (1513)
Luther makes "Tower of Discovery": "the just shall live by faith" (between 1513 and 1517)

Letters of Obscure Men published (1515)

Leo X and Francis I sign Concordat of Bologna (1516)

Luther posts *Ninety-Five Theses* attacking indulgences (1517)
Oratory of Divine Love founded at Rome (c. 1517)
Erasmus publishes Greek New Testament (1517)

Election of Emperor Charles V (1519)
Luther engages in Leipzig debate with Eck (1519)
Zwingli begins to preach at Zürich (1519)

Luther excommunicated, writes three great treatises (1520)
Revolts of *communeros* and *germanias* in Spain (1520–22)

Diet of Worms meets, declares Luther a rebel (1521)
Luther at Wartburg; translates New Testament into German (1521)
Reformation begins in Wittenberg (1521)
"Conversion" of Ignatius of Loyola (1521)

Knights' Revolt in Germany (1522–23)

Zwingli's Reformation accepted in Zürich (1523–24)

Anabaptism appears in Zürich (1524–25)

1525–

Peasants' Revolt in Germany (1525)
Thomas Münzer executed (1525)
Lutheranism becomes state religion in Saxony (1525)

Rome sacked by soldiers of Charles V (1527)

Marburg Colloquy between Luther and other Protestant leaders (1529)

Zwingli killed at battle of Cappel (1531)

Henry VIII declared Head of Anglican Church (1534)
Calvin "converted" to Protestantism (1534)
Paul III elected pope (1534)

For 1505–1525 see also Major Events, Part VII.

Paul III accepts report of Cardinals' commission on state of Church (1536)

Calvin publishes first edition of *Institutes of the Christian Religion* (1536)

Calvin with Farel at Geneva (1536–38)

Calvin with Bucer at Strasbourg (1538–40)

Calvin in Geneva; his *Ecclesiastical Ordinances* adopted (1541)

Society of Jesus founded (1541)

Regensburg meeting between Catholics and Protestants fails (1541)

Roman Inquisition established (1542)

Schmalkaldic War in Germany (1546–47)

First meeting of Council of Trent (1545–47)

Death of Luther (1546)

Archbishop Cranmer publishes first Book of Common Prayer (1549)

1550– Jesuits found colleges throughout Catholic Europe (1550's)

Second meeting of Council of Trent (1551–52)

Servetus burned at Geneva (1553)

Catholic reaction under Mary in England (1553–58)

Peace of Augsburg legalizes Lutheranism in Germany (1555)

Calvinist missionary activity begins (1555)

Abdication of Charles V (1556)

Spanish defeat French at St. Quentin (1557)

Elizabeth becomes queen of England (1558)

Treaty of Cateau-Cambrésis between Spain and France (1559)

Calvin publishes final edition of *Institutes* (1559)

Congregation of the Index established by papacy to censor books (1559)

Wars of Religion begin in France (1561)

Third meeting of Council of Trent (1562–63)

Death of Calvin (1564)

1 Martin Luther and the Protestant Revolution

Nobody believes anymore that either God or the devil caused the Protestant Reformation. But many historians in the past have accepted such a single, all-embracing cause. The growth of the nation state, the "commercial revolution," the Renaissance ideal of "individualism": each of these and more have been offered to explain the religious movements of the sixteenth century. In recent years, however, most historians have come to realize that the Reformation was immensely complex, that its causes were numerous and difficult to define. They have concentrated on close studies of individual cases. Where a sincere spiritual conversion might have turned a German prince to Protestantism, a victory of one political faction over another might have caused a French town to do so. Where one man might have joined an Anabaptist sect out of religious conviction, another might have done so as an extreme form of social protest. In each case, whether involving kingdoms, principalities, towns, or individuals, a variety of influences was at work, and nowhere were they exactly the same. Students, therefore, must be wary of glib and over-simple explanations.

THE CHURCH ON THE EVE OF THE REFORMATION

Corruption and Reform A good example of oversimplification is the traditional Protestant view that the success of the Reformation was due largely to the moral and spiritual collapse of Catholicism. "Abuses" within the old Church were a secondary issue to Luther, Zwingli, Calvin, and most of the Protestant leaders. Their criticism went much deeper, to the fundamental doctrines on which the Church was founded: the nature and efficacy of the sacraments, the roles of faith and good works in salvation, the legitimacy of the priestly function and of the papacy itself. But to most Europeans, generally orthodox in their beliefs, corrupt churchmen and questionable rites and practices were most important. Almost any observant European in 1500 could point to a bishop who had bought his office for its income and prestige and who allowed self-serving underlings to run it, to a parish priest who hardly knew the Mass and demanded money for administering the sacraments, to a monk whose easy life was far removed from the Rule of St. Benedict, to a friar who bilked a gullible public by hawking spurious relics and misrepresenting indulgences—indeed, to popes whose chief interests were Renaissance culture and advancement of their own families. But these kinds of abuses were not much different from those of a century before. There may even have been fewer of them.

The difference was that now the voices calling for reform were louder and more numerous and their audience larger and more responsive. Those who spoke out were mostly churchmen, determined to restore the dignity and sanctity of the great institution to which they belonged. Erasmus and many of the Christian humanists were of this sort, and their program of personal spiritual renewal and return to the simplicity of the Apostolic

These woodcuts by Lucas Cranach constrast Christ's treatment of the money-changers with the attitude of the pope. Such simple illustrations of complex issues were used by both sides during the Reformation and Counter-Reformation to influence illiterate and semiliterate people. (The Pierpont Morgan Library.)

Church had enormous appeal among clerics and laymen alike. The books and pamphlets of the Christian humanists, easily available because they were now printed cheaply by the thousands, were read especially by educated nobles and patricians of the towns. For nonreaders there were preachers and printed pictures. This was the first great age of visual propaganda. Explicit, often crude and unfair, etchings and woodcuts set forth ideas and events in the graphic form that illiterate people could best understand.

The call was for reform, and the logical initiator and leader was the pope. But the Renaissance popes, as we have seen, were creatures of their age, politicians, patrons of the arts, worldly men with worldly concerns. They worked diligently to reinforce their spiritual autocracy and secure their temporal authority in Rome and the Papal States. Moreover, they deeply feared a resurgence of Conciliarism, an idea still very much alive despite its condemnation as heresy a half century before. To call a free and open, European-wide council to begin reform was a gamble they dared not take. In 1512, Pope Julius II convened the Fifth Lateran Council in response to mounting criticism within and without the Church, but both he and his successor, Leo X, saw that it met in Rome under tight papal control. It dragged on until 1517, accomplishing little of real significance and satisfying almost nobody.

The other possible initiators and leaders were the secular rulers, particularly the kings, to whom the papacy had surrendered important prerogatives relating to ecclesiastical discipline, appointment, and taxation. Indeed, it was the secular rulers, not the pope, who had the authority to reform their own churches. But there was little inclination among them—with the exception of Queen Isabella of Spain—to alter the status quo and thereby threaten a lucrative source of revenue and an important way to award political favors.

Spain—or more specifically Castile—was an exception. Under the leadership of Cardinal Francisco Ximenes de Cisneros, Archbishop of Toledo and Primate of Spain—and with the whole-hearted support of Isabella, whose confessor he had been—a thoroughgoing reform program was carried out between 1495 and 1517. A man of wisdom and zeal, of learning and exceptional administrative ability, Ximenes rebuilt the Church of Spain. He fearlessly righted abuses among the regular clergy of every religious order, eliminating one Franciscan house entirely and distributing its houses and land to orders he considered more worthy. But the secular clergy was his primary concern and with rare energy he threw out bad bishops and priests and replaced them with good ones. To provide clerical education at all levels, he founded the great University of Alcalà in 1498. In each of his activities, Ximenes had the full support and encouragement of Ferdinand and Isabella whose political as well as religious aims were served by a strong, upright, and loyal Church. Although they could not know it, such a church was to be the best possible defense against the infection of Protestantism.

But few churchmen attacked the problem so well and on such a broad scale as Ximenes or had such positive and lasting results. Other bishops made some progress in diocesan reform elsewhere in Europe but their programs were not coordinated, and there was nothing that can be termed a general movement for reform. Among the regular clergy, the rigorous discipline of the Augustinian monks at Windesheim in the Dutch Netherlands had a wider influence. But the entire pre-Lutheran reform effort was only a beginning. Some Roman Catholic historians have suggested that internal reform was so far advanced by 1517 as to soon embrace the entire Church, in other words, that a Catholic Reformation was about to occur before the Protestant Reformation intervened. Evidence in favor of this suggestion is scanty; the Catholic Reformation, as we shall see, was partly of independent origin but was largely a response and a reaction to the dangers posed by Protestantism.

Popular Religion Meanwhile, many laymen and priests, feeling themselves abandoned by the organized Church, sought salvation in a more individualistic way. For a number of reasons, the years before the Reformation were a time of extraordinary religiosity in Europe: a morbid fascination with death as an aftermath of the Black Death of 1348–1349 and the lesser plagues that followed (manuals on the *Art of Dying* were best sellers); the greater availability of the Bible and popular devotional writings because of the spread of printing; a sense of disquietude and insecurity generated by the disintegration of medieval society under economic and political pressures; and the influence of Christian humanist ideas. This religiosity was stimulated by growing dissatisfaction with the papacy and Church hierarchy, their unwillingness to reform, and their apparent lack of concern for the spiritual lives of men; not surprisingly it was often of a highly personal kind with distinct anti-sacerdotal overtones. The most characteristic manifestation was the *devotio moderna* whose adherents, as we have seen, strove for a mystical union with God through love and "methodical prayer." They put great stock in reading the New Testament and in performing the devotional exercises set down in the *Imitation of Christ.* Both Erasmus and Martin Luther were exposed to the "new devotion" because they studied in the schools of its founders, the Brethern of the Common Life.

No less pious, though less individualistic, more conventionally orthodox, and hence ultimately less dangerous to the organized Church, were the religious orders and societies devoted to charity which sprang up in Italy in the first and second decades of the sixteenth century. The first of these was the Oratory of Divine Love, an association of priests and laymen organized at Rome about 1516. The Oratory numbered among its members Giacopo Sadoleto, a leading Christian humanist, Gian Pietro Caraffa, Bishop of Chieti, and later Pope Paul IV. Besides extreme personal sanctity, achieved by frequent confession and acceptance of Holy Communion and by prayer, they devoted their lives to the performance of good works as an aid to the love of God. The "Clerks Regular" were the Oratory's heirs. These men were neither monks nor friars, though they took the traditional vows of poverty, chastity, and obedience. Rather they were secular priests dedicated to service, whose vocation was to teach, administer the sacraments, and care for the sick and poor. They emphasized *good works,* the sacraments and acts of charity in combination with *faith* as the means to salvation, in direct opposition to the Protestants, who insisted that *faith* alone was sufficient. Among the Clerks Regular were the Theatines (founded 1524); the Barnabites (founded 1533); the Ursulines (an order of teaching nuns, founded 1535); and most famous, the Jesuits (founded 1540). Their role in bringing renewed life to the old Church during the Catholic Reformation was of immense importance, as we shall see in a later chapter.

Among the ignorant, this strong revivalist spirit often took distorted forms. Accepted doctrines and practices were twisted and larded with superstition and quasi-paganism. Veneration of the saints, for example, degenerated into worship of lesser deities, while the Virgin assumed most of the attributes of a goddess. Cults grew up around many of the most popular saints and their relics were in great demand. The pious Elector of Saxony, later Luther's protector, is said to have had over five thousand relics of various kinds in 1509, including a tooth of St. Jerome, a bit of cloth from Christ's swaddling clothes, a piece of bread from the Last Supper, and a twig from Moses' burning bush. Sales in relics were brisk and cynical, and unscrupulous churchmen made handsome profits.

Profits from indulgences were even better. Introduced first as a reward for Crusaders fighting in the Holy Land, the indulgence had become a recognized part of popular religion by the later Middle Ages. Its object was to remit temporal punishment (that is, punishment in Purgatory) for sins, properly confessed and forgiven through the sacrament of Penance. Theological justification derived from the idea that Christ, the Virgin Mary, and the saints because of their extraordinary goodness had stored up a *Thesaurus*

Hawking Indulgences. This was an issue that Luther made much of in the beginning, first because it troubled him and then because it was good anti-Roman propaganda. Once he had rejected papal authority and Penance as a Sacrament, indulgences as doctrine or as propaganda ceased to interest him.

Meritorum, a "treasury of merits," in heaven which could be drawn upon by the pope. No serious theologian taught that indulgences forgave sins outright or permitted additional sinning, but, as with most complex doctrines, the orthodox meaning was lost on the average man. An indulgence was a passport to paradise, either for the purchaser himself or for a loved one in Purgatory. Like relics, indulgences were not "sold" but were granted in return for contributions to worthy charities. They were great moneyraisers and an important source of papal revenue. But this fact, too, became confused in the public mind, and a favorite jingle ran:

As soon as a coin in the coffer rings
A soul from Purgatory springs.

LUTHER'S GERMANY

The Catholic Church's failure to minister adequately to the souls entrusted to it helps explain the immediate response to Luther's teachings. But the failures of the Church and the needs of its flock are not enough in themselves to account for the transformation of Luther's attack on the indulgence traffic into a religious revolution or to explain the revolution's character and course. Precursors of Luther, men like John Wyclif a hundred years before, had preached a substantially "protestant" doctrine that appealed to many, but the Christian Commonwealth remained intact. Therefore, to find the additional elements essential to revolution, we must examine briefly Luther's Germany.

Decline of Imperial Authority The elements for revolution were there. As we have already seen, Germany's distinguishing political feature was particularism. Imperial authority had broken down. Despite attempts by the Emperor Maximilian and the Imperial Diet to establish some sort of police system for maintaining law and order, many parts of the country were prey to banditry and to the petty aggression of political opportunists. Tensions ran high. At the same time, Germany was feeling the effects of economic and social change. Though agriculture was still the way of life for most Germans, trade was expanding and so too were banking and large-scale industries such as mining. The towns were active and growing and a capitalist class was taking its place beside the traditional peasants and nobles of medieval society.

The great secular princes made use of this situation to begin shaping their feudal domains into rudimentary states. The free cities basked in their independence; in the citizens' minds, prosperity and retention of their ancient rights and privileges went hand in hand. Lesser princes and nobles immediately below the princely rank had managed to hold their own. Their properties were extensive enough to provide a cushion against a relative decline in agricultural income and their overlords had not yet succeeded in usurping their aristocratic privileges.

Discontent and Rebellion The imperial knights, the peasants, and many artisans were less fortunate. A changing world had left them behind. The knights, of which there were about two thousand, were poor and land-hungry; some 250 square miles served them all. Schooled only in warfare, they lived by robbery, by selling their swords as mercenaries, and by whatever small secular and ecclesiastical benefices they could scrape up. The peasants and artisans were confused and left insecure by the transformation of the medieval agricultural and industrial order. The peasants in particular resented the efforts of profit-hungry lords to reimpose feudal dues and services long fallen into disuse. Their concern was less with their economic position than with their loss of status and pride. The knights, the peasants, and the artisans looked to an imagined past of high-minded emperors who upheld tradition and respected customary law, when every man, regardless of his station, had a function and enjoyed a certain dignity. Their discontent found expression in violent rejection of authority. The knights lived outside the law; the lower classes frequently took up arms in blind rebellion, overrunning the countryside, burning castles and monasteries, and demanding restoration of the old ways.

It was inevitable when religion was still at the center of men's lives that discontent often focused on the Church. There was little quarrel with doctrine, except perhaps among a few followers of Erasmus. All classes of German society, from the great secular prince to the lowest peasant, condemned the worldliness, the corruption, and the oppressive financial and judicial practices of the pope and the high clergy. Bishops and abbots, many of them secular rulers as well as churchmen, were envied their lands and their luxuries and resented for their disinterest in spiritual matters. The papacy, whose powers of taxation and justice were greater in Germany than anywhere else in western Europe, was denounced for stripping Germans of their wealth to glorify Rome and for subjecting them to judgment by Italians in cases of canon law. The indulgence traffic which netted the pope several hundred thousand good German crowns a year was cited as an example. Thus, religious grievances and a strong anti-papalism were linked to a kind of German nationalism. Patriotic humanists such as Ulrich von Hutten, imperial knight and author of *Letters of Obscure Men* (1515), combined patriotism with Christian humanism in a program to reform the Church and revive imperial power. His views were shared by most devotees to the "New Learning" in Germany. Humanism, as we have seen, had early made a strong impression on the intellectuals of Germany.

MARTIN LUTHER

Martin Luther, with his gift for sensing the shifting winds of public opinion, made brilliant use of this patriotic sentiment. In his *Address to the Christian Nobility of the German Nation* written in the summer of 1520, he seemed to articulate the German mind and heart. The *Address* is a direct appeal to the emperor and the princes to cleanse the Church and rescue Germany from the "distress and oppression" brought on by the "avarice," "wickedness," and "tyranny" of the "vermin" at Rome. The secular authorities, Luther asserts, have the right, indeed the duty, to force the Church to reform if it is unwilling to reform itself. "We are all one body, yet every member has its own work, whereby it serves every other. . . ."[1] The work of the secular authority is "to punish evil doers and protect them that do well . . . without respect of persons, whether it affect pope, bishops, priests, monks, nuns, or anybody else." All men are priests, and all have an equal right with the pope to interpret scripture and to convene a general council of the Church. The latter, he believes, is the best way to restore the health of Christendom and to free Germany from enslavement to Rome. In Luther's hands, priests would lose their miraculous powers, the Church would cease to be a special institution outside secular society, and the pope would have

[1]These quotations are taken from the translation of C. M. Jacobs in *Three Treatises by Martin Luther* (Muhlenburg Press: Philadelphia, 1943).

become, not the Vicar of Christ on earth, but a minor administrative functionary. It was a summons to revolution.

And it was heard. For by 1520, the development and spread of the printing art made possible mass distribution of tracts such as this. The first edition of the *Address,* four thousand copies in German, was sold out in three weeks and many other editions followed. Luther's other works, the *Ninety-Five Theses,* the *New Testament* in German, the theological tracts, did equally well. For the first time in European history the inflammatory ideas of a great revolutionary leader were made available quickly to everyone who could read or was willing to be read to. This was of decisive importance in making possible the rapid expansion of the German Reformation. Indeed, without printing, the German Reformation might never have occurred.

The revolutionary nature of Martin Luther's reform program contrasts with the very personal nature of his religious experience. The doctrines that distinguish his theology from Roman Catholicism were worked out by a lonely and sorely troubled man seeking his own salvation. Only after he was convinced of their validity and at peace with himself and his God, did he turn to the more general problem of the salvation of his fellow man. Even then, he remained essentially an individualist in religious matters, despite occasional outbursts of fiery intolerance. He did not intend to destroy the existing Church and found a new one; the suggestion would have horrified him. Nor did he consider himself a rebel or heretic. His sole aim

View of Wittenberg during Luther's Time. (Lutherhalle, Wittenberg.)

was to reform the religious practices, to deliver the Church from evil and set it once again on the path of righteousness and truth. But he was a stubborn man, uncompromising in his beliefs, and when the papacy took an equally stubborn and uncompromising stand against him, his instinct was to fight. He became a rebel and a heretic more by circumstance than desire.

Luther's Early Years Luther's quest for spiritual relief began in 1505 when he abandoned his legal studies to join the congregation of Augustinian Hermits at Erfurt in Saxony. He was twenty-two years old, a tormented young man whose strict upbringing had exaggerated his natural sensitivity. His father, a peasant turned businessman, had ambitions for the boy and was bitterly disappointed when he abandoned a professional career for religion. In 1507, Luther became a priest and moved from Erfurt to the Augustinian house at Wittenberg, there to study and teach at the little university founded a few years before by Elector Frederick the Wise of Saxony.

But monastic life did not appease Luther's troubled spirit. "I was a good monk," he recalled later, "and I kept the rule of my order so strictly that I may say that if ever a monk got to heaven by his monkery it was I." He fasted for days, mortified his flesh by suffering cold and forsaking sleep, spent hours examining his conscience and more hours confessing his sins. He prayed continually. But none of these "good works" satisfied him; he was a man, hence depraved and wholly unable to assuage God's wrath by his own feeble efforts. "Love god?" he asked, "I hated him!"

At the suggestion of his superior, Johann von Stauptiz, vicar-general of the Saxon Augustinians, he began to study and teach the Bible. After he received his doctorate in 1512, he gave a series of Biblical lectures which attracted wide attention and brought a certain fame to himself and the university. His scholarly technique was traditional, but like the Christian humanists he "glossed" the Bible itself, not its commentators. To the Bible he brought a sound knowledge of scholastic philosophy and of St. Augustine and the Fathers. In the next years, he searched continually for the answer to his problem: how can sinful man achieve the state of moral perfection demanded by God? He found it in a phrase in St. Paul's *Epistle to the Romans,* "the just shall live by faith." Much later he told of his discovery:

Night and day I pondered until I saw the connection between the justice of God and the statement [of Paul]. Then I grasped that the justice of God is that righteousness by which through Grace and sheer mercy God justifies us through faith. Thereupon I felt myself to be reborn and to have gone through the open doors into paradise. . . .

Luther no longer "hated" God, for God was not full of wrath but full of love and mercy. God, after all, had made grace available to man so he might have faith and through faith salvation. For Luther, faith was not merely belief in the doctrine of Christianity, but a wholehearted, childlike trust in Christ as Savior. Faith could not be gained without grace, which was a "free gift" of God, not a reward for "good works," and was not given to all men. This doctrine, based chiefly on St. Augustine, caused Luther to be accused of denying man free will by humanists like Erasmus who believed in the dignity of man and in man's ability to contribute to his own salvation. It also, naturally enough, aroused the ire of churchmen, for it made the Church, dispenser of good works, an unnecessary institution.

Albert of Brandenburg. The Hohenzollern prince's loan from the Fugger bank to buy the archbishopric of Mainz was partly repaid by the selling of indulgences. In this engraving by Albrecht Dürer, Albert seems worldly and well-fed, exactly the sort of churchman Luther despised. (Lutherhalle, Wittenberg.)

Luther's Theses Luther posted his *Ninety-Five Theses* on the door of the castle church in Wittenberg on the eve of All Saints' Day, October 31, 1517. Religious revolution was farthest from his mind; he was simply following accepted custom for one who wished debate with fellow theologians. Written in scholar's Latin, his *Theses* were an attack on the indulgence traffic, specifically the recent activities of Johann Tetzel, a Dominican preacher who was carrying on a thriving trade in the neighboring lands of Albert of Brandenburg. Pope Leo X had granted the rights of sale to Albert in return for half the profits which Leo planned to use to complete construction of the Basilica of St. Peter's in Rome. With his share, Albert planned to pay the heavy debt he had incurred to the Fugger bank in purchasing the Archbishopric of Mainz; indeed a Fugger representative accompanied Tetzel on his rounds. It was a thoroughly sordid business. Many thoughtful men of the time condemned it, as have both Catholic and Protestant historians.

The *Theses* were a direct outgrowth of Luther's doubts about the efficacy of "good works" as a means to salvation and the power of the pope to draw on a "treasury of merits." But they also reflect his anger that money was being "sucked" out of Germany "into this insatiable basilica." "We Germans," he complained, "cannot attend St. Peter's. . . . Why doesn't the pope build the basilica out of his own funds?" Since indulgence-selling was a well-established practice, clerical conservatives considered the attack unwarranted and close to heresy. But Germans, when they read the translation that was quickly published and circulated throughout Germany, were delighted. Luther voiced their deepest spiritual and patriotic feelings. They took him to their hearts and made him a revolutionary leader in spite of himself.

The Church's Response to Luther Luther's sudden notoriety surprised him but he took advantage of it to elaborate his ideas. He followed up the *Theses* with several tracts and sermons which also reached a wide audience. Each tended to take a more radical anti-papal position than the last, in part because of Luther's natural inclination, in part because the obstinate and hot-headed monk was replying in anger to attacks from the papalists themselves who had chosen to adhere uncompromisingly to the status quo. He refused Rome's demand that he retract his writings and submit to papal judgment in Rome for suspected heresy, and was supported by his prince, Elector Frederick the Wise who promised him a fair trial in Germany. In

July 1519, Luther engaged in a public debate at the University of Leipzig with the Dominican Johann Eck, a third-rate theologian but a man of formidable forensic skill. Eck badgered his less clever opponent into admitting theological doctrines very similar to those held by the heretics Wyclif and Hus. In June 1520, Pope Leo X issued the bull *Exsurge Domine,* condemning many of Luther's doctrines and ordering their author to recant within sixty days on pain of excommunication.

But Leo had waited too long. Tolerant, a lover of beauty and pleasure, this son of the great Lorenzo de' Medici was a victim, in a sense, of his own heritage. He had little respect for Germans and was bored by Luther's rantings. Failing at first to see the threat the reformer and his teachings posed, he delayed decisive action until all Germany was aflame. Moreover, he allowed direction of the battle, once it had been joined, to pass into the hands of men whose loyalty to the papal cause did not compensate for their stupidity and lack of imagination. Their heavy handedness did much to drive Luther further into heresy and alienate his sympathizers. Finally, political considerations, particularly a desire to placate Elector Frederick the Wise, caused Leo to vacillate indecisively between toughness and conciliation. Luther, meanwhile, gained adherents: humanists such as Philip Melanchthon, knights such as Ulrich von Hutten, princes such as Frederick and Ludwig of the Palatinate, and many common people. They responded both to his spiritual vigor and to his patriotism. Jerome Aleander and other papal agents sent from Rome to post the bull of excommunication were met by an aroused Germany. Aleander reported to Leo that "all Germany is in an upheaval. Nine out of every ten people shout 'Luther,' and the tenth . . . shouts 'Death to the Court of Rome!'"

Luther's most valuable allies were the princes. Orthodox in religion and conservative in politics, they may have been dubious of Luther's theology, though many later became Lutherans, and were certainly opposed to doctrines that might encourage social revolution. But they saw merit in his heartfelt cry for reform, and their conservatism and patriotism made them determined to guarantee Luther's "ancient rights" as a German. They would not permit him to be thrown to the Roman jackals; he would be given a fair hearing in Germany before an impartial German tribunal. These were the reasons why Frederick the Wise protected Luther, and why the papacy was powerless to do anything about it.

During the summer of 1520, while Luther waited in security for his hearing, he wrote and published his most important works. One of them, the *Address to the Christian Nobility of the German Nation,* we have already examined. Two others of great importance were the *Babylonian Captivity of the Church* and *The Liberty of the Christian Man.* In the *Babylonian Captivity,* Luther repudiated sacerdotalism and the sacramental system, the theological foundations on which Catholicism had been built. On Scriptural grounds, he cast doubt on all but two sacraments, Baptism and Holy Communion, and he changed the character of these. Neither sacrament operated by a power within itself (*ex opere operatio*) as Catholicism taught, but both were dependent for their efficacy on the faith of the receiver. Further, Holy Communion was not a miracle, and the bread and wine did not become in substance the body and blood of Christ (transubstantiation) during mass; rather Christ was present in an indirect, mystical way (consubstantiation). Finally, wine should be given to the laity. The Church became not a separate organization of hierarchy, priests, and lay members but merely the union of all men with faith. This argument was the theological parallel to the political argument contained in the *Address to the German Nobility.* The *Christian Man* was a more popular treatise explaining the doctrine of justification by faith alone. A Christian is free, Luther declared, because he has faith (only men with faith were "Christians" for Luther), and wants for nothing. At the same time he is bound to God and to other men; he is a responsible member of society who every day performs good works. "Good works do not make a good man, but a good man does good works." These good works serve society and glorify God: that is their purpose.

Luther Condemned at Worms Luther was finally called before the Imperial Diet assembled at Worms in the spring of 1521. Granted safe conduct by Emperor Charles V, Luther arrived at Worms in mid-April, his journey from Wittenberg having assumed the aspects of a triumphal tour. His first appearance left a bad impression. To the question of whether he had written the books shown him he answered, yes. But he mumbled and asked time to consider when commanded to retract the heresies they contained. On the following day he was better prepared. Straight and calm before young Charles V and the great men of Germany, he delivered his famous speech, concluding:

Since Your Majesty and your lordships desire a simple reply, I will answer without horns and without teeth. Unless I am convicted by Scripture and plain reason—I do not accept the authority of popes and councils for they have contradicted each other—my conscience is captive to the word of God. I cannot and I will not recant anything, for to go against conscience is neither right nor safe. God help me. Amen.[2]

The Emperor's blunt reply was equally sincere and unbending: Luther was a "notorious heretic" and it was the duty of every good Christian to hunt down and eradicate his ideas. How could "a single friar who goes against all Christianity" be right?

Luther was declared a rebel in May by the Edict of Worms, to which Frederick the Wise of Saxony and Ludwig of the Palatinate (two of the seven electors) did not subscribe since they had already gone home. The rebel himself was delivered safe at the secluded Wartburg Castle in Saxony by

[2] The earliest printed version added the words "Hie stehe ich; ich kan nicht anders. Got helffe mir" (Here I stand, I cannot do otherwise, God help me) but their authenticity has never been established.

Luther in the 1520's by Lucas Cranach (left). (Brown Brothers.)

Young Charles V (right). Charles must have looked like this when he faced Luther at Worms in 1521. (Borghese Gallery, Rome/Alinari-Scala.)

agents of Frederick. There he grew a beard and took the name of "Junker George." Between bouts of indigestion and deep melancholy, he completed his magnificent translation of the New Testament into German, setting a standard for the language much as Dante had done for Italian. The work was quickly printed and its impact was immense. Now, the Scriptures, with their revolutionary ideas of communal property, of social equality, of the dignity of the individual man, were made available to all who could read or were willing to listen.

THE ESTABLISHMENT OF LUTHERANISM

While Luther was at the Wartburg, the "reformation" began at Wittenberg. His followers, eager to translate the master's words into action, aroused the townspeople to an orgy of iconoclasm. Churches were attacked, images and ceremonial objects destroyed, and recalcitrant priests driven out. Carlstadt and Zwilling, the leaders, preached against clerical celibacy, Carlstadt himself setting the example of marrying. On Christmas Day, 1521, Carlstadt said Mass in black scholar's robes and administered both bread and wine to the laity. The Wittenberg town council approved, passing an ordinance in support of changes. Luther and the conservative Elector Frederick the Wise were troubled by the extremism. At the Elector's request and with his promise of protection, Luther returned to Wittenberg in March, 1522. Under his moderate guidance the people were calmed and the "enthusiasts," as the extremists were called, were curbed. Indeed, some of the old practices were restored. This satisfied Frederick the Wise, but it infuriated Carlstadt and the radicals. They had not realized how abhorrent to Luther was rapid, uncontrolled social change.

The Lutheran Church, as established by Luther in Saxony during the next few years and carried by his followers to other parts of Germany and Scandinavia, was a conservative Church. Its fundamental theology was

Protestant, justification by faith, establishment of the Bible as absolute authority in doctrinal matters, the priesthood of all believers. But in practice, and this was true of all Protestant sects, interpretation of the Bible was left to learned experts and diversity of opinion was discouraged, even forbidden. Outward ceremonies, about which Luther showed less concern, remained close to Catholicism. Ornaments and music, which Carlstadt had thought belonged only in theaters, were restored to the churches. Luther himself composed a number of hymns, including the popular "A Mighty Fortress Is Our God." The Mass, no longer a sacrifice, became "Sunday service" and was spoken in the vernacular with emphasis on reading and explaining passages from the Bible. Much of the medieval liturgy was retained. Baptism and the Lord's Supper, the latter taken in both kinds,[3] were the only official sacraments; but, in time, confirmation, marriage, and ordination took on a quasi-sacramental character. The clergy was freed from its vow of celibacy and encouraged to marry. Luther married a former nun in 1525. Finally, Church administration passed from the now-defunct Catholic hierarchy to the princes. The Lutheran Church became a state church both in Saxony under Elector John, who succeeded his father in 1525, and in every other state where it was established. Its administration was in the hands of state officials, its charitable function a state responsibility, and its buildings and clergy paid for out of state funds.

Luther concurred in this arrangement because he was by nature a conservative in his political and social views. Moreover, because of what he saw happening in Germany in the 1520's, he came to regard the princes as the only reliable guardians of peace and the traditional order he believed in. First was the Knights' War of 1522–1523. This abortive revolt of the imperial knights was led by the mercenary Franz von Sickengen and the erstwhile humanist Ulrich von Hutten. Their aim was to secularize the ecclesiastical lands of the archbishop of Trier, but a coalition of Catholic and Lutheran princes defeated them easily. Luther was horrified at this use of his teachings for materialistic ends and when he heard of Sickengen's death in battle he proclaimed, "God is a just and wonderful Judge!"

Sectarianism and the Peasants' Revolt The reformer was also surprised and frightened by the rapid multiplication of sects. He found it hard to understand why everyone did not interpret the Bible exactly as he did. While Luther was at the Wartberg, the so-called Prophets of Zwickau appeared at Wittenberg. These men, weavers by trade, were imbued with an emotional religiosity, complete with visions, that has come to be known as Spiritualism. Luther was horrified by them, including them in his tirade *Against the Heavenly Prophets* (1524). The greatest and most influential of the Spiritualists was Thomas Münzer (c. 1490–1525).

Münzer was a Saxon priest, heir of the German mystics and of the millenarian tradition of the late Middle Ages. He was not really a Protestant at all, for although he knew his Bible and his theology, he believed them unnecessary; he relied on direct contact with God through revelations and

[3] That is, in bread and in wine.

visions, and on a peculiar kind of natural religion in which the relationships of men and animals were compared to the relationship of man and God. He was also a social radical, who took up the cause of the oppressed, becoming a leader in the Peasants' Revolt of the mid-20's. He was captured, tortured, and put to death in 1525, a troubled victim of the forces of conservatism led by the princes and cheered on by Luther.

The Peasants' Revolt of 1524–1525 was an outburst of long pent-up dissatisfactions, a kind of mindless plea for social and economic justice. It was ascribed by contemporaries to the egalitarian doctrines contained in the Bible. At first Luther sympathized with the commoners' cause. But after he had tried to reason with some of them, only to be vilified and threatened with physical violence, his sympathy turned to fury. Damning the rebels as "mad dogs," he called on the princes "to smite, to stab, to choke," to suppress them mercilessly. The princes did so but at the cost of terrible bloodshed and devastation. Luther lost the support of most peasants and many artisans, and Lutheranism lost much of its popular appeal.

Peasants Attack a Knight in a Woodcut of the Peasants' Revolt.

The Spread of Lutheranism By the close of the 1520's Lutheranism had spread to other parts of Germany, to Prussia, Brandenburg, Brunswick-Lüneburg, Schleswig-Holstein, Mansfeld, Silesia, Hesse, and to a number of free cities, notably Augsburg, Nürnberg, and Hamburg. This was possible only because Germany lacked any central authority to stop it. Emperor Charles V, who stood firmly by the old Church and might have rallied the Catholic powers, left Germany for Spain and did not return until 1531. By that time, religion had become a political matter and Protestant and Catholic "leagues" for mutual protection had been formed.[4] Not until the mid-1540's did Charles take time out from his Spanish affairs and his wars with France and Turkey to seek to restore German religious unity. But he was too late; Lutheranism was too deeply entrenched. The Schmalkaldic War of 1546–1547, named for the Protestant Schmalkaldic League, was a standoff and Germany remained divided.

[4]The term "Protestant" was applied to the Lutheran princes who "protested" the majority ruling of the Diet of Speyer (1529) outlawing their creed.

The Peace of Augsburg of 1555 recognized the situation. The princes and free cities were permitted to choose between Catholicism and Lutheranism, according to the principle *cujus regio, ejus religio* (each prince may decide the religion of his realm), but no other Protestant sect was recognized. The princes could demand religious conformity but free cities could not persecute a Catholic minority. By the so-called "ecclesiastical reservation," any ecclesiastical prince becoming a Lutheran had to forfeit his office and his benefice. The Peace of Augsburg marked the high point of Lutheran strength in Germany. Thenceforth, Lutheranism began to give way before the forces of revived Catholicism and the new, more militant faith of John Calvin.

FURTHER READING

Accounts of the Protestant Reformation are legion and all must be read with a critical eye. For the origins, see the excellent J. R. Hale, * *Renaissance Europe, 1480–1520* (1971); and, more controversial, J. Lortz, * *How the Reformation Came* (1964). Two standard histories in English are P. Smith, * *The Age of the Reformation* (1920), and H. Grimm, *The Reformation Era* (1954). The latter contains an excellent bibliography. A good short introduction is E. H. Harbison, * *The Age of Reformation* (1955); another, even better, is G. Mosse, * *The Reformation* (3rd ed., 1963). A more detailed survey from the Catholic point of view is P. Hughes, * *A Popular History of the Reformation* (1957), and an interpretative account by a well-known Protestant scholar is R. Bainton, * *The Reformation of the Sixteenth Century* (1952). Best by far of recent works are A. G. Dickens, * *Reformation and Society* (1966), a fine synthesis emphasizing religious questions, but excluding the Catholic Reformation; and G. R. Elton, * *Reformation Europe, 1517–1559* (1963). More conventional is O. Chadwick, * *The Reformation* (1964). A fascinating narrative of the Reformation by contemporaries is H. Hillerbrand, ed., *The Reformation* (1964). *The New Cambridge Modern History*, II, is adequate for reference.

There are many biographies of Martin Luther. The most interesting are G. Ritter, *Luther* (1963); and L. Febvre, *Martin Luther: A Destiny* (1955). The most readable Protestant account is R. Bainton, * *Here I Stand: A Life of Martin Luther* (1950). E. G. Schweibert, *Luther and His Times* (1950), contains much valuable information on Luther's milieu, particularly the teachers and teaching at the University of Wittenberg. E. G. Rupp, * *Luther's Progress to the Diet of Worms* (1951) is good on the early years. The best Catholic biography is H. Grisar, *Martin Luther: His Life and Work* (1955). A fascinating attempt to psychoanalyze Luther is E. Erikson, * *Young Man Luther* (1962). The best, most solid summary is A. G. Dickens, * *Martin Luther and the Reformation* (1967). P. S. Watson, *Let God be God!* (1947) presents Luther's theology. An excellent and easily available selection of Luther's writings is J. Dillenberger, ed., * *Martin Luther, Selections from His Writings* (1961). Luther's principal assistant is the subject of C. L. Manschreck, **Melanchton the Quiet Reformer* (1958).

*Books available in paperback edition are marked with an asterisk.

2 The Revolution Spreads

Martin Luther died in 1546. His active reforming days had ended long before. Mellowed by success and a happy family life, grown heavy on the good German food served him by his beloved wife, Katherine, Luther was content to spend his last years at home in Wittenberg, preaching, writing, and reminiscing with his friends and disciples. His place on the Protestant battlefield was taken by others. Of these, the greatest was John Calvin, whose bleak, bearded figure dominated the Reformation after Luther. Calvin was a systematizer, an organizer, an administrator, a crusader of the Lord, and his church was incomparably the most influential of all Protestant churches. But two lesser-known reformers were influential, too, directly on Calvin and on the reform movement as a whole. They were Huldreich Zwingli and Martin Bucer. And all the reformers were confronted by and responded to the radical sectarians called Anabaptists.

NEW FORMS OF PROTESTANTISM: ZWINGLI, BUCER, AND ANABAPTISM

Huldreich, or Ulrich, Zwingli (1484–1531) was a Swiss priest and scholar who began preaching a moderate evangelical doctrine at Zürich in 1519. Son of respectable country folk who were prominent in Church and civic affairs in their small Alpine community, Zwingli received an excellent education in medieval philosophy and classics, both pagan and Christian. He also gained considerable practical knowledge of the world by studying contemporary politics and by visiting Italy twice as a chaplain with a body of Swiss mercenaries. His Italian experiences turned him into a vehement opponent of the Swiss practice of selling their young men into mercenary service. An ardent patriot, he was also a thorough Erasmian; hence his political ideas reflect a deep devotion to his native land and his religious ideas a powerful humanist bent. At first Catholic, he moved swiftly to the left. His compelling personality and his fiery sermons aroused the Zürichers, and by the mid-1520's, he had "reformed" the city, becoming its leading ecclesistical and political figure.

Zürich Zürich, located in north central Switzerland, was one of thirteen "cantons," or provinces, joined together in a loose political union called the Swiss Confederation. Against pope and emperor, their old religious and

Greek and Hebrew to go with his Latin, and reading widely in the pagan and Christian classics. He even wrote a humanist *Commentary* on Seneca, demonstrating great erudition and a fine Latin style but little originality. In 1532, he received his doctorate of laws. Up to this time, he had shown little evidence of what he would later become. Pious, but not troubled over his own salvation as Luther had been, studious, but not wholly dedicated to the law, he was little different from many young lawyer-scholars. If he stood out from his contemporaries, it was because he was a bit austere and withdrawn.

Calvin's Conversion Sometime in the early 1530's Calvin became interested in the youthful Reformation. France was alive with religious controversy in those years. Ideas drawn from Erasmus, from Luther and Zwingli, from the radical Protestants, and from other foreign sources were blended with native mysticism and the teachings of French Christian humanism into a potpourri of heresy and near-heresy. French "protestantism" was too ill-defined to be termed a movement, and since it did not threaten the established order was tolerated by a curious and broadminded King Francis I. Calvin was familiar with the new ideas and seems to have examined them carefully in his scholarly way, but his traditional faith remained unshaken—evidence of "obstinacy," he said later. In 1533 or 1534, however, he experienced a "conversion," the exact nature of which we do not know.

John Calvin in Early Middle Age. An aloof and austere man, Calvin in the few pictures he allowed to be made of himself, displays zeal and intelligence but little of the warmth and humanity of Luther.

It was Calvin's temperament that once convinced, he was without peer in strength or depth of faith. Immediately, he began preaching and writing, travelling about France and gaining a reputation for brilliance and zeal. In 1536, he published the first edition of his great *Institutes of the Christian Religion.* It would undergo many revisions before reaching its final form in the edition of 1559. Already Calvin had been cited for associating with heretics. The evangelicals had become too active, and Francis I could no longer maintain his air of amused detachment in the face of open insults to the old Church and to his own person. In 1534, placards inveighing against the Mass had been affixed to the king's bedroom door. Forced into hiding, Calvin fled France. In the summer of 1536, he reached Geneva.

Geneva was being "reformed" by William Farel, an energetic and dedicated French Protestant, when Calvin arrived. This lovely lakeside city resembled Zürich in its social and economic aspects. It too was ruled by an urbane patrician class devoted to liberty and Erasmian humanism. The Genevans had accepted a Zwinglian form of Protestantism, mostly for political reasons. Bern, Geneva's chief ally and protector, was Protestant, and the Genevans treated their new faith largely as a political matter. Farel was frustrated in his bid to introduce theological innovations along more evangelical lines and to remove the church from under the thumbs of the politicians. He appealed in desperation to Calvin for help. The two reformers gained many supporters, but they gained many enemies as well from among the conservatives, mostly the wealthy. In 1538, the conservatives won a majority in the city councils, and Calvin and Farel were asked to leave the city. Calvin went to Strasbourg where he became Bucer's chief assistant.

CALVIN'S RELIGIOUS AND POLITICAL DOCTRINES

Calvin was not so much an originator as a systematizer of theology. To him fell the task of taking ideas from the Bible, the Church Fathers, Erasmus and the Christian humanists, Luther and Bucer, and shaping them into a logical and coherent body of doctrine. In its logic and coherence lies the strength of Calvinism. Calvin's church was also patterned along lines suggested or put into practice by earlier reformers. This is not to say that Calvin's religious, ethical, and political system was merely a rehash; its very completeness made it different from anything that had gone before and at the same time more influential than any system except Catholicism.

The Doctrine of Predestination At the core of Calvin's theology was his belief in the omnipotent majesty of God and the weakness and utter degradation of man. God is sovereign and man is subject to him absolutely. From this foundation, Calvin's doctrine of predestination and his insistence that men devote their lives to rendering homage to God's glory follow logically. God created man out of his infinite goodness and love but man betrayed this trust. By Original Sin, Adam and all his heirs became corrupt, driven by their natures to sin and sin again. God, however, in His infinite mercy, offered man a chance to redeem himself through Jesus Christ, His Son. Absolute obediance to Christ's teachings as revealed in Scripture and unswerving faith in His saving powers are the necessary requisites to salvation.

But not all men are able to obey and believe, however hard they try, for they have not been granted God's great gift of grace. Predestination enters here. At the instant of creation, God set the course of the world and of mankind. On some men, he bestowed grace, by which they gained the power and the desire to obey and believe. These are the "elect," few in number,

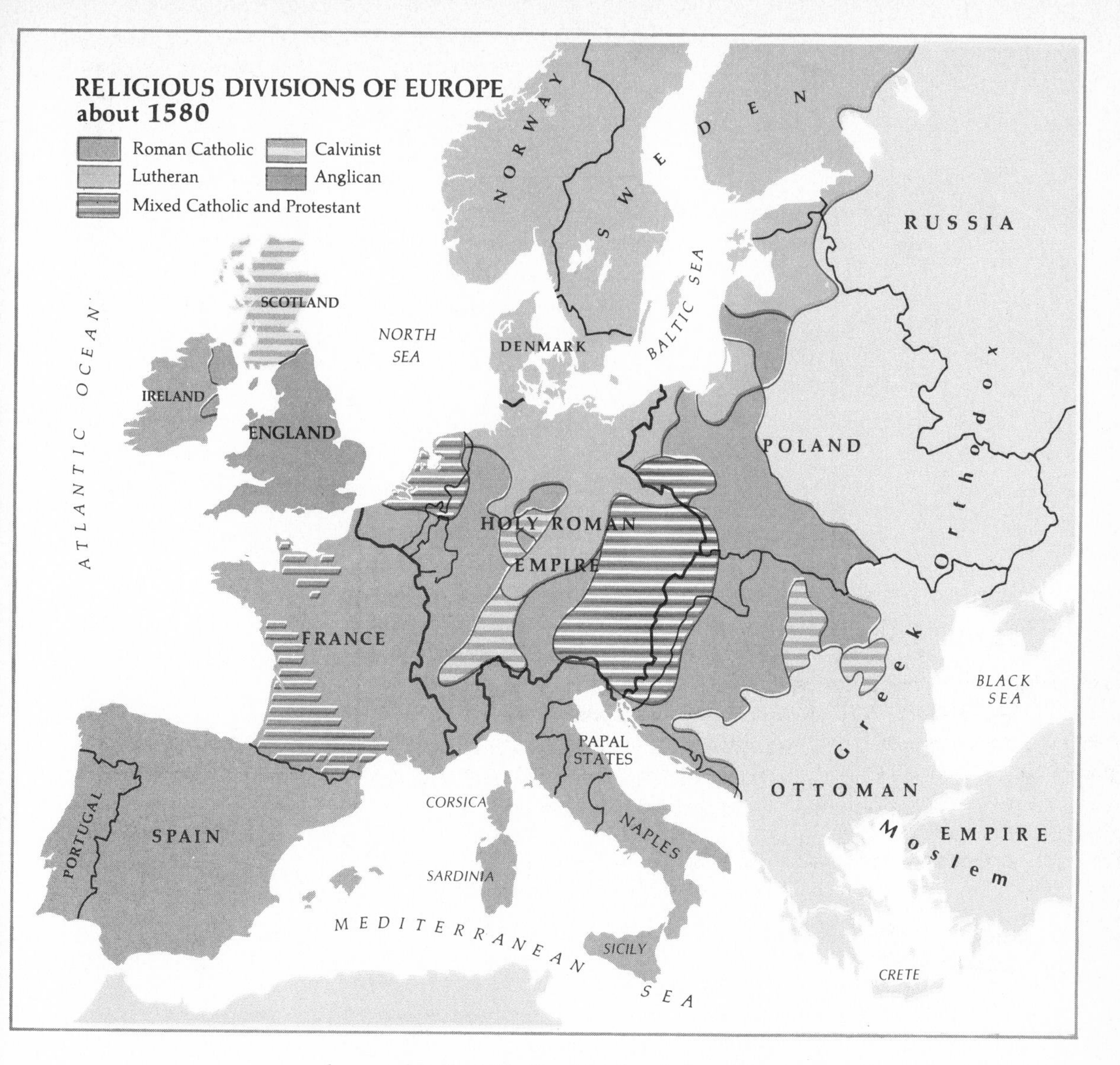

who would sit at God's right hand through eternity. From the rest of men he withheld grace and these are the "reprobates," helpless to act in their own behalf, destined inevitably for hell fire. Calvin emphasized that God's choice was entirely His own; man was helpless to influence it in any way. Calvin had gone as far as possible from the Catholic position, which holds that grace is attainable through man's "good works."

For Calvin, predestination as such was not the central issue. It was not evidence of God's wrath but simply of His nature: since God is all-knowing, He must know the ultimate fate of all men; since God does nothing indiscriminately or unreasonably, He must have made a choice. He must have determined for all time who would be saved and who damned. A dilemma that had confronted theologians from the earliest days of Christianity, squaring God's foreknowledge with man's free will, was settled by Calvin in God's favor.

"Good Works" One might think that the doctrine of predestination would have encouraged a spirit of fatalism and moral irresponsibility among the Calvinists as it did among adherents of some ancient predestinarian sects, but rather the reverse was true. Calvin taught that men must live their everyday lives in conformance with God's commands as set down in the Scriptures. Humility, austerity, subjugation of fleshly desire, regular attendance at church and participation in Holy Communion: this was the ideal mode of life as Calvin envisaged it. "Man," he wrote in the *Institutes,* "being taught that he has nothing good left in his possession, . . . should, nevertheless, be instructed to aspire to the good of which he is destitute, and to the liberty of which he is deprived. . . ." In this way man bears witness to God's glory, and, since God's goodness is manifested in the good works of His people, man gives evidence of membership in the elect. Positive identification of the elect is impossible, of course, for God's inscrutable will can never be fully comprehended. In later Calvinism, among the Dutch, and the English and American Puritans especially, evidence of salvation often came to consist of success in business and the amassing of wealth, though an austere mode of life was still emphasized. Calvin would have rejected this interpretation of his doctrine.

God, Calvin taught, helps men do good works by giving them the Bible and the church. The Bible is God's Word. It is divinely inspired and the sole authority in matters spiritual and temporal. All that man can ever know about God and his commandments is contained therein. Calvin never thought of *The Institutes of the Christian Religion* as any more than a manual, a key to understanding the Bible. The church is the divine institution through which God's word is interpreted and disseminated. It is the minister of souls, the receptacle of doctrine, and the judge of right and wrong actions on earth; it is the spiritual and moral arbiter of society. In its invisible form, it consists only of the elect, but through necessity caused by man's ignorance, its visible form must include reprobates as well. We must remember, however, that Calvin never considered the church indispensable for salvation: God's decree has already been made and man is powerless to alter it. In matters of ceremony, the Calvinists stressed simplicity and evangelism. Traditionally, services consisted of prayers, hymn singing, and a sermon on some appropriate passage from the Bible, conducted in austere surroundings. At regular intervals, Holy Communion was celebrated. This for Calvin was neither a sacrament nor a purely symbolic act, but a means to spiritual union of the faithful with Christ and with each other. The only other sacrament to be admitted was Baptism, which was necessary for salvation.

Calvin's Concept of Church and State Considering Calvin's conception of the church's role in men's lives, it is not surprising that he devoted much thought during his life, much more than had Luther, to ecclesiastical organization and discipline. Most important were the clerical functionaries: the "pastors," trained and licensed theologians who interpreted the Bible and administered the sacraments; the "doctors," also trained theologians, who taught; the "elders," who maintained discipline and oversaw public and private morality; and the "deacons," who managed church finances and supervised care of the sick and poor. The elders and deacons were laymen, testimony to Calvin's belief that the laity should take an important part in church affairs. The administrative structure of Calvinist churches varied slightly from place to place according to local needs, but in general it followed the pattern set down in Calvin's *Ecclesiastical Ordinances* (1541). Under the *congregational* system, which prevailed most notably in England, control was wholly decentralized, each congregation enjoying autonomy. Under the *presbyterian* system, for which Scotland is the best example, there was a kind of administrative hierarchy for supervision of the entire church. But under both systems, individual members of each congregation—including women—worked closely with their pastors and had much influence in the day-to-day conduct of church affairs. This "democratic" character of the Calvinist churches was one of its strongest appeals.

Calvin was also deeply concerned about the relationship between church and state. Man is subject to two authorities, Calvin said, ecclesiastical and civil, the latter embodied in the state. The state's chief end was "to cherish and support the external worship of God [and] to preserve the pure doctrine of religion." But it also served more mundane purposes: to dispense justice, to maintain property, and to establish peace and tranquillity within society. For Calvin, as for Bucer (but compare Luther and Zwingli), the church and state were separate and equal partners in the supervision of men's lives. Each played its role, ordained and defined by God, through its functionaries, pastors and magistrates, and neither should interfere with the other. Being of divine character, civil government once instituted could not be overthrown. However, a certain group of governors, whom he ambiguously called "magistrates," possessed the right to disobey a heretical and tyrannical king, and this single idea ("magistrates" were defined in several convenient ways) was picked up and used to justify revolution by all Calvinist churches of Europe. In practice at Geneva, as we shall see, Calvin tried to adhere scrupulously to his ideal of separation of church and state.

CALVIN'S GENEVA

Calvin was invited to return to Geneva in 1540, following the victory of his supporters at the polls. He was now able to win a constitution for his church, the *Ecclesiastical Ordinances,* which passed the councils in 1541. If the *Institutes of the Christian Religion* are the foundation of Calvinism, the *Ordinances* are the framework around which the structure was built. Like the *Institutes,* they are distinguished by clarity, completeness, and above all universality. They are adaptable to almost any political and social situation, hence could be made to serve aristocratic reaction in France or middle-class democracy in the New England colonies of America. This was their great strength.

The Consistory Ecclesiastical offices created by the *Ordinances* have already been described. The two chief organs of church government were the Venerable Company of Pastors and the Consistory. The former was an assembly of all the Genevan ministers, which gathered periodically to formulate doctrine, discipline offending brothers, and examine prospective recruits to its ranks. The Consistory also included the Genevan pastors, together with twelve elders. The elders were selected by the city councils, an arrangement calculated to bring the council's influence to bear on church affairs. The Consistory's function was disciplinary, enforcement of the beliefs and practices which Calvin considered requisite for sanctity and which the politicians thought necessary for good citizenship. Among the hundreds of sins a man could be cited for were dancing, cardplaying, drunkenness, adultery, and profanity. Punishment ranged from a dressing-down to excommunication. The latter was fear-inspiring, for it meant expulsion from the church, virtual proof of damnation, as well as exile from Geneva. It required concurrence of the civil authority and was rare. Discipline was universal and unsparing; even Calvin's brother-in-law was cited. The character of Genevan society was completely transformed. A gay city, full of frivolous people, indulgent of gambling, of roisterous parties, of the theater, became "puritanical" through vigorous application of Calvin's moral precepts by a dedicated Consistory.

Calvin's Opponents But the task was not an easy one. For fifteen years Calvin struggled against opponents on the left and right, against arguments theological and political, before he could rest secure in the knowledge that his reform had conquered Geneva. For part of that time his opponents held a majority of seats in the city councils. Conservative in their politics, but liberal in their attitude toward religious belief and moral conduct, a great many Genevans regarded Calvin as a tyrant and little better than the papist bishops they had rid themselves of with such difficulty. "Libertines," Calvin called them, and applied all his energy and fervent spirit to defeating them.

Opponents of his theology also plagued the reformer. In our eyes, most of them appear "modern" in their views, broad-minded, forgiving of differences of opinion. But to Calvin, righteous and convinced, they were heretics. One of them was Sebastian Castellio, an Erasmian humanist and early advocate of religious toleration, who shocked Calvin by reading the Song of Solomon literally, as a love poem rather than as an allegory of Christ and His Church. Another was Jerome Bolsec, a refugee from France, who quarreled with the doctrine of predestination—a Calvinist rock on which many liberals foundered. Both Castellio and Bolsec were sent into exile. But the opponent whose heterodoxy has gained the greatest fame was the Antitrinitarian Michael Servetus, who was the most notorious religious radical of his time, a bold controversialist who dared to question the divinity of Christ and thus the Trinity, to deny Original Sin, and to proclaim his belief in the intrinsic goodness of man. He was also arrogant and unstable, always spoiling for a fight. Apparently unmindful of the consequences, he travelled to Geneva in 1553 to face Calvin in person. With full agreement of the city councils, Calvin had him condemned and burned for heresy. Most Protestant leaders, including Melanchthon, Luther's moderate successor, applauded Servetus' death.

The Conversion of Geneva By 1555, Calvin was at peace with Geneva. A massive immigration of French Protestants fleeing King Henry II's persecution helped increase and solidify his support; but much of his success Calvin owed to his own efforts. He won the victory by persistence, hard work, and an unquenchable confidence in his cause. His spiritual domination of Geneva was so complete that historians have often described the city as a "theocracy." By the dictionary definition and by Calvin's own lights, it was not. The clergy did not govern; Calvin had no civil authority. Church and state were clearly separate; sometimes, during the Wars of Religion which began in France in 1561, for example, they pursued different foreign policies. But even with these reservations, no one can deny that Geneva in these years was largely oriented toward religion, that religion pervaded everyone's thoughts and actions, or that the religion was that of John Calvin. Moreover, the state, Calvin taught, was duty bound to preserve the church and to see that Genevans followed in the footsteps of Christ and the Apostles. And Calvin himself was duty bound to see that the state did so. Hence, while Calvin did not rule Geneva in a legal sense, his spiritual power was a sufficient substitute.

The Spread of Calvinism In the years after 1555 until his death in 1564, Calvin focused his energies on spreading his faith throughout Europe. The Venerable Company of Pastors, of which he was the head, became the central coordinating body, the headquarters of the missionary effort. It trained and dispatched many pastors to mission churches particularly in France but also in the Low Countries, Scotland, and parts of Germany. The Scot John Knox studied at Geneva as did Philip van Marnix de St. Aldegoude, chief propagandist for William of Orange in his fight for Dutch independence. Except in places where Lutheranism had caught firm hold as in Northern Germany and Scandinavia, Calvinism gathered together all the separate forces of ill-defined religious dissent, knitting them into a mighty army against Catholicism. Political, social, and economic dissent proved powerful allies, and Calvinism became a true revolutionary movement. Almost always the movement drew on the traditions of feudal "liberty" and privilege in opposing the forces of strong monarchy. Clashes and ultimately civil wars were the inevitable result. We shall examine some of these in Chapter 4.

THE REFORMATION IN ENGLAND

The English Reformation in its beginnings was not a "religious" reformation as were the Lutheran and Calvinist reformations; rather it was an affair of state. King Henry VIII (1509–1547), with the sanction of Parliament and the acquiescence of the English people, simply cut the tie of allegiance that bound the Church of England to Rome and declared himself "Supreme Head" in place of the pope. Henry made no doctrinal changes. The theology, the ceremony, the customary practices remained as they had been. Indeed, the old doctrines were restated in explicit terms. Henry, to the end of his life, thought of himself as a pious and orthodox Catholic who had restored the independent authority of the Church of England usurped centuries before by the bishop of Rome. The fact remained, however, that Henry had joined the Protestant rebels on the continent in their destruction of Christian unity, and hence his action, like theirs, was revolutionary.

The first Tudors, though more autocratic than most English monarchs, were not wholly unrestricted in the exercise of their power. Henry had to reckon with Parliament and with a politically conscious public opinion. Both Parliament and most of the public, however, were as eager as he to break with Rome. The spiritual and moral condition of the English hierarchy and priests was no better than that of their continental counterparts; indeed, it may have been worse, particularly among the regular clergy. Many Englishmen looked with envy on the vast lands being wasted by the monasteries and nunneries. Like the Germans, the English were strongly anti-papal and anti-clerical and for many of the same reasons. They resented any attempt by the pope to interfere in English affairs. For centuries they had resented papal taxation and resisted ecclesiastical justice, which compared unfavorably with their notions of justice by common law. Efforts by the crown to limit papal influence had achieved only partial success. Hence, there was a strong strain of patriotism which found an outlet in opposition to Rome. It was reinforced in the 1520's by hatred of Cardinal Wolsey, Henry's chancellor and the papal legate who seemed to personify all that was secular and grasping in the clergy.

Further, Christian humanism, under the aegis of John Colet, Sir Thomas More, and others, had had considerable influence on both laymen and the clergy. After 1517 or 1518, the writings of Luther and then Zwingli found their way across the channel. Christian humanism and the new heresies reinforced Lollardy, a native heresy that had maintained a clandestine existence since the days of John Wyclif a hundred years before. This is not to say that England was seething with heresy in the 1520's, but heresy was widespread enough to cause the authorities concern. King Henry himself had taken special cognizance of it, composing a small treatise against Luther for which the pope awarded him the title "Defender of the Faith." Still, in spite of these things, England might have remained faithful to Rome had not King Henry wanted a divorce.[1]

The King's Divorce Henry VIII was the kind of self-indulgent, egotistical man who could make himself believe whatever pleased him. By 1527, he

[1]Divorce in that day meant annulment. Marriage, of course, was a sacrament, sacred and inviolable. However, if it could be shown that a sacrament had not taken place, then the marriage was not a true one and could be invalidated by the pope.

was convinced that for eighteen years he and his wife, Catherine of Aragon, the daughter of Ferdinand and Isabella of Spain, had been living in sin. Catherine had been married first to Henry's brother, Arthur, a sickly boy who had survived the wedding only a few weeks. Both Catherine and contemporary witnesses had sworn the marriage had never been consummated and a papal dispensation to that effect had been easily obtained. But Henry, who fancied himself a theologian, had suddenly taken seriously the Biblical injunction against a man's marrying his brother's wife. Specifically, he pointed to Leviticus XX, 21: ". . . if a man shall take his brother's wife it is an unclean thing. . . . They shall remain childless." This was doubtless the reason, he declared, that of all Catherine's children only little Mary had survived. The marriage was displeasing to God.

Henry seems to have been sincerely troubled in his conscience. But there were more mundane considerations. He had become infatuated with

Young Henry VIII, Beginning to Run to Fat, by Joos van Cleve. Henry was a pious man and an intelligent one, and had the reputation of a good amateur theologian, as the scroll he is holding suggests. (Her Majesty the Queen. Copyright Reserved.)

Anne Boleyn, the daughter of an ambitious man who had risen high in court circles and who wished Anne to become queen. The girl tantalized Henry by refusing to play the common role of mistress. Moreover, Henry was determined to have a son to inherit his throne. The memory of his father's long struggle to secure the new Tudor dynasty was fresh and he feared for its future in the hands of a woman. Thus, the scruples of Henry's conscience coincided neatly with the desires of his heart and the realities of politics. He decided in 1527 to divorce Catherine and marry Anne.

European kings had got divorces before, most recently Louis XII of France, who had shed his first wife of three decades earlier to marry Anne of Brittany, widow of his predecessor. All that was necessary was a papal pronouncement that the marriage was invalid, based of course on satisfactory evidence. Everything might have gone smoothly for Henry VIII had he chosen another time and another man to do the job for him. Cardinal Wolsey was too sure of his skill, too arrogant and high-handed. Hoping to gain a decision quickly, Wolsey took it upon himself, as papal legate in England, to act in the pope's name, angering Pope Clement VII. Moreover, Clement himself was hardly free to find in Henry's favor even if he had wished. Since the sack of Rome in 1527, imperial troops had occupied the Holy City and the pope had been a virtual prisoner of the emperor. Charles V was a nephew of Catherine of Aragon, and a man sensitive to his relatives' predicaments. Clement, weak and devious by nature and trapped by forces beyond his control, chose delay as his tactic. The affair dragged on for two more years until Henry, frustrated and furious, discharged Wolsey and took matters into his own hands.

Henry VIII does not seem to have planned at first to break completely with Rome, but rather simply to fortify his authority over the Church in England while leaving the pope as nominal head. He soon found this impossible, however, because the pope's headship was inextricably bound up with the financial and judicial prerogatives that Henry wanted for himself. Hence, the series of acts that Henry and his new chief minister, Thomas Cromwell, proposed to the Parliament beginning in 1531 had the practical effect of establishing an independent English Church, free entirely of papal control or influence. In 1534, the English clergy, cowed by Henry and Cromwell, accepted the inevitable conclusion that "the Bishop of Rome . . . has no greater jurisdiction in the realm of England than has any other foreign bishop." Two years later, Parliament declared it treason to hold the contrary opinion. Meanwhile, in 1533, the Archbishop of Canterbury, Thomas Cranmer, had pronounced the marriage of Henry and Catherine invalid; Henry had quietly wed Anne Boleyn and Anne had become Queen of England. In the same year, Anne bore an heir to the throne, not a boy, for which Henry yearned, but the future Queen Elizabeth.

ESTABLISHMENT OF THE ANGLICAN CHURCH

The substitution of king for pope as "Supreme Head" of the Church of England, set parliamentary precedents that would eventually redound to that body's advantage; not an action had been taken by the king without Parliament's assent. But it brought an immediate increase in royal power. It gave Henry the legal right to manage ecclesiastical business much as he saw fit. With support of Parliament, he filled high church posts with his supporters and favorites, reorganized finances to the crown's advantage, and began a systematic dissolution of monasteries and convents. This last was accomplished under the shrewd guidance of Thomas Cromwell who made the most of monastic waste and corruption to win over public opinion. Lands, plate, jewels, even lead from the roofs and windows of the houses were confiscated and sold. Most of the land found its way into the hands of the gentry,

Archbishop Thomas Cranmer of Canterbury, before he was burned at the stake in the reign of Queen Mary, did more than any man to set down the doctrine and establish the practice of the Anglican Church. Cranmer's was the middle way, much influenced by the moderate good sense of Ulrich Zwingli. (National Portrait Gallery, London.)

strengthening that class and giving it a material stake in Henry's Reformation. The total profit to the crown was not nearly so much as it would have been if the land had been worked or rented and not sold.

But the English Reformation during King Henry's lifetime was wholly of this administrative kind. Dogma and practice remained unchanged despite efforts by Cromwell, who wanted to curry favor among the Lutheran princes, and by Archbishop Cranmer, who admired Zwingli's ideas, to introduce a few changes. Henry's views were written into law in 1539 by the "Act Abolishing Diversity of Opinions," which reaffirmed under pain of heresy the Catholic doctrines of transubstantiation, confession and penance, and clerical celibacy. But administrative separation was bound to be followed by doctrinal separation as well. People were intensely interested in religious matters and despite legal prohibitions read the new English Bible of Tyndale and Cloverdale and the works of the European reformers. Calvinism began to gain many adherents by the late 1540's. Protestants were a large minority by the time the boy Edward VI ascended the throne in 1547.

English Protestantism after Henry During Edward's reign (1547–1553), Archbishop Cranmer was the most influential religious figure in England. This contradictory man had held his tongue while Henry VIII lived; but now his Protestant tendencies found full expression. He prepared two prayer books, the first in 1549 quite conservative in tone, the second in 1552 definitely Protestant with a strong flavor of Zwingli. Both were made official by act of Parliament and the second with only minor changes is the Book of Common Prayer still in use by the Church of England. Its wording was vague enough to permit a broad range of interpretation, thus giving rise to the "latitudinarianism" so characteristic of Anglicanism.

But Protestantism had not triumphed in England; Mary Tudor, Edward's successor, was the daughter of Catherine of Aragon and was loyal to her mother's faith and her mother's native Spain. Pious, sincere, not very clever, Mary spent her short reign (1553–1558) futilely trying to redress her mother's grievances. She married Philip of Spain to assure an alliance with the great Catholic power, and directed her energies at home to bringing the English Church once more into the Roman fold. In both actions she was blind to the temper of Parliament and the English people, who wanted no part of Spain and were satisfied with their moderate Protestantism. To overcome her people's obstinacy, she instituted a policy of harsh persecution which remains her best-known legacy and which earned her the soubriquet "Bloody Mary." Although England was nominally Catholic for a few years, the ultimate result was to strengthen rather than weaken the Protestant cause. Elizabeth, who became queen in 1558, was able to reestablish Henry VIII's independent Church of England with the monarch at its head, but now with a latitudinarian attitude toward theology which left a place for everyone but the most violent extremists.

FURTHER READING

Little enough has been written on Zwingli and Bucer in English, but there are two good biographies: J. Courvoisier, * *Zwingli: A Reformed Theologian* (1964); and H. Eels, *Martin Bucer* (1931). The radical Protestant sects have been studied more thoroughly in recent years. Basic is the encyclopedic G. H. Williams, *The Radical Reformation* (1962), which treats both Anabaptists and Spirituals. See also F. H. Littell, *The Anabaptist View of the Church* (1958); and, for those with German, O. H. Brandt, *Thomas Müntzer: Sein Leben und seine Schriften* (1932). S. Kot, *Socinianism in Poland* (1957), is concerned with antitrinitarianism. A standard work on Calvinism in Europe is J. T. McNeill, * *The History and Character of Calvinism* (1954). On Calvin, the man and his thought, see W. Walker, *John Calvin* (1906); J. McKinnon, *Calvin and the Reformation* (1936); Q. Breen, *John Calvin: A Study in French Humanism* (1931); and above all, F. Wendel, *Calvin* (Eng. trans., 1963). An excellent study of Geneva and Calvin's impact on it is E. W. Monter, * *Calvin's Geneva* (1967).

The question of the relationship between Calvinist social doctrine and the evolution of the capitalistic spirit has stimulated much writing, the most important being M. Weber, * *The Protestant Ethic and the Spirit of Capitalism* (1930); and R. H. Tawney, * *Religion and the Rise of Capitalism* (1926). Samples of the literature may be found in R. W. Green, ed., * *Protestantism and Capitalism: The Weber Thesis and Its Critics* (1959).

A good introduction to the political side of the English Reformation, though somewhat interpretive, is F. M. Powicke, * *The Reformation in England* (1941). Another more general introduction, of greater length and of high scholarly merit, is T. M. Parker, *The English Reformation to 1558* (1950). A more recent Protestant account is A. G. Dickens, *The English Reformation* (1964). The Catholic view is provided by P. Hughes, *The Reformation in England,* 3 vols. (1950–1954). Henry VIII has been the subject of two excellent recent biographies: J. J. Scarisbrick, *Henry VIII* (1968); and L. B. Smith, *Henry VIII* (1971). Good is J. Ridley, *Thomas Cranmer* (1962).

G. Mattingly, * *Catherine of Aragon* (1941), is a beautifully written and scholarly life of the tragic queen.

*Books available in paperback edition are marked with an asterisk.

3 Catholicism Revived

The Catholic Church responded slowly and hesitantly to the problems of Protestantism and self-rehabilitation. More than two decades elapsed between the day Martin Luther posted his *Ninety-Five Theses* and the opening session of the reform Council of Trent, and it was another two decades before the Council's work was done. The first period was spent in determining what form the Catholic Reformation should take and who should direct it, the second in reformulating doctrine and setting up machinery of discipline and propagation. Even at the end, the old Church had not become a wholly new one. Only a part of the abuses had been eliminated and not all the clergy had been restored to sanctity. France refused to accept the decrees of the council; Spain accepted them only with reservations. Other states honored them more in the breach than the observance. In spite of these qualifications, however, the Catholic Church emerged from its reformation immeasurably stronger than before.

THE PAPACY AND REFORM

As we have noted in an earlier chapter, a general Catholic Reformation was impossible without papal leadership and no pope was willing to lead until the mid-1530's. Neither Leo X, who died in 1521, nor Clement VII, who reigned from 1523 to 1534, had the character or the inclination to do so. They were men trapped by their heritage, with minds rooted in the Renaissance past, essentially secular in their view of the papacy and the Church, insensible if not indifferent to the burning spiritual issues Luther raised, naively trusting in political cleverness to solve everything. It is doubtful whether they appreciated the religious ferment in the north for what it truly was, a spiritual revolution and a mortal danger to their Church. They were ill served by a College of Cardinals and a Curia filled with worldly and self-seeking professionals, whose interest was to preserve the status quo and who fought every effort to reform.

Leo did almost nothing to combat the northern heresies. Clement was well meaning, but weak and equally ineffective. He appointed a few good bishops, listened sympathetically to the pleas of the Christian humanists, and spent most of his time playing at the intricate game of international diplomacy for which as a Medici he considered himself especially qualified. He resisted pressure to call a great reform council of the Church with all his strength. Still fresh in his memory was the Conciliarist challenge, which he was fearful of reviving. His fear was compounded, and with good reason, by his conviction that a council would serve merely as a political tool in the hands of King Francis I or Emperor Charles V. For both monarchs, the religious issue was an element in their political rivalry and neither was willing to give his wholehearted and disinterested support to a bold and far-reaching reform program under papal direction. The idealistic and ineffectual Adrian VI, a Fleming and former tutor of Charles V who was pope for twenty months between Leo and Clement, was proof that personal sanctity and good intentions were not enough. Not only the popes, but the entire papal bureaucracy would have to change before a general reform could begin.

CONCILIATION OR COUNTER-REFORMATION

But the Church was not without reformers in the years before 1517, and there were more of them in the 1520's and 1530's. We have looked at the work of the Spanish Cardinal Francisco Ximenes de Cisneros. There were other churchmen with similar zeal and devotion, although their efforts, unsupported by the likes of Queen Isabella, were necessarily on a smaller

The Visit of Pope Leo X to Florence in 1514, Depicted on a Majolica Plate. In the foreground are troops of the Swiss guard, on the left flies the banner of the Medici. (Victoria and Albert Museum.)

scale—a single diocese instead of a nation. These pioneers who ventured into the wilderness of ecclesiastical corruption and papal inertia were Erasmians almost to a man: Reginald Pole, an English nobleman; Giacopo Sadoleto, a famed humanist, and Gasparo Contarini, a learned Venetian layman, each of whom received cardinal's hats in the mid-1530's. They were idealists who believed that individual bishops would in time regenerate the entire Church and the papacy. They were also deeply pious but liberal in their doctrinal views, being uninterested in fine theological distinctions. Some critics accused them of "Lutheranism." Hence, they were willing to compromise somewhat with the tenets of Protestantism in the interests of religious harmony and, above all, to restore the unity of Christendom.

Charles V and Pope Clement VII by Titian. An emperor and pope of the old school, the Protestant Reformation was for them an essentially political problem, to be solved by diplomacy and war. (Palazzo Vecchio, Florence/Alinari-Scala.)

Conciliation Under the influence of these "conciliationists," reform began when Paul III (1534–1549) ascended the papal throne. Paul's reign was a period of transition for the papacy and for the pope himself. In the beginning, he seemed little different from his predecessors, a lover of beauty and comfort, a patron of Michelangelo, a man of the Renaissance. Among his first acts was one aimed at securing favors for his shiftless nephew. But Paul also exhibited intelligence and character in comprehending the problems that faced him and courage in trying to solve them. For the first half of his reign he favored the conciliationist approach. He nominated an outstanding group of cardinals including, besides those mentioned, Giovanni Morone who would lead the papal forces at the Council of Trent, and Gian Pietro Caraffa, later Pope Paul IV. Curial opposition to reform, which had frustrated Adrian VI, was largely removed. Paul also appointed reforming bishops and he himself began to put his own diocese of Rome in order.

In 1536, he directed a commission of prelates, headed by Contarini, to assess the condition of the Church and recommend correctives. Its report was brutally frank, citing terrible abuses and laying most of them at the door of an indifferent papacy and hierarchy. The recommendations were equally blunt, nothing less than renovation of the Church from top to bottom. Paul was admonished to imitate the charity of the Apostle whose name he had taken ". . . to heal our ailments, to bring back the flock of Christ into one fold, to remove from us the wrath of God. . . ."

Paul was attracted at first by the idea of reconciliation with the Protestants. In this he was joined, not only by the liberal Catholics like Contarini, but by a number of liberal Protestants like Melanchthon and Bucer and by the Emperor Charles V. Indeed, Charles was willing to go far toward theological compromise to return Germany to one religion. Unlike Charles, however, the pope was as reluctant to convene a general council as earlier popes had been. For Charles the best way to reunite the Church was to let German Catholics and Protestants get together and thrash their differences out. However, for Paul this remained a danger to the papacy unless the council could meet in Italy under papal control. Further, for Protestants to attend a council required at least *de facto* recognition of the northern heresies, hardly something the papacy in good conscience could grant. Paul's tactic, therefore, was delay. Without much enthusiasm he summoned a council at Mantua in 1537 from which Protestants would be excluded, but an unfavorable political situation and meager attendance caused its early dissolution. Meanwhile, he supported a series of less formal discussions with the Protestants; these culminated in a conference of leaders of the two faiths at Regensburg in 1541.

Cardinal Gasparo Contarini. Scholar and diplomat, this Venetian aristocrat was a leader of the liberal Catholics who sought reform of the Church and reconciliation with the Protestants in the 1530's. (Courtesy of the Trustees of the British Museum.)

The conference came to nothing although it began hopefully enough with tentative agreements on the questions of original sin, free will, and justification. Cardinal Contarini, the papal legate, did everything in his power to effect a compromise. But Melanchthon, then Luther's chief assistant, refused to accept the authority of general councils in matters of faith and both he and Bucer rejected Contarini's Catholic interpretation of transubstantiation. This last was the rock on which the conference foundered.

Counter-Reformation The failure of the conference of Regensburg discredited the idea of reunion and the men who advocated it. Paul III turned to men of less conciliatory temper, men who would fight Protestantism rather than compromise with it, and the Catholic Reformation went forward thereafter under their direction. It became in effect a *Counter*-Reformation. Significantly, the leadership of Protestantism fell almost simultaneously to John Calvin, a man whose temper was much like his opponents'. The days of peacemaking were over.

First among the rigorists was Cardinal Gian Pietro Caraffa, an early member of the Oratory of Divine Love and one of the founders of the Theatine order of "clerks regular." Caraffa had begun his clerical career as a moderate, but by 1541 he had become a theological conservative and a rigid moralist whose driving ambition was to purge the Church of heresy and corruption. His nature and his Dominican training caused him to distrust the easygoing tolerance of such liberals as Contarini. He believed reform must be imposed from the top, by force if need be. The Protestants he regarded not as lambs strayed from the fold, but as irredeemable heretics to be fought with the weapons of persecution, censorship, and propaganda. His inspiration was the Church of Spain, upright, austere, disciplined, resembling as much a military as a religious organization.

The Roman Inquisition and the Index In 1542, at the urging of Caraffa and others of Caraffa's persuasion, Paul III established the Roman Inquisition (officially the Congregation of the Holy Office). This differed from the medieval inquisition, still in existence after two centuries though rusty with age and disuse, in that its administration was in the hands of the pope and his agents. The idea of centralization was borrowed from the Inquisition of Spain with the papacy replacing the crown. Also borrowed from the Spanish model were all the severe, to modern eyes unjust, methods of search, arrest, interrogation, and trial. Secret prosecution witnesses, admission of rumor and hearsay as evidence, and torture were regularly used to secure conviction. On the other hand, our judgment must be tempered by the realization that the inquisitors were honestly seeking to recover lost souls, that in their view heretics were traitors against God and the foulest of criminals. Censorship and close control of the printed book were also imposed by the new Inquisition. Since books and pamphlets were the chief instruments for spreading heretical doctrines, the inquisitors kept careful watch over suspect presses, burned questionable books, and brought persons possessing such books to trial for heresy. In 1559, the censorship procedures were regularized with the appointment of a permanent commission of cardinals, the Congregation of the Index, to pass on all books and keep lists of those condemned up to date.

In theory, the Roman Inquisition applied to all of Christendom. But in practice, no Catholic ruler outside Italy, not even the king of Spain, accepted it in undiluted form, for none was willing to permit such direct papal intervention in the internal affairs of his realm. Spain preserved its native Inquisition. Suppression of heresy elsewhere, in France, the Low Countries, the Austrian lands of the Habsburgs, remained a responsibility of the crown. In most of the Italian states, Venice being a partial exception, the new institution was formally accepted. But opposition of governments made it largely ineffective outside the Papal States and the few other Italian states that cooperated. In fact, there was little for it to do. There were very few Protestants in Italy and, except for a time at Lucca, no organized Protestant movement. The Congregation of the Index was more successful in applying the *coup de grace* to an already dying Renaissance. Henceforth, Italy's creativity was largely Catholic in inspiration.

SOLDIERS OF THE CHURCH

Ironically, it was not the rigorist Caraffa but the liberal Contarini who was chiefly responsible for bringing into existence Rome's most potent instrument of Counter-Reformation. The Society of Jesus was founded in 1540 by a reluctant Paul III. Religious orders had acquired a bad reputation in the recent past, and many Church leaders, among them Paul and most of the rigorist party, were dubious of a new one. The obstinate Caraffa, even as Pope Pius IV, refused to admit the Society's value. Contarini, however, was attracted to the idea of a missionary order, the aim of whose members was to propagate and defend the faith among all peoples anywhere in the world. This the Society proved to be; in places as widely separated as Germany and Goa, Jesuits carried on their missionary labors, converting the heathen and the infidel and stemming the rising tide of Protestantism. Indeed, they began to roll the tide back in many places, retrieving lost ground even from the Calvinists.

Ignatius of Loyola.

Ignatius of Loyola The Society of Jesus was the inspiration of Ignatius of Loyola. Born in 1491 in the Basque country of Spain, Don Iñigo Lopez de Loyola was an *hidalgo,* a member of the lower nobility. Like most Europeans of his class, he was a soldier, and like many soldiers he was crude, badly educated, a swashbuckler, and something of a dandy. But Ignatius was also a Spanish soldier, heir of the *Reconquista.* For all his rough ways, he was imbued with the ancient crusading tradition, that compound of the warlike spirit with the instinct to serve God and the Church. This heritage shaped his life and gave the Jesuits their unique character.

His military career ended when he received a serious leg wound in 1521. During long months of recuperation, he read popular religious books and contemplated his future. On recovering, he went into seclusion to work out his personal religious problems (he had discovered his conscience while convalescing) in preparation for the life of a monk. Beset with many of the same doubts and fears as Luther, he met and mastered them in quite a different way. Where the German scholar, trained in theology and exigesis, looked to the Scriptures, reinterpreting them in the light of his own needs, the Spanish knight, possessed of a simple faith, accepted orthodox Catholicism and the whole vast structure of popular piety without question. He relied instead on mystical illumination, self-induced and carefully controlled by sheer force of will. Ignatius' ability to discipline his mind was remarkable. In spirit, he relived Christ's Passion and experienced the joys of heaven and the pangs of hell. To guide himself, he developed his famous system of disciplined asceticism and methodical prayer which he later set down in the *Spiritual Exercises,* the manual of the Jesuit order.

Ignatius very soon abandoned his plan to enter a monastery, convinced he could serve God best in the world by preaching, teaching, and caring for souls. To qualify himself, he began an arduous course of study in the fundamentals of Latin (he attended classes with children) and theology that took him to several Spanish universities and finally to the University of Paris in 1528. Very soon he gathered around him a group of like-minded younger men, most of them Spanish or Portuguese, among them the Spanish knight Francis Xavier (the "Saint of the Indies"), and Diego Laynez and Alfonso Salmerón, first in a long line of great Jesuit theologians. In August 1534, these men took informal vows of poverty and chastity, since not all were priests, and pledged their lives to converting the Muslims. They would go to the Holy Land; failing this, they would offer their services to the pope.

The Jesuits War between Venice and the Turks forced them to take the second course. In 1537, they went to Rome, where they gained the favor of Paul III who set them to teaching and preaching in Rome and other parts of Italy. Their experiences showed them the condition into which the Church had fallen and alerted them to the dangers of Protestantism. Reluctantly, they abandoned hopes of reaching the Holy Land though not their resolve to Christianize Muslims; instead they formed themselves into a brotherhood to which they gave the military appellation "Company of Jesus" (the Latin is *Societas,* usually translated more loosely as "Society"). They asked Paul to regularize it in 1539.

Paul was sympathetic but not wholly convinced that establishment of a new religious order was justified. Furthermore, the charter Ignatius submitted contained provisions that clerical conservatives viewed as dangerous novelty: excluded were daily singing of the Office in choir, strict rules about fasts and other penitential acts, and a requirement to wear distinctive dress—traditions of a thousand years. To add to the conservatives' distress, a special vow to the pope was introduced "by which the companions are to be so bound that they must immediately, without any shuffling or excuse, undertake whatsoever His Holiness commands appertaining to the progress of souls and the propagation of the faith, whether he sends us to the Turks, or the New World, or to the Lutherans or to others whomsoever, infidels or Catholics. . . ." Paul took two years to decide whether to authorize the new order, pressed on the one side by the conservatives and on the other by Cardinal Contarini, who envisioned great things for the Society. Contarini won out and, by the bull *Regimini militantes Ecclesiae,* published September 27, 1540, the charter was accepted with the condition that membership would be held to sixty. In 1544, Paul III removed the restriction on membership and in the next years he and his successors approved the Society's constitutions.

Ignatius himself wrote the constitutions and they are very personal, a blend of their author's militancy, mysticism, and common sense. Everything was aimed toward service to God and mankind. Ignatius believed this could be best accomplished by abandoning most of the traditional monastic rules and establishing a quasi-military organization, centralized and authoritarian. He placed a "general," elected for life at the head, with subordinate commanders appointed by the general below. He saw the individual members as soldiers of the Church, whose duty was not to prepare their own souls for the hereafter like monks, but "to procure salvation and protection of one's neighbors." He believed the chief qualifications for membership to be piety, humility, and zeal, but also intelligence, good manners, ability to speak, and an attractive personality. Obedience without question was essential; the Jesuit "must let himself be carried and ruled by his superior, as if he were a dead body." But like any good military leader, Ignatius encouraged individual intiative and decision making on the battle line. "Be all things to all men," he advised, ". . . let us follow the method adopted by our enemy, the devil, in his dealings with a good man, he all for evil purpose, we all for good."

Each new member had to pass severe tests of character and temperament and undergo thorough intellectual training during his novitiate. Only the best were admitted to the Society's ruling elite, the "Professed of Four Vows" who took, in addition to the three usual vows of poverty, chastity, and obedience, the special vow to the pope. Others took only the three vows and were assigned to lesser tasks befitting their abilities. By the nature of the Society and its work, it attracted recruits mostly from Europe's lesser nobility and upper middle classes, cosmopolitan young men who would fit in and be at ease on any social level. Many of them in the first decades were Spanish, a fact that led most contemporaries to identify the Society with the political ambitions of the king of Spain. This was a superficial judgment, for only where Spanish policy advanced papal interests did it coincide with Jesuit policy; the Spanish crown and Church distrusted Jesuits for their loyalty to Rome.

Although not founded for the express purpose of fighting Protestantism (Francis Xavier's great missionary work in the Orient was the Jesuit ideal), this shortly became the Jesuits' most pressing task. They carried it out in two important ways: by propagating the Catholic faith through education of young men and pastoral care of the poor and sick, and by pressing the papal cause among the Catholic rulers of Europe. Beginning in 1542 at Padua in Italy and Coimbra in Portugal, the Society had founded, by the death of Ignatius in 1556, thirty colleges and secondary schools in various parts of Catholic Europe, several at Rome to train Catholic exiles. Though humanities and philosophy were offered, the core of the curriculum was orthodox Catholic theology. Modern teaching methods were used, some borrowed from the humanists and Calvinists. After 1556, the number of institutions continued to expand until the Society had virtually preempted education of upper-class Catholic youth. At the same time, many Jesuits became scholars in theology and philosophy, contributing significantly to revitalizing Aristotelian and Thomistic scholasticism in the later sixteenth and seventeenth centuries.

The Jesuits did their most effective and lasting work for the Catholic Reformation in the field of education, but they gained their greatest fame in politics. Realists and men of this world, they knew that much of Catholicism's strength depended on the continued loyalty of Catholic princes and governing classes. Hence, they sought to influence public policy along lines most favorable to Catholic and papal interests. They did this by becoming confessors to monarchs and nobles and by supplying the Catholic cause with propaganda and ideology. The kings of Portugal, the electors of Bavaria and several Habsburg emperors accepted Jesuit confessors very early. Henry IV of France, when he converted to Catholicism in the 1590's, allayed the pope's doubts about his sincerity by taking a Jesuit as his spiritual guide. Jesuits were prominent on the Catholic side in the French Wars of Religion. In treating their highborn charges, the Jesuits were sympathetic and forgiving, emphasizing self-rehabilitation through good works rather than the threat of damnation. They were positive thinkers: "Send no one away dejected," Ignatius had advised, "God asks nothing impossible." This point of view raised the ire of zealous Catholics such as the Jansenists, who accused them of spiritual laxness. Naturally enough, Protestants feared and hated them, but so too did many leaders of the "national" churches of France and Spain because of their unswerving devotion to the "internationalist" papacy. Thus, they made enemies wherever they went, and around their political activities a black legend grew up. In fact, they were neither so successful as they themselves believed nor so sinister and scheming as contemporaries pictured them.

THE COUNCIL OF TRENT

It was left to the Council of Trent to state the doctrine that the Jesuits and other Catholic proselytizers would teach, and at the same time lay the foundations of internal reform on which a new, more vigorous, more deeply spiritual Catholic Church could be built. This great council opened in late 1545 at a little town in the Italian Alps. It completed its business in three separate periods or assemblies, the first in 1545–1547, the second in 1551–1552, the last in 1562–1563. The third was followed by a papal proclamation giving legality to the council's work.

The most important part of this work concerned doctrine. The beliefs of orthodox Catholicism were defined with clarity and precision, the differences with Protestantism specified. The doctrine was eventually accepted throughout the Catholic world and is in force today. In matters of ecclesiastical administration, finance, justice, and discipline, the council's work was less impressive. In a general way, the most notorious abuses were condemned and ordered eliminated; but as in the past there was no way the orders could be enforced. Execution depended on the zeal of popes, princes, and prelates. If contemporary princes were still guided largely by political motives, prelates were more spiritual minded than their predecessors, and the popes of the second half of the sixteenth century were reformers. In the hands of men like Pius V, Trent's weak decrees became formidable weapons against evil.

Pope Paul III issued the bull convoking the Council of Trent in May 1542. He still feared the possible consequences of his action. The spectre of anti-papal Conciliarism continued to haunt him, and the power struggle between Francis I and Charles V and between Charles and the Lutheran princes of Germany could pose a danger to a council's independence.

Pope Paul III. The man most responsible for setting papal reform in motion in the 1530's and '40's, Paul was hesitant to act at first. He grew bolder and brought his reign to a climax by calling the Council of Trent. (Alinari-Scala.)

Nevertheless, he had become reconciled to the need for a council now that the conference of Regensburg had demonstrated the practical impossibility of reunion with the Protestants. However, he wanted a council on his own terms, free from interference by politicians and under strict papal control. He had his way, but not without difficulty. No sooner had he summoned churchmen from all parts of Catholic Europe than war between Francis and Charles resumed, forcing postponement of the council for three more years. In the meantime, he won Francis' support and reached an agreement with Charles regarding the Lutherans. Though dissatisfied that the Lutherans were not participating, Charles was willing to allow the council to go ahead. The Lutherans, he believed, could be brought in later, after their obstinacy had been softened by force of arms. This aim he would achieve by decisive defeat of the Protestant Schmalkaldic League.

Titian painted this final session (1563) of the Council of Trent. (Alinari-Scala.)

The Curialists and the Ultramontanes The Council began to sit in December 1545 with only thirty-one bishops present. The pope himself was not in attendance, but as presiding officers he assigned three cardinals. Immediately, a parliamentary struggle erupted between the Curialists, as the papal party was named, and the Ultramontanes, the delegates who wished to challenge papal authority by asserting the rights of the episcopacy.[1] The latter were Frenchmen, Spaniards, and Germans, heirs of the Conciliar tradition and often mouthpieces for the king of France and the emperor. The Curialists, who were in the majority, included the papal representatives and most of the Italians. Although the struggle continued through all three assembly periods, the Curialists won a decisive victory at the very start. With their Italian allies, they determined that the rules of previous councils would be abandoned; voting would be by head, not by "nation" as at Constance; and only bishops, generals of religious orders, and representatives of monastic congregations actually present could take part. The Curialists counted on circumstances, chiefly the difficulties of travel over long distances, to keep the number of Ultramontanes relatively low. They were right as it turned out, though in later sessions more northerners attended and on one or two key issues a few Italians changed sides. The opposition never won a majority but on several occasions the vote was close enough to force the Curialists to compromise. On the whole, however, it is fair to say that the voting rules permitted the papacy to direct the council from start to finish.

[1] "Ultramontane" translates "the other side of the mountains," understood to be the Alps. At Trent, the designation referred to northern Europeans, including Spaniards, but later on it was used by northerners in exactly the opposite sense, to mean papalists.

The second important victory for the Curialists was the council's decision to deal simultaneously with questions of doctrine and problems of Church reform. The Ultramontanes wanted to eliminate abuses first and consider doctrine later. In this they reflected the preference of Charles V and Francis I. The two monarchs still hoped somehow to accommodate Catholic belief to the beliefs of their native heretics and saw clerical abuse as the heretic's strongest ally. The Curialists, on the other hand, had accepted the opinion of rigorists like Cardinal Caraffa, who wanted to restate Catholic orthodoxy in the boldest possible terms, indeed accentuating its differences with Protestantism. The Council's decision had this result but it also tended to limit discussion of reform.

The most significant battles for the future constitution of the Church were fought out in the first and last assemblies. They revolved around the technical question of the residency of bishops in their diocese. All agreed that residency was obligatory; the argument arose over whether residency was a divine ordinance (*jus divinum*) or whether it was merely ecclesiastical law and hence dependent on papal authority. If it was the former, then bishops were equal to the pope in God's eyes; if the latter then the pope was superior. The Ultramontanes had dressed out the old Conciliarist ideas in a new guise, one that attracted some of the more devout Italians. The Curialists held the balance, however, but only after agreeing to a compromise; papal primacy was upheld but the pope, in a personal letter to Philip II of Spain, had to pledge his intention to undertake thoroughgoing measures of reform. The last Curialist victory came when the council voted to submit all its conclusions to the pope for approval and promulgation. The Conciliarist movement was finally laid to rest. Though the idea cropped up here and there, notably in the French Church in the next century, it was no longer a threat to the papacy.

Definition of Catholic Doctrine As we have noted, the council's principal business was the definition of Catholic doctrine. The delegates' mood was rigorously orthodox from the beginning; both Curialists and most Ultramontanes were aligned solidly against compromise with the doctrines of Protestantism. This was made clear by the first decision of the first assembly:

The sacred and holy, oecumenical and General Synod of Trent, lawfully assembled in the Holy Ghost . . . following the examples of the orthodox Fathers, receives and venerates with an equal affection of piety, and reverence, all the books both of the Old and the New Testament—seeing that one God is the author of both—also the said traditions, as well as those appertaining to faith as to morals, as having been dictated, either by Christ's own word of mouth, or by the Holy Ghost, and preserved in the Catholic Church by a continuous succession. . . .

Scriptura et traditio, the Bible and the teachings of the Church, were to be treated as equally authoritative in doctrinal matters. The Vulgate translation of the Bible was confirmed as the authentic version, though susceptible of correction by authorized scholars, and only the Church could interpret it. Each of these declarations was directly contrary to the Protestant position.

No less contrary were declarations on justification, the nature of man, the role of the Church and its clergy, and the character of the sacraments and the Mass. Good works, it was declared, are as necessary to salvation as faith. Man is not "wholly depraved": after Baptism he retains only the taint of the "consequence of sin." Man is saved by God's grace, but grace is not a free gift. It is offered to man as reward for the merit he gains by performing good works. Man has free will, for he may reject the grace offered. The Church is indispensable to salvation. It is the fountainhead of doctrine and the dispenser of the sacraments, the vehicle through which God's grace passes to man. The seven sacraments were retained with their traditional qualities. The Mass is the occasion of the miraculous transubstantiation of the bread and wine into Christ's body and blood. A proposal by the German delegates in the second assembly to permit communion in both bread and wine was flatly rejected because it smacked of the Lutheran heresy. The last assembly issued decrees on purgatory, indulgences, the veneration of saints, relics and images. Payment of money for indulgences was allowed, though the attendant evils were condemned. "It is a good and salutary thing to invoke the Saints; their relics must be honored by the faithful," as must their images be, "not because [they] possess a supernatural virtue," but because of the holy men and women they represent. Conservative orthodoxy triumphed all along the line.

Administrative and Disciplinary Reforms The measures for administrative and disciplinary reform were also conservative, a disappointment to the zealous. There was little novel in the decrees regarding preaching and alms-taking, the broad duties of bishops, the granting of appointments and benefices, and the general education and supervision of secular priests and regulars. There was one innovation in the field of clerical education, however, which had a profound effect on the character of the clergy. A seminary to train young men for the priesthood was ordered established in every diocese. That action, a modern Catholic historian has observed, ". . . more than anything else has made all the difference between the health of the Church in the last four centuries and its chronic state in the Middle Ages. . . ."[2] Furthermore, the other measures, taken together, had an effect outweighing their individual significance. They created a mood of reform throughout the Church, even in those countries like Spain and France where royal influence in ecclesiastical affairs was powerful. Doubtless they contributed, together with the doctrinal decrees, to the "Catholic revival," the awakened spirituality in Catholic Europe, of the late sixteenth and early seventeenth centuries. In more explicit terms, they strengthened the hand of the bishop in his diocese by giving him practical disciplinary and administrative prerogatives

[2]P. Hughes, *A Popular History of the Reformation* (Doubleday: Garden City, N. Y., 1960), p. 258.

that traditionally had been reserved to the pope. The most notable example concerned certain classes of clerics who had been "exempted" from episcopal authority. Thus, zealous bishops, of which there were many in the next years, now possessed effective weapons of reform.

Pope Pius IV issued the bull *Benedictus deus,* proclaiming as law the council's decrees on January 26, 1564. But the bull was not accepted everywhere in Europe. The Italian governments accepted it, as did Emperor Ferdinand I for his hereditary Austrian lands, the kings of Poland and Portugal, and the Catholic princes of the Empire. Philip II of Spain, the "Catholic King" but no papist, accepted it only after adding the reservation "without prejudice to the rights of the crown." France refused under any conditions, maintaining the decrees infringed on the prerogatives of the Gallican Church.

THE REFORMED PAPACY

The Council of Trent left reform of the Holy See and the Curia to the popes themselves. This was another concession to papal primacy, and fortunately for the Church's future the popes were worthy of the responsibility. From the reign of Paul III, who died in 1549, to the end of the century, the Chair of Peter was filled by men dedicated to the Catholic Reformation. Paul himself had made a start and his successor, Julius III (1550–1555), despite peasant origins, was a first-rate administrator and canon lawyer. He applied his skill to the overgrown papal bureaucracy, seeking to eliminate the graft and favoritism connected with papal exemptions. These were waivers of ecclesiastical regulations, usually awarded in return for money. Paul IV (1555–1559), the awesome Cardinal Caraffa, completed Julius III's work of curial reform. A ferocious and fanatical man, with a will of iron and a passionate belief in his mission, he struck out at corruption and immorality without regard to individuals or concern for the financial consequences. Austere himself, he made the papacy austere. He subjected Rome to puritanical rule, turning it into a model of rectitude. He was particularly hard on the wandering monks and absentee bishops who frequented the Holy City in search of amusement and favors. During Paul's pontificate, the Council of Trent did not meet. He simply refused to summon it, believing Church reform wholly a papal affair.

Pope Sixtus V. One of the most effective of the Counter-Reformation popes, Sixtus was a man of great force and character. He pressed the Catholic cause everywhere in Europe. It was said that he admired only two of his contemporaries, Queen Elizabeth and (the later canonized) Philip Neri. (Courtesy of the Trustees of the British Museum.)

Pius IV (1559–1565) guided the Council of Trent to a conclusion and confirmed its decrees. As a person, he was something of a nonentity after Paul IV, friendly, easy-going, a lover of Renaissance culture. But he carried the work of reform forward, compiling and publishing the Index of forbidden books, supervising preparation of the Roman Catechism for the use of parish priests, and addressing himself to revision of the standard breviary and missal. He was ably assisted by his nephew, the saintly Cardinal Charles Borromeo (1538–1584), Archbishop of Milan, whom he made his secretary of state. Under Borromeo's direction, Rome remained free of vice and worldly diversion. Pius V (1565–1572) was a throwback in some ways to Paul IV. A paragon of virtue and correct doctrine (he was canonized in 1712), he was wholly ruthless in his treatment of heretics and sinners. In his hands, the Index and the Inquisition became fearful instruments of orthodoxy. Neither Gregory XIII (1572–1582) nor Sixtus V (1585–1590) was so vigorous in his approach as Pius V. Gregory concentrated on administering the papal bureaucracy and reviving the diplomatic service. He also gave the Church a new edition of the canon law. More impressed than his predecessors by the work of the Jesuits, he encouraged them and contributed liberally to their Roman colleges. We owe our calendar, the "Gregorian" calendar, to him. Sixtus was also a skilled administrator. His fields of activity were the Curia, where he made several innovations, and the Papal States. The latter were the papacy's chief source of revenue, and he sought to control them more firmly and make them prosperous.

Beginning shortly after the middle of the century, the popes once more took an active role in international politics, supporting the Catholic cause in France, England, the Netherlands, and wherever there were Protestants. But the aim of their diplomacy had changed. It was not that of the head of Christendom trying to enforce order on a fragmented and unruly society—the Middle Ages were past, and the states had taken over that job. Nor was their aim that of a Renaissance prince, secular and self-seeking. Protected from threats to their small temporal domain by the power of Spain in Italy, the reformed papacy could now direct itself to the spiritual aim of Counter-Reformation. Although the losses Catholicism had sustained hurt their prestige and badly weakened their influence, there were some notable successes. Using the Jesuits as shock troops, Catholic forces fought Lutheranism to a stand-still in most of Germany and won back Poland, the Austrian lands of the Habsburgs, and eventually Bohemia and Hungary. They held French Protestants to a minority and kept the southern half of the Netherlands. Where they failed, in Scandinavia, England, and the northern Netherlands, the reason was usually political, as we shall see in a later chapter.

FURTHER READING

Many of the works cited for the previous two chapters contain information on the Catholic Reformation. Best, even compared with longer works, for its sensitivity and scholarship is A. G. Dickens, **The Counter Reformation* (1969). P. Janelle, **The Catholic Reformation* (1949), is useful, but suffers not from its Catholic viewpoint but from its failure to elaborate the role of the Jesuits and the sources of the religious revival of the late sixteenth century. H. Daniel-Rops, *The Catholic Reformation*, 2 vols. (1962), is also the work of a distinguished Catholic historian. H. O. Evennett, **The Spirit of the Counter Reformation* (1968), is excellent. An older Protestant work is B. J. Kidd, *The Counter-Reformation* (1937), which treats the movement largely as a reaction against Protestantism.

On reform before Trent, two recent biographies of "conciliationists" are useful: W. Schenk, *Reginald Pole* (1950), and R. M. Douglas, *Jacopo Sadoleto,*

*Books available in paperback edition are marked with an asterisk.

1477–1547 (1959). Much has been written for and against the Jesuits. The best Protestant treatment is P. van Dyke, *Ignatius Loyola* (1926), eminently fair but uninspired. Far more lively, and equally scholarly if one recognizes the author's Catholic faith, are the two works of the Jesuit Father J. Brodrick, * *The Origin of the Jesuits* (1940) and * *The Progress of the Jesuits* (1947). Among other books on the great figures of the Catholic Reformation, one might consult M. Suclair, *St. Teresa of Avila* (1953); M. Jouhandeau, *St. Philip Neri* (1960); and E. A. Peers, *St. John of the Cross* (1946).

On the Council of Trent, all previous historical work has been superseded by the monumental H. Jedin, *A History of the Council of Trent,* 2 vols. (1957, 1961). On the Church after Trent, see P. Hughes, *The Church in Crisis* (1961); and L. Willaert, *Après le Concile de Trente* (1960).

4 The Age of Charles V

The election of Charles of Habsburg as Emperor Charles V of the Holy Roman Empire in 1519 cost over 850,000 gold florins and climaxed fifty years of brilliant dynastic politics. In the person of young Charles was joined the heritage of a half-dozen complex and scrupulously chosen marriage alliances of which the most important were Castile with Aragon, Burgundy with Habsburg, and Burgundy-Habsburg with united Spain. By his Burgundian inheritance Charles received the Free County of Burgundy and the Netherlands, which he rounded out to seventeen provinces. By his Habsburg inheritance, Austria, Carinthia, Styria, Carniola, and Tyrol came under his control. With his Spanish inheritance, he gained Spain itself, Naples, Sicily, and the New World. No Christian prince since Charlemagne had possessed so extensive a realm.

CHARLES AND HIS EMPIRE

It was inevitable because of his great inherited power and wealth that Charles should be put forward as a candidate for Charlemagne's crown. His grandfather, Emperor Maximilian I, prepared the diplomacy, and to secure the necessary electoral votes the Fugger and Welser banks were persuaded to loan 500,000 florins, to which Charles himself added 350,000. The chief rival, Francis I of France, could not match this huge sum, nor were the electors particularly favorable to Francis anyway. Charles was chosen unanimously.

He was nineteen years old at the time of his election, a slender boy of medium height, with close-set eyes and a badly undershot jaw which tended to hang open, giving him a deceptively stupid appearance. He soon learned to mask his "Habsburg jaw" with a beard, a fashion he bequeathed to his similarly disfigured heirs. In reality, Charles had better than average intelligence which he utilized to its fullest, as well as considerable common sense. A deep feeling of personal responsibility and an insatiable appetite for hard work were additional compensations. Charles was raised in the Netherlands, amid all the late medieval splendor of the court of Burgundy. There he learned the life of a Burgundian nobleman, affected, provincial, with special emphasis on horseback-riding and the joust. He was quite ill-prepared by education, and it must have seemed, by personal qualities as well, to assume the enormous tasks thrust upon him. But assume them he did, and for more than thirty-five years he was the most energetic and effective administrator, soldier, and diplomat in Europe.

But Charles never really lost the spirit of Burgundy; indeed, in some ways he was a living anachronism who fought a rearguard action for the Middle Ages throughout his life. He never thought of his empire (contemporaries called it his "monarchy") as a "state" in the modern sense, or even in the sense that Machiavelli used the term, as an autonomous, omnicompetent entity, binding together the people of a particular geographical area and having a meaning and an end entirely within itself. Such a concept was wholly outside his ken; rather his empire was simply a group of territories united in his person. Nor did Charles have a concept of "nation." To him Italians, Spaniards, Flemings were alike his subjects, owing him loyalty, although he granted and usually respected their individual differences in matters of local government.

Charles' aims and ambitions were founded on his attitude toward his empire. In part (how large a part is still a matter of historical controversy) they were narrowly dynastic—to save the empire for his heirs at any cost. The greatest danger, he believed, came from France, with which he warred throughout his life. On the other hand, his aims and ambitions were of heroic scope. Deeply religious in an old-fashioned way, he believed himself the leader and inspiration of a great Christian crusade against Islam, represented by the Ottoman Turks, and the defender of Catholicism against the heresies of Martin Luther. His long reign was consumed in advancing these aims and ambitions, usually, though he regretted it, by means of war. He undertook campaign after campaign against France over Italy and the Netherlands, launched sporadic attacks against German Protestantism, and sent expeditionary forces against the Turks. When he abdicated his offices in 1556, he could say, not that he had been successful, but only sadly that he had done his best.

Charles' realms were scattered over Europe, and included many peoples speaking many languages, living under a variety of constitutions, and having diverse and sometimes conflicting interests. Over each realm he appointed a regent, a viceroy, or governor whose job it was to rule in his stead. Generally, this official's most important job was to extract as much revenue from the lands under his authority as possible without forcing the inhabitants into obstinacy or rebellion.

The Netherlands Closest to Charles' heart was the conglomeration of duchies, counties, and bishoprics comprising the Netherlands. The separate areas or provinces existed in virtual independence one from the other. Each had its own representative body, or "states," which voted taxes and administered expenditures. Delegates from the provincial states met in the States General, a body dating only from the late fifteenth century, which gave the provinces a certain amount of centralization. But the amount was very small, for the delegates to the States General had no right to take action unless authorized by their home provinces. Their principal function was to hear

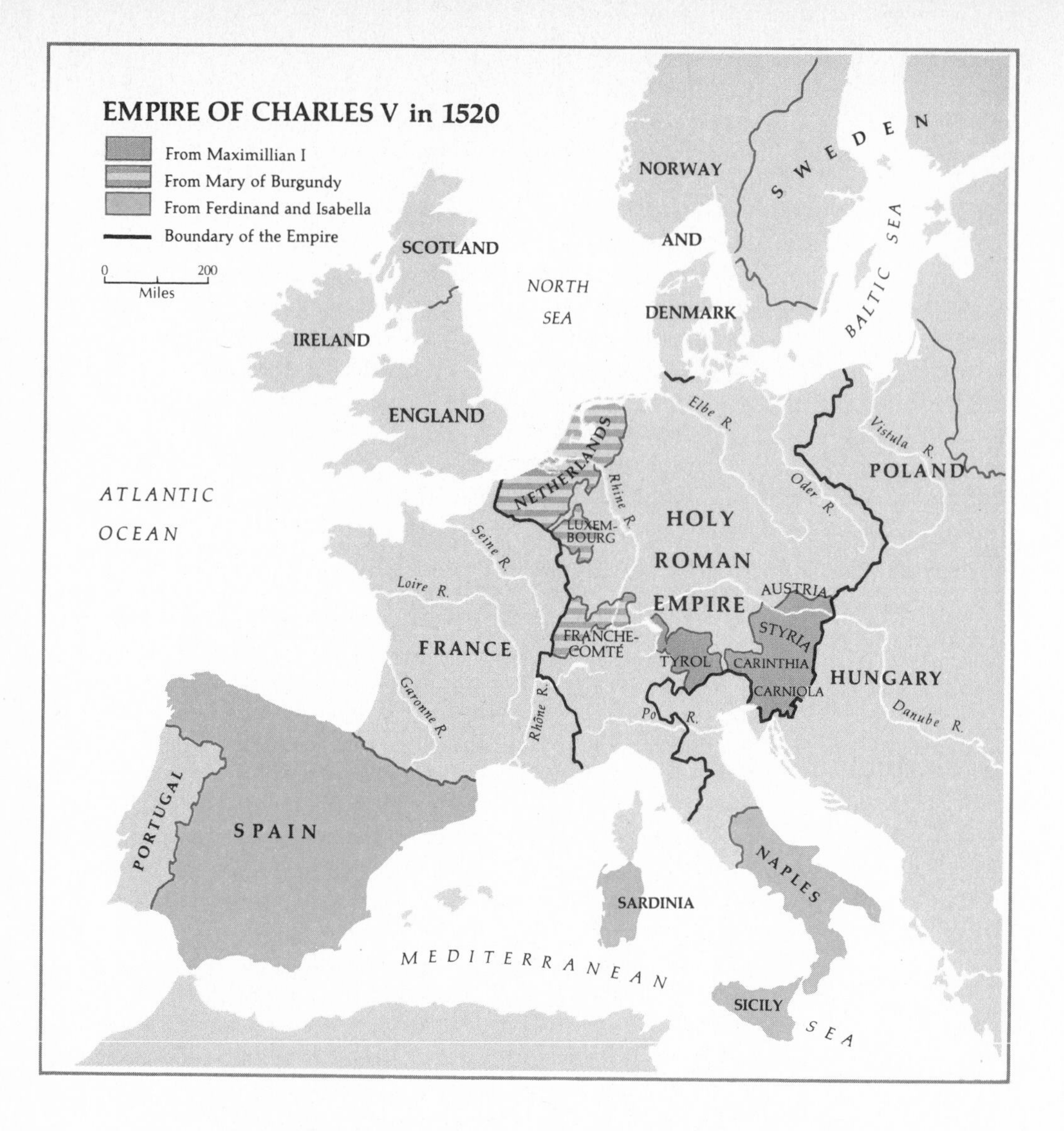

and report the request of the crown. The crown was represented by a regent, first Charles' aunt, Margaret of Austria, then his sister, Mary of Hungary, and finally his illegitimate daughter, Margaret of Parma. The regent was assisted by several councils composed mostly of local magnates. Under the regents, the provinces prospered, despite high taxes. Charles treated the traditions of provincial and local liberty gingerly, and the people loved and respected him.

Italy In Italy, where at first only Naples and Sicily, old Aragonese crown lands, belonged to Charles, viceroys were appointed. For Charles, the two realms were little more than sources of revenue. He had little interest in or understanding of them, nor did he make any serious effort to change their institutions. But he allowed the viceroys considerable leeway in their actions and provided them with troops. The result was that for the first time in centuries the bellicose baronage was pacified and Naples and Sicily enjoyed order and tranquility. An attempt to establish the Spanish Inquisition in Naples provoked a rebellion and was abandoned, but a similar attempt in Sicily was successful. Milan, when it was annexed in 1540, became a province of Spain and was administered by a governor. But again the crown's chief interest was in tax revenue and the old ducal institutions of government remained essentially unchanged. Over the rest of Italy, the shadow of Spanish power hung heavily. Spanish troops were stationed in several places in nominally independent Florence, which became a duchy in the 1530's, and Spanish troops assisted the Florentines in their conquest and absorption of Siena in 1555. Thereafter, the old states of Florence and Siena constituted the grand duchy of Tuscany. The proximity of Rome to Spanish Naples and the leading role played by Spain in the Counter-Reformation made Charles Europe's most influential Catholic layman. Genoa, by the end of Charles' reign, had fallen within the Spanish orbit too, and within another generation Genoese bankers were Spain's chief source of loans. Venice and Savoy alone held to their independence, though Venice was deprived of any significant role in Italian politics and Savoy was not yet ready to step onto the European stage.

Austria The Austrian Habsburg lands were turned over by Charles to his younger brother Ferdinand for himself and his posterity in 1521. Charles retained superior authority in name only. These lands were truly disparate in character. In the best of situations, the hereditary lands (Austria proper, Carinthia, Styria, Carniola, and Tyrol) were joined under a single head who was also elected King of Bohemia and Hungary. In Charles' and Ferdinand's time, however, the hereditary lands were still subject to division among several Habsburg sons and the elective kingdoms were only Habsburg by custom. Even the beginnings of centralization and consolidation would have to wait until the seventeenth century. Once given his responsibility, Ferdinand, who had grown up in Spain, set his capable mind to becoming a good Austrian and to protecting his lands against the invading Turk, who threatened Vienna itself. He and his successors remained remarkably loyal to overall Habsburg policy.

Spain Spain was unquestionably the most important of all Charles' dominions and the one over which he exercised the closest personal control. And the Spanish accepted Charles less readily than any of his other subjects for this reason. Charles brought to Spain a greater degree of governmental centralization and autocracy than Ferdinand and Isabella had dared. At the same time, he brought Spain glory, making it the most prestigious and powerful state in Europe and thereby winning the eventual respect, if not the love, of his people. But glory cost money, and in Spain as elsewhere, Charles found himself concerned chiefly with revenues.

Charles' introduction to the Spanish people in 1518 set the tone of his reign; he made financial demands of the several Cortes. Already he had earned the Spaniards' displeasure by delaying his first visit to the Iberian kingdom for eighteen months after his succession. Further, he was preceded by a body of rapacious Flemings bent on replacing the natives in top posts of government and church. These men became his chief aides and advisors, and one of them, amid cries of outrage, was made Archbishop of Toledo, Primate of Spain. The Flemings continued to rule after Charles had gone off to northern Europe to seek the imperial crown, and through them he made another request for money in 1520. The Spanish answered by revolting, first the townspeople of Castile, whose citizens set up independent "communal" governments (*comuneros*), then the common people of Valencia and Majorca, who organized themselves into "brotherhoods" (*germanías*).

The revolt of the *communeros* and *germanías* was a serious if short-lived threat to royal government. Many noblemen and clerics supported the *comuneros* at first, and it looked as if all of Castile had turned on its new king. But class quarrels and promises of favor by Charles brought the upper classes over to his side, and crown and aristocracy joined in general suppression. The Cortes was confirmed in its impotence; the towns were placed once again under the close supervision of royal officials, the *corregidores.* The last flicker of old Castilian liberty was snuffed out. Defeat of the *germanías* did not have such autocratic results. The lesser Spanish realms, including Aragon, Valencia, Catalonia, and Majorca, retained most of their provincial freedoms, for Charles was obliged to guarantee the traditional political arrangements to gain allies against the revolutionaries. The Cortes in these places remained obstinate and tight-fisted, and much local government was kept in local hands. Charles, like Ferdinand and Isabella before him and the Philips after him, was a truly effective monarch only in Castile.

Castile Castile was the keystone of the Spanish monarchy and, indeed, of the Habsburg Empire. It was Castile that felt the full effects of Habsburg policy, for this small, relatively poor Iberian kingdom supplied much of the money to finance Charles' (and his son's) wars, and in time Castile was sucked dry. Charles' policies were incredibly short-sighted. Taxes rose steadily, but more important, payment fell most heavily on the non-noble, non-clerical classes. Agriculture, industry, and commerce, although fairly prosperous during Charles' reign, could not keep pace. The crown took little interest in encouraging economic growth, refusing to recognize the danger to farming of uncontrolled sheep raising, imposing high sales taxes on manufactured goods, failing to exploit the American treasure and expanding American trade, and generally favoring noble, non-mercantile elements in town and countryside. Not to do productive work became the hallmark of Spanish gentility, and, as the saying went, every man wanted to be an *"hidalgo como el rey, menos dineros"* (a gentleman like the king, but not so rich). At the same time, prices rose steadily because the Castilian economy could not increase its agricultural and industrial production to meet the demands of empire and because of the influx of precious metals into Spain from the New World. Many people were impoverished, and the gulf between the few very rich and the great number of poor widened. The small middle class virtually disappeared. Already the seeds of Spain's later decline were beginning to germinate.

Along with the revenues from Castile and the treasure from the New World, Charles could count on taxes from the Netherlands and Italy. But still he was constantly short of funds. He began to depend more and more on German and Genoese bankers, sliding deeply into debt and even declaring partial bankruptcy several times. The discovery of rich mines at Potosí in upper Peru in 1545 brought only momentary respite. The fact was that Charles had set himself a mission too vast and too expensive for the relatively meager resources at his disposal. But neither he nor his son, Philip II, looked at it that way. Castile above all suffered for it.

CHARLES, THE LUTHERANS, AND THE TURKS

A large part of this mission was to defend the Catholic Church against heretics and infidels. It was a huge undertaking, and Charles' limited funds and armed forces, combined with his distracting struggle with France to preserve the Habsburg family interests, prevented any real success. His greatest failures came in Germany, where the office of Holy Roman Emperor gave him a heavy traditional responsibility but very little real power. Lutheranism spread rapidly in the 1520's. But Charles' problem was not so much the religion itself, which the effective application of inquisitorial methods might still eliminate or contain, but rather the independent political power of the great princes who used the religion to further their non-religious ambitions. Charles' war against them was motivated largely by spiritual zeal, for he had no desire to transform Germany into a monarchy on the French or English style. In contrast, their war against him was almost wholly political in intention. It would seem that their motive drove them the harder; Charles, for all his devotion to his Church, was unwilling to sacrifice his family to it. Within a short time after the Diet of Worms in 1521 at which Luther was declared an outlaw, Charles left Germany. He remained away, settling his Spanish affairs, fighting France and the Turks for most of two decades. Lutheranism took root freely among the people and demonstrated its political advantages to the princes and free cities. In 1530, the princes and cities that had taken up the new faith felt themselves strong and numerous enough to form the Schmalkaldic League. The League's purpose was mutual protection and preservation of the Protestant claim that choice of religion was up to the individual ruler or ruling body, a privilege granted by the Diet in 1526 but withdrawn later. The Catholic princes, still fearful of an emperor, even a Catholic emperor, were unable to form a similar alliance until 1539. In the intervening years, the Protestants, who were led by the intelligent, mercurial Philip of Hesse, pretty much had their way in Germany, and Lutheranism made significant gains by winning Brandenburg and most of northern Germany. By the end of the 1530's, four of the seven imperial electors were Protestant. Protestants allied themselves to the "Most Christian" king of France, who found them most useful in his war against Charles.

Charles V by Titian. The emperor is shown here at the Battle of Mühlberg in 1547 where he defeated Protestant forces. (The Granger Collection.)

Charles' Struggle in Germany After 1544, Charles was in a position to give more attention to Germany. He made alliances with the pope, with the Catholic princes, and even with a few of the Protestant princes. After some delay, the so-called Schmalkaldic War opened in 1546 and Charles' forces did well. Without leadership (Philip of Hesse had been disgraced by a bigamous marriage), and concerned more about protecting their own lands than fighting the common foe, the Protestants were beaten fairly easily. Charles spoke authoritatively about reuniting the faith by force, but he could not match his words with action. Still in the forefront of his mind was the hope that reunion could be achieved by judicious theological compromise between the opposing parties and a thorough-going reform of abuses in the German Catholic Church. But neither side was amenable, and since Charles could not carry out his threats of armed suppression, the only realistic solution was recognition of the religious and political status quo. This was forcefully demonstrated by a new war begun by the Protestants and prosecuted with success in the early 1550's. Charles, in effect, gave up the fight, turning over his German responsibilities to his brother Ferdinand. Ferdinand was a seeker of peace at any price. After several years of negotiation he agreed to the Peace of Augsburg in 1555, establishing the principle of *cujus regio, ejus religio,* which confirmed the right of each prince and city council to determine the religion to be practiced in their own territories.

War Against Islam In reality, the Ottoman Turks presented a more dangerous threat to western Europe and to Charles' personal empire than did the Lutheran princes of Germany. For two centuries this new, strong people of Islam had been expanding their territories and their influence in the Near East. Their greatest victory had come in 1453 when they had captured the city of Constantinople. They had not halted, however, but had continued to march north into the Balkans as well as east into Syria and Palestine, south into Egypt, and west along the coast of North Africa. The Turks were a strong power by 1520, when the greatest of them, Suleiman the Magnificent, became sultan. Within two years, Suleiman was threatening Hungary and Rhodes; the capture of the latter would be a heavy blow to western European commerce. In 1526, he overwhelmed King Louis II of Hungary at the battle of Mohács, and the long struggle between Habsburgs and Turks began. After some difficulty, Ferdinand got himself elected king of Hungary and went to the defense of his lands. He succeeded in beating off Suleiman's siege of Vienna, giving Austria a momentary respite, but could achieve no real victory. In the next years, most of Hungary was swallowed up. In 1547, Ferdinand and Charles recognized the situation and a precarious peace was established. Meanwhile, Charles tried to head off Turkish advances in the Mediterranean by attacking North Africa. In 1535, he took Tunis, but failed to take Algiers in 1541.

Charles considered his war against Islam a crusade, but as with all his wars he was unable to prosecute it singlemindedly because of his many other pressing affairs. The princes and the Diet of the Empire were only reluctantly cooperative, providing some troops and money. But they were devoid of a crusading spirit and unwilling to support wholeheartedly what they considered a private Habsburg war. And France was busily engaged in promoting the Turkish cause as part of a complex anti-Habsburg diplomacy. The activities of France in favor of Lutherans and Muslims against fellow Catholics is the best possible evidence of how far Europe had moved toward a purely secular view of politics by the sixteenth century. Any pretense to the "unity of Christendom" was now abandoned.

Habsburg Against Valois Charles' longest, most costly war, and the only one that could be called successful, if success be measured solely in terms of territory won, was against the Valois, Francis I and Henry II of France. In part it was a continuation of the Italian wars begun by the French in 1494, for much of it was fought in Italy and the stakes, control of the rich duchy of Milan, were those of the previous generation of rulers. But the nature of Charles' empire led to territorial disputes in other parts of Europe. Fighting took place in the Netherlands, in northern France, in Germany, and along the Franco-Spanish border, while diplomacy involved England, the German Lutherans, and the Ottoman Turks. This Habsburg-Valois war was the first great European power struggle, foreshadowing the later great national wars in its scope, its intensity, and the sophistication of its military and diplomatic arts.

It was not a national war, however, but a dynastic war, a war between two great ruling houses motivated by family pride, jealousy, and acquisitiveness. Since he never conceived of his empire as a "state," "reason of state" did not enter into Charles' calculations. For the kings of France, whose realm more nearly resembled a "state" in the modern sense but whose political ideas were as dynastic as Charles', the goals were nevertheless essentially the same. Conflict arose because both sides claimed the same pieces of land: Milan, Burgundy, Flanders, the kingdom of Navarre. But, though to the participants this was a war of dynastic rights, it inevitably affected the states that were to evolve—France and Spain.

In a general way, the needs of this war helped to develop further the state system we have seen arising on the foundations of feudal monarchy. For, whatever pseudo-feudal motives prompted Charles, Francis, and Henry to make war, the means and methods by which they fought were quite modern. Armies, for example, lost most of the vestiges of medievalism. They were now permanent, royal armies, paid by the crown and loyal to it. Soldiers were not knights fighting for fun and personal profit, but professionals engaged in a serious, bloody business. The decisive tactical change that made the cannon the dominant weapon and replaced the heavy, armored cavalry with closely disciplined infantry completed the armies' transition from feudal levies. Diplomatic apparatus also underwent rapid development, for governments came to realize that quick communication and accurate information were indispensable to policy making in foreign affairs. It would be an exaggeration to say that policy makers of the time thought in terms of such an advanced concept as "balance of power"; but they were beginning to realize that Europe was breaking down into an agglomeration of separate, sovereign states and that diplomatic negotiation was the only way one political entity could talk to another.

Within each state were forces of centralization and unity, which the war stimulated. While feudal wars were traditionally paid for out of the king's own purse, with only emergency assistance from his subjects, the Habsburg-Valois wars were financed by the subjects themselves, making them national wars in this respect at least. The commoners were taxed immoderately, and even the nobles and clergy contributed something. In practice, the crowns borrowed on "expectations" from bankers, Charles from the bankers of Genoa and Germany, Francis and Henry from the bankers of Lyon. Necessarily, the machinery of collection and disbursement, the royal administration, became more centralized and complex. European banking, naturally enough, grew apace. Both sides emerged from the wars exhausted in spirit and material resources, but with the institution of monarchy stronger than before.

The first phase of the war went to Charles. No sooner had he gained the imperial throne than he asserted his claims to Milan, to the duchy of Burgundy, and to Flanders and Artois, all in French hands. He attacked in Italy first, driving out the French forces and routing a counter-attack mounted by King Francis himself at Pavia in 1526. Francis was ignominiously captured and forced to sign the treaty of Madrid acquiescing to all Charles' demands. "All is lost save honor," Francis wrote his mother, Louise of Savoy, who governed France in his absence. A huge ransom bought his release,

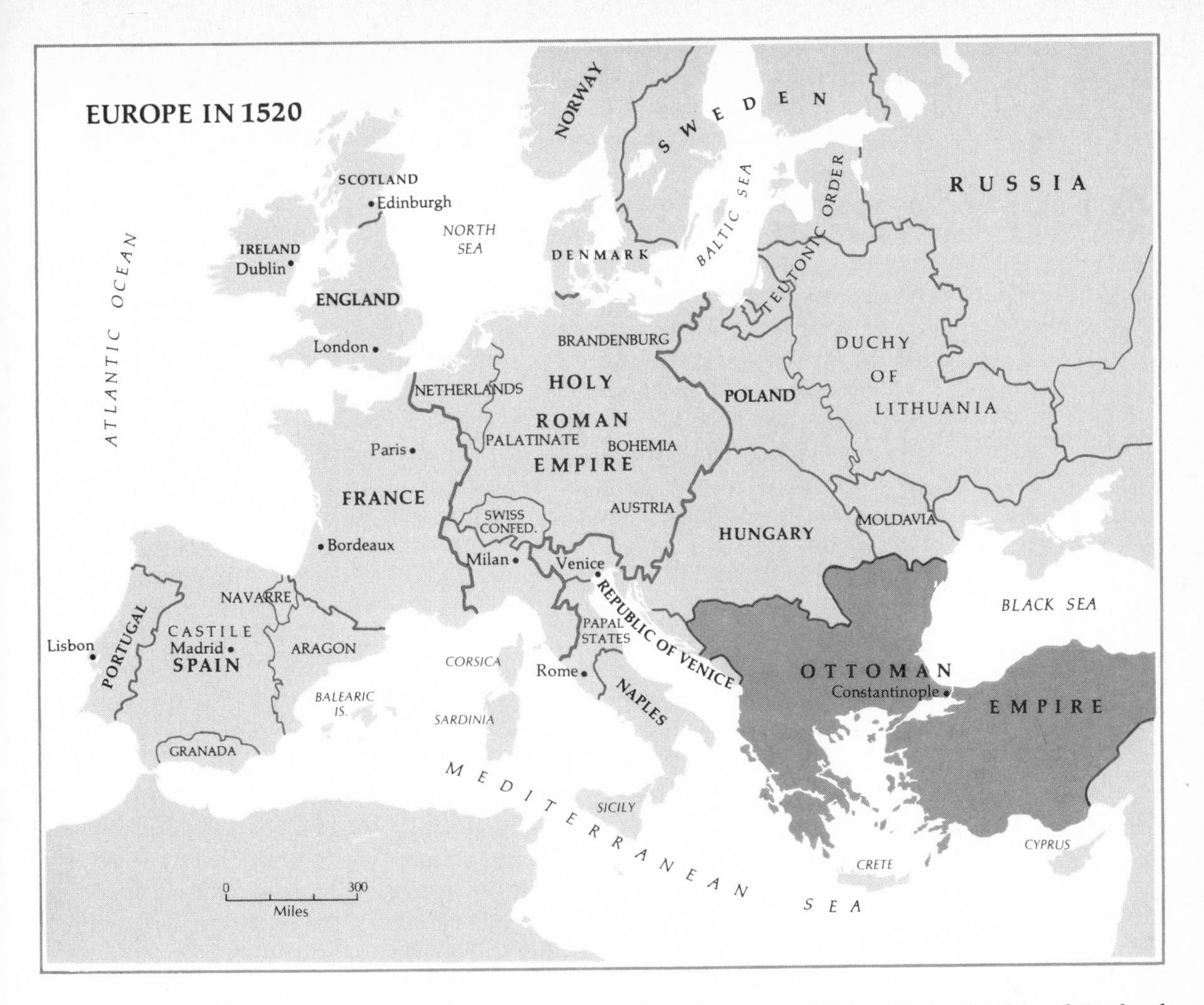

and once home he repudiated the treaty. Under the leadership of England and the papacy, an anti-imperial coalition, the League of Cognac, was formed, and France had a short breathing space. War broke out again, however, and again it went badly for Francis. In 1529, he agreed to the Treaty of Cambrai, the so-called "Ladies' Peace" because it was arranged by Charles' aunt and Francis' mother, in which he renounced all claim to Milan, Flanders, and Artois, retaining only Burgundy, and promised to marry Charles' sister, Eleanor of Portugal. Charles was at the height of his prestige and power.

But Francis had not given up the fight. He made alliances with the Schmalkaldic League and the Turks, to the horror of conservative Catholics, and he and Charles carried on intermittent and indecisive fighting along the border of France and Germany from Groningen in the north to Savoy in the south. France made some temporary gains in Savoy and Piedmont and suffered some losses in the northeast. But on Francis' death in 1547, neither side could claim clear victory. Henry II continued his father's policies, and for fourteen more long years the war dragged on, mostly by diplomacy, but intermixed with sporadic fighting. Both combatants were weary and near bankruptcy by the mid-1550's. Charles perceived that a definitive treaty to bring the much-needed peace was inevitable. He could not face it, as he could not face the religious Peace of Augsburg. In 1556, he abdicated, confirming his Austrian possessions to Ferdinand, who became Holy Roman Emperor, and leaving the remainder of his vast empire to his son, who became Philip II of Spain. Returning to Spain, Charles dragged out the last two years of his life in a monastery, old before his time, spent and disillusioned by what he considered his failures. His son Philip, imbued with his father's pride of family, sense of responsibility, and crusading spirit, would attack many of the same problems, not as an emperor, however, but as king of the greatest state in Christendom, Spain. He was of a newer breed than his father, but like his father, he was the outstanding figure of his age.

Hence, it was Spain rather than Charles' empire that finished off the wars. At St. Quentin in northeastern France in 1557, the Spanish armies won a great victory, only to follow it up with losses to a revived French army under an excellent soldier, Francis, Duke of Lorraine—again a stalemate. Finally, in 1559, Henry and Philip agreed to peace terms, ostensibly so that both might take measures against the Protestant heresies that were infecting their lands. France abandoned all its claims in Italy, but kept several fortresses in Piedmont and Savoy, including Turin, Saluzzo, and Pignerol. The Italian question was settled in Spain's favor, and Spain remained dominant in the peninsula for a century and a half. France also kept the famous "Three Bishoprics" of Metz, Toul, and Verdun on its eastern border. These had been handed over by the German Protestants a few years before. Thus, France, though without substantial influence in either Italy or Germany, had a toehold in both places, useful and tempting for future aggression. Philip of Spain was confirmed in his possession of all the Netherlands, Milan, and Naples. He also agreed to his own marriage with Elizabeth of Valois, daughter of Henry II. This peace, legitimatized as the Treaty of Cateau-Cambrésis, signaled the rise of Spain as Europe's foremost power.

FRANCE: FRANCIS I AND HENRY II

Francis I (1515–1547) was a tall, muscular, and, according to contemporaries, handsome man, brimming with charm and good humor. He was fond of the traditional royal sports, particularly hunting, but he also had a taste for the culture of the Italian Renaissance. He looked and acted like a king, and though at times his policies seemed somewhat immature, on the whole he ruled with determination and did much to advance the cause of monarchy. His son, Henry II (1547–1559), was a big, blond man, morose and somewhat dullwitted, who lacked most of his father's best qualities. He was dominated by favorites: his mistress, Diane of Poitiers; the careful Constable Montmorency; the scheming Guise family.

The Renaissance monarchy in France, as we have seen, was built on the crown's financial independence, which permitted a paid royal army, a sumptuous court, and an adventurous foreign policy. Indeed, throughout

Francis I of France by Jean Clouet. (Giraudon.)

Europe, the French king was envied his resources. The *taille* was the keystone, and long before, the crown had won the right to set the amount of this tax on non-noble property and to collect it at will. "Does the king wish to increase the *tailles* on his people?" the Venetian ambassador asked rhetorically. "However heavy the charges he imposes on them, they pay without question." The Estates General did not meet during the reigns of Francis I and Henry II, and the provincial estates were usually amenable to the king's requests. Furthermore, the Concordat of Bologna, which we shall discuss below, put much of the wealth of the French Church at their disposal. Even so, Francis and Henry experienced severe money problems. They raised taxes, and resorted to borrowing from bankers at high interest rates and selling royal offices by the score. This last practice was employed by every future king of France whose purse was depleted, and helped to strengthen an already numerous office-holding class, the so-called *noblesse de la robe* (nobility of the robe) alongside the old *noblesse de l'épée* (nobility of the sword). But Henry was always short of money, and his successors had not only family rivalry but virtual bankruptcy to plague them.

Both Francis and Henry were personal rulers, relying on a small group of advisors and a still-simple administrative staff. Government in the provinces was delegated to great nobles who acted as "governors" or "lieutenants-general." Francis perceived more clearly than his successors the tendency of these officials to act independently and consequently he withdrew most of their non-military powers. Royal justice and the administration of the crown's affairs in the royal domain remained in the hands of bailiffs and seneschals. Greater unity of the realm was achieved by the ordinance of Villers-Cotterets (1539), which placed all of France under the jurisdiction of the royal courts, eliminating the last enclaves of feudal law, and made French the language of the courts. Henry II issued edicts early in his reign which regularized the office of "secretary of state." There were four secretaries, their duties limited almost entirely to preparation of the king's correspondence at this time. But in the troubled years ahead, these loyal functionaries would begin to assume a policy-making role.

As one of the first acts of his reign, Francis brought the French Church under royal control. By the Concordat of Bologna, a kind of contract negotiated between himself and Pope Leo X in 1516, he agreed to accept the spiritual and theological leadership of the papacy in return for the practical right of appointment to most of the Church benefices in France. The *Parlement* of Paris and many conservative French churchmen protested that the "liberties of the Gallican Church," the right of local election of prelates, had been usurped; but the king's will prevailed. The Gallican Church became a virtual appendage of the crown, a rich reservoir of money and offices which the crown could tap, and remained so down to the end of the Old Regime. In return, the crown became the unswerving champion of the Church. Thus was eliminated the lure that tempted other princes to turn Protestant.

If royal authority was strengthened and consolidated in France during the reigns of Francis I and Henry II, it was still far from "absolute." The realm still harbored powerful forces opposed to unlimited monarchy, forces that had the intellectual if not the material support of many thoughtful men. In the 1520's, for example, Francis' cousin, Charles, Duke of Bourbon, withdrew his allegiance from Francis and went into the service of Charles V. He accused Francis of breaking his feudal contract by trying to dispossess him of his extensive lands in central France. Francis, in turn, charged him with *lése majesté,* treason against the crown. Parlement sympathized with the duke as did most of the nobility, and Francis had a most difficult time forcing through the court an order of condemnation and confiscation. Under Henry II, as we have noted, great families rose to prominence as advisors of a fundamentally weak king. On one side were the Guise, with the Duke of

Henry II of France in the Year of his Succession to the Throne. He is posed here as a Roman general, for the classical Renaissance tradition was well established in France by this time.

Guise and Cardinal of Lorraine the leaders, on the other the heirs of Charles of Bourbon. Both clans were ambitious and selfish, their aim not to prevent tyranny in the interests of public welfare but to increase their own wealth and power. They found eventual support, not as their earlier counterparts had done in landed wealth and provincial loyalties, but in religion. They used Protestantism and Catholicism to serve political ends. The strength of tradition when buttressed by religion and the still-considerable weaknesses of royalty were measured in the terrible domestic chaos into which France fell during the reigns of Henry's unfortunate sons.

ENGLAND: FROM HENRY VIII TO ELIZABETH I

Henry VIII (1509–1547), like Francis I, was a big man but not so big that Francis could not throw him, which he did in an impromptu wrestling match on the Field of the Cloth of Gold in 1520. He was handsome, gay, cultured, a talented musician, and a self-styled theologian. He was fond of games

Field of the Cloth of Gold Painted by an Unknown Artist. Henry VIII arrived in France (left) in 1520 to discuss matters of state with Francis. Colorful tents were set up, and pageants, tournaments, and sporting events were held to entertain the pair of kings. The Lord Chamberlain, St. James Palace.

and parties, and he had a feeling for magnificence and display that came as a welcome relief to Englishmen tired of the stingy ways of his austere father, Henry VII. From his father, he inherited a reasonably secure throne, an overflowing treasury, and a tradition of royal authority, but no great interest in the day-to-day business of government. The problem of an assured succession troubled him. As we have seen, fear of not having a male heir influenced his decision to divorce his first wife, Catherine of Aragon. But by the end of his reign, even a woman could safely inherit. He looked upon money as something to spend. He spent it on himself and on raising English prestige abroad. Most of his foreign policy schemes were unrealistic and, from the standpoint of those who thought like his father, stupidly wasteful. But they managed to win Scotland and make England's presence felt among the greater powers on the Continent. Meanwhile, his accession as head of the Church of England did much to enhance royal authority. Actual rule he left to others throughout most of his life, first to the diligent but too-ambitious Cardinal Thomas Wolsey, then to the clever royalist Thomas Cromwell, becoming his own "first minister" only after 1540.

The great affair of Henry's reign was his divorce and the separation of the English Church from Rome, which occupied the decade and a half after 1527. Prior to this date, Wolsey pursued his diplomacy of grandeur to please his royal master and advance his own fortunes. He may actually have tried to head off the Habsburg-Valois collision by the Treaty of London (1518), but much of his policy was aimed at pure dynastic aggrandizement. On the whole, he failed. If England's stock as a kingdom rose slightly, its purse shrank alarmingly. Wolsey's domestic policy was equally unproductive. He employed most of the methods of government introduced by Henry VII. The "Star Chamber," where heavy fines and imprisonment awaited

Henry VIII in 1544. By this time Henry had settled into his role as head of the English Church, and was spending his remaining years contentedly in company with his sixth and last wife, Catherine Parr.

over-mighty nobility, and the Court of Requests, where the lowly could be heard, were the chief instruments of royal justice. In the counties, the justices of the peace were becoming better established as local agents of the crown. Routine central administration remained in the hands of middle-class men, lifted to high positions to replace the untrustworthy nobility. Thomas Cromwell, an administrator of great skill, did much to regularize this administration during his ten years of office.

Henry VIII and his ministers also depended on established sources of income, though they increased them in various ways. The most important were levies of various kinds, on income and property, on imports and exports, and so on. The crown encouraged the commerce and industry on which most taxation fell, and the economy prospered. Exports of cloth from London, for example, doubled during Henry VIII's time. Confiscations produced additional revenue, particularly those resulting from the dissolution of the monasteries, though the crown realized only a fraction of the value of the monastic lands by selling them quickly and cheaply. Finally, Henry, in the 1540's, began to debase the currency, a desperate expedient which in this case, as in others, brought immediate dividends, but caused in the long run more harm than good.

Henry, like his father, avoided asking the Parliament for money. Rather, and this was also like his father, he made the Parliament serve a strong monarchy. Scrupulous in his adherence to constitutional procedures, he demanded and received Parliamentary approval of all his acts. He achieved this partnership between himself and the representative body by influencing elections, by careful management of debate, and by skillful lobbying, but mostly because the bulk of the English people were favorable to his policies. Under Henry VIII, England seemed to be moving purposefully forward, leaving behind the bad days of Lancaster and York and the Wars of the Roses. Parliament was becoming more institutionalized all the time, but the time had not yet come for it to assert its claim to rule in the king's stead.

Edward VI of England Painted by an Unknown Artist.

Henry VIII's only son, Edward VI (1547–1553), and eldest daughter, Mary (1553–1558), reigned briefly and brought to near-disaster the work of the first two Tudors. Edward never ruled. He ascended the throne at nine years and died at fifteen. The two regents, the dukes of Somerset and Warwick, were neither particularly capable men. Somerset was a liberal in his theology and a conservative in his economic and social thought, determined, on the one hand, to make the English Church "Protestant," and, on the other, to protect the "poor commons" from the great landowners who were enclosing good farmland to raise sheep. He alienated religious extremists, both Catholic and Protestant, and all landowners, wool merchants, and cloth manufacturers to whom sheep were the chief means to wealth. Warwick overthrew him and reversed his economic policy, while continuing the religious shift away from Rome. Warwick was a self-interested man, more concerned with feathering his own nest than with good government. His regime was crumbling when young Edward, a tubercular, died in 1553.

Mary Tudor as a Young Woman. Raised by her firmly Catholic mother, Catherine of Aragon, Mary was pious and plain-looking. She sincerely, and in the best way she knew how, sought throughout her reign to return England to the Roman fold.

Edward's half sister Mary was the second child of Henry VIII to ascend the English throne. The daughter of Catherine of Aragon and a pious Catholic, she spent her reign in a clumsy, though well-meaning, effort to return her country to the Roman fold. She provoked resentment first and then open rebellion by her ill-advised stand. The rebellion failed, but the resentment grew in the fires of Smithfield, where many Protestants, including

Archbishop Cranmer himself, were burned. Her marriage to Philip II of Spain alienated her further from her subjects, most of whom were anti-Spanish. They identified Catholicism and Counter-Reformation with Spain while Protestantism became linked in their minds with English patriotism. Mary's success, therefore, was minimal. Parliament resisted full surrender to papal allegiance, insisting that English civil laws were superior to Church laws and that monastic lands that had been confiscated should remain in private hands. Mary's pro-Spanish policy also proved a failure. At Philip's behest, she aligned England against France; but in the war that followed, she lost Calais, last English foothold on the Continent. Her greatest frustration, however, was her inability to bear a child by Philip. She left as heir her half sister Elizabeth, with the fear that all she had tried to accomplish for Catholicism and Spain would soon be undone.

FURTHER READING

There are several biographies of Emperor Charles V. The best is K. Brandi, * *Charles V* (1939), which sees Charles as a dynast who failed to develop a coherent "German" policy. E. Armstrong, *Emperor Charles V,* 2 vols. (1902), is still useful if used along with Brandi. R. Tyler, *The Emperor Charles V* (1956), is good. Charles' Spanish policy is best treated by J. H. Elliot, * *Imperial Spain, 1469–1716* (1964); and J. R. Lynch, *Spain under the Habsburgs,* I (1964); but see also R. Trevor Davies, * *The Golden Century of Spain, 1501–1621* (1937). B. Chudoba, *Spain and the Empire, 1519–1643* (1952), looks at Charles from the Austrian Habsburg point of view.

The most recent general work on the period of Charles' reign is G. R. Elton, ed., *The New Cambridge Modern History,* vol. II, which contains a chapter on each of the continental European states. On the whole, it is disappointing. Much more useful are G. R. Elton, * *Reformation Europe, 1517–1559* (1963); and E. F. Rice, * *The Foundations of Early Modern Europe, 1460–1559* (1969). H. G. Koenigsberger and G. L. Mosse, *Europe in the Sixteenth Century* (1969), is broader but good, and contains an excellent bibliography. For the particular states, in addition to books cited in Part VII, Chapter 4, consult: J. D. Mackie, *The Earlier Tudors, 1485–1558* (1952), for England; L. Batiffol, *The Century of the Renaissance* (1916), for France; and for the Low Countries, the first chapters of P. Geyl, * *The Revolt of the Netherlands* (1958). C. Petrie, *Earlier Diplomatic History, 1492–1713* (1949), is a most useful handbook.

*Books available in paperback edition are marked with an asterisk.

PART IX

We have seen the beginnings of the transition from the medieval form of western civilization to its early modern form. The era of the Renaissance and the Reformation introduced striking new elements of a religious, esthetic, political, and geographic nature into western culture. These were not quickly or easily absorbed, and the result was more confusion, disorder, and conflict.

By the middle of the sixteenth century—when this section begins—equilibrium had still not been achieved. By the end of it, as we shall see, certain matters were in the process of resolution. By 1609, it was already becoming clear that the Roman Catholic Church could not stamp out Protestant heresy while Protestantism would not overwhelm Roman Catholicism. The Habsburgs and the Spanish monarchy had passed the peak of their influence, and the rulers of Catholic France, Protestant England, and an independent Netherlands were seizing the reins of power.

The period of time from about the middle of the fifteenth century (1450) through the first decade of the seventeenth (150 years) was an expansive one for Europe. Population increased dramatically. Europe expanded geographically, as well, exploring by sea the outer edges of all the other continents of the world and establishing colonial empires on these peripheries. Partly because of this physical expansion, commercial activity in Europe quickened and prices rose. Faced with more mouths to feed, European agriculture failed to expand significantly or to improve its techniques. Thus, the supply of food and fiber remained approximately stable, while prices rose, so that the standard of living of the average European probably fell.

Historians have characterized the second half of the sixteenth century under several rubrics, none of which seems entirely satisfactory. Since Philip II of Spain was the dominant figure in European politics from 1556 until his death in 1598, this period is often called "The Age of Philip II." Since it was during these years that the Roman Catholic Church rose to meet the persistent and spreading challenge of Protestantism, some historians choose to refer to this period as the "Era of the Counter-Reformation." Finally, the towering achievements of the scientists who followed after Copernicus (d. 1543)—Tycho Brahe, Kepler, and Galileo—have led others to speak of this span of time as the "Age of the Scientific Revolution."

The first two chapters of this section will describe the long-term economic and social changes—including the so-called Overseas Expansion—that marked this transitional period of early modern Europe. The fifth and last chapter will treat the intellectual developments, especially those in the scientific realm, whose effects were less immediately felt by most Europeans but would eventually change their world nonetheless. In these three chapters, we shall not be limited to the last fifty years of the sixteenth century, but will move forward or backward with our chronology as necessary to give coherence to our story.

The third and fourth chapters of this section will fill in the political and, of necessity, the religious story of the turbulent period from 1559 to 1609, dominated by the figure of Philip II of Spain. The year 1559 is the year of the Treaty of Cateau-Cambrésis, which brought to a temporary halt the dynastic struggles of the early sixteenth century. In 1609, a temporary truce in the Netherlands marked, in many respects, the end of the hegemony of Spain and the emergence of France, England, and the United Provinces of the Netherlands as the dominant powers of seventeenth-century European civilization. In this age of Spanish hegemony, a great European civil war was in progress, in the course of which Christians continued to persecute and kill one another in the name of Christ, as well as in pursuit of power, prestige, and territorial gain.

SEVENTEENTH-CENTURY DUTCH SHIP

NEW FRONTIERS IN AN EXPANSIVE ERA

LEGACY OF THE PAST

In response to Protestantism, some Roman Catholics adopted an approach to religion as a direct, personal experience available to the humblest of men. Caravaggio (1573–1610) was an Italian who depicted the Virgin Mary (in the words of a contemporary) "like some filthy whore from the slums." This style, now called "baroque," spread quickly to north and central Europe. (Louvre.)

During these years the great Spanish and Portuguese empires in the Americas were firmly consolidated, laying the historical basis for what is called "Latin" America. A new dimension to the multiracial societies of America was added by the large-scale importation of black African slaves to the western hemisphere. Henceforth, black people would play a basic role in the history of "Latin" America and later of North America. Overseas expansion also stimulated the growth of a vital new commercial capitalism in northwestern Europe, and this commercial capitalism would spur the further economic expansion of the next two centuries.

It was during this period that the two main powers of northwestern Europe, England and Holland, established their identity as independent Protestant powers. The outcome of this struggle helped to guarantee that nearly all of northern Europe would become Protestant, and Roman Catholicism could no longer be the almost universal religion of the Western world.

These years also bequeathed major new intellectual and artistic achievements: new scientific investigation highlighted by the "Copernican revolution" in astronomy; the baroque culture of the Catholic Counter-Reformation, climaxed by a new realism in painting and major architectural achievements such as the building of St. Peter's Cathedral in Rome; and two great, though quite different, national literatures: the Spanish literature of the "Golden Age," which reached its apex in Cervantes, the world's first great modern novelist, and the splendors of English Elizabethan literature, culminating in the work of William Shakespeare.

MAJOR EVENTS, 1550-1610

	Overseas Expansion	*Philip II's Problems*	*France and Britain*	*Science and Culture*
1550–	End of the *Conquista* era; consolidation of Spanish Empire in the New World		Rapid growth of Protestantism in Britain and France (1547 on) d. Edward VI; accession Mary Tudor (1553) Persecution of English Protestants (1553)	
1555–	Portuguese Empire at its height	Philip m. Mary Tudor (1554) Philip II vows to build the Escorial Palace (1557) d. Charles V (1558); Philip king Philip m. Elizabeth of Valois (1559)	d. Mary Tudor; accession Elizabeth (1558) d. Henry II of France; accession Francis II (1559)	St. John's College, Oxford, founded (1555) Work begins on the dome and nave of St. Peter's, Rome (1558)
1560–	Spanish take Philippines; Spanish drive French from Florida (1564)	Extirpation of Protestantism in Spain (1559–60)	d. Francis II; accession Charles IX (1560) Mary Stuart to Scotland (1561) 39 Articles of the Anglican Church (1563)	Michelangelo dies at age 89 (1564)
1565–		Incident of the Beggars in the Netherlands (1565) Turkish assault on Malta (1565) Alva and blood in the Netherlands (1567–1573) Revolt of the Moriscos in Spain (1568–70)	Mary Stuart flees to England (1569)	Breugel paints the "Triumph of Death" (1568) C. Plantin begins publication of *Polyglot Bible* (1569)
1570–		Battle of Lepanto (1571)	Massacre of Huguenots in France (1572) d. Charles IX; accession Henry III (1574)	Palestrina made choirmaster at Julian Chapel, Rome; Benvenuto Cellini dies (1571)
1575–	Drake's circumnavigation (1577–1580)	Pacification of Ghent (1576) Duke of Parma in the Netherlands League of Arras and Union of Utrecht (1579)		El Greco moves to Spain (1575); Titian dies, aged 99 (1576)

	Overseas Expansion	*Philip II's Problems*	*France and Britain*	*Science and Culture*
1580–		Begin Spanish captivity of Portugal (1580)		Montaigne's first books of *Essays* published (1580)
		Murder of William of Orange (1584)		
1585–			Elizabeth sends troops to the Netherlands (1585) War of the Three Henries (1585–89)	Will Shakespeare moves to London (1585)
		The Armada (1588)	Execution Mary Queen of Scots (1587) Murder of the Duke of Guise (1588) Murder of Henry III; contested accession of Henry IV (Bourbon) (1589)	
	Hakluyt's *Principal Navigations* (1589)		War in France—League *vs.* Henry (1589–98)	
1590–		d. Alexander Farnese (Parma) (1592)	Henry IV abjures Protestantism (1593)	
1595–	Dutch East Indian expedition (1595); conquest of the Portuguese East Indian Empire	d. Philip II; accession Philip III (1598)	Edict of Nantes (1598)	A new "Globe" theater opens in Bankside on the Thames (1599)
1600–	British East India Company founded (1600) Dutch East India Company founded (1602)		d. Elizabeth; accession James VI of Scotland (Stuart) as James I (1603)	J. Kepler joins Tycho Brahe in Prague (1600) Giordano Bruno burned at the stake in Rome (1600)
1605–	Settlement of Jamestown (1607)			
	Foundation of Quebec by French (1608)	Expulsion of the Moriscos (1608–11) Twelve Years' Truce in the Netherlands begins (1609)		Cervantes' *Don Quixote* published in Madrid and Lisbon (1609)
1610–			Assassination of Henry IV; accession of Louis XIII (1610)	Galileo publishes first pictures of moon as seen through a telescope (1610)

War in the Netherlands

Civil War in France

1 Continued European Expansion

By 1559, the Overseas Expansion of Europe was well under way. It had been started by the Portuguese, who had gone over the water to attack the Moor in North Africa (1415) and then had explored the West African coast, rounded the Cape of Good Hope, and established a commercial empire that reached as far as the Spice Islands and China. Late in the fifteenth century, the Portuguese were joined on the high seas by the Spanish Castilians. Thus, the Expansion was at first an Iberian monopoly.

We have seen that, immediately upon da Gama's return from India in 1499, the Portuguese began to reap rich returns from their empire. Not so the Spaniards. By the time of Columbus' death in 1506, Cathay, Japan, and the Indies had not yet been found to the west, and the mysterious lands he had discovered yielded little gold or silver and no spices.

In the decades after Columbus' first voyage, however, Cortes penetrated Mexico and laid his avaricious hands on the Aztecs' accumulation of precious metal. The delayed rewards began finding their way to Spain where they brought joy to the new young Habsburg king and emperor, Charles V. During the 1530's, Pizarro overthrew the Inca in Peru and acquired a room full of gold. Thus, what had been for so long a disappointment became an empire rivalling and perhaps surpassing that of the Portuguese in value.

Then, in the mid-1540's, the advancing Spanish *conquistadores* opened a veritable mountain of silver on the eastward slope of the Andes in what is today Bolivia. Soon a roaring mining town developed at Potosí (altitude nearly 13,000 feet), which by the early seventeenth century achieved a population of 150,000, larger than all but two European cities. Swelling the product of the great Mexican and Peruvian mines, silver from Potosí flowed over the ocean to Spain and thence across Europe, where it measurably increased the supply available for coinage.

Meanwhile, as we have seen, other *conquistadores* were at work subduing Indians and competing with one another. As a result of their work and as a result of the efforts of royal administrators who took over from the *conquistadores,* by the year 1559 Castile held sway over much of South

Mariner's Mirrour. The frontispiece of a compendium of Dutch nautical information, "The Mariner's Mirrour," was published in England in 1588, the year before Hakluyt's "The Principal Navigations. . . ." Note the various marine instruments, the coat of arms of Queen Elizabeth below the celestial map. The book included a description of the exploits of Sir Francis Drake. (Folger Library.)

America, Central and Caribbean America, and parts of North America. The age of conquest was over and the era of consolidation was at hand. Spain was able to consolidate and hold on in America; but, as we shall see, the Portuguese found their resources unequal to the task of keeping what they had won. Meanwhile, other competitors for empire and gold were moving in.

CONSOLIDATION OF THE SPANISH EMPIRE

As we have seen, the Spanish conquest in America took some of the forms of the medieval *reconquista* (reconquest) in Iberia itself. In that earlier, centuries-long operation, during which the Moor was driven south and eventually off the peninsula, the work had often been done by *adelentados* or frontier military governors who bore the expenses of the conquest and the brunt of the fighting. Their rewards were great power and wealth in the newly conquered territory. This arrangement worked equally well in America for a time. But, as a base for the future organization of the empire, this feudal pattern ceased to harmonize with the realities of the sixteenth century.

With the troublesome nobles of Castile in mind, the Spanish crown discouraged the development of vast hereditary estates in the New World, doing everything in its power to keep control in the hands of officials appointed by and responsible to the central government. In this effort the crown was successful up to a point. In its second effort, the Christian monarchy listened to the counsels of the Spanish Catholic Church, which tended to think of the American natives as souls to be won rather than as workers to be exploited. But the efforts of humanitarians in Spanish America

Potosí. Situated in the Andes nearly 13,000 feet above sea level and 400 miles from the nearest seaport, Potosí, in present-day Bolivia, was one of the most amazing of all colonial cities. By the end of the sixteenth century, its population neared 150,000. Thousands of Indians worked at forced labor in the silver mines, and mules in endless columns brought the mercury required to process the ore from a point 800 miles away. (Hispanic Society of America.)

generally gave way before the pressure of demands for cheap labor.

Such men as the Dominican, Bartolomé de Las Casas (1474–1566), the first priest to be ordained in the American colonies, devoted their lives to mitigating the plight of the Indians, especially in the West Indies. Despite nearly heroic efforts, Las Casas met with disappointment at every turn. Even his well-meant efforts to encourage the importation of African slaves as substitutes for the Indians he tried to protect was a disaster, as he himself came to realize.

As early as 1501, the Castilian crown had authorized the importation of Africans to the colonies. At first, a small but flourishing traffic in both white and black slaves among Arab, Portuguese, and other European traders in the Mediterranean (who profited from selling prisoners taken in African tribal wars), the capture and sale of blacks for shipment to the New World began in earnest in the sixteenth century. As the Indians languished, died out, or were exterminated, blacks were brought in to work the sweltering sugar cane fields of the Caribbean islands, to man the mines, and to do other heavy chores the Spaniards were too lazy or too proud to undertake. Thought to be better able to withstand the heat and primitive living conditions and accustomed to a meagre diet, those blacks who survived being crowded into the filthy holds of sailing vessels for the Atlantic voyage were sold in slave markets to Spanish landlords and miners who regarded them as less than human.

Still, in some ways, slavery in the Spanish New World was less harsh than forms that developed elsewhere. Slave codes required minimum standards of food and care and established age limits for work. Branding and mutilating of slaves was prohibited. Slaves could purchase their own freedom for a price fixed by courts without reference to the price that had originally been paid for them. Intermingling of the races, while discouraged, did occur. The numbers of blacks imported into the Spanish colonies are difficult to document, since few records have survived. But the trickle of blacks brought to the New World in the early sixteenth century turned into a river of "black gold" in the seventeenth.

Well before the end of the sixteenth century, then, the main lines of Spanish colonial administration and policy as they were to shape the America's until the 1820's were established. By and large, the result was a remarkable achievement, from the Spanish point of view. Able administrators in Peru and Mexico tried to regularize affairs in the name of the king of Castile according to the centralizing ideas of modern royal absolutism.

From the homeland, the empire continued to be administered and regulated by two central agencies: the *Consejo de las Indias* (Council of the Indies) and the *Casa de contratación* (House of Trade). The former body consisted of royal appointees who legislated for the colonies, approved appointments of all colonial officials, and served as the final court of appeals for legal processes originating in the Indies. Subordinate to the Council, the *Casa de contratación* supervised and controlled all commerce with the West Indies. Anyone who wanted to export a bag of nails or a ball of wax to the colonies had to apply to the *Casa* for a permit. Both agencies were kept very busy dealing, on the Spanish side, with job seekers and would-be entrepreneurs and, on the colonial side, with regulating administrators thousands of miles from Madrid or Seville and from each other.

The regulation was intended to be close. Only nine ports—all depending on the crown of Castile—were permitted to send ships to America. All homeward-bound ships were required to put in at one port, at first Cadiz and later Seville, where the *Casa de contratación* was located. Only Roman Catholic Castilians (and not other Spaniards) could engage in the colonial trade or emigrate to America.

Securing the Sea Lanes If this regulation was intended primarily to maintain the security of the empire, it succeeded. Year after year the "plate fleet" (convoys of ships carrying precious metals) arrived safely at Seville or Cadiz, where the king's agents took the crown's share, the royal fifth (*quinto*). The fact that the plate fleet was able to reach home almost every year, and the fact that Spain was able to keep its American empire for nearly three hundred years were the result of another kind of consolidation, namely the organization of communications and the defense of the sea lanes between Spain and the various parts of Spanish America. For by the middle of the sixteenth century, Spanish control was being severely challenged.

The Caribbean, the Gulf of Mexico, and the Florida Strait became favorite haunts for French, Dutch, and English freebooters who sought to steal the treasure that the Spaniards were taking home from Mexico and

Peru. Havana, a crucial port and the gathering place for homeward-bound Spanish fleets, was twice sacked by buccaneers. In 1562, a group of French adventurers claimed Florida for France; and in 1564, a French settlement was founded at the mouth of the St. John's river (near present-day Jacksonville). John Hawkins, English slaver, trader, and pirate, organized four predatory expeditions to Spanish-American waters, and Francis Drake led two raiding parties. In the course of one of these he managed to intercept a Spanish mule-train carrying silver from Peru across the Isthmus of Panama.

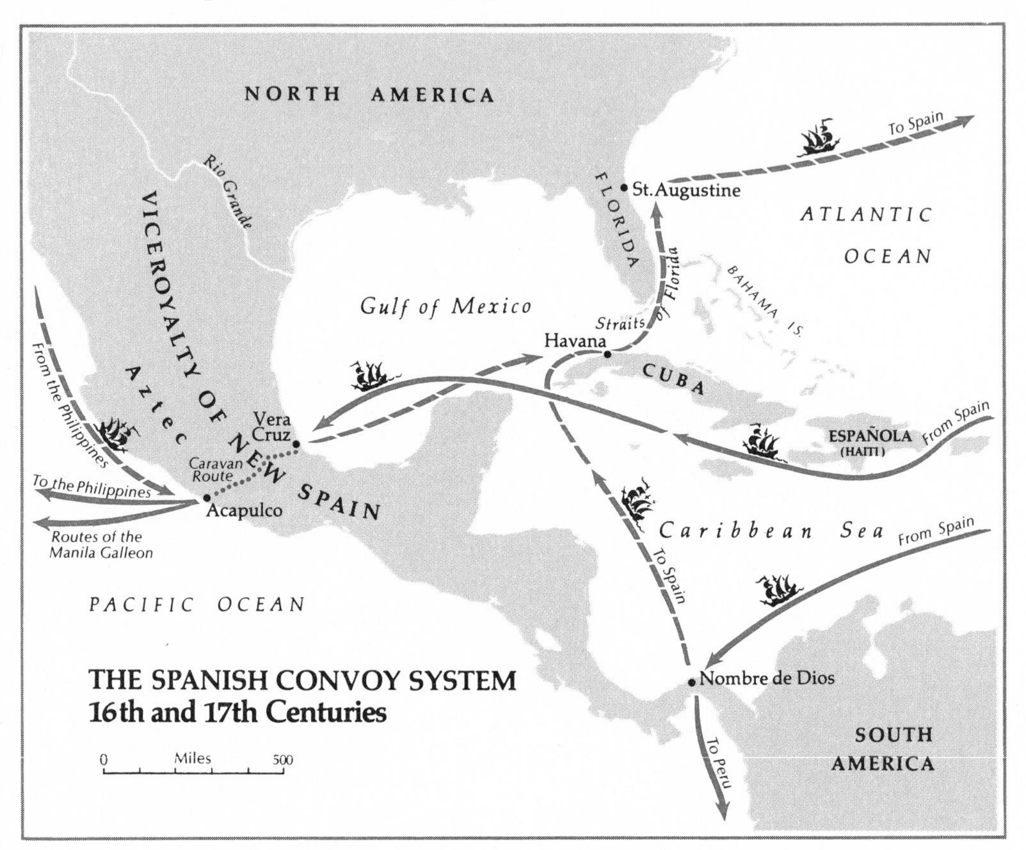

To meet these threats, an able admiral, Pedro Menéndez de Aviles, organized a comprehensive convoy system and constructed fortifications at vital spots. The system he developed provided that the homeward-bound ships from Mexico should sail in late winter from Vera Cruz to Havana. There they were met by the fleet that sailed from the Isthmus of Panama carrying silver from Peru. Then, together and under convoy they beat northward through the strait between Florida and the Bahamas before turning east when they encountered a westerly wind. Given the wind patterns of the area, this was the only practicable route for sailing vessels to pass from the Gulf of Mexico to the Atlantic. Thus, Havana, the hinge of the whole system, and the Florida Strait assumed great strategic importance.

To secure Havana, Menéndez and his successors built strong fortifications (Punta and Morro Castle) that kept Havana safe, despite frequent attack, for nearly two hundred years. To protect his convoys as they navigated the Florida Strait, Menéndez attacked the French settlement on the east coast of Florida and killed the entire garrison. To prevent further intrusions he established forts at St. Augustine and at four other spots along that vital coast.

The Spaniards did not establish effective control north of Florida in eastern North America, nor did they attempt to under Philip the Prudent. In a very real sense, Menéndez' work saved the Spanish American empire and forced the northern Europeans to do most of their empire building elsewhere in America, if they were to do it at all.

The Philippines Despite his caution, Philip II did add to Spain's imperial holdings by acquiring, during the late sixteenth century, the islands in the Pacific named for him: the Philippines. These islands had been earlier claimed for the crown of Castile by Ferdinand Magellan, a Portuguese navigator in the service of Philip's father, Charles, in the course of the first recorded circumnavigation of the globe. Charles ordered several other expeditions to the East—Charles was much more interested in overseas expansion and conquest than his son—but these attempts were so unsuccessful that in 1529 he had agreed to a treaty with Portugal establishing a new line of demarcation that left the Philippines in Portuguese territory.

Despite this agreement, the Spanish crown persisted in attempts to secure a foothold in Asia. The work of conquest was begun by the Spaniard Miguel Lopez de Legazpi, who sailed from the west coast of America with four hundred men and a number of friars. The motives behind this move are not entirely clear. Possibly Philip felt that a holding on the western side of the Pacific Ocean would contribute to the security of his American empire; possibly he took the Philippines simply to prevent another power from taking these islands.

Unlike the earlier *conquistadores,* Legazpi conducted himself with considerable finesse, and the peoples of the islands received him fairly cordially. The friars made converts with great success. In 1571, Legazpi founded the city of Manila as his capital after defeating a native ruler in battle. Gradually, thereafter, subjugation of the various inhabitants of the islands continued until by the middle of the seventeenth century a large number of the over seven thousand islands in the archipelago were under Spanish control.

The Spanish government did not encourage trade between the Philippines and the rest of the world, nor even with Spain and the rest of the Spanish Empire. Contact between the islands and the Spanish world was limited to one or two galleons per year, which sailed on schedule from Manila to Acapulco on the west coast of Mexico. From there cargoes and

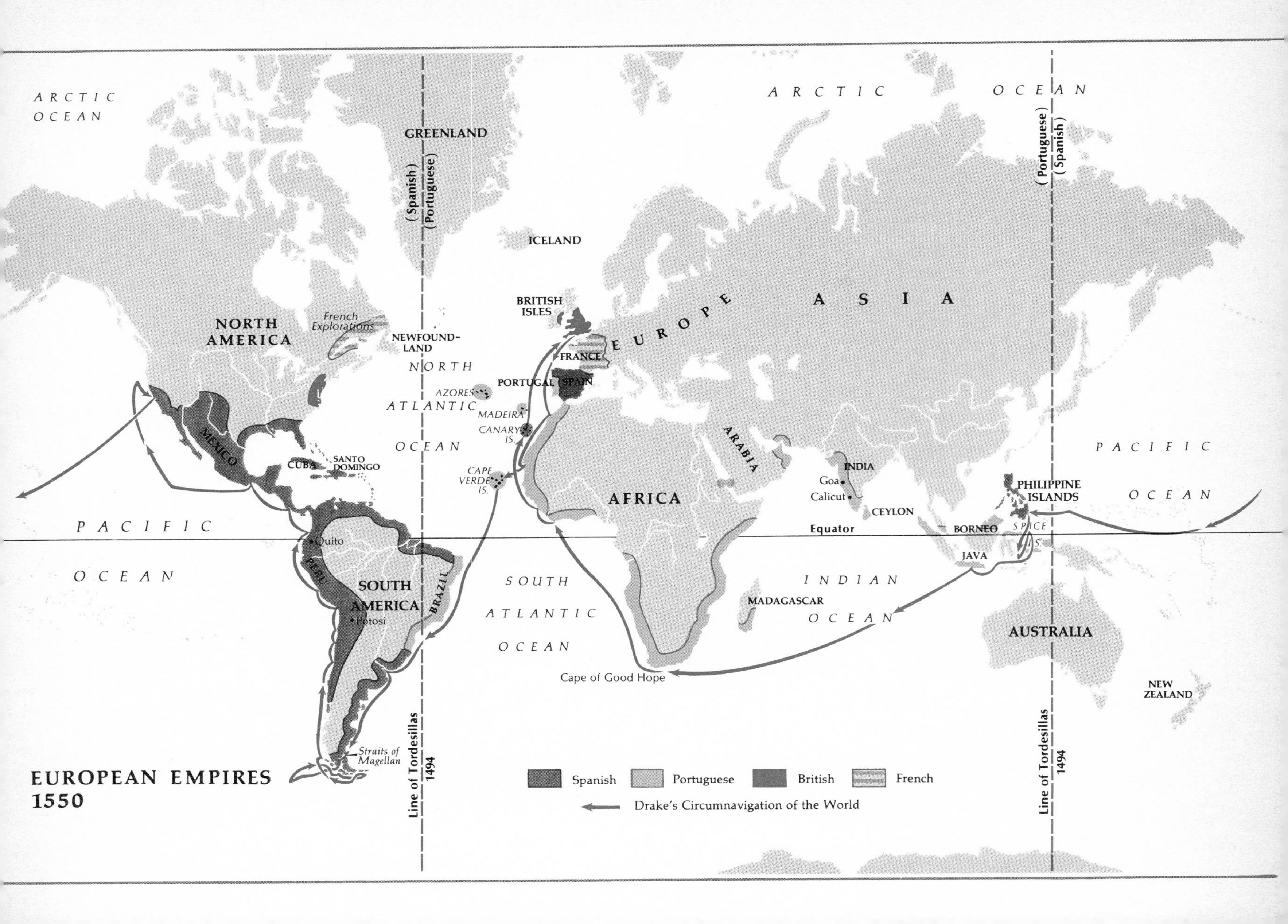
EUROPEAN EMPIRES
1550
ARCTIC OCEAN
GREENLAND
(Spanish)
(Portuguese)
ICELAND
NORTH AMERICA
French Explorations
NEWFOUND-LAND
NORTH ATLANTIC OCEAN
BRITISH ISLES
EUROPE
ASIA
FRANCE
PORTUGAL
SPAIN
AZORES
MADEIRA
CANARY IS.
CAPE VERDE IS.
MEXICO
CUBA
SANTO DOMINGO
ARABIA
INDIA
Goa
Calicut
CEYLON
AFRICA
PHILIPPINE ISLANDS
BORNEO
SPICE IS.
JAVA
PACIFIC OCEAN
Equator
Quito
PERU
SOUTH AMERICA
Potosi
BRAZIL
SOUTH ATLANTIC OCEAN
MADAGASCAR
INDIAN OCEAN
AUSTRALIA
NEW ZEALAND
Cape of Good Hope
Straits of Magellan
Line of Tordesillas 1494
Spanish
Portuguese
British
French
Drake's Circumnavigation of the World

passengers went overland to Vera Cruz to join the regular convoys to Spain. Most of the Spanish emigrants to the Philippines were Augustinian and Dominican friars and Jesuits who worked at converting the natives to Roman Christianity, taught some of them to read and write, and introduced new crops and methods of agriculture.

As usual, the Spanish government issued many admirable decrees that were intended to ensure that the natives should be treated humanely and justly; but, equally as usual, the Spanish governors-general behaved very much as they wished. It is probable, however, that the Filipinos suffered less at the hands of their European rulers than did the Indians of North and South America. Because few Spaniards settled in the islands, there was relatively little pressure to drive away, enslave, or exterminate the natives. Because very little in the way of precious metal was discovered, the Filipinos were not driven down into mines, as were the Indians of Mexico and Peru.

Spain held the Philippines for more than three centuries, until the islands were "liberated" in 1898 by the United States of America. During this period of time, the overwhelming majority of Filipinos became Christians, nominally, at least, thanks to the efforts of the friars.

THE DECLINE OF THE PORTUGUESE EMPIRE

In 1559, the Portuguese Asiatic empire, the work of da Gama, Almeida, and Albuquerque, was at its height. Thereafter it declined precipitously. What were the reasons for this decline? Simply put, Portugal did not have the human and material resources to maintain and defend a world empire.

Established and organized early in the sixteenth century, this empire included Brazil, posts on the west and east coasts of Africa, bases at strategic points in the Indian Ocean, in India itself, the Spice Islands, and a trading station near Canton in China. The Portuguese objective was to control the export trade of this vast region.

The Portuguese Empire remained essentially a commercial empire, and the Portuguese tended realistically to stay out of local politics except when intervention was required for commercial or naval reasons. They were directed by the papal grant of 1493 to convert the heathen; and they did attempt to convert the natives, build churches, and establish monasteries. But there was no significant expansion of Christianity as a result of Portuguese missionary endeavors.

Even when their imperial tide was at the flood the Portuguese were not able fully to enjoy the fruits of their accomplishments. They shipped spices and other merchandise as far as Lisbon, but were unable to manage the European distribution of their Asiatic imports. This was taken in hand by Dutch, Flemish, and Italian carriers who took them to Antwerp, in the Netherlands, which city became the great European market center for the Eastern trade. The profits accruing to the middlemen were probably as great as those of the Portuguese who had taken the great risks and made the long voyages.

The Portuguese continued to dominate their overseas empire until the seventeenth century, despite the fact that a great Muslim power grew up in India—the Mogul Empire—and despite the emergence in the East Indies of powerful Muslim sultanates that threatened Portuguese bases. By virtue of their command of the eastern seas, the Portuguese were able to hang on.

The debacle began in 1578 when King Sebastien of Portugal, the last of a dynasty, undertook a romantic crusade in North Africa. He was soundly beaten by the Moors at Alcazar-el-Kebir and was killed in the defeat. When his successor, an aged great-uncle, died two years later, Philip II of Spain decided to press his hereditary claim to the Portuguese crown. (Philip's

The Portuguese port of Lisbon with its wide and deep natural harbor was and still is the westernmost seaport of the continent of Europe. In the sixteenth and seventeenth centuries, Spanish, Dutch, and English sea captains vied for access to its busy wharves. Philip II gained control of the port in 1580, and his Invincible Armada sailed from Lisbon in 1588. (Folger Library.)

mother had been a Portuguese princess.) By judicious use of propaganda and bribery and by force of arms Philip became King of Portugal and, therefore, master of its Atlantic port, Lisbon, and its overseas empire.

If he had been able to unite the Portuguese Kingdom with his Spanish kingdoms and to coordinate the overseas empires under a single administration, Philip would have ruled a realm mightier than the sum of its component parts. However, the union was only a personal one, and the Spaniards placed more emphasis on the protection of their American empire and upon their struggle for European hegemony than on defending the Portuguese commercial realm in the East. Therefore, when strong European maritime rivals entered their waters, the Portuguese were finished.

English and Dutch Competition In the same year that Portugal fell under Spanish domination (1580), Francis Drake returned triumphantly in the

Golden Hind to Plymouth, England, after his circumnavigation of the globe. The English queen had invested her own funds in his adventure of nearly three years, which had involved a good deal of piracy at the expense of the Spaniards. Drake had visited the Spice Islands and been cordially received by one of the local rulers. After his return, Queen Elizabeth knighted Drake on his own quarterdeck, despite protests from Philip of Spain. After the Spanish Armada had been defeated (1588), Elizabeth authorized an English expedition to Malaya with the intention of interloping in the spice trade. By and large, however, little came of English adventures in the East at this time. It was not until the eighteenth century that the English were to penetrate Asia in force.

When the crowns of Portugal and Spain were placed on one head, another northern power, the United Provinces of the Netherlands, was stimulated to compete with the Portuguese in Asia. Since the 1560's, the Netherlands had been in revolt against their Spanish master, Philip II. The Dutch financed their revolutionary war, in important part, with the profits they derived from the carrying and distribution of Portuguese Asiatic goods from the port of Lisbon to all the rest of Europe. After the unification of the Iberian crowns, the Spanish government quite naturally moved to close this strategically located port to the Dutch. As a result, the latter were quickly inspired to replace the Portuguese on the long haul from Asia so that they could continue their lucrative European distribution trade.

The Portuguese had tended to be close with the secrets of navigation on the sea road to the Indies, secrets they had patiently accumulated over nearly two centuries of exploration. Fortunately for the Dutch, a Netherlander, Jan Huyghen van Linschoten, had spent six years with the Portuguese in India. He published a very informative book of sailing directions. Equipped with this guide, in 1595 a Dutch expedition financed by a group of Amsterdam merchants and commanded by an adventurer named Cornelius Houtman sailed for the Indies. Some of Houtman's ships returned two years later with interesting news about the weaknesses of the Portuguese position and a commercial treaty with the Sultan of Bantam on the Island of Java. Dutch capitalists responded by fitting out a large number of expeditions—sixty by 1602. In 1598, they tried a scientific experiment to determine which was the better route: that of Diaz and Da Gama around the Cape of Good Hope or Magellan's and Drake's route around South America. Nine ships tried the Straits of Magellan and all but one came to grief; thirteen sailed around the Cape of Good Hope and all but one arrived safely. This latter fleet traded successfully and was well received by the Sultans of the Spice Islands, who seem to have been glad to be able to deal with someone besides the Portuguese. In 1601, a Dutch fleet fought Portuguese men o' war off Java and won.

The Dutch captains and traders who were responsible for these adventures in the late sixteenth century did not differ significantly from the Spanish *conquistadores.* Violent and aggressive men, they fought with one another, as well as with the Portuguese and with the natives. The result

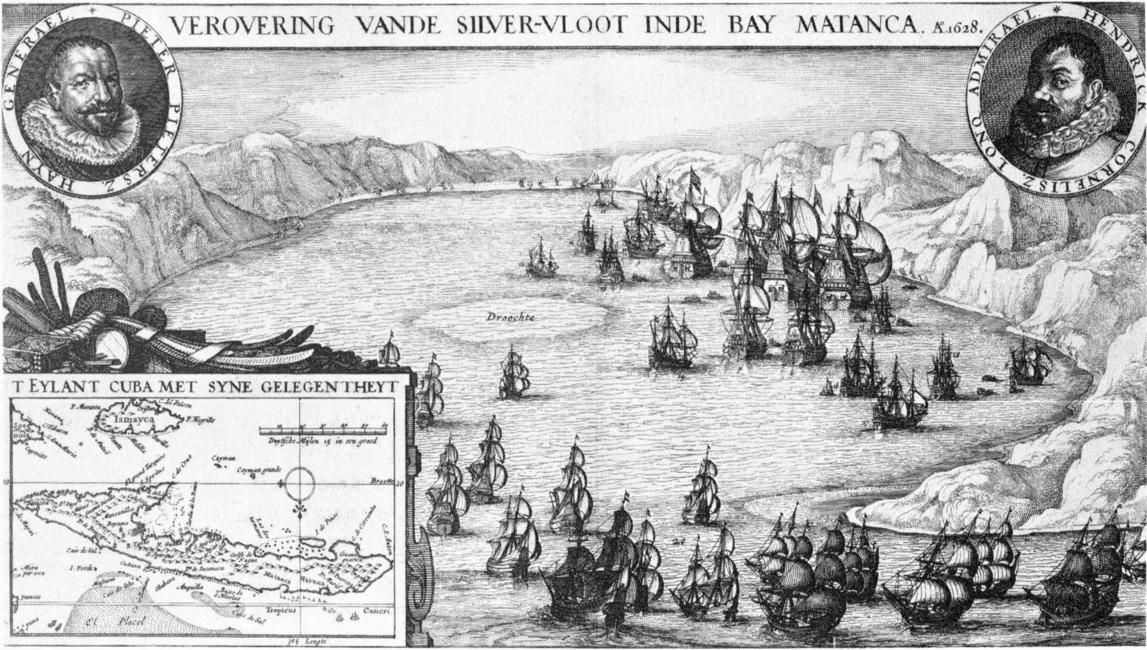

was competitive disorder which disarranged the supply and also the prices of eastern goods and unsettled the affairs of Dutch capitalists. The Dutch States-General (parliament) accordingly agreed in 1602 to establish a monopolistic corporation to handle the far eastern trade. The result of this agreement was the Dutch East India Company, one of the most successful

(Top, page 672) Dutch explorers visited Nova Zembla, an island off the frozen coast of Siberia, as early as 1597. (Bottom, page 672) Dutch capture of the Spanish plate fleet off the southern coast of Cuba in 1628. At right is a seventeenth-century view of the Cape of Good Hope, with sailing vessels belonging to the Dutch East India Company and a fort defending the harbor. (Ryksmuseum/Schultmeijer, *De Gouden Eeuw.*)

and enduring business organizations of all time. Some sixty years after its establishment, it was paying annual dividends of 40 percent; its agents had driven the Portuguese from the East Indies; it supported a colony at the Cape of Good Hope, which served as a watering and victualling station for its fleet of nearly 200 ships; and it commanded an army of 10,000 men. For a short period, the Dutch East India Company was threatened by its slightly older rival, the British East India Company, but the Dutch managed to drive the English out of what we now call Indonesia and Malaya. During the seventeenth century, the English had to be content, as did the French, with a few trading stations along the Indian coast, where the Portuguese also kept a toehold.

Relative late-comers to the business of exploration and empire building, the Dutch made a very good thing of it once they became involved. Their Asian empire proved to be the most durable of all.

OTHER LATE-COMERS AND THE NORTHERN PASSAGES

It should be remembered that to the early explorers and conquerors an empire was valuable chiefly and almost only if it produced high-value goods. The early explorer or conqueror was not looking primarily for timber, fish, wheat, meat, or a place to settle. He was interested in securing those commodities that were part of the traditional interregional trade pattern: gold, silver, spices, and other exotic merchandise. Colonization for its own sake did not inspire empire building; gold and pepper did. Because of the monopoly of the Spaniards and Portuguese over the sources of supply of the desired commodities, early Northern European efforts overseas tended to take the form of piracy rather than parallel imperial activity in other parts of the world such as North America. Later, as they gained confidence, the

Northerners began to think of exploiting directly the good things and places that the Spanish and Portuguese had found.

We have seen that the Dutch borrowed Portuguese navigational secrets to find their way to the Indies in the later sixteenth century. Writing during the latter part of the reign of Henry VIII, an English merchant, Roger Barlow, published a volume by means of which he hoped to turn English attention to the great profit, honor, and glory that would follow once English mariners had found their way to the new worlds. But he felt that it was not possible to compete with the Portuguese via their southern and eastern route nor with the Spaniards by the west. He suggested that the English focus their energies on finding an alternate route. Why not sail over the North Pole to Asia?

Northern Explorations Men of many nations pursued the idea of the northern passage as though it were a new Holy Grail. Many perished in the attempt to reach Asia by sailing north. But despite their failure, the voyages to the north in the end proved to be quite as creative as the southern voyages to the Far East.

Sir Walter Raleigh, the entrepreneur and patron of the first, if very short-lived, English colonies on Roanoke Island in present-day North Carolina (1585–1587), obtained his charter from Queen Elizabeth by way of inheritance from his half-brother, Sir Humphrey Gilbert. Gilbert was an intellectual follower of Barlow and in 1576 wrote a long pseudo-scientific treatise on the possibility of finding a Northwest Passage. In the same year, he invested in the first of Martin Frobisher's three voyages. Gilbert took to the sea himself in 1583 and sailed to his death in search of the Passage. Ostensibly, Raleigh was carrying on the same endeavor.

That Raleigh did not effectively push forward the search for the Northwest Passage is but one symptom of a change that came over the expansive efforts of the northern nations during the last decade and a half of the sixteenth century and into the early seventeenth century. We have already noted that the Dutch dared to attack the Portuguese frontally in Asia, which they reached by sailing the traditional routes. Drake made his circumnavigation during the late 1570's without recourse to a northern passage, and English sea power managed to defeat the Spanish Armada in 1588 without appreciable help either from the weather or from luck. Although the battle of the Armada was not a crushing defeat for Spain nor a crucial victory for England, as is sometimes claimed, it certainly increased English self-confidence on the high seas.

One of the most important books in the history of English expansion, *The Principall Navigations, Voiages, Traffiques and Discoveries of the English Nation,* by Richard Hakluyt (1552–1616), was published in London the year after the Armada. A compilation of accounts of voyages, this book, like Hakluyt's earlier and later writings, was intended to stimulate interest not only in discovery but also in colonization in North America. In the preface to the 1589 edition, Hakluyt exploded Barlow's notion that an easy passage to Asia

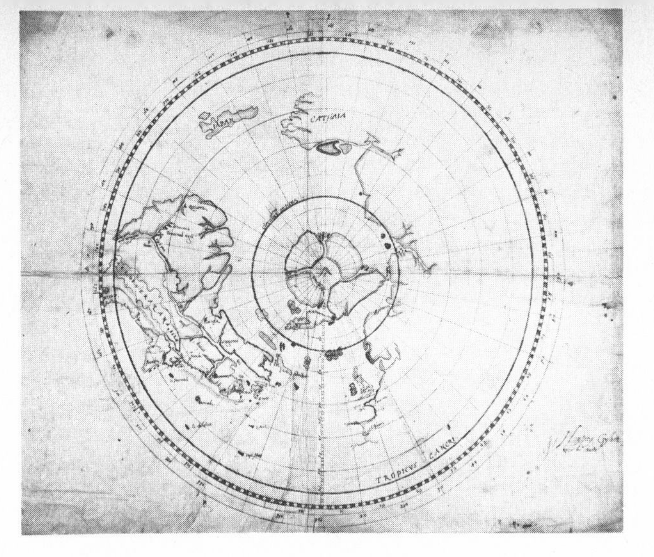

Sir Humphrey Gilbert's Map of the Polar Regions. Drawn by the English explorer in 1582, it shows a passage (left) through North America to Japan and China (top). The next year Gilbert took possession of Newfoundland. (Elkins Collection, Free Library of Philadelphia.)

EARLY QUESTS FOR A NORTHERN PASSAGE TO INDIA

c. 870–c. 1300 Numerous voyages by Norsemen around the North Cape and to the West—Iceland, Greenland, North America.

1497 John Cabot, in English service, sailed to the mouth of the St. Lawrence.

1524 Verrazano, in French service, to Newfoundland.

1534–1541 Three voyages of Jacques Cartier, French, in Gulf of St. Lawrence.

1553 Willoughby and Chancellor around North Cape.

1576–1578 Frobisher's voyages to Canada.

1583 Sir Humphrey Gilbert took possession of Newfoundland.

1585–1587 John Davis in Davis Strait between Greenland and Baffinland.

1594–1597 William Barents and Cornelius Nay, Dutch, around North Cape.

1603 Pontgravé and Champlain along the St. Lawrence River.

1607 Henry Hudson, in English service, set out for China *via* the North Pole—reached Spitsbergen.

1608 Henry Hudson reached ice pack near Spitsbergen.

1609 Henry Hudson, in Dutch service, to Hudson River.

1610 Henry Hudson to Hudson's Bay.

1611 Champlain to Lake Huron.

Attempts to find the Northern Passages did not stop in the early seventeenth century; but later expeditions were inspired more by scientific curiosity than by the hope of finding a practical route to Asia. The Northeast Passage was not forced until 1878–1880, when Nordenskiold sailed with a scientific expedition around North Cape and across the top of Siberia, then south through Bering Strait. The Northwest Passage was made in 1906 by the great Norwegian explorer Amundsen, who froze a small sloop into the ice among the islands of northern Canada and was carried by the drift from the Atlantic to the Pacific, but very slowly.

could be found in the north. Rendering high tribute to the hardy adventurers of all nations who had exposed themselves "unto the rigor of the stern and uncouth Northern seas," he said that the time had now come for realism and self-confidence:

But it is high time for us to weigh anchor, to hoist up our sails, to get clear of the boisterous, frosty and misty seas, and with all speed to direct our course for the mild, lightsome, temperate, and warm Atlantic Ocean over which the Spaniards and the Portuguese have made so many pleasant, prosperous and golden voyages.

EUROPEAN COLONIZATION IN NORTH AMERICA

The late-comers were ready to take hold. But, because they were late and because they had been directed toward the northern part of North America by the dream of a northern passage and by effective Spanish defenses, their empires turned out to be quite different from either the Portuguese Asian empire or the Spanish American empire.

Shortly after the turn of the seventeenth century, four northern European peoples and states began to colonize various parts of North America. It is interesting to note that three of these colonizations—those of the French, English, and Dutch—began at very nearly the same time; and they probably took place for the same reasons. Sweden came somewhat later.

Although Spain claimed all of America west of the 1494 line of demarcation, it became obvious from events that Spanish power could defend only the areas that it had effectively occupied. It also became apparent that there was nothing to fear from Spain in Virginia, nor in what came to be called New England and Canada. Further, sailors from these three northern countries had gained much experience in American waters as a result of the quests for a northern passage and the exploitation of American fisheries.

Dutch and Swedish Colonies One of the early colonizers in North America was also one of the smallest "states" to become involved in the competition for empire in the New World. This was the United Provinces of the Netherlands, which were just winding up their revolt against Spain. The extraordinary energies of this little congeries of lowland provinces were sufficient to generate colonization in the West at the same time that they were wresting an empire from the Portuguese in Asia.

In 1608, the Dutch lured a veteran English navigator, Henry Hudson, to work for them and sent him off in the *Half Moon,* once again to try to find a northern passage to Asia. Hudson, who had braved a good deal of ice in previous attempts, found that his crew agreed with Hakluyt that the frozen North should be abandoned for more temperate climes. His change of direction led him to Sandy Hook and the river that now bears his name. The mouth of this river had been visited by Verrazano, while in French service, as early as the 1520's; but nothing had come of this discovery. The Dutch, however, followed up on Hudson's claiming voyage. Almost immediately, Dutchmen appeared in the Hudson river valley to trade in furs with the Indians. In 1614, a company was formed to handle this trade; and in 1621, a new company, modeled after the Dutch East India Company, was chartered to control American trade and colonization. This company dealt in furs and other trade goods, including slaves.

The new company, the Dutch West India Company, sent out the Prussian-born Peter Minuit. Minuit, who had a good eye for real estate, purchased in 1626 a likely tract from the natives on the island of Manhattan, and proceeded to construct the essentials of a colony: a fort, a mill, and a warehouse. Settlers were soon established there and up the Hudson River at what is now Albany. It did not take the Dutch in New Netherlands long to develop a highly lucrative fur trade with the Iroquois Indians along the Hudson and its tributaries.

Another northern European country that became interested in the New World during the first half of the seventeenth century was Sweden. Swedes, too, became involved in overseas expansion at a time when they were active in other theaters. Under the rule of the house of Vasa (1523–1660), little Sweden became a great European power, dominant in the Baltic region. And during the reign of Gustavus II Adolphus (1611–1632), Swedish armies played crucial roles in the Thirty Year's War.

At the suggestion of a disaffected Dutchman, King Gustavus Adolphus chartered a colonizing company shortly before his death. Later, the New Sweden Company was formed. Under its aegis Peter Minuit, who had by this time left Dutch service, founded in 1638 a settlement on Delaware Bay. The Dutch had already settled further up the Delaware. For a while, the Dutch and the Swedes got along with each other well enough; but as time went on the competition for furs became more intense and led the Swedes to attack and capture the Dutch fort at Camden on the Delaware. The Dutch retaliated in 1655 by forcibly taking over all Swedish posts, thus eliminating the Swedish enclave in America. Most of the Swedish settlers remained, however. They gave to colonial America one of its most characteristic structures—the log cabin—which became the characteristic shelter of the westward-moving frontiersman.

The Dutch administrator in New Amsterdam who urged and carried out the move against the Swedes was Peter Stuyvesant. A few years later (1664) an English fleet appeared off Manhattan island and Stuyvesant was forced to surrender the Dutch colonies in North America to another power as the process of bigger fish swallowing littler fish continued in European competition for the New World. The Swedish colony endured for only seventeen years. New Netherlands became New York, in English hands, after only about fifty years as a Dutch colony.

The English Colonies After the death of Queen Elizabeth (1603), Hakluyt's pro-colony propaganda was reinforced by economic and social considerations that stimulated a drive to colonize in America. American fish from the Grand Banks off Newfoundland and along the American coasts were needed to feed a growing English population. American timber and naval stores were thought by the government to be useful in maintaining the English fleet in case supplies of these strategic materials from the Baltic region should be cut off. Mounting religious tension at home led some Englishmen, who did not wish to conform to the Established Church of England, to think of emigrating to the New World. Finally, America came to be thought of as a place to which the excessive numbers of sturdy beggars and paupers who plagued the realm could be exported. The result was that lasting settlements were established in America. Successful colonization required the conjunction of governmental and private interests. The government granted authorizing charters and provided naval and military protection. Private interests got together the necessary capital, supplied the ships, the personnel, and the supplies.

In 1606, two groups of Englishmen were granted related charters by the crown to colonize in North America. The first of these, the Virginia Company of London, was given the territory from about the latitude of Cape Fear (in southern North Carolina), north to about the latitude of what is now New York City. The second company, the Virginia Company of Plymouth, was given overlapping territory from the latitude of Lubeck, Maine, south to that of Charlottesville, Virginia. No western boundary was set.

In 1607, under the auspices of the London Company, Jamestown became the first English colony to take root in America. No gold was discovered there and the fractious settler-adventurers made great difficulties for their energetic but stern leader, John Smith. This colony struggled along on the edge of abandonment until the introduction of tobacco culture in 1614 gave

Roanoke Island. This map-picture of the coast of "Virginia" (present-day North Carolina) indicates the dangerous shoals off Cape Hatteras on which so many sailing vessels foundered. Note that the ships in the foreground have anchored well offshore. The rendering in this 1590 volume shows Indian settlements on Roanoke Island and at Secotan, above left, which appear to have been taken from John White's original drawings (see illustrations p. 689). (Folger Library.)

it an economic reason for existence that led to growth, prosperity, and Negro slavery.

In 1620, the Pilgrim Fathers, religious dissidents, came ashore on their famous rock, survived the "starving time," and became a viable if tiny colony. Nine years later, a new corporation, Governor and Company of Massachusetts Bay in New England, received its charter from King Charles I. The stockholders of this company were mainly Puritans who, unhappy with the established church in England, emigrated—charter, officers, and all—to Massachusetts Bay. There they were joined in the period from 1630 to 1642 by 16,000 other colonists, most of them Puritans. Before mid-century, there were English settlements in Maine, New Hampshire, Massachusetts, Rhode Island, Connecticut, Maryland, and Virginia.

In the 1660's the crown granted the Carolinas to a group of aristocratic proprietors, and some twenty years later William Penn received a proprietary charter and founded his colony. By the 1680's, therefore, having eliminated the Dutch, England was the more-or-less bemused mistress of a good share of the eastern seaboard of North America. Since Spain had given up trying to expand to the north of Florida, the only remaining competitor in the northern part of the New World was France.

New France Early in the sixteenth century, French mariners began to sail to American waters to fish and hunt whales. The Italian, Verrazzano, who was in French service when he discovered the entrance to New York harbor, was followed by Jacques Cartier, who made several voyages of exploration along the coasts of Labrador and Newfoundland and into the Gulf of St. Lawrence.

No successful French settlements were established during the sixteenth century after the 1564 colony on the Florida coast, probably because a wracking civil war going on in France restricted the energies and resources necessary for successful colonization. After 1600, when internal peace had been achieved, the French became more active overseas. King Henry IV granted a monopoly privilege in those parts of America that had been claimed by France to a group interested in fur-trading. This group employed one of the most indefatigable heroes of New World exploration, Samuel de Champlain, the founder of Quebec in 1608. From Quebec, the French fur-traders and missionaries moved westward along the St. Lawrence River and the Great Lakes. At times (1642–1653, 1665–1666, and 1684–1689) French expansion and trade in America were limited or halted by warfare with the Iroquois Indians who were stirred up against France first by the Dutch and later by the English. The men of the Iroquois Five Nations were fierce enemies; but the struggling French establishment in America survived, and the French pushed on with ever more grandiose projects.

As with the Netherlands and Sweden, the expansive efforts of France were greatest at times when she was most active on the European scene and engaged in European wars. Competition among European countries was

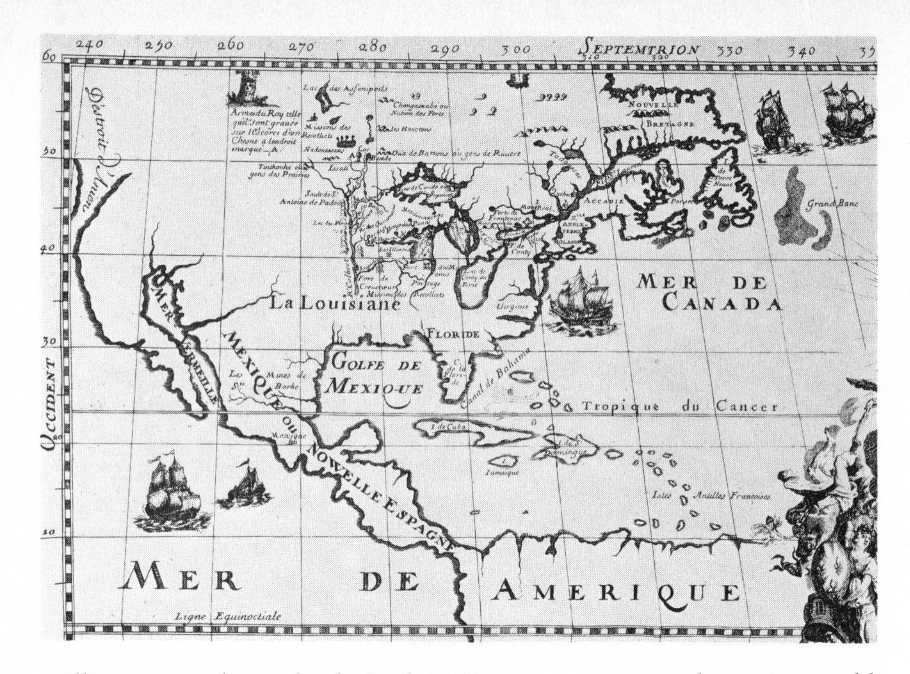

spilling over to distant lands. In short, European wars were becoming world wars.

In 1642, Montreal was founded at the falls of the St. Lawrence River and became the center for the French fur trade. By the 1660's, French missionaries had pushed to the western end of Lake Superior; and, in the 1670's, Marquette and Joliet descended the Mississippi River as far south as present-day Arkansas. This French exploration of the interior of the North American continent took place almost a century before the English colonists left tidewater and began to feel their way into and over the Appalachians.

In 1669, one of the world's most ambitious and most determined empire builders appeared upon the Canadian scene, René Robert, Sieur de La Salle. He envisioned a French American empire reaching from Acadia (Nova Scotia) on the east to the infinitely far west and south along the Ohio river valley and the Mississippi to the Gulf of Mexico. La Salle's first task was to make peace with the Iroquois. Succeeding in this, he and his companions travelled through the Ohio country south of Lake Erie, built a ship on the same lake, constructed a fort on the Illinois river, and, in 1682, paddled down the Mississippi to its mouth. He took possession of the entire region, which he called Louisiana, for Louis XIV of France. Later, in order to make good the claim, La Salle sailed from France with a small fleet to the Gulf of Mexico in order to establish a post from which the French could attack Spain in Mexico. On this voyage, La Salle missed the mouth of the Mississippi, landed instead on the coast of Texas, and was subsequently murdered by his own men.

The map on page 680 is from an account of La Salle's voyages by Louis Hennepin. A Franciscan who traveled with the explorer, the missionary published his work after his return to France in 1682. Maps from later editions of Hennepin's work show the Mississippi all the way to its mouth, which the author later falsely claimed to have discovered. The illustration at right is from one of Hennepin's later, amplified accounts of La Salle's travels. It shows the "Unhappy Adventures of Sire La Salle." (LCRB and LCPP.)

Despite La Salle's failure in his last adventure, France was able to establish colonies on the Gulf coast of Louisiana (1699); and, in 1718, New Orleans was founded. But the French empire in North America did not live up to La Salle's grandiose dream. Had it done so, United States citizens might well be speaking French today.

As things turned out, not enough French men and women came to the New World to populate and develop the immense territories explored and claimed for France. Combined with what seemed to be a general French disinclination to leave home was the influence of the French government,

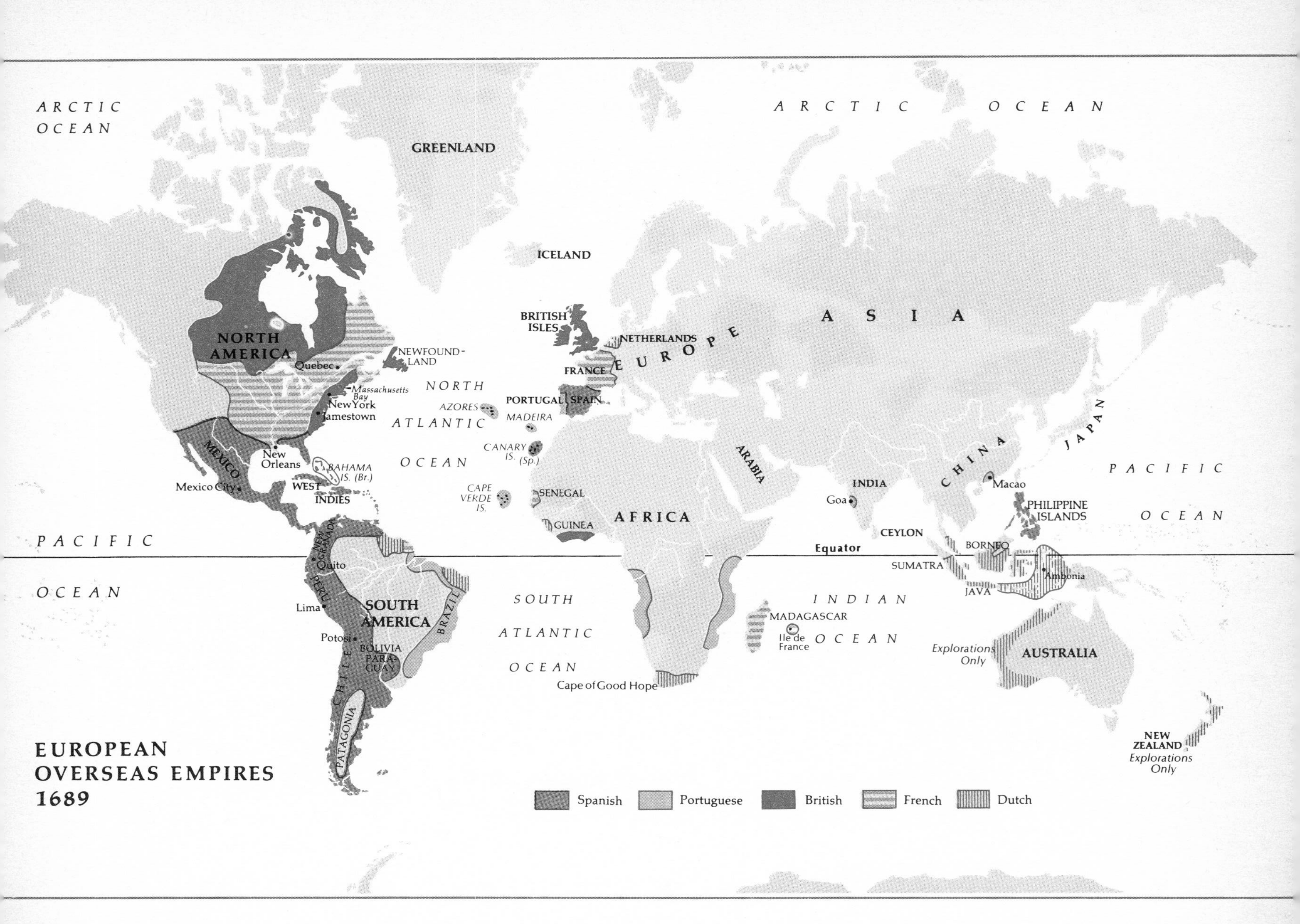

EUROPEAN OVERSEAS EMPIRES 1689

which tended to discourage large-scale emigration. French religious dissidents such as the Huguenots were forbidden to emigrate to New France in Canada. Thus, the French empire in North America remained essentially a trading and missionary empire. The English American empire, on the other hand, was a colonial empire with a growing population of farmers, plantation owners, slaves, fishermen, ex-convicts, indentured servants, and merchants from many nations.

CONCLUSION AND A LOOK AHEAD

What, then, was the situation of the overseas empires of the major western European powers in the last decades of the seventeenth century? The Portuguese pioneers had been pushed out of their Asiatic empire by the Dutch, who, though they were experiencing some pressure from the French and English, were holding on in southeast Asia. The Spanish had made good their claims in Central and South America and in parts of southern and western North America, as well as in the Philippines. Despite both official and piratical attempts at encroachment by other powers, the Spanish were solidly in control of their empire. The French had established a great and potentially very valuable empire along the lake and river systems of North America and in the Caribbean, and had important claims and holdings in Asia, particularly in India. The English were coming to be deeply interested in Asia (including India), in the Caribbean, and, if perhaps more casually, in the plantations along the eastern seaboard of North America.

The geographical juxtaposition of the imperial interests of France and England in several parts of the world made a clash between them likely even if there had been no other cause of enmity between these neighbors. The stage was set for the second act of the drama of competition among European powers for overseas hegemony—the eighteenth-century wars between France and England. But before approaching that struggle, let us look closely at some of the economic, social, and political forces that were driving Europeans to spread themselves across the globe.

FURTHER READING

For the expansion of Europe, there is no nearly satisfactory overall treatment. Over half a century ago, Professor W. R. Shepherd, author of the most famous English-language historical atlas, wrote a three-part article for the *Political Science Quarterly,* Vol. 34 (1919), emphasizing the significance of European expansion and suggesting how its history might be organized and written. As he then said, the greatest of historical subjects awaits the "master hand." It still waits.

There is, however, an immense literature on bits and pieces of the story, including some good material in paperback form. B. Penrose, * *Travel and Discovery in the Renaissance, 1420–1620* (1955), recommends itself immediately,

*Books available in paperback edition are marked with an asterisk.

as do J. H. Parry, * *Establishment of European Hegemony, 1415–1715: Trade and Exploration in the Age of the Renaissance* (1961); C. E. Nowell, * *Great Discoveries and First Colonial Empires* (1954); Sir Percy Sykes, * *History of Exploration* (1934); and, in hard-back form, J. N. L. Baker, *A History of Geographical Discovery and Exploration* (1937). See also J. B. Brebner, * *The Explorers of North America* (1935). A handy collection of writings by several experts is R. G. Albion, ed., *Exploration and Discovery* (1965).

For the Portuguese empire, see C. R. Boxer, *Four Centuries of Portuguese Expansion* (1961). The first volume of A. H. De Olivera Marques, *History of Portugal,* (1972), contributes to an understanding of the Portuguese expansion. Still the basic study of Spanish expansion is R. B. Merriman, *The Rise of the Spanish Empire in the Old World and the New,* 4 vols. (1918–1934). Also see Ruth Pike, *Aristocrats and Traders: Sevillian Society in the Sixteenth Century* (1972), good social history for the background of Spanish overseas empire. B. W. Diffie, *Latin-American Civilization: Colonial Period* (1945), and C. Haring, * *The Spanish Empire in America* (1947), are general treatments. See also C. Gibson, * *Spain in America* (1966); and J. H. Parry, *The Spanish Seaborne Empire* (1966), which is good for the impact of expansion on the mother country. L. Hanke, * *The Spanish Struggle for Justice in the Conquest of America* (1949), deals with Spanish intentions regarding the native Americans.

H. I. Priestly, *France Overseas* (1939), is convenient for French expansion; for French America it should be supplemented by G. M. Wrong, *The Rise and Fall of New France* (1970), in two volumes; R. G. Thwaites, *France in America* (1968); and J. F. McDermott, ed., *The French in the Mississippi Valley* (1965). The work of one of America's greatest historians, Francis Parkman, is the classical treatment of French efforts in America and of the competition between the French and the English: *France and England in North America,* in many volumes and conveniently digested in S. E. Morison, ed., *The Parkman Reader* (1955). Admiral Morison's recent study, *Samuel de Champlain: Father of New France* (1972), is disappointing in some respects, but well written and worth a glance.

For the Dutch in Asia there is B. H. M. Vlekke, *Nusantara: A History of the East Indian Archipelago* (1943); A. Hyma, *The Dutch in the Far East* (1953); and J. J. van Klaveren, *The Dutch Colonial System* (1953). G. Masselman, *The Cradle of Colonialism* (1963), ranges from the building of the Dutch dikes to the Dutch East India Company. C. R. Boxer, *The Dutch Seaborne Empire, 1600–1800* (1965), is recent and most useful.

Nearly everything one wishes to know about British expansion can be found in the eight volumes of *The Cambridge History of the British Empire* (1929–1936), and more briefly in C. E. Carrington, *The British Overseas: Exploits of a Nation of Shopkeepers* (1968). J. A. Williamson, *The Age of Drake* (1938), is a successful introductory study. George Thomson, *Sir Francis Drake* (1972), is a fine adventure story. On England and the search for northern passages: D. B. Quinn, *The English and the Discovery of America, 1481–1620* (1973); E. S. Dodge, *Northwest by Sea* (1961), which traces the search for a northwest passage from the fifteenth to the twentieth century; and A. L. Rowse, *The Elizabethans in America* (1959).

C. M. Cipolla, * *Guns, Sails and Empires, 1400–1700* (1965), helps explain how Europeans were able to carry off the great adventure. P. D. Curtin, * *The Atlantic Slave Trade: A Census* (1969), deals with an important by-product of the expansion.

2 Early Modern Economics

The Overseas Expansion of Europe during early modern times was one of the great creative forces shaping European civilization in the sixteenth, seventeenth, and eighteenth centuries. What were some of the effects of this expansion to Africa, Asia, and America on people at home on the continent of Europe? The horizons of most Europeans were only gradually broadened by the expansion. But if the early overseas adventures did not make a strong and immediate impact on general European culture, they did contribute not only to substantial economic growth but also to the development of two phenomena that are often called "revolutions:" the so-called "commercial revolution" and the "price revolution." The former involved changes in traditional trade routes and centers of commerce; the latter was an inflation that we know had severe social repercussions. Our discussion of these two concurrent revolutions will lead us to a description of new developments in capitalism and of some of the ways in which the emerging states of the early modern era involved themselves in the economic life of their peoples.

CHANGING TRADE PATTERNS

Late medieval and early Renaissance trade patterns may be represented by three interlocking circles. On the east was the great complex of Asiatic trade, touched at points on its western perimeter by Italian merchants. In the center was the circle of Mediterranean trade dominated by Venetians and Genoese but participated in by other Italians and by Spaniards, Portuguese, Netherlanders, and Frenchmen. On the northwest was the circle of Baltic trade with English commerce as a part. The circles overlapped in the Netherlands, particularly at such Flemish ports as Bruges, and in the ports of the Near East.

Trade Patterns in the Late Middle Ages and Early Renaissance

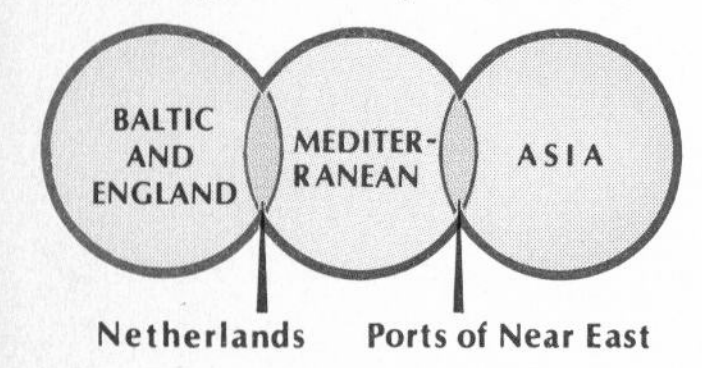

From the European point of view, the Mediterranean was central to this world trade pattern. A great share of European interregional trade passed at one time or another through the hands of merchants in Genoa, Venice, Barcelona, and Marseilles, or was carried through the Mediterranean area. The most important banking houses were located either in Italy or in south Germany and southeastern France on the overland trade routes from the Mediterranean region into the rest of Europe.

Flemish Household by M. van Cleve. The decline of Mediterranean trade brought increased prosperity to the Netherlands in the sixteenth century. This view of the interior of a village home shows that peasant life, while often cramped for space, could be comfortable, even opulent. (Kunsthistorisches Museum, Vienna.)

Although this pattern changed after the Portuguese reached the Indies by sea—Lisbon became the principal port of entry for eastern goods and Antwerp the center of distribution—all Venetian merchants did not, of course, close their counting houses overnight and sell their ships, nor did the Medici bankers in Florence suddenly call in all loans. The decline of Mediterranean commerce was gradual and relative: cities like Seville, Lisbon, Antwerp, and, after 1585, Amsterdam, grew rapidly in economic importance while some Mediterranean centers declined slowly and relatively. By 1609, when the Bank of Amsterdam was founded, Amsterdam was on its way to becoming the financial and commercial capital of Europe. The centers of political power, likewise, began to move gradually from the Mediterranean basin to western and northern Europe.

Stock Companies Whether launched from the Mediterranean or from the English Channel, a maritime expedition to Asia or to America required an enormous investment of capital. To send four ships with cargo to the Far East required, at the beginning of the seventeenth century, a capital of over

Dutch West (left) and Dutch East (right) India Houses. Dutch joint-stock companies copied and then rivalled the British. While the Dutch West India Co. was mounting armadas to attack the Spanish plate fleet in the Caribbean, the East India Co. was attempting to drive the English and the Portuguese out of the Pacific. (*De Gouden Eeuw.*)

half a million dollars; although the profits were often great, so also was the likelihood of loss. Single entrepreneurs, even royal ones, no longer could provide the funds nor assume the risks involved.

At first, businessmen who engaged in overseas trading ventures met their capital requirements by using the *partnership* device to concentrate the available capital of two or more individuals. An outgrowth from partnership was the *regulated company,* which brought together a group of people with funds to invest as active participants in an enterprise. The regulated companies usually received monopolistic privileges by way of a charter from the civil authorities; then the participants pooled their resources to buy ships, hired captain and crew, and went off on the expedition, trading on their own account and using space assigned to them in the ships to carry their goods. This scheme worked well enough, but it had its drawbacks. The participants were, in effect, competing against one another within the framework of the regulated company. The amount of capital available was limited to the number of active traders.

The *joint-stock company* was an improvement over the regulated company since it provided a way for many investors—even those with small surpluses and no special interest in business—to put their money to work by buying shares of stock. At first, joint-stock companies were formed for one voyage only. The books were closed after the ships returned home, the goods were sold, and the profit or loss per share calculated. Francis Drake's circumnavigation and freebooting expedition of 1577–1580 was organized and financed in this fashion. Later the joint-stock company was organized in perpetuity with a permanent capital rather than with capitalization for one venture only. The British East India Company was established (1600) first as a joint-stock company for one voyage and was changed later (1657) to a company with permanent capital. The great importance of this device to the economic development of western civilization need not be labored here. It is enough to say that gradually this form of organization was applied to manufacturing and banking enterprises (the Bank of England, for instance) as well as to overseas trading adventures.

New Commodities Another noteworthy aspect of European overseas expansion was the introduction of new commodities into European trade. These commodities had a tonic effect on commerce and eventually stimulated European industry as well. Among these, perhaps none had more impact than Negro slaves. The Portuguese imported considerable numbers of African slaves during the course of their expansion, but the largest number of Negroes were carried by Europeans to America to man plantations and mines. However immoral, the traffic in slaves was an extremely lucrative one for European slave-traders—otherwise it would not have flourished as it did. The profits from this trade, carried on principally by the English, Dutch, French, and Portuguese, could be and were used at home in Europe to finance important new enterprises.

Other new commodities were tobacco, which became culturally significant near the end of the sixteenth century; maize (American corn); tea, brought by the Dutch in the early seventeenth century and arriving in England about 1650; and coffee, which appeared in Europe in the early seventeenth century. The potato, which later came to change the dietary habits of millions of people, found its way into European agriculture as early as the latter part of the sixteenth century.

Porcelain from China, cotton textiles from India (called "calicos" in

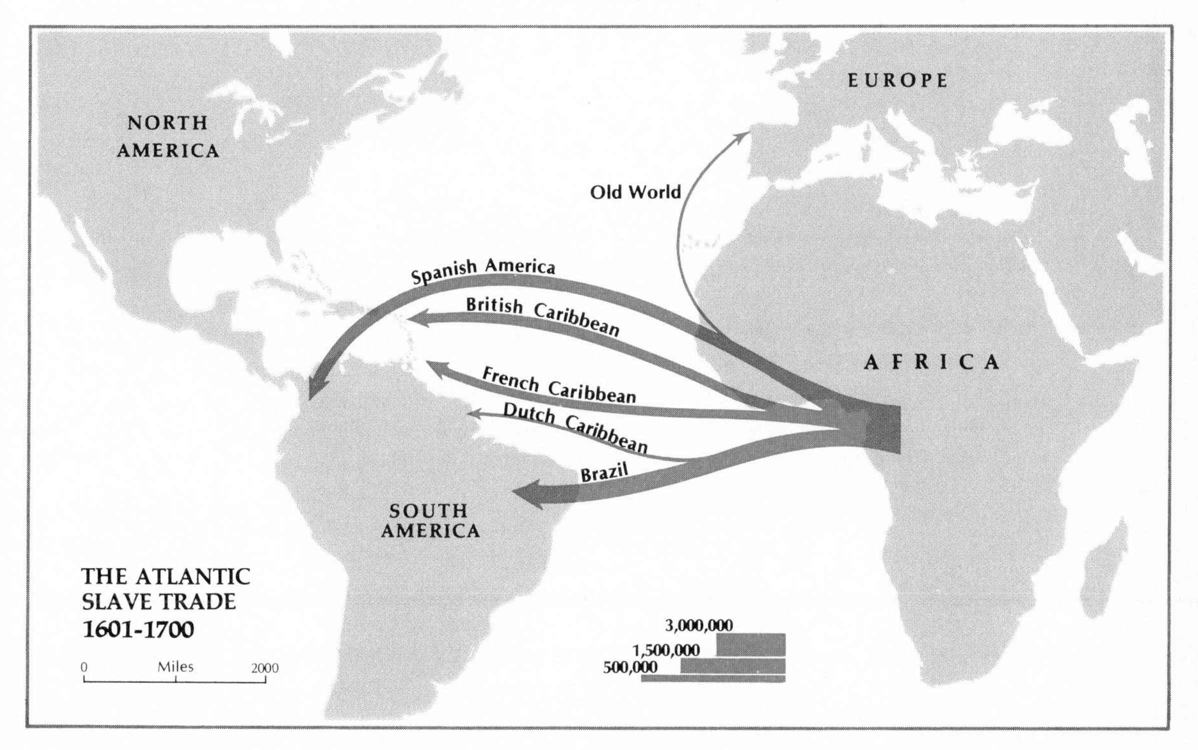

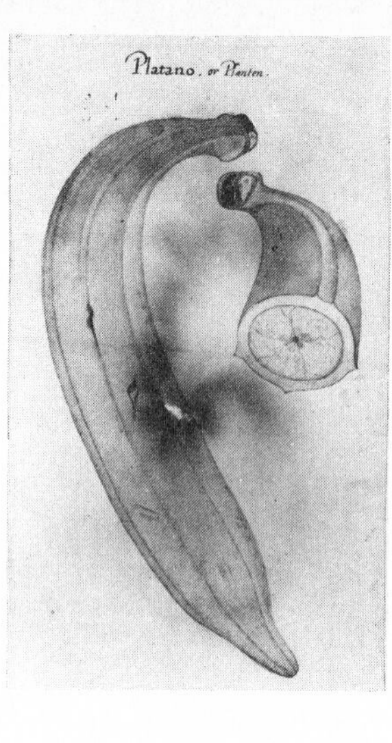

The English crown sent the artist John White to the Virginia colony and elsewhere to record the strange things that he saw, such as the pineapple and plantain shown here from the West Indies. White's rendering of the Indian village of Secotan on the coast near Roanoke Island shows Indian corn, then unknown in Europe, in three stages of growth. (Courtesy of the Trustees of the British Museum.)

England because the Indian port of Calicut shipped large quantities to Europe), codfish, tomatoes, turkeys—all began to take their places among standard articles of consumption. Quinine and opium found their way into the western physician's bag of medicines. Indigo, a brilliant blue dye, replaced the more delicate European pastel or woad in the textile industry. Insofar as these products were used, they indicate a development of tastes that were true results of the "homeward" aspect of European overseas expansion.

Were these changes in European tastes, in the centers of commercial and financial activity, and in the nature of business organization, *revolutionary*? Probably not, if a revolutionary development is defined as one that takes place over a short and limited period of time. The commercial effects of the expansion were gradual. The modern corporation with its concept of "limited liability" was not fully rounded out until the nineteenth century; the relative economic decline of Venice and other Mediterranean ports took place at a dignified pace; and the new commodities came into use over a period of two hundred years. Thus, these developments could hardly have seemed "revolutionary" to contemporaries.

BULLION AND POPULATION

When Overseas Expansion began, Europe had been short of precious metals for centuries. Moreover, as the late medieval trade with Asia developed, the Europeans imported from Asia goods in greater value than they exported there, so that there was a steady flow of gold and silver out of Europe. The resulting dearth of specie made the purchasing power of a small silver coin grow throughout most of the fifteenth century. However, silver production from European mines gradually increased and the Portuguese began bringing home gold from West Africa in larger quantities. In the early sixteenth century, the booty from the Spanish *conquista* arrived from America; then, by mid-century, the great product of the Mexican and Peruvian silver mines began to arrive. Quite suddenly, therefore, something like a monetary revolution took place as the European supply of precious metal for coinage swelled dramatically.

At the same time, and for mysterious reasons, European population, which had been in decline during the fourteenth and early fifteenth centuries, began to grow again. Estimates (based of necessity on inadequate data, for there were no census takers at that time) vary; but it appears that over the hundred and fifty years from 1450 to 1600, Europe witnessed a population increase of twenty to thirty-five million people, roughly 50 percent. This increase took place despite continuing attrition resulting from war, pestilence, and famine. Within this general population increase there was a striking growth in urban centers. In 1500, there were only four European cities with populations greater than 100,000. In 1600 there were ten such cities and two with populations greater than 200,000.

The Rise in Prices Accompanying the increase in population and growth of the money supply was a spectacular rise in prices. An indication of the magnitude of this price-rise is given by the fact that between 1550 and 1600 in parts of Spain prices about doubled. The price of grain in Paris was fifteen times greater in 1650 than it had been in 1500.

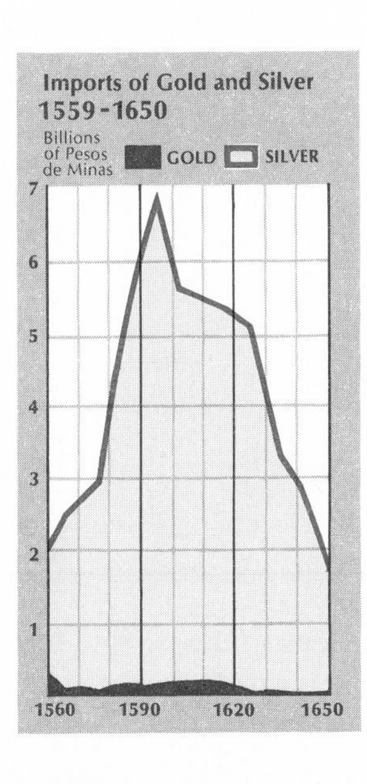

In eastern Europe, prices rose less dramatically than in the west, but they rose nonetheless. This pattern of inflation is called the "Price Revolution" because it violently reversed the falling price trend of the fourteenth and early fifteenth centuries.

Contemporaries and recent scholars have tried to account for this price-rise. Those who have argued that the influx of American treasure caused inflation—by making money less dear in relation to goods—point out that there seems to have been a tendency for the rate of rise in any locality to vary inversely with the distance from Seville, the official port of entry for Spanish-American bullion. Others consider the population increase to be responsible. They argue that the dramatic rise in the price of foodstuffs, especially grain, while the price of manufactured goods increased more slowly, indicates that the Price Revolution was produced by the growing number of European mouths to feed.

In dealing with such historical problems, the multicausative approach is perhaps best. The increased quantity of money in circulation, enhanced principally by American treasure, made money less valuable in relation to commodities. And the increasing population made for more competition for goods, thus driving prices up. It is probably true, however, that without the influx of American bullion the price rise would have been less drastic and, therefore, less nearly "revolutionary" than it was.

We are accustomed today to an even more violent upward price movement, but we can perhaps comprehend what an economic and social shock this sixteenth-century price-rise must have been to a civilization that had probably never before experienced, on such a wide scale, a comparable fluctuation. The shock registered differently upon different groups of people. Manufacturing entrepreneurs profited because wages rose more slowly than prices of goods (as is usually the case in a period of rising prices), producing profit inflation. Merchants who participated in the growing interregional trade saw their stock of goods increase in value from year to year and were able to build great fortunes. On the other hand, workers (artisans and journeymen), finding that their wages did not keep pace with the inflation, suffered a decline in their standard of living. Hunger became an even more serious problem than usual; urban populations, weakened by want, succumbed to pestilence by the hundreds of thousands—perhaps half the population of Paris, or 120,000 deaths in one year (1580), for example. Facts such as these render the remarkable sixteenth century population growth difficult to understand but pay tribute to the tenacious and expansive vitality of European peoples.

Change in Status of Lord and Peasant One of the outstanding changes wrought by the price-rise was the change it brought about in the well-being and status of the landholding classes and of the peasants. By the early sixteenth century, there were few serfs in western Europe. Throughout the thirteenth, fourteenth, and fifteenth centuries the desire of landlords for cash to purchase goods not available from manorial production had been so great that the payments in kind and labor rendered by the peasant to his lord had been changed or "commuted" in many localities to annual money payments. These contractual relationships, once established, were not easily changed. Consider, then, the plight of the sixteenth-century landed noble whose ancestors had succeeded in imposing a money rent upon the peasants of his estates. Suddenly, within a few decades, prices of basic commodities doubled and, in some localities, tripled. What had been a substantial money income became, through the action of the price-rise, an inconsequential handful of silver!

The more fortunate nobles still received payments in kind and had, therefore, an income in goods that rose in value as prices mounted. But many of those who were injured by the price-rise went to work again to change the "system."

In England, for example, the rise in wool prices brought about an "enclosure movement." Usually through unilateral action or agreement with the more substantial peasants, landlords managed to enclose—that is, to put fences around—the common land upon which many peasants depended for pasturing livestock. The enclosed common was used for running sheep that the lord could manage and profit from with the aid of a few hired shepherds. Landlords also sought, most nearly successfully in England, to change their peasants' inheritable tenure on the land to a short-term leasehold, so that the rent could be raised as prices of commodities rose.

Unemployment in England Undoubtedly, the price-rise and the resulting defensive actions of landlords helped contribute to one of the most talked-about problems of the sixteenth century: pauperism. Beggars, vagabonds, and crime came increasingly before the public eye. In 1531, an English Act of Parliament provided that, except for indigent persons who belonged to the parishes in which they lived, all beggars and vagabonds should be whipped and then encouraged to go somewhere else, preferably to the place where they were born. Over the next fifty years in England, several statutes were passed designed either to punish or to provide for the needs of the poor. In 1598, towards the close of Elizabeth's reign, Parliament promulgated an "Act for the Relief of the Poor" that was intended to abolish begging and vagabondage entirely by making poor relief, including the building and maintenance of poorhouses, a charge on each parish. Unemployment was a continuing and rising problem, especially in England.

Hanging Thieves by Jacques Callot. "These base and fallen thieves, hung in the end like ripe fruit on a tree . . . ," begins the caption for this picture of a mass hanging. Punishment for petty crimes became increasingly severe as the number of criminals grew in the early seventeenth century. The priests in the foreground and on the ladder are administering the last rites. (LCPP.)

Factors other than the price-rise and the enclosure movement played their parts in making the problem of unemployment acute. First, the dissolution of the monasteries in 1539 and the abolition of the regular clergy had eliminated the agencies that traditionally gave succor to the poor.

Second, the Tudor monarchy, relatively efficient and modern, was more inclined to establish order in the kingdom than had been its predecessors. The poor had always been with the English as with all Europeans, but now it seemed reasonable for the state to do something about them just as it seemed proper for the state to levy taxes.

Thus, not only did the influence of the Expansion make for movement and dislocation in European social and economic life, but the reaction of Europeans to this influence produced further change. Altogether, the result was a remarkable change in the nature of capitalism. At this point, it may be well briefly to review what the term "capitalism" means.

CAPITALISM AND THE CAPITALIST SPIRIT

Capitalism is generally defined as the use of capital for private profit. A developing and changing thing, capitalism was not the same in 1800 as it was in 1600; it is not the same today as it was in 1914 or in the middle of the nineteenth century when Karl Marx gave its modern name to a kind of economic system he thought would disappear. Karl Marx did not, of course, originate the phenomenon of capitalism, any more than he created socialism.

For the capitalist system to function, several conditions are necessary. The first of these is the existence of a generally positive attitude toward work and wealth and personal profit. What is more, this attitude must be socially approved.

Second, for capitalism to flourish there must exist the possibility of accumulating various forms of capital. In a society where land is the principal badge of power, and where land can be acquired only through inheritance, as in medieval Europe, motivation for the accumulation of other capital assets—such as money, ships, warehouses, factories—is lacking.

Other requirements for capitalism are an impersonal market, interregional trade, and the use of money to pay wages to workers for performing rather specialized tasks. Capitalism is, therefore, impossible in a localized economy where goods are exchanged mainly through barter, where most labor is used to till the soil, and where each family or social unit tends to be self-sufficient. Finally, capitalism is accompanied by all sorts of techniques to collect, transfer, and use capital, to exchange goods and to extend credit.

Historically, European capitalism developed in four fairly discernible stages. The first was the era of *petty capitalism,* which was marked by the activities of late medieval itinerant merchants. Exceptions in their own day, these men had the capitalist spirit: they bought and sold in an impersonal market; they traded interregionally; they used money and various credit devices; they reinvested their profits to buy more pack-animals and to increase their stock in trade. But they operated on a very small scale. Eventually some of them settled down in the *faubourgs* (suburbs) of old towns and became sedentary merchants.

At some point in the later Middle Ages, the activities of these people expanded to the point where capitalism could enter into its second stage—that of *commercial capitalism.* The era of commercial capitalism spanned the fifteenth, sixteenth, seventeenth, and most of the eighteenth centuries. During this period, the most important accumulators and exchangers of capital and the most important entrepreneurs were those who bought and sold goods (merchants). Where industry existed, it was generally dominated by commercial men who did manufacturing as a sideline. Banking, though important, was subsidiary to commerce and, again, many people who engaged in banking were primarily merchants or goldsmiths.

During the eighteenth century, as we shall see, a new kind of capitalist appeared and before long took first place: the "Captain of Industry" who ushered in the era of *industrial capitalism.* Much later, in the nineteenth century, the banker came into his own in the age of *financial capitalism.*

Many economists and historians think that the essential nature of capitalism lies in its spirit or attitude, that the other elements described above are merely techniques through which this spirit finds expression. If this interpretation is correct and if it is true that, although the capitalist spirit did exist in the Middle Ages, it did not achieve general social approval until early modern times, how, then, and why, did an appetite for personal wealth and accumulation of capital come to receive social approval in the sixteenth century?

Protestantism and Capitalism Possibly this change in attitude was a result of the Protestant Revolt of the sixteenth century. Certain of the reformers of the period, notably John Calvin, are said to have preached a doctrine that not only would free the Christian from religiously imposed restrictions upon his economic activity but would also stimulate him, as a Christian, to greater effort in business. The Protestants, some scholars argue, removed the stigma from usury and encouraged banking as a legitimate form of business activity. Calvin presented a doctrine of hard work. Whereas the medieval Church expected the individual merely to maintain himself through economic activity, the Protestant churches, it is held, spurred the faithful on to unceasing toil as part of his duty to God.[1]

Some critics of this point of view deny that Protestantism had anything significant to do with the development of capitalism. Protestant reformers, they believe, tended to adjust their doctrines, where they bore upon economics, to ideas and attitudes that were already in the air, thus assuring the success of their heresies. Another group of critics takes the stand that such important tenets of the capitalist credo as the idea that hard work is good for its own sake, that accumulation of wealth is desirable, and that it is necessary to plan carefully and to keep accounts derive not from Protestantism at all but from the activities and attitudes of some of the

[1] R. H. Tawney, author of an influential volume called *Religion and the Rise of Capitalism,* has presented data from Protestant sermons and writings to show the creative relationship between Protestantism and the capitalistic spirit. Critics of Tawney (and of Tawney's predecessor, the German sociologist Max Weber) point out, however, that he found most of his supporting material in the work of seventeenth-century preachers like Richard Baxter (1615–1691), and not in the era of the Reformation itself.

regular Roman Catholic clergy. Specifically, monastic orders like the Benedictines worked hard at farming, sheep-raising, and other forms of production but were forbidden by their vows to spend their profits. Thus, they tended to accumulate capital and set an example for laymen. This is a fairly plausible argument.

Recently, other explanations for the change in outlook, only indirectly related to religion, have been suggested. A mass attitudinal change such as the adoption of the capitalistic outlook by the European business community may perhaps be explained in purely psychological terms. Having survived the castastrophic experiences of the Black Death and the political turmoil of the late fourteenth and early fifteenth centuries, Europeans entered into a more hopeful world in the later fifteenth century. Evidence of this worldly optimism was to be found in the way population began to increase after 1450. One way to express hope in this world is to work hard in it and to strive to accumulate and to invest one's substance for the benefit of future generations.

Whatever the sources of the new spirit, by the later part of the seventeenth century many Christians were being exhorted by their clergy to live quietly and chastely, and to walk soberly before their God. At the same time, they were led to believe that money making and wealth do not close the way to salvation and that it is the Christian's duty to God to work as hard as he can at his worldly calling. To paraphrase some old hymns, one should not stand idle on the harvest plain; one should give every fleeting minute something to keep in store and "work, for the night is coming when man works no more." On the other hand, one did not dare to waste on frivolous pleasures the wealth gained by hard work. What should be done with this new wealth? The answer was simple: it should be invested, that is, turned into capital with which to generate greater income.

Of course, any reasonably alert reader who has travelled in Europe and who has visited a few museums and palaces may well question the notion of capital accumulation through frugality. Over the whole span of early modern times in much of Europe, kings and nobles lavished their time and money not investing in productive enterprises but in what was later to be called "conspicuous consumption." Royal officials, judges, ecclesiastics, bankers, and merchants all tended to emulate their betters in this kind of consumption. Palaces containing hundreds of rooms, all furnished and decorated most luxuriously, fine clothing, magnificent carriages, and an opulent dinner table hardly seem to be the outward signs of walking soberly before God in order to pile up capital for investment. Rather, on the surface of things, these luxurious habits would seem to have led to the opposite of capital accumulation.

But at least one student of such matters, Werner Sombart, has pointed out that this demand for grand houses and luxury goods was an important stimulus to the development of capitalism as we have described it. Many of the materials for this luxury trade (spices from the East Indies and silks from China, for instance) had to be brought from far places, thus contrib-

Syndics of the Cloth Guild by Rembrandt, 1662. "The prodigious increase of the Netherlands in their domestic and foreign trade, riches and multitude of shipping," wrote an Englishman in 1669, "is the envy of the present and may be the wonder of future generations." Dutchmen were justly proud of their achievements, and liked to see themselves portrayed in group portraits like this one commissioned by woolen cloth inspectors of Amsterdam. (Rijksmuseum.)

uting to interregionalism. By and large, luxury goods had to be paid for, stimulating the use of money. Often they were purchased on credit, thus furthering the development of capitalistic techniques. Many luxury goods could be produced only under something like factory conditions—tapestries, brocades, and books, for example—and this fact led to a rationalization of manufacturing procedures. These highly sophisticated goods could be produced only by specialists, thus contributing to capitalistic division of labor. Finally, those who supplied the luxury goods—merchants, craftsmen, incipient industrialists—put into circulation money that the spenders—kings, princes, nobles, royal officials, and aspiring bourgeois—might otherwise have locked away in strongboxes or have spent on destructive wars.

All this is not, however, a contradiction of the interpretation that sees Protestantism as a spur to the capitalist horse or of the idea that a mass psychological change contributed significantly to the development of a capitalist outlook. Rather, it is a supplement. For any historical phenomenon as complicated as capitalism, it is a mistake to insist on a single interpretation. Religious factors, both Protestant and Catholic, played their parts; so did human greed. The state, too, played an important part in the shaping of early modern capitalism, as we shall now see.

Early Mercantilism During the sixteenth and seventeenth centuries, because of the urgency imparted to religious questions by the Reformation, religious ideas played a greater part in determining the nature of nonreligious activities—including economic activities—than they do today. But civil governments also shaped men's behavior and often guided the economic lives of their subjects in highly creative ways. The particular forms that governmental economic policies took during the period from about 1500 well into the eighteenth century are lumped together by historians under the rubric *mercantilism.* A rough definition of mercantilism is that it was the economic aspect of early modern state making.

In the political realm, during the period we have been discussing, one of the major continuing historical processes, as we have already seen, was that of state making. European princes were endeavoring to expand and consolidate their power over larger areas, to elevate themselves at the expense of the nobility, and to gain advantages over neighboring princes. As they expanded their territorial monarchies, these rulers, who were actually if unwittingly engaged in creating the bases for the later nation-states, strove to unite their kingdoms. To this end, they worked for political, legal, and administrative unity, religious unity, and, not the least important, economic unity.

This is not to say that these princes or their advisors had any clear sense of nationality; and mercantilism should not be equated with nineteenth- and twentieth-century economic nationalism, though the two are similar in many respects. It should not be forgotten that early modern rulers did not necessarily think of themselves as rulers of nations. The populations under their control, these princes thought, existed simply and mainly to support them and their dynasties in their power. This power required police and an administration faithful to a central government so as to ensure that the king's writ would be enforced in all parts of the realm. A bureaucracy was necessary, also, to carry on diplomacy and to generate military and/or naval forces to support the rulers' external ambitions. Such a modern governmental apparatus costs money, available from a prince's subjects through taxation, extortion, or contribution, but only if money existed within

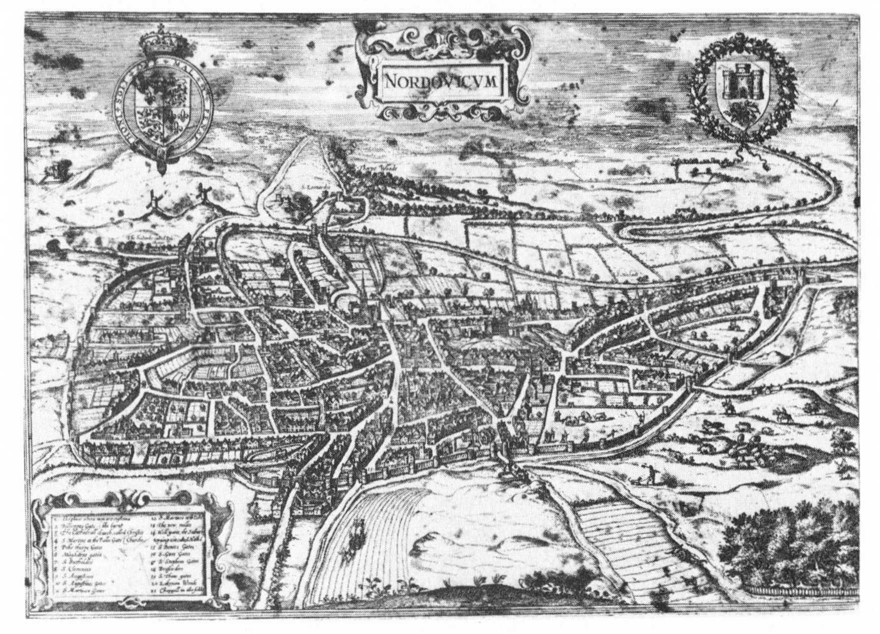

Norwich, 1577. Provincial towns like Norwich on the east coast of England prospered from the troubles in the Lowlands during the sixteenth century. In 1577 its population was over one-third foreign-born. Strongly Protestant, it was the center of English textile manufacture. Queen Elizabeth welcomed skilled Dutch and Flemish artisans of all kinds. (Courtesy of the Trustees of the British Museum.)

his realm. Thus, the ambitious prince tried to see to it that his subjects should prosper. In addition, he strove to prevent his subjects from engaging in any sort of economic activity that might threaten his power.

Mercantilism can be seen as the attempt of a state to control the entire economic activity of a realm for reasons of state. This attempt involved encouragement of some kinds of economic activity, discouragement of others, and, very often, the fostering of policies that would tend to keep a healthy supply of gold and silver within the country.

Was mercantilism an innovation? In one important respect it was, because the early-modern, centralizing monarchy was an innovation at that time. In another respect it was not innovative because the monarchy took up the kinds of local restrictions and regulations that had been commonly imposed by municipalities and guilds in the later Middle Ages, and endeavored to apply them uniformly over an entire kingdom. When this attempt was successful—and it was not so everywhere—it made for larger and more efficient politico-economic units. By creating larger markets within one political unit, mercantilism contributed to the development of capitalism. But the mercantilists' tendency to restrict trade between their subjects and the peoples of other jurisdictions had quite the opposite effect.

Bullionism As we have noted, the historic process of centralized state-making began in the period when Europe was experiencing a shortage of gold and silver. This shortage had from time to time troubled the medieval feudal monarchs, but they had had other ways of providing administration and of raising armies than by paying cash for them. For the new monarchs, however, this shortage represented a crisis. The centralizing prince was quite understandably preoccupied with the problem of seeing to it that sufficient gold and silver be available in his kingdom so that his government could carry out its plans. An ambitious monarch tended to equate bullion—a medium of exchange—with wealth, because to him it meant freedom of action.

To achieve this kind of "wealth," the Portuguese and Spanish governments single-mindedly pursued a policy designed to pile up hoards of gold and silver in their treasuries. The Portuguese policy took the form of exploitation of the empire entirely for the benefit of the mother country, regulating all trade so that the value of exports should exceed that of imports. Gold and silver would thus flow into Portugal to redress the balance of trade and payments. Spanish policy was similar but simpler, because the Spanish empire actually produced large quantities of silver. Despite close governmental control of trade between the colonies and Spain—the export of gold and silver was long forbidden—a great deal of precious metal did find its way out of Spain to the rest of Europe.

This mercantilist attitude and policy toward gold and silver and external trade is called *bullionism.* It is easy to criticize the bullionist for his simple-minded concept of wealth and to point, with all the advantages of hindsight, to the historical fact that those countries pursuing a most nearly bullionist course (Portugal and Spain) in early modern times suffered the greatest

French bullionists like the merchant of Bordeaux, France, on the right insisted upon payment in specie. "I bring gold from England for wines," says the English trader as his men unload sacks of gold ducats, crowns, and other coins for the counting table. The cartoon is from a volume published in 1580. (Folger.)

decline. But if we remember that, in the early period of statemaking, the shortage of specie was a confining and restrictive reality, we can at least understand the motives behind bullionism.

If carried to its logical but ridiculous extreme, bullionist policy would eventually have brought all interregional trade to a halt and would, therefore, have terminated the development of capitalism. It never was carried to such an extreme. A number of mercantilist governments quite early cast off the gold and silver fixation and developed more economically sophisticated policies.

The Dutch, for example, although basically mercantilist, did not adopt a strict bullionist position. Netherlandish statesmen clearly recognized that their wealth was derived from trade. Governmental regulation was, therefore, devoted to increasing the volume of Dutch commerce. There were almost no import or export duties, and the Dutch permitted the exportation of gold and silver to buy goods for trade. This is not to say that Dutch merchants were not regulated by their government. Trade with the colonies was in the hands of a state-directed company; and the Netherlands attempted to monopolize trade with its colonies.

English Mercantilism Another example of a mercantilist state that early abandoned pure bullionism for a more sophisticated form of mercantilism was England.[2] Although the English did not give up the belief that it is better to export than to import, they bound their mercantilist package with other strings.

[2]Much of what is said here about England also applied to France. French mercantilism will be discussed in more detail later, in connection with King Louis XIV (1643–1715) and his finance minister, Colbert.

English mercantilist policy was in part directed toward enhancing the maritime strength of the island kingdom. In Elizabeth I's reign, the smelting of iron with charcoal was forbidden within a certain distance from the coast in order to ensure a supply of timber for shipbuilding. The eating of fish on fast days was enforced by law in order to guarantee a thriving fishing industry that would serve as a training school for merchant sailors; in turn, the merchant marine served as a recruiting ground for the naval fleet.

But Elizabethan mercantilism did more than foster English naval power: it also encouraged production and trade. Foreign craftsmen, notably refugee textile workers fleeing from the wars in the Netherlands, as well as metallurgical workers from various parts of Europe, were encouraged to emigrate to England. Subsidies, monopolies, and other kinds of official encouragement were given to entrepreneurs who would manufacture sails and rope for the merchant marine and the navy, and to those who would engage in mining.

During the seventeenth century, England continued to elaborate its productive mercantilism. Protective tariffs insulated English industry from foreign competition; Navigation Acts (1651, 1660, 1663, and 1673) restricted English colonial trade to English ships; and, finally, direct governmental assistance was given to English traders in their competition with Dutch carriers. Twice in the late seventeenth century the English fleet fought naval wars with the Dutch, during a period when the political situation in Europe tended rather to align the two countries than to separate them, and naval war against the Netherlands continued so long as Dutch competition seriously threatened English maritime commerce.

In the late sixteenth century, William Cecil, Queen Elizabeth's principal secretary of state, seems to have made characteristically English mercantilist decisions without benefit of intellectual guidance from others. In the early seventeenth century, Thomas Mun, a director of the British East India Company, wrote a pamphlet defending the Company against bullionists who criticized it for exporting silver to Asia in order to buy goods.

Bullion, Mun insisted, is not wealth in itself. England's wealth, he said, was represented by the stock of goods it had to sell. This should be increased not only by increasing English production but also by using gold and silver to buy goods for resale, thus stimulating English shipping and further increasing the wealth of England. After Mun, other English economic writers produced a small library of books and pamphlets reiterating that the object of governmental economic policy should be ever-greater economic activity, rather than the amassing of specie. Until the middle of the eighteenth century, however, very few questioned the basic principle of mercantilism, namely, that the government should direct, regulate, and encourage the economic life of the country, for whatever reasons, which, even in England, were principally reasons of state.

CONCLUSION

In general, the sixteenth and seventeenth centuries saw a substantial growth of European capitalist economic activity. Much of this growth resulted from the effect of the Overseas Expansion of Europe on economic life. The outstanding developments in early modern European economic history were, first, the shift of the principal commercial and financial centers from the Mediterranean region to the Atlantic seaboard; second, the dramatic price rise; third, the spread and acceptance of capitalist attitudes and techniques; and fourth, the social dislocations resulting from all these changes. Crucial to these developments was the role assumed by the emerging states as mercantilist supervisors and regulators of economic life during the era of early-modern commercial capitalism. In the next two chapters, we shall explore the personalities of some of the rulers of these states to see how they shaped the political and military aspects of the early modern period.

FURTHER READING

Two surveys of European economic history are H. Heaton, *Economic History of Europe* (1948); and S. B. Clough and C. W. Cole, *Economic History of Europe* (1952). For the period discussed in this chapter, see E. E. Rich and C. H. Wilson, eds., *The Economy of Expanding Europe* (1967), Volume IV of *The Cambridge Economic History of Europe.* R. Davis, * *The Rise of the Atlantic Economies* (1973), touches on the relation of the expansion to economics.

J. U. Nef's stimulating * *War and Human Progress: An Essay on the Rise of Industrial Civilization* (1968), presents interesting material for early modern times. The same author's * *Industry and Government in France and England, 1540–1640* (1957), shows that mercantilist policy was applied to industry as well as commerce. A great book on mercantilism is E. Heckscher, *Mercantilism* (1955), in two volumes. A summary of Heckscher's argument can be found in his article on the subject in *The Encyclopedia of the Social Sciences.* C. W. Cole, *French Mercantilism 1683–1700* (1965), deals with France. In the Heath series, see W. E. Minchinton, ed., * *Mercantilism: System or Expediency?* (1969). For economic thought as a whole, E. Roll, *A History of Economic Thought* (1956), is a good beginning. On the poor, see W. K. Jordan, *Philanthropy in England, 1480–1660* (1959).

L. B. Packard, *The Commercial Revolution* (1927), is still the best introduction to the topic. The matter of prices is treated in E. J. Hamilton, *American Treasure and the Price Revolution in Spain, 1501–1650* (1965), a markedly influential study. On capitalism, see the incisive introduction by Henri Sée, *Modern Capitalism: Its Origin and Evolution* (1928); the more recent M. Dobb, * *Studies in the Development of Capitalism* (1964); and F. L. Nussbaum's adaptation of W. Sombart in *History of Economic Institutions of Modern Europe* (1935). See also V. Barbour, * *Capitalism in Amsterdam in the Seventeenth Century* (1962). L. A. Clarkson, *The Pre-Industrial Economy in England, 1500–1750* (1972), is a fine, up-to-date synthesis.

A point of view on the highly controversial question of the relation of religion to capitalism is presented in R. H. Tawney, * *Religion and the Rise of Capitalism,* first published in 1926. A summary of this issue can be found

*Books available in paperback edition are marked with an asterisk.

in the Heath pamphlet, R. W. Green, ed., * *Protestantism, Capitalism, and Social Science: The Weber Thesis Controversy* (1973).

In early modern times, nearly everyone was a peasant farmer who lived on, and on what he could raise from, the land. For an understanding of rural matters, see B. H. Slicher Van Bath, *The Agrarian History of Western Europe, A.D. 500–1850* (1963); R. H. Tawney, * *The Agrarian Problem in the Sixteenth Century* (1970); R. Trow-Smith, *Life from the Land: The Growth of Farming in Western Europe* (1967); and J. Blum, * *The European Peasantry from the Fifteenth to the Nineteenth Century* (1960), American Historical Association Pamphlet, number 33.

Finally, H. Kamen, *The Iron Century: Social Change in Europe, 1550–1660* (1972), is an important, revisionistic essay in "quantitative social history," relevant to this chapter and those that follow.

3 Philip of Spain: Troubled Titan

Spaniards call the hundred years from 1559 to 1659 their "Golden Century" (*siglo de oro*). Golden it was in many respects, with heavy touches of silver. Bullion from America, imports of which reached a high point in the last decade of the sixteenth century, was the most spectacular but more fleeting aspect of Spanish treasure produced in the *siglo de oro.* More lasting and more valuable, in the end, was the work of the great Spanish artists of this period, including two of the western world's finest painters: El Greco (1540–1614) and Velasquez (1599–1660). Spanish literature reached unsurpassed glories in what is probably one of the most popular and enduring of books, Cervantes' *Don Quixote* (1605), and in the hundreds of plays, not to speak of other works in like quantity, of Lope de Vega (1562–1634). Philosophy and theology were strongly and ardently represented in Spain by the Jesuit thinkers Suarez (1548–1617) and Molina (1535–1600), while Christian mysticism reached its finest expression in the work of Saint Theresa of Avila (1515–1582) and Saint John of the Cross (1542–1591).

During the first fifty years of the *siglo de oro,* corresponding to the second half of the sixteenth century, Spain was not only culturally brilliant; Spain was also the political leader of Europe. Its Habsburg king, Philip II (reigned 1556–1598), came through inheritance and conquest to rule over more of the surface of the globe than had any ruler since the beginning of time.

Philip did not inherit the eastern part of the Habsburg heritage, which went to his uncle Ferdinand. But the Spanish crowns brought with them rule over Milan and Naples in Italy; the Balearic Islands, Sardinia, and Sicily in the Mediterranean; Oran, Tunis, and other *presidios* in Africa; the Netherlands and Franch-Comté as well as Spain in Europe; Spanish America and the Philippines overseas. Philip acquired the Portuguese crown in 1580 and thus came to rule over the great spread of the Portuguese empire as well.

To control these widely dispersed territories, the Spanish king commanded not only a flotilla of ships greater than any yet seen, but a respected and feared land army recruited from all over Europe. Popes and princes almost literally cowered before the power of the Spanish crown. Yet, by

the time Philip II's remains had rested only sixty years in his carefully prepared tomb, Spain had become a second-rate European nation.

How and why did such a rapid Spanish decline come about? Was Philip in fact the prudent ruler he is said to have been? Why should this solitary monarch have become so embroiled in political quicksands that he seems to us more nearly like a royal Don Quixote than like Philip the Prudent? As we shall see, the answers to these questions lie partly in the ferment of the times and partly in the character of Philip himself.

I, THE KING

During Philip's youth, his father, Charles V, Holy Roman Emperor, had tried to inculcate in the boy a deep sense of responsibility. The burden of Charles' counsel was that a prince must see to everything himself, that he should not permit the nobles of his realms to have any real power.

Philip liked flowers and bird-watching. He was tenderly affectionate with at least two of his four wives and with all but one of his children. Most of his portraits reveal a tall, dark-haired man, looking rather like a monastic clerk, his lower jaw a bit more out-thrusting than his father's. Actually, Philip was short and fair. He had little taste for dancing, war, sport, or hunting. As king, he revealed a deadly seriousness and a monumental capacity for work. Nearly every report or request or suggestion from no matter what part of his empire found its way to his work table, where Philip read it, annotated it, thought about it, put it aside, then thought about it some more. If in the end he did send a reply, he signed it simply *Yo, El Rey* (I, the King).

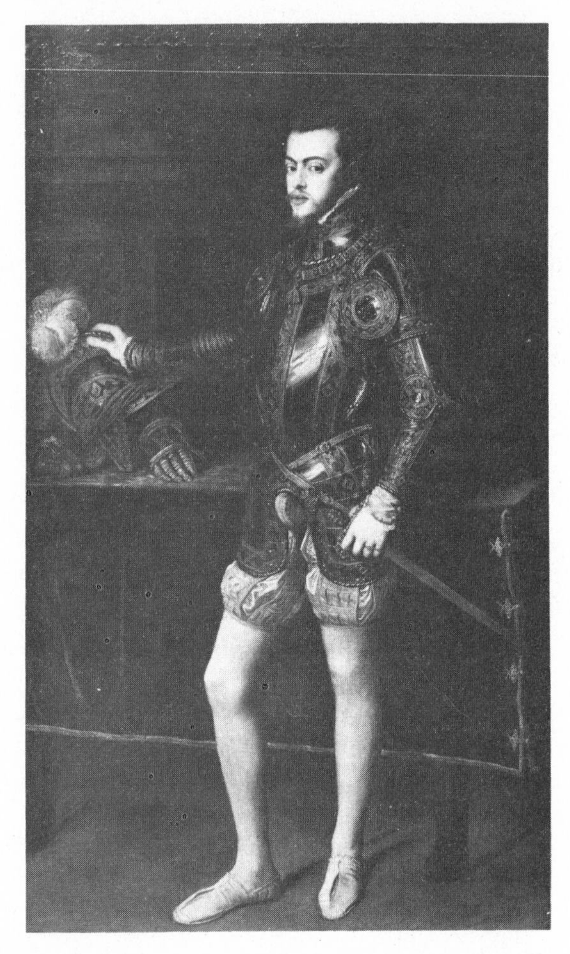

Painted by Titian in 1551 in Augsburg, Germany, at the request of Charles V, this portrait of young Prince Philip is one of the best we have of the man who was to rule the Spanish Habsburg empire for most of the latter half of the sixteenth century. Mary Tudor, Queen of England, whom Philip married in 1554, is said to have been reassured by the portrait in advance of the royal wedding. (Prado, Madrid.)

His desk was located in an enormous tomb-palace that he built for himself and his family high on an isolated and arid shoulder of the Guadarrama mountains. San Lorenzo de Escorial was more than a tomb. It was

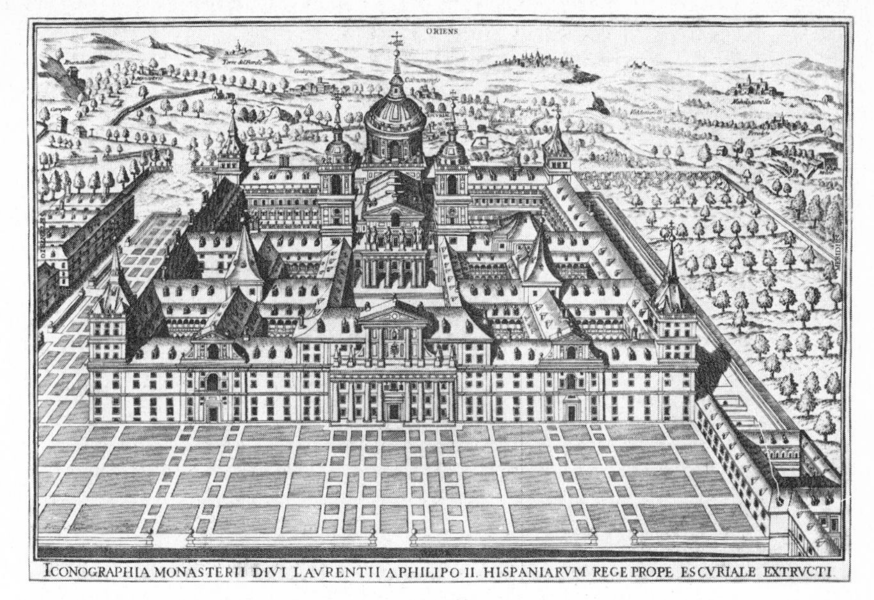

The Escorial. Philip's modest apartments were just to the right of and above the high altar under the domed apse of the church in the center of the complex. From his bedroom he could look down unobserved upon priests officiating at mass. Hieronymite monks lived in the long dormitories on the right or southern side. (LC RB.)

also a monastery centered about a great monastic church. On one side of the church, above the altar, was a modest apartment where Philip lived and worked. There was room in the Escorial for the coffins of Philip's ancestors, for the monks, and for Philip's secretaries; and there was space to hang the tapestries, sculpture, and paintings that Philip's agents bought for him in Spain, Italy, and the Netherlands; but there was little place for courtiers and diplomats. In a period when most monarchs lived, ate, and slept amongst a throng, Philip, *El Rey,* sat late over his candle-lit papers and brooded all alone over the destiny of his empire. Those who had business with the greatest monarchy in Christendom crowded and strained the facilities of Madrid some thirty miles away.

Philip was not a good man; nor was he a bad one. He was a suspicious and thoroughgoing clerk, truly devout. Despite his title, "the Prudent King," Philip was led by circumstances, ambition, and his Christian conscience into some highly imprudent adventures.

PHILIP AND SPAIN

Actively occupied with governing his many realms and in leading his armies during the series of wars concluded by the Treaty of Cateau-Cambrésis (1559), Philip's father had spent only part of his time in Spain. In order to guarantee his tax revenues from that country, Charles V generally had followed a policy of conciliation with his Spanish subjects and respected what was left of their traditional rights and liberties.

Philip was, on the contrary, a Spaniard, living near the geographical center of Iberia. During his reign, Spain was centralized and more closely supervised. This supervision was administered by a hierarchy of Councils (*consejos*), one of which, the *Consejo de las Indias,* we have already described (see Chapter 2 in this section). At the top of the council system was the

Council of State, which deliberated on matters that concerned the empire at large. Next, there were subordinate councils, one for each of the component kingdoms of the empire (Castile, Aragon, Italy, etc.). Under the regional councils there was a complicated, expensive, and cumbersome system of administration and justice. Other councils dealt with particular functions: e.g., the Councils of War, Inquisition, Orders, and Finances. At the top of this structure sat the king, who was willing to permit his councils to discuss almost indefinitely so long as decision making was left to him. The *Cortes* or parliamentary bodies continued to exist and draw up petitions, but they had little legislative power or control over taxation.

A large part of the money needed to support this governmental apparatus, as well as the court and Philip's armies, navies, and foreign policy, came from Castile, whose peasants were probably the most heavily taxed of any in the sixteenth century. Other substantial sources of revenue were the rest of Spain, the Netherlands, Italy, and the Indies. The royal fifth of precious metals coming from America in 1559 amounted to about one third of the tax income the crown derived from Spain. This annual charge of raw bullion had an important psychological effect: it enabled the Spanish government to borrow freely from bankers, who, seemingly dazzled by the glitter of so much gold and silver, kept on lending to the Spanish crown despite its unfortunate habit of repeatedly declaring bankruptcy. For example, the greatest sixteenth-century banking house in Europe, the Fugger bank, was ruined by Habsburg bankruptcies, three of which occurred during Philip II's reign.

In theory, all of Philip's Iberian realms except Aragon were unified into a great system supervised by himself. In fact, the centralization was only apparent. For geographic and other reasons, Spain was unsuited to administrative unification; Spanish localism and regionalism were (and still are) strong. The crown's attempts at centralization did little more than stultify political life while increasing the expenses of government. Moreover, Philip's system served to reduce the royal income by eliminating, for all practical purposes, parliamentary bodies to which the king might have appealed for funds in time of need.

Racial and Religious Uniformity Administrative unification was not the only aim of Philip's internal policy. Religious unity and racial uniformity were also to be achieved. These were uncommonly difficult to impose in Spain.

During ancient and medieval times, the Iberian peninsula had been one of the great racial and religious "melting pots" of the world. During most of the *reconquista* both Moor and Christian had been remarkably tolerant of racial, linguistic, and religious differences, and intermarriage had been relatively common. Jews had concentrated their efforts in trade, science, and scholarship; the "Moors" became great artisans and developed one of the best agricultures in Europe; the Christian Spaniards manned the Church and filled the honorific positions. This fruitful collaboration came to an end

Detail of El Greco's View of Toledo. The painter Domenikos Theotocopoulos (1541–1614) of Crete came to Spain early in Philip II's reign but failed to win the king's favor. "El Greco" settled in Toledo, where he had received a commission. The city at this time had a mixed population of converted Jews, Moriscos, and foreigners, as well as Christian Spaniards. (The Metropolitan Museum of Art, Havemeyer Collection.)

during the reigns of the "Catholic Monarchs," Ferdinand and Isabella, when they turned against the Jews and then the Moors in the last decade of the fifteenth century (ca. 1492). Jews and Moors were given the choice of conversion to Christianity or emigration. Those who chose to remain in their homes at the expense of enforced conversion were known respectively as *Marranos* and *Moriscos.* The converted Jews (*Conversos*) who remained in Spain were fairly easily absorbed into Spanish life. (For example, the second head of the Society of Jesus, Diego Laynez, was a Christian of Jewish origin.) The *Moriscos,* on the other hand, tended to be geographically and culturally isolated, and thus more vulnerable to attack.

Early in his reign, Philip moved against the Protestants, who were few in number. In 1559 and 1560, nearly all Protestant or even reforming religious leaders were arrested by the Holy Office, condemned, and burned with great solemnity in "acts of faith" (*autos da-fe*), which were attended by the king himself.

The *Moriscos*—perhaps a half million industrious people, living in southern and eastern Spain close to their north African compatriots—remained a problem. After hesitating for several years, Philip gave the order in 1565 to the authorities in Granada (the eastern part of Andalusia), to see to the effectiveness of their conversion. Accordingly, *Morisco* children were to be taken from their families and placed in Christian schools; their parents were ordered to learn the Castilian language within three years.

The *Moriscos* responded to this treatment by organizing themselves and rising in rebellion (1568). A Spanish army came from Italy and for three years hunted down the peasant rebels in defiles of the Sierra Nevada, while the Spanish fleet prevented the *Moriscos* from escaping to Africa or receiving aid from that quarter. The peasants fought bravely against what was then the best army in the world, led by Philip's half-brother, Don John of Austria, and lost. Thousands of men, women and children were killed, and the survivors were scattered. Under Philip's successor, Philip III (1598–1621), all *Moriscos* living outside Andalusia were ordered to leave the country. Thus, through the death or expulsion of some 275,000 of its most industrious and useful citizens, the Spanish kingdom made another step toward racial purity, religious uniformity, and decadence.

PHILIP AND THE TURK

Spanish policy toward the *Moriscos* within Spain was not entirely an internal religious matter. It was closely linked with Philip's war against Islam and with the need to protect or secure Spanish and Christian communications in the Mediterranean.

At mid-sixteenth century, the Ottoman or Turkish empire was the great naval power of the Mediterranean. Islamic pirates were a threat to Christian towns along the coasts of the inland sea as well as to Christian shipping. In order to defend its Mediterranean seaports and to protect the sea lanes to the Balearic Islands, to Naples, and to Sicily, Spanish policy had been to establish fortified posts along the Tunisian and Algerian coasts of North Africa and to see to it that the island of Malta, at the junction of the eastern and western Mediterranean, should be held by a friendly power. Charles V had turned Malta over to the crusading knights of Saint John (the Knights of Malta), but realized that sooner or later the Turks would try to drive them off their strategic rock.

Opposite Malta, just off the Tunisian coast, was the island of Djerba, which, if held in conjunction with Malta, would have given the Christians something like control of the passage between the two parts of the Mediterranean Sea. In 1559, a combined Spanish, Genoese, Papal, Florentine, and Maltese fleet, dispatched to capture this strategic island, was surprised and wiped out by a Turkish fleet. Islam continued its counterattack and reconquered most of the Spanish strongholds in North Africa. In 1565, Suleiman I, the Magnificent, in the last year of his reign, unleashed his forces on Malta. Ably and heroically defended by the Knights of Saint John, the island barely managed to hold out. Five years later, counseled by Don Joseph Nassi, a refugee Spanish Jew who lent his great wealth and wisdom to Turkish causes, Selim II (reigned 1566–1574) took Cyprus from Venice.

In all, Christian fortunes in the Mediterranean did not seem promising in 1570. Turkish power was growing rather than shrinking. Christian states, divided by religious and dynastic controversies, found it difficult to coalesce to meet the common danger, and skillful Turkish diplomacy helped to keep the Christian powers apart. Pope Pius V and Philip of Spain wanted a Holy Crusade against the Turks. Fearing that a holy war would disrupt commerce for centuries, the Venetian Republic wanted a limited war only—to regain Cyprus and to secure Venetian trade in the eastern Mediterranean. France and England would join no coalition against Philip's enemies. Even Philip's imperial cousin, Maximilian (Habsburg) of Austria, was willing to achieve peace with the Turk by paying him tribute.

Nevertheless, a naval campaign was mounted. The driving spirit behind the enterprise was Pius V, the most rigorous, austere, and single-minded pontiff of the Roman Catholic Counter-Reformation. The only really enthusiatic ally Pius could find was Philip, but Venice and Genoa contributed ships and men to Pius' Holy League. Philip named the grand commander, his half-brother Don John of Austria. Eventually, after some false starts, on October 7, 1571, a great Christian fleet of 208 galleys met a Turkish armament of 286 galleys in the Bay of Lepanto near the mouth of the Gulf of Corinth. It was a bitter and bloody fight: 38,000 men were killed on both sides. Of the Turkish vessels only 40 escaped. The victorious Christians freed 15,000 galley slaves from the enemy ships.

Never before had Christendom won such a victory over Islam. Young Don John of Austria was wounded, as was another Spanish soldier, Miguel de Cervantes. The latter, though sick with fever on the day of the battle, fought bravely, was wounded three times, and lost the use of his right hand. (This helped to turn the future author of *Don Quixote* from war to literature.)

What other results? The reconquest of Cyprus, the main objective of the enterprise, was not achieved, nor was any other strategic base taken. After the great victory, the Christian fleet broke up into its component parts. Don John managed to take Tunis—but in the next year a rebuilt Turkish fleet took it back. By 1574, despite the Christian triumph three years before at Lepanto, the Turk was more nearly the master of the Mediterranean than ever. In the meantime, Philip was musing over reports of a troublesome rebellion in the Spanish Netherlands.

PHILIP AND THE NETHERLANDS

The Netherlands, Philip's *pays d'embas,* was a complicated congeries of seventeen provinces which he sometimes did not even call by their right name.[1] It seems clear that he did not fully understand his Netherlandish subjects nor their stubborn determination to rid themselves of Spanish rule.

[1]The word "Netherlands" means lowlands or "Low countries" (in French, *pays bas*), and is descriptive of the territory near the mouth of the Rhine River. Much of the land there was, in fact, lower than sea level, having been reclaimed from the sea. In referring to it, Philip tended to use the insulting phrase, *"mes pays d'embas"* (my provinces down there).

The peoples of the Netherlands included some, the Walloons, who spoke French. Others spoke Dutch and Flemish, essentially the same Germanic language. The language of the aristocrats was French, a language in which Philip was never fluent.

Philip's father, Charles V, had spent considerable time in the Low Countries and seems to have identified himself more closely with them than with any other part of his realms. It was he who had assembled all of the provinces under one rule and tried to impose some sort of political order on the area, as administered for him by his female relatives. He had created a council system, and from time to time he had called together States General representing all the provinces. On one occasion, the heavy taxes that Charles imposed upon the Netherlands as well as his determination to see to it that Protestantism should gain no foothold amongst his Dutch, Flemish, and Walloon subjects had given rise to opposition and even to rebellion, as in

The Battle of Lepanto by no means drove the Turks from the Mediterranean. In this remarkable drawing by a Neapolitan artist of the early seventeenth century a Turkish galleon or sailing vessel is shown ramming an oar-driven Christian galley. (The Louvre.)

the case of the city of Ghent. One of the important European manufacturing and trading centers, proud of its traditional political liberties, Ghent refused in 1539 to pay taxes levied upon it and expelled the Emperor's representatives from the town. A year later, with a sufficient army at his back, Charles chastised the city by executing the ringleaders of the rebellion and revoking all of the rights and charters of the city.

After his accession, Philip did not change his father's policies regarding the Netherlands. He, too, was represented there at first by a female relative; he, too, was determined to stamp out heresy. His financial needs and requests were of the same general order. But there were important differences between the rule of Charles and that of his son Philip. The latter's attachment to Spain antagonized the Netherlandish nobles; and Philip, as we shall see, seemed to have a knack for using force and terror as instruments of policy at the wrong times and on the wrong people.

Leadership of the Netherlandish nobility was in the hands of Lamoral, Count of Egmont, one of the wealthiest and most attractive men of his day, the Count of Horn, another wealthy noble, and the even richer William, Prince of Orange, who possessed lands in southern France and in the Empire as well as in the Netherlands. A brilliant but cautious man, William was called "the Silent" because he tended to think carefully before making a statement about anything whatsoever. Neither Egmont nor Orange represented the common people of the Netherlands, of course. They were essentially leaders of the local aristocracy. As such, they could only be opposed to the sort of reforms that Philip undertook to impose by remote control.

Philip had visited the Netherlands twice as a young man and again at the time of the ceremony of his father's abdication in Brussels in 1555. When he quit the Low Countries for good in 1559, Philip left Margaret of Parma, his natural half-sister, in charge, to be assisted by his own confidential advisors. One of these confidants was Antoine Perrenot, Sieur de Granvelle, a Burgundian dedicated to the service of the Habsburgs, who later became cardinal and twice an archbishop.

Perrenot (or Granvelle) and his colleagues were expected by Philip to exercise the real power in the interests of the Spanish crown. Margaret presided over the three Netherlandish governing councils set up by Philip's father Charles: the Council of State, the Council of Finances, and the Privy Council. The councils were to see to it that the Protestants were suppressed and that Philip's demands for funds were met.

Even before Philip left for Spain, financial need had led him to call the Estates General (Parliament) of the Provinces. The deputies complained about their taxes, about the presence of Spanish troops in the Netherlands, and about Philip's attempts to unleash the Inquisition upon his Flemish, Walloon, and Dutch subjects. In no position to enforce his will at this time, Philip agreed to withdraw his troops in return for the supply of money he requested, and eventually (1561) the Spanish soldiers left.

The Beggars Margaret of Parma and Granvelle were thus left to carry on a highly unpopular reform program and to collect taxes without military backing. At first, the nobles tried to carry on a dignified and loyal opposition policy. Some of them joined together in 1565 to sign an agreement opposing Granvelle and his administrative and ecclesiastical reforms. These nobles were, at least ostensibly, Roman Catholics and all professed fealty to the crown.

If Spain were to keep the Netherlands as a Spanish province and a fruitful source of revenue, wise policy probably would have been for the crown to ally itself with the local nobility. Acting on bad and arrogant advice, however, Margaret chose to reject a petition submitted to her by about three hundred nobles objecting to the religious persecution. In giving her his opinion, Margaret's advisor happened to say that she need pay no attention to a cupful of beggars (*tas de gueux*). The name caught on, and soon all those who were opposed to Spain and to Philip started proudly to call themselves "Beggars."

The Spanish general Francisco de Toledo, Duke of Alva (above), was sent by Philip II to pacify the Netherlands after the rioting of 1566 and the sack of Antwerp cathedral. As his troops moved systematically to punish rebellious towns and re-establish the Inquisition, Alva's name became synonymous with Terror. So successful was his campaign that when William of Orange-Nassau (below) invaded the Netherlands two years later not one town dared to come to his assistance. (LCRB.)

Calvinist Resistance Aristocratic resistance to centralization was not the only opposition encountered by Philip and his servants in the Netherlands. There was also a developing revolutionary movement centered around the growing Calvinist religious congregations. These consisted of people from all walks of life—from nobles, bourgeois merchants, and bankers down to unemployed workingmen—drawn together by religious conviction and organized as an underground movement by their pastors, many of whom had learned the techniques of covert resistance to authority during their training in Geneva. In the Netherlands, as in France and Germany, Calvinist minority groups were able to survive and even to grow in the face of governmental opposition. When the power of the government was temporarily weak, as was the case in the Netherlands after 1561 when Philip recalled the Spanish troops, they were able to launch an offensive of their own in order forcibly to impose their views on the majority.

Quite soon after the incident of the "Beggars" (spring, 1566), the results of Calvinist subversive activity became vividly apparent as the congregations acquired noble supporters. These, with their military skills and their armed followers, protected the Calvinists against interference by the authorities and enabled the heretics to meet openly rather than in secret cellars. During the summer Calvinist successes were marked by violent riots. In an orgy of iconoclasm, in churches and monasteries, statues, stained-glass windows, and other "idols" were smashed. The interior of the magnificent cathedral at Antwerp was virtually gutted.

These riots led to some political changes. The Netherlandish upper nobility, as represented by Egmont and William of Orange, recoiled from the spectacle of mob violence. Egmont decided to wash his hands of any taint of opposition; William of Orange left the country for temporary retirement. Margaret of Parma, deciding that the time had come for firmness, called in German mercenary troops. In the spring of 1567, she proceeded to repress this religious uprising through mass executions. Philip II came to the same conclusion as had his sister and dispatched one of his more thoroughgoing generals, the Duke of Alva, with ten thousand troops of the famed and feared Spanish army to the Netherlands.[2] Alva replaced Margaret as regent and proceeded to try to complete the repression. Egmont, though still loyal to Philip, was arrested. A special new council was created which soon acquired the name "Council of Blood." Supplied with human material by an active group of police agents, it hastily condemned religious and political dissidents to death.

Revolt in the Netherlands The upshot was war. William the Silent and his brother, Louis of Nassau, raised armies and invaded the Netherlands. They were defeated by Alva, who took this opportunity to have Egmont and Horn beheaded (1568). With this victory behind him, Alva, who was constantly in need of money, proceeded to impose in the Netherlands the Castilian tax system, including a 10 percent sales tax, the *alcabala,* on every transaction, whether wholesale or retail. Bad enough in Spain, such a tax was disastrous in a commercial and industrial country where economic activity consisted largely of the turnover of goods. Thus, by 1569, Alva's tactics had succeeded in arousing the business community as well as political and religious dissidents. His execution of Egmont widened the already serious breach between the Netherlandish nobility and the Spanish crown. In short, Alva guaranteed that the revolt in the Netherlands should become a revolution.

The nobles who led the early Netherlandish resistance to Philip had been, nevertheless, willing to accept the overlordship of the king of Spain. William of Orange, who coveted the title of *stadholder* (governor) of all the Netherlands under Spanish sovereignty, had been trying to play the part of the moderate leader opposed to active foreign Spanish control and military occupation. He had tried to keep religious issues, which he saw as potentially divisive, in the background. (He had, therefore, been embarrassed by the untidy intervention of the iconoclasts.) But as time went on and as Alva's heavy-handed religious persecution, taxation, and mass confiscations made it all too clear what the Netherlands could expect from Spanish rule in the future, he and others came to believe that revolution was their only alternative.

A Divided Netherlands Revolutions or rebellions undertaken by unorganized groups have seldom succeeded. A successful revolution requires a disciplined organization inspired by an ideology or principle sufficiently compelling to lead people to sacrifice their tranquility, their possessions, and eventually their lives in the prosecution of the revolution. In more recent times, territorial revolutions have found their principle in the ideology of nationalism. Ahead of his time, William of Orange seems to have intended to base the Netherlandish revolt on national pride or patriotism.

[2]By 1574 the Army of Flanders numbered 86,000. Geoffrey Parker, *The Army of Flanders and the Spanish Road, 1567–1659* (1972), p. 6.

But the collection of provinces recently assembled by Charles V was not a unit. Some of the nobles tended to identify themselves with France and some with the German Empire. There was economic rivalry among the towns. Because the necessary linguistic, economic, and cultural bases of nationality did not exist, there was no nation. Although there was near universal opposition to the Spanish king, his henchman, the Duke of Alva, and the Spanish armies, there was as yet no spirit of nationality in the Netherlands. This was demonstrated when, in 1568, the Netherlandish towns failed to rise in support of William's invasion.

Yet, if nationalism did not exist, there was another strong unifying ideology in the late sixteenth century: religion. As time went on and as more and more blood flowed, Calvinism came to serve as a driving revolutionary principle. The presence of thousands of Spanish troops made it difficult for heresy to flourish in the south. Less effectively policed, and with access to the open sea, the north became the locus of the rebellion.

Revolt in the North As Calvinist theology supplied the revolutionary spirit, Calvinist congregations supplied the organization. At first unarmed and underground, then, in the early 1560's acquiring the military capabilities of some of the lesser nobility, this minority was soon to develop a navy.

William of Orange and Louis of Nassau, his Calvinist brother, issued letters of marque (privateering licenses) to Dutch sea captains, some of

Two Chained Monkeys, Signed and Dated 1562. In this year the artist, Pieter Brueghel, the printer, Christopher Plantin, and many others were obliged to leave Antwerp to escape persecution. The painting shows two monkeys chained to a window of the newly erected Spanish citadel, Fort Philip, overlooking Antwerp. (Berlin State Museum.)

whom had taken refuge from Alva's terror by sailing their vessels to French Huguenot ports. Joined by adventurers of all nations, these Dutch sailors fared forth in ships specially designed with shallow drafts—the famous "flyboats"—to navigate the shallow coasts and estuaries of the Netherlands. Quite soon they succeeded in paralyzing Spanish sea communications and trade in northern waters. In the spring of 1572, they captured the town of Brill and several other ports along the Dutch coast and began to take on the appearance of a regular navy, with their own ports in the ostensibly Spanish Netherlands. Then the Sea Beggars, as they came to be known, moved on other towns in Holland, Zeeland, Gelderland, and Utrecht, and by land and sea took control there. In many cases, these towns did not welcome the extremist Calvinist minority and resisted the "Beggars" as valiantly as they had tried to resist Alva's troops. Often the barbarities inflicted by the Calvinists in these towns on Roman Catholics—especially priests, monks, and nuns—were fully as horrible as those perpetrated by Alva.

Alva reacted characteristically to the Beggars' successes. Force should be met by overwhelming force. In the summer of 1572, forty thousand troops were unleashed on Malines, Zutphen, and Naarden.[3] The surrender of these towns was marked by unspeakable pillage to reward the soldiers for their efforts—and to compensate them, for their pay was far in arrears. In the next summer, when Alva chose to stop them from sacking the town of Haarlem, the troops mutinied. Alva submitted his resignation.

The Pacification of Ghent In the full flush, then, of the afterglow of his victories over the Turk at Lepanto and over the *Moriscos* in Granada, Philip was made vividly aware, as he pored over reports in the Escorial, that he had serious problems on his hands in the north. He tried a new governor-general, Don Luis Requesens, who modified Alva's policy somewhat but who died less than two years after taking office. Still unpaid and now without a leader, the Spanish troops once again mutinied. While William of Orange was attempting to unify all of the provinces under his leadership, the Spanish soldiers proceeded unofficially but thoroughly to sack the city of Antwerp. Just ten years after the iconoclasts' orgy in that city, this so-called "Spanish Fury" galvanized the representatives of the several provinces into joining in an agreement—the so-called "Pacification of Ghent" (1576)—whereby they all united, regardless of religious differences, to expel the foreigner. This was a great triumph for William the Silent, but, for reasons suggested earlier, this union was a shaky one at best.

The revolution and the union of the provinces according to the terms of the Pacification of Ghent survived the short rule of a new and famous Spanish governor, Don John of Austria, whose string of victories came to an end, however, in the Netherlands. He died in 1578. Philip now found,

[3]Though under command of the king of Spain, the Flanders army, as it was called, consisted mainly of non-Spanish soldiers. In 1572, in the total army of 67,000, there were about 9,000 Spanish infantrymen, 24,000 Germans, and 19,500 Netherlanders (Walloons).

too late, the man who could do his work in the Low Countries. This was the supple and elegant Alexander Farnese, son of his half-sister Margaret of Parma (and, therefore, grandson of Charles V). The prince of Parma was at once an able soldier and an accomplished statesman, a worthy contemporary of Elizabeth of England and at least the match of William of Orange.

The Separation of the Two Netherlands By the time Alexander Farnese arrived, several foreign princelings had sensed the possibility of an open sovereignty or empty throne in the Netherlands and had presented themselves as willing and able to take the place of the old dukes of Burgundy. Elizabeth of England became involved by providing one of the aspirants with money to hire troops; later she made money and men available to William of Orange and his successors. Another interloper, Matthias of Habsburg, Archduke of Austria, had been invited to intervene by malcontent southern Roman Catholic nobles. The latter were becoming more and more convinced that a union with Calvinist extremists, as agreed to in the Pacification of Ghent, was not in their best interests.

The behavior of the Calvinist minorities in towns that they came to control in the middle ground between the North and South Netherlands—Ghent, Brussels, Bruges, Ypres, for example—was often fanatical. A kind of class struggle was interjected into the religious conflict. To religious

Brueghel's "The Massacre of the Innocents," dated about 1567, exists in two versions. This one shows Spanish soldiers sacking a village in the Netherlands. The page on horseback (right, center) wears on his tunic the bifurcated eagle of the House of Habsburg. Another version is closer to the biblical story, showing the soldiers killing the newborn. (Hampton Court.)

intolerance was joined demagoguery, as the Calvinists came increasingly to rely on the rootless and the poor for support. Mobs completed the gutting of churches; monks and nuns were mistreated; people of wealth began to take fright. Farnese sensed the new division among the Netherlands and proceeded to encourage it.

He contrived to make the Roman Catholics of the south forget the atrocities perpetrated by Alva and the Spanish troops and to encourage them to believe that they had more to fear from wild Calvinists than from Spain.

In the first days of the year 1579, his efforts were rewarded when the malcontents of a number of the southern provinces in effect withdrew from the union agreed upon in 1576 and formed the League of Arras for the defense of the Roman Catholic religion. In return for Farnese's promise that their traditional political rights would be respected, these provinces professed loyalty to the Spanish crown.

Those in the north, beyond Farnese's immediate reach, soon responded by making a new agreement of their own. With the Union of Utrecht (January 1579), they bound themselves together to repel the foreign enemy and to preserve their historic rights and liberties. William the Silent, who still dreamed of uniting all the Netherlands, was saddened by this development, the work of one of his brothers. But as time went on he was led more and more surely to the position of being the leader of a northern rebellion only. Two years later (1581), the northern provinces declared their independence from Spain and installed William as hereditary *stadholder.* A *stadholder* was something like a military governor and not a sovereign.

With the deposition of Philip of Spain, it became necessary to find a new sovereign. At William's suggestion the Dutch settled upon a French interloper-prince, Francis, Duke of Anjou, who was solemnly installed early in 1582 as Duke of Brabant. William's idea was that Francis should serve only as a convenient figurehead. Francis had other ideas, however, and resolved to seize full power with the help of French troops through an armed *coup.* The attempt failed completely, but this experience with what they called

One of the most frightening paintings ever conceived, "The Triumph of Death" is now dated 1568, the year of the height of Alva's Terror and the defeat of William of Orange. Brueghel himself died the following year. (Prado, Madrid.)

"the French Fury" and others like it convinced the northern Netherlanders that they would have to find and hold their own sovereignty.

Meanwhile, William's worthy adversary, Alexander Farnese, after having secured most of the southern provinces, had gone on the offensive, joining force and terror to persuasion and diplomacy. With a new army of 31,000 men, he attacked, besieged, and took the essentially Dutch city of Maastricht. Farnese went on to attack and eventually take the southern and mainly Walloon stronghold, Tournai, near Lille, where the victorious army was allowed to massacre no one and the defeated garrison was given full honors of war. Next, the Duke began to conquer all of the principal towns of the middle ground between the Dutch and the Walloons: the towns of the regions of Flanders and Brabant (Bruges, Ghent, Brussels, and, eventually, Antwerp, which fell in 1585). His base of operations south of the Rhine and the Meuse (Maas) thus secured, Farnese was ready to press his offensive into the provinces to the north. Meanwhile, William the Silent had been assassinated by an adventurer seeking the 25,000 *thalers* and title of nobility that Philip had offered as a reward to anyone who would perform this deed.

There is little doubt that, given sufficient support in the form of men and money from Philip of Spain, the Duke of Parma would have been able to complete the conquest of the eastern and "mainland" provinces of the northern Netherlands. Whether such conquest would have led to the eventual domination of the maritime provinces, Holland and Zeeland, relatively secure behind their dikes and canals and equipped with sea power with which the Spaniards never were able to cope, is a question that must remain unanswered. Events outside of the Netherlands, over which he had no control, and decisions made by Philip II in the Escorial, combined to deprive Farnese of the opportunity to make a serious attempt to enter the northern Netherlands. The result was that the split between north and south became permanent. Where there had been no nation before, two nations began to take shape, their respective parameters determined by the fortunes of war.

Calvinists and others who for one reason or another felt that they could not or did not wish to live under Spanish rule emigrated to the north in ever-increasing numbers. They were passed *en route* by equally large numbers of Roman Catholics and other malcontents from the north moving south. Over the years thereafter, Calvinist churches in the Dutch provinces, through education, propaganda, and coercion, gradually won the majority of the population over to the new faith. The dominant culture of the northern provinces thus became Protestant.[4] In the south, the continuation of Spanish rule and the tendency of anti-Calvinist Netherlanders to congregate there led to the development of a Roman Catholic culture markedly different from that of the Dutch provinces only a few miles away. The United Provinces to the north became a prosperous and bustling republican federation dominated by the more substantial Protestant businessmen.

[4]The present population of the Kingdom of the Netherlands is Protestant by roughly half, that of Belgium is overwhelmingly Roman Catholic.

Within a few years, the principal city of Holland, Amsterdam, was the commercial and financial capital of Europe.[5] The Dutch pursued the war against the Duke of Parma and, after Parma's death in 1592, against a succession of Spanish generals. It was during these wars that the Dutch began, as we have seen, to wrest control of the East Indies from the Portuguese. Thus, the King of Spain, who was now also King of Portugal, lost not only the vast sums that he had to spend to maintain the Army of Flanders but also the larger part of the Portuguese overseas empire, not to speak of the lives of his soldiers and subjects. But loss of human life was of no

[5]The decline of southern Netherlandish ports contributed to the economic decline that followed. Great old ports like Bruges had long since been rendered useless by the silting of their rivers. The new port of Antwerp was effectively closed by a Dutch naval blockade at the mouth of the Scheldt. Later, in 1648, the *de facto* closing of the river Scheldt was legalized by international agreement in the Peace of Westphalia.

great matter to European rulers when population was growing rapidly. The financial losses were more serious. At the time of Philip II's death in 1598, two-thirds of the Spanish government's revenues (including those from Spanish America) were swallowed by interest on the royal debt. Much of this debt had been incurred by the expenses of the war in the Netherlands.

Shortly after the turn of the century, Spain was forced to suspend the war for a variety of military, diplomatic, and financial reasons, some of which we shall discuss in the next chapter. In 1609, a twelve-year truce was signed between Spain and the northern Netherlands. In the end, Philip's efforts in the Low Countries resulted in the more-or-less permanent political division of the country into two parts. The south was made safe for Roman Catholicism while the north was "lost" to Protestantism.

But we move ahead of our story. Let us backtrack to see how Philip II's trials in other parts of Europe—for example, in France and in England—contributed to the decline of Spain.

FURTHER READING

The best general work on this period is H. Hauser, *La prépondérance espagnole, 1559–1660* (1948), in the *Peuples et civilisations* series. There is nothing in any other language to match it, though the reader can refer to textbooks like H. S. Lucas, *Renaissance and Reformation* (1960), for some aid in English. Part of one of the most stimulating works in sixteenth-century multidisciplinary history, F. Braudel, *La méditerranéen et le monde méditerranéen à l'époque de Philippe II* (1949), has been translated as *The Mediterranean and the Mediterranean World in the Age of Philip II* (1972); this is an exciting book.

Spanish history in the period can best be studied in J. H. Elliott, **Imperial Spain, 1469–1716* (1963). J. Lynch, *Spain under the Habsburgs,* Vol. I, *Empire and Absolutism, 1516–1598* (1964), is a fuller study. Older, but still useful, is R. B. Merriman, *The Rise of the Spanish Empire in the Old World and the New,* 4 vols. (1918–1934), already mentioned. On the Inquisition, consult H. C. Lea, **A History of the Inquisition in Spain,* an abridgement of a four-volume work published in 1906. Lea also dealt with the Morisco problem in *Moriscos of Spain: Their Conversion and Expulsion* (1901), still the best treatment. For the Marranos, see C. Roth, **History of the Marranos* (1963). On Spanish sheep-herding, see J. Klein, *The Mesta* (1920), the only work of its kind in English on this fascinating subject.

On the Netherlandish revolt, P. Geyl, **The Revolt of the Netherlands* (1932), and *The Netherlands Divided* (1936), translations from a larger work in Dutch history, supersede all other studies. Two massive works by one of America's greatest historians of the nineteenth century, recently reprinted, may still be read with pleasure and profit: J. L. Motley, *The Rise of the Dutch Republic,* 5 vols., and *History of the United Netherlands,* 5 vols. C. V. Wedgwood,

*Books available in paperback edition are marked with an asterisk.

William of Nassau, Prince of Orange (1960), again presents her subject at its best.

To understand how William, Alva, and Parma fought, see C. W. C. Oman, *A History of the Art of War in the Sixteenth Century* (1937). The problems of Spanish communications with the Netherlands are most interestingly laid out in Geoffrey Parker, *The Army of Flanders and the Spanish Road, 1567–1659* (1972).

To check on the present writer's prejudices regarding Philip II the reader should consult the volume in the Heath series, "Problems in European Civilization," edited by J. C. Rule and J. J. Te Paske, * *The Character of Philip II—the Problem of Moral Judgements in History* (1963); and C. J. Cadoux, *Philip of Spain and the Netherlands: An Essay on Moral Judgements in History* (1969). By all means do not omit the most delightful book in late sixteenth-century European history, G. Mattingly, * *The Armada* (1959).

4 Spanish Hegemony Checked

During the late 1550's, the Scots religious reformer John Knox published a pamphlet in which he expressed the following sentiment:

. . . to promote women to bear rule above any realm is repugnant to nature, contumely to God, a thing most contrarious to His revealed will and approved ordinance; and finally it is the subversion of good order, of all equity and justice.

Aptly entitled *First Blast of the Trumpet Against the Monstrous Regiment* [*Rule*] *of Women,* Knox's "blast" was inspired by what he considered the melancholy state of affairs in England, where Queen Mary's single-minded Roman Catholicism was lighting the doleful fires at Smithfield,[1] and in Scotland, where another woman, Mary of Guise (also known as Mary of Lorraine and acting as regent for her daughter, Mary, Queen of Scots), was also persecuting Protestants. When he wrote his pamphlet, Knox could not have known what part another lady, Catherine de'Medici of France, was soon to play in one of the most outrageous persecutions of an outrageous age. And in addition to the three Mary's and one Catherine, there was soon to be a fifth female ruler, Elizabeth of England, whom Philip II of Spain tried unsuccessfully to master, first through marriage and then by military conquest.

In the pages that follow we shall describe "what mighty woes to [Spain's] imperial race from woman rose" in France, Scotland, and England. We shall see how these relations, combined with the problems of the Netherlands described in the previous chapter, attained a sort of climax in the Armada of 1588 and how the wreckage of Philip's foreign policy during the "Monstrous Regiment of Women" helped to establish some of the basic political characteristics of early modern European civilization.

THE CRACK IN THE VALOIS DYNASTY

We have seen that during the reign of the dull-witted but athletic French king, Henry II, the French domain expanded significantly, even though the Treaty of Cateau-Cambrésis (1559) had seemed a victory for the Habsburgs.

[1]Smithfield was the place in London where the objects of persecution were burned alive. Some of Knox's earlier activities and writings stimulated persecution of Protestants under Mary.

Henry II of France (above, left) died in 1559 in the course of a jousting tournament (shown in the inset below the portrait). His wife, Catherine de'Medici, is shown (right) as she appeared shortly after the king's death and his succession by his eldest son, Francis, a lad of fourteen, below. (LCRB and the Uffizi, Florence.)

Under the leadership of two powerful French families, Coligny and Guise, French arms had secured the three bishoprics of Metz, Toul, and Verdun and thus pushed the eastern boundary of France farther toward the Rhine River. French forces, led by Francis, Duke of Guise, had conquered Calais, the last English foothold on French territory. Finally, although the French relinquished most of their Italian claims to Spain, they did keep some fortresses on the other side of the Alps. While Spanish triumphs in widely separated parts of Europe had multiplied Philip's commitments in areas that were to prove a source of endless difficulties for him in the future, the French crown emerged from the wars of the early sixteenth century in a tightly consolidated position, its territorial integrity intact and its internal power seemingly unchallengeable.

Soon after the signing of the Treaty of Cateau-Cambrésis in 1559, and to celebrate the marriages of his daughters and of his sister, Henry arranged a grand series of festivities in Paris. In the course of these, he donned armor to joust with the Count of Montgomery. As the galloping horses came together, Montgomery's lance broke, a splinter penetrated the king's eye, and some ten days later Henry died, aged forty. He left a widow, Catherine de'Medici, descended from a family that had made its original reputation in Italian banking circles, and many children, four of them boys. None of the latter was over fifteen years of age.

One after another these princes came to the throne as France went through one of its most painful ordeals in modern times. Philip II of Spain, unable to resist the temptation offered by the French dynastic failure, stirred the French cauldron—and was scalded in the process. Unfortunately for Spanish interests, Philip's intervention in France, like so many of his enterprises, proved unsuccessful. In the end, for Spain, the result was humiliation and diminished prestige accompanied by severe financial loss.

HUGUENOT VERSUS CATHOLIC IN FRANCE

Henry's eldest son, Francis II, had been married in 1558 at age fourteen to the beautiful sixteen-year-old Mary Stuart, Queen of Scots, whose mother, a member of the prominent and powerful Guise family, acted as regent for Mary in Scotland. The principal objective of the Guise family at this moment was more power; the death of Henry II in the prime of life before any of his sons had grown to manhood offered an opportunity that this ambitious and aggressive family was quick to seize. For outside help they tended to look to the pope at Rome and to Philip of Spain. They were committed to the subsidiary policy of repressing Protestantism which, especially in its Calvinistic form, had already made large inroads in France.

Although its administrative and spiritual capital was in Swiss Geneva, Calvinism was the characteristically French form of Protestantism. Calvin was French; most of his early associates in religious reformism had been French; the first edition of his great book, *The Institutes of the Christian Religion* (1536), had been dedicated to a king of France; and many of the preachers who received their training in Geneva were French. Located as it was at the point of a salient jutting out into French territory, Geneva served as a convenient transmitter of the new faith into France.

At first, during the 1540's and 1550's, Calvinism had appealed mainly to unemployed workers, artisans, small businessmen, and other out-groups who were suffering from rising prices, heavy taxation, and the economic dislocations of the wars of the first half of the sixteenth century. Later, during the late 1550's, numbers of petty nobles, also injured by the price rise, began to flock to the secret meetings of the Calvinist preachers. After the conclusion of the wars in 1559, unemployed soldiers, including many nobles, joined the movement, adding, as was the case in the Netherlands at the same time, their military skills and bringing their armed retainers to what had been essentially a religious, economic, and social movememt. Among these old fighters was one of the foremost soldiers of France, Admiral Gaspard de Coligny (1519–1572), and two disaffected "Princes of the blood," the king of Navarre and the prince of Condé. The presence of these recruits transformed the Huguenot[2] religious community into an armed political party, less and less under the control of Calvin's Geneva-trained pastors and more and more dominated by dissident nobles.

[2]Huguenot, a word of mysterious origin, came into use to designate the French Calvinist community. Later it designated a party and, still later, a religious community again.

As was the case in the Netherlands, the Calvinists were able to grow as a party and to become powerful because of governmental weakness, in this case the crack in the Valois dynasty after the death of Henry II. The Huguenots illegally took over towns, especially in the south and west where Calvinist influence and the distance from the center of legitimate French government were both great. They sacked churches, persecuted Catholic monks and nuns, imposed and collected taxes, and even minted their own coins. With support from Protestant Germany and England, in the course of time they raised their own army.

This detail of a contemporary painting shows Catherine de' Medici presiding over a court ball with her effeminate third son, King Henry III. Twenty-five years after her husband's death, Catherine still wears a plain black dress and a cap with a widow's peak, in sharp contrast to the lavishly-dressed courtiers around her. (Louvre.)

To oppose the Huguenots, there arose a Catholic party which, for France, corresponded to the Spanish power in the Netherlands. As early as 1560, local Catholics who were being terrorized by the Huguenots formed leagues here and there. Eventually, these local leagues came together under the leadership of the Guise family to form a nation-wide union known as the Holy or Catholic League. Founded in 1576 with the support of the pope and the king of Spain, the League was particularly strong among the more conservative Catholic nobility.

Both the Huguenot party and the League looked outside France for guidance and support. Both parties were centrifugal forces tending to tear France apart again after the promising start toward centralization begun at least as far back as the time of Charles VII and patiently carried on by royal administrators in the century thereafter.

CATHERINE DE' MEDICI

Between these two parties, each with its foreign allies, stood the French crown. During most of this period (1559–1589) royal power was exercised by the queen mother, who was prepared to use any method to hold the kingdom together for her male children, one of whom she vainly hoped would eventually provide her with a grandchild. Though a Roman Catholic, she was not a fanatic. She was willing to compromise with the Huguenots for the sake of peace and the maintenance of royal power in France. Thus, she served as a centripetal force counteracting the centrifugal tendencies of the Huguenots and the Leaguers.

During the five-month reign of her eldest son, Francis II, the Guise family exercised great power at court through the young queen, their niece. After Francis' death (1560), the Guises were shunted into the wings. Catherine, as regent during the minority of her second son, Charles IX, tried to steer a moderate, middle course between Roman Catholic and Protestant as the two parties fought savagely for primacy in France. For example, she refused to accede to the Guise's demand for vengeance following the assassination in 1563 of Francis, Duke of Guise, by a Huguenot. In 1570, she assented to the Peace of St. Germain, which granted the Huguenots a general amnesty, liberty of conscience, and control of a number of fortified towns. One of the principal Huguenot military leaders, Admiral de Coligny, was welcomed at court and included in the royal council.

Once at court, Coligny soon gained the confidence of the young king and urged him to make war on Spain. Catherine was disturbed at the prospect of being displaced by Coligny as the power behind the throne. She was terrified by thoughts of what disastrous effects war with mighty Spain would have on royal power in an already fractured France. She now turned against Coligny and gave her approval to a plot put forward by the Guise family, still seeking revenge on the Huguenots for the assassination of Francis of Guise.

St. Bartholomew's Day Massacre The occasion for wider violence was provided by one result of Catherine's earlier policy of reconciliation with the Huguenots, the marriage of her daughter Margaret to a Protestant leader, young Henry Bourbon, king of Navarre. To celebrate the marriage, nearly all the Huguenot leaders, feeling secure in the provisions of the Peace of St. Germain, congregated in Paris. A few days after the wedding, an attempt to kill Coligny failed when the assassin's bullet merely wounded the Admiral. What happened the next day is not fully known, but it seems that there was a meeting in the royal palace, attended by Catherine, during which it was decided that nearly all the Protestants (the king of Navarre and some others excepted) in Paris should be killed. King Charles gave his assent, and plans for the executions were laid.

Early on St. Bartholomew's day (August 24, 1572), Henry of Guise revenged the death of his father Francis by sending his hirelings to murder Coligny. Then the church bells rang, and all over Paris prominent and ordinary Huguenots were slaughtered. In the days that followed, what had been intended as a fairly conventional political *coup* designed to eliminate a threat against the interests of the state became a social movement. Over most of France and for weeks, Roman Catholics moved against local heretics. Before the massacre was over some twenty thousand (estimates vary greatly) persons had been killed. The queen mother wrote triumphantly to her son-in-law, Philip II of Spain, the news of how her son had dealt with rebels. Philip replied with his congratulations, and the pope had a medal struck in honor of the occasion. But in London, after hearing the news, Elizabeth, in a typical theatrical gesture, dressed in mourning clothes to receive the French ambassador.

If the St. Bartholomew's Day massacre was intended to eliminate the Huguenot party, it failed. Henry Bourbon and many other Huguenot leaders were spared or escaped, and their party was strengthened by the blood of martyrs. Two years after the massacre, Catherine's second son died and was succeeded by his younger brother, Henry III, Catherine's favorite son. Despite certain effeminate characteristics, this last of the Valois kings of France was a good soldier and something of a statesman. At the time of his succession, he was serving as the elected king of Poland, an honor that his mother had gained for him. After his return to France as king in 1575, he found himself and the crown in the difficult middle position that Catherine had been trying to hold. Like her, he found it impossible to maintain an independent policy. Quite early, he and his mother decided the crown could not defeat the Huguenots and made peace with them in 1576, once again legalizing Protestant worship.

It was this royal concession to the Huguenots that caused the separate local Catholic Leagues to coalesce as a national movement in opposition to the crown, as well as to the Huguenots. Under Henry of Guise's leadership and supported by Spanish gold, the League soon became so powerful that Henry of France was forced to revoke his concessions to the Huguenots. Then he declared himself the head of the League and abolished it. For a few years thereafter, he and his mother tried to rely for support on a middle-of-the road group known as the *politiques,* who, like Catherine, were willing to compromise on religious matters in order to achieve unity and peace. The difficulty with this posture was that the middle was not organized while the Catholic and Protestant extremes were. By associating himself with the middle, Henry III subjected himself to attack from both extremes. A weaker man would probably have taken the easier course of siding with one or the other of the extremes; but as a matter of royal pride Henry refused to give into Guise pressure to join the Holy Leaguers and the king of Spain in an all-out repression of Protestantism in France. On the other hand, he would not tolerate an absolute victory of the Huguenots. Childless though he was, this last of the Valois was determined to pass on his kingdom and his royal prerogatives as nearly intact as possible.

THE WAR OF THE THREE HENRIES

The French political crisis of the sixteenth century had begun in 1559 with the death of Henry II. The climax of the crisis was ushered in by the death without issue in 1584 of Henry III's younger brother, the duke of Anjou (whom we last encountered in the Netherlands). This event clearly indicated that Henry III, who could not or would not have any children, was really the last of his line, and threw open the question of succession. The person with the most nearly direct claim to the French throne was Henry Bourbon, king of Navarre. But Navarre was a Protestant; and the threat of a heretic as king caused fanatical Catholics in Paris to revive the Holy League. Once again, Henry of Guise assumed the leadership of the League. The Guise and League candidate for king was the elderly Charles, Cardinal of Bourbon, who was also supported by Philip. The king of Spain agreed to pay a large subsidy for the purpose of keeping Henry of Navarre from the French throne. The pope published a "Bull of Deprivation" in which he declared Henry of Navarre ineligible, as a heretic, to accede to the throne of France. Henry of Navarre denounced the bull as contrary to the French constitution, and the war was on again.

So great was the influence of Henry of Guise and the League at this time (1587) that Henry III was forced against his will to take their side against Henry of Navarre and the Huguenots. The humiliation of the French crown seemed complete when, in 1588, Henry III was forced to flee from Paris in response to demonstrations organized by the League. But Guise underestimated the determination of Henry III of France—who would and could

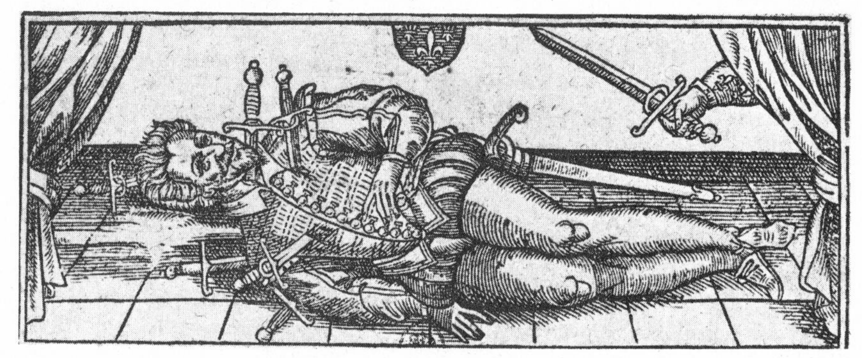

The Assassination of Henry of Guise at Blois, from a French Woodcut. (Bibliothèque Nationale, Paris.)

fight for survival. Taking advantage of Guise's presence at a meeting of the French Estates General (parliament) at Blois, the king had his bodyguard assassinate Guise in his presence. The next day Duke Henry's brother, the Cardinal of Guise, was also murdered. When the king told his mother about his triumph, she is said to have expressed her fears for the future.

A few months later, a fanatical Leaguer disposed of the king in the same fashion. As he lay dying of an abdominal stab wound, Henry of Valois named Henry of Navarre as his successor—on condition that he become a Roman Catholic.

Henry Bourbon, King of Navarre, did succeed as Henry IV of France. He was the beneficiary of Henry III's labors as well as of his own superb military prowess and good luck. The new king, born a Catholic but raised a Huguenot, decided that if he were to be king of France, and, particularly if he were to be ruler over the fanatically Roman Catholic and Leaguer stronghold of Paris, he would be wise to shift to the old faith. This was small comfort to the king of Spain, who had made an immense investment in the project of keeping Henry Bourbon off the French throne and of making France a satellite of Spain.

Young King Henry of Navarre, before his Accession to the Throne of France. (Bibliothèque Nationale, Paris.)

Meanwhile, in the north, the duke of Parma had been calling on Philip for money to complete his subjugation of the Netherlands. Since 1585 he had been contending not only with the Dutch forces but also with an expeditionary army sent to the Netherlands by the Protestant queen of England. For Philip, the whole affair was like a giant jig-saw puzzle. By inserting just the right piece he thought he could solve all of his French, Netherlandish, and English problems at once. This "piece" was known to Philip as "The Enterprise of England"; we know it as the launching of the Spanish Armada. Before we can consider the Armada, however, it is well to look back, shifting the scene to the Britain of Mary, Queen of Scots, and of Elizabeth I; for it was the intertwining of Philip's fate with that of these two female rulers, as well as with France and the Netherlands, that stirred the prudent Spanish king to mount his historic attack on the British Isles.

MARY OF SCOTLAND

Before his father's abdication, and in an effort to link the Spanish to the English throne, Philip had been married to Queen Mary Tudor of England (who was his first cousin once removed). Philip spent some months on two occasions in England counselling Mary on the best ways to stamp out Protestantism. But unfortunately for Spain, this marriage lasted only four years. In 1558, Mary died and her half-sister Elizabeth, then 25, succeeded to the English throne.

François Clouet made this drawing of Mary Stuart as a young lady of seventeen in the French court shortly before her return to Scotland. Two years later she claimed the throne of England as well. She thus embarked on a collision course with Elizabeth I. (Bibliothèque Nationale, Paris.)

Three years later, Elizabeth's young second cousin, Mary Stuart, now dowager queen of France after the death of her husband, Francis II, returned to Scotland, a land she barely remembered. Aged nineteen, this young lady had already begun to style herself Queen of England as well as of Scotland and to assert that she, not Elizabeth, was the legitimate heiress of Mary Tudor. By Roman Catholics, Elizabeth was considered to be an illegitimate child of her father.

Mary Stuart was a remarkable young woman, about whom it is easy to romanticize. Even when one discounts the flattery that crept into descriptions of her, Mary seems to have been extraordinarily beautiful, though tall for a girl—perhaps six feet. She was a thoroughgoing Roman Catholic, a good lover, and a magnificent hater. Politically she was certainly unwise, as events proved.

During much of Mary's sojourn in France, Scotland was ruled in her name and in French interests by her mother, Mary of Guise. Ostensibly, Scotland still adhered to its traditional French alliance; in fact, the marriage of young Mary with the French *dauphin* (heir to the throne) had made the Franco-Scottish connection even closer and pointed toward the time when the two kingdoms should be united under one ruler. But religious changes that had been taking place in Scotland during the regency made such a result more and more unlikely.

John Knox and the Scottish Reformation Just before the middle of the sixteenth century, one of the greatest Protestant Reformers, the Calvinist John Knox, began to make headway in convincing the Scots nobles that they should take religious matters into their own hands, more or less as Luther had appealed to the princes of Germany. Following his advice, a group of dissident nobles made a "Covenant with God" (1557) and became a revolutionary-military-religious organization similar to the Dutch Beggars and the French Huguenots. The noble leaders of this movement styled themselves the Lords of the Congregation. Their vassals and retainers as well as Protestant zealots made up the revolutionary army. Knox assumed the spiritual as well as diplomatic leadership of the movement.

The army of the Congregation attacked the Catholic regent, Mary of Guise, and her French troops in Edinburgh but were no match for the trained French soldiery. It soon became obvious that without help from abroad the Scottish rebels would fail. In this crisis, Knox made a dramatic move. He communicated with the new English queen to suggest that traditional English policy toward Scotland was out of date; that at this moment the interests of the Scottish Protestants and those of the English coincided; that it was time for Scotland to cast off its French liaison; and that, in return, the English queen should send military assistance. Elizabeth herself would not deal with Knox because she had, understandably, taken offense at the remarks he had written about the "Regiment of Women"; but she did not forbid her principal secretary of state from continuing the correspondence. The negotiations were spurred when the Lords of the Congregation formally renounced their allegiance to the regent. Eventually, Elizabeth's English troops arrived to help drive the French into their ships and away.

From this point the Scottish Reformation proceeded very rapidly, especially among the nobles and the townsfolk of the Lowlands, although probably the majority of the population still held to the old faith. The new church was Calvinist in theology and organized on a presbyterian rather than episcopal basis.[3] The nobles profited from this Reformation by taking over the church lands.

Thus, by the time Mary Stuart arrived in Scotland in 1561, this Reformation was already far advanced and John Knox was a dominant figure in Scotland. Mary came quickly to understand that there was little that she could do immediately to undo the new Scottish church and that the reorientation of Scotland away from France and toward England was a reality she had best accept. She made no attempt to restore to the old church the property that the Protestant lords had plundered. She limited her religious complaints to an assertion that she should be allowed to hear mass in private at Holyrood House palace. Knox objected, but she heard mass.

Mary's End as Queen of Scotland There is little doubt that Mary thought of the Scottish throne as a stepping-stone to the crown of England. She remarkably improved her chances, or those of her future children, of achieving that goal when she married her cousin Henry, who was next in

[3]An episcopal church is governed by a hierarchy of bishops as in the case of the present-day Church of England. A presbyterian church is governed by presbyteries or councils of priests and elected laymen.

line, after her, to the English throne. Henry, Lord Darnley, was also a great-grandchild of Henry VII. Darnley's main function, from a historical point of view, was to get Mary with the child who eventually became James VI of Scotland and James I of England. Darnley, an opportunist, repeatedly betrayed his wife in a number of political schemes. His less-than-chivalrous attitude toward Mary was colored by what he thought was her unfaithfulness. As Darnley's deviousness became more and more apparent, Mary seemed to come under the influence of her Italian secretary, David Rizzio. One of Darnley's plots led to Rizzio's being dragged from Mary's dinner table and murdered by a band of noble Scots conspirators, one of whom was Darnley himself. Thereafter—and understandably—Mary's dislike of her husband reached the point where she was determined to be rid of him. At the same time, as a young woman trying to rule a country in which the chief nobles often acted like highwaymen and constantly indulged in private warfare, she needed a male, noble protector who could hold his own in a savage environment.

She thought she found such a man in James Hepburn, the earl of Bothwell, a well-bred ruffian, famous for his raids on England, for his sexual exploits, and for his ambition. Whether Mary actively conspired with Bothwell and others to murder her husband is not entirely clear; but Bothwell almost surely participated in Darnley's assassination (February 1567). Shortly thereafter, Bothwell was brought to trial in a civil action initiated by the Earl of Lennox, Darnley's father. Inasmuch as Bothwell brought 4,000 armed men with him to the trial, it is not surprising that no one, not even the plaintiff, would testify against him and that he was found innocent. Despite the fact that he had been declared legally innocent, nearly everyone believed Bothwell guilty. Therefore, when, within a shockingly short period of time, Mary married her late husband's murderer, her position in Scotland rapidly deteriorated. Public opinion ignored the fact that Bothwell forcibly abducted her before the marriage.

Nobles who had been squabbling among themselves now coalesced in opposition to Mary and Bothwell; and Mary was left with only Bothwell to support her. He was not equal to the task. Mary was taken and imprisoned in a castle on a loch island. Eventually, she was able to escape to England (1569), where she threw herself on the mercy of her cousin Queen Elizabeth. Elizabeth incarcerated her and, as we shall see, eventually consented to her execution. Bothwell also escaped from Scotland and ended his days insane as a prisoner of the king of Denmark.

Mary left behind her in Scotland an infant son in whose name a series of regents governed tempestuous Scotland as the new church, or kirk, tried to consolidate its position. When he came of age, James Stuart lent his learned mind to the task of trying to transform Scotland into a modern and centralized absolutism. Though a Protestant, he came into conflict with the Presbyterians over the question of how the kirk should be governed. James believed strongly that an episcopal organization of the kirk was necessary to support the kind of monarchy that he had in mind. In this regard, his ideas were the ones entertained by most contemporary monarchs, whether they were Protestant or Roman Catholic. Later, after little success in Scotland, James was to try to apply these notions on the larger stage of English affairs.

ELIZABETH OF ENGLAND

The ruler who was Mary Stuart's unwilling hostess for eighteen years owed her accession and her very life to the influence of her brother-in-law, Philip of Spain. During the English Mary's reign, an attempted rising against the queen had been put afoot without Elizabeth's knowledge but in her name. The result was that Mary, who had been tenderly kind to Elizabeth during her young girlhood, turned against Elizabeth, banished her from court and later committed her to the awesome fortress of the Tower of London. It had seemed highly likely for a time that Elizabeth's candle would be snuffed out.

After the marriage of Mary Tudor and Philip of Spain, however, the Spanish prince came to realize that his wife would probably not live long and that if Elizabeth were dispatched, the next in line for the throne of England would be Mary of Scotland who was also, at that time, Queen of France. Because of Mary Stuart's French connections, her accession to the English throne would have been far less than ideal from the Spanish point of view. Combined under one ruler, France and England could easily have driven the Spanish out of the Netherlands and would have seriously threatened the power of Spain in the European world. In short, the union of the two kingdoms would represent a strategic and diplomatic disaster for Spain. Moreover, Philip did not fail to remark the obvious popularity among the English people of the young princess who was so much her father's daughter. He realized that Elizabeth would probably make an effective ruler, that he would do well to be on good terms with her, and that Mary would only injure herself by persecuting Elizabeth. Accordingly, Philip advised his bride to reconcile herself with Elizabeth. (He also cautioned Mary regarding the wisdom of burning quite so many heretics.)

And so it was that one of the most intelligent and best educated persons of her time survived and came to rule over England. Elizabeth was not only bright and well educated; she was also rigorously trained in the hard school of English royal fortunes. One result of a series of macabre girlhood experiences was that Elizabeth, who was endowed with the lively imagination that usually accompanies a sensitive intelligence, developed a certain ambivalence regarding love and marriage. Throughout her reign, her great and abiding love affair was with the English people—upon whom she lavished her womanly wiles, always in touch and in sympathy. As time went on, the English came more and more to appreciate their queen, who so artfully sought to amuse them and so sturdily defended their interests.

From the beginning, Elizabeth surrounded herself with extraordinarily able men, most of them of humble origins. William Cecil, Francis Walsingham, and Christopher Hatton served steadily and sometimes magnificently

This painting of Elizabeth I of England is said to be one of the few portraits of her painted from life. The queen was in full command of her powers in 1575 (age 41). Her regal presence was tempered by a warm and sometimes impulsive nature. (National Portrait Gallery, London.)

in the Privy Council. Nobles like Robert Dudley, Earl of Leicester, gave less useful service. Often, Elizabeth's councilors were at odds with one another, but they were usually ready to join ranks when danger threatened the queen.

The situation immediately upon Elizabeth's succession was one of severe crisis. The Spanish alliance was unpopular. Religious divisions rent the realm. Internal peace had vanished as Protestants and Roman Catholics fought one another during the reign of Edward (1547–1553), and Mary (reigned 1553–1558) burned several hundred Protestant victims at the stake. The currency was depreciated; the royal treasury stood empty; and economic activity was at a low ebb. The sorry internal condition of England was matched by its external situation. Calais had been lost to the French; the fleet had been neglected; and England herself stood almost defenseless against the very real danger of foreign intrusion.

The tasks that lay before Elizabeth and her council were therefore fourfold: (1) to spur the economy, (2) to settle the religious strife, (3) to re-establish the prestige of the crown, (4) and to maneuver until such time as English defenses were sufficient to maintain the security of the realm. These were great tasks, and the remarkable fact is that Elizabeth and her servants managed to perform all of them during her reign.

Economic Development Elizabeth's government contributed to the economic recovery of England through its mercantilist policies and by exploiting to English advantage the contemporary difficulties in the Netherlands. Thousands of skilled textile craftsmen, refugees from Alva's Spanish terror, were encouraged to come to England where they settled down, mainly in the eastern counties, taught their skills to the English, and contributed to the development of a growing textile industry which Elizabeth observed with lively interest. English wool growers gained a new and more reliable market for their product. English woolen goods, which had been known mainly for their sturdiness, became noted for their fineness. The value of English exports rose.

The prestige of the crown was re-established partly through Elizabeth's masterful handling of Parliament and the English people. She made it plain that she was "mere English" and that she would make no alliance, by marriage or otherwise, that was not in the English interest. The currency was re-established at full value and kept that way through careful management. Elizabeth tried to spend no more money than she had—and she never had much, never over half a million pounds per year. Parliament at no time supplied her with more than one fourth of her income. The money she had she laid out very carefully. She was willing to spend money for warships, but she was reluctant to keep these ships in commission, their crews requiring pay and food at the queen's expense. On the eve of the battle with the Spanish Armada she kept most of her fleet in harbor, manned only by skeleton crews, while the rest of the men lived ashore at their own expense and while her admirals chewed their beards in apprehension. Later, when the cannonading between the fleets had barely stopped, she ordered the

Elizabeth won the hearts of her subjects by being a highly visible and hardworking ruler. In the print above, she is being borne through the streets by six noblemen to attend the wedding of two of her subjects. At right, she presides over the House of Lords. The Queen was dependent on Parliament for money, which she succeeded in getting despite the fact that she consulted that body as little as possible. (Folger.)

decommissioning of substantial portions of the fleet before it was entirely clear that all danger of invasion had passed.

The Religious Settlement The religious settlement was characteristically Elizabethan in that it was not doctrinaire. During the first months of her reign, there was some apprehension that caution would lead Elizabeth in the Roman Catholic direction; and indeed it would have been unwise for Elizabeth to provoke an open break with the pope and his mighty Spanish defender at this time. Elizabeth herself was a Protestant of sorts, but she was not Puritan. The fact was that details of religious dogma made very little difference to her. But she realized that within her kingdom there was a wide range of religious views and she sought an Establishment—it went without saying that an established church was necessary—that would be as nearly national as possible: catholic but not Roman Catholic, Protestant but still episcopal. To this end, her moves were made in cooperation with Parliament. First, an Act of Supremacy (1559) repudiated all foreign jurisdictions and made Elizabeth "Supreme Governor" of the Church of England. (Her father had been styled "Supreme Head.") Second, the Act of Uniformity set the nature of the established church. Cranmer's Prayer Book of 1552 was restored with some minor changes. The Thirty Nine Articles of the Anglican Church and the Act of Uniformity were (and are) sufficiently flexible so that services can range from something rather like a Roman Mass down to a very simple Protestant service. Like most compromises, this arrangement did not satisfy everyone. Extreme Puritans grumbled about the vestiges of popery and attacked the Anglican episcopate with pamphlets; diehard Roman Catholics hid their priests behind their chimneys and continued to hear mass; but the majority of the nation conformed. To do otherwise was treason.

That there was not a Roman restoration was not due to lack of effort on the part of the Roman Catholics. Seldom has a ruler lived in such nearly constant danger of assassination as did Elizabeth. The pope, Philip II, Jesuits, English Roman Catholics, and the imprisoned Mary Stuart, all together and separately, hatched plots against her life. There was also continuing danger of outright attack on England by Spanish fleets and armies. Elizabeth greatly feared the results if Philip were to throw his full influence against her and her realm. This intelligent fear goes a long way toward explaining the deviousness of her diplomacy, her refusal to break off with Philip at the same time that her subjects were clamoring for war and were raiding Philip's empire. These apprehensions also explain why she was reluctant to give aid to the Netherlandish revolutionaires and why she held out against her Parliaments, against the City of London, and against her Privy Councilors, all of whom urged and begged her to execute Mary, Queen of Scots, as the intriguing focus of all plots against Elizabeth.

Elizabeth and Mary Her relationship with Mary was a delicate subject with Elizabeth. The year after Mary Stuart fled to England, the earls of the north of England, lawless and feudal, rose against Elizabeth with the intention of putting Mary on the English throne. Involved in this plot was a man very close to Elizabeth: Thomas Howard, the Duke of Norfolk. He had been in communication with Philip of Spain and with the Duke of Alva, who promised an invasion force of Spanish infantry. The armed rebellion was crushed; Norfolk's part in it was later discovered by Elizabeth's councilors (who had to spend a great deal of time acting as counter-intelligence agents), and Norfolk, who had been intended as a husband for Mary, was executed in England in the same year as the Massacre of St. Bartholomew (1572) in France.

About this time, Elizabeth gave up talking about marriage with Philip and began flirting with French princes. Then, in 1580, Philip acquired Portugal with its Atlantic harbors, thereby increasing his capacity to attack England by sea and further alarming Elizabeth. She realized that as she sided more and more openly with the Netherlandish rebels, she increased her terrible danger from Spain. The fact that this danger not only existed but was increasing made her all the more determined *not* to execute Mary Stuart.

Why should Elizabeth struggle to preserve the life of Mary, around whom developed plot after plot against Elizabeth's life? Was it honor—the duty of the hostess to the unfortunate guest? Partly. But mainly it was that Elizabeth knew that as long as she lived Mary served as a hostage assuring that Philip would not undertake war with England.

So long as Elizabeth felt that England's defenses were not strong enough to repel a Spanish attack she would risk the personal danger implicit in assassination plots against herself in order to spare her realm.

It was a dreadful gamble; and some of Elizabeth's councilors were nearly beside themselves with anxiety as Walsingham patiently collected information regarding the plotters who were in communication with Mary, the Duke of Parma, and Philip during the year 1587. Eventually, Walsingham sprang his trap on what is known as the Babington Conspiracy, in which Mary was thoroughly implicated.

Even then Elizabeth was reluctant to sign Mary's death warrant. At one point she suggested that someone quietly might do Mary in; but no one volunteered for the task. Eventually, she did sign the warrant, though afterwards she insisted that one of her secretaries of state had delivered the warrant against her wishes. The unfortunate man was locked up in the Tower, but Mary was executed nonetheless. The country was relieved and, as Elizabeth had foreseen, Philip of Spain was galvanized by this execution to put his final approval on "The Enterprise of England." It was to be a tremendous effort of staggering cost.

THE ARMADA (1588)

By the time Philip made up his mind it was too late for success. The decades that Elizabeth had saved by her ploys and gambits had given the English time to build what proved to be the ablest and best-armed fighting fleet the world had ever seen. Before the Armada left port it was defeated, and would have been so even if the Englishman Drake had not played havoc with his raids on the Spanish preparations. Though commanded by a man of great courage and manned by valiant soldiers and sailors, nothing short of a miracle could have carried the Spanish fleet to victory.

The plan was that the Armada should sail into the Channel, meet and, if possible, defeat the English fleet, and cover the Duke of Parma's crossing from the Netherlands with his troops. Parma, who was nothing if not a realist, did not prepare seriously for an amphibious operation. He knew that the Dutch Sea Beggars could sail their shallow-draft "flyboats" where the great Spanish ships could not go and thus blast invasion craft before they could reach deep water and the protection of the Spanish fleet.

The Armada. These two schematic views of the great contest have been woven into tapestries in the House of Lords. They show (left) the approach of the Spanish fleet to the English Channel and (right) the engagement of the Spanish by the English vessels sailing from Plymouth harbor. Since the wind was blowing from the Atlantic, the English warships had to sail a zig-zag course against the wind (to "tack") in order to come upon the Spanish from the rear. The crescent-shaped formation of the Armada was well-nigh invulnerable. (Folger.)

The Armada and the English fleet came together toward the end of July 1588. For several days, they fought along the Channel, in an artillery gunners' battle for which the English were much better prepared. Eventually, the two fleets fought a last engagement in the North Sea, after which contact was broken and the Duke of Medina Sidonia, the Spanish commander, decided to circumnavigate the British Isles and return to Spain. To his credit is the fact that despite the terrible pounding his fleet had received from English guns and fierce storms, he managed to sail home two-thirds of his first-line fighting ships.

After having received some enthusiastic but false early reports about the success of the enterprise, Philip was told of the failure. Before the year was over, he was informed of the assassination of his French ally, Henry, Duke of Guise. In the north, Parma realized that the tremendous effort expended on the Armada had robbed him of the opportunity to subjugate the northern Netherlands. Developments in France required him to divert troops from the Netherlands in an unsuccessful attempt to keep Henry Bourbon from ascending to the French throne after the assassination of Henry III. And, perhaps worst of all from the Spanish point of view, Parma died in 1592 at the age of forty-seven of wounds suffered in battle.

In all, things had not gone well for Philip. But he was able before his death in 1598 to put together a new and stronger fleet; and the war with England dragged on until 1604. The dreary affair in the Netherlands con-

Don Quixote *Frontispiece, 1605.* Although Cervantes began to write the adventures of the knight Don Quixote of La Mancha as a parody on the chivalric romances of the sixteenth century, it was soon recognized as a commentary on all aspects of life in this transitional period. The idealistic knight continually fights against reality and loses every contest. This woodcut is from a pirated edition which appeared in Lisbon in 1605 shortly after the first edition appeared in Castile. (LCRB.)

tinued until a truce was signed in 1609. At the time of Philip's death, Spain was still a very great power. But the English were very much alive on the sea and at home; and, on the continent, the wealth, power, and prestige of France were waxing. Never again was Spain to play as great a part in the world's affairs as it had under Philip the Prudent.

During this period, when the overwhelming Spanish predominance was checked, changes were taking place in the intellectual realm. These changes produced a revolution as pregnant with significance for the future as the geographic, economic, and political shifts described in the four chapters above.

FURTHER READING

The very best book to read in connection with this chapter is the late G. Mattingly's * *The Armada* (1959), previously listed, a scholarly delight, though intended for "the general reader." The Folger booklet by the same author, * *Invincible Armada and Elizabethan England* (1963), illustrated, is also recommended.

For Scotland, Mary, and Knox, see A. M. McKenzie, *The Scotland of Queen Mary and the Religious Wars* (1936); and P. H. Brown, *John Knox,* 2 vols. (1895). Knox wrote a history of his own times; the best edition is W. C. Dickinson, ed., *John Knox's History of the Reformation in Scotland,* 2 vols. (1949). Antonia

*Books available in paperback edition are marked with an asterisk.

Fraser's fascinating study of the star-crossed Queen of Scots, * *Mary Queen of Scots* (1969), is available in paperback.

On Elizabeth and her England there is much to read, some of it excellent, including J. B. Black, *The Reign of Elizabeth, 1558–1603* (1959); and J. E. Neale's * *Queen Elizabeth First* (1959). E. Jenkins, * *Elizabeth the Great* (1959), is popular while also sound and challenging. C. Read, * *The Tudors* (1969), on "personalities and practical politics" is fine; as are Read's other studies of Elizabeth's councilors. S. T. Bindoff, *Tudor England* (1973), is an excellent introduction. More exciting is A. L. Rowse, *The Elizabethan Age,* 2 vols. (1950–1955). The first volume has appeared in paper as * *The England of Elizabeth* (1961). Elizabeth's relations with her Parliaments are treated by J. E. Neale in his * *Elizabeth I and Her Parliaments,* 2 vols. (1958). Readers interested in Elizabeth, with pictures, will like N. Williams, *The Life and Times of Elizabeth I* (1972), with an introduction by Lady Antonia Fraser.

J. E. Neale has also turned his skillful hand to French subjects. His * *The Age of Catherine de' Medici* (1943) is now available in paperback. R. M. Kingdon, *Geneva and the French Protestant Movement* (1967), is crucial to this discussion. See also F. C. Palm, *Calvinism and the Religious Wars* (1971), a brief study; J. W. Thompson, *The Wars of Religion in France, 1559–1576* (1958), is still useful; as is A. J. Grant, *The Huguenots* (1934). S. L. England, *The Massacre of St. Bartholomew* (1938), and the more recent and popular H. Noguères, *The Massacre of St. Bartholomew's* (1962), will serve for their depressing subject. N. M. Sutherland, *The Massacre of St. Bartholomew and the European Conflict, 1559–1572* (1973), is illustrated and expensive, as well as revisionistic, regarding the motivation for the massacre. The decline of Spain in this period and that which followed can be studied in J. H. Elliott, *The Revolt of the Catalans: A Study in the Decline of Spain* (1963).

5 The Scientific Revolution

From the sixteenth to the seventeenth century, a great change came over the way educated men saw their world. This change has traditionally been called the "Scientific Revolution," and rightly so: the discoveries of scientists from Copernicus to Newton revolutionized man's relation to nature. They subjected the universe to a single set of laws, and opened the prospect that man's inventions might conquer the physical environment. They transformed disciplines like medicine; created a division of labor among philosophers and started an international exchange of ideas. The discoveries in science were in part responses to demands from the practical world: of military men for more accurate guns or of navigators for more reliable maps. But while they turned out to be immediately useful, they were also intellectually revolutionary, and threatened the Christian account of man's relation to God that had ruled Europe for a thousand years. The great revolutionaries themselves were good Christians; few seventeenth-century thinkers echoed John Donne's lament that "New Philosophy calls all in doubt." When Newton died in 1727, the struggle between science and religion was just beginning to be a factor in European culture. Yet the preconditions for that struggle had been laid before, during the span of the scientific revolution itself.

The Middle Ages had not been indifferent to science. The intellectual revival of the twelfth and thirteenth centuries, tied to the influx of Arabic learning, led to an expansion of technical knowledge, the meticulous study of optics and biology, and ambitious pronouncements on the methods of science. Robert Grosseteste (ca. 1168–1253), an English Franciscan scholar and bishop, who lectured and wrote on a wide variety of scientific matters, did much to familiarize Christian Europe with Greek and Roman scientific thought. Roger Bacon (ca. 1214–1292), another English Franciscan, who had studied with Grosseteste, developed in rudimentary form the canon of scientific method: he proclaimed the goal of science as power over nature and mathematics as the instrument of scientific knowledge, classified various sciences by their objects of study, and extolled experimentation. Grosseteste and Bacon were the greatest, but by no means the only scientific minds of their age: to think of the Middle Ages as steeped in mystical devotion or superstitious practices is to repeat a slander invented in the Renaissance and popularized in the Enlightenment.

Still, a close study of medieval science reveals the persistence of mental habits hostile to scientific progress. Experimentation was proclaimed as a method but not practiced. Astrology and astronomy, alchemy and chemistry, magic and mathematics were not clearly separated. The rediscovery of

Hans Holbein the Younger's Portrait of the Astronomer Nicolas Kratzer, 1528. (Louvre/Giraudon.)

Aristotle and other ancient treatises led to learned discussion and fresh thinking, but even the best minds of the thirteenth century relied on authority and were mainly concerned with the religious significance of nature. Clergymen like Grosseteste restated the general principles of Greek science and made contributions of their own within the firm boundaries of Christian theology, for to many thoughtful Christians, the world science disclosed only confirmed the glory of God. Yet the religious boundaries were there, and in the fourteenth and fifteenth centuries they became ever more oppressive. The late Scholastics concentrated on sterile academic disputes. Even the Renaissance made little direct contribution to the scientific revolution. The Humanists were so worshipful of the ancients and so devoted to pure literature that few of them took much interest in science. Roger Bacon's prophetic pronouncements were not followed up for three centuries.

THE PIONEERS

The scientific revolution was launched by the epoch-making discoveries of the sixteenth century. The Renaissance Humanists translated the available corpus of ancient learning, supplying the scientific inquirer with rich factual and theoretical materials, while their criticism of the "dark Gothic ages" fostered independent habits of mind even though it was made in the name of antiquity. The Protestant Reformation, although concentrating on matters of doctrine and on restoring earlier, "purer" forms of worship, gave further impetus to independence.

Copernicus The first great breach in the accepted view of the universe was made by Nicholas Copernicus (1473–1543), a Polish astronomer and mathematician, whose masterpiece, *Concerning the Revolutions of the Celestial Spheres,* was published in the year of his death. The Copernican revolution was simple but far-reaching. It opposed the Ptolemaic system, which had prevailed since its formulation in the second century A.D. According to Ptolemy, the earth is the stationary center of the universe. Some medieval scholars had suggested that it is at least possible that the earth, although at the center of the world, described a daily rotation around its own axis. Copernicus now went further, and argued that the earth at once revolved around its axis and around the sun, in circular orbit.

Like Ptolemy's system, Copernicus' theory was designed to "save the appearances," to give a plausible mathematical account of the observed motions of the planets. But it also offered a rational theory of how they actually moved. This was a complicated problem, for the visible paths of the planets are tantalizingly irregular. To account for them, Ptolemy had resorted to an extremely involved theory, describing the planets as moving around the earth in a series of progressive epicycles, little circles which make up a large circle traveling around the earth, with a point near the earth as its center. Copernicus did not give up the epicycles. But for Copernicus, the hypothesis that the sun is in the center of the world was more rational and more beautiful than Ptolemy's geocentric theory: "In the middle of all there sits the Sun on his throne."

Copernicus' heliocentric astronomy proved subversive of a central assumption of Christianity: it deprived man of his place at the center of the universe. But it took many years and much further speculation before the churches felt threatened by it. Indeed, some leading scientists of the

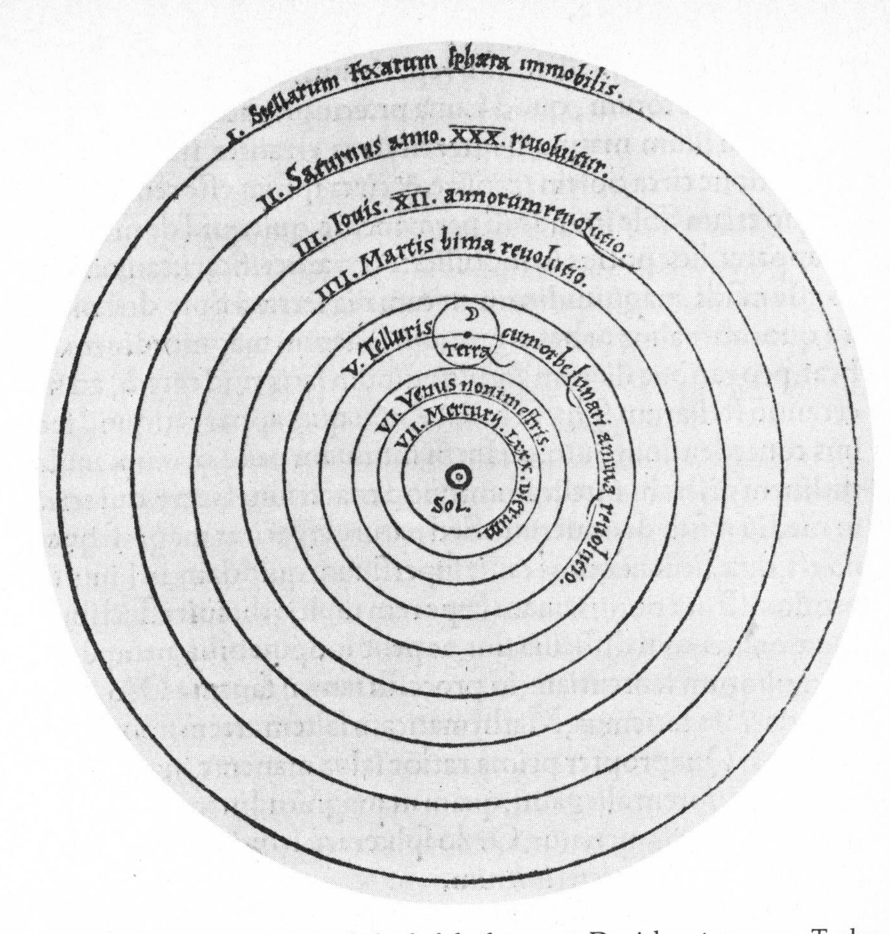

The Copernican System. (Courtesy of the Trustees of the British Museum.)

sixteenth century remained doubtful: the great Danish astronomer Tycho Brahe (1546–1601), whose observations of the planets were far more accurate than any made before him, was never a wholehearted Copernican. When Kepler and Galileo accepted Copernicus, they did so not only because his hypothesis was plausible, but also because they found it aesthetically satisfying. Copernicus had drawn on ancient Greek philosophy, especially Plato, who had seen the universe as a marvelous cosmos mathematically ordered, and who thought the sun most worthy of holding the central position. Such notions strongly appealed to Kepler and Galileo: far from distinguishing mysticism and science, they built a scientific universe on mystical foundations.

Kepler Johann Kepler (1571–1630), whose three laws of motion were the next great advance in the scientific revolution, seems to have lived in a perpetual state of ecstatic excitement, a curious and fruitful combination of antique number mysticism and the most painstaking scientific patience. To Kepler, the regularities of the universe were beautiful, and observable deviations, such as the erratic orbit of Mars, were a challenge to further labors. A German, he moved to Prague as imperial mathematician to Emperor Rudolph II, and at Prague he met and worked with Brahe. Using Brahe's observations, and after many years of exhausting calculations and painful failures, Kepler came to the conclusion that Copernicus' circular orbits could not be rescued. It was only after he had abandoned the circle that he was ready to formulate his three laws: (1) planets travel in elliptical orbits with the sun in one focus; (2) the speed of the planets varies with their distance from the sun; (3) the squares of the revolution of any two planets are proportional to the cubes of their mean distance from the sun.

It was the third law, tying the planets into a harmonious system, that made the universe perfect and Kepler's delight complete. "Eighteen months ago the first dawn rose for me," he wrote, "a very few days ago the sun, most wonderful to see, burst upon me. Nothing can hold me back; I will let myself go in divine rage." This exclamation was not merely the effusion of an enthusiast: it throws much light on the motives of the scientific pioneers. As they saw it, their work was a revolution in behalf of Plato against Aristotle.

SCIENTIFIC PHILOSOPHY

By the beginning of the seventeenth century, there was sufficient ferment in natural philosophy to demand a systematic statement of the nature and possibilities of science. Kepler had published his first two laws in 1609 and the third law ten years later. Also in 1609, Galileo Galilei (1564–1642) had perfected Dutch lenses and constructed a telescope; and in January 1610, he saw through it the rough surfaces of the moon, the stars in the milky way, and the satellites of Jupiter. In the same period, William Gilbert (1540–1603), court physician to Queen Elizabeth I of England, had revolutionized the study of magnetism in his *Concerning the Magnet* (1600); and in 1628, William Harvey (1578–1657), an English physiologist and anatomist, helped to liberate the study of the human body from its slavery to the ancients by announcing his theory of the circulation of the blood. Galen had dominated physiology from the second century A.D., and served as an undisputed authority until he was challenged in the sixteenth, and finally overthrown in the seventeenth century by Harvey's patient dissection of the hearts of animals.

Bacon The meaning of these discoveries was first canvassed by Francis Bacon (1561–1626), essayist, jurist, statesman, and philosopher. Bacon has been called the prophet, the poet, the propagandist of science, and dismissed as a visionary. It is true that despite all his vigorous propaganda for the "new learning," he failed to do justice to the work of his contemporaries: he rejected Copernicus, thought little of Harvey, misunderstood Galileo, and underestimated the role of mathematics in science. Bacon's greatness lies in his vision of himself as a pioneer of new ways of thinking: he called himself "a bell-ringer which is first up to call others to church."

Bacon memorably expressed the need for a new method of mastering nature. The first step in that direction was to remove the obstacles that language and habit put in the way of knowledge. He developed his case in the *Advancement of Learning* (1605); in the *Great Instauration* (1620); and in his scientific utopia, the *New Atlantis,* written in his last years and published in the year of his death, 1626. His case may be briefly stated: the touted learning of the Scholastics had been about words, not things; they were philosophical debates over meaningless distinctions and unprovable notions. All this must be replaced by the search for usable knowledge: "I am labouring to lay the foundation, not of any sect or doctrine, but of human utility and power." The methods to be used for this search are (1) diagnosis: the identifying of "idols" that govern and twist men's thinking; (2) induction: the patient collection and careful sifting of facts; (3) experimentation: testing, refining, and guiding observation; (4) division of labor; and (5) organization: the new learning must be public, cooperative, and cumulative, until the world is run by a community of benign scientists who will alleviate man's estate.

Bacon's program has often been deprecated as naive and vulgar, and it is a little of both. No scientist has ever discovered a great truth by induction alone, by piling up instance after instance; scientific thinking is a complicated mixture of acting on hunches, collecting evidence, confirming notions by experiment, and appreciating a mathematical equation for its beauty rather than its utility. Bacon slights both the playfulness of the scientist and the dignity of the pursuit of knowledge for its own sake. But Bacon was engaged in a polemic: his writings point to a new civilization in which men would be masters and not victims of the environment. While his ideas on method were not followed out literally, scientific organizations and communication were to follow his lead and invoke his name.

Descartes In the eighteenth century, the followers of Bacon battled against the followers of Descartes, but in their time, Bacon and René Descartes (1596–1650) were engaged in the same enterprise and shared the same vision. Descartes' most famous work, the *Discourse on Method,* was published in 1637 as a guide for "correctly conducting the reason and seeking truth in the sciences." It was full of optimism about the new learning, and spleen against Scholasticism:

It is possible to obtain knowledge that is highly useful in life . . . instead of the speculative philosophy taught in the Schools we can have a practical philosophy with which . . . we may make ourselves the masters and possessors of nature. This is desirable, not only with a view to inventing an infinite number of skills that would enable us to enjoy the fruits of the earth and all its conveniences without heavy labor, but above all for the preservation of health.

The Cartesian Method Descartes planned to make a decisive contribution to this scientific utopia by means of a fresh method of thinking, and by sharing that method with the educated public—significantly, he wrote his *Discours de la méthode* in elegant French. In his hands, scientific method became a radical weapon. In the autobiographical sections of his *Discourse,* Descartes expresses his dismay at discovering that despite centuries of argument, nothing in science seemed solid, nothing in his Scholastic education seemed helpful. "I had no choice but to look to myself for guidance." Trusting to his reason, fully aware of the pitfalls in its path, he devised a set of four rules to give himself, and thus mankind, clarity and certainty: (1) to accept as true only ideas that are clear, distinct, and obviously true; (2) to divide each difficulty into "as many parts as may be necessary for its adequate solution"; (3) to arrange ideas in a step-by-step sequence, with the simplest first; (4) to make both enumeration of instances and review of thinking as complete as possible.

Portrait of the Philosopher René Descartes by Frans Hals. Hals' best work was of lusty subjects and scenes of life round about him, but he painted a large number of portraits of local burghers and men of note, such as Descartes, to eke out a meager living. (Louvre, Paris.)

While Descartes cautiously, and doubtless sincerely, claimed that his method was not hostile to theology, it contained the seeds of skepticism and materialism. But these seeds ripened only after Descartes' death: in his time, many rational Christians used Descartes' method to establish the existence of God.

Using the method for himself, Descartes demonstrated that "established truths" are in reality far from certain. Beginning at the beginning, Descartes found one incontrovertible truth: *cogito, ergo sum*—I think, therefore I am; the most determined doubter cannot doubt that there is something that does the doubting: the mind. With this disciplined method, on this slender foundation, Descartes built his world. Moving step by logical step, Descartes proved to his satisfaction the existence of God, of matter, and of motion. God must exist since man's mind can conceive of something more perfect than itself, and this conception can spring only from that more perfect being. Matter in motion is a palpable reality. From these propositions, Descartes deduced other propositions, which were to arouse considerable controversy. He reasoned that there can be no void, because void is space, space means extension, and extension presupposes extended matter. Similarly, the universe cannot be finite, because limits to the world are inconceivable and hence do not exist.

Descartes' deductive method, proceeding from an indisputable general principle to specific applications, has often been contrasted with Bacon's inductive method. The contrast should not be exaggerated. Just as Bacon saw the uses of generalization, Descartes was not blind to the scientific work done around him. But his deductive method involved him in an extravagant cosmology, which is no more than a scientific curiosity today, although it was firmly accepted throughout much of the seventeenth century and had many supporters in France even after Newton's work. In his *Principles of Philosophy* (1644), Descartes argued that the earth is embedded in a material aether, which whirls around the sun in vortices. Thus he managed to combine the Copernican theory with the Ptolemaic theory. This was typical of Descartes; it illustrates his mixture of boldness and caution. Boldly he thought his way through to far-reaching conclusions and accepted the latest scientific discoveries; cautiously he avoided publishing ideas that might get him into trouble with Church authorities. Galileo had been condemned by the Vatican in 1633 for insisting on his Copernicanism; Descartes, who knew of this condemnation, had no desire to share Galileo's fate.

If Descartes had done nothing but devise his method, which cut through the accumulations of philosophic speculation, his place in the history of the scientific revolution would be secure. But he did much more. His writings advanced research in optics, physiology, physics, and astronomy. Even more important is his contribution to mathematics, which places him in the first rank of the theorists of science. His invention of analytical geometry, which permitted the application of algebra to geometry, made science subject to mathematical description. The coordinates on which Descartes plotted his equations are still called "Cartesian coordinates" in his honor. They liberated scientists from crude models and prepared the way for the Newtonian synthesis.

SCIENTIFIC COMMUNICATION AND ORGANIZATION

Bacon and Descartes had insisted that scientific progress depended not only on sound method, but also on the labors of many hands. By the middle of the seventeenth century, scientists began to act on this suggestion: they communicated with one another and created an international community of scholars. The poets of their age delighted in the new discoveries and dwelled, in typical Renaissance fashion, on exhilarating analogies between man and nature, the circulation of the blood and the circle in mathematics. But the scientists themselves, spurred on by Bacon's warnings against "idols" and by the cool, impersonal language of mathematics, became more cautious with their metaphors, more precise in their theories, and more cooperative in their researches.

The Accademia del Cimento The most effective instruments of communication were the scientific academies that sprang up all over Europe in the seventeenth century. One of the earliest was the short-lived Accademia del Cimento (that is, the Academy of Experiment) of Florence. It consisted of a fraternity of nine scientists, some of them disciples of Galileo, who accumulated an impressive collection of scientific instruments and made scientific experiments which they later published. This Academy did not last, but in the ten years of its existence, from 1657 to 1667, it demonstrated that seventeenth-century science required experiment, publication, cooperation, and expensive equipment.

The Royal Society While the Accademia del Cimento was the creation of the grand dukes of Tuscany, its more durable sister institutions, although sponsored by their governments, grew from the enthusiasm of private men. As its founders proudly proclaimed, the Royal Society of London for the Improving of Natural Knowledge was the direct descendant of Bacon. Its informal beginnings came about 1645, when some "worthy persons, inquisitive into natural philosophy and other parts of human learning, and particularly of what has been called *New Philosophy* or *Experimental Philosophy*" met in London to discuss common concerns, buy instruments, and "consider Philosophical Enquiries and such as related thereunto; as Physick, Anatomy, Geometry, Astronomy, Navigation, Staticks, Magneticks, Chymicks, Mechanicks, and natural Experiments; with the state of these studies, as then cultivated at home and abroad." These are the words of John Wallis (1616–1703), a fine mathematician, characteristic of this early group. When the Royal Society was founded in 1660 and received its charter from King Charles II in July 1662, Wallis was one of its charter members.

With royal patronage and a distinguished membership, the Royal Society built a laboratory, collected a "Musaeum" of rare natural specimens, performed, repeated, and reported experiments, and improved scientific instruments. Even more significant than this work was the publicity that the Society gave it, in both the voluminous correspondence of its secretary with foreign scientists, and its celebrated publication, the *Philosophical Transactions,* which first appeared in March 1665. The *Transactions* proved invaluable: it reviewed books, acquainted scientists with new instruments, publicized experiments and carried on controversies. Its issues were widely read in England, and on the Continent where it appeared in Latin. England's greatest scientists published in the *Transactions,* and published or lectured under the auspices of the Royal Society. Isaac Newton (1642–1727) was only the greatest of its great members. There is, therefore, only a little extravagance in the accolade of the English scientist Thomas H. Huxley, who wrote late in the nineteenth century: "If all the books in the world except the *Philosophical Transactions* were destroyed, it is safe to say that the foundations of physical science would remain unshaken."

The Académie Royale des Sciences Like its English counterpart, the French society began as a private enterprise. Then, in 1666, under the patronage of Louis XIV and with the support of his chief minister Colbert, the *Académie royale des sciences* was established in Paris, with generous stipends and well-equipped laboratories. The vicissitudes of the reign affected its fortunes, and the *Académie* was not firmly settled until 1699; but even before then its members did significant experiments in acoustics, dynamics, and several other fields, and published their findings to the world.

Louis XIV Founding the French Academy of Science. (Palace of Versailles.)

The example of these academies was imitated by societies elsewhere, while science was made palatable to a wider public through journals and popularizations. The pursuit of science was growing more technical, but the divisions between amateur and professional, and among specialized areas of competence, were not yet very deep. The most professional of scientists called themselves "natural philosophers": the great chemist Robert Boyle (1627–1691), today remembered as the discoverer of Boyle's law of gases, was chemist, physicist, philosopher, man of letters, and theologian all at once. Blaise Pascal (1623–1662) was a great mathematician, a fine physicist, a brilliant polemicist, and a profound philosopher of religion. Yet for all this versatility, all was not smooth in the scientific community: ugly fights over precedence of discovery and ugly charges of plagiarism marred the concord of the fraternity. But by the end of the seventeenth century, the character of science as public, international, self-critical, and self-corrective, was widely accepted.

THE NEW DYNAMICS

The most spectacular discoveries of the age were in astronomy, and by the second half of the seventeenth century hundreds of amateurs peered through telescopes to confirm the Copernican theory of the heavens. But the decisive step toward modern science was taken in the related field of dynamics. The towering geniuses of the scientific revolution, Galileo, Descartes, and Newton, devoted themselves to discovering laws of motion that would apply equally to heavenly and earthly bodies. Their labors culminated in the laws of motion announced in Newton's *Mathematical Principles of Natural Philosophy*, and the year of its publication, 1687, marks an epoch in the history of modern science.

The problem of motion had dominated scientific thinking ever since the Greek philosophers. Aristotle, whose views on dynamics governed science until the seventeenth century, had postulated a qualitative distinction between the celestial motion of perfect heavenly beings and the terrestrial motion of imperfect earthly beings. He had argued, first, that a body will keep in motion only as long as it is pushed, since its "natural" condition is rest; and second, that bodies will fall with speeds proportionate to their weight, since "light" bodies tend upward and "heavy" bodies tend downward.

Galileo's Telescope. Although Galileo was not the first to make a telescope, he made such crucial improvements in it that he has been given much credit for its development. His first instrument (1609) had a convex lens at one end of a long tube and a concave lens at the other.

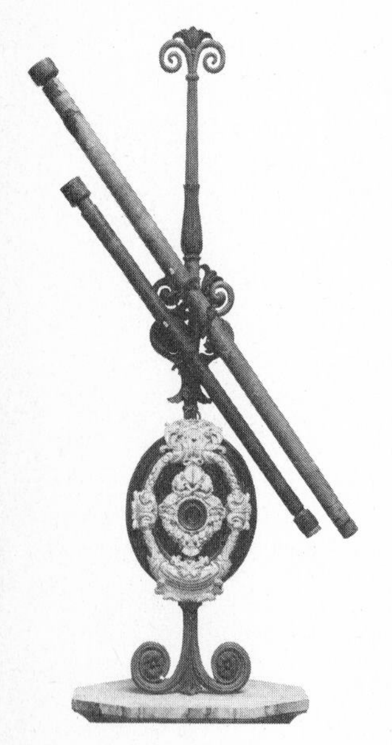

This kind of thinking was wrong in its conclusions and unscientific in its method, since it intruded religious, metaphysical, or aesthetic considerations into areas in which quantitative and not qualitative judgments are central. By the time of Kepler, this kind of thinking was already under pressure: if it was true that planets traveled in elliptical orbits, which were far less "perfect" than circular orbits, it seemed at least possible that Aristotle's physics and astronomy needed to be discarded altogether.

Galileo It was Galileo, preoccupied with the problem of motion throughout his scientific career, who conclusively refuted Aristotle. Improving on some earlier experiments, and following his intuition that the universe must be subject to a single set of mathematical laws, Galileo established that bodies fell with speeds not in proportion to their weight but in proportion to their time of fall. After years of reflection and experimentation, Galileo produced the principle of inertia, announced in its final form in his *Dialogues and Mathematical Discourses Concerning the Two New Sciences* (1638). The principle of inertia holds that a body at rest, or moving with constant speed on a straight line, will persist in its rest, or in its course, without change. A force is needed not to keep the body going (as Aristotle had argued) but to stop it or deflect it from its course. Galileo thus made the crucial distinction between velocity and acceleration. He applied the principle to celestial and terrestrial bodies, to planets moving in their orbits and to stones dropped from a height. Galileo, then, freed science from the qualitative thinking of Aristotle and his innumerable followers, and prepared the way for Newton's work.

Galileo made immense contributions to science, not only by what he discovered but by how he discovered it. His assumption that all parts of the universe followed the same laws and were open to the same methods of inquiry put emphasis on the discovery of regularities rather than on hierarchies of value or beauty. This helped to free science from irrelevancies. At the same time, Galileo extolled both observation and what we might call freedom from observation. By his biting ridicule he has preserved for posterity the professors who would not look through his telescope. They were men, he wrote to Kepler in disgust, who "close their eyes to the light of truth," and search for authorities in books. But observation was not everything, since the senses give misinformation about the universe. Scientists like Copernicus, Galileo wrote, had been willing "to commit rape upon their senses." They had made the sun stand still when it appears to be moving. Finally, Galileo firmly insisted on the uses of mathematics in science. The curved path of a projectile described a parabola, and other physical events, too, can be described in mathematical language.

Newton Galileo's principles and discoveries, shared and refined by Descartes, were fused into a system by Isaac Newton. Unlike many other pioneers, Newton was greatly admired in his lifetime and nearly deified after his death: Voltaire argued that he was the greatest man who ever lived, and many thought Voltaire was right. The impact of Newton's *Principia Mathematica* on England was immediate and decisive. It took longer to conquer the Continent, but by the 1750's there were few educated amateurs and almost no scientists who professed Descartes' vortex physics or deductive method.

Newton, of course, was a genius, but he cannot be understood in isolation. His work represents the culmination of two centuries of scientific labors: it confirmed Copernicus's astronomy, and universalized Galileo's dynamics. Newton's method, too, leaned on great predecessors: it shows the mark of Bacon's distrust of system, Descartes's passion for mathematics, Galileo's and Boyle's respect for experimentation. Newton's *Principia Mathematica* does more than state laws of nature or offer a wealth of empirical evidence; it also makes important observations on scientific method that became the slogans of the scientific community. Newton eloquently warned against "hypotheses," rash generalizations or speculative conjectures, and urged that the "experimental philosopher" deduce his principles from the phenomena. To Newton, mathematics and experiment were two branches of a single inquiry: observation yielded general principles that could then be stated in universal, mathematical language and proved by experiments.

The Newtonian system is a superb achievement. It united disparate discoveries, like Galileo's laws of falling bodies and Kepler's laws of motion, and explained a variety of familiar phenomena, like the tides and the precession of the equinoxes. Significantly, Newton could not create his system until he had the mathematical language for it, and since it was not available, he invented it. Newton's "fluxions," today called the differential calculus, allowed him to express change mathematically, and to bring together the phenomena of the physical world under the universal law of gravitation.

The Law of Gravitation This law was a necessary development from Galileo's principle of inertia: if a moving body will persist in its motion unless acted on by an external force, there must be a force compelling the planets to move around the sun in regular orbits. This force Newton showed to be gravitation, which inheres in all particles of matter. All particles attract all other particles with a power proportional to their mass and inversely proportional to the square of their distance. The calculations required to prove this law were immensely difficult, for the location of the gravitational force in large bodies was mysterious, and the power of the force in small bodies almost negligible. Newton succeeded in showing that the force required to keep the moon in its orbit around the earth was identical with the gravitational pull exerted by the earth on an apple. Thus the action of the moon on the tides, of the earth on the moon, of the sun on planets or comets was all one: gravitation.

The theory of gravitation allowed the laws of motion to take their place in a complete dynamic system, and Newton's three laws of motion ruled the world of physics until Einstein. But the idea of gravitation was not without its irony, which the supporters of Descartes's vortices were not slow to exploit: Newton had expressed contempt for "occult qualities," the favorite device of the Scholastics in their speculations about nature. But was this mysterious gravitational force not an occult quality? What was more speculative than action at a distance through empty space? Newton faced the question boldly: we must assume the existence of gravitation because the notion works—it serves to explain the most disparate phenomena in the simplest manner. Yet its nature was, and would probably forever remain unknown: "The Principles," Newton wrote in his late masterpiece, the *Opticks,* "I consider not as Occult qualities, supposed to result from the specifick form of Things, but as general Laws of Nature, by which the Things themselves are form'd; their Truth appearing to us by Phaenomena, though their Causes be not yet discovered." Here Newton announced another step in the liberation of science from philosophy: the scientist could proceed with his measurements and calculations even when the mysteries of nature remained impenetrable to him.

THE MEANING OF THE REVOLUTION

Newton's work meant that Europe was on the threshold of modernity. The intellectual creation of a new physical universe was accompanied by intellectual changes in other fields. But the scientific revolution, one of the greatest revolutions in history, was both less extensive and less intensive than has often been thought. Millions continued to live as though Galileo or Newton had never written a line, and even those who were most deeply touched by science in the seventeenth century did not for a moment consider the new discoveries a danger to their religious beliefs. Newton was a Christian mystic who spent much time ruminating over Biblical chronology. Similarly, Robert Boyle expended his best energies proving the concord of theology and natural philosophy—in his will he left the handsome sum of £350 to have sermons delivered on the truth of Christianity. Yet, while religion remained unchallenged in the minds of most men, and even of the scientists themselves, the world was changed by the new discoveries. More unwittingly than deliberately, the scientific revolution set the stage for the Enlightenment.

FURTHER READING

The most satisfactory general account of the scientific revolution is A. R. Hall, * *The Scientific Revolution* (1954), which covers the years from 1500 to 1800. A. C. Crombie, * *Medieval and Early Modern Science* (2nd ed., 1959), brilliantly covers the earlier background and includes Newton. Herbert Butterfield, * *The Origins of Modern Science* (1949), is a persuasive collection of lectures on crucial selected topics. In his *The Mechanization of the World Picture* (1961), E. J. Dijksterhuis offers a rigorously organized account of the rise of the scientific world view from the Greeks onward. It should be read in conjunction with Charles C. Gillispie's *The Edge of Objectivity* (1960), an original, stimulating treatment of scientific thinking from Galileo to Einstein. For the intellectual implications of the scientific revolution, see Alexander Koyré, * *From the Closed World to the Infinite Universe* (1957); and E. A. Burtt, * *The Metaphysical Foundations of Modern Physical Science* (2nd ed., 1932).

On the giants of the revolution, see the recent treatment of Copernicus's achievement, placed in its historic environment, by Thomas S. Kuhn, * *The Copernican Revolution* (1957). For Galileo, see F. Sherwood Taylor, *Galileo and Freedom of Thought* (1938). L. T. More, * *Isaac Newton* (1934), is standard but not wholly satisfactory. On the philosophers of science, see F. H. Anderson, *The Philosophy of Francis Bacon* (1948). For Descartes, see especially the collection of essays by Norman Kemp Smith, *New Studies in the Philosophy of Descartes* (1952). The scientific academies of the seventeenth century are dealt with by Martha Ornstein, *The Role of Scientific Societies in the Seventeenth Century* (3rd ed., 1938).

*Books available in paperback edition are marked with an asterisk.

PART X

Inconclusive warfare between the Netherlands and the Spanish crown came to a temporary halt with a truce (signed for twelve years) in 1609. Elizabeth of England had died a few years earlier (1603) and a new king, foreign and Scottish (James VI of Scotland, James I of England), ruled the "scept'red isle." In the next year (1610), Henry IV of France would feel the assassin's steel. Overseas, Frenchmen and Englishmen had recently founded tiny settlements (1603–1607) that were to develop into colonies and empires in the next century and a half. As we have seen in the earlier discussion of European expansion English, French, Dutch, and Swedish people in considerable numbers moved to the New World during the early seventeenth century.

It is not easy for today's historians to analyze or even describe the social, economic, and demographic changes that occurred during the first decades of the seventeenth century. Nevertheless, the present state of the art or science of history indicates that near the beginning of this period European population, which had increased steadily and significantly from 1450 to 1600, now levelled off or began to decrease. At the same time, the stimulating flow of precious metal from the Spanish overseas empire in the Americas began to dwindle. Thus, at the beginning of the period under consideration here, an expansive era ended and a period of unease set in. The religious problems held over from the sixteenth century were still far from resolution; and the political structure of Europe was still confused.

What happened between 1609 and 1715 seems more than usually chaotic. The first half of the seventeenth century was a time of great disorder within the emerging states and especially within the Holy Roman Empire. The so-called Thirty Years' War in the Netherlands and the Germanies, the fronde *in France, and the, Civil War in England, not to speak of many other contemporary upheavals, were not mere perturbations of domestic tranquility; they were paroxysms of civil strife and warfare which some modern historians liken to the "crisis" period in a disease. The "patient" would either have to get well or die. In this case, the "patient" Europe appeared to rally in the 1660's, but shortly thereafter suffered a relapse and cannot be considered to have returned to something like stable health until after the death of Louis XIV.*

The turbulent seventeenth century was also a "Century of Genius" accompanied by the "Golden Age" of baroque painting. While Galileo observed the movements of the stars through a homemade telescope and Newton measured the refraction of light through glass prisms, the painters Velazquez and Vermeer studied the reflection of light from children's hair and gleaming pearls. Rembrandt retold the Christian story in direct, moving terms. While Dutch and English ships plied the ocean lanes, William Harvey was demonstrating the circulation of blood through the veins and arteries of the human body. Philosophers explored the bases of man's social and political associations while rulers and their armies were shaping the geographic boundaries of the modern nation-states.

Yet this cosmopolitan world was quite a different one from that of 90 percent of the population. The peasant tilled his fields in the autumn and spring only to have his crops trampled by marauding soldiers in summer. Plague and famine continued to take enormous toll. Witch-hunting and superstition flourished in many parts of Europe and England as well as in Salem, Massachusetts.

PARADE HELMET MADE FOR LOUIS XIV OF FRANCE. (The Metropolitan Museum of Art, Rogers Fund.)

CENTURY OF CRISIS AND GENIUS

LEGACY OF THE PAST

The baroque artist Jan Vermeer (1632–1675) painted intimate scenes with great artistry but little emotional or religious content. Such paintings were collected by wealthy Dutch merchants who admired the play of light on the beautiful objects their new overseas empires had brought them. (National Gallery, Washington, D.C.)

The "Century of Crisis and Genius" left lasting changes in the field of government. The system of constitutional monarchy was established in England, the first example of what were to become the standard "modern" political institutions of a later Europe. In France, internal conflict was ended by the establishment of highly centralized government under authoritarian, so-called "absolute," monarchy. For the next hundred years, the French system would be more highly admired and imitated than that of England. In the Germanies, the remains of the medieval Holy Roman Empire disintegrated, leaving a fragmented Germany without political or religious unity. The resultant division and power vacuum in central Europe has lasted throughout most of modern history, save for the brief era of unified Germany between 1870 and 1945.

Overseas, the English colonization of eastern North America began early in the century and soon took firm root. This laid the basis for what became a new national culture and later a world power—the United States.

The seventeenth century bequeathed new and enduring accomplishments in art and intellect. It was during this time that the technique of "scientific method" was firmly established and that the idea of "social contract" was first stated. The period saw the climax of baroque painting and of the classical revival in esthetics, with the founding of the modern French cultural academies.

MAJOR EVENTS, 1600-1715*

	Wars and Diplomacy	France, Internal	England, Internal	Science and Culture
1600–	Last phases, Dutch war of independence	Sully and Laffémas	d. Elizabeth I; accession James I (1603)	
1605–	d. Duke of Cleves (1608) Twelve Years' Truce (1609)	d. Henry IV; accession Louis XIII (1610)	Gunpowder Plot (1605)	"King James" or Anglican version of the Bible completed (1611)
1610–	Defenestration at Prague (1618)	Estates General (1614)	James' troubles with Puritans and Parliament	
1615–	Bohemian Phase, 30 Years' War (1618) Ferdinand II, Emperor (1619)			Death of William Shakespeare (1616)
1620–		Richelieu in King's council (1624)		First newspaper published in England (1621) First folio edition of Shakespeare's plays published (1623)
1625–	Danish Phases, 30 Years' War (1625)	Defeat of Huguenots at La Rochelle (1628) Richelieu principal minister (1629)	d. James I (1625); accession Charles I Petition of Right (1628) Assassination of Buckingham (1628)	William Harvey publishes work on circulation of the blood (1628) Bernini appointed architect of St. Peter's, Rome (1629)
1630–	Swedish Phase, 30 Years' War (1630)			
1635–	Ferdinand III, Emperor (1637) Active French intervention in war	French Academy (1635)		Corneille writes *Le Cid* (1636) Descartes' *Essay on Method* (1637) Poussin appointed painter to the French Court (1639)
1640–	Fall of Olivares (1643)	d. Richelieu (1642) d. Louis XIII (1643) Regency of Ann of Austria	Long Parliament (1640) Strafford executed (1641) Civil War	Milton's *Areopagitica* (1644)
1645–	Treaties of Westphalia (1648)	The fronde (1648) French clergy condemns Jansenism	Charles executed (1649) Commonwealth Protectorate	Royal Academy of Arts founded in Paris (1648)
1650–				Hobbes' *Leviathan* (1651)

The Wars of Fifty Years

Interregnum

	Wars and Diplomacy	*France, Internal*	*England, Internal*	*Science and Culture*
				c. 185,000 slaves sent to Brazil (1651–1675)
1655–				Velasquez paints "Maids of Honor" (1656)
	Peace of the Pyrenees (1659)		d. Cromwell (1658)	Rembrandt completes "The Night Watch" (1660)
1660–			The Restoration (1660) Legislation against Non-conformists	Work begun on Versailles Palace (1662) Royal Society of London founded (1662)
		d. Mazarin; begin personal reign of Louis XIV (1661)	Great Plague of London (1665)	
1665–	War of Devolution (1667)			
1670–		Colbert: reforms and mercantilism Louvois: army reforms	Secret Treaty of Dover and resulting subsidies from Louis XIV (1670)	Pascal writes *Pensées* (1670) Moliere publishes "Le Malade Imaginaire" (1673) c. 102,500 slaves sent to Spanish America (1676–1700)
1675–	Treaties of Nimwegen (1678)			Paul Bunyan writes *Pilgrim's Progress,* Part I (1678)
1680–			Exclusion Bill (1679)	William Penn publishes *General Description of Pennsylvania* (1683)
	French invade Spanish Netherlands (1683)	d. Colbert (1683)		
1685–		Revocation of Edict of Nantes (1685)	d. Charles II; accession James II (1685)	
1690–	War of the League of Augsburg (1688)		The Glorious Revolution (1688)	John Locke completes *Essay Concerning Human Understanding* (1690)
		d. Louvois (1691)		
1695–			d. Mary (1694)	
	Treaties of Ryswick (1697)			
1700–	d. Charles II of Spain War of the Spanish Succession		d. William II; accession Anne (1702)	
1705–				Excavations begin at Pompeii and Herculaneum (1706)
1710–		Destruction of Port Royal (Jansenist center)		Alexander Pope publishes *The Rape of the Lock* (1712)
	Treaties of Utrecht, etc. (1713)	Unigenitus (1713)	d. Anne; accession George I (1714)	
1715–		d. Louis XIV; accession Louis XV (1715)		

The Wars of Louis XIV

*For 1600–1610 see also Major Events, Part IX.

1 The Thirty or Fifty Years' War

In 1638, Peter Paul Rubens, the painter-diplomat of Antwerp, described to its Italian purchaser a figure in one of his allegorical paintings, as follows:

That lugubrious matron, clad in black and with her veil torn, despoiled of her jewels and every other ornament, is unhappy Europe, afflicted for so many years by rapine, outrage and misery.[1]

The painter expressed the hope that his work would arrive safely in Italy, passing as it must along certain roads that had only recently been battlegrounds. The student may well share Rubens' concern for "unhappy Europe" as he plunges into the history of the Thirty Years' War.

The series of struggles known as the Thirty Years' War involved the chief European rulers—at different times, on one side or another—in hostilities across most of the continent of Europe. It destroyed populations in many areas of Germany, causing untold suffering and forcing huge migrations of people. Were these wars the most "meaningless" in all history, as they have been termed by some historians? Or were they decisive battles in a continuing European civil war that had begun at least as early as the previous century?

Since the struggles of the sixteenth century between Philip of Spain and Elizabeth of England and the Henries of France may still be fresh in the reader's mind (Part IX, Chapters 3 and 4), it may be helpful to return first to Spain as we attempt to distinguish between the centrifugal and centripetal forces at work in Europe in the opening decades of the seventeenth century.

THE FAILURE OF CENTRALIZATION IN SPAIN

When Philip II of Spain died at the end of the sixteenth century, the Habsburg realms, much of which passed to his son Philip III, may be roughly compared to the shape of a lobster. The forked tail of this huge lobster was in Mexico and South America, its hypothetical body stretched in a line of

[1]Letter of March 12, 1638.

ships across the ocean to Spain and the Mediterranean islands including the boot of Italy. One claw reached northward across the Alps to the headwaters of the river Rhine and thence to the Spanish Netherlands, where it menaced France. The other claw stretched from the Alps eastward along the Inn and the Danube Rivers to Vienna.

Under the terms of Emperor Charles V's abdication, the right or eastern claw belonged to a different branch of the family, the Austrian Habsburgs. But Spanish gold continued to provide the glitter at the court of Vienna; soldiers in Spanish pay fought for the eastern Habsburgs in the Germanies; and Philip II's daughter Isabella ruled the Spanish Netherlands as the wife of an Austrian Habsburg prince.

Spain in the seventeenth century experienced a misfortune in her rulers. Both Philip III (1598–1621) and Philip IV (1621–1665) were uninterested in politics and left the conduct of state affairs in the hands of favorites. This misfortune was magnified during the reign of Philip IV by the fact that the king's favorite over more than twenty years (1621–1643), the Count-Duke Olivares, happened to be an extremely unlucky, though energetic, statesman.

The Count Duke Olivares, chief minister of Philip IV, was instrumental in getting his fellow townsman, Diego Velasquez de Silva (1599–1660) to come to Madrid as court painter. Velasquez served the crown for 37 years, painting the king's family, courtiers, and historic events. Shown here are a detail from his great portrait of the royal family, "Las Meninas" (1656), and part of an equestrian portrait of Olivares (c. 1634). (Prado.)

He advised the king to refrain from summoning the *Cortes,* while at the same time he imposed new taxes and cut down on expenses by quartering armies on the Spanish populations and suppressing pensions. He tried manfully to raise money and troops outside of Castile (in Aragon, Catalonia, Valencia, and Portugal, for instance) for what were essentially Castilian foreign wars; and he replaced local administrators with his own followers. Everywhere outside of Castile—and even in some respects within that kingdom—these recommendations and actions were unpopular. Likewise unpopular was Olivares' imperialist foreign policy, which seemed to put the interests of the crown of Castile before the traditional rights or privileges of other Spanish groups.

What followed was disaster for Spain. Castile itself was picked bare of men and substance by the demands of far-flung wars. The other Iberian kingdoms managed fairly successfully to avoid contributing to the war effort. When pressed hard by Olivares, the Catalans revolted in 1640, as did the Portuguese. Portugal succeeded in permanently dissolving its personal union with Spain and elevated John of Braganza to the throne, while Catalonia maintained something like independence for twelve years (with French support) and was not officially returned to the Spanish monarchy until 1659.

A pathetic figure, Olivares tried to pit his strength against an indolent court, a faction of the Church, an entrenched conservative nobility, and the separatist movements within Spain and failed. (Even for Don Quixote, one windmill at a time was sufficient!) The defeat of the Spanish army by the French at Rocroi in 1643—said to be the first failure of Spanish infantry in battle—marked a turning point in Spain's destiny. The outward sign, defeat in battle, was bad enough. The defeat of the monarchy, symbolized by the disgrace of Olivares (as engineered by Spanish conservatives and separatists), was a surer sign of declining Spanish Habsburg power in the early modern world.

CENTRIFUGAL AND CENTRIPETAL EUROPE: FRANCE, ENGLAND, AND THE NORTH

The same problems of internal dissension and strife that beset Spain in the first half of the seventeenth century were experienced by her friends and enemies to the north and east. Like Philip III and Philip IV of Spain, Louis XIII of France left a great deal to his ministers, the most important of whom was Cardinal Richelieu. In France, Richelieu's ministry (1624–1642) almost exactly paralleled that of Olivares (1621–1643). Richelieu, like Olivares in Spain, encountered internal opposition from various important groups: Huguenots on one side and nobles, Roman Catholic clergy, and judges on the other. Most of these groups resented any attempt at royal centralization and struggled against it in different ways at one time or another. But despite the resistance of French opposition factions, Richelieu survived; and we shall see that at the end of the Thirty Years' War France emerged triumphant over Spain.

In the newly liberated Dutch provinces, a struggle broke out between Maurice of Nassau, the leader of the extreme war party, who was accused of having personal ambitions for the crown, and a party of moderates, led by John Oldenbarneveldt and supported by the Estates of Holland, who were in favor of peace and continued local authority. As we shall see in the next chapter, the civil war of mid-century England was largely an expression of the resistance of the English gentry to the centralizing policy of the Stuart kings.

Along the Baltic, in Lutheran Denmark and Sweden, the aristocracies were also fighting the centralizing powers of their respective kings.[2] Christian IV (1588–1648) of Denmark increased his power both at home and abroad through his control of both sides of the Sound, on the commerce of which he levied ever larger dues, filling his royal treasury so that he might subdue a largely agricultural nobility.[3] He became involved ultimately in the Thirty Years' War not only in defense of Protestantism but also to defend his control of the Sound. He hoped, as well, to unite, or at least to distract, his unruly nobility through foreign war.

In contrast to Christian IV, Gustavus Adolphus of Sweden (1611–1632) preferred to compromise with the nobility, while keeping in his own hands the modernized administration he had inherited as well as substantial control over the courts, education, and commerce.

The Germanies and the Holy Roman Empire Last mentioned by us in connection with the election to the imperial title in 1519, the Holy Roman Empire moved a hundred years later to the center of the stage set for the Thirty Years' War. It was the most unwieldy administrative entity in western civilization. Independent factions continued to maintain themselves, as we have indicated, within all European countries; but in the Empire the particularists possessed real power. The Holy Roman Empire was composed of more than 300 different political units, of which about 80 played a major role in the determination of its fate. In theory, it comprised the German nation but included Czechs, Poles, and Italians. It was governed, also in theory, by an elected emperor and by the imperial diet (council) at Ratisbon. The ecclesiastical and lay princes of the Empire were expected to send representatives to the diet every ten years, but actually it sat most of the time, since it could seldom come to a decision—not even on a motion to adjourn. An imperial tribunal (the *Reichsgericht*) could render judgments but had no force with which to see that its edicts were put into effect. Thus all decisions had to be enforced by some individual member of the Empire.

The emperor's power was severely limited by the fact that some of his princes, supposedly loyal to him and under his command, were outsiders, parts of whose domains happened to lie within the imperial boundaries. For example, the king of Spain held lands along the Rhine, in the Netherlands, Franche-Comté, and the Tyrol; and the king of Denmark held the duchy of Holstein within the Empire. The elector of Brandenburg, on the other hand, was a prince of the Empire, but also a vassal of the Polish king, from whom he held Prussia, which was outside the Empire. Even princes whose lands, large or small, lay entirely within the Empire, pursued their own ends, usually supporting decentralization for the Empire as a whole

[2] Denmark at this time included the territory of Norway and some of southern Sweden.
[3] The Sound is the strait between Denmark and Sweden connecting the Kattegat with the Baltic Sea.

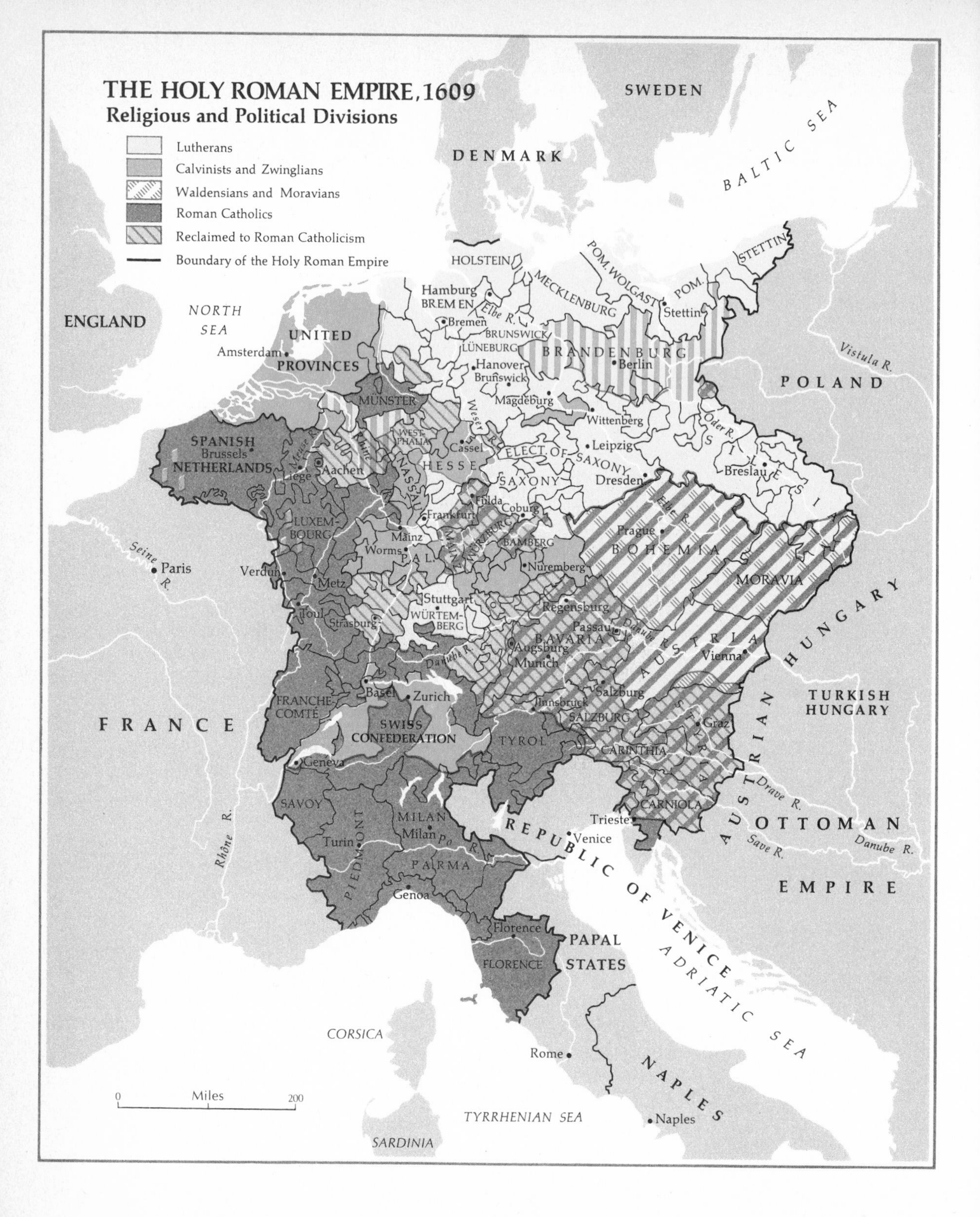
THE HOLY ROMAN EMPIRE, 1609
Religious and Political Divisions
Lutherans
Calvinists and Zwinglians
Waldensians and Moravians
Roman Catholics
Reclaimed to Roman Catholicism
Boundary of the Holy Roman Empire
SWEDEN
DENMARK
BALTIC SEA
ENGLAND
NORTH SEA
UNITED PROVINCES
Amsterdam
SPANISH NETHERLANDS
Brussels
HOLSTEIN
MECKLENBURG
POM. WOLGAST
POM.
STETTIN
Stettin
Hamburg
BREMEN
Bremen
Elbe R.
BRUNSWICK
LÜNEBURG
BRANDENBURG
Berlin
Hanover
Brunswick
Magdeburg
Wittenberg
Vistula R.
POLAND
Oder R.
MÜNSTER
WESTPHALIA
Cassel
HESSE
NASSAU
Rhine R.
Meuse R.
Weser R.
Aachen
Liège
ELECT. OF SAXONY
SAXONY
Leipzig
Dresden
SILESIA
Breslau
Fulda
Coburg
Frankfurt
LUXEMBOURG
Mainz
Worms
PAL.
BAMBERG
Prague
BOHEMIA
MORAVIA
Nuremberg
Seine R.
Paris
Verdun
Metz
Toul
Strasburg
Stuttgart
WÜRTEMBERG
Regensburg
Passau
BAVARIA
Augsburg
Munich
Danube R.
AUSTRIA
Vienna
HUNGARY
FRANCE
FRANCHE-COMTÉ
Basel
Zurich
SWISS CONFEDERATION
TYROL
Innsbruck
Salzburg
SALZBURG
STYRIA
Graz
CARINTHIA
CARNIOLA
TURKISH HUNGARY
AUSTRIAN HUNGARY
Geneva
SAVOY
PIEDMONT
Turin
MILAN
Milan
Po R.
PARMA
Genoa
Rhône R.
Trieste
Venice
REPUBLIC OF VENICE
Drave R.
Save R.
OTTOMAN EMPIRE
Danube R.
Florence
FLORENCE
PAPAL STATES
ADRIATIC SEA
CORSICA
Rome
NAPLES
Naples
TYRRHENIAN SEA
SARDINIA
0 Miles 200

and centralization within their own domains. Both Protestant and Catholic imperial princes alternated between seeking strong allies and leaders of their own faith within the Empire, at one moment, and fearing any strong leadership as a threat to their particular power, at the next.

Within the Catholic camp, the Habsburgs, holders of the imperial crown and probably the most powerful princes within the Empire, should have been the natural leaders. Since the time of Charles V, however, the Habsburgs were distrusted because of their supposed subservience to Spanish policies. The non-Habsburg German prince who came closest to fulfilling the requirements for a Catholic leader was Duke Maximilian of Bavaria. Although his family (Wittelsbach) was more ancient than the Habsburgs, his power did not seem a threat to other German princes. Maximilian had ruled Bavaria since 1597 and through careful organization had amassed enough gold in his coffers to make him independent of the Bavarian estates and able to pay the expenses of any League he might head. He was an ardent Catholic in his own right, but willing to compromise with Protestants within the Empire. In general, throughout the period of the Thirty Years' War, the Catholic German princes wavered between supporting the Habsburg emperors or the anti-Habsburg duke of Bavaria.

The divisive forces operating within the Holy Roman Empire were counteracted by the fact that the German princes could usually be relied on to unite in the face of common danger. When faced with a number of threats all at once, however, they often found it impossible to decide just where the greatest danger lay.

The elected ruler of this collection of principalities in 1609 was an aging and insane Habsburg (Rudolph II) whose own hereditary domains shared all the difficulties of the German Empire. Within his realms were many different nationalities. The Czechs in Bohemia and the Hungarians showed distinct separatist tendencies. Both Bohemia and Hungary had been separate kingdoms until early in the sixteenth century, when, under the Turkish onslaught, they had lost their desire and capacity for independence, accepting protection from and then domination by Austria and/or the Ottoman Empire. In the early seventeenth century, with the Turks busy in Persia, the pressure on eastern Europe declined and the separatist spirit reasserted itself. By this time the disruptive process of the Reformation had created in both Bohemia and Hungary strong Protestant groups seeking independence or at least virtual autonomy within the Habsburg domains.

Added to the problems of centralization versus separatism, Catholic versus Protestant, which in some degree or another were common throughout Europe, the Germanies suffered from their peculiar position at the focal point of trade and diplomacy. For centuries, this region had profited from being at the crossroads of Europe, its highways leading in all directions. Now it was to pay the price by becoming a diplomatic pawn and a battleground in the contest for hegemony between France and Spain.

COMMUNICATIONS AND DIPLOMACY

In 1609, the Spanish empire was global in scope. If it was to prosper or even survive, it required a satisfactory system of communications. Although

THE HOUSE OF HABSBURG

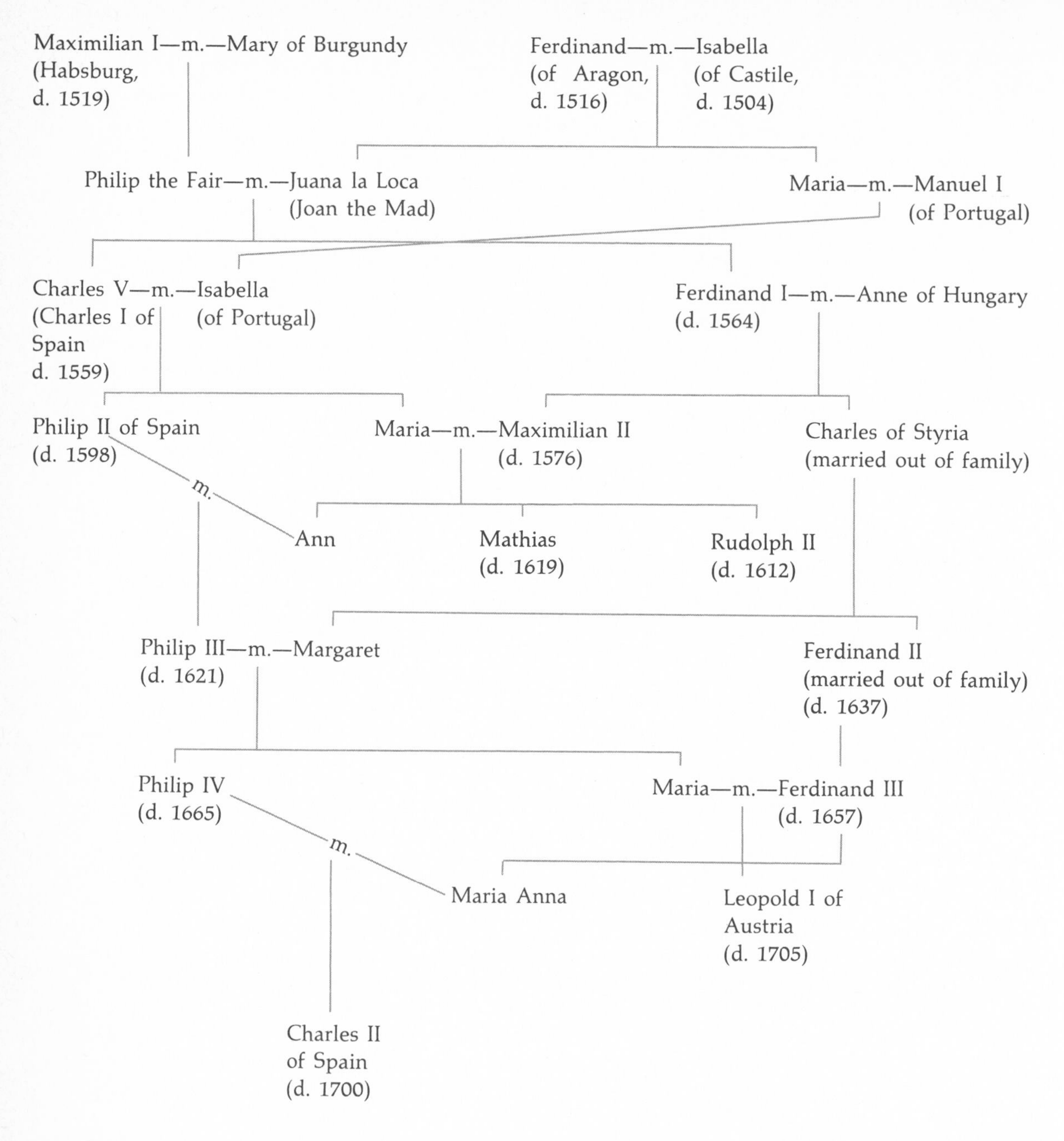

Spain was able to organize and maintain contact with the American and Asiatic parts of the empire across the seas, communications within Europe—with the Spanish Netherlands and with the Habsburg cousins in Austria—were more difficult. After the 1560's, the Spaniards hardly dared to use the water route across the Bay of Biscay and the English Channel to reach the Netherlands; and the sea road by way of the Mediterranean and the Adriatic was constantly subject to threat from the Turks and from the Republic of Venice. Therefore, to reach the Netherlands and Austria, Spain was forced to move on land.

In 1567, when the Duke of Alva marched his army to the Low Countries, he had followed the "Spanish Road": by sea from Barcelona to the friendly port of Genoa; thence to Spanish Lombardy (Milan), through the Duchy of Savoy, passing over the Mont Cénis pass; and thence through Franche-Comté (Habsburg territory) and Lorraine (neutral) to the Spanish Netherlands. After 1601, expansive French power threatened this route and by 1622 French diplomacy had persuaded the Duke of Savoy to deny Spain the right of passage. The Spaniards were, thereby, forced to develop another land route for men, money, and supplies: from Genoa to Lake Como in the foothills of the Alps (see map); then the trail wormed its way with the Adda River along the Valtelline, a narrow valley bordered on the south by the Republic of Venice (hostile to Spain), and through the territory of the Swiss League of the Grisons. The Valtelline leads to the Solda River which leads to the Inn which, in turn, runs eastward to the Danube and Vienna. But at Landeck, in the Tyrol, the Spaniards could turn north and west and, travelling through Habsburg-controlled lands, reach Lorraine and the Netherlands.

The viability of this communication system depended primarily upon Spanish control of the Valtelline—which the French also needed to maintain contact with their ally Venice—and secondly on the right of passage through the Duchy of Lorraine. On two occasions (1624 and 1635), French forces seized the Valtelline for brief periods, thus seriously disrupting Habsburg military operations. When, in 1633, the French occupied Lorraine, the Spanish Army of Flanders was cut off. This event foreshadowed the defeat of that same army in 1643 by the French at Rocroi.

RELIGIOUS DIVISIONS

Although the struggles for secular power among the rulers of Europe at the opening of the seventeenth century were as intense as they were complicated, religious strife was equally fierce. Since the religious Peace of Augsburg of 1555, Catholic toleration of Lutheran heretics had been regarded as a necessary evil, a price to be paid for political gain, for temporary peace in order to be able to proselytize and convert the opponent.

The Peace of Augsburg had proved unsatisfactory from a religious as well as from a political point of view. The motto *cujus regio ejus religio* ("He who rules, his, the religion") made no provision for the Calvinists at all and was a hardship for Protestants or Catholics who happened to disagree with the religious ideas of their respective rulers. More unsatisfactory still was

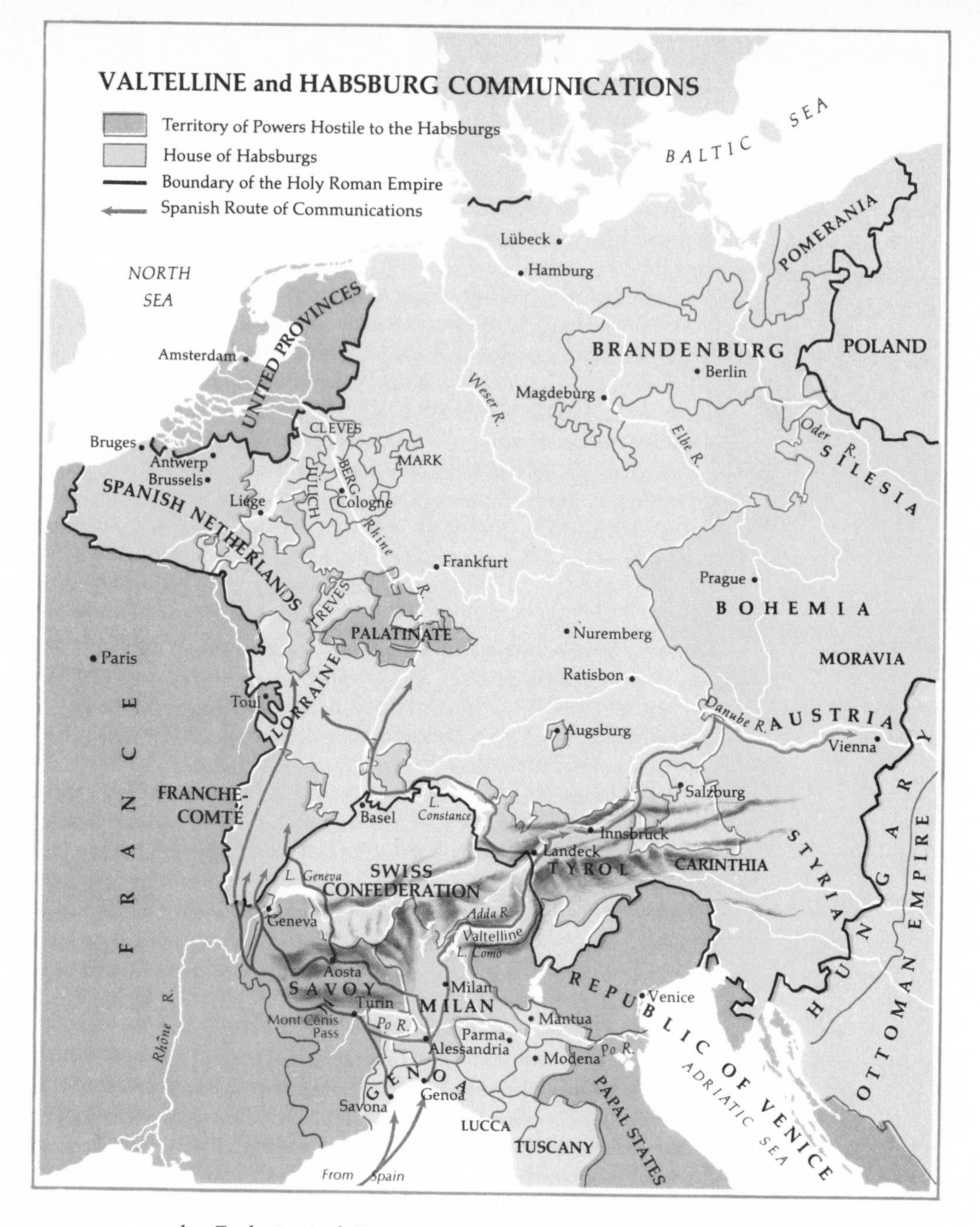

the Ecclesiastical Reservation, a provision that the lands of prelates who should be converted to Protestantism should revert to the Roman Catholic Church. This last simply brought up once again the age-old question of the relationship between the secular and religious duties of churchmen. It might be unfair to have a Catholic bishop turn Protestant and be maintained in his Catholic bishopric; but if he were ousted, changes in the imperial balance of power would surely result.[4]

At every turn we find questions of religion and politics closely intertwined, even—or perhaps especially so—within the Roman Catholic camp. As we have already seen, the Catholics were sharply divided into French and Spanish, Habsburg and Wittelsbach factions, and even the religious orders and the papacy were involved in the political aspects of the struggle. The pope as the leader of the Roman Catholics should have been overjoyed with the crusading spirit of the Spanish and Austrian princes. But the pope was not only the prince of the Church, he was also a powerful Italian ruler. As such, he both resented and feared any extension of Spanish and Austrian power in Italy. Thus the Vatican moved steadily away from the Habsburgs and toward the Bourbon cause of France.

The Protestants, too, were divided. In England, as we shall see in the next chapter, Protestant religious sects proliferated like jackrabbits. On continental Europe, while there were many new interpretations of dogma, the Christians who refused to accept the pope as spiritual leader had separated into two readily distinguishable groups: the Lutherans and the Calvinists. The inheritance of Martin Luther had spread north from Wittenberg in Germany to Denmark and Sweden. Geneva in Switzerland was still the center of Calvinist thought, but Calvinism was strong in the Netherlands, especially in the Dutch provinces, and in France. Minority groups in Catholic countries, such as the (Calvinist) Huguenots in France, openly proclaimed their spiritual—and political—independence of Rome. Meanwhile, Lutherans and Calvinists attacked each other in sermons and pamphlets as bitterly as they attacked the pope at Rome.

Between 1609 and 1621, Europe moved from one crisis to another while waiting for the twelve-year truce between the Spanish and Dutch to expire, at which time everyone expected that full-scale hostilities would resume. All parties concerned, Spain, France, Austria, Roman Catholics and Protestants alike, looked back upon the political and religious settlements of the previous century as temporary and unsatisfactory. Such agreements merely gave time to prepare for the wars that were certain to come.

THE BEGINNING IN GERMANY, 1608–1618

Before the truce in the Netherlands was even signed, violence broke out on the Danube. The first manifestation was in Donauwörth on the Danube where Protestants and Roman Catholics rioted in 1608, the Protestants winning temporary control of the city. The imbroglio was discussed at length in the imperial *Reichshofrat,* but there was no imperial army to step in. After lengthy wrangling, the subjugation of the Protestants and the town was delegated to Maximilian of Bavaria, who did a thorough job of it. The

[4]It should be noted that in the Free Cities of the Empire (for example Hamburg, Bremen, Lübeck, and Frankfort-am-Main), which were, in effect, republics, the principal of *cujus regio, ejus religio* could not prevail. Accordingly, the Treaty (or Peace) of Augsburg provided that in the Free Cities Lutherans and Roman Catholics were to "live quietly and peacefully" with one another. This was probably a more nearly satisfactory arrangement than that applied to the rest of the Empire.

successful attack on Donauwörth caused a number of Protestant German princes to band together in a Union under Frederick IV, Elector of the County Palatine on the Rhine. (Frederick, at this moment, stood in need of friends to defend him from the Spanish-Italian General Spinola who was planning to move in on Frederick's principality.) To counter this Protestant Union, a number of Roman Catholic princes fell in behind Maximilian of Bavaria in a new Catholic League.

The year 1609 saw an uprising in Bohemia, which forced the doddering Emperor Rudolph II to promise religious freedom there. In this same year

Reformed Church, Nuremberg and Bernini's Baldacchino, St. Peter's. The stark interior of a Calvinist church in Nuremberg, Germany (right), is the total antithesis of Catholic Counter-Reformation church decoration as it was developing in Rome under the great sculptor-architect, Gianlorenzo Bernini (1598–1680). The *baldacchino* or canopy (on page 774) was designed by Bernini to cover the high altar of St. Peter's. (Germanisches Nationalmuseum, Nuremberg and Alinari-Scala.)

the Duke of Cleves died without an heir. His lands, the provinces of Jülich, Cleves, Mark, Berg, and Ravensberg, formed a scattered group along the Rhine, from the Dutch frontier to Cologne, and were of great strategic value. Both legitimate claimants to the duchy were Protestants; but the emperor occupied the area, ostensibly to maintain order until all claims were settled. To the Protestant powers and to France, however, this seemed a direct expansion of Habsburg power in a strategically dangerous area; and Henry IV of France began immediate preparations for war in Germany. Full-scale war was averted by the assassination of Henry in 1610, and Europe settled down again to wait for 1621, the year of the expiration of the truce between Spain and Holland. The next crisis, in Bohemia in 1618, seemed relatively minor, yet it touched off the European powder keg.

The Bohemian Phase, 1618–1624 Ferdinand of Styria, an able and vigorous man, was elected King of Bohemia in 1617; King of Hungary in 1618; and, after the death of his cousin Mathias, in 1619, he acceded to the full eastern Habsburg heritage. Immediately, he showed himself an apt student of the Jesuits and a firm adherent of their doctrines of centralization and Counter-Reformation. He had already stamped out Protestantism in his realms of Styria; now he started the same process in Bohemia. In 1618, Ferdinand sanctioned the closing of Protestant churches in Branau and Prague and installed Roman Catholic governors over the predominantly Protestant Bohemian nobles. On the 23rd of May 1618, a revolt broke out. The castle of Prague, the Hradsin, was taken by the Protestant rebels and two of Ferdinand's governors were heaved bodily from a window. The opportunistic

Duke of Savoy, whose territory had recently been invaded by Spanish troops, sent Count Mansfeld, a soldier of fortune, with two thousand men to the aid of the rebels. He recruited more troops from among Bohemians and Protestant Germans and was reinforced by the Hungarian nobility under Bethlen Gabor, Prince of Transylvania, who hoped to regain independence for Hungary. The rebel forces won an initial victory and then marched on Vienna. The Bohemians formally deposed Ferdinand and elected to his throne Frederick V, Elector Palatine, the Protestant son-in-law of James I of England, and, at this point, leader of the Protestant Union of German Princes.

Thus, even before he had come into his Austrian heritage (1619), Ferdinand was in serious trouble. The new emperor found himself with a major political, national, and religious war on his hands. The besieging troops of his enemies were at the gates of Vienna, and his most immediate subjects (the Austrians) were making trouble. It was evident that if the Catholic power were to survive in Germany, Ferdinand would have to receive support from outside his own realms. This he obtained from Maximilian of Bavaria and the Catholic League, which, in spite of its opposition to the Habsburg monarchy, could not tolerate the absolute triumph of Protestantism. The Spanish crown, committed to the support of the Habsburg family, also offered to intercede.

The Spanish army in the Netherlands, which had been mobilizing in anticipation of the expiration of the truce, was dispatched to Frederick V's Palatine territory on the Rhine. The army of the Catholic League marched to Bohemia, where, at the Battle of the White Mountain (1620), its general Tilly (an able soldier who had received his military training in the Netherlands) defeated Frederick V and proceeded to "pacify" Bohemia by revoking Protestant political and religious liberties, executing rebels, and confiscating their property for the crown. Frederick now acquired the derisive title of "Winter King" (the Jesuits having said that he would not last a winter). He not only lost his new Bohemian kingdom but also his lands on the Rhine and his position as Elector of the Empire. This title passed to the Catholic hero of the hour, Maximilian of Bavaria.

By 1623, it seemed that Roman Catholic and Habsburg victory in Germany was assured: the Bohemians had been defeated; Frederick had fled; the Catholics had gained while the Protestants had lost an imperial elector; and the troublesome Hungarian and Austrian rebels had been subjugated without compromise. Ferdinand's star rode high.

In 1624, imperial prospects became even brighter. The emperor found a commander who was willing to fill the gap in the imperial power structure by creating an army directly responsible to the emperor, thus relieving him of the necessity of relying on his Spanish or Bavarian allies. This commander, Albert of Wallenstein, a Bohemian of Protestant family but strict Catholic upbringing, was made Duke of Friedland in 1624 and proceeded to recruit a large army of mercenaries for the emperor. Previously, the major stumbling block to the creation of such an imperial army had been the emptiness of the imperial coffers; Wallenstein solved the problem not by raising money but by developing an army that paid for itself—he made haphazard looting and requisitioning by soldiers into a system. His soldiers stripped the German villages and countryside so bare that little was left for the inhabitants to do but to join his army and hope to recoup their losses by looting somewhere else. Wallenstein's army thus seemed to be a free gift to the emperor—save, of course, for the ambitions of Wallenstein. The emperor rewarded Wallenstein by offering him the duchy of Mecklenburg (on the Baltic coast east of Denmark), hoping that he would develop the area into a strong naval base. This transfer of Catholic and imperial power to that area brought on the second phase of the war—Danish intervention.

Danish Intervention, 1625–1629 Christian IV, King of Denmark, was also duke of Holstein and president of the Saxon Circle, one of the ten administrative circles of the Empire. He had an interest in the affairs of the Empire both as a legal member and as a good Protestant wishing to advance Protestant interests. Inasmuch as he was interested in protecting the Sound at the entrance to the Baltic, from whence his Danish crown derived its only independent revenue, any project for the creation of an imperial Baltic fleet—which now seemed a possibility—alarmed him. All of these interests led Christian to invade Germany in 1625. It seemed a propitious moment for intervention, for French forces had recently thrown confusion into

Detail from the Surrender at Breda by Velasquez. Breda in the Netherlands burns in the distance as Justin of Nassau hands the keys to the fortress to the Spanish General Spinola. This incident of 1625 marked the high tide of Spanish fortunes in the Thirty Years' War. The chivalrous attitudes of both generals were typical of seventeenth-century military traditions. (Prado, Madrid.)

Habsburg communications by taking over the Valtelline. But in 1626, Richelieu had to recall French troops to deal with a Huguenot rebellion at home; and once again Spanish treasure and Italian recruits moved through the Alpine passes to defend the eastern Habsburgs.

Christian of Denmark advanced into Thuringia and Brunswick between 1625 and 1626. By 1626, Tilly had succeeded in starving out Mansfeld and Gabor and brought about a truce which led to their withdrawal into Hungary. He then moved upon Christian and defeated him at the battle of Lutter-am-Barenberge in August 1626. With Wallenstein, he proceeded to drive the Danes back to Jutland, reconquering Schleswig-Holstein and Mecklenburg on the way. They advanced as far as Stralsund, which was saved only by the heroic defense of its citizens.

These victories seemed to have cleared the field at last of Protestant opposition, leaving the German Catholics free to reap the fruits of victory and to quarrel over the spoils. But once again Habsburg and Roman Catholic ambitions overreached themselves. In the same year (1629) that he signed the Treaty of Lübeck with Denmark (whereby Christian agreed to withdraw from Germany and cease all interference in imperial affairs) the emperor saw to the passage of an Edict of Restitution. This provided for the restoration of all ecclesiastical estates confiscated by the Protestants since before the 1555 Peace of Augsburg and for the breaking up of all Protestant sects save that of the Lutherans. The far-reaching edict affected 2 archbishoprics, 12 bishropics, and about 120 monasteries and religious foundations. It marked one of the high points of Catholic and imperial victory. But it had the effect of rekindling the war spirit of the Protestant party. It gave almost every Protestant ruler of Germany a vested interest in ousting the Habsburgs, since the confiscated Church lands had in most cases been taken over by the Protestant rulers.

Further, with the Protestant danger seemingly under control, old quarrels flared up within the Catholic party. The new independence of the emperor, supported as he was by Wallenstein's army, was deeply resented by both the Bavarian anti-Habsburg party in Germany and by Spanish diplomats at the Austrian court. Both of these made use of complaints against Wallenstein to force his dismissal in 1630. Meanwhile, the question of who should take over North Germany and the Baltic was still open. At this point, Sweden's Gustavus II Adolphus moved in.

The Swedish Phase, 1630–1635 At home, Gustavus Adolphus had managed to bind the Swedish aristocracy to the crown by granting liberties to the estates and conducting almost continuous and successful foreign wars. During a period of internal chaos in Russia (1604–1613), Sweden had repeatedly intervened in that country, and as a result had succeeded in sealing off Russia from the Baltic. This left Sweden with only two major opponents in the north—Denmark and Poland. At the end of an eight-year war in 1629, Poland was defeated by Sweden and had ceded Livonia, not only strengthening Sweden's position in the Baltic but also providing an

Gustav II (Gustavus Adolphus). The Swedish king was looked upon as a savior by the Protestants of north Germany, even though he was technically a foreign invader. This allegorical print shows him after his death in the battle of Lützen in 1632—a Swedish victory. The print is unusual in that it shows a female form standing over the dead monarch. The Virgin Mary was not normally depicted by German Lutherans and Calvinists. (LCPP.)

important source of grain. The same year, as we have seen, the Treaty of Lübeck signaled the defeat of Denmark in Germany. If the Catholic-Habsburg threat could be eliminated from northern Germany, Sweden would be the mistress of the Baltic.

Having secured his position in the north and provisioned a well-drilled army, Gustavus Adolphus invaded northern Germany in 1630. He spent most of that year in fortifying captured Mecklenburg and Pomerania, his major objectives in the war. Next he united with the new leader of Protestant Germany, John George of Saxony, to defeat Tilly at the Battle of Leipzig in 1631 and proceeded to advance into Germany toward the Rhine. This new crisis drew the Catholic forces together and resulted in the recall of Wallenstein, but too late to prevent another resounding Swedish victory at Lützen in 1632, in which Gustavus Adolphus lost his life. The "Great White Knight of the North," as he became known, disappeared in the mist during a wild *mêlée* and was found later under a heap of cadavers, killed by four musket wounds and a dagger thrust.

Germany now had two strong fighting forces on her soil—the imperial army built by Wallenstein and the Swedish force, led by the Swedish chancellor Oxenstierna after the death of the king. Both the Catholic and Protestant parties were resentful and fearful of the strength of their respective champions and ready to reach a compromise if only to be rid of them. As a result, John George of Saxony, hitherto the champion of the Protestant princes, and the emperor concluded the Treaty of Prague (1635). Although it did not grant religious toleration to all Protestant sects, this treaty at least confirmed the secular rulers in their possession of ecclesiastical property for the following thirty-two years, thus rescinding the Edict of Restitution for all practical purposes. The old enemies of Wallenstein at the imperial court, the Spanish and the Bavarian parties, prevailed once more, accusing him, justly it seems, of independent negotiations with the enemy and of a desire to carve out for himself a dukedom or even a kingdom in Germany. As a result, Wallenstein was relieved of command and eventually murdered (1634). Ferdinand rewarded the assassins.

The Active French Phase, 1635–1659 It is conceivable that if its complex structure had been concerned merely with the internal religious and political configuration of the Empire, the war would have ended at this point, with all parties exhausted and ready to compromise. But perhaps the most important aspect of the conflict was the great struggle between France and Spain, to which we now return.

The French and Spanish parts of the wars were unmarred by religious complications. Throughout the end of the sixteenth century, France had seen herself threatened by territorial encirclement by the Habsburg Empire. Further, not content with encirclement, the Spanish kings had consistently interfered in French politics by trying to gain the French crown for a candidate subservient to Spanish policies. With the success of Henry of Navarre (Henry IV) and the establishment of the Bourbon dynasty in France, this policy had failed, but the territorial encirclement continued to grow.

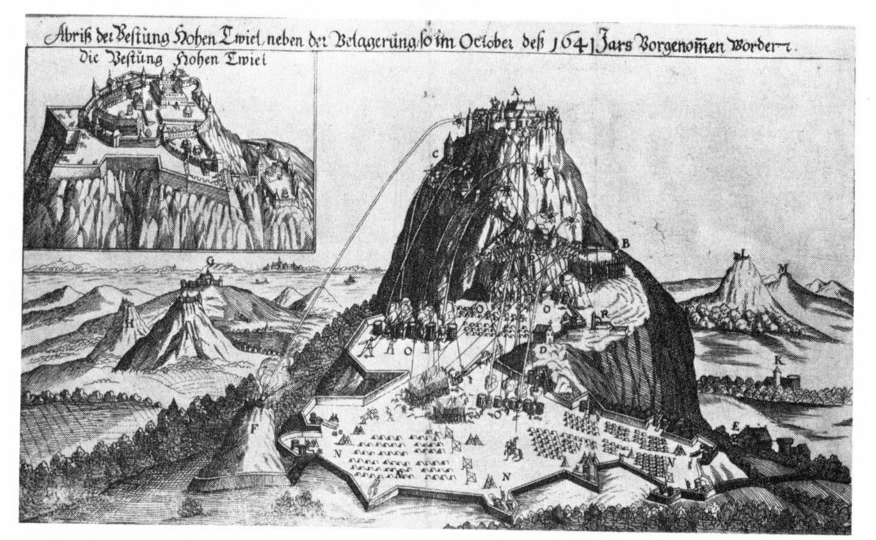

During the Thirty or Fifty Years' War, warfare was more and more a science rather than an art or sport of kings. In this print a Catholic force assaults a hilltop bastion in Protestant hands. Cannonballs explode like daisies in the air after having been shot from heavy artillery below. (LCPP.)

The French entered the war, therefore, to gain three principal objectives: to capture and hold the Alpine passes from Italy into the north so as to disrupt Spanish communications and trade and facilitate French contacts with Venice; to capture and hold the Spanish lifeline along the Rhine in Germany; and to oust the Spanish from the Netherlands. As part of this struggle, the Catholic crown of France supported the Protestant forces in Germany and the Catalan insurgents in Spain, while Spain supported the French Huguenots and antiroyal movements in France.

Officially, Spain and France were not at war until 1635, when the French sent a herald to Brussels to announce a declaration of war. But the coming of the war had been announced previously in other ways. The struggle over the Valtelline had started in 1620, when the Spaniards had succeeded in capturing the valley—then officially part of the Swiss Confederation—with the aid of a local Catholic faction, although the Protestant cantons had sent an army to assist the local Protestants. In 1625, the valley was seized by Swiss forces in French pay who succeeded in hampering Spanish movement in that area. In the north, Richelieu sent a force to cooperate with the Dutch against the Spanish Netherlands. In theory, the Brabanters and Flemings should have rejoiced at their liberation from Spanish oppression, but the Spanish had not repeated in the southern Netherlands the administrative and other mistakes they had made in the north. Through just and reasonable government they had succeeded in gaining the good will of the majority of the population in the south, which, far from feeling liberated, organized an uprising against the French and Dutch forces. Then the Spanish army made ready to invade France from the north. By 1635, the French attempt to break the Spanish encirclement seemed a failure.

French Victory In reality, and despite a Spanish invasion of France in 1636, France was soon in the ascendant. The French army had received valuable training, but had not been exhausted, in a victorious campaign against the Huguenots culminating at La Rochelle and concluded in 1628. Because Richelieu successfully minimized Huguenot resentment by inviting some of the Protestant leaders to join the government in high offices, this victory contributed substantially to French unity. In 1640, on the other hand, the Spanish Habsburgs were faced by the great Portuguese and Catalan revolts. Spain was approaching the end of Olivares' attempts at reform. Her allies in Germany were exhausted and disinclined to continue the struggle. In 1637, the single-minded Ferdinand II was succeeded as German emperor and Austrian ruler by his son, Ferdinand III (1637–1657). Though he shared his father's commitment to the Roman Catholic cause, the new Austrian Habsburg was anxious for peace and willing to settle for a position as an Austrian rather than a German sovereign. His devotion to Spanish interests in western Germany was, therefore, not so strong as that of his father.

Spain had hoped to profit from noble opposition to the centralizing tendencies of Richelieu in France; but Richelieu had managed to destroy a Spanish-backed plot against him in 1641 and to carry on his foreign policy unchanged. Spain had further hoped that the outbreak of a war between Denmark and Sweden over the possession of North Germany would force the Swedes to withdraw permanently from German soil. That hope came to nothing in 1645 when peace was reestablished in the north. From 1645 to 1648, the Swedes and the French together proceeded to defeat the Bavarian and imperial forces in Germany. A second revolt of the French nobility did not occur until 1648, during the peace negotiations in Westphalia, and too late for Spain to profit from it. For eleven years after the Peace of Westphalia, however, the French and Spanish continued intermittent warfare, maneuvering for positions in Italy, along the Rhine and in the Netherlands. This was largely a war of attrition, in which the French were successful in further weakening the Spanish lines of communication. This continuation of the Thirty Years' War was not brought to an end until eleven years later in 1659 with the signing of the Treaty of the Pyrenees. In its broader sense, then, starting with the disturbances of 1608–1609 and lasting until 1659, the Thirty Years' War was in fact a half-century of European warfare.

The Peace of Westphalia The part of the wars that lasted forty years (1608–1648) took five years of negotiations to end. The mere question of the seating of the delegates to the peace conferences that met in Westphalia consumed upwards of six months. Because the Protestants and Catholics refused to sit together, the representatives of France, the emperor and the German Catholics ended up meeting in Münster, while the Swedes and the German Protestants met at Osnabrück with representatives of the Empire. The Habsburg emperor Ferdinand III had hoped to have the purely German questions settled at a meeting of the deputies of the imperial princes, but as it turned out the peacemaking was done—except for the later settlement of the French-Spanish conflict—at these two international congresses, the first of their kind.

The Treaties of Osnabrück and Münster dealt with the German and imperial aspects of the conflict. Some of the most important territorial gains within the Empire were made by outsiders like France and Sweden. The latter gained a good portion of the Baltic coast (western Pomerania) east of Jutland and reaching to the mouth of the Oder River. French sovereignty over the border bishroprics of Metz, Toul, and Verdun was recognized after nearly a century of *de facto* control, as well as rule over the lands and cities in Alsace that had belonged to the Habsburgs. There was considerable shuffling and dealing among imperial insiders as well. The Bavarian Wittelsbachs, for example, kept the Upper Palatinate and the electorate that went with it; a new electorate, the Rhenish Palatinate, was created for another branch of the Wittelsbach family, descendants of Frederick V. Abbeys and bishoprics were pushed around: the Hohenzollern elector of Brandenburg gained a number of important bishoprics (Halberstadt, Minden, Kammin, and Magdeburg) in compensation for the loss of part of western Pomerania to Sweden. The several treaties signed at Osnabrück and Münster in 1648 are known collectively as the Peace of Westphalia.

RESULTS OF THE THIRTY YEARS' WAR

What were the overall consequences of this half-century of war? The major parties concerned began and ended the conflict on more or less equal footing. There was, in fact, no clear victor and no vanquished. Some of the results might be considered as having been positive: The peace treaties legalized political facts already well established—but not recognized—at the beginning of the wars: the boundary lines of Europe and especially of Germany; the independence of the Swiss and the Dutch; and the virtual independence of the German princes within the Empire. Since the pope, who still had pretensions to being the arbiter of the nations of Europe, was forced to accept

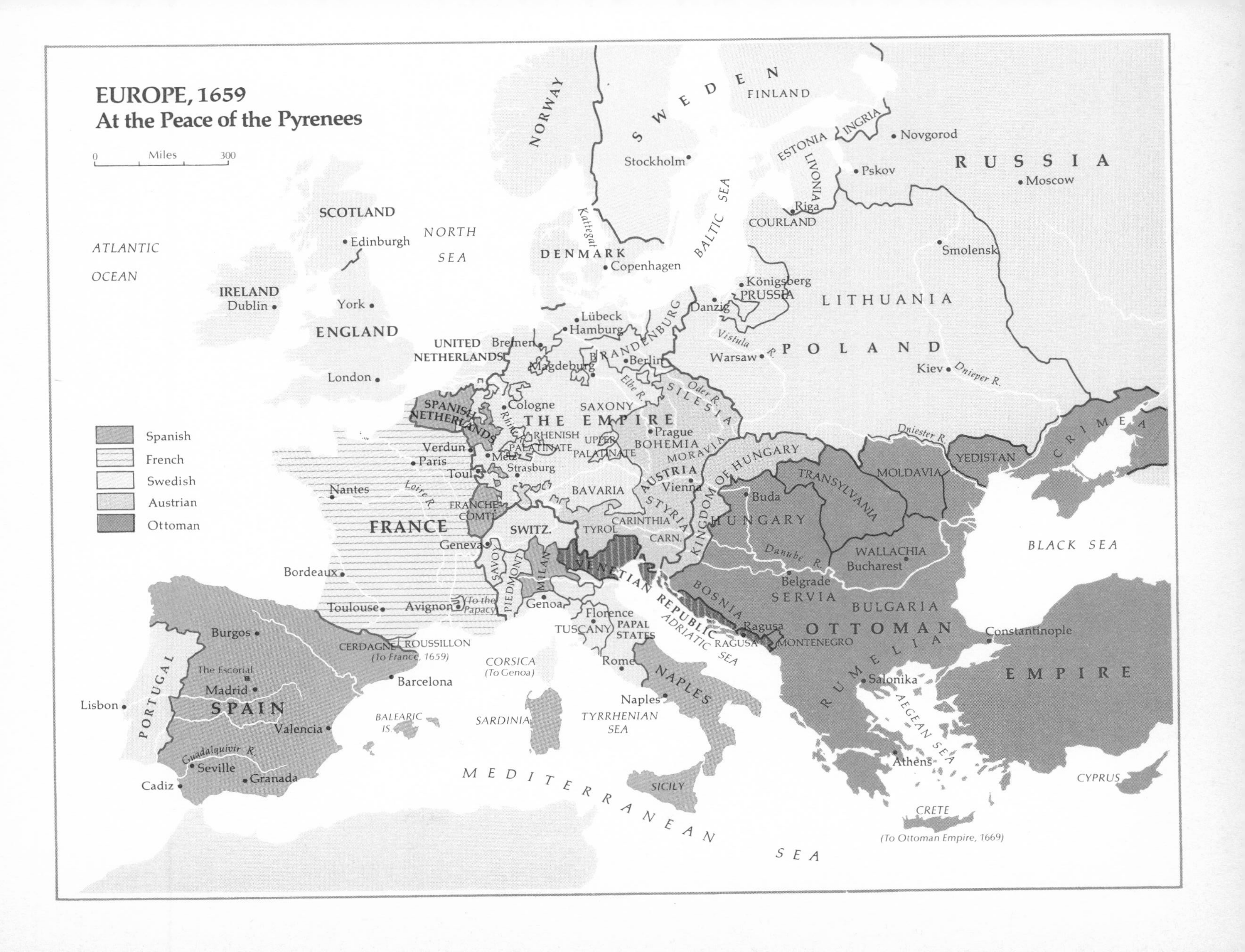
EUROPE, 1659
At the Peace of the Pyrenees
0 Miles 300
Spanish
French
Swedish
Austrian
Ottoman
ATLANTIC OCEAN
NORTH SEA
BALTIC SEA
BLACK SEA
MEDITERRANEAN SEA
ADRIATIC SEA
TYRRHENIAN SEA
AEGEAN SEA
NORWAY
SWEDEN
FINLAND
Stockholm
Kattegat
DENMARK
Copenhagen
ESTONIA
INGRIA
LIVONIA
Riga
COURLAND
Novgorod
Pskov
RUSSIA
Moscow
Smolensk
Königsberg
PRUSSIA
Danzig
LITHUANIA
POLAND
Warsaw
Vistula R.
Kiev
Dnieper R.
Dniester R.
SCOTLAND
Edinburgh
IRELAND
Dublin
York
ENGLAND
London
UNITED NETHERLANDS
Bremen
Lübeck
Hamburg
BRANDENBURG
Berlin
Magdeburg
Elbe R.
Oder R.
SILESIA
SPANISH NETHERLANDS
Cologne
Rhine R.
THE EMPIRE
SAXONY
Prague
BOHEMIA
MORAVIA
RHENISH PALATINATE
UPPER PALATINATE
Verdun
Metz
Paris
Toul
Strasburg
AUSTRIA
Vienna
BAVARIA
STYRIA
CARINTHIA
CARN.
TYROL
Nantes
Loire R.
FRANCHE COMTÉ
FRANCE
SWITZ.
Geneva
SAVOY
PIEDMONT
MILAN
Genoa
VENETIAN REPUBLIC
Bordeaux
Toulouse
Avignon
(To the Papacy)
Florence
TUSCANY
PAPAL STATES
Rome
NAPLES
Naples
CORSICA
(To Genoa)
SARDINIA
SICILY
CERDAGNE
ROUSSILLON
(To France, 1659)
Barcelona
BALEARIC IS.
Burgos
PORTUGAL
The Escorial
Madrid
SPAIN
Lisbon
Valencia
Guadalquivir R.
Seville
Granada
Cadiz
KINGDOM OF HUNGARY
HUNGARY
Buda
TRANSYLVANIA
MOLDAVIA
YEDISTAN
CRIMEA
WALLACHIA
Bucharest
Danube R.
Belgrade
SERVIA
BOSNIA
Ragusa
RAGUSA
MONTENEGRO
BULGARIA
OTTOMAN EMPIRE
RUMELIA
Constantinople
Salonika
Athens
CRETE
(To Ottoman Empire, 1669)
CYPRUS

his position as one ruler among many, the Peace of Westphalia is often called "a secular charter for Europe." Although the Austrian Habsburgs were effectively detached from Spanish policy, they were not ousted from the Empire, where they continued to enjoy an ineffectual primacy. Likewise, the treaties confirmed the religious diversity that had been a European reality in 1609. Calvinism won recognition as a faith in Germany, and it was established that neither Roman Catholicism nor Protestantism would overwhelm the other.

All of these results might be considered as having been positive. In social terms, however, the effect was devastation. Even in areas free from the wars, human misery reached great depths during the first two-thirds of the seventeenth century. The general level of European nutrition fell significantly while outbreaks of disease (plague, typhus, cholera, dysentery,

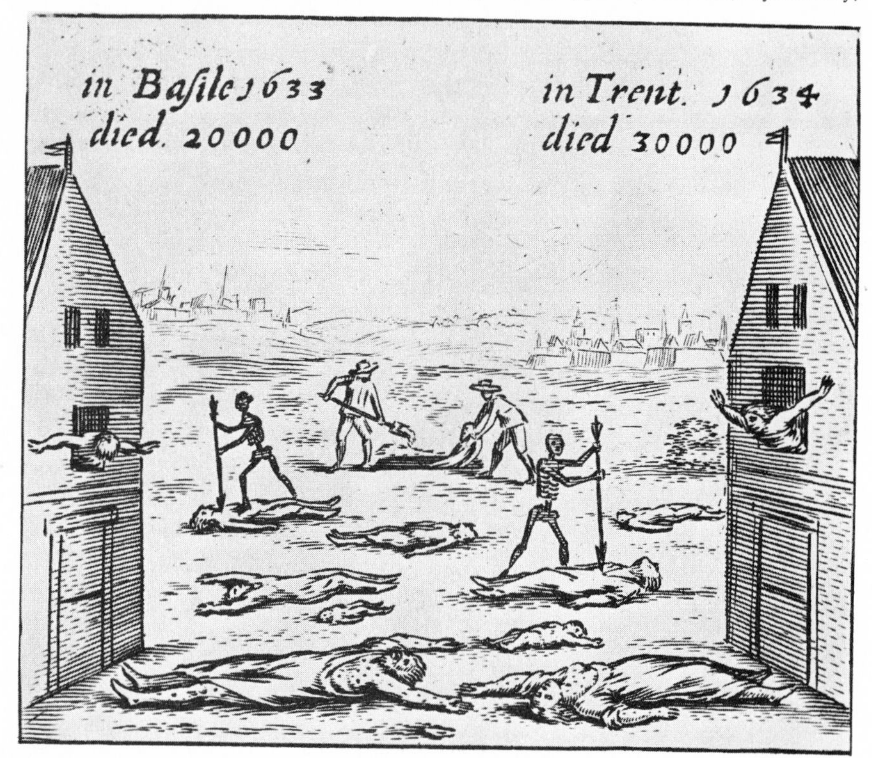

Plague Victims. In this print (c. 1638), victims of a smallpox epidemic lie waiting to be buried. Death figures give them the *coup de grace.* Whole villages and even cities were wiped out by such pestilences, which were often spread by the moving armies. (Folger.)

among others) took dreadful and increasing tolls of human life. Even before the Great Plague of 1665, London lost one quarter of its inhabitants to this disease at least three times; and in one year, 1630, a million and a half people (probably well over 10 percent of the total population) died of the plague in Italy. All of Germany was subject to the same biological disasters; and, in addition, parts of the Empire were seats of war and objects of pillage by marauding armies for fifty long and doleful years. There were some spectacular incidents of warfare: in 1631, for example, the city of Magdeburg on the Elbe River was assaulted by Imperial troops and completely destroyed with the loss of twenty thousand persons. Such sensational atrocities, however, probably did less overall damage than did the systematic plundering by the various armies. Some parts of Germany were untouched by war; but in other areas, although it is difficult to assign proportional responsibility among war, disease and emigration, 15 to 80 percent of the population was lost. Whatever the figures, the impact of the war on Germany was great and tragic.

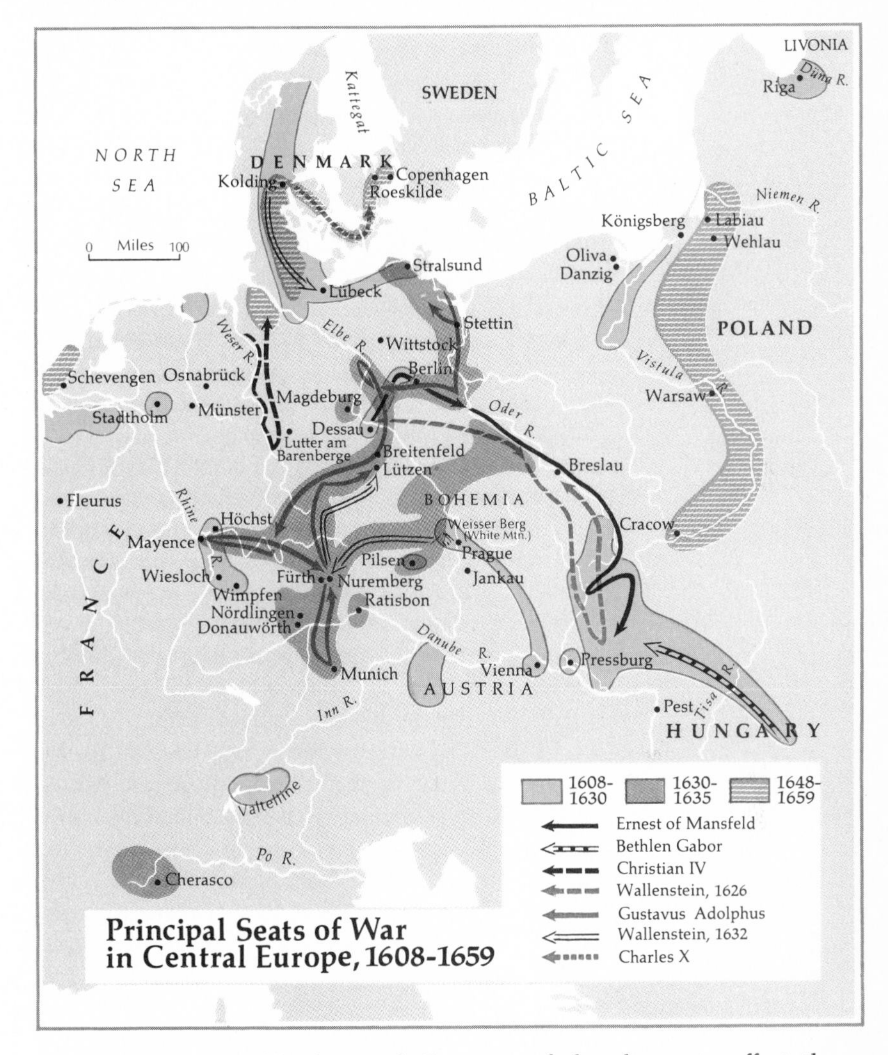

Principal Seats of War in Central Europe, 1608-1659

The war probably deprived Germany of the chance to effect those political and economic changes that could have made the Empire a major power in Europe. Continued fragmentation set back the political and economic development of Germany for years to come. No one, Habsburg or Wittelsbach, Protestant or Catholic, had succeeded in uniting the German princes. What economic and centralizing reforms were made in Germany throughout this period were undertaken by local rulers with an eye to fortifying their own positions against their immediate neighbors and against imperial power.

As a result of the war and the Peace of the Pyrenees in 1659, French ascendancy in Europe was clearly established. Territory was gained by France in the south and east and the northern frontier was advanced, giving Paris more safety than it had ever possessed. More important from the French point of view was the breaking of Habsburg encirclement. Habsburgs still controlled territory north, south, and east of France. But the Habsburg at Vienna was now more a ruler over a congeries of lands on the middle Danube than a German Emperor; and the two branches of the Habsburg family were effectively divided. Spain's power in the Spanish Netherlands and northern Italy was diminished. Moreover, despite Olivares' efforts, Spain had failed to embark on the road to administrative and economic progress that was to be followed by the great powers of the late seventeenth and eighteenth centuries.

The Thirty Years' War had demonstrated fairly clearly the advantage of an organized army that could be maintained in the field for a long period of time. The difficulties of provisioning and disciplining large numbers of men had been one of the major problems of all participants in the war. Often, troop movements, victories, and withdrawals were the result less of clearly planned strategy than of starvation and lack of discipline among the troops. The fact that for nearly fifty years almost every major European power was in constant need of finding large amounts of cash and provisions for troops in the field had stimulated widespread fiscal reforms. From 1660 on, large-scale movements of troops gave way increasingly to economic warfare, the mercantilist attempt to defeat the enemy before he ever put troops in the field. The ultimate victory in this type of struggle was to go to those countries that had effected the change most quickly from feudal anarchy to the modern centralized state.

The Thirty or Fifty Years' War thus set the stage for the Age of Louis XIV. With Spanish predominance broken, Spain and Austria effectively separated, and Germany and Italy politically splintered, a French monarch with a large, loyal and expanding population could hope to dominate the European stage. Meanwhile, during the entire period of the continental wars of fifty years, a revolution had been in progress across the channel in England.

FURTHER READING

This series of conflicts can best be approached on the pan-European plane. An outstanding general work, again, is H. Hauser, *La préponderance espagnole* (1933), already cited. C. J. Friedrich, * *The Age of the Baroque, 1610–1660* (1952), gives good coverage, especially of intellectual and artistic history, and comes equipped with a fine bibliographical essay, as do the other volumes in the *Rise of Modern Europe* series. Beginning and advanced students should become familiar with these bibliographies.

*Books available in paperback edition are marked with an asterisk.

Other general studies include D. Ogg, * *Europe in the Seventeenth Century* (1961), a dull, all-round treatment; while G. N. Clark, * *The Seventeenth Century* (1947), is a brilliant series of essays on European institutions and culture. R. B. Mowat, *A History of European Diplomacy, 1451–1789* (1971), is very good for this period.

The most readable book on the wars is C. V. Wedgwood, * *The Thirty Years' War* (1962); though it may not be the last word in interpretation, it is a charming book by a distinguished historian. More recent is S. H. Steinberg, * *The Thirty Years' War and the Conflict for European Hegemony, 1600–1660* (1967). Still more recent, and sharply at odds with C. V. Wedgwood, is J. V. Polisensky, *The Thirty Years' War* (1971), a serious study based on Czech sources, translated by Robert Evans. For background on the Empire, see J. Bryce, * *Holy Roman Empire* (1961), now in paperback, a tiresome classic. C. R. L. Fletcher, * *Gustavus Adolphus and the Thirty Years' War* (1963), is another paperback that may prove useful for those interested in the Swedish phase, as will A. T. Anderson, *Sweden in the Baltic: A Study in the Politics of Expansion under King Gustavus Adolphus and Chancellor Axel Oxenstierna* (1947). W. Kirchner, *The Rise of the Baltic Question* (1954), is pertinent here. J. H. S. Birch, *Denmark in History* (1938), handles the Danish aspect of the wars. F. Watson, *Wallenstein: Soldier under Saturn* (1938), is good on that adventurer though it rather exaggerates Wallenstein's role.

For the French part in the wars, see especially C. V. Wedgwood, * *Richelieu and the French Monarchy* (1966). A brief study by a German of the Peace of Westphalia is M. Braubach, *Der Westfälische Friede* (1948). Some of the ideas set forth in this chapter were derived from an article by S. H. Steinberg, "The Thirty Years' War: A New Interpretation," published in *History* (1947). Steinberg's interpretation is sharply at odds with that of Miss Wedgwood. For a collection of different interpretations of the war see T. K. Rabb, ed., * *The Thirty Years' War* (1972), a Heath pamphlet.

During the past fifteen years or so, many historians have been tussling with the notion that somewhere in early modern times (late sixteenth and early seventeenth century, mid-seventeenth century, or what have you) European civilization underwent a "crisis." H. Kamen, *The Iron Century: Social Change in Europe, 1550–1660* (1972), already cited, deals with this matter. T. H. Aston, ed., * *Crisis in Europe, 1560–1660* (1965), is a stimulating collection of essays from the English multidisciplinary journal *Past and Present* by such people as J. H. Elliott, Pierre Goubert, E. J. Hobsbawm, R. Mousnier, and H. R. Trevor-Roper. A. D. Lublinskaya, an able Soviet scholar, attacks Hobsbawm (also a Marxist) and Trevor-Roper as regards the "general crisis" of the seventeenth century theory in her *French Absolutism: The Crucial Phase, 1620–1629* (1968). D. Bitton, *The French Nobility in Crisis, 1550–1640* (1969), also touches on the crisis theory.

Students who wish to get the feel of the period from primary material might read a new translation of a famous seventeenth-century novel that bears on the Thirty Years' War: H. J. Von Grimmelshausen, * *Adventurous Simplicissimus* (1973).

2 England in the Seventeenth Century: Revolution and Resolution

REGICIDE!

On a somber afternoon at the end of January 1649, a sense of dread had settled over Westminster and the city of London beside the leaden river Thames. The palace of Whitehall was filled with a silent throng guarded by grim-faced soldiers. One of the tall windows of the Banqueting Hall (recently decorated at the king's request by the painter, Peter Paul Rubens) had been removed to form an exit to a scaffold draped in black. On the platform was a headsman's block. A double line of soldiers hand-picked from Oliver Cromwell's New Model Army held the open space between the palace of St. James and the spectral scene in Whitehall.

Early that morning, Charles I, king of Great Britain, Scotland and Ireland, had listened gravely as an Anglican bishop read to him from the 27th chapter of Matthew. The reading of Jesus' trial and passion had been followed by the ministering of Holy Communion. In mid-morning, led by halberdiers, Charles had been moved to the Banqueting Hall, traditionally the site of so much gaiety, for the dreadful wait. Across the Channel in Paris, Charles' wife, Queen Henriette, was lodged in an apartment in the Louvre, blockaded by the opening battles of the *fronde.*

For three hours the king waited. At last he was brought out for a final confrontation with his people. On the scaffold, two black-masked executioners awaited him. The composure of the king, his steadfastness in this extremity, need not have been unexpected by his enemies. Although his continual duplicity had convinced his opponents that no agreement could be reached with him, he had dealt with all sides with but one intent—to maintain the absolute power of the crown unfettered by Parliament or common law or by those who used these institutions to challenge his royal will. Standing near his executioners, the king began his last futile defense. The Rump of the House of Commons which had tried him, he said, was an illegal body. The Army, which now held power in England, was an

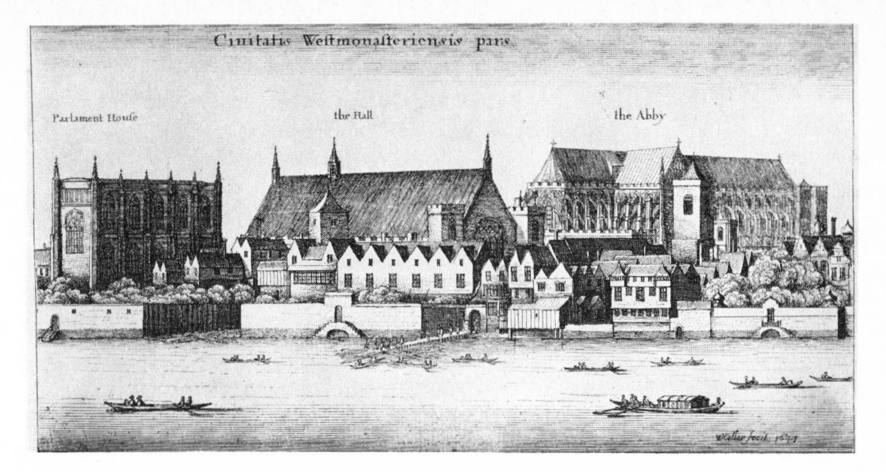

A View of Westminster in Old London from the River Thames. From left to right: Parliament House, the great hall of Westminster, and the Abbey church. A great fire in 1666 destroyed most of the city. (Folger.)

usurping government, a tyrannous element backed by force alone. A common lieutenant-general was the unlawful chief of state. It was he, Charles I, who sought to uphold the English tradition, now ruptured by this monstrous insurgency. His last words were: "I am the martyr of the people."

The king's cloak was removed. He was placed on the block; the axe rose and fell. After a moment of shocked silence, one of the headsmen raised the bloody remnant to the sky. Thus, on a wintry afternoon ten years before the end of the fifty years of warfare on the continent of Europe, an English king was executed by one of the new popular armies of the seventeenth century.

In Europe, during the preceding forty years, minor kings had been driven out of their realms; the ministers of one ruler had been thrown from a palace window; at least one monarch had been killed in battle; and Henry III and Henry IV of France had been assassinated by fanatics. Only in England had a king been brought to trial for high crimes against the state and condemned to death.

Why was it that, instead of being ignored by a supreme monarch, as were the Estates General in the France of Louis XIV, the seventeenth-century English House of Commons played the decisive role in destroying and then making kings? How was it that Great Britain could undergo two "revolutions" in one century and emerge, as we shall see, more united than ever before?[1] How was it that just when the theory of the absolute and divine right of kings emerged triumphant in the person of Louis XIV in France, the English succeeded in establishing a constitutional monarchy limited by a Bill of Rights? Let us look at the political, economic, social, and religious developments in England from the end of Elizabeth's reign through the "Glorious Revolution" of 1689 to find some partial answers to these questions.

[1] The British have traditionally referred to the events of 1640–1649 (see below) as the "Great Rebellion," and the *coup d'état* of 1688 as the "Glorious Revolution." Today, historians tend to merge the whole affair into one great revolutionary process.

THE DIVINE RIGHT OF KINGS: JAMES I

The English kings had long been the effective rulers over their realms. The Tudor monarchs, Henry VII, Henry VIII, Edward VI, Mary, and Elizabeth, in their several ways ruled in an arbitrary manner—although through cajolery, tact, and craft they often avoided head-on clashes and mesmerized their subjects into feeling that they were being led rather than pushed. Not even Henry VIII managed to build up royal power without relying on parliamentary support. James I, who came to the English throne from Scotland in 1603 following the death of Elizabeth, was not content with the *de facto* possession of almost limitless power. In fact, he had already written his credo, *The Trew Law of Free Monarchies: Or the Reciprock and Mutuall Dutie Betwixt a Free King and His Naturall Subjects.* It stated the divine right of kingship, declaring that "Kings are called gods by the prophetical King David because they sit upon God His throne in earth and have the count of their administration to give unto Him." Upon his accession he proudly announced that since God made kings, only kings could make the laws.

As the son of Mary Stuart, Elizabeth's enemy, James I was an unattractive figure to his new subjects. Further, his years of political intrigue in Scotland and his bitter struggles with the Presbyterians there made him overly wary of the moderate Puritans in England.[2] Naturally tactless and undignified, he did not conceal his contempt for others and especially for members of Parliament. The latter were no more willing to accept his exalted notions about monarchy than the religious dissidents were willing to accept his insistence upon religious conformity. As time went on, his penchant for handsome but frivolous courtiers like George Villiers (1592–1628), whom he made first Duke of Buckingham, disgusted more responsible ministers of state.

"No Bishop, no King," was one of James' typically curt remarks to a group of Puritans who petitioned for more freedom for the lower orders of the clergy. He was equally determined to enforce penalties against the Roman Catholics. One upshot of his stand was that a Catholic group conceived the idea (in the famous "Gunpowder Plot" of 1605) of blowing up the whole Establishment—King, Lords, and Commons—at once. They very nearly succeeded, and Britishers still celebrate "Guy Fawkes Day" in honor of the gentleman who was to have touched off the explosion under the Houses of Parliament. The Puritans did succeed in persuading the king to command a new translation of the Bible (published in 1611). What Americans call the King James version of the Bible became known in England

[2] "Puritan" was a word of changing meanings during this period of English history. Throughout much of Elizabeth's reign "Puritans" observed the Anglican forms but wished and worked for a simpler ceremonial and a more democratic organization of the Church. In theology they leaned toward Calvinism, but they had not yet broken from the Established Church of England. Increasingly, in the first half of the seventeenth century, and especially after the Hampton Court Conference of 1604 (which resulted in the punishment of many who deviated from established practices), the word "Puritan" came to refer to non-Roman Catholic Christians outside the Church of England: Presbyterians, Independents or Congregationalists, Anabaptists, and many other proliferating sects.

as the "Authorized Version" because it was authorized by the bishops to be read in the Anglican church.

James I's troubles with Parliament stemmed from his need for money combined with his unwillingness to justify his expenditures. He called only four Parliaments during his reign of twenty-two years, resorting instead to expedients such as levying fines for encroaching on the royal forests, and settling titles of nobility.[3] Whereas his predecessor Elizabeth lived frugally and sent able ministers to defend her requests to Parliament, James appeared to squander money on his family and his favorites and treated members of Parliament with contempt. His—and especially Buckingham's—foolhardy efforts to embroil England in continental wars and politics courted disaster at a time when new English commercial classes perceived their true interests to be in building their colonial empire and overseas trade and collecting profits from home industries.

THE
HOLY
BIBLE,
Conteyning the Old Teſtament,
AND THE NEW:
Newly Tranſlated out of the Originall
tongues: & with the former Tranſlations
diligently compared and reviſed, by his
Maieſties ſpeciall Cōmandement.
Appointed to be read in Churches.
Imprinted at London by Robert
Barker, Printer to the Kings
moſt Excellent Maieſtie.
ANNO DOM. 1611.

James I of England (below) was a pedant who wrote continually, both before and after his accession to the throne. Besides his analyses of the character of monarchy (see text, p. 790) he composed essays on the evils of tobacco, on demons, and other matters. He approved the new translation of the Bible which today bears his name (the "King James" or "Authorized" version published in 1611) whose title page appears here. (National Maritime Museum, London/Yale University.)

[3]Strictly speaking, the English crown enjoyed independent income only from (1) property owned by the crown (crown lands), (2) feudal dues, and (3) tariffs and duties on foreign trade. For any other monies the king was supposed to approach Parliament for grants of supply.

ROYAL PREROGATIVES VS. ENGLISH COMMON LAW

The sale of patents or monopolies had long provided a supplement to royal income. Complaints about crown-oriented monopolies, such as the exclusive right to manufacture and sell wine and spirits, had been voiced to Elizabeth in one of her last Parliaments, and the queen had promised to look into the problem. James characteristically ignored it. In 1615, for example, Sir Robert Mansell purchased a royal patent in the glass industry. Although he made no improvements and introduced no new processes, he had complete control over the production and sale of glass in England. At last, Parliament officially denounced such abuses in a Statute of Monopolies (1624). "Monopolies, commissions, grants, licenses, charters and letters patents . . . for the sole buying, making, working, or using of anything within this realm" the legislature declared contrary to law. Only "first and true . . . inventors" should have these benefices.

Legal arguments proliferated in an atmosphere of mutual distrust. Edward Coke (1552–1634), for example, who had, under Elizabeth, been a strong supporter of royal prerogatives, became, under James I, the champion of the power of Parliament. He tangled with James early in his reign when, as chief justice of the common pleas (courts where civil cases were tried by jury according to English common law), he resisted the king's attempt to withdraw a case. He hurled his defiance at the crown, stating that the common law was supreme and that "the king in his own person cannot judge any case." This was sharply at variance with the legal system that had grown up under the Tudors, wherein special courts, such as the Court of the Star Chamber and the Court of High Commission, were responsible directly to the king, and in effect made their own rules. Coke's doctrine was, of course, incompatible with James' version of himself as the source of all law. As we shall see, Coke and his disciples were to overturn the foundations of English royal authority before the century was out.

At the beginning of the seventeenth century, the character of the English Parliament was changing rapidly. The divisions between the English House of Lords and the Commons were becoming much less rigid. A "rising gentry," composed of "improving" landholders or squires and enterprising city merchants (who might be the same persons) was displacing the impoverished monarchy and hereditary nobility at the seat of political power. The late R. H. Tawney, an English historian, pointed out that these men generally held Puritan religious views. They were highly distrustful of a divine authority linked to a nearly bankrupt and incompetent monarch and an established church which they viewed as corrupt.[4] Some of them lived and acted very much like peers of the realm, and others earnestly prepared themselves for public service by attending universities and/or studying at the Inns of Court (law schools).

[4] Tawney equated this "rising gentry" with a "middle class" or bourgeoisie. Tawney's thesis has been disputed or elaborated upon by H. R. Trevor-Roper, who distinguishes between the "fat" court gentry which profited from royal favors and the "depressed" country gentry which was economically in decline. The latter tended to be more radical.

CHARLES I AND THE PURITAN REVOLUTION

James I's son Charles had absorbed all the political and religious notions of his father. "King and subject are clean different things," is one of the remarks for which he is remembered. Shortly after he became king in 1625, all the troubles that had been brewing under his father boiled to the surface.

Charles was diminutive in person and not without charm and ability. He brought into his government remarkably competent men—Thomas Wentworth, Earl of Strafford, and Archbishop William Laud, for instance—who worked closely with the king to centralize and rationalize the monarchy. They successfully devised new ways to increase crown revenues: imposing special fines on gentlemen who neglected to be knighted and forcing loans. As English foreign trade increased, so did that part of the royal income that came from import and export duties.

Charles I by the Flemish Artist Van Dyck. The English monarch wears on his sleeve the red Cross of St. George surrounded by an aureole of silver rays, symbol of the royal hereditary Order of the Garter. Charles was greatly interested in preserving the trappings of knighthood and chivalry. (Dresden, Staatliche Kunstsammlungen.)

Unfortunately, Charles retained Buckingham as his chief minister for foreign affairs. The latter soon proved himself worthy of public distrust by embroiling Britain in war with both Spain and France. When a naval expedition against Cadiz in 1625 proved a disaster, the Commons tried to impeach Buckingham for treason. Charles parried this by dismissing Parliament. Next, an expedition led by the Duke against the French coast near La Rochelle to aid the Huguenots there was decisively repulsed and the king's fortunes ebbed. The expenses of these expeditions forced him to ask Parliament for funds again, and this time the Commons was ready with a list of grievances and a "Petition of Right" to which the king was forced to assent in order to get the subsidies he required. In the furor, Buckingham was assassinated. When Charles dismissed his fourth Parliament in as many years he hoped it was for good.

From 1629 to 1640 Charles ruled without help from that body. These eleven years of personal rule or "Eleven Years Tyranny," as they were known to Charles' opponents, were a period of domestic happiness for the king and of relative prosperity for his subjects. But when trouble came again it was clear that this surface tranquility covered wounds that had not healed but rather continued to fester and swell.

In 1637, Charles, at the urging of Archbishop Laud, decided to impose upon Scotland a new Anglican liturgy based upon the Book of Common Prayer. The Scottish Presbyterians resisted by force of arms. To impose his will, Charles again needed armies—and subsidies from Parliament. Two Parliaments called in 1640 (the "Short" and the "Long" Parliament respectively) breathed fiery hostility. Their leader was John Pym (1584–1643). One of the country gentry described earlier, Pym had studied at Oxford and at Middle Temple (a "law school") and sat in the House of Commons whenever it was in session from 1615 to his death in 1643. There he had heard Coke expound the doctrine of common law and attack the royal prerogatives. Pym was not an ardent Puritan, but he knew how to exploit the present crisis and was an effective parliamentary manager. He succeeded in turning the king's initiatives in Scotland and at home into irresponsible innovations in the public eye, calling for a return to the country's "first institution and ordinance."

John Hampden (1595–1643), another well-to-do, well-educated member of the English landed aristocracy, helped lead the fight in parliament and out. He made his greatest mark through his opposition to Charles' attempt to increase his revenues by exacting "ship-money." Since the thirteenth century, the kings of England had had the right to require certain port towns to supply warships for the defense of the realm. As time passed, it became customary to levy this tax in money terms in time of war or imminent danger. Charles and his advisors decided to innovate as regards "ship-money" by levying it in 1635 when England was at peace and applying it to all inland counties as well as to seaports. The idea occurred to some that this gambit was not only unconstitutional (of course, Charles thought it was constitutional because he willed it); it was also very dangerous. If successful, it would put the king entirely out of the reach of Parliament.

Four men who played critical roles in the sequence of events that led to England's civil war: (1) the Duke of Buckingham, fop and favorite under James I and Charles I; (2) Archbishop Laud, whose attempts to suppress Puritanism in England and impose the "Bishop's" religious forms on Scotland brought on the crisis; (3) John Pym, leader in Commons; and (4) Oliver Cromwell, who would fill the power vacuum left by the execution of the king. (Uffizi, Florence/LC/City Museum and Art Gallery, Birmingham.)

Hampden refused to pay his share (one pound) of the "ship-money" levied in his county of Buckinghamshire (he had earlier been imprisoned by the king for refusing to contribute to a forced loan), and he argued in court that the king had no right to collect such money unless the country was in clear danger, as determined by Parliament. Hampden lost the case, but public attention had been focused on the danger of arbitrary royal taxation, and resistance to Charles and his advisors mounted.

Also in Parliament during this crisis was Hampden's cousin, Oliver Cromwell of Huntingdonshire (1599–1658). Cromwell had left Cambridge at the age of eighteen, but not before he had absorbed the Puritan ideas that were circulating in his college at the time. He quietly managed his modest acres and enjoyed riding and hunting throughout the eleven years of Charles' personal rule. He was returned to the House of Commons in 1640. He spoke little, but when he did it was to criticize what he thought of as "High Church" innovations in the Anglican ceremonies and to rail against the bishops. Religious questions were not uppermost in the minds of those in Parliament at this time, however, and it was not until he became a military leader that his convictions found a receptive audience.

Radical Religion It has been frequently suggested that the Reformation came to England not in the sixteenth century when it separated from Rome but in the seventeenth century under the Stuarts. In the sixteenth century, the split had been between a Protestantism of sorts and Catholicism. Now, the important divisions were among several categories of Protestantism, and the level of intensity about the differences was much higher than it had been.

Three broad shades of opinion and practice in England may be distinguished in the religious ferment under the Stuarts. The conservatives were the "church types," who wished to establish or maintain one church (their own) as the national religion buttressed by the state and with absolute authority in all spiritual matters. Presbyterians, Anglicans, and Roman Catholics were "church types." The "sect type," on the other hand, believed in complete separation of church and state and in the autonomy of his sect. He tended to idealize the primitive Christian church and was led by inspired preachers rather than ordained ones. Independents such as Congregationalists and Anabaptists (later called Baptists) were "sect types." Finally, those who rejected all secular authority in spiritual matters, even from those of like persuasion, were the "spiritual types" who received individual revelations from God. The primitive Quakers and the "Diggers" were the most notable examples of the latter.

The program of the Presbyterian "church types" was the most influential in the House of Commons. The army as it later developed under Cromwell, on the other hand, was dominated by the "sect-type" Independents or Congregationalists, of which Cromwell was one. Another "sect-type" group was the "Levellers," whose most eloquent spokesman was John Lilburne. Lilburne translated Christian doctrine into political terms, advocating radical reform of Parliament through extension of the suffrage. The Levellers were organized as a "party" with a mass membership, weekly newspapers, and a color—sea green—to distinguish adherents. A looser organization was the "spiritual-type" Society of Friends or "Quakers," formed by George Fox. Quakers sought God "experimentally"—as a personal experience. Fox referred contemptuously to Cambridge University, for example, as the place where apprentices learned the "trade" of preaching. To him, education was neither necessary nor desirable for spiritual well-being or leadership. Any man, carpenter or shoemaker, could, if inspired, come to understand God's word. To the left of the Quakers were the spiritual communists, the "Diggers," whose leader was Gerrard Winstanley. Winstanley appeared in 1649 with a few followers on St. George's Hill in London and began to dig the commons to sow parsnips, carrots, and beans, saying that God had told him that only those who labor in the earth could enjoy its fruits. Wilder spirits among the religious personalities began to question conventional views of morality and the ownership of property.

Thus, as Lilburne and the Levellers attacked traditional English political institutions, Winstanley and the Diggers threatened the social order. Fox and the Quakers attacked Church authority and the educational system. Some of their exaggerated ideas frightened the more conservative reformers in Parliament.

In 1640 and 1641, the objectives of the active dissidents in Parliament were to impose, first, some limitations on the king's power, and second, a Presbyterian system (free of the hierarchy of bishops and archbishops but still tightly organized) on the church. This opposition was still, therefore, quite moderate. Gradually, the situation moved out of moderate control.

The Long Parliament and Civil War We have seen that hostility between crown and Parliament began to become acute as a result of the troubles that arose out of Charles' and Laud's attempt to impose Church of England usages on Scotland. In order to get the money necessary to deal with the Scots insurgency, Charles called a parliament in early 1640, expecting them to grant supply. The members refused unless the crown agreed to a redress of grievances. Charles dissolved the Parliament, as was his prerogative; and the Puritan-Parliamentary party was in a difficult situation. If the crown, served by able administrators, could continue to increase the royal income without calling upon Parliament, it would soon be entirely out of control. Something like the centralized absolutism that was forming across the channel in France would be a distinct possibility for England.

Obviously an immediate crisis was required to force the king to have recourse to Parliament. Fortunately—and perhaps by design—the crisis appeared in the form of an invasion of northern England by a Scottish army. A royal force could not drive them out; and the Scots said that they would not retire until they were paid £850 per day until a final settlement was reached. Because Charles did not have the money, he was forced to call another Parliament—the Long Parliament, as it has been called—in November 1640.

Under the leadership of men like Pym and Hampden, this Parliament pressed hard to capitalize on its advantage. Before supplying the money to settle the Scots affair, they forced the king to agree to an act (the Triennial Act) that would require that Parliament should meet every three years, as well as to the abolition of the Courts of Star Chamber and High Commission—the royal prerogative courts. Further, they moved against Charles' two principal ministers, Strafford and Laud. Strafford was the first victim. Tried on a Bill of Attainder, he was beheaded on May 12, 1641, while a delighted London crowd watched and roared.[5] Such was the temper of the day that although treason was never proved, Strafford himself urged the king to sign the bill rather than to allow his own person to come between the king and his people.

Then, in the autumn of 1641, another crisis intervened, this time in Ireland. Despite Strafford's considerable achievements as Lord Deputy of Ireland during the 1630's, tensions increased there between more-or-less native Catholics and English Protestants. In 1641, the Catholics in Ulster rose up and slaughtered as many as 30,000 Protestants. Obviously, the matter had to be attended to; but neither Parliament or the king was willing to trust the other with an army. Parliament now decided to create its own militia. Under Pym's leadership, a "Grand Remonstrance" or list of grievances was passed and offered to the king. Charles responded by ordering the arrest of one lord and five members of the House of Commons whom he suspected (and probably correctly) of having colluded in the Scottish invasion of the North. On January 4, 1642, at the head of 400 troops, he attempted to carry out his own order. The accused escaped and took shelter in the hospitable city of London. Charles fled to the north with a band of

Once organized and disciplined, the soldiers of Cromwell's New Model Army had the twin advantages of personal belief in the rightness of their cause and willingness to learn new techniques of warfare. This illustration is from a text on cavalry warfare published in England in Cromwell's day but based on techniques developed in the Netherlands. (Folger.)

[5] When approved by Lords and Commons and signed by the king, a Bill of Attainder permitted the execution of an accused person without benefit of trial.

loyal peers and commoners and in August raised the royal banner at Nottingham. The civil war had begun.

In London, Parliament appointed a committee of public safety and proceeded to raise an army. Charles' queen sailed to the Netherlands where she bought arms for the king's forces by selling some of her jewels. Oliver Cromwell, who had had no previous training as a soldier, at first recruited men and material and then was given a command in the parliamentary forces. In the next few years he rose rapidly, although he came under frequent personal attack for his radical religious views. At first, the inexperienced parliamentary forces fared badly against the royalists. Eventually, Cromwell in Parliament proposed a total reorganization under a commander divorced from politics. Parliament agreed, and, although he had resigned his previous command, Cromwell himself was put in charge of organizing the "New Model Army."

Cromwell's army was composed in large part of yeomen (small farmers or freeholders), many of them from the east of England (East Anglia) which county supplied most of the Puritan fathers of Massachusetts Bay. It quickly became an effective military force characterized by discipline, purpose, and efficiency. Its chaplains assumed the role of prophets. Its leader, profoundly religious as were his men, saw the hand of Providence in even his most cruel and unnecessary acts. The ideas of Cromwell and his soldiers on religious matters were more independent than those of either the Puritan squires or the Presbyterians. In fact, Cromwell's soldiers became disenchanted with the leadership in Parliament when they learned that this body thought of replacing Anglicanism with Presbyterianism as the established religion of England.

The story of how the royalists were eventually defeated and the king captured, tried, and executed as the "grand author of our troubles" need not detain us here. Charles I maintained to the end that "a king cannot be tried under any superior jurisdiction on earth."

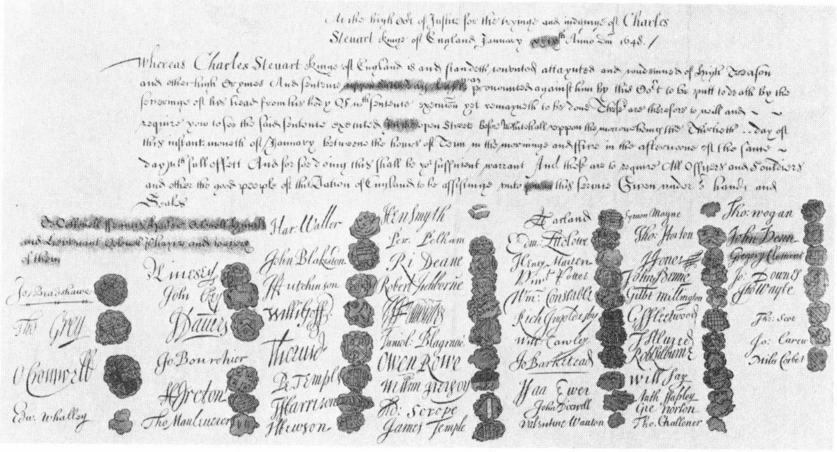

THE INTERREGNUM

The English revolution had reached its zenith with the execution of Charles, which left England without a ruling monarch. Begun in a moderate way by legalistically inclined country squires, the revolt had turned into a democratic and religious revolution in which the ends were thought to be social justice and reform of the whole order of society. The sectaries and the soldiers threatened to overwhelm the original objectives of the gentry. Now it was Cromwell who checked these trends and stabilized the revolution. He agreed to the Army's request for the removal of the king—"Cruel necessity," he is said to have murmured over the monarch's coffin. The year before, he had purged the Presbyterians from Parliament, leaving a "Rump" of Independents. Subsequently he eliminated the most radical elements from the Army. Cromwell was not a power-mad dictator, but rather thought of himself as cast by fate to preside over a tragic and bloody transition. Intolerant as a younger man, he now advocated freedom of worship for all save Roman Catholics. And having fought the king, he proceeded to carry on many of his imperial projects. Thus, the "Interregnum" of eleven years when England did not have a king or queen did represent a sort of continuity in English history.

Impeachment and Trial of King Charles I. In this illustration taken from the official record the king (center, foreground) sits with his back to the viewer, facing the presiding officer (chief judge) of the Lords (High Court). The king refused to plead, that is, to enter a plea of guilty or not guilty. Charles' death warrant, with the seals of the judges, is shown on page 798. (Photos by John Freeman London.)

Ireland is a case in point. Before 1640, Charles, through Strafford, his Lord Deputy, had been trying to rationalize Irish affairs. These were—and remain—chaotic because of the colonization of an essentially Gaelic island by Anglo-Normans since at least as far back as the twelfth century. In Elizabethan times and later, large numbers of Protestants had emigrated to Ireland, especially in the northeast (Ulster). By and large during the Civil War, Irish sympathies—especially Roman Catholic—had been with the king; and the threat of an important invasion of England by Charles' Irish supporters was a real one. Even after Charles I's execution, the situation in Ireland was fluid and his son was proclaimed as Charles II by most of the Irish. Shortly after the execution of the king, Cromwell was appointed Lord Lieutenant of Ireland by Parliament. In August 1649, having disposed of some left-wing resistance in England, he sailed to Ireland, massacred (September) some 2,800 royalist Irish at Drogheda, north of Dublin, and had "knocked on the head" every Irish Catholic priest that his troops could catch. Royalist and Roman Catholic landlords were dispossessed, and their estates given to Cromwell's soldiers and to creditors of the English Parliamentary government. This Irish policy was in line with what Strafford had tried to effect in the 1630's, though Strafford's execution of it had been considerably less brutal.

Another case in point was Cromwell's approach to mercantilism and foreign policy. The Navigation Act of 1651, which decreed that all English imports must be carried in English bottoms or in vessels belonging to their country of origin, continued and strengthened English mercantilist policy. This Act led to a trade war with the Netherlands (1652–1654), and another war with Spain (1656–1659), both of which Cromwell vigorously pursued.

On the domestic front, Cromwell had his own difficulties with representative government. He found the "Rump" Parliament, which had voted to try the king, impossible to get along with. A new Parliament was no better. Eventually (1653), a written constitution, called the "Instrument of Government," was prepared (England's first and last). It gave Cromwell executive powers as Lord Protector and specified that Parliament was to be elected every three years. Even with his new powers, he thought of the assertive parliamentarians (who seemed to throw Scripture at him with one hand and constitutional arguments with the other) as representing anarchy, which he hated even more than arbitrariness. Accordingly, Cromwell sent his second Parliament home—just as Charles I had done on several occasions.

To keep order, Cromwell was forced to move further and further toward a military dictatorship. The realm was divided into twelve military districts, each in charge of a major general who supervised morals, closed alehouses, enforced religious observance, levied taxes, and arbitrarily imprisoned and transported suspects. Cromwell did not believe that his regime was the right one for England; but he could not arrive at a desirable alternative. He continued to see God's hand at work. "These issues and events," he said, "have not been forecast, but were providences in things."

Cromwell died in 1658, after nearly ten years of rule. The title of Lord Protector passed, by previous arrangement, to his son, Richard, who was soon persuaded to resign his title. A confused situation developed which ended with the calling of a special Convention Parliament that decided to call the son of the beheaded Charles from exile in the Netherlands to the English throne as Charles II. The Interregnum was over.

THE RESTORATION

A supple, buoyant spirit, tall and graceful, possessed of considerable courage and few scruples, Charles II arrived in London on his thirtieth birthday in late May of 1660, determined never to travel again. The country, relieved of its austere and omnipotent major generals, welcomed its errant, wenching king.

If he were to remain and keep the loyalty of his new subjects, it was necessary for Charles II to make some sort of accommodation to the changes that had taken place since 1640. A thoroughgoing Restoration should have seen the gutters running with the blood of Charles' father's enemies. Instead, the fountains ran with wine; and only a handful of the most prominent regicides were executed. Charles' main preoccupations were his health, which was excellent, and his mistresses, who were numerous.

Charles II of England in the Ceremonial Robes of the Order of the Garter (compare the portrait of Charles I on p. 793). Charles II was generally short of funds, but succeeded through an odd combination of indolence, cynicism, and craft in keeping his subjects reasonably content. He accepted Roman Catholicism on his deathbed. (LCRB.)

Other changes had overtaken the crown. The Prerogative Courts had disappeared; the common law courts were sovereign. The "mystery" of absolute monarchy no longer inhibited the will of the subject. Arbitrary rule was no longer possible. Parliament had to be recognized as a permanent reality; thus royal ministers congenial to it recommended themselves.

Charles was politically astute and realized that he had to adjust to these changes and accept Parliament more or less as he found it. But he was determined not to be at the mercy of Parliament in money matters. Therefore, he took some characteristically devious steps to gain a certain measure of financial independence. These steps had an important effect on British foreign policy.

Foreign Policy We have noted that English mercantilism tended in the seventeenth century to lead to competition and war with the Netherlands. The aggressive and far more powerful monarchy of Louis XIV in France could be viewed as a more serious or, at the very least, an equal competitor. From 1664 to 1667, the English found themselves fighting both at once. On the high seas, the English fared well, winning two naval battles against the Dutch; but in 1667, England suffered the humiliation of seeing a Dutch fleet sail up the Thames and into the Medway where it destroyed English warships at anchor on July 1, 1667. One month later the Dutch and English made peace.

French aggressiveness in the War of Devolution (1667–1668) inspired the English diplomatic establishment, represented by Sir John Temple, to negotiate a treaty of triple alliance among England, Holland, and Sweden against the power of France. English commercial interests had come to the point where they considered France a greater threat than the Netherlands. But Charles II had his own ideas and his own needs. The king privately reversed official English policy by agreeing to assist Louis XIV in his preparations to attack the Dutch in what came to be known as the Dutch War (1672–1678). In return, Louis XIV promised Charles a large annual subsidy (£200,000). Thus the English king gained a kind of independence from Parliament while becoming a pensioner of the king of France. In the years that followed, the power of the Dutch declined to the point where they were indeed an insignificant threat to English mercantile prospects, while the power of France increased.

The King's Religion With the return of the English king came the return of the bishops. The old Prayer Book was restored; and some 1,760 ministers and 150 university dons were ejected as dissenters. The Anglican Church was reestablished. The bishops did not, however, retrieve their former political influence. In 1600, the bishops had formed nearly a third of the House of Lords; by 1700 their number had been reduced to one eighth.

Religious passions seemed to cool as reaction set in against the former fanatic spirits. Once again the townspeople dared to laugh at the broad humor of what we today call "Restoration Comedies." There were masked balls at the Court of St. James, and people danced in the streets of London.

Although too solidly rooted to be destroyed, the ascetic Puritan sects that had proliferated during the Interregnum suffered in this new generation. The Corporation Act of 1661 and the Act of Uniformity of 1662 denied to Nonconformists (i.e., Non-Anglicans, including the Presbyterians), the right to hold public office, and the universities were closed to their sons. The wheel had turned full circle and nobody seemed to care.

One of the great problems of the Restoration was the religion of the king. Charles was secretly a Roman Catholic. This was bad enough for those who knew the situation, but the fact that the next in line to the throne, James, Duke of York, the king's brother, was an avowed Roman Catholic was a more serious matter. During the reign of Charles II, a bill was introduced in Parliament (1679) that would have had the effect, if passed and accepted by the crown, of excluding James from the succession. One element in Parliament, the Whigs, led by the brilliant Earl of Shaftesbury, supported the bill, whereas the Tories opposed it. Charles was determined to forestall the bill and roused himself sufficiently to employ his considerable political skill and influence in engineering its defeat. The opposition, however, did not need to feel that this loss was serious. After all, James was all of 46 years of age, and his two children were both Protestant. It seemed unlikely that he would have any more children by his new and Roman Catholic wife.

James II and the "Glorious" Revolution Eventually (1685), Charles died in bed and still king of England. His brother and successor, who ruled for three years (1685–1688) only, was not so fortunate. James II had all the instincts of his father and grandfather, even to the point of reasserting absolute monarchy by divine right. He played into the hands of the opposition by appointing Roman Catholics to university and governmental posts and by asking for a larger army. To confuse the issue he pressed for toleration for Protestant Nonconformists as well as for Roman Catholics. But James II's greatest crime was to beget, late in life, a healthy male, Roman Catholic child. There was nothing for it except that the king had to go. Thus, under James II, the crisis that Charles II had avoided precipitated itself, rather like a distorted and accelerated playback of the reign of the first James some eighty years before.

There were, however, certain basic differences. In the opening phases of the English Revolution, the drive had come from men of the lesser aristocracy joined by others in the middle and lower orders of society. In the situation of 1688–1689, it was the great aristocratic grandees who directed the delicate operation of forcing James into flight rather than martyrdom. In the early stages of this nearly century-long revolutionary process, there had been basic disagreement on constitutional, economic, religious, and social questions. Now the real anxiety turned on whether James would make the boat at Dover! When a bumbling patriot caught and triumphantly returned James to London, the action verged on slapstick comedy.

The English leaders who had originally supported James had already made contact with James' daughter, Mary, in the Netherlands. Mary, a Protestant, had married William of Orange, *stadholder,* popular leader, and successful soldier. The couple were invited to ascend the thrones of England, Scotland, and Ireland as co-rulers. William and Mary accepted the invitation; William organized one of the few successful invasions of England; James was allowed to flee to France; and England appeared to have permanently resolved its long period of difficulties with a "Glorious" or "Bloodless" revolution.

William and Mary of England, from a Medal Struck in Honor of their Coronation in 1689. (LC.)

To make certain that there would be no return to arbitrary power, the new monarchs were asked to accept a "Declaration of Right," which later became the original "Bill of Rights" guaranteeing a Protestant monarchy with strictly limited powers. It was almost entirely a negative document, a list of things the British rulers could not do. On the positive side, however, it said that "Parliaments ought to be held frequently" and, to make sure, Parliament made the traditional Mutiny Act, which gave the king the right to enforce discipline and, therefore, control the military, effective for only one year at a time. Parliament's assent was, henceforth, to be required for all levying of taxes, and for the maintenance of a standing army. The so-called "Toleration Act" of 1689 granted religious freedom to Protestants of all sorts (but not yet to Catholics or Unitarians), though Dissenters (as non-Anglican Protestants were called) were still technically excluded from political life and public office.

The Revolution of 1688–1689 was "Glorious" mainly because it was accomplished almost without bloodshed and by the "right" people: members of Parliament, lords and commoners, all people of substance. When James left, as a loyal noble put it at the time, "it became necessary that government should be by somebody, to avoid confusion." No one of radical political or religious philosophy was allowed to participate in this *coup d'état.*

Thus, a nearly farcical but truly conservative "revolution" finally established some of the important political ideas put forward in the days of Pym: authority would be vested in Parliament with kingship a revocable trust. Certainly the king was not turned into a figurehead by the Revolution of 1689, but a substantial step toward such a royal condition was taken. The more radical ideas expressed by the Levellers, Diggers, and others during the civil war of the 1640's found no implementation in the "Glorious Revolution" of the 1680's and had to wait until the nineteenth and twentieth centuries for further exploration. For the immediate future, England was to be governed by the crown in partnership with the great landed aristocracy known as the "Whig Oligarchy." In 1711 membership in Parliament was limited by law to persons who had large incomes from land.

The more active of the husband and wife team of rulers, William quickly led England into the great European coalition that was fighting against Louis XIV's France. The people who had made the Glorious Revolution of 1688 were willing to follow him and to finance him on this course partly, as we shall see, because aggressive French expansion threatened English commercial and colonial interests and partly because Louis XIV harbored the expelled and deposed James II, continued to recognize him as king of England, and backed James in his attempts to regain the English throne.

Shortly after his flight in the last days of 1688, James landed in Ireland with French troops, hoping to use that troubled island as a base from which he could descend on England. Irish Roman Catholics rallied to him. As soon as he could, William of Orange crossed to Ireland, defeated James in the battle of the Boyne (July 12, 1690), and proceeded to a thoroughgoing repression of the Irish people. So it was that the Irish became the principal losers in the "Glorious Revolution."

In 1694, Mary died, leaving William III to rule alone until 1702. In 1701, an Act of Settlement provided that on William's death he was to be succeeded by Princess Anne Stuart, Mary's younger sister, and after her by Sophia of Hanover, a Protestant granddaughter of James I and daughter of Frederick, the Elector Palatine (the "Winter King" of the opening phase of the Thirty Years' War) and her issue. England was determined not to have another Roman Catholic king.

Queen Anne (1702–1714) presided over the grandeur of the Duke of Marlborough's campaigns on the continent in the War of Spanish Succession. A great event in the reign of Anne was the parliamentary union of England and Scotland (1707) as the kingdom of Great Britain. Politically the country was split between Whigs and Tories, though the difference between these two groups can easily be exaggerated. The Whigs, an alliance of great aristocrats and leading businessmen, considered themselves the defenders of the Revolution of 1688. They tended to dominate the House of Lords whereas leadership in the Commons shifted sides from time to time.

England took nearly the whole of the seventeenth century to work its way through crisis. Throughout this period, England was still near Europe but not of it. Although moved by most of the same economic, social, and religious currents that swayed the continent, Britain reacted in special and insular ways with rather different political results, as we shall see when we turn to the story of France in the seventeenth century.

FURTHER READING

The subject matter of this chapter has been receiving very sharp attention during the last decades, so much so that it is difficult to decide on what to mention in a short reading list. The century as a whole is conveniently treated in M. Ashley, * *England in the Seventeenth Century* (1958). For readers with a penchant for the old-fashioned Whig interpretation of England's most exciting century, G. M. Trevelyan, * *England Under the Stuarts* (1961), (which has gone through 21 editions), is still probably the best one-volume account. C. V. Wedgewood's three volumes are narrative history at a very high level: * *The King's Peace, 1637–1641* (1955); *The King's War, 1641–1647* (1959); and *A Coffin for King Charles: The Trial and Execution of Charles I* (1964). An excellent

*Books available in paperback edition are marked with an asterisk.

survey of English society and institutions during the early part of the turmoil is W. Notestein, * *The English People on the Eve of Colonization, 1603–1630* (1954).

The heavy and interesting debate on the causes of the English civil disturbances can be sampled in the Heath pamphlet edited by Philip Taylor, * *The Origins of the English Civil War—Conspiracy, Crusade, or Class Conflict?* (1960). Some of the stakes at issue in the Rebellion are revealed in J. R. Tanner, * *English Constitutional Conflicts* (1973), and G. P. Gooch, * *English Democratic Ideas in the Seventeenth Century* (1955), which are old and somewhat dated but still essential to an understanding of what some Englishmen were fighting about. Newer and more sociological is C. Hill, * *Puritanism and Revolution* (1964). For nobles and the "rising gentry," see L. Stone, * *The Crisis of the Aristocracy, 1558–1641* (1965), by an important historian of seventeenth-century England, and the same author's * *Social Change and Revolution in England, 1540–1640* (1965). Essential reading is J. H. Hexter's "Storm over the Gentry," in his collection of essays, * *Reappraisals in History and Society in Early Modern Europe* (1961). Related is P. Zagorin, * *The Court and Country: The Beginning of the English Revolution* (1970).

C. V. Wedgewood has also done an important biography of Wentworth in which she suggests that he was not a tyrannical monster: *Strafford* (1936). Hers is probably the most readable * *Life of Cromwell* (1938, revised and updated 1973). See C. Hill, * *Oliver Cromwell, 1658–1958,* an historiographical pamphlet of the Historical Association (1958). A fairly recent paperback on the "dictator" is M. Ashley, * *Oliver Cromwell and the Puritan Revolution* (1959); but the most recent biography is by Antonia Fraser, *Cromwell* (1973). Regarding the Civil War, see A. Woolrych, *Battles of the Civil War* (1966), illustrated, and L. F. Solt, *Saints in Arms: Puritanism and Democracy in Cromwell's Army* (1971).

For the Restoration, see G. N. Clark, *The Later Stuarts, 1660–1714* (1955); D. Ogg, * *England in the Reign of Charles II,* 2 vols. (1955), a good, old standby, as well as the same author's * *England in the Reigns of James II and William III* (1969); and M. Ashley, *Charles II, The Man and The Statesman* (1971). The best place to begin the study of the Glorious Revolution is G. M. Trevelyan, * *The English Revolutions, 1688–1689* (1965), a brief essay that should be supplemented by G. M. Straka, ed., * *The Revolution of 1688—Whig Triumph or Palace Revolution?* (1963), another Heath pamphlet.

The great diarist of the Restoration, Samuel Pepys, should be explored by everyone. Try O. F. Morshead, ed., *Everybody's Pepys, The Diary of Samuel Pepys, 1660–1669* (1973), a good selection, illustrated.

3 The Grand Monarchy and the Hegemony of France

Though not comparatively large, populous, or militarily strong today, France is in many ways still the arbiter of western European taste and politics. The foundations for this pivotal role were laid in the seventeenth century. Then it was that France developed the remarkable civilization that enabled her to dominate European culture until long after her real political and military might had declined. To a wholly novel degree, the "style" of French life in the seventeenth century, as we shall see, was determined by the royal court in Paris and Versailles. Individual Frenchmen—nobles, soldiers, priests, businessmen, scientists, artists and other craftsmen, and even the peasants—no doubt made many contributions to France's "Splendid Century." But it should not be forgotten that it was the French government, commanded by its Bourbon kings, that orchestrated this extraordinary cultural flowering.

To better understand the history of this period, we shall trace the steps by which the French monarchs, aided by such servants of the crown as Sully and Richelieu, established their political authority and began to shape the French economy in the first half of the seventeenth century. After this, we shall proceed to the era of France's greatest "glory" (*gloire*) under the Sun King, Louis XIV.

HENRY IV

When last we considered French affairs (Part IX, Chapter 4), we left France in a shocking state of disorder. The Wars of Religion had undone the centralizing and organizing work begun in the late fifteenth century; and the Valois dynasty, in the person of Henry III, had perished ignominiously. After that assassination (1589), the Huguenot Bourbon, as Henry IV, began the long process of gaining control over his kingdom. Realizing that if he were to be king in fact he would have to command the support of the moderate Catholic majority in France, he renounced the Protestant faith and became a Roman Catholic. That done, he was crowned at Chartres and was allowed to enter Paris, saluting pretty women as he came.

The amiable and witty Henry IV (top) and his hard-working civil servant, the Duke of Sully, succeeded in restoring order to a France sorely tried by years of civil and religious strife. Sully, a Huguenot, favored the king's conversion to Catholicism in the interests of peace. He and Henry dreamed of a "Grand Design" for Europe in the form of a confederation of Christian republics. (Bibliothèque Publique et Universitaire, Geneva/Bibliothèque Nationale, Paris.)

Then Henry turned to the matter of dealing with the leaders of the Holy League, who still did not recognize his sovereignty and who controlled substantial parts of the country. Instead of trying to subdue them by force, Henry chose to buy off the Leaguers. The duke of Mayenne accepted three and one half million livres for Burgundy; Normandy cost four million livres; and, before he was done, Henry had paid out vast sums to the rebels. When Henry's friend and collaborator, the duke of Sully, objected to this expensive bribery, Henry is said to have replied, "If we fight for it, it will cost us ten times more."

The Edict of Nantes The League thus taken care of, Henry IV turned to the Huguenots. Henry's conversion had left these Protestants feeling deserted and threatened; they were still under arms and represented a possible source of continued civil war. In this case, Henry's "bribe" took the form of the Edict of Nantes (1598). The king was fairly sure that the rest of the country would not follow him if he granted complete religious toleration. He proposed, therefore, a measure very like the one in 1570 that preceded the St. Bartholomew Massacre. The Huguenots could worship on their own estates and in those towns where Protestantism had been the prevailing mode of worship before 1597, as well as in at least one town in every *baillage* in France, provided that no Protestant worship should take place in or around Paris nor in any episcopal town. The Huguenots were promised admission to all employments, representation in law courts, and educational opportunities for their sons. To guarantee that these promises would be fulfilled, the Huguenots were given control of about one hundred fortified places, their garrisons to be paid by the crown.

Compromise though it was, the Edict of Nantes was a great step for the time and was recognized as such by its opponents. The pope and the French Roman Catholic clergy thundered against it. The *parlements* (whose assent was necessary before the edict could become law) drew back from a measure that would officially condone heresy. But the king put it before them as the only alternative to continued civil war. When he succeeded in drawing the Jesuits into his camp by pointing out that the Edict of Nantes would have the effect of containing and preventing any further expansion of Protestantism in France, the recalcitrant *parlements* came around. Happily, this experiment in religious toleration worked, at least for the time being.

End of War Between France and Spain To confirm his sovereignty, Henry had next to deal with Spain and Philip II, now an old man, whose troops were still on French soil. The death of Philip's ablest general, the duke of Parma, had been a boon; but the real reason for the termination of the war between France and Spain was the fact that neither Henry nor Philip (the latter, it should be remembered, was also at war with the English and Dutch) had the resources to keep it up. Henry apologized to Elizabeth of England for deserting the alliance against Spain and made peace at Vervins (1598) in a treaty that substantially repeated the provisions of the Treaty of

Cateau-Cambrésis of 1559. Four months after signing this treaty, Philip died. Henry proceeded to the rejuvenation of France.

ECONOMIC RECONSTRUCTION

There was much to be done. War had been nearly constant since 1562. The country had been overrun and pillaged by Germans, Swiss, Spaniards, Italians, English, and Walloons. One late sixteenth-century French authority stated that the French people lost the equivalent of 423,510 mule-loads of gold during the wars. Be that as it may, there is no doubt that the economy was virtually at a standstill, that the country was plagued with unemployed soldiers who knew no trade save destruction. The task of economic reconstruction was taken in hand by the king counselled by two outstanding servants: the duke of Sully and Barthélemy de Laffémas. These two advisors complemented one another: Sully concentrated on finance and agriculture while Laffémas turned his attention to commerce and industry.

Sully (1560–1641), a Calvinist soldier and military engineer during the French Wars of Religion, took well to peacetime occupations. He was made superintendent of finances about 1600. In this capacity, and without changing the basic tax system that had come down from the days of Charles VII and Louis XI, he put his efforts to seeing to it that the taxes should actually be collected, that the taxes find their way to the treasury, and that nearly all expenditures be accounted for. He also increased the royal revenue by reclaiming vast parts of the royal domain that had been alienated during the religious wars.

Henry IV made great efforts to rebuild French agriculture, going so far as to suggest that there should be a "chicken in every peasant's pot." "The Milkmaid's Family" (below, left) by Louis Le Nain (c. 1593–1648) shows a typical peasant group of northern France. Henry's search for new industries resulted in the encouragement of the silk industry, carried on by women in small factories such as this one from an early print. (Hermitage, Leningrad/ Bibliothèque Nationale, Paris.)

Like many people of his time, Sully was a convinced agrarian. Agriculture, he believed, was the source of all wealth and the womb that produced the robust recruits needed for the army as well as increasing numbers of taxpayers. To promote order and prosperity on the land, therefore, he policed the countryside. To eliminate brigandage would be to enable the peasants to work and to sell their produce. At his instigation, the crown decreed that the peasants' working livestock and tools could not be seized for debt. Great public works were undertaken: roads, canals, and bridges, all of which gave employment to peasants and ex-soldiers and facilitated the marketing of agricultural products. Sully's program, like the Edict of Nantes, worked; and within a short period of time rural France was a smiling land, comparatively speaking, populated by industrious if still poor peasants and prospering landlords.

Laffémas and Mercantilism Unlike Sully, who sprang from the country nobility, Laffémas (1545–1611) was of humble, bourgeois origin. He became Henry's *valet de chambre,* wrote several treatises on economics in bad French and was eventually appointed controller general of commerce. One of the most creative of mercantilist statesmen, Laffémas set the mold for French mercantilist policy for many years to come. He deplored the loss of gold and silver resulting from the import into France of luxury goods, especially Italian silks. He did not propose to abolish consumption of luxuries; rather, he intended to make France the supreme producer for all of northern Europe. Under his lead, the government stimulated cultivation of mulberry trees and silk worms, as well as manufacturing enterprises to make silk goods. In this effort Laffémas had the cooperation of Sully, who approved of the stimulating effect that silk production would have on the rural economy.

Laffémas firmly established the principle that the government should take the lead in economic development. His office became a central bureau, supervising, stimulating, and regulating trades and crafts, setting standards for quality, testing new machines and tools, giving subsidies to enterprises that seemed useful to the state. He aided Henry IV in putting afoot an early project in urban renewal—the Place Royale, now the Place des Vosges—in Paris and installed there a silk factory for all the world to see.

The collaboration of Henry, Sully, and Laffémas produced results. During the twelve years between the Treaty of Vervins (1598) and the death of Henry IV (1610) what had been a war-ravaged country became one of the great economic powers of Europe. Amazed contemporary observers commented, as they bought French luxury goods, on the tremendous resiliency of France. Was this economic rebirth primarily the result of governmental activity? The indications are that it was. Further, the remarkable durability of mercantilist policy and practice over the years to come may well have stemmed from this early example of French success.

Death of Henry IV Unfortunately, this bright French internal promise came to a halt in 1610, and probably would have done so even had Henry IV not been assassinated, as he was, in that year. For when an assassin's dagger struck Henry down, the king was preparing for war in Germany. The opening phases of what was to be fifty years of war were at hand, and the prospects for hopeful developments diminished as bellicosity increased. France was thrown into another period of internal confusion and turmoil.

After Henry's murder, the kingdom was once again presided over by an Italian, widowed queen-mother Marie de' Medici. As regent during the

Louis XIII was a boy of nine when his father was assassinated in 1610. Henry IV's wife, Marie de' Medici became regent of France. The queen invited the famous Flemish painter, Peter Paul Rubens, to execute a series of paintings celebrating her life with the late king. Rubens flattered the heavy-set Marie, shown (left) after the birth of her son and (right) as she appeared in widow's garb at the time the series was undertaken. (Louvre/Prado.)

minority of her young son, Louis XIII (whom she seems deliberately to have kept in a state of ignorance) Marie resumed her husband's early policy of bribing malcontents. She discharged Sully (who could have collected the funds she needed to pay the bribes) and disbanded the army. Marie and her advisors temporarily reversed Henry's foreign policy. By marrying her son and daughter to a Spanish princess and prince respectively, she allied the French crown with the Habsburgs.

Great nobles once again intrigued and fought. They insisted upon the calling of an Estates General (1614). The Estates met, but, like the fractured monarchy, failed to take a coherent position and was sent home—not to meet again for 175 years. One important result of the calling of this assembly was the rise to prominence of a representative of the clergy, Armand Jean du Pléssis de Richelieu (1585–1642), Bishop of Luçon, who entered the queen mother's service to work with her Italian favorite, Concini.

Eventually (1617), the young king, who had been declared of age some time before and who resented being put in the background by his mother and by Concini, stirred himself to have Concini shot. At the same time, Henry IV's religious settlement broke down. Roman Catholics began to persecute Huguenots; Protestants in Béarn and Gascony rose in open revolt; great Huguenot nobles took up arms and even tried to separate the region around La Rochelle from France as a Protestant "United Provinces" under the willing protection of England. Religious war again bloodied the land. In this threatening situation, it was Richelieu, now a cardinal, who was charged with restoring order (1624).

RICHELIEU'S USE OF POWER

Richelieu met Huguenot force with force. Driving off the English soldiers and ships of the duke of Buckingham, he laid siege to La Rochelle. Upon its capitulation (1628), he voided the special military and political provisions of the Edict of Nantes. Henceforth, the Huguenots were to be tolerated in their religious faith but not as an armed political party. As regards nobles, he tried with some success to discipline them. He put great emphasis on a campaign to end the practice of duelling. Through careful intelligence work he was able to uncover noble plots against his life and to put them down. He ordered the destruction of nobles' fortified castles. To counter the influence of noble governors in the provinces, he expanded the system of using royal *intendants* as the principal administrators of the crown and selected these important officers from his own following. In this fashion, he contributed to the development of a centralized bureaucracy.

By and large, these internal achievements seem small when compared with his tremendous success in foreign affairs. For Richelieu's greatest contributions to French royal power lay in the policies and actions that led eventually to the humbling of the Habsburgs in the Thirty or Fifty Years' War (see Chapter 2). Thus it was that Richelieu went to his deathbed in 1642 declared a great success, while his vigorous Spanish opponent and contemporary, Olivares, was discharged in defeat.

Louis XIII, who had been steadfast in support of Richelieu, died in the following year, leaving as heir a young son, aged five years. It would be pleasant to be able to say that by this time the French state had been brought to the point where the death of a king and the succession of a child would not lead to disorder; but this was not the case. Within a few years, France sank once again into civil turmoil, as various groups seized the opportunity offered by the new crack in the dynasty to reassert themselves against royal centralizing tendencies.

MAZARIN AND THE FRONDE

The new uprising, known as the *fronde,* occurred at the expense not only of French unity but also of Richelieu's successor, Cardinal Jules Mazarin.[1] A gallant Italian and extremely able diplomat, Mazarin had entered French service under Richelieu. After Richelieu's death, Mazarin was acknowledged as principal minister by the ailing Louis XIII at the same time that he acquired the affectionate support of the queen. Mazarin used his position as the means of creating immense fortunes for himself and his family. The exigencies of the moment, added to his personal unpopularity, gave rise to a rebellion.

The *fronde* began in 1648 as a direct reaction to increased taxation resulting from the war with Spain. The *parlement* of Paris, aping the English House of Commons joined the resistance and proclaimed a kind of constitutional monarchy in which the *parlement* should act as a check upon the crown. Later, a number of great princes and nobles mounted their own

The chief stronghold of Huguenot power in the seventeenth century was La Rochelle, a port on the west coast of France. Richelieu decided to lay siege to the city, shown here in a contemporary painting. The city was forced to capitulate in 1628 when all its food and ammunition were exhausted. (Versailles.)

[1] A *fronde* was a child's slingshot. The application of this word to the noble aspect of this rebellion is properly descriptive.

The supple but determined Cardinal Richelieu won complete control of the French government in 1624 when Louis XIII became convinced that he alone could maintain order in France. After silencing opposition at home, Richelieu led the successful French intervention (1631–1648) in the Thirty Years' War. This handsome portrait is by Philippe de Champaigne. (Louvre.)

rebellion against Mazarin; and under their leadership the *fronde* degenerated into a farce. Some of the nobles fought for the sheer love of excitement; others changed sides from time to time as directed by their ladyloves. Eventually, they went so far as to make treasonable arrangements with Spain.

Unlike the monarch across the Channel, Mazarin was able to weather the storm. In fact, he did more: as the *frondeur* rebels wore themselves out, Mazarin managed to put together a new middle-of-the-road, royalist party that rallied behind young Louis XIV. By 1653, the *frondeurs* were discredited in the eyes of the French people, who had had their fill of irresponsible civil strife. Thus the *fronde* and Mazarin's handling of it helped lay the base for the extraordinary enthusiasm for the monarchy that seems to have marked French opinion during the three or four decades after 1653. And before his death in 1661, Mazarin was able to complete the negotiations leading up to the Treaty of the Pyrenees (1659) by which France acquired important territories in the south and along the northern frontier. Under the terms of the treaty, young Louis XIV was married to the Infanta Maria Theresa, eldest daughter of Philip IV of Spain. The union was to be cemented by a huge Spanish dowry. The fact that this dowry was never paid was to become politically significant later on.

LOUIS XIV AND THE GRAND MONARCHY

This bust of the young king, Louis XIV, was made by the great Italian baroque sculptor, Bernini. Bernini's flamboyant style profoundly influenced the French architects and decorators who created the setting for the splendid world of the "Sun King" at Versailles. (Versailles.)

Mazarin's death was a lingering one, and during the cardinal's last days Louis had time to contemplate the role that he would assume. Early on a March morning, 1661, he was informed that Mazarin was dead. A few hours later the 23-year old king summoned all heads of departments in his government and the secretaries of state. Standing in front of his chair, his hat on, he read them a lesson. "Gentlemen," he said, "I have had you meet . . . so that I might tell you that until the present I have been willing to let my affairs be managed by the late Cardinal. It is now time that I manage them myself. You will assist me with your advice when I ask you for it." Louis went on to say that in the future his secretaries of state were to sign nothing, not even a passport, without his permission and that they were to report to him daily with their accounts. From that moment onward, Louis plunged into the task of trying to oversee every aspect of French administration personally. In this respect, he showed himself to be the true descendant of his great-grandfather, Philip II of Spain.

Many of the king's guiding principles and much of his adult behavior can be explained as reactions against his boyhood and adolescent experiences. Louis XIV had been dominated and patronized by his mother and by the chief minister for eighteen years. His humiliating experiences during the *fronde,* when a Parisian mob invaded his bedchamber, had made an indelible impression on him. He frequently spoke of an aversion to having a chief minister and to having churchmen of any kind in his government. Further, he resolved never to let himself be dominated by women (a resolve he was not able to fulfill). He determined to keep the nobility in a subservient position and to exclude them whenever possible from his ministry. Finally, he developed such dislike for the city of Paris that he removed himself from it at the earliest opportunity.

Louis XIV was well-made, strong, and graceful. He could be remarkably courteous in formal relations, and he was almost neurotically conscientious. But he was poorly educated and intensely distrustful. His greatest concerns were for his dignity, glory, greatness, and reputation, especially the last. In addition, he liked women and food. He tended to choose his officials, people he had to work with every day, from the legal profession and the middle class. This was not a bad idea, since that class supplied faithful and efficient counselors whom he could pit against rebellious nobles and clergy if need be. Some nobles accused him, however, of surrounding himself with humble people so as always to be seen to best advantage.

Versailles and the Court In the provinces, Louis and his counselors permitted the noble governors to continue to hold their offices and titles. But increasingly the work of provincial administration came into the hands of the bourgeois *intendants,* professional administrators, supervised by a Council of State and responsible directly to the crown, with or without cooperation from the governors. Louis pressed the higher nobility into a great courtly dance centering around his person. The almost incredibly grand palace that Louis built for himself at Versailles was conceived for three purposes: first, to give the king a residence safely outside of turbulent Paris; second, to serve as a proper setting for the incomparable royal person; third, to provide housing for the greater nobles so that they could be kept under observation and harmlessly occupied. Building upon the work of Henry IV and Richelieu and profiting from the results of the *fronde,* Louis' scheme of emasculation worked. Instead of plotting uprisings against royal authority, descendants of old warrior families vied with each other for royal favor, the outward signs of which were better apartments in the *château* at Versailles, titles like "Master of the Royal Wardrobe," and the right to enter the king's bedroom in the morning to watch him dress.

Despite his reputed reluctance to bring into his government men who might outshine him, Louis did make use of two able ministers: Jean Baptiste Colbert (1619–1683) and François Le Tellier, who became Marquis of Louvois (1639–1691). Colbert took charge of financial affairs; Louvois became minister of war. Together, these two men were responsible for most of the internal reforms and military changes for which the reign of Louis XIV is noted.

COLBERT AND FRENCH MERCANTILISM

The inexperienced young king stood in need of the kind of support and counsel that Colbert could give. Once again the crown's revenue was in question, for the promising work in financial and economic development under Henry IV, Sully, and Laffémas had been set back by thirty years of war and eighteen years of royal weakness. As controller-general of finances, Colbert soon dominated every department of the government except war and foreign affairs. Colbert did not have original ideas—indeed, much of what he did had been anticipated by Sully and Laffémas under Henry IV—but so great were his industry and achievement during the first twelve years of Louis' active reign (1661–1683) that the French label his brand of mercantilistic activity "Colbertism."

Like other mercantilists, Colbert wished to increase the power of the state—in this case the monarchy of Louis XIV. Though of bourgeois origin, he had no quarrel with his master's desire for "dignity, glory, greatness, and reputation." But he was aware that achievement of these qualities would be expensive, and he set about arranging the royal finances and the national economy so that the necessary funds should be available.

In his view, the economic activity of the country must contribute to the welfare of the state, and the state's welfare depended upon its ability to gather taxes. Since there were few legal or constitutional obstacles to tax collecting in France, the capacity to gather taxes depended first, on the administrative machinery of the state, and second, on the economic health of the country. Colbert worked with some success to improve both areas. He arbitrarily reduced the *rentes* (interest on the royal debt) and attempted to reduce graft and corruption. He stopped up leaks in the tax-collecting apparatus and imposed more rigorous accounting in the government. In 1664, he lumped a number of small customs areas in north-central France into one big customs union, known as the "Five Big Farms." This reform made tariffs easier to collect and facilitated commerce.

As a mercantilist, Colbert was closer to the mercantilism of England than to that of Spain. Certainly, he desired that France should acquire ever-greater supplies of gold and silver. But, lacking the Spanish king's overseas mines, he realized that the desired bullion could only be obtained by stimulating French production and seeing to it that an increasing part of that production be sold abroad. Conversely, he believed that French consumption, especially of manufactured goods, should be supplied primarily by French enterprise so that bullion should not flee the realm in paying for imports. To these ends, he labored to improve every aspect of French economic life. Thus he worked not only to increase manufacturing and foreign trade but also to facilitate internal trade. Internal tariff reform was one step in this direction. Others included continuing the digging of canals as begun or projected under Henry IV and Richelieu (such as the Canal of Two Seas that connects the Atlantic with the Mediterranean) and beginning new ones. He pushed a system of royal highways (useful for troop movements as well as for commerce) that came to radiate from Paris like the spokes of a wheel.

Trade and Industry As regards foreign trade, Colbert lowered tariffs on certain goods in order to encourage Frenchmen to invest in shipping. He urged the king to permit nobles to engage in maritime commerce without losing their noble status—an innovation at the time. He encouraged the construction of a navy to protect French sea trade. Subsidies were offered to French shipbuilders. Colbert urged French capitalists to found chartered companies for trade in and exploitation of Madagascar and the East and West Indies. Accordingly, the French East India Company and the French West India Company were founded in 1664. The Company of the North was created (1669) for trade in the Baltic and the Levant Company for commerce between French Mediterranean ports and the Near East (1670). None of these projects was an unqualified success, but some of them went on to achieve importance in the eighteenth century.

Industry, like trade and shipping, was the recipient of much solicitude. Again, the technique was to encourage desired enterprises by prodding investors and entrepreneurs and by giving subsidies, monopolies, and tariff protection to favored enterprises. Skilled workers were lured from abroad and French artisans were forbidden to emigrate. Tapestries, laces, woolens, fine cloth, stockings, and a host of other products were manufactured in increasing quantity and improved quality. Colbert worked to achieve quality through minute industrial regulation by government inspectors working through the guilds and town governments, and by establishing industrial codes to specify standards.

On occasion, Louis XIV's grandiose schemes, especially his determination to build the ultimate palace, vexed Colbert. The amounts of money required were immense; and the needs of the *château* threatened to undermine his bullionist policy. The project of the Hall of Mirrors at Versailles, for instance, troubled Colbert because he was loath to spend abroad the great sums required to purchase mirrors in Venice, where, alone in the world, the secret of mirror making was understood. Thus, we have the picture of one of the greatest statesmen in Europe negotiating through spies to lure Venetian mirror makers to France. Eventually, Colbert was able to see to it that the mirrors were, indeed, made in France, and a new French industry was the result. As the Versailles project went forward, it became a showcase for the French luxury goods that Colbert was so anxious to sell abroad. The grandeur of it all, the high style of court life, as regulated by the most impressive of kings, caught the eye of all Europe. Kings and princelings abroad began to build their own "Versailles" and to import French mirrors, tapestries, dishes, decorations, furniture, and fashions. In this way, staggeringly expensive though it was, the *château* may have paid for itself in the end.

Although Colbert's total program was too vast to have been an unmitigated success, it did result in certain definite achievements over the short run. First, it revitalized French economic life and settled French manufacturing in the pattern of producing a high quality of luxury goods. Second, it made France a strong naval power and a competitor for overseas colonies. Third, it succeeded in producing the revenues necessary for Louis' ambitious projects, diplomatic, military, and vainglorious.

ARTS AND LETTERS

It was not commercial activity nor royal grandeur but "the progress of the human spirit," wrote Voltaire, that was the supreme achievement of the era of the Sun King. Voltaire admitted that the French were not equally successful in every line of intellectual and artistic endeavor during the reign of Louis XIV. In science, for instance, they were surpassed by the English and, in music, by the Italians. But on the whole, especially in the plastic and literary arts, he thought Louis' achievements a remarkable model for future generations.

Far from being the haphazard expression of spontaneous creativity, French cultural growth was carefully planned, cultivated, and nurtured by the French state. From early in the seventeenth century, cultural affairs received as much royal attention as did the army, navy, industry, and the highways. And from this effort the state—and the king—reaped a rich harvest of prestige.

The French Academies About 1630, a group of congenial friends in Paris were in the habit of meeting regularly to discuss literary topics. Richelieu, who made it a point to know nearly everything that went on, heard of these meetings and suggested to the group that it accept his protection and incorporation under the crown. Because all meetings except those permitted by the crown were forbidden, the members had no choice but to accept the offer. The result was the French Academy, founded in 1635. The principal function of this body was to "give certain rules to our language, and to render it pure, eloquent, and capable of treating the arts and sciences." Thus the Academy entered upon its great work of disciplining and forming the French language so that it became the precise and flexible instrument that it is today. The influence of the Academy was exercised through its control of the French dictionary, which it has been in the process of making ever since.

In the years after 1635, academies of different kinds, all under governmental tutelage, proliferated. Mazarin decided that supervising bodies could do for the plastic and musical arts what the original Academy was doing for language and literature. The result was the Academy of Fine Arts (later, the Royal Academy of Painting and Sculpture), founded in 1648 to supervise the training of artists and to reward the worthy with scholarships for study in Italy (the *Prix de Rome*), and the Academy of Music (1645), which established opera under government patronage in Paris. The Academy of Science (1666) was the creation of Colbert, as was the Academy of Inscriptions (1663), founded to help him and Louis prepare devices and legends for the all-important medals, statues, and monuments that were the hagiography of the new centralized state. Colbert himself, who was interested in history and antiquities, met with this latter group. Eventually it developed into a kind of national historical society, though it continued its functions as the brains behind the elaborately contrived ritual of royal and state aggrandizement.

Writers and Artists A brief look at the careers of the principal French artists and writers of the seventeenth century may help us to understand the extent of the participation of the state in cultural endeavors. Pierre Corneille (1606–1684), author of *Le Cid, Horace,* and *Cinna* and by all odds one of the greatest poetic dramatists in any language, was never in easy circumstances, but he survived well enough. In addition to the modest income that he derived from his literary works he enjoyed a pension from Richelieu and in the 1660's he was on the government payroll. Louis XIV ordered a revival of his plays in 1676. Jean Racine (1639–1699), the master tragedian of the late 1660's and early 1670's, enjoyed pensions from the government. Molière (1622–1673) was applauded by the king and given a theater in which to produce his comedies, while the crown protected him against his detractors. The satirist La Fontaine (1621–1695), although never congenial to Colbert, kept a government job and was eventually accepted by the king on a promise to "be good" in the future.

For nearly thirty-five years the Italian-born musician, Jean Baptiste Lully (1632–1687) composed music for the French royal court. He became "secretary to the king," a position reserved for aristocrats. The Gobelins tapestry works, which Colbert purchased for the crown, were supervised for many years by the painter Le Brun (1619–1690), later ennobled by Louis XIV. Le Brun was also head of the Academy of Painting and Sculpture and generally arbiter of taste in painting in France through most of his life. He was responsible for the interior decoration and furnishing of the palace at Versailles as construction went forward under the architectural direction of Jules Hardouin-Mansart. The magnificent formal gardens and fountains were laid out by Le Nôtre. Almost daily, Le Brun, Le Nôtre, and Mansart met with the king to discuss progress and to lay plans. In 1682, Louis and his court moved into the new *château,* but construction continued for years.

The system was authoritarian: censorship was freely exercised; indiscreet or irreverent writers faced prison terms; and without a doubt worthy intellects and talents were excluded from the various academies. After 1682, French creative endeavor became increasingly repetitive and sterile as the hold of the Sun King and his ministers on every phase of French life turned into a sort of strangulation. Nevertheless, the "Grand Style" was emulated throughout Europe; the French language replaced Latin as the principal international language; and the foundations were laid for French eighteenth- and nineteenth-century scientific achievement. French culture, wit, and wisdom were the envy of all Europe; and, as Voltaire put it, "Not only were great things done in [Louis'] reign, but it was he who did them."

PERSECUTION AND WAR

Louis XIV and the Huguenots Between ages twenty-three and forty-five Louis XIV went through a series of mistresses, by whom he had a number of children. When middle age caught up with him, his current mistress was a forceful bluestocking and devout Roman Catholic convert, Madame de Maintenon, who persuaded Louis to marry her after the death of his wife and queen in 1683. Then she proceeded to encourage Louis to atone for his youthful sins and return to his childhood piety. The influence of Madame de Maintenon was so great that Louis seems to have given up his earlier resolve never to let women dominate his affairs. The atmosphere at Versailles became extremely pious. At the same time, Louis was subjected to increasing pressure from the Roman Catholic clergy, which called upon the state to impose religious orthodoxy on the entire population. In truth, Louis needed little urging to move to eliminate a sect that could not be relied upon to support the state in case of war with a Protestant power. Further, Louis could not logically continue to tolerate religious deviants while preaching that throne and altar are the two fundamental supports of the state.

Accordingly, shortly after 1683, Louis agreed to an intensified missionary campaign intended to convert the Huguenots to Roman Catholicism. This campaign took many forms: first, Protestants were offered money as a reward for conversion. When this approach developed a group of professional, repeater converts, the state resorted to more rigorous methods. Protestant schools and churches were suppressed; Huguenots were barred from certain occupations; and, finally, soldiers (dragoons) were billeted in Huguenot homes and encouraged to make life miserable for their unwilling hosts. By the tens of thousands, Louis was told, the Protestants responded to these *dragonnades* and other persecutions by forsaking their faith. Louis was also aware that for years Huguenots had been leaving the country in ever-increasing numbers. Believing—or, at any rate, stating—that these developments had in fact made of France an entirely Roman Catholic country, in 1685 Louis revoked the Edict of Nantes as an unnecessary anachronism. Thus, the step toward religious toleration taken by the first Bourbon (Henry IV) was reversed by the third. Many Huguenots remained in France despite continued persecution, but as many as two hundred thousand Protestants, including large numbers of merchants, manufacturers, and craftsmen, went to England, Prussia, the Netherlands, and America where they contributed markedly to the economic development of their adopted countries. Colbert, who had died in 1683, would have been upset by this outcome.

Militarism Under Louis XIV The mercantilism of Louis' great economic minister Colbert was, as we have suggested, aggressively competitive. He believed that maritime commerce was limited in volume. Therefore, the only way for one country to increase its foreign commerce was to take trade away from another country. He estimated that in the 1660's the maritime trade of the world was carried in twenty thousand ships, of which the Dutch owned about three quarters, the English about one quarter, and the French only a tiny fraction. Reasoning that the only way that France could improve its position on the high seas was at the expense of the Dutch, Colbert encouraged Louis to undertake the Dutch War (1672–1678). This was one of the long, wearying, and, by and large, fruitless series of wars engaged in by the French during the reign of the Sun King. Until 1683, Colbert supplied the money for these military ventures. But oversight of the army was in the hands of his ministerial colleague and competitor, Louvois.

Louvois and Military Reform Louvois has been described as Louis XIV's "evil genius," who offset Colbert's productive and constructive tendencies and led the king into warlike pursuits. If what has been said above about Colbert's theories on foreign trade is true, however, it would seem that the finance minister contributed as much as Louvois to Louis' aggressive bent. Louvois' contribution as minister of war was important—he did supply Louis with a fine army—but, in fact, the ultimate decisions were Louis' own. And to Louis, success on the battlefield was essential to his greatness.

As we have noted earlier, the armies of the early seventeenth century were almost literally ravenous and ravening hordes. Between battles they pillaged for food, fodder, and loot, as well as for amusement. In France, colonels and captains acquired their regiments and companies by purchase, and were paid, in turn, by the crown, a certain sum per soldier put at the crown's disposal. There was no reliable way of ascertaining whether the proprietors kept their units up to strength.

Louis XIV bowed to Catholic pressure to harass and discourage the Huguenots and then revoked the Edict of Nantes in 1685. The Huguenot church (top), erected in 1624, was destroyed (at right), along with other remnants of Protestantism. The bottom print shows the miserable Huguenots being escorted to waiting boats by the king's men. (Copenhagen Library/Bibliothèque Nationale, Paris/LCRB.)

When, in 1661, the colonel-general of the French infantry died, Louis seized the opportunity to take over this post personally. Thenceforth, every infantry officer held his commission directly from the king; and Louis, with the assistance of Louvois as minister of war, concentrated military control into his own hands. Louvois was greatly concerned with improving the human material in the army. He was never able to solve the problem of attracting good men to the ranks, but to train officers he established nine military schools for cadets. Officers were closely supervised and their units frequently inspected. In order to reduce desertions, Louvois tried to insist that the men be treated, if not gently, at least fairly. The king supplied uniforms for the soldiers, specified rations, and established military hospitals for old, sick, or wounded soldiers. (The *Invalides* in Paris is the most conspicuous example of these.) Arsenals were built to supply weapons and gunpowder, and weaponry was improved. The army grew dramatically in

Deserters were shot on the spot when caught by seventeenth-century armies. Louis XIV and his generals tried other means of encouraging his soldiers' loyalty (see text). The executioners, shown here in an etching by Jaques Callot, fire an early version of a musket, the *harquebus.* The weapon was so heavy it needed extra support. Louvois' soldiers fired a much lighter *fusil.* (LCPP.)

size. In 1667, on the eve of the War of Devolution, it consisted of 72,000 men, of which only half were effectives. At the beginning of the Dutch War (1672) there were 120,000 soldiers; by the end of the war in 1678, there were 279,000. Thereafter, the French Army never fell below 200,000 in war or peace.

Soldiering lost some of its romantic individuality and began to be conducted "by the numbers." Louvois supplied standard manuals for drill, formation, and tactical procedures. While the king animated the army by his frequent presence in its midst, capable generals supplied strategic direction. A corset of thirty-three fortresses was constructed along the frontiers of France. Combined with the royal highways, which enabled troops to move quickly from the center of France to any threatened point on the periphery of the kingdom, these fortresses made the defenses of France well-nigh impregnable. Despite the fact that in two of his wars Louis XIV was fighting against coalitions of all the other great European powers, France was not invaded during her "Golden Age."

The Wars of Louis XIV What did Louis XIV achieve with this military apparatus? A glance at the tabulation below will show that during his active reign of fifty-four years, Louis was at war for a total of more than thirty years. His announced purpose was to gain reputation for himself and to expand French territory to the Pyrennes, the Mediterranean, the Alps, and the Rhine. For the last war, there was the additional purpose of putting a member of the Bourbon family, his grandson, on the throne of the extinct Habsburg line in Spain. With the exception of Franche-Comté (acquired as a result of the Dutch War) and a strip of territory in the North stretching from Dunkirk towards Rocroi and parts of Alsace, the substantial French territorial gains were made either before 1661 or after 1715—that is, before or after the active reign of the Sun King. Nevertheless, French armies covered themselves with what was of greatest concern to Louis: glory and prestige.

The Early Wars Louis' first war, against the Spanish in the Netherlands, was a failure, mainly because England, Holland, and Sweden, fearing French expansion, formed a triple alliance against Louis. The second war (the Dutch

THE WARS OF LOUIS XIV
(Active Reign, 1661–1715—54 years)

1667–1668	War of Devolution *result:* France gained some towns in the Netherlands at the expense of Spain (Treaty of Aix-la-Chapelle)	*1+ year*
1672–1678	Dutch War *result:* France gained Franche-Comté and more of the Spanish Netherlands (Treaties of Nimwegen)	*6 years*
1683–1684	Invasion of the Spanish Netherlands *result:* France gained Luxembourg and Strasburg for a period of 20 years	*1 year*
1688–1697	War of the League of Augsburg *result:* France gained parts of Alsace (Treaty of Ryswick)	*9 years*
1701–1714	War of Spanish Succession *result:* No significant gains or losses for France in Europe, although Louis' grandson Philip was confirmed as King of Spain; France lost some territory in America (Treaties of Utrecht, Rastadt, and Baden)	*13 years*
		30 years

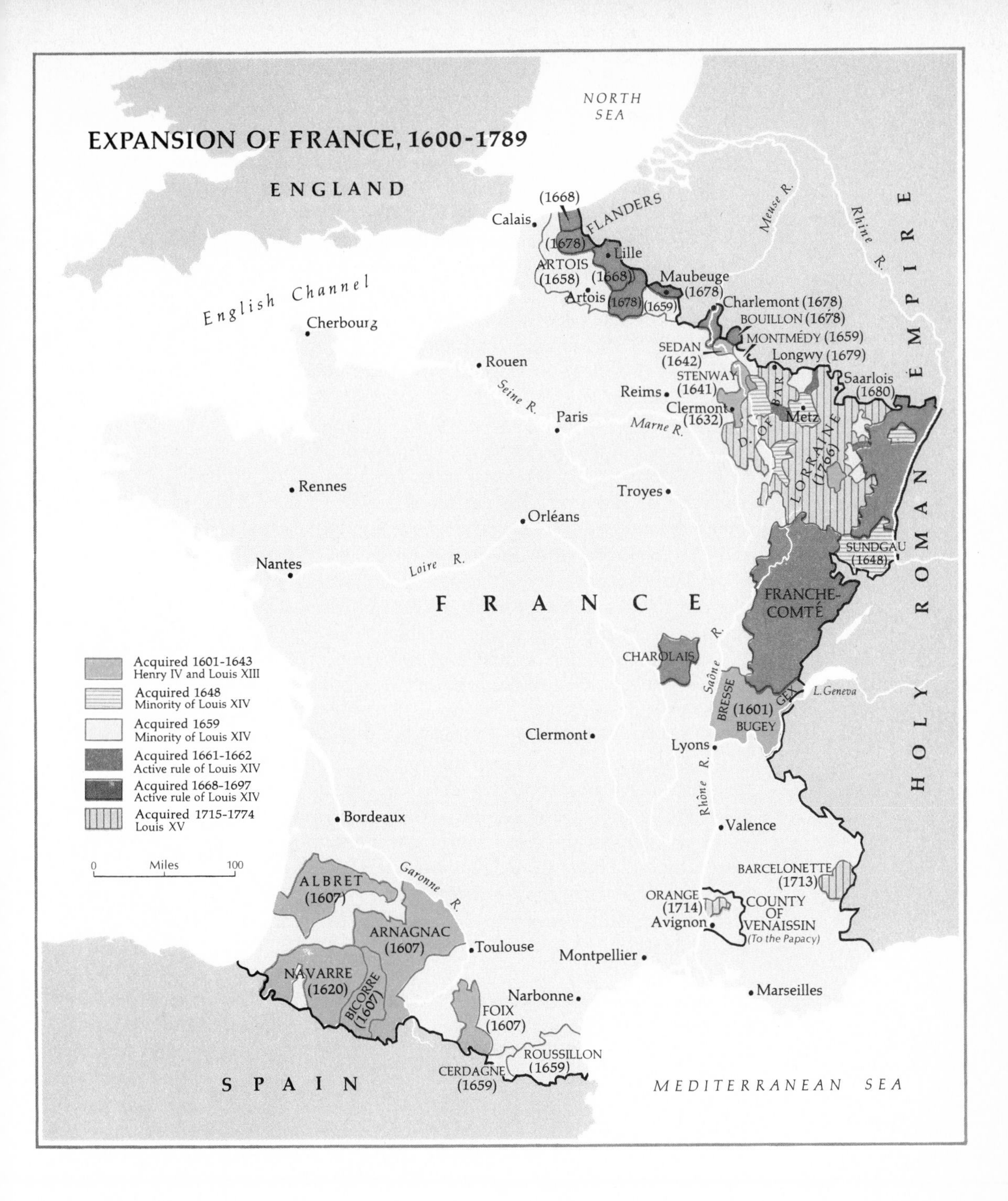

EXPANSION OF FRANCE, 1600-1789
NORTH SEA
ENGLAND
English Channel
FRANCE
SPAIN
HOLY ROMAN EMPIRE
MEDITERRANEAN SEA
FLANDERS
(1668)
(1678)
Calais
Lille
ARTOIS (1658)
(1668)
Artois
(1678)
(1659)
Maubeuge (1678)
Charlemont (1678)
BOUILLON (1678)
MONTMÉDY (1659)
SEDAN (1642)
Longwy (1679)
STENWAY (1641)
Saarlois (1680)
Reims
Clermont (1632)
Metz
D. OF BAR
LORRAINE (1766)
SUNDGAU (1648)
FRANCHE-COMTÉ
CHAROLAIS
BRESSE
(1601)
BUGEY
GEX
L. Geneva
Cherbourg
Rouen
Paris
Seine R.
Marne R.
Meuse R.
Rhine R.
Troyes
Rennes
Orléans
Nantes
Loire R.
Saône R.
Clermont
Lyons
Rhône R.
Valence
Bordeaux
Garonne R.
ALBRET (1607)
ARNAGNAC (1607)
NAVARRE (1620)
BICORRE (1607)
Toulouse
Montpellier
Narbonne
FOIX (1607)
ROUSSILLON (1659)
CERDAGNE (1659)
BARCELONETTE (1713)
ORANGE (1714)
COUNTY OF VENAISSIN (To the Papacy)
Avignon
Marseilles
Acquired 1601-1643 Henry IV and Louis XIII
Acquired 1648 Minority of Louis XIV
Acquired 1659 Minority of Louis XIV
Acquired 1661-1662 Active rule of Louis XIV
Acquired 1668-1697 Active rule of Louis XIV
Acquired 1715-1774 Louis XV
0 Miles 100

War) was an attempt to eliminate Holland as a power. To prepare for this war, in 1670 Louis made a secret agreement, the Treaty of Dover, with King Charles II of England whereby, in return for a cash subsidy, the English crown agreed to support Louis against the Netherlands. Once again, Louis' aggression inspired the development of a coalition against him; and, after six years of war, peace was made at Nimwegen, with relatively little achieved for France as far as Holland was concerned.

Five years later (1683), another war involved another invasion of the Spanish Netherlands. Once again, little more was accomplished, but the other European powers became convinced that the France of Louis XIV was a serious threat to peace and stability. Shortly after this affair, the revocation of the Edict of Nantes and continuing French persecution of the Huguenots reinforced the idea—at least in Protestant countries—that France was a serious menace.

War of the League of Augsburg The result of this seeming threat was a new coalition (1686) against France engineered by William of Orange, *Stadholder* of Holland. This coalition, known as the League of Augsburg, linked the emperor, the kings of Sweden and Spain, the electors of Saxony and the Palatinate with the United Provinces of the Netherlands and the pope! War began again in October 1688, with a French invasion of the Rhenish Palatinate, which territory the armies of Louvois and Louis thoroughly devastated. In the next months, as we have seen in the previous chapter, the principal architect of the League of Augsburg, William of Orange, became King of England and soon led his new monarchy into the anti-French alliance. For nine years thereafter, soldiers of many tongues fought in the Netherlands, in Italy, and in western Germany, but mainly in the Netherlands. What it all proved was that France alone was a match for a Grand Alliance of nearly all the rest of Europe but that France could not defeat a united Europe. The Treaty of Ryswick (1697) put an official stamp on this conclusion as for the first time territories conquered by France were returned. France gained only parts of Alsace in return for the prodigious efforts of its soldiers and taxpayers. Perhaps the most fruitful clause in the Treaty of Ryswick was one that declared the Rhine River free for commerce and navigation.

The War of Spanish Succession Louis' greatest and last war involved all the major European powers as well as many minor ones. It meshed in with a contemporaneous Great Northern War (1700–1721) among Sweden, Russia, Denmark, Saxony, and Poland and Prussia. And throughout the period of the War of Spanish Succession, Austria, Venice, and Russia were, from time to time, at war with the Turks. The armies involved in all these wars were often large; and, although the military art as practiced by most generals involved much maneuvering for position, these thirteen years of war in the west were punctuated by a number of what one of the English generals, the duke of Marlborough, called "very murdering" battles.

Louis XIV took personal charge of some of his early battles, taking care, like most of his generals, not to get too close to the firing line. Above, a courier brings him a message. Right, a civilian supervises the recruitment of soldiers by lot, a French innovation. About this time (1705), Saint-Simon reported that men were intentionally maiming themselves rather than serve in the crown's armies. (Bibliothèque Nationale, Paris.)

The trouble started before 1700 when it became obvious that the European balance of power was about to be upset, or, at least, disarranged, by the impending extinction of the Spanish Habsburgs. Charles II, who had ascended the Spanish throne in 1665 at age four, was mentally and physically deficient and, though twice married, seemed unlikely to produce an heir. Toward the turn of the century, he was not expected to live for many years. Moreover, he had no brothers to take over the Spanish crowns, the disposition of which preoccupied all European statesmen, some of whom were personally interested in the problem.

Louis XIV was one of the most interested. His son, the dauphin, was more Habsburg than Bourbon and thus had an excellent claim to the Spanish heritage. Although the dauphin's Habsburg mother and grandmother had expressly renounced their rights of succession to the Spanish throne in their marriage contracts, Louis XIV felt that his family had a legal claim because the Spanish Habsburgs had not fulfilled their part of these treaties by paying the agreed-upon dowries. He maintained, therefore, that the renunciations of the Spanish princesses were null and void. Supported by a party of French-oriented Spaniards, Louis proposed his grandson, Philip of Anjou, as the best candidate for the Spanish throne.

The Austrian Habsburgs were also intimately concerned with the future of the Spanish crown. Like Louis, Emperor Leopold I was the grandson of

THE PROBLEM OF THE SPANISH SUCCESSION, 1700

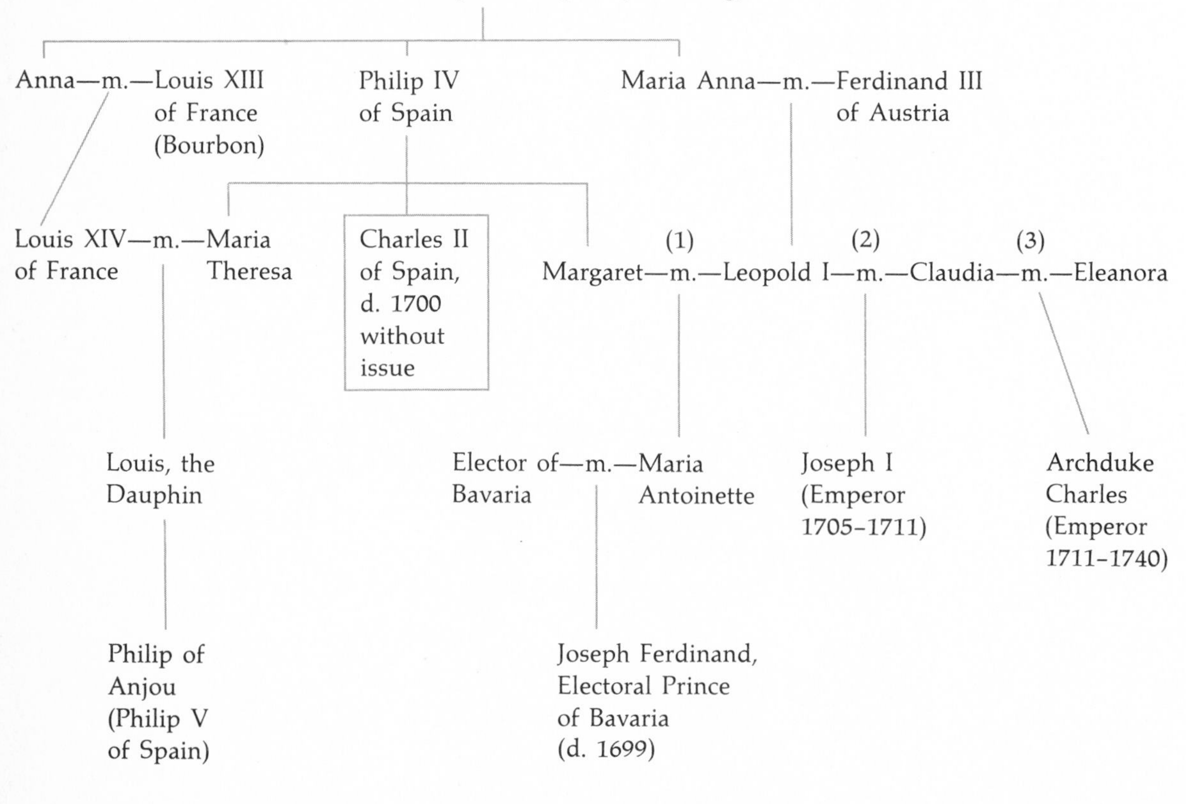

Philip III of Spain, and he, too, had married a sister of Charles II of Spain. Furthermore, neither his Habsburg mother nor his wife had renounced their rights of inheritance—they had, in fact, expressly reserved them. Therefore, Leopold and his sons and grandson felt they had claims to the Spanish throne a bit better than those of Louis and his son and grandson.

Although they had no candidates for the Spanish throne, the English and the Dutch were nonetheless vitally concerned with the balance of power in Europe. English and Dutch statesmen felt that the interests of their states would be seriously hurt were either the Austrian Habsburgs or the French Bourbons to gain the entire Spanish heritage. The only tolerable disposition, they believed, would be a partition. Louis XIV was perfectly willing to talk about a partition with the English and the Dutch while, at the same time, he attempted to win over Spanish courtiers to the idea that Spanish interest would best be served by a Bourbon king who could draw upon French military and diplomatic assistance to keep the Spanish empire intact.

Diplomats from all of the interested states conferred at length and agreed, between 1698 and 1700, to a number of interesting ideas regarding partition of the Spanish Habsburg heritage; but before his death in 1700 Charles II decided to accept the arguments of the French party at the Spanish court and to name Philip of Anjou, Louis XIV's grandson, as his sole heir.

One week later the Spanish ambassador to France told Louis the news of Charles' last will and of his death and asked whether the King would accept the settlement in the name of his grandson. Louis recoiled. If he accepted the Spanish crown in the name of his grandson would he be in for another great war against another Grand Alliance? The outcome of such a war would be uncertain to say the least. Moreover, he had just signed a treaty of partition with the English and the Dutch. It was time to take counsel. He listened to various arguments and, finally, after what was probably more than simply feigned hesitation, he decided that Philip should accept the Spanish crown. A week later, as Philip of Anjou (now Philip V of Spain) prepared to depart for his new kingdom, the elated Spanish ambassador remarked that the Pyrenees had melted away.

As Louis had anticipated, several powers disagreed with this assessment and prepared to defend their view by force of arms. The war that ensued was fought ostensibly over Spain and its northern boundary; but the fighting took place on the peripheries of France: in the Netherlands, in Italy, in the Rhineland and in Germany, as well as in Spain. This fact illuminates allied objectives—which were not so much to secure Spain as they were to render France incapable of again upsetting the balance of European affairs. French armies fought those of the new Grand Alliance well; but the allies fought better. Eventually, the French were driven out of Italy in the south and back toward French territory in the north. By 1708 it was obvious to Louis that a war against all the rest of Europe, except Spain, was more than his resources and arms could stand. Willingly, therefore, Louis entered into peace negotiations even though he was not in a favorable bargaining position. He agreed to all allied stipulations until the allies demanded that the French army drive Philip V, his grandson, out of Spain. At this point Louis broke off negotiations. He appealed successfully to the French people to carry on the war; Philip made a similar appeal in Spain; and the hostilities continued. The French armies fought better than they had in the first seven years of the war. At Malplaquet (1709) they literally destroyed the Dutch army, killing some twenty thousand men, and repulsed allied attempts at invasion.

Then, in 1711, the Grand Alliance began to fall apart. English taxpayers and parliamentarians, bleeding almost as freely from their pocketbooks as Marlborough's soldiers were bleeding on the field, overthrew the Whig ministry that had been supporting Marlborough.[2] Also in 1711, the Habsburg emperor Joseph (who had succeeded his father Leopold in 1705) died, so that Archduke Charles became heir to all the Habsburg possessions. Thus, if the allies were to win the point they had been fighting for since 1701 (to achieve the Spanish throne for this same Charles), the balance of power would be completely destroyed and the old sixteenth-century empire of Charles V would be reconstituted on an even grander scale! Quite naturally, therefore, the Dutch and the English quickly lost interest in the war and negotiated for peace. This time, the French bargaining position was considerably improved by the success of French arms in Spain and the Netherlands and by lack of unity among the allies. The resulting Treaty of Utrecht (1713), with the separate treaties signed at Rastatt and Baden in 1714, made for some revisions of European political geography and established the map of Europe substantially as it was to remain throughout most of the eighteenth century.

THE TREATIES OF UTRECHT, RASTATT, AND BADEN, 1713–1714

The cause of all the trouble—the Spanish succession—was now no longer a matter for concern on the part of the maritime powers. The treaties permitted Philip V (Bourbon) to keep the Spanish throne for himself and his heirs, with the important proviso that the crowns of France and Spain should never be united. This settlement satisfied everyone except the eastern Habsburg, Charles, who, however, could do nothing about it. To compensate him for the loss of Spain, he was given the Spanish Netherlands (roughly comparable to present-day Belgium and Luxembourg), as well as Milan, Naples, and Sardinia, while Sicily went to Savoy, which had fought for the allies. This arrangement was not acceptable to the new king of Spain who tried after 1713 to take back Sardinia and Sicily. Once again the balance-keepers, now joined by France and Austria, went into action (1718), and an English fleet drove Philip's troops out of Sicily. This adventure and the Great Northern War concluded (1721), the European "family" of states settled down to a fairly long period of peace—twelve years—until the outbreak of the War of Polish Succession in 1733. But that is another story for another chapter.

The English were the great gainers from the treaties of Utrecht, Rastatt, and Baden. All France achieved was the privilege of having a relative of

(Page 831) *The Sun King in all his Magnificence, 1701.* (Louvre, Paris.)

[2]John Churchill, the first duke of Marlborough (1650–1722), was the son of one Winston Churchill and the ancestor of another.

its king confirmed in his Spanish title. England acquired two strategic points from which it could protect and expand English interests in the Mediterranean: Gibraltar and Minorca, both gained at the expense of Spain. Even more important, as we shall see, the overseas branch of the struggle, known as Queen Anne's War, gained for England—at the expense of France—Newfoundland, Nova Scotia, and the Hudson Bay territory. As one of the best historians of the reign of Louis XIV has written, "This was the beginning of the end for the French American empire. . . ."

CONCLUSION

It was clear enough in 1714 that the principle of balance of power had won out over the principle of European empire. Internally, in several states, the rulers were increasing their hold on their countries; but for Europe as a whole, the anarchical charter that had been signed in Westphalia in 1648 was reconfirmed. Europe was to remain a congeries of sovereignties and states arranged in a condition of tension, moving from balance to imbalance as changes took place within them. Within this kaleidoscope, France could dominate Europe only intermittently or indirectly.

Shortly after the 1713 treaties were signed, Louis XIV died. It was the seventy-second year of his reign and the seventy-seventh year of his life. By this time there were few who regretted the passing of this grand monarch—who had survived all but one of his legitimate children, grandchildren, and great-grandchildren. The populace of Paris made the royal funeral the occasion for a celebration of deliverance. The road to St. Denis, the burial place of French kings, was lined with onlookers who cursed the royal bier as it passed.

France had gained much glory and great prestige under the Sun King; and French government had become the outstanding example of centralizing absolutism. But for Louis, it all ended in the grave; and since 1683 the French population had probably declined, agriculture and industry had seriously deteriorated (Colbert's work in the early part of the reign notwithstanding), and French royal finances had fallen to low estate. Even the vaunted absolutism was more apparent than real, as Louis' successors were to discover.

FURTHER READING

Again one should see C. J. Friedrich, * *The Age of the Baroque, 1610–1660* (1952), as well as the next two volumes in the "Rise of Modern Europe" series: F. L. Nussbaum, * *The Triumph of Science and Reason, 1660–1685* (1953); and J. B. Wolf, * *The Emergence of the Great Powers, 1685–1715* (1951). The usual fine bibliographies are present. In addition, there is M. Beloff, * *The Age of Absolutism, 1660–1815* (1966), a fast-moving survey.

To what has already been suggested for Henry IV, add G. E. Slocombe, *The White Plumed Henry, King of France* (1931). General treatment of or introductions to seventeenth-century France include J. R. Boulenger, *Seventeenth*

*Books available in paperback edition are marked with an asterisk.

Century in France (1973), a translation of a volume in one of the big French national histories; A. L. Guérard, *France in the Classical Age: The Life and Death of an Ideal* (1970), a highly readable treatment of the classic style in France from the sixteenth century to the eighteenth. L. Battiol, *Marie de Médicis and the French Court in the XVIIth Century* (1972), recently reprinted, is sufficient for a starter on that subject. C. V. Wedgewood, * *Richelieu and the French Monarchy* (1966), and G. Treasure, *Cardinal Richelieu and the Development of Absolutism* (1973), will serve for the great cardinal.

P. R. Doolin, *The Fronde* (1935), considers that revolt and assesses to what degree the French monarchy was absolute. A recent major study of the *fronde* is A. L. Moote, *The Revolt of the Judges: The Parlement of Paris and the Fronde, 1643–1652* (1971). See also P. Knachel, *England and the Fronde: The Impact of the English Civil War and Revolution on France* (1967), a Folger Library monograph.

On Louis XIV and his age there is a mountain of books. The beginner might well start with L. B. Packard, * *Age of Louis XIV* (1969), a very brief survey. More recent is M. Ashley, * *Louis XIV and the Greatness of France* (1946). For Colbert and French Mercantilism look in the pertinent chapters of S. B. Clough and C. W. Cole, *Economic History of Europe* (1952), as well as in C. W. Cole's *French Mercantilism, 1683–1700* (1965). H. Hauser's important article, "Characteristic Features of French Economic History from the Middle of the Sixteenth Century to the Middle of the Eighteenth Century," may be found in H. Ausubel, ed., *The Making of Modern Europe,* Vol. I (1951). W. C. Scoville, in his important study, *The Persecution of the Huguenots and French Economic Development* (1960), concludes that the harassment of the Huguenots had less of an economic impact on France than is usually maintained.

Finally, a series of essays by W. H. Lewis, * *The Splendid Century: Life in the France of Louis XIV* (1971), is popular history on a high plane. One may come to grips with the Sun King in M. Ashley, * *Louis XIV and the Greatness of France* (1965); and J. B. Wolf, * *Louis XIV* (1968), a good big book by the leading American student of seventeenth-century France. Probably the best and most interesting short treatment is: P. Goubert, * *Louis XIV and Twenty Million Frenchmen,* translated by Anne Carter (1972). Goubert is more concerned with French men, women, and children than with Louis. Unfortunately, this translation from the French original is far from perfect. J. E. King, *Science and Rationalism in the Government of Louis XIV, 1661–1683* (1973), gives an idea of the relationship between the French state and science; R. M. Isherwood, *Music in the Service of the King: France in the Seventeenth Century* (1973), does the same for music.

J. C. Rule, ed., *Louis XIV and the Craft of Kingship* (1969), contains essays by such seventeenth-century experts as R. Hatton, H. C. Judge, A. Lossky, A. L. Moote, O. Ranum, H. Rowen, and P. Sonnino. Rule's bibliographical introduction is particularly valuable. See also R. Hatton, "Louis XIV: Recent Gains in Historical Knowledge," a review article in the *Journal of Modern History* (June 1973); and W. F. Church, ed., * *The Greatness of Louis XIV: Myth or Reality?* (1972), another Heath pamphlet.

4 New Currents of Thought in the Seventeenth Century

While seventeenth-century scientists carried through their revolution, it cannot be repeated often enough that they did not think of themselves as subversive. They were certain that the capacious tent of Christian philosophy could contain both traditional theology and Newtonian physics. The moralists, too, continued to profess their orthodoxy, while they rebelled only against "Scholasticism." In the midst of revolution, medieval ways of thinking persisted.

THE REVIVAL OF ANCIENT PHILOSOPHY

This persistence marks the Elizabethan dramatists and poets. To medieval man, the world was a series of hierarchies. God was creator and King of the universe; He was the head of a hierarchy that ran from the Divinity through the angels, to man, animals, and inanimate beings. And this hierarchy was mirrored everywhere: social life was regulated by a pattern of higher and lower orders, cosmology celebrated heavenly above earthly bodies. This view of the world remained intelligible to the playgoers of Shakespeare's time. In play after play, Shakespeare's theme is the divinely ordained order disrupted by criminal action: Hamlet is the prince who finds that "the time is out of joint," and it is his grim but exalted task to set it right. In a famous speech in *Troilus and Cressida,* Shakespeare expresses this vision of a world order:

> *The heavens themselves, the planets,*
> *and this centre*
> *Observe degree, priority, and place,*
> *Insisture, course, proportion,*
> *season, form,*
> *Office and custom, in all line of order.*

Then troubles arise and shake divine order, and these troubles are mirrored in earthly commotions:

Oh, when degree is shak'd,
Which is the ladder to all high designs,
The enterprise is sick.

With the rediscovery of the classics in the Renaissance, the ancient roots of these medieval ideas were clearly exposed. By itself, therefore, classical philosophy offered no challenge to the Christian world view. But the conflicts of ancient thinkers with one another, coupled with the incompatibility of some ancient with Christian thought, created an atmosphere conducive to doubt. It was in this atmosphere that modern versions of ancient Stoicism, skepticism, and Epicureanism achieved a certain popularity. The modern Stoics or skeptics who studied their Seneca or Pyrrhus were anything but anti-Christian; but as their erudition coalesced with the discoveries of the scientists, there arose a formidable competitor to Christian thought.

Montaigne The most effective transmitter of ancient thought in a Christian world, and the greatest moralist of the age, was Michel de Montaigne (1533–1592). His essays, garrulous, long-winded, moving, and brilliant in turn, exercised enormous influence. They burst with classical citations and anecdotes from Greek and Roman life, and show wide reading in ancient sources. Montaigne never renounced the Catholicism of his birth, but his concern was man, not God; his main witness was himself; his favorite method of research was introspection, not prayer, and the study of pagan rather than Christian books. In early essays, Montaigne shows the influence of Stoic doctrine: to philosophize is to learn how to die; to live well is to be free from emotional involvement. In his middle years, skepticism became his predominant mood, and his essays stressed man's ignorance. It was at this time that he coined the famous motto, *Que scais-je?*—What do I know? An affirmative philosophy, a mellow, humane, unsystematic view of life emerged in his last years, when he could proclaim that "our great and glorious masterpiece is to live appropriately."

The Stoics Less famous, but only slightly less influential, were the Christian Stoics of Montaigne's age. The Flemish scholar Justus Lipsius (1547–1606) is typical of them: he popularized such Stoic doctrines as tranquility, constancy under suffering, conformity with nature, and humanity toward fellow men. Lipsius presented Stoicism as an ethical system thoroughly compatible with Christianity. He candidly admitted irreconcilable differences, but held that these the modern Stoic could readily resolve: when Christian revelation clashed with Stoic reason, reason must give way to revelation. Stoicism thus seemed harmless: an extension, or rather an anticipation, of Christianity. Despite such claims to innocuousness, modern Stoicism pointed the way to a large-scale mental readjustment. This is shown by Hugo Grotius (1583–1645), the father of modern international law. Grotius, a Dutchman, was a religious though not sectarian Protestant; in his legal writings he

Michel de Montaigne (1533–1592). Montaigne's *Essays* is a random collection of his thoughts and observations on a great variety of subjects. They reflect a man of great intelligence, who was at home with intellectuals and men of action (he was mayor of Bordeaux for a number of years). (Giraudon.)

derived the law of nature, in characteristic Stoic fashion, from the nature of things and of man. Its rules, he said, would hold good even if there were no God. Christian theologians of the Middle Ages had incorporated the Stoic law of nature into their hierarchy of laws emanating from God. With Grotius, the law of nature was once again emancipated from religion.

Epicureanism Epicureanism was far harder to reconcile with Christianity than Stoicism. Yet this is precisely what Pierre Gassendi (1592–1655), a French cleric and mathematician, tried to do. The Epicureans had the reputation of materialists and atheists. Not without reason: according to ancient Epicurean doctrine the world is made up of atoms, and the gods live in a realm of their own, far from human concerns. Gassendi revived this atomism, but tried to make it respectable by imputing the creation of the atoms to God. Gassendi's influence seems to have been considerable. His insistence on empirical methods was later taken up by Locke; his atomism impressed scientists like Boyle and Newton. Thus, one more ancient strand of thought was woven into the seventeenth-century mind.

Art and Literature This complex mixture of paganism and Christianity was mirrored in art and literature. To be sure, the seventeenth century is too rich to be reduced to a formula—it was, after all, the age of Shakespeare and Milton, Donne and Dryden, Rembrandt and Vermeer, Bernini and Wren. Yet most of the great productions of the age bear the stamp of an enlarged Christian sensibility, a Christianity first enriched, later subverted, by pagan elements.

The Triumph of Flora by Nicolas Poussin, painted about 1630. As was frequently done during the Renaissance, Poussin chose as the subject of his painting a Greek myth. Flora was the goddess of flowers and of regeneration. Poussin attempts to convey the stress placed at the time upon vigor and upon the desire for a rebirth of classical culture. Note that a light seems to play across the canvas from left to right and accentuates elements of the scene; this technique was known as *chiaroscuro.* (Louvre.)

Consider Pierre Corneille (1606–1684), who achieved fame with the *Cid* (1637), a play that aroused a great controversy over the so-called classical rules. In imitation of these rules, a play was supposed to obey the unities of place, time, and action. Corneille argued that his stormy drama had actually observed these unities; in any event he observed them more literally in his later work. *Horace* and *Cinna*—both written in 1640 and both, be it noted, on antique Roman subjects—scrupulously confine their action to a single day, a single scene, and a continuous story. At first glance, obedience to these rules might seem a triumph of pedantry over life; but in the hands of great playwrights like Corneille or Jean Racine (1639–1699) they were the vehicles of a great tension—between passion, which seeks to break barriers, and reason, which seeks to maintain them. The plays of Corneille and Racine were called "Neo-Classical" for several reasons: the rules they obeyed could be traced back to Aristotle, their preoccupation with order reminded audiences of the calm regularity of antique architecture, and the moral problems they explored had been the common coin of Stoic speculation. At the same time, these plays were not vehicles of unbelief. Corneille and Racine were good Christians. While Racine wrote some of his greatest plays on Greek themes, and while his work broods on the tragedy of forbidden love, his plays never lost their Christian imprint. Neo-Classicism in art, drama, and philosophy furnished the seventeenth century with a new vocabulary, and some important alternatives, but trouble for religion was to arise, paradoxically enough, in religion itself.

THE TROUBLED WORLD OF RELIGION

The Middle Ages had been filled with religious controversy. Heretics had tried to modify Christian dogma; reformers had periodically renewed the dedication of the early Christians by founding new monastic orders purging clerical institutions. This activity could be absorbed as long as Europe was religiously unified: challenges to religious institutions could be turned back by the Inquisition or by excommunication; clerical reformers often did their work in the protective shadow of Rome. But with the success of the Protestant rebellion and the permanent disruption of Christian unity, each further controversy appeared as a danger to the stability of the Christian world. The danger was all the greater since these controversies took place in the midst of the scientific revolution coupled with the renewed interest in ancient philosophy.

The Controversy over Grace The most virulent religious controversy of the seventeenth century involved a question that had agitated thoughtful Christians almost since the founding of their religion: grace. One view, first systematically stated by St. Augustine, held that grace was conferred by God alone, and that not all men would be elected to salvation. A form of this severe view had, in fact, been adopted by the Protestant Reformation. But there was a more relaxed view of grace, which was championed by the Jesuits: according to this interpretation, grace was indeed a divine gift, but it required man's willing cooperation. This was far less austere than Augustine's interpretation, because it emphasized the part human effort might play in salvation, and made it at least possible that all men might be saved. There was no reconciling these views, and at the end of the sixteenth century the papacy entered the controversy. It failed, however, to pacify the combatants. Early in the seventeenth century, the controversy was embittered, not by anti-Catholic theologians, but by Catholic clerics who rejected the very Protestants whose teachings they echoed.

Jansenism The most significant opponent of Jesuit teachings was Cornelius Jansen (1585–1638), after whom Jansenism was named. Jansen was an irreproachably orthodox Catholic theologian, who taught at the University of Louvain and ended his days as Bishop of Ypres. But two years after his death there appeared Jansen's book *Augustinus,* the fruit of a life-long study. It reiterated Augustine's views on grace in their purest form. The quarrel *Augustinus* kindled was made all the more intense by the activities of Jansen's two chief supporters, Jean Duvergier de Hauranne, Abbé of St. Cyran (1581–1643), and Antoine Arnauld (1612–1694). St. Cyran—as he is usually called—entered the convent of Port Royal near Paris as confessor, and spread Jansenist ideas there. They were taken up by Angélique Arnauld, Mother Superior of the convent, and began to spread. In 1643, Antoine Arnauld, Angélique's brother, published *Concerning Frequent Communion,* which gravely offended the Jesuits who assumed, rightly enough, that it was aimed at them. Arnauld attacked priests who allowed their penitents to enjoy a gay social life while holding out the hope of heaven to them; there were evil priests, he said, who condoned worldly pleasures as long as each lapse was confessed and then purified by frequent communion. In the course of his polemic, Arnauld reiterated the doctrines of Jansen and the fulminations of St. Cyran against a relaxed Christianity. The battle was joined.

Its first result was the condemnation of Jansenism by Pope Innocent X in 1653. The pope asserted that *Augustinus* denounced propositions that were perfectly orthodox: the Jansenists, he said, claim that it is heresy to hold that man can cooperate in obtaining grace or that he can resist grace, and to say that Christ died for all men. The Jansenists' claim that these statements were heretical, the pope said, was itself heretical. This condemnation put the Jansenists in a quandary. They did not want to disobey the pope, whose authority they recognized, and they did not want to associate themselves with the Protestants. The Jansenists thought themselves good Catholics. They had two lines of defense. First, they agreed that the propositions condemned by the pope were indeed heretical, but they argued that these propositions could not be found in *Augustinus.* This was sophistry, for while they were not in the book word for word, they did fairly summarize the Jansenist position.

Pascal's Defense Their second defense was counterattack, under the generalship of the Arnauld family. Its strongest weapon proved to be Pascal's brilliant polemic, the *Provincial Letters* of 1656, a merciless assault on the Jesuits. After his career as a mathematician, Pascal had turned to the philosophy of religion, and in his later years collected notes for a comprehensive "Apology for Religion." These notes were published after his death in fragmentary form. His *Pensées* remain a masterpiece of religious thought and French prose. They deal with fundamental questions: man's greatness and impotence, man's anguish in a mysterious universe, man's search for the hidden God.

In his *Provincial Letters,* Pascal used his unsurpassed style against the enemies of Jansenism. Pascal had come to Port Royal early in 1655; without formally joining the order, he had made the Arnaulds' cause his own. The Jansenists could use an eloquent champion: in 1656, Arnauld was expelled from the Sorbonne for his views. Pascal defended his friends from censure and assailed their enemies. The controversy over Pascal's *Provincial Letters* is unending. There is little question that he selected the most damaging passages he could find, attributed more evil motives to the Jesuits than the facts warranted, and imputed to the Jesuits alone what was practiced by other Christians. His central target was casuistry, a practice that had been developed by the Jesuits as a guide to confessors. It set up imaginary situations and tried to determine what sort of conduct was permitted, what kind of contrition was adequate, what was sinful and what mere honest error. This kind of legalistic speculation opened the way to abuse, and the Jesuits doubtless tried to adjust their moral precepts to the needs of their fashionable penitents. For Pascal, such quibbling was a betrayal of Christian morality, inviting the twisting of words and condoning crime. To the Jesuits, he wrote, religion was nothing more than the empty observance of outward forms. Cheating, adultery, even murder could be justified by lax confessors armed with casuistic arguments.

Jansenism and the State While the Jesuits rightly objected that their casuists did not abet crime, Pascal's attack was the heartfelt outcry of the truly religious man, of the man who will not compromise with the world. But the sincerity of Pascal's passion and the power of his style did the Jansenists little good. The nuns of Port Royal were subjected to persecution, until, in 1669, the argument was temporarily settled by an ingenious formula devised by Pope Clement IX and reluctantly accepted by the Jansenists. For more than a decade the Jansenists seemed safe, especially since respectable circles in French society took their side, not so much for the sake of their austere theology as for the Jansenists' implicit resistance to Rome. The legal nobility of the robe, concentrated in the *parlements*, adopted Jansenism as a political rallying cry against the undue influence of the papacy. Indeed, in 1682, the French clergy issued its "four Gallican articles," following the direction of King Louis XIV. These articles declared the French king independent of ecclesiastical jurisdiction in temporal matters, General Councils superior to the papacy, the relations between the papacy and France governed by local French custom, and papal decrees binding only when the Church as a whole accepts them. For a while at least the Jansenists could find shelter under the anti-Rome policies of the French state.

But their position remained precarious. When, in 1693, the outstanding disagreements between Louis XIV and the papacy were settled, their subversive theology once again called attention to itself. Some years before, in 1678, the Oratorian priest Pasquier Quesnel (1634–1719) had published *Moral Reflections on the New Testament*, reiterating the most extreme Jansenist assertions on grace. The book caused no scandal on its appearance, but in the 1690's the aging Louis XIV decided to wage war on the near-heretics in his realm. In 1709 and 1710, the two nunneries of Port Royal were closed, the nuns dispersed; leading Jansenists went into exile or fell silent. Finally, in 1713 Pope Clement XI issued the Bull *Unigenitus* on the urging of Louis XIV; it condemned 101 propositions drawn from Quesnel's book. Political Gallicanism protected the Jansenists for several years: the French Church did not accept *Unigenitus* until 1730. But as an intellectual and spiritual movement Jansenism had died long before that. What remained was a fanatical and political Jansenism that plagued France through much of the eighteenth century.

Protestantism Protestantism had been born in controversy, and with its insistence on the authority of the Bible and the priesthood of all believers, it encouraged continuing controversy. To be sure, in most Protestant states, controversy was tepid or repressed: the sect of the ruler was generally the sect of the country as a whole. Most German states, like Brandenburg-Prussia, Saxony, and Württemberg, were Lutheran; Scotland, the Dutch United Provinces, and the Protestant sections of Switzerland were Calvinist. But during the seventeenth century, the question of grace, which had exercised Catholics, troubled Protestants too, and led to outbursts of rhetoric and repression. In Great Britain, the Civil War of the 1640's (see Chapter 2) was intimately connected with religious differences among Puritans, and between Puritans and Anglicans. In the Dutch Republic, fighting for its independence against Spain, austere Calvinists came face to face with liberal Protestants. Here the pressure of the new ideas was brought to bear on older religious ideas. Late in the sixteenth century, the Dutch theologian Jacobus Arminius (1560–1609) developed a liberal theology which came to be named after him. It opposed the rigorous, logical theory of Predestination of the dominant Dutch Reformed Church, and held that every believer might be saved and might participate in taking or rejecting grace. In 1610, shortly after Arminius' death, his supporters addressed a "Remonstrance" to the States of Holland, setting forth their Arminianism but insisting that they had no intention of stirring up conflict. Yet conflict was inevitable. In 1618 and 1619 the Synod of Dort suppressed the Remonstrants, exiled their leaders and closed the churches to them. It was only in the 1630's that toleration prevailed once again.

Few other Protestant countries imitated Dutch toleration, but the rationalist influence of Arminius grew later in the century. In some areas of the Protestant world, like Scotland, rigor persisted into the eighteenth century, but elsewhere there was a marked shift toward modernity. "Enthusiasm" or firm belief in Predestination came to be taken as characteristic of the lower classes. The Church of England moved toward "Latitudinarianism," which greatly reduced the severity of the Christian message, questioned most miracles, and treated revelation as an extension of reason. Early in the eighteenth century a bishop of the Church of England could preach a sermon arguing that good will alone could get a Christian into heaven. Such extreme views were typical of a few, and strongly resented by many. The religious spirit was eroding, but slowly.

SKEPTICS AND CRITICS

Hobbes Religious skeptics, for all their later fame, were a small and notorious minority in the seventeenth century. The greatest of them was Thomas Hobbes (1588–1679), one of England's most vigorous thinkers. As a materialist, Hobbes treated the study of man, the state, and the universe as the study of particles in motion. With pitiless clarity and energetic English, Hobbes expounded a universe in which spiritual were reduced to material forces. Christianity got short shrift in such a system, as can be seen from Hobbes's pithy definition in his *Leviathan:* "Fear of power invisible, feigned by the mind or imagined from tales publicly allowed, Religion; not allowed, Superstition."

In addition to attacking religion by means of such sarcasms, Hobbes advanced the cause of skepticism by his attitude toward the Bible. For more than a thousand years, this sacred book had been studied and interpreted, but always with the respect due a divine message. During the Renaissance, there had been scholarly attempts to establish a definite text (the so-called textual, or lower criticism). Then, with the Reformation, a new kind of criticism (the so-called historical or higher criticism) began to emerge. Its object was to place biblical statements in their historical context, discover the authors of the various books of the Bible, and lay bare the editorial work done by later compilers. In the hands of a believer, the higher criticism was the pious study of the complex history of God's word. But in the hands of an unbeliever like Hobbes it led to skepticism about miracles recounted in the Sacred Book. In the *Leviathan* (1651), Hobbes boldly argued that the scholar must address himself to evidence offered by the words of the text itself. If he does so freely, he will discover contradictions, especially in chronology, and it will become clear that Moses did not write the whole Pentateuch, and that such books as Kings, Chronicles, Judges, and others were written much later than had been commonly supposed.

Spinoza This secular manner of reading sacred texts was developed further by the Dutch philosopher Baruch (or, after his expulsion from the synagogue, Benedict) Spinoza (1632–1677). Unlike Hobbes, Spinoza built his philosophical system on God, although his God was so intellectual a construction that for a century Spinoza was called an atheist. The misunderstanding of Spinoza's philosophy, which was in fact saturated with religious feeling, was due to its mathematical rigor. All beings, Spinoza taught in his *Ethics,* are aspects of the perfect Being, which is God or Nature. Man's freedom lies in understanding the unalterable plan of an orderly universe, and in following the laws of which he is a part. Man's highest activity, therefore, is an unceasing search for knowledge and dignity, the "intellectual love of God." It was for such views that he was excommunicated in 1656, and he quietly lived in various Dutch towns, grinding lenses and perfecting his philosophical system.

Spinoza's principles for reading the Bible were laid down in several chapters of his *Political-Theological Treatise* (1671). Spinoza urged that Scriptures be interpreted in the light of natural reason: "The method of interpreting Scripture does not greatly differ from the method of interpreting Nature—in fact, it is almost the same." In accord with these principles, Spinoza argued that the ethical prescriptions set down in the Bible apply to a specific nation at a specific time, and not necessarily to all men; that since the laws of nature are unalterable and the Bible contains all sorts of tales in which these laws are broken, these miraculous tales must be later interpolations; that the Pentateuch is encumbered with duplicate sets of narratives and chronological inconsistencies. In a word, the Bible is a fallible human production, a book like other books.

Simon Less serene in temper than Spinoza, and less generous in controversy, the French biblical critic Richard Simon (1638–1712) pursued a similar path. In several books, most notably his *Critical History of the Old Testament* (1682) Simon brought together the results of earlier criticism and added ideas of his own. There was nothing new in his assertion that Moses could not have written all of the Pentateuch, but his observations on variations in style pointing to diversity of authorship were an advance in method.

By the end of the seventeenth century, biblical criticism had constructed a respectable set of principles. But it was too specialized and too technical to arouse the wrath, or even the interest, of more than a handful of theologians. Polite society learned its unbelief through other channels: the elegant Epicureanism of Saint-Evremond, and the ponderously witty skepticism of Bayle. Charles de Marguetel de Saint Denis, seigneur de Saint-Evremond (1616?–1703), had served with distinction in the French army but was exiled in the early 1660's and never returned to France, preferring a life of ease in Dutch and English society. In his mode of living, his letters, and his sparkling essays, he embodied and spread a doctrine of tolerant indifference to religious questions, and of sensual enjoyment as an end in itself. He did not attack religion; he enjoyed himself too much to get angry. Instead, he laughed at it, setting a pattern for ridiculing the sacred which was to become widespread in the Enlightenment.

Bayle Pierre Bayle (1647–1706) was more serious. The son of a French Huguenot minister, he briefly converted to Catholicism, and ended up a Pyrrhonist—that is, embracing an extreme form of skepticism named after the ancient Greek philosopher Pyrrho who had held that true knowledge was impossible. Bayle was as unpopular with austere Protestants as he was with Catholics. He made himself unpopular first with his *Miscellaneous Thoughts on the Comet of 1680*, published in 1682 in Holland, whither he had fled after the French government had begun its persecution of Huguenots. The comet of 1680 had aroused much superstitious fear; Bayle described it as a natural event. This gave him a platform for an assault on credulous belief in miracles, and led him to the conclusion that superstition is the most dangerous enemy of civilization—more dangerous than atheism. Employing the formidable erudition that was to make him proverbial, Bayle showed history filled with religious men who had been scoundrels and with atheists who had lived decently and governed reasonably.

Such views involved Bayle in unending controversy, a situation he much enjoyed. The mounting persecution of Protestants in France, culminating in the Revocation of the Edict of Nantes in 1685 and enveloping Bayle's family in grievous suffering, turned Bayle's attention to toleration. The result was his moving and powerful *Philosophical Commentary on the Words of Jesus Christ, "Compel Them to Come In."* It assailed the Catholics for their cruelty to the Protestants, their brothers, and then launched into a brief for toleration. The persecutor, Bayle wrote, is not only evil but irrational, for he supposes that one religion is true and all others are false. But this can never be proved. What is worse, the persecutor twists a few words in the Bible for the sake of his criminal inclinations. To compel men to believe only leads to hypocrisy: it is the antithesis of, not the path to, true religion.

Bayle explored these themes in other works. His most famous production is the *Historical and Critical Dictionary,* first published in 1697. It purports to be a biographical dictionary of famous people in history, mythology, and the Bible. But most of the work is a sly attack on superstition and an indirect plea for toleration. It includes some indecent anecdotes to hold the reader's attention, uses a complicated system of footnotes and cross references to make oblique hits against religious orthodoxy, popular gullibility, and celebrated figures hitherto untouched by criticism, like King David. Bayle's immense learning always served the same message: man can never know anything with certainty, and his acknowledgment of ignorance ought to lead him to tolerate other men, his fellow-ignoramuses. Bayle's genial Pyrrhonism and devious methods had great influence all over Europe. The English Deists, the French *philosophes,* and such monarchs as Frederick the Great of Prussia were Bayle's avowed disciples.

While Bayle's skepticism was a destructive force, his campaign for toleration pointed the way to a positive policy. It implied a new respect for fact, and looked to a political community organized on secular rather than religious principles. Bayle's writings thus direct our attention to seventeenth-century developments in political theory.

THE MAKING OF MODERN POLITICAL THEORY

One traditional problem of political theory is the problem of political obligation: why, and whom, must man obey? In the sixteenth century, the question arose with special urgency. The rise of the state brought with it the erosion of feudal obligations and demanded new justifications for obedience. Moreover, the Protestant revolt had left large religious minorities in several countries. For these minorities—Roman Catholic in Britain, Protestant in France—the question of obedience could become an agonizing dilemma. All men agreed that rebellion against constituted authority was a criminal act, but what was a true believer to do if his prince ordered him to forsake his faith? If obedience to God clashed with obedience to man, who should have preference, God or man? And even if the choice was God, what did this mean in practice: passive endurance, heroic resistance, or active rebellion?

Medieval political thinkers had been concerned with the relation of papacy to emperor, but not in any central fashion with the duty to obey. Theologians like Thomas Aquinas had differentiated tyranny from legitimate rule, and defined the latter as government limited by law and the ruler's conscience. But neither Aquinas nor any other medieval thinker had gone beyond general assertions of a Christian man's right to resist the tyrant.

Sovereignty and Social Contract In the sixteenth and seventeenth centuries, the rights of the state over the subject and the right of the subject against the state were thoroughly redefined, and produced a theory of sovereignty and a theory of social contract.

France, ravaged by thirty years of fratricidal wars, was a good laboratory for political speculation. Huguenots, shaken by the massacre of St. Bartholomew's Day in 1572, developed the first modern theory of resistance. François Hotman (1524–1590) argued in his *Franco-Gallia* (1573) that the French monarchy had never been absolute, and that the consent of the governed was the foundation of royal power. This was wrong as history, but pseudohistory has always been an important weapon for political theorists. Another significant Huguenot document of the Religious Wars was *Vindiciae Contra Tyrannos,* published in 1579 over the ringing pseudonym "Stephen Junius Brutus." It justified the right to resistance by postulating a double contract: between God and men, establishing a religious community; between ruler and people, creating the state. In the latter, the king undertook to rule justly, and the people agreed to obey as long as the king fulfilled his obligations.

Such contractual theories were not the sole property of Protestants: Catholics developed similar ideas, allowing Catholic subjects to appeal from their king to Rome under extreme provocation. But these contractual theories were neither democratic nor libertarian: the *Vindiciae* expressly forbids private citizens from taking the law into their own hands, insisting that the signal for disobedience must be given by the elders of a Huguenot community. Nor were these notions full-fledged theories of the state. These came from other quarters, notably from Jean Bodin (1530–1596), whose *Six Books of the Republic* (1576) is a landmark in the history of political thought. Bodin belonged to a small group of French lawyers and statesmen known as the "politiques," men sick of civil war and doctrinaire claims. For the politiques, the solution for disorder was the power of the state, a legal institution that could claim the obedience of all its subjects regardless of their religion. Bodin was both rationalist and mystic, a scoffer at superstition and a believer in witchcraft. But behind its verbosity and contradictions, Bodin's *Six Books* discloses a most important idea: sovereignty. The sovereign state is the central institution in society. All associations, including religious ones, are inferior to it. Bodin did not draw his conclusions unequivocally: while he defines the sovereign as "unrestrained by law," he insists that the sovereign is bound by his obligations to God, natural law, and such traditional restraints as the constitution of France.

Bodin was trying to define something being born before his eyes, the modern state, and to reconcile the clashing claims of order and freedom. Three-quarters of a century after Bodin, Thomas Hobbes developed a political theory in which the social contract was subsumed under sovereignty with iron consistency.

Frontispiece of the Leviathan *published by Thomas Hobbes (1651).* The life of Thomas Hobbes reflects the intellectual interests of his time. He was a classical scholar, mathematician, philosopher, and political scientist. During the civil war in England he was in exile in Paris and there wrote the *Leviathan.* Note in the inserts the possible forms of "power" and their instruments for exercising their wills on others. (Granger Collection.)

Hobbes's "Leviathan" English political thought, like French political thought before it, flowered in a time of civil strife. James I and Charles I had claimed that they were governing by divine right: government, James I said, was a mystery entrusted by God to rulers alone, and not only disobedience but even criticism or inquiry into royal conduct were unlawful. The Civil Wars of the 1640's destroyed these theories, and created a great debate in which democratic ideas of equal representation competed with aristocratic views. By far the most remarkable product of the period was Hobbes's *Leviathan* (1651). Hobbes was eager to support the royal cause, but not on mystical grounds. A rigorous logician and radical materialist, he derived his political theory from the nature of man. Man is driven by desire and restrained by reason—that is, the rational calculation of his advantage: "I put for a general inclination of all mankind, a perpetual and restless desire of power after power, that ceaseth only in death." In a world in which goods are scarce and the powers of individuals relatively equal, men are in a brutally competitive situation. In the absence of a power to overawe them, there is a "war of every man against every man." In this state of nature, as Hobbes put it, "there is no place for industry; because the fruit thereof is uncertain: and consequently no culture of the earth; no navigation, nor use of the commodities that may be imported by sea; no commodious building; no instruments of moving, and removing, such things as require much force; no knowledge of the face of the earth; no account of time; no arts; no letters; no society; and which is worst of all, continual fear, and danger of violent death; and the life of man, solitary, poor, nasty, brutish, and short."

The only help for this condition is enlightened self-preservation: the contract that hands all power to a central government, a "great Leviathan." That may be a king or an assembly, but whatever it is, it must be obeyed. Hobbes was aware that this is an extreme method of conquering anarchy, but "covenants, without the sword," he argued, "are but words, and of no strength to secure a man at all." He anticipated the obvious objection that subjects might be miserable under the great Leviathan. "The state of man," he replied, "can never be without some incommodity or other; and . . . the greatest, that in any form of government can possibly happen to the people in general, is scarce sensible in respect of the miseries, and horrible calamities, that accompany a civil war, or that dissolute condition of masterless men, without subjection to laws, and a coercive power to tie their hands

from rapine and revenge." Civil war is the worst scourge in the world, far worse than tyranny.

Hobbes neither prescribed nor desired tyranny. His private preference was for a moderate kingship that left wide latitude to the individual. It is worth noting that Hobbes justified absolute power on pragmatic grounds: he rejects tradition, divine right, hierarchy. Men obey because, and only as long as they are protected. Hobbes, the proponent of absolutism, is thus also a father of modern liberal thought. But in the extreme rigor of his logic, Hobbes made no provisions for the rights of the subject.

John Locke. (Green Studio, Dublin.)

Locke These rights played a central part in the thought of John Locke (1632–1704), whose political theory reflects the new conditions confronting Englishmen after 1660. For several years before his accession in 1685, James II had aroused the antipathy of his future subjects by his narrow Catholicism. The attempt was made to exclude him from the throne, and when that failed, to remove him. All this political activity once again raised the question of a ruler's religion, and John Locke's celebrated *Two Treatises of Government* were written during the Exclusion controversy in the early 1680's, and then published in 1690, after William and Mary had succeeded James II on the throne.

Locke's first treatise was a scathing refutation of *Patriarcha* (1680), a posthumous pamphlet by the extreme royalist Sir Robert Filmer (d. 1653). Locke demolished this defense of divine right with little effort, and then proceeded, in his second treatise, to delineate a political theory of his own. While Locke was more optimistic about mankind than Hobbes, he too had grave reservations about human nature. He postulated a state of nature in which men might live in peace, but the absence of impartial judges and the threat of endless warfare made the state of nature at best an inconvenience and at worst a disaster. Hence man is driven into making a social contract, the society thus formed invests an authority with the power to govern. That power was strictly conditional: it rested on the consent of the governed expressed through rational political institutions, and could be overthrown once it became tyrannical. The central task of the government is to protect man's "property"—a word by which Locke meant life and liberty as well as physical possessions. A subject must not be deprived of his property without his consent: he must live under due process of law.

Locke's thought, with its emphasis on the conditional grant of power to the state and on the right to resist, is a landmark in the history of European liberalism, and clearly distinguishes liberal from democratic political thought. Locke did not preach the doctrine of "the fewer laws the better." In his system, the government was invested with the prerogative power, which gave it the authority to act without, and even against, the laws in emergencies. Locke combines hard-headedness with libertarianism, a combination that makes him, with Newton, one of the fathers of the Enlightenment.

FURTHER READING

The most satisfactory work on the revival of classical thought remains Sir J. E. Sandys's classic 3-volume *History of Classical Scholarship* (3rd ed., 1904). Gilbert Highet, * *The Classical Tradition* (1949), may be used for facts. Much scattered information can be gathered from the series "Our Debt to Greece and Rome."

In the vast literature on individuals, consult especially Donald M. Frame, *Montaigne's Discovery of Man* (1955), compact and persuasive. Jason L. Saunders, *Justus Lipsius* (1955), is a pedestrian but helpful introduction to Neo-Stoicism. The Renaissance world view is brilliantly analyzed in Theodore Spencer, *Shakespeare and the Nature of Man* (1942); and E. M. W. Tillyard, * *The Elizabethan World Picture* (1943). On general intellectual currents, see these illuminating studies by Marjorie Nicolson: * *Science and Imagination* (1956), * *Mountain Gloom and Mountain Glory* (1959), and above all, *The Breaking of the Circle* (rev. ed., 1960). On religion, see N. Abercrombie, *The Origins of Jansenism* (1936); A. L. Drummond, *German Protestantism Since Luther* (1931); G. R. Cragg, *From Puritanism to the Age of Reason* (1950); and the opening chapters of Cragg's popular * *The Church and the Age of Reason* (1960).

The best general survey of the political thought of the times remains George H. Sabine's *History of Political Theory* (2nd ed., 1950). See also Julian H. Franklin, *Jean Bodin and the Sixteenth-Century Revolution in the Methodology of Law and History* (1963); Michael Oakeshott's brilliant "Introduction" to Hobbes's *Leviathan* (1947); Stuart Hampshire, * *Spinoza* (1951), a clear introduction to a difficult thinker. While Bayle is being reevaluated, Howard Robinson's *Bayle the Skeptic* (1931) remains standard. For Locke, see Richard I. Aaron, *John Locke* (2nd ed., 1955).

*Books available in paperback edition are marked with an asterisk.

PART XI

The next two parts are devoted to the history of Europe in the eighteenth and very early nineteenth centuries, the period of the Enlightenment, the French Revolution, and Napoleon. The first of these sections will sketch the political events of the period between the Peace of Utrecht of 1714 to the end of the Seven Years' War in 1763. But because this is the century of the French Revolution, we shall try to do much more: we shall try to discover and describe the wellsprings of those forces that erupted in the cataclysm of the closing years of the century. We shall be studying what the French, in hindsight, call the ancien régime, *or "Old Order" of European society which was destroyed after 1789.*

Why should we devote so much attention to a social system that no longer exists? Living in a century that has seen a Russian Revolution, a Chinese Revolution, two World Wars and the Atom Bomb, why do historians still argue—as they do—about the nature of society in the eighteenth century, about the motives and actions of its leaders, and about the order of events? One answer may be that the dam that broke in 1789 loosed waters which are still flowing, still sending out ripples to affect our lives today. For the eighteenth century was not only the century of the French Revolution, it was the Era of the Enlightenment and an Age of Reason. The "Enlightened Despots" who tried to rule according to rational principles (as they understood them) are dead and gone, but the ideas that swayed them are still very much alive.

We shall attempt, first, to describe the "winds of change" that were affecting the social patterns of Europe under the Old Regime, and some of their economic foundations. In doing this, we shall devote special attention to those at the base of the pyramid—the peasants who tilled the soil and tended the livestock from the moors of Scotland to the plains of Hungary. Especially in England alternatives were being sought for the traditional practices of agriculture and handicraft methods of manufacturing.

Awareness of the epochal scientific discoveries of the sixteenth and seventeenth centuries spread beyond the small circle of learned men to an "enlightened" world of reformers, philosophers, and popularizers—especially in France—from many walks of life. Drawing their own implications—especially a belief in man's perfectability on earth—from the discoveries and theories of such men as Newton and Locke, these intellectuals urged the overhaul of the society they had inherited. Among those who listened to their ideas were the rulers of two relative newcomers on the European stage—Prussia and Russia. We shall pause in Chapter 3 to fill in some of the background of the rise of these two states.

In Chapter 4 we shall take up the thread of political history in the West with the death of Louis XIV of France in 1715. In their external affairs the new European rulers continued to seek to add to their territories by guile and force of arms and thereby increase their power and prestige in traditional ways. Throughout this century, France remained the arbiter of western European civilization, albeit, as we shall see, on increasingly weak underpinnings. It was England that challenged French primacy in what has been called a "Second Hundred Years' War."

While the monarchs of Europe were reassessing their traditional foreign alignments and forming new coalitions abroad, at home, as "enlightened despots," some were not only attempting to consolidate and increase their powers but also to effect social change. How these rulers reacted to the heady ideas of the day, and how their subjects reacted to some of the reforms that were set in motion, may help us to a better understanding of the revolutionary era described in the next part.

"THE COMTESSE DU CAYLA" BY HOUDON. (The Frick Collection.)

THE ANCIEN REGIME AND THE ENLIGHTENMENT

LEGACY OF THE PAST

The chief bequests of the eighteenth century were the ideas of the Enlightenment and their dissemination through a considerable part of the western world. Attitudes toward religion, politics, science, and philosophy have never been entirely the same since, even though some of the new concepts merely led to confusion and conflict. A minor legacy of the period was that women, at least a handful of educated upper-class women, participated in cultural affairs.

During this century the British empire rose to the highest rank among overseas empires, a position that it retained until the middle of the twentieth century. In central and eastern Europe, the main legacy of the period was the emergence of the Russian empire and the kingdom of Prussia as major powers.

This era produced fundamental advances in modern technology on which later science and industry built. In northwestern Europe agriculture began to assume the form of a scientifically managed business, creating a basis for future economic growth.

The Salon of Madame Geoffrin by Lemonier. The *salon* (literally, drawing-room) of a woman such as Mme. Geoffrin (right of center) was the meeting place of the intellectuals of the French Enlightenment. Here the arts of conversation, wit, and criticism were perfected, making French the language of cultivated persons the world over. It is still the preferred language of diplomacy. (Giraudon.)

MAJOR EVENTS, 1700-1763*

	Politics	*Enlightened Thought and the Arts*	*Economics, Technology, Expansion*
1700	Battle of Narva: Charles XII defeats the Russians		
			Methuen Treaty (1703)
		John Locke dies (1704)	
1705			
	Union of England and Scotland (1707)		
	Peter defeats Swedes at Poltava (1709)		Darby cokes coal (1709)
1710			English South Sea Company (1711)
	Accession Fred. Wm. I of Prussia (1713)		Asiento Treaty (1713)
	Louis XIV dies; accession Louis XV (1713)		
1715			
		Leibnitz dies (1716)	John Law establishes bank in France (1716)
1720			The South Sea bubble bursts (1720)
	Robert Walpole becomes "prime" minister (1721)		
		J. S. Bach: *Well-tempered Clavicord* (1722–1723)	
1725	Peter the Great of Russia dies (1725)	Voltaire to England (1725)	
	George I dies; accession George II (1727)	Sir Isaac Newton dies (1727)	
		Handel musician to the English royal family (1727)	
		John Gay, "Beggar's Opera" (1728)	
1730			
	War of Polish Succession** (1733)	Voltaire's *Philosophical Letters* (1733)	Kay's flying shuttle (1733)

1735	Peace of Vienna—end of War of Polish Succession (1735)	English laws against witchcraft repealed (1736) John Wesley starts Methodist revival (1738)	
1740	Accession Frederick the Great of Prussia and Maria Theresa of Austria (1740) War of Austrian Succession (1740–1748)	Torture abolished in Prussia (1740) Hogarth: "Marriage à la Mode" (1744)	Dupleix, French governor in India (1741) Clive arrives in India (1744)
1745	The "Forty-Five": Bonnie Prince Charles (1745–1746)	*Sans Souci* palace built, Potsdam (1745–1747) T. Smollett. *Roderick Random* (1748) Montesquieu's *Spirit of the Laws* (1748) Condillac's *Treatise on Systems* (1749) H. Fielding: *Tom Jones* (1749)	W. Cooke invents heating by steam (1745)
1750		Publication first volume of the *Encyclopèdie* (1751)	
1755	French and Indian War (1754–1763) The "Diplomatic Revolution" (1756) Seven Years War (1756–1763) Jesuits expelled from Portugal (1759)	Hume: *Natural History of Religion* (1755) Birth of Mozart (1756) Helvetius: *On the Mind* (1758) Suppression of the *Encyclopèdie* (1759)	Battle of Plassy (India) (1757) Quesnay's *Economical Tables* (1758) Wolfe takes Quebec (1759)
1760	George II dies; accession George III (1760) Jesuits expelled from France (1764)	Rousseau: *Nouvelle Heloise* and *Social Contract* (1761–1762) Haydn joins Esterházy court (1761) Voltaire's *Philosophical Dictionary* (1764)	Blast furnace (1761) Hargreave's spinning jenny (1760's)
1765	Jesuits expelled from Spain (1767)	Blackstone's *Commentaries on the Laws of England* (1765–1769)	Watt's first steam engine patent (1769)
1770		Holbach's *System of Nature* (1770) First edition of the *Encyclopedia Britannica* (1771)	

*For 1700–1715, see also Major Events, Part X.
**For other wars, see Major Events, Part XII.

1 Winds of Change in the Eighteenth Century

Historians have often been accused of paying more attention than they should to courts, kings, and diplomats, to popes, parliaments, treaties, and wars, and not enough to the common people, to—in a poet's phrase—the "short and simple annals of the poor."[1] If this accusation is well founded, it is partly the result of the fact that many historians would agree with an American politician's view that if you have seen one slum you have seen them all, or with Thomas Hobbes, who wrote that the life of uncultivated man is "solitary, poor, nasty, brutish, and short." In other words, until fairly recently, most historians have felt that the "short and simple annals of the poor" were not worth relating.

In this chapter we shall attempt to make up for any lack of attention to the common man by assessing the present state of our knowledge of the way the vast majority of the people lived in Europe in early modern times. We shall go on to see how a general rise in population and prices in the eighteenth century caused a new interest in agriculture and technology, which led to some important innovations.

THE HISTORICAL SOURCES

Some historians have believed that the annals of the poor do not exist. The history of European civilization, as they see it, is based on the written word. In the early modern world, and throughout the eighteenth century (under consideration in this section) eighty to ninety percent of the population consisted of peasants. Even in the most progressive of western European areas very few peasants could read or write and, therefore, tended not to leave written accounts of their activities. Further, some members of the upper and literate classes simply took the peasantry for granted, paying less attention to them than they did to their horses or their dogs. In short, the "common man" of early modern Europe has been supposed to have had no history.

[1]Thomas Gray's "Elegy in a Country Churchyard," circa 1750.

Fairly recently, however, these negative attitudes toward the history of lower classes have been eroded as social historians have moved to the forefront of the profession and have begun to use all sorts of new materials and methods to study early modern society in all its aspects. As a result, the previously neglected humble people are now finding themselves posthumously reconstructed, counted, analyzed, and run through computers, as we move toward "total History."[2]

Some of our sources for social history derive not from written records but from pictures. Occasionally we may receive marvelous visual flashes of peasant life through paintings like those by Pieter Brueghel the Elder (late sixteenth century) and Louis Le Nain (early seventeenth century) or of the urban poor through the paintings and engravings of William Hogarth (mid-eighteenth century). At least one contemporary French social historian (Philippe Ariès) has imaginatively used artworks as historical sources (iconography) to trace the evolution of the nuclear family and changing attitudes toward children in early modern times.

Other, more nearly conventional sources of historical information about the submerged sectors of humanity are the records of those within the literate world who, though they had very little interest in how peasants lived and loved, were intensely interested—for economic reasons—in the fact of the peasants' existence. The landlord, insofar as he (or his bailiffs) could read, write, and cipher, kept records of his relationships with the peasant as they pertained to rents or dues owed. Large numbers of these estate (or manorial) records still exist in local repositories, and more and more they are being studied by social historians.

STATE AND CHURCH

The early modern state, also, was interested in the members of the lower orders of society as potential soldiers and as the principal taxpayers. Therefore, as the state apparatus grew in size and sophistication during early modern times, it endeavored with increasing success to count (short of mounting a regular census) its people and to determine their capacity to pay taxes. The records resulting from these endeavors—tax rolls, for instance—have been preserved in considerable quantity. Although they are difficult to work with, the historian who has patience can learn from them much about what peasants were willing to tell the government about their economic situation. This information is less reliable than most present-day income tax returns and must be handled with care. For instance, in France, rich peasants could and did proclaim their poverty and live in absolute squalor—no windows, pig under the bed, etc.—to avoid exhibiting a wealth that would make their taxes go up.

The Church was interested in the peasants and the lower orders of society generally as souls to be saved and also as tithe and revenue producers (the Church owned, of course, much rural real estate). In most European

[2] R. and E. Forster, eds., *European Society in the Eighteenth Century* (1969). The Introduction to this collection of documents is a fine brief description of the aims and methods of the social historian.

countries during early modern times, the Church was responsible for maintaining vital statistics: births (indicated by baptisms), marriages, and deaths (burials). In theory, a priest or minister had to preside over all these stages in the progression of a soul through life and to record these events in his parish register. In spite of fire, flood, and human destruction, tens of thousands of these registers still exist. Scattered over the face of Europe,[3] they are difficult to use; but they provide the best indication we have of what was happening to European population in early modern times. And we can learn more from these registers than simply whether population was going up or down. Suppose, for instance, that in a particular parish or group of parishes we note that the marriage rate held steady or increased over a period of time while the birth rate fell. What does such evidence mean? Possibilities: young married couples were emigrating; married couples were practicing some form of birth control; stillbirths and abortions were increasingly common; illegitimate births were decreasing; people were drinking too much gin (as was the case in England during the early eighteenth century); priests were becoming more lax about recording births than marriages; infants were being killed at birth and hidden from the authorities; or any combination of the above. Obviously, to deal with these possibilities and to try to understand what was going on, the social historian must address himself to a variety of factors: the state of the economy, the morals or social habits of the day, public health, and administrative efficiency.

With this by way of introduction to the general topic, let us see if we can answer the question, What was happening to European population—all of it—during the century of the Enlightenment?

DEMOGRAPHY

The upsurge of European population that began about 1450 ended in most parts of Europe in the 1630's and was followed during the next hundred years or so by decline, stagnation, or, at best, by very slow growth, depending on the area. The most obvious reasons for the seventeenth-century decline were disastrous and repeated visitations of bubonic plague, the widespread ravages of warfare (the Thirty Years' War and the wars of Louis XIV), and frequent crop failures with resulting famine and increased susceptibility to diseases like typhus, typhoid, smallpox, dysentery, and cholera. Confronted with such depressing conditions, men and women tended to marry later, if at all, thus reducing fertility; adult as well as infant mortality rose, while births fell. For example, in one much-studied English parish (blessed with extraordinarily complete parish registers) burials tended to surpass baptisms from the 1640's until the late 1730's.

A turnabout in this parish—and in much of Europe—occurred somewhere between 1720 and 1740. The upward curve of population that began then became steeper after the middle of the eighteenth century. The angle became even more acute after 1760, especially in parts of Scandinavia and

[3] The Church of Jesus Christ of Latter Day Saints (Mormon) of the United States has copied for religious reasons, great numbers of European parish registers. The photographic copies are deposited in Salt Lake City, Utah.

The taste for an alcoholic beverage known as "gin" was brought to England from the wars in the Netherlands by British soldiers. Flavored with juniper berries (*genever* in Dutch, shortened to "gin" in English), the distillate was soon locally produced and became a popular drink among the working classes. Some results of its abuse in eighteenth-century London are shown in this eloquent engraving by William Hogarth (1697–1764). (British Museum.)

the Low Countries, Russia, England, Wales and Ireland, and in parts of Germany. In Spain, Italy, and France, the rate of increase was smaller but still significant. Why, we might ask, did this marked increase in population come about at this particular time?

Causes of Population Increase Historical demographers and social historians are by no means agreed on the answer to this question. Some argue for increased fertility and others for reduced mortality; and within each camp there are differing interpretations as to why fertility might have increased or why mortality decreased. There is no doubt that during the eighteenth century the most spectacular killer disease—bubonic plague—effectively disappeared from Europe. The last important west European epidemic of this disease hit southern France in 1720.[4] But there were plenty of other biological killers—tuberculosis, smallpox, typhoid, typhus, dysentery, and European cholera, among others—ready to take over in times of famine and other natural or man-made disasters. Yet population increased.

Did improvements in medical knowledge and practice and in public health measures permit more infants and their mothers to survive childbirth and enable adults to achieve longer lives? There is little evidence to sustain this notion. Eighteenth-century physicians, if they were honest, admitted that they were powerless to deal with infection; and many informed Europeans believed, with reason, that a sick man who put himself into the hands of a medical doctor would be lucky to survive the treatment. The obstetrical forceps was invented in the late seventeenth century but its use in the hands of the practitioners of the day was nearly sure to produce a dead or deformed child. Hospitals, while becoming more numerous in urban centers during the eighteenth century, were sinks of contagion. Such matters as assuring sanitary public water supply and sewage disposal were not attended to in the eighteenth century, any more than they had been in the seventeenth and sixteenth centuries; and the city of the Enlightenment was probably a less healthful place than had been the medieval town. As cities became larger and more populous, buildings became higher and closer together, wells more polluted, and the air more fetid. In a small town or city without high buildings, the gatherers of night-soil (human excrement and garbage) could remove it to outlying farms where it was used as fertilizer or food for pigs. A person living in an eighteenth-century "high-rise" urban slum was not likely to walk down several flights of stairs with a potful of excrement and deposit it on the neighborhood pile for the scavengers. Rather, he would throw it out of the window—pedestrian beware! An eighteenth-century king of Spain, as we shall see, tried to prohibit this practice in Madrid; but there is no evidence that he succeeded.

It has been argued that, in the eighteenth century, because innoculation (with live smallpox virus) was practiced, the incidence of smallpox declined. Actually, such innoculation was done on a very small scale and was highly dangerous because the innoculated patient contracted a real case of smallpox—which he, in turn, could and often did transmit to those about him. The practice was forbidden, in many areas, in the interest of public health. It was not until after 1800 that Edward Jenner's vaccination with cowpox

[4]Various theories are put forward to explain the disappearance of plague from Europe. (1) The black rat liked to live in human habitations and was the most efficient carrier of the plague bacillus (which was spread from the black rat to human beings by a species of flea that liked to live on black rats). In the early eighteenth century, the black rats were killed off or driven away by immigrant brown or grey rats. These newcomers did not like to live with people, and their fleas were not efficient transmitters of plague to human beings. (2) Changes in house construction (greater use of brick instead of wood or mud for walls and substitution of tile and slate roofs for thatch) made it more difficult for rats (and their fleas) to enter human habitations. (3) Europeans developed immunity to the plague bacillus. (4) Quarantine regulations prevented the plague from reaching Europe from India and other parts of the world where it remained endemic.

Crop failures could spell disaster and even starvation for thousands of peasants, who had no reserves of food to carry them over difficult times. City-dwellers were even worse off in times of famine. Here the hungry are shown receiving a hand-out from the royal stores in Paris in 1693. (Bibliothèque National, Paris.)

virus for immunization against smallpox—a much safer procedure and one to which most of us have submitted—was introduced. After the early nineteenth century, in civilized areas, smallpox was a less serious killer; but during the eighteenth century there were no significant impediments to its ravages.

If this were the end of possible analysis, we would be required to conclude that European population did not increase because it could not. But increase it surely did. Therefore, let us look farther. It seems more than likely that the economic advances already discussed in connection with the early modern commercial revolution made increased subsistence available. The growth of trade, creation of larger markets, and improvement of transport made it possible to deliver food more efficiently and cheaply while, at the same time, providing employment for the increasing population.

Warfare and Weather Another possible explanation of eighteenth-century population growth is that warfare was less destructive than it had been in previous periods. The eighteenth century from 1715 to 1789 was marked by many wars, but also by two extended periods of peace in parts of Europe (1720–1734 and 1763–1778). Further, we have already seen that, beginning in the late seventeenth century, armies began to come under stricter control. Because soldiers were fed, clothed and housed by the state, they were not expected to loot for their subsistence. In the eighteenth century, in western Europe, at any rate, local populations often welcomed the presence of armies in their neighborhoods as being good for business. Though armies continued to grow in size, generals were becoming more wary of pitched battles. Maneuver, march, and countermarch were the order of the "scientific" warfare of the day. Losses through casualties in combat were minor in comparison with losses through desertion. One contemporary observer commented that "wars were going out nowadays, from their mildness."[5] Moreover, soldiers were increasingly recruited from those social groups (criminals, vagrants, debtors) of least economic value, the "dregs" of the people. Their absence from civilian life was no great loss to society and might have been a benefit. Thus militarism and war failed to restrain population growth in the eighteenth century as they had in the seventeenth. On the contrary, the fact that war seemed less terrible might very well have lessened the prudential restraints on population growth by encouraging couples to marry earlier.

Finally, it is probably true that after the first decade of the eighteenth century the weather was more favorable to the principal European crops (small grain, especially rye and wheat) than it had been during the preceding many decades.[6] France experienced a number of crop failures after the first decade of the century, most of them resulting from excessive dampness, but nothing like the terrible famines of 1693–1694 or of 1709–1710 when as many as a million people died of starvation and related disease. Even

[5]Quoted in M. S. Anderson, *Europe in the Eighteenth Century, 1713–1783* (New York, 1962), p. 130.

[6]Pierre Goubert has pointed out that one of the reasons for repeated crop failures and consequent famines in much of Europe was the fact that the principal food crops (winter rye and wheat) came from the Near East and "did not adapt easily to a maritime climate with cold wet summers . . ." *Louis XIV and Twenty Million Frenchmen* (Vintage, 1969), p. 23.

the great grain crisis of 1787–1789, at the onset of the French Revolution, was not so severe as the earlier disasters. Thus it appears that nature smiled on the eighteenth century, relatively speaking, and permitted the production of more food to feed a growing population, even given an almost static agricultural technology.

RURAL LIFE AND TRADITIONAL AGRICULTURE

During the sixteenth and seventeenth centuries, some notable improvements in the techniques of farming had been made in certain areas (particularly the Low Countries). However, peasant life and peasant farming were organized and carried on very much as they had been since the "agricultural revolution" of the high middle ages in northern Europe, when the two-field system (leaving half of the plowland fallow every year) gave way to the three-field system in which two-thirds of the arable land was planted, while only one-third was left fallow.

The three-field system was a great advance over two-field cultivation and provided one of the agricultural bases for late medieval population increase. This was not, of course, a system of crop rotation in the modern sense. Overwhelmingly, throughout most of the eighteenth century, the northern European peasant continued the three-field system on the better lands. Poor soil in the north (the Breton peninsula of France, for instance) and most land in the south was still cultivated according to the ancient Roman two-field system. In much of Europe the arable open fields were still divided into strips in the north or squares in the south. Food grains, notably rye and wheat, were still the most important crops on the best land

Harvest Scene by Pieter Brueghel the Elder. Farming methods had changed little since the sixteenth century, when Brueghel painted this harvest scene. Peasants used long-handled scythes to cut wheat which was then bound (often by women) in sheaves arranged tent-like to dry. The short-handled sickle, while less efficient than the scythe, was the preferred harvest implement in some areas since it left a higher stubble which could be gleaned by the poor (see text). (Metropolitan Museum of Art, Rogers Fund.)

of the plains. In mountainous regions, peasants grazed livestock; and in many areas, particularly in the south, grapes, fruit, and olives were vital to the peasant economy. In some of the more primitive parts of France, peasants lived principally on wild chestnuts and berries.

Plowing was still done as it had been in the thirteenth century, though the moldboard plow was probably in wider use than it had been five hundred years earlier. Grain was still sowed broadcast by hand; and the harvest was still accomplished with sickles. Brueghel's late sixteenth-century painting of a harvest scene (see illustration) may show reapers working with the more efficient scythes; but Flanders, where Brueghel worked, was one of the most technologically advanced provinces of Europe at that time. In parts of France, reaping grain with scythes was forbidden, on the grounds that the scythe cut the stubble so short that little was left in the field for poor people to glean.

Most peasants still lived in nucleated villages in the shadow of their church steeples. In some areas, their houses may have been a bit more substantial than the huts of their thirteenth-century ancestors; and the landlord's house was probably considerably grander and more liveable than the medieval manor house. But a thirteenth-century person reincarnated in, say, the mid-eighteenth century would have found, at first glance, little to surprise him in the villages of continental Europe.

Landholding and the Status of Peasants Looking a bit deeper, however, he would have noticed some changes. If he were reincarnated in Russia, he would note that, whereas in the thirteenth century Russian peasants had been free to move about, now they were serfs, attached to the land. In France, Germany west of the Elbe, or England, our visitor would be surprised to find that serfdom had virtually disappeared. By the eighteenth century, the breakdown of the manorial system was nearly complete in the west, while in eastern Europe the status of peasants had degenerated to a point where they were nearly slaves.

In the west, some peasants actually owned land; but most of them were tenants of one sort or another. The most nearly secure peasants enjoyed an indefinitely inheritable right to a cottage and yard, along with the right to farm a certain number of strips in the open fields and to use the village common and fallow fields to pasture their livestock. The most substantial peasants in this category held enough land to support themselves and their families (in good years) and sometimes have a surplus for sale. In return for their right to use the land these peasants paid to their landlords certain dues in money or in kind and often rendered services, as had the medieval serf. Unlike the medieval western and modern eastern serf, however, all but a handful of peasants west of the Elbe River were free to leave the land if they chose to do so.

Many western European peasants—the majority—did not hold sufficient land to support themselves by farming. In order to subsist, they were forced to hire themselves out as day-laborers to the landlords or to more substantial peasants. Often they and their families engaged in manufacturing—spinning or weaving, for instance—as organized by the putting-out industry. Some peasants held no land at all, not even a cottage garden. They too toiled for others or became sharecroppers, working land belonging to a landlord who supplied tools, seed, and working livestock in return for half the product. At the other end of the peasant scale were the money renters, who supplied their own capital. Often the latter were substantial people who could afford to pay enough rent to keep their landlords happy and to make a profit. This sort of peasant capitalist was to be found on the best land, especially in the neighborhood of large urban markets.

THE PRICE RISE

Like those noble and other landlords who were fortunate enough to receive their fixed rents in kind rather than in cash, large-scale peasant farmers stood to profit from the movement of prices in the eighteenth century. For, as population was increasing, prices were rising. After a period of roughly seventy years (1660–1730) during which the price trend had been downward, prices in France started to go up and showed a steady if gradual increase to about 1763, when they increased sharply. Between 1730 and 1789, French grain prices increased 60 percent. As we have previously noted, among those who suffer most from price increases are those who live on fixed money incomes or wages or those (as in the case of landed aristocrats) whose revenues are set contractually over long periods of time and cannot rapidly be adjusted to the changing price structure. In a period of rising prices, especially when a growing population produces a larger supply of labor, wages tend to rise less rapidly than prices, and consequently the opportunities are attractive to entrepreneurs who can make great profits under such circumstances. In fact, while prices in France increased 60 percent between 1730 and 1789, wages increased only about 22 percent. This situation helped to prompt would-be entrepreneurs—many of whom in the Age of the Enlightenment tended also to be "do-gooders"—to take new interest in agriculture.

East and West Europe Although there were many similarities in the lives of peasants in eighteenth-century Europe, it should be clear from the above that the peasant community was, in fact, becoming less of a community as the century progressed. It appears that the lot of the statistically "average" English peasant did not worsen greatly in the eighteenth century; French peasants who controlled land were probably better off in the second half of the century than in their recent past; but more and more peasants, even in the northwest, were becoming landless. The burdens laid upon the west Elbian German peasant were probably not more than he could carry. In the south and east, however, in Iberian Spain and Portugal, in southern peninsular Italy, in Germany east of the Elbe, in Danubian Europe (Bohemia, Austria, and Hungary) and across the plains of Poland and Russia, most peasants were sunk in servitude and poverty, their lot tending to become worse rather than to improve. A sign of the difference between peasants' condition of life, east and west, is the fact that while there were very few, and no important peasant uprisings west of the Elbe River during the eighteenth century until the summer of 1789, Russia experienced seventy-three known local risings from 1762 to 1769, followed by a huge peasant revolt in 1773–1775 led by the Cossack Pugachev. In 1796–97 there were 278 recorded peasant revolts in Russia. The Habsburg lands (Bohemia and Transylvania) also experienced serious peasant uprisings in the eighteenth century.

WINDS OF CHANGE IN AGRICULTURE

Most historians are now convinced that the eighteenth-century "agricultural revolution" that was served up in school books to the present writer's generation was an evolutionary, rather than a revolutionary process. There is no doubt that vast changes occurred on the land; but it is equally clear that temporally these changes stretched from the sixteenth century to the twentieth. Traditional land-tenure and farming techniques were not overthrown in a sudden "Revolution" during the period of the eighteenth-century Enlightenment; rather, the pace of change was quickened.

For example, in the sixteenth century, English landlords succeeded in fencing common pastures in order to engage in rationalized grazing of sheep. By the end of the seventeenth century, nearly half of all English plowland had been enclosed. In the latter half of the eighteenth century, an intensified effort began to enclose all the remaining plowland. Landlords were reacting in understandable ways to the facts of rising population, rising prices for agricultural products, and the increasing profitability of farm real estate. These conditions encouraged many of the large landholders to produce more crops—especially grain—for sale at home or abroad in the regional or interregional markets rather than for local consumption.

For the English landlord, the effect of enclosure was to liberate him from the traditional patterns of farming in those fields that he could enclose. Substantial peasants who had controlled large numbers of strips before enclosure were compensated with large, consolidated holdings; and, if they could resist the temptation to sell out to the noble landlords, they could profit from the rearrangement by rationalizing their own farming methods and developing a market orientation—in short, by becoming agricultural capitalists. On the other hand, those peasants who had held little land before enclosure very often found that the new arrangement worsened their condition. The costs of fencing their new consolidated holdings might be beyond their means; and in the process of enclosure they lost whatever right they had to common pasture. They were then faced with the problem of raising both their own food and feed for animals on the equivalent (or less) of their previous strips. Moreover, in many cases, the creation of consolidated holdings made the nucleated village obsolete and required the peasant to build a new dwelling. Faced with these problems, many poorer peasants sold out and became hired hands or moved to the already swollen cities, where they often fell to the level of paupers.

In eighteenth-century France, in many parts of the continent west of the Elbe River and south in parts of Italy and Spain, the pressure on the land had almost exactly the opposite effect on landholding from that we have described in England. In this vast area, the greater lords were wont to depend for their incomes largely on money payments or dues from their peasants rather than on the crops they raised. Peasants were closely attached to the land they worked by tradition, arrangements with the lords, and law. Under these circumstances, the lords endeavored to get larger payments in money or kind from the peasants rather than taking over the land for themselves.[7] This situation fostered deep antagonisms that became overt in France in the course of the French Revolution.

TECHNOLOGICAL CHANGES IN AGRICULTURE

Winds of change on the land blew in the realm of technology as well as on rural social relationships. During early modern times, in parts of the Netherlands, Dutch farmers had developed an agricultural style known as "high farming." They found by trial and error that, when they alternated or "rotated" certain crops (turnips, peas, clover) with grain, the land did not deteriorate as it did when grain was grown in the same field every year. Further, having little unused land, they tended to confine their farm animals in barns and fenced fields, thereby controlling their breeding and collecting manure with which to enrich the soil. Putting such experiences together, a number of "improving landlords" in eighteenth-century England began to create what was known as the "new husbandry" on their enclosed fields.

One of these English aristocrat-farmers, Viscount Townshend (1674–1738), began to experiment with crop rotation and with the use of lime soil (marl), wood ashes, soot, and manure on the soil. As rotational crops, he tried legumes like clover, peas, and lucerne (alfalfa), which return some nitrogen to the soil, and turnips. He became, indeed, such a strong advocate of turnips in the rotation process that he was nicknamed "Turnip" Townshend. He had enough success so that he acquired followers who continued his work. The most famous of them was Coke of Holkham (1752–1842), who developed a technique of four-crop rotation that came to be known as the Norfolk System. This permitted the cultivation of all the land every year, thus doing away with the fallow system entirely.

While men like Townshend and Coke were experimenting with the rotation of crops, other landowners interested themselves in problems of tilling the soil and in improving breeds of farm animals. Thus Jethro Tull (1674–1740) improved the "horse hoe", that is, a horse-drawn cultivator for removing weeds from between rows of crops, which had been in use in the vineyards of Languedoc in the south of France. Robert Bakewell (1725–1795) devoted himself to improving the qualities of cattle and sheep. Although he knew little about genetics, he did know that promiscuous mating of animals turned out by peasants in common pastures meant that good animals might be bred by the scrubby ones and that the results were

[7] This generalization does not apply to the land beyond the Elbe, especially in East Prussia, nor to the great estates called *latifundia* in southern Italy and Spain. In both of these places peasants usually had little land and worked for the lord in large-field cultivation of grains, especially wheat.

undesirable. Hence he advocated breeding those animals that were by outward appearances the best, keeping males out of the common pastures, and more stabling of animals. Then others made improvements on the plow, especially the coulter in front of the share, which would cut heavy sods, and the moldboard for turning over the sods in the furrow.

Word of the new agriculture spread rapidly. Arthur Young (1741–1820) traveled in Europe, observing farm practices and writing extensively about what he saw, judging everything by the latest developments in England. King George III of England (nicknamed "Farmer George") was intensely interested in new agricultural methods and wrote for Young's journal, *Annals of Agriculture,* under the pseudonym of Ralph Robinson. In France, interest was great in certain circles, as the plates on agricultural machinery in the great *Encyclopédie* and the works of Duhamel du Monceau attest. Queen Marie Antoinette "played" at farming at her Swiss-type cottage, Le Hameau, in the park at Versailles, and Louis XVI tried to improve Merino sheep on his estate at Rambouillet. Catherine the Great in far-off Russia and George Washington and Thomas Jefferson in America extolled the virtues of farm life and admired the progress that was being made in farm techniques.

Among the more important developments in agriculture was the extension of the use of the potato, for no other plant produces so much nutrition per acre at so low a cost and under so many and varied conditions of soil and climate. By the sixteenth century, this humble immigrant from the New World was being grown in Spain and the Germanies; in the eighteenth century, it became the principal nourishment of an exploding Irish population. Thanks to the efforts of a propagandist named Parmentier, the tuber was in the process of being accepted by Frenchmen (who learned to do many things with potatoes besides frying them!).

While they made significant beginnings, these reformers and publicists did not immediately revolutionize farming as practiced on west European—or even English—farms. What was most important in this work was the development of a new mind-set regarding agriculture that carried over into the nineteenth and twentieth centuries.

BEGINNINGS OF THE INDUSTRIAL REVOLUTION

More spectacular for the future were some innovations in manufacturing techniques made in the eighteenth century, especially in England. Behind the decisions made by innovators in industry were the same stimuli that inspired the "improving landlords": population growth, rising prices, expanding local and interregional markets, and desire for personal profit.

What began in eighteenth-century England and later spilled over to the continent, and eventually to the whole world, was what we call, more-or-less loosely, the "industrial revolution." Like the agricultural revolution, this was a long-range affair and is still in progress; but it did have its initial "take-off" in late eighteenth-century England. The leap from the springboard involved increased mechanization and new sources of power in manufacturing processes.

Frontispiece from Systema Agriculturae. Interest in improving agriculture was already in evidence in seventeenth-century England, and indeed even earlier in Italy and the Low Countries. The rhymed inscription to the book whose frontispiece we see here points out that

"Plenty unto the husbandman, and Gains,
Are his Rewards for's Industry and Pains . . . ."

The work was published in 1669 by the Englishman John Worlidge. (LCRB.)

It is not surprising that the initial breakthroughs took place in England. The island kingdom had a particularly lively colonial trade, and the largest urban market in the western world was London. The English also had a high concentration of demand for goods, thanks to their active overseas and coastwise shipping trade. Further, England had an advanced monetary system and was accustomed to the use of money for exchange and for investment, as well as considerable knowledge of the productive arts, especially coal mining, metallurgy, and textile manufacture. And England was experiencing rapid population growth, with plenty of people seeking employment.

Similarly, it is not surprising that the first innovations occurred in the textile, ferrous metal, and power-producing industries. The demand for the product of these industries was great; profits from them could be very large; and the state of technology in each was such that relatively minor alterations in the method of production could cause major changes in quantity and quality of output.

Textiles In the textile trades, for example, the hand loom and the spinning wheel had, by the early eighteenth century, reached a high stage of development. This relatively advanced textile machinery was sufficiently simple and inexpensive to enter nearly every rural household and give employment to women and children in "spare time" and even to men when they could not work in the fields. Thus a great many people were familiar with the problems of making cloth and a great many carpenters and handymen were engaged in constructing or repairing machinery. Moreover, many men in business were well acquainted with the technical problems of the trade, as well as with the profits to be derived from it. In fact, cloth merchants had begun to buy machinery, rent it out to workers, furnish them with the raw materials to process, and then collect the finished products for which a wage was paid. This "merchant-employer", "putting-out", or "domestic" system, as it has been variously called, was highly developed in the textile trades. Furthermore, in a small but significant number of instances enterprising businessmen had brought workers together in workhouses or "factories" in order to reduce costs, guarantee a steady supply of the product and/or ensure quality control.

Given this general familiarity with textile manufacture, people were forever making new contributions to its technology. One of the first techniques to make a crucial impact on the volume of production was the "flying shuttle," invented by the Englishman John Kay in 1733. Kay was a loom maker and workman and had already made several minor innovations on the loom. But the flying shuttle, a simple device, was of major importance. With it, the operator could pull a string that would activate a hammer that would hit the shuttle and send it flying through the shed of the warp (the threads running the long way of the cloth) to the other side of the loom. Then, by pulling another string, he could drive it back again. This greatly increased the output of the weaver and, at the same time, allowed him to weave wider pieces of stuff, for previously width had been limited by how far he could manually push (the technical term is "throw") a shuttle from one side to the other.

This advance created a demand for more thread, but already tinkerers were at work trying to improve methods of spinning, carding and combing (preparing fibers for spinning), and fulling and dyeing (finishing by shrinking and coloring). In the early 1730's John Wyatt, along with Lewis Paul, the son of a French refugee, developed a machine to make thread by a system of rollers running at different speeds, with much the same effect that one gets in trying to roll fibers into thread with the fingers. But their machine, patented in 1738, was not much of a success. It was for James Hargreaves, a weaver, carpenter, and millwright of Lancashire, to effect the great breakthrough (1770). His "spinning jenny", named affectionately after his wife, was a relatively simple variation on the spinning wheel.

Hard on these inventions came efforts to activate the machines by mechanical power. Richard Arkwright produced the water frame (1769), which was a spinning machine on the jenny principle driven by water power; Samuel Crompton produced the "mule," which combined spindles and rollers in one machine (perfected about 1779, but not patented because Crompton was too poor to seek a patent); and Edmund Cartwright applied power successfully to the loom in 1785. From then on improvements in textile technology came thick and fast, in America and continental Europe as well as in England.

Cotton Inasmuch as these various machines and techniques were used first and for some time mostly for cotton, the demand for cotton grew enormously. Cotton had traditionally been procured primarily from India; but, because that source of supply had been reduced by internal disturbances and foreign war, cotton raising was attempted in the English colonies in southern North America. Southern plantation owners soon discovered that they could raise cotton more profitably than tobacco or indigo and turned rapidly to it. Negro slaves were acquired to do the work. Capital for expansion was furnished by Englishmen who wanted cotton or by Americans who had saved their profits from tobacco-raising or land speculation. Progress was, however, slow. As late as 1784 eight bags of American cotton were seized by customs officials at Liverpool on the grounds of allegedly false declaration of origin, for the officers thought that so much cotton could not be grown in America. Yet American output of cotton did go up, especially after Eli Whitney invented the cotton gin (1793). This machine greatly reduced the labor and cost of picking seeds from the bolls.

The new textile and harvesting machines resulted in the production of cloth at lower prices and made possible the substitution of cotton for wool (too hot and itchy in warm weather), more expensive linen, and almost prohibitively priced silk. By 1800, England's exports of cotton exceeded in value those of any other product.[8]

[8] In this connection, mention should be made of the fact that no further fundamental changes in textile techniques were made until the development of rayon in 1884 and of nylon in 1938.

Iron Important as were these early advances in the textile trades, industrialization would have had a precarious future if machines had continued to be made of wood, which is not strong enough to stand great stress and cannot endure much friction of moving parts. What was needed was a strong "building material," and this is why the development of iron and later, steel was so crucial for the subsequent development of mechanized industry.

Iron had, of course, been in use since some time around the beginning of the first millennium B.C., but its use had been limited because smelting iron ore with charcoal was expensive and had to be carried on near forest supplies, which were continually being depleted. What was needed was a new fuel for the smelting process. In the seventeenth century, coal was tried as a substitute for charcoal, but it was not successful, for it left too much sulphur in the iron, giving a product that was too brittle and had too many flaws. To render coal more suitable for smelting it was necessary to burn off its impurities, much as the impurities of wood were burned in the making of charcoal. The person who was first (1709) successful in thus reducing coal to coke was Abraham Darby, an ironmaster of Shropshire, England, a place to which the smelting industry had moved in search of cheap wood and where coal was available. Gradually coke fires were made hotter by the use of stronger drafts from piston pumps (1761) rather than from bellows, by the use of a hot-air rather than cold-air blast, and by higher blast furnaces. Next, Peter Onions, an ironmaster, and Henry Cort, a contractor for navy supplies, discovered at about the same time (1784) that if the molten mass were stirred, or "puddled" as it was called, during the smelting process more impurities would be burned off.

The product from coke smelting was pig iron, named from the shape of the molds into which it was run. This hard but brittle material had to be reheated and hammered in order to drive out sulphur and carbon and to produce wrought iron. This laborious task was greatly facilitated by the invention in the 1780's of a steam hammer, in principle something like a pneumatic drill, and by Henry Cort's invention of the rolling mill (also in the 1780's), similar in type to the rollers of a washing machine, which squeezed out excess carbon and produced iron sheets that could be used for boilers, the sides of ships, and armor, or that could be run through a slitting mill to produce rods for nails, bolts, and screws. The availability of better iron and—eventually—steel, and general economic expansion combined to bring into existence a great number of new metal-working and metal-using machines and tools, and dramatic improvements in the implements of warfare.

Steam Power The new industries required great amounts of power for water and air pumps, spinning mules, and power looms. In many instances, power from falling water was unavailable, and the windmill was an uncertain and unsatisfactory resource. Thus, the imperative search for new sources of power turned to the expansive power of steam. The principle of the power of steam had been known for many centuries, and had actually been employed by Hero of Alexandria about 50 A.D. Then it seems to have been pushed into oblivion for many centuries until Solomon de Caus (1576–1630) discovered that a partial vacuum could be created in a pipe by filling it with steam and then condensing the steam, and Giovanni Branca (1629) designed a machine on the principle of the turbine. In 1663, Edward Somerset, later the Marquis of Worcester, was given a patent monopoly for a contraption which was able to raise water a hundred feet.

The need to pump water out of coal and iron mines was responsible for the next innovations. Thomas Savery improved Somerset's device for the purpose of pumping water out of mines by creating a vacuum in a tank by condensing steam in it, then allowing the air pressure outside to raise water via a pipe from the mine to the tank, and then blowing the water out of the tank up another pipe by the use of steam. This Savery "atmospheric" engine was not without some success, but it was only practical for light work. What was needed was a machine that would lift great quantities of water from mines. This need was met by Thomas Newcomen, an iron monger, about 1708. He got up-and-down motion by using a piston within a cylinder. The piston was attached to a long beam resting on a fulcrum. By the use of a weight and low-pressure steam, the piston was raised. By condensing the steam behind it and thus creating a vacuum, air pressure applied above the piston would push it back down. The beam was attached to an ordinary atmospheric water pump which lifted water out of the mine.

Newcomen's engine attracted considerable attention, even among academic people. In fact, a professor at the University of Glasgow, who wanted to demonstrate the Newcomen engine, asked a technical assistant by the name of James Watt (1736–1819) to repair and set up a model of Newcomen's machine. It was in the performance of this task that Watt became interested in the steam engine and that he was launched in an endeavor to improve it. His great contributions were that he arranged for the condensation of steam in a separate chamber (not in the cylinder) and, by an ingenious device known as the "sun and planet" system, was able to get rotary motion from the action of the piston going up and down. Rotary power was just what was needed to activate a host of machines which, up to that time, had been driven by water, animal, or even human power.

The development of the Watt steam engine (patented 1769) was marked with many hardships and near failures. Watt's first partner, John Roebuck, lost a fortune in an effort to perfect and market the engine. His successor, Matthew Boulton, a well-to-do manufacturer of Birmingham, invested heavily before the machine became a financial success. It finally caught on and was used to pump water uphill to activate waterwheels on the way down. It was soon applied to machinery needing rotary power, including textile machinery, steamboats, and railway locomotives.

Thus, by the end of the eighteenth century, the power source for the nineteenth-century industrial and transportation revolutions was available.

Revolutionary Changes that Occurred in Power Sources in the Eighteenth Century. (Top) the early Newcomen steam engine being used to raise water from a mine or well; and (bottom) 1788 model of Boulton and Watt's steam engine, which utilized gears to transmit steam power to industrial machinery. (Science Museum, London.)

"Prometheus was unbound."[9] All this is not to say that in the eighteenth century a full-fledged economic and social revolution remade the western world. In fact, it is safe to say that until well into the nineteenth century most Europeans were unaware of the industrial and agricultural changes

[9]The most important recent book on the industrial revolution is David Landes, *The Unbound Prometheus* (1969).

that were afoot. In the eighteenth century, the new industry was localized in parts of England, France, and Belgium; and not until the 1790's did industrialization really "take off," even in those advanced areas. But eighteenth-century agricultural innovators and industrial entrepreneurs set the world on a seemingly irreversible course toward capitalistic exploitation of mechanical inventions, urbanization, and the breakup of the Old Order.

SOCIAL CONSEQUENCES OF CHANGE AND NEW ECONOMIC THEORY

With the greater use of machines in production for profit, western civilization entered a new stage of economic history—industrial and agricultural capitalism—where the entrepreneur owned the means of production, hired labor for wages, and produced goods for sale in an impersonal and uncertain market in the hope of making a profit. This change gave rise to a new type of businessman and a new body of economic theory. Leaders in business now came more frequently from the lower classes than had previously been the case and they had much less culture and social polish than had their predecessors. They were less interested in the classics; they drove themselves harder; and they were willing to undertake extraordinarily large projects for personal gain.

Among other things, these men wanted conditions that would favor their activities. Thus they were inclined to be hostile to existing mercantilist theory and practice, much of which, as we have seen, had been inspired by monopolistic guilds and ambitious absolutist states. In general, they wanted to be free of controls that would restrict their freedom to make profits. And, in good eighteenth-century fashion, they wanted to find those natural, eternal, and immutable laws of economics, which, they believed, must exist, as they seemed to exist in the physical world described by Sir Isaac Newton.

One of the first of the new schools to break sharply with the old traditions of economic theory was Physiocracy—meaning, literally, "the rule of nature." The leader of this school was a Frenchman and physician to Madame de Pompadour, Dr. François Quesnay (1694–1774). He had become much interested in William Harvey's theory of the circulation of the blood and came to believe that there must by analogy be a system controlling the circulation of wealth in society. In a famous economic treatise, *Le Tableau Économique* (1758), Quesnay contended that all wealth came originally from the land and then "circulated" through other groups in society. This did not mean that industry and commerce were to be neglected, but it did mean that production from the land should be increased by all possible means, including the new agricultural technology. More importantly, all man-made impediments to the "free" flow of wealth should be removed. Quesnay and his followers popularized the famous slogan of *laissez passer, laissez faire,* which became the byword of the new business community.[10]

[10]Physiocratic doctrine was also the taking-off point for tax reform, especially notions of a single tax. If land were the only source of wealth, it was argued, then only land should be taxed. Manufacturers, bankers, and commercial men were not likely to oppose such a conclusion.

Thrift, moral rectitude and respectability were the virtues cultivated by the new commercial and manufacturing classes, who contrasted themselves favorably with what they saw as the extravagant, profligate nobility. The joys of *bourgeois* family life were celebrated, and children were enjoyed for their own sakes, as in this intimate luncheon scene, "Le Dejeuner," by Francois Boucher (1703–1770). (Louvre.)

Hard upon the Physiocrats and to some extent influenced by them came a group of English writers who began to question the old mercantile principles and to propound what they thought were "laws" of economics. One of the first to do this was Adam Smith (1723–1790), whose *Wealth of Nations* (1776) is a masterpiece of style and analysis—and is still one of the most widely read and studied works in all economic literature. Smith contended that the true wealth of a state is not to be measured by the land it exploits or the gold and silver that it possesses but by the amount of goods and services that it furnishes. This point established, he went on to show the means by which goods and services can be increased. He thus took an opportunity to advocate the use of machines, the division of labor, the development of transportation, the investment of capital in new plants, and the better training of labor. Especially did he advise a policy of governmental "hands-off" business at home and free trade among nations. He believed that each economy should concentrate on the production of those things in which it had a competitive advantage. Smith's work laid the groundwork for the "classical" school of economics of Malthus and Ricardo, about whom we shall hear more later.

CONCLUSION

The eighteenth-century "coin," in its social and economic aspects, presents contrasting surfaces. On the obverse of this coin we see a picture of a pyramidal society still consisting of nobles and clergy at the apex, supported by a very large remainder. Part of that remainder consisted of a middle class; but most of the common people were still peasants who were bound to traditional ways. This is the picture of the *ancien régime.* The reverse of the coin, however, shows a shifting pattern caused by population growth and the tendencies of middle-class or noble entrepreneurs to innovate in agriculture and industry, thereby stimulating social change. Now, it is time to try to penetrate the interior of the coin, into the thought of the eighteenth-century intellectuals whom we call the *philosophes* of the Enlightenment. Their thought and the dissemination of their ideas were perhaps the most dynamic features of this century of contradictions.

FURTHER READING

The best general single volume on Europe in the period under consideration in this section is M. S. Anderson, * *Europe in the Eighteenth Century, 1713–1783* (1961 and 1970). Also useful are the pertinent volumes in the Rise of Modern Europe series: P. Roberts, * *The Quest for Security, 1715–1740* (1947 and 1973); W. Dorn, * *Competition for Empire, 1740–1763* (1940 and 1973).

During the past twenty years the history of population, or demographic history, has become a growth industry as scholars try, first, to discover population trends; second, to explain why population increased or decreased; and, third, to understand the effects of population change. A handy introduction to this fascinating set of topics is D. Glass and R. Revelle, eds., *Population and Social Change* (1972), as well as D. Glass and D. Eversley, eds., *Population in History: Essays in Historical Demography* (1965); J. Chambers, *Population, Economy, and Society in Pre-Industrial England* (1972); H. Habakkuk, * *Population Growth and Economic Development since 1750* (1971); E. Wrigley, *Population and History* (1969).

P. Laslett, * *The World We Have Lost* (1965), deals with the size and structure of the domestic household in England, as does P. Laslett and R. Wall, *Household and Family in Past Time* (1972). The latter work treats not only England, but France, Serbia, Japan, and North America. P. Ariès, * *Centuries of Childhood: A Social History of Family Life* (1962 and 1973), has

*Books available in paperback edition are marked with an asterisk.

already been listed. Another item in this literature is D. Hunt, * *Parents and Children in History: The Psychology of Family Life in Early Modern France* (1970 and 1972). Hunt offers a depressing picture. Also see T. Rabb and R. Rotberg, eds., * *The Family in History: Interdisciplinary Essays* (1973). O. and P. Ranum, eds., * *Popular Attitudes toward Birth Control in Pre-Industrial France and England* (1973); and E. Wrigley, "Family Limitation in Pre-Industrial England," in *Economic History Review,* 2nd series, 19 (1966), deal with the pre-pill situation.

For the long view of the role of climate in history, see E. L. Ladurie, *Times of Feast, Times of Famine: A History of Climate since the Year 1000,* trans. by B. Bray (1971). Related is W. Shelton, *English Hunger and Industrial Disorders* (1973). On disease and famine see F. Hirst, *The Conquest of Plague* (1953); J. Shrewsbury, *A History of Bubonic Plague in the British Isles* (1970); and A. Appleby, "Disease or Famine? Mortality in Cumberland and Westmoreland, 1580–1640," *Economic History Review,* 2nd series, XXVI, no. 3 (August 1973).

On social classes, see R. Mousnier, *Social Hierarchies, 1450 to the Present* (1973); A. Goodwin, ed., * *The European Nobility of the Eighteenth Century* (paper 1973); R. Forster, *The Nobility of Toulouse in the Eighteenth Century* (1960 and 1971), a fine book; F. Ford, *Robe and Sword: The Regrouping of the French Aristocracy after Louis XIV* (1953); G. Rudé, *Europe in the Eighteenth Century: Aristocracy and the Bourgeois Challenge* (1973); and E. Barber, * *The Bourgeoisie in Eighteenth-Century France* (1955). R. and E. Forster, eds., *European Society in the Eighteenth Century* (1969), is a superbly edited collection of readings on various aspects of society. P. Goubert, *The Ancien Régime: French Society, 1660–1750* (1973), recently translated, is of great interest and should be read.

For the industrial revolution, T. Ashton, * *An Economic History of England: The Eighteenth Century* (1972), and the same author's * *The Industrial Revolution, 1760–1830* (1948), recommend themselves, as does E. Lampard, *Industrial Revolution: Interpretation and Perspective* (1957), an American Historical Association Pamphlet.

Agrarian and agricultural history are the subjects of J. Blum, * *The European Peasantry from the Fifteenth to the Nineteenth Century,* and B. H. Slicher Van Bath, *The Agrarian History of Western Europe,* both previously cited. Recent works on the agricultural revolution are G. Mingay, * *Enclosure and the Small Farmer in the Age of the Industrial Revolution* (1968); and J. Chambers and G. Mingay, *Agricultural Revolutions, 1750–1880* (1966).

Interesting recent studies in economic history include P. Curtin, * *The Atlantic Slave Trade: A Census* (1969); and R. Davis, * *The Rise of the Atlantic Economies* (1973).

Finally, J. Laver, *The Age of Illusion: Manners and Morals, 1750–1848* (1972), deals with a special kind of social history.

2 Enlightened Thought

In 1784, the German philosopher Immanuel Kant (1724–1804) wrote an article entitled "Answer to the Question: What Is Enlightenment?" Better than a lengthy treatise, Kant's answer sums up the meaning of this movement. "Enlightenment," he wrote, "is man's emergence from his self-imposed nonage. Nonage is the inability to use one's own understanding without another's guidance. This nonage is self-imposed if its cause lies not in lack of understanding but in indecision and lack of courage to use one's own mind without another's guidance. *Sapere aude—Dare to Know!* 'Have the courage to use your own understanding,' is therefore the motto of the Enlightenment."

THE TASK OF THE ENLIGHTENMENT

For Kant, as for the other men of the Enlightenment, its task was to discredit time-honored myths and outworn institutions, and to create in their stead a new view of the world and a new society. In calling themselves *philosophes* (the French word) the men of the Enlightenment emphasized the power of philosophical, critical thought. Man's critical mind, extended into all areas of human activity, could change the world.

This was an ambitious program, and the Enlightenment offers an exhilarating but bewildering spectacle of strenuous intellectual and polemical activity. *Philosophes* of various countries were in touch with one another; many of them were friends. Frenchmen learned from Englishmen, and in turn taught the rest of Europe. Montesquieu (1689–1755) visited England and used English institutions as a model in his masterpiece, *The Spirit of the Laws* (1748). The long-lived Voltaire (1694–1778), too, went to England, admired its House of Commons, its appreciation of literary men, and its civil liberties, and helped to popularize Newton and Locke on the continent. Denis Diderot (1713–1784), perhaps the most versatile genius of the Enlightenment, went to school to English philosophers. The great Scottish thinker David Hume (1711–1776) traveled widely and was a particular favorite among the *philosophes* of Paris, while Hume's friend and disciple, the economist Adam Smith (1723–1790) was indebted to the French school of economists, the physiocrats, and in turn taught continental economists. There were other connections. Jean Jacques Rousseau (1712–1778), the "bad boy" of the Enlightenment, had an immense influence in France, Germany, and England, with his radical educational and political theories. Among those he influenced was Immanuel Kant, who learned to respect the ordinary man by reading Rousseau, just as reading Hume had revolutionized his view of philosophy.

These men, and others like them, made distinctive contributions to political thought, educational theory, dramatic and art criticism, psychology, sociology, the short story, the play, the novel, the writing of history, and technical philosophy. Yet we may discern order in this fruitful chaos: the Enlightenment is unified by its assumptions; it shows development with a dramatic turning point; it had a recognizable enemy; and it propagated a relatively clearcut program.

Gersaint's Sign (1720) *by Antoine Watteau.* Gersaint, the owner of an art shop in Paris, is shown putting a portrait of the Sun King in a box, as though that were the end of him. At the right, he is showing his customers the more pastoral scenes, of which Watteau was a master. The painting symbolizes the transition from the classical world of Louis XIV to the more "natural" world of the Enlightenment. (Staatliche Schlosser und Garten, Berlin.)

THE ASSUMPTIONS OF THE *PHILOSOPHES*

Locke For all their differences, the *philosophes* shared a certain outlook. They were the disciples of Newton's *Principia Mathematica,* and hence enemies to system-making, and admirers of science; of Bayle's *Historical and Critical Dictionary,* which fed their religious skepticism; and of Locke's *Essay concerning Human Understanding,* with its emphasis on experience. Locke argued in the *Essay* that man has no innate knowledge at birth, but acquires the materials for knowledge through his senses, and then kneads these materials into shape by reflection. Locke followed scientists like Galileo and Newton in distinguishing "primary" and "secondary" qualities in our experience. Primary qualities like extension, shape, and motion inhere in the outside world; secondary qualities, like color, smell, and taste, are supplied by the observer. Knowledge, to Locke, consists not of a faithful copy of external realities, but of a correspondence of ideas to the outside, and of a clear view of this correspondence.

Locke's theory of knowledge, developed by the *philosophes,* directed the Enlightenment toward science and away from the system-making of Scholasticism or seventeenth-century philosophy. Locke and the *philosophes* ridiculed metaphysics as a meaningless activity. Man is ignorant and can reduce his ignorance only by first acknowledging it, and then following the tested methods of the sciences. To expand Newtonianism to areas other than physics and astronomy was one of the *philosophes'* favorite hopes. David Hume subtitled his philosophical masterpiece, the *Treatise of Human Nature,* an "attempt to introduce the experimental method of reasoning into moral subjects."

Condillac To be sure, the pose of philosophical "modesty" was often little more than a pose. But it was grounded in the sincere conviction that men have wasted far too much time contending over words and grasping at phantoms, and that philosophizing must alleviate men's estate. That is why the *philosophes* made jokes about "metaphysics": metaphysics, Voltaire wrote, resembles the minuet—the dancers expend much energy, move about gracefully, and end up where they started. The task of thinking, for the *philosophes,* was as much to unmask pretentious philosophizing as it was to advance knowledge; the unmasking preceded the knowing.

The most thoroughgoing attack on metaphysics is the *Treatise on Systems* (1749) by the Abbé Condillac (1715–1780). In this essay, Condillac reviewed the philosophical constructions of the previous century and dismissed them as the presumptuous speculations of hasty men. The true method was patient empiricism. That this concern with method was not merely academic becomes evident in the polemics the *philosophes* mounted in the second half of the eighteenth century: for the Enlightenment the task of philosophical activity was, above all, practical.

The Enlightenment's rejection of metaphysics threw a heavy burden on the theory of knowledge, which, in turn, rested on psychology. The central philosophical question had become, How do we know anything? and the answer seemed to lie not in ruminations or constructions, but in careful observation of psychological operations. While the Enlightenment did not profess a single psychology, the roots of its various views were in Locke's rejection of innate knowledge. In his *Treatise on Sensations* (1754) Condillac pushed Locke's sensationalism to the limit: he resolved reflection into the sensations that give rise to it. The simplest sensations, he argued, produce the most complex thoughts, and "uneasiness" is the source of all psychological activity.

Hume Condillac's psychology was radical, but in some respects David Hume was even more radical. For Hume there is no entity called "mind." When we look closely into ourselves, tracing the path of our mental activity, all we find are discrete impressions. To be sure, we think about connected wholes in space or time—organized groupings or historical sequences—but these are created simply by mental habits. In his celebrated analysis of causation, Hume argued that we can never conclusively know the bond between cause and effect. The bond we feel, and on which we act, is supplied by habit. As we experience events in conjunction, we come to expect this conjunction in the future. Such expectation, Hume said, is reliable enough for men to live by, but it never reaches the absolute certainty of mathematical reasoning.

Hartley Closely related to this analysis is the doctrine of Association, which achieved wide popularity in the eighteenth century. It had first appeared in a late edition of Locke's *Essay,* but became a prop of the new science of psychology with *Observations on Man* (1749), by David Hartley (1705–1757). Hartley tried to give a Newtonian account of all mental phenomena, including reverie, memory, and the growth of ideas. He argued that the repeated association of certain sensations with one another give each of them such "power" that the sight or memory of one would give us the idea of the others. Thus man's mind moves from one image, sensation, or idea, to others in a natural, mechanical progression.

Ethics The psychological doctrine has obvious import for morals. If man's thinking can be studied with as much precision as can the motion of bodies, man's moral nature must be open to scientific investigation. The *philosophes* did not all subscribe to a single ethical doctrine, but their views did not differ widely. Until Rousseau suggested, and Kant developed, a stern morality of duty, the *philosophes* generally held to some version of hedonism. Psychologically, hedonism—the view that man seeks pleasure and flees pain—is almost self-evident. But as an ethical doctrine—that man should in fact seek pleasure and flee pain—it is far from obvious. Indeed, many *philosophes* softened this glorification of selfishness in one form or another. Diderot, joining a whole school of Scottish philosophers, argued that men have sympathy for others as instinctively as they have love for themselves. Others followed Claude Helvétius (1715–1771), who preached a rudimentary Utilitarianism—a kind of hedonism that holds that pleasure should be extended as widely as possible. It was Jeremy Bentham (1748–1832), who developed Utilitarianism into a comprehensive philosophy. Carrying the Enlightenment into the early nineteenth century, Bentham became a great legal reformer on the basis of utilitarian doctrine: the increase of pleasure and the decrease of pain involved certain social policies, including humane punishment of criminals. It also involved education, for the ignorant and vicious mistook certain acts for pleasures, or indulged in certain pleasures that would later give them grave pains. Thus, in Bentham as in other *philosophes,* warm humanitarianism was dressed up in the cool vocabulary of science.

These assumptions of the Enlightenment, in philosophy, psychology, or ethics, have this in common: they are secular. They dispense with supernatural, religious justifications of human activity. Even for the *philosophes* who believed in God, their God was no more than the inventor of the rules of the game; but the game itself had to be played by man alone.

These assumptions were subversive of the Christian view of the world. Yet during the first half of the eighteenth century, the writings of the *philosophes* had evoked much amusement and little retaliation. Locke's writings had been subjected to scathing criticism by conservative clergymen, but his freedom was never in danger, and good Christians found that even if they could not accept all of Locke's *Essay*, they could read and even learn from it. In the decades after Locke's death, David Hume referred to himself as an "infidel," but was dismayed to discover that his works caused almost no scandal at all.

Voltaire In France, Voltaire's prosperous career was testimony that radicalism could pay, if it was witty. The son of respectable middle-class parents, François-Marie Arouet had been intended for the law, but chose poetry instead. Not long after he graduated from the fashionable Jesuit school Louis-le-Grand, where he met the sons of leading Paris families, he began to frequent elegant, impious circles. There he exercised his wit, to his own advancement and the amusement of others. After an eleven-months' arrest in the Bastille for impudent verses against the Regents he emerged with a tragedy, *Oedipe*, and with a new name, "de Voltaire." The tragedy was a

J. A. Houdon's bust of Voltaire reveals the keen intelligence and astonishing vigor of the subject. Like so many of the influential writers of his time, Voltaire was a prodigious worker. The first edition of his complete works filled seventy octavo volumes, and his subject matter embraced social criticism, drama, the short story, legal reform, politics, philosophy, and history. (The Louvre.)

success, so was the name. A few years after *Oedipe*, "the successor to Corneille and Racine" turned to the epic. During the 1720's, he published several versions of his *Henriade*, a rapturous paean on his favorite French king, Henri IV. But his career took a more serious turn through a petty quarrel with a dissolute aristocrat in the winter of 1725–24. This adventure landed him in the Bastille once again. Freed after several weeks of comfortable imprisonment, Voltaire went to England, and there experienced the pleasures of a free government and a relatively open society. The result of his stay was his conversion to Newtonianism, a close knowledge of English Deism, admiration for liberal political institutions, and commitment to free speech and religious toleration. All these impressions were collected in his book on England, the *Philosophical Letters*, published in France in 1734. These "letters" poured forth wry praise for Quakers, extolled religious diversity and toleration, idealized a society dominated by a House of Commons, and described the enviable life led by English men of letters. The book got him into trouble, but not for political reasons: Voltaire had appended a lengthy refutation of Pascal's "misanthropy," which struck the authorities as irreligious. But Voltaire was not imprisoned. He left town and spent several blissful, hardworking years at the château of his bluestocking mistress, Madame du Châtelet. With her, he studied the Bible, Newton and Leibniz, and modern history. During the 1730's and 1740's, Voltaire's urge to publish irreverent works became more irresistible than ever. But his popularity and his wealth increased. While his notorious irreligion kept him out of the coveted *Académie française* until 1746, and while he learned to cloak his most dangerous views, it can hardly be said that the opinions of the Enlightenment were being stifled in France.

Deism and Materialism Voltaire, like most of the other *philosophes* of the early generation, was a Deist. Deism, in some aspects an offshoot of latitudinarian Protestantism, in others a reflection of antique pagan speculation, ridiculed miracles, derided special Providence, uncovered contradictions in the Bible, and set up a short list of simple, rational dogmas: the universe is as orderly and intricate as a watch; it had been created and set in motion by a Great Watchmaker; the moral law under which men live is almost self-evident, derived from the nature of man and the universe, and hence everywhere the same.

While Voltaire always remained a Deist, the younger generation pushed the Enlightenment further. David Hume developed a skeptical theory of knowledge, first in the masterly *Treatise of Human Nature* (1739 and 1740) and later in more accessible works, which were devastating critiques not only of Christianity but of Deism as well. Another rival to Deism was materialism, which had been implied in Descartes, playfully developed in the Epicureanism of the late seventeenth century, and was now established as a full-fledged philosophical alternative to Christian or Deist explanations of the world. Materialism emerged as a serious philosophy in the witty, doctrinaire *Man a Machine* (1748) by the French physician La Mettrie

(1709–1751). Here all phenomena were derived from matter, nature was postulated as a self-sufficient whole, and the Divine Watchmaker was dismissed as unnecessary. In the second half of the century, materialism recruited some of the most notable of *philosophes,* including Diderot and the baron Holbach, who published the atheist tracts of others and a whole series of materialist works of his own, most notoriously the *System of Nature* (1770), to which Diderot lent his literary skills.

Diderot and the Encyclopedia This growing radicalism in religion was at once the expression and the cause of a growing tension between the Enlightenment and the Old Regime. The first signs of serious troubles came

Diderot by Louis Michel Van Loo (1767). Not only famous as the editor of the *Encyclopédie,* Denis Diderot was also the author of *Le Père de famille,* which became a model for "bourgeois drama," *La Religieuse,* a psychological novel, and *Le Neveu de Rameau,* a satire in dialogue form. One may wonder at the output of a man working with pen and ink, with no typewriter or copying machine! (The Louvre.)

in France, with the imprisonment of Diderot. In 1749, Diderot was sent to Vincennes (a far less palatable place of detention than the Bastille) for several of his materialist writings, especially his *Letter on the Blind.* Diderot was the son of a prosperous provincial craftsman, and had early thought of entering the Church. But he soon lost his religious vocation and came to Paris, where he made an uncertain living as a journalist and translator from the English. A fine classicist, a bold intellectual adventurer, Diderot moved from Catholicism to materialism. After several weeks of solitary confinement and less stringent imprisonment, Diderot was released, largely upon pressure from a group of publishers for whom he had been editing an Encyclopedia since 1747.

Generally writing an Encyclopedia is a harmless chore, a piece of tedious drudgery for the editors and ponderous information for the reader. This Encyclopedia, too, was drudgery for Diderot, who wrote many articles and supervised many contributors. True, for several years he had the able assistance of Jean le Rond d'Alembert (1717–1783), mathematician and *philosophe,* but most of the editorial labors rested on him. As Diderot conceived of it, his Encyclopedia was anything but innocuous; rather, it was a machine to "change the general way of thinking." With more or less candor—usually with less—the authors, who included most of the celebrated *philosophes,* Montesquieu, Voltaire, and Holbach, covertly championed toleration, slyly ridiculed religious practices, and scorned superstition. But in their hundreds of straightforward articles on crafts, industry, and science, they also popularized Newtonian physics and Newtonian methods, encouraged the use of modern techniques and a rationalist view of the world.

The first volume of the Encyclopedia came off the press in 1751, and until 1757 (down to Volume VII) all went fairly well. Then came the turning point, not only in the history of the Encyclopedia, but of the Enlightenment itself. Early in 1758, d'Alembert decided to withdraw from the enterprise. He had written an appreciative article on Geneva that had aroused much criticism. D'Alembert had praised the Genevan clergy for their intelligent freedom from superstition, and described them as if they were practically all Deists. There was some truth in this description, but it was hardly politic to broadcast it in a reference work that had by then acquired a great reputation. Shaken by d'Alembert's desertion, Diderot determined to persevere. Then, in July, there appeared Helvétius's *On the Mind,* a psychological and ethical treatise committed to hedonism. The book had been approved by a royal censor, but more alert readers objected to its philosophy. Helvétius's book is not a masterpiece, but it demonstrated to the defenders of the old order just how far irreligion might go. The censor who had approved the book was fired, and authority after authority fulminated publicly against philosophic impiety. Helvétius was coupled with the Encyclopedia, and in 1759 the Encyclopedia was suppressed. Work on it continued underground.

Intellectuals and the State These events were only the most startling symptoms of an approaching crisis between the forces of stability and the

Quentin de la Tour's Portrait of Madame de Pompadour. Madame de Pompadour was one of Louis XV's favorites. Elegant and cultivated, she helped to found the royal porcelain factory at Sèvres and took great interest in the Gobelin tapestries. This pastel portrait shows her surrounded by the trappings of the Enlightenment, including a volume of the controversial Encyclopedia (next to the globe), which had recently been published. (The Louvre.)

forces of change. The temper of this crisis varied from state to state, but it emerged everywhere. Great Britain had had its Revolution, and British writers could publish their works on theology, economics, and aesthetics with relative impunity. Yet even here David Hume's timid friends held him back from publishing his *Dialogues Concerning Natural Religion.* In the Italian states, in which the ideas of the Enlightenment had considerable popularity, these ideas were translated into policy in the 1760's. In the German states, with their severe authoritarian regimes, the *Aufklärung,* as the Enlightenment was called, had no opportunity for political action. Thus in this critical period, men like Gotthold Ephraim Lessing (1729–1791) poured their reforming energies into liberating the German stage from French influences and arguing fine points of classical scholarship or Christian theology. It was in France, where the contest between authorities and *philosophes* was most closely balanced, that the Enlightenment was most aggressive.

THE ENEMY OF THE ENLIGHTENMENT: CHRISTIANITY

Among educated men and women, religious fervor was on the decline in the eighteenth century. Yet, despite this decline, and in some respects because of it, the *philosophes* launched a serious assault on Christianity in the 1760's. Rich *philosophes* like Holbach ran a factory turning out anti-Christian tracts. Keen analysts like Hume uncovered the weakness of evidence for miracles. Fervent humanitarians like Rousseau denounced a religion that relied on force and external observances. Even the Germans developed a religion of humanity far removed from the Christian story.

The most notorious antireligious campaign was launched by Voltaire shortly after the suppression of the Encyclopedia, with the slogan *Écrasez l'infâme.* The "infamous thing" was superstition, clerical power, the Inquisition, the influence of priests over education. Voltaire, in a word, was an anticlerical, picturing the priests of all religions as lazy, vicious, intolerant, and ignorant. But he went further: everything that goes beyond the practice of natural religion (that is, the worshipful acknowledgment of a creator and the rational exercise of decency) is superstition. Even at its mildest, superstition is a disease; all beliefs that foster superstition, and all institutions that sustain it, must be destroyed or closely supervised. Voltaire's *infame,* then, is any organized religion, both as system of beliefs and as institution.

To wipe out this *infame,* Voltaire and his allies employed many techniques. Voltaire wrote simply, repeated his message, tied his attacks to specific anecdotes, and kept his readers' interest with his wit and his unsurpassed ability to tell a story. The most effective weapon was the *Philosophical Dictionary,* published in 1764 and reissued in larger editions in the following years. This was an alphabetical compendium that ridiculed miracles, denigrated saints, exposed contradictions in biblical history, attacked the Jews of the Bible, preached toleration, and denounced the persecuting spirit of the religious mind. Thus the *philosophes* pushed their civilization further in the direction of secularism.

THE PROGRAM OF THE *PHILOSOPHES*

To many critics of the Enlightenment, then and now, such an effort appeared merely negative. But to the *philosophes,* destruction and construction went hand in hand. Reason could not triumph until unreason had been unsaddled; the advent of toleration must wait upon the conquest of intolerance. "What shall we put in its place, you ask," Voltaire threw at a defender of Christianity. "What shall we put in its place? What! A ferocious beast has sucked the blood of my family; I tell you to get rid of that beast, and you ask me what shall we put in its place!"

But the *philosophes* did have something to put in its place. Their writings offer a program of social and political betterment, which can be summed up as toleration, secularism, reasonableness, humanity, and freedom.

The *philosophes'* demand for toleration reflected the intellectuals' need to speak freely and their conviction that all men are ignorant and interdependent. If men are brothers in a mysterious universe, they must learn to live in peace by respecting the opinions of others. In practice, this meant guarantees for free speech, the abolition of censorship, cessation of persecution for ideas, and the elimination of the very idea of heresy. To be sure, the *philosophes* themselves were often intolerant of their critics, but at least some of that was intolerance of the intolerant: they were mainly attacking those who would prevent them from expressing themselves.

This demand for toleration flowed from the conviction that men are brothers, and from the absence of belief: religious indifference. In fact, the *philosophes* were secularists. While their prescriptions varied slightly, most of them considered the eighteenth-century Church of England, with its polite ceremonial and political innocuousness, as an ideal institution. The *philosophes* desired not only the creation of a secular society, but also propagation of a belief in a secular universe governed by unalterable laws. Just as the natural sciences were eliminating the need for supernatural explanations, so the advance of rational statecraft and the emergence of a reasonable public opinion were now, in the *philosophes'* view, eliminating the need for a strong clergy.

Implied in both toleration and secularism was reasonableness. This idea introduces a difficult and controversial point of interpretation. The Enlightenment is generally called "The Age of Reason," and, used with care, this label accurately describes the age. But it is usually taken to imply, first, that the *philosophes* had a naive faith in the power of reason, expressed in an optimistic theory of progress, and second, that the *philosophes* disdained emotion. Passion had to be, as it were, rediscovered by the Romantics. In truth, few *philosophes* had a theory of progress. The historians among them, like Voltaire and Edward Gibbon (1737–1794), saw the past as a register of crimes and follies, and the present as a mixture of reason and superstition. Most of the *philosophes* were ready to express a moderate optimism about the conquest of ignorance and suffering, but, with few exceptions, their hope was held back by a realistic appreciation of the power of habit.

A similar caution holds for the *philosophes'* attitude toward passion. Most of the *philosophes* had a sensitive appreciation of the place of emotions in conduct. The observation that reason is, and ought to be, the slave of the passions was the foundation of David Hume's philosophy. In one of his first philosophical writings, Denis Diderot expressed a similar view: "People think that reason will be wronged if we say something in behalf of its rivals; nevertheless, it is the passions alone—and great passions—which can lift the soul to great things." This high valuation of the passionate side of man runs through Diderot's work. And it plays a significant part in most philosophic speculation of the age.

Rousseau's Thought The vexing question of the relation of reason to passion brings up the tormented genius of the Enlightenment, Jean Jacques Rousseau. He was the most famous representative of the "sentimental" wing of the Enlightenment, and he has often been taken as the harbinger of the Romantic movement. Nevertheless, though he quarreled with his fellows, Rousseau belongs with the Enlightenment. Like the other *philosophes,* Rousseau loved the Greek and Roman classics, and he joined the anticlerical campaign of the 1760's. Like many *philosophes,* he was a Deist. But unlike them, he engaged in a profound critique of civilization.

Born in Geneva, as a young man he led a wandering life full of turmoil, which included a temporary conversion to Roman Catholicism, and a liaison with an older woman—"Maman." In the early 1740's, he came to Paris. There he mingled in philosophic circles, became Diderot's close friend, wrote articles on music for the Encyclopedia, and began a life-long association with an ignorant servant girl. By the late 1750's, after his essays on civilization had made him famous, he became estranged from his erstwhile associates, and the rest of his life was an unhappy series of flights from shelter to shelter, and of miserable quarrels. Always extremely sensitive to his surroundings, self-questioning, volatile, Rousseau's neurotic instability made him an exciting but difficult companion when he was young; his psychotic delusions of persecution made him a perpetual outcast in his later years.

Not all of Rousseau's fears of persecution were imaginary. His writings expressed, with a boldness and fervor unmatched in the century, the discontents of sensitive souls with the artificial and mendacious society of their time. The book that made Rousseau famous, his *Discourse on the Progress of the Arts and Sciences* (1750), was a prize-winning answer to a question set by the Academy of Dijon. Rousseau argued, with more rhetoric than logic, that man's innate goodness had been corrupted by the advances of culture. In a second essay, the less successful but far more discriminating *Discourse on the Origin of Inequality* (1754), Rousseau developed a hypothetical history of civilization, in which the origin of property appears as the clue to much that was evil in the eighteenth century. This *Discourse* has given Rousseau the reputation of a primitivist, but he never used the phrase "the noble savage." Rather, he distinguished between several prepolitical states of mankind, and deplored the passing of the one in which men had lived in a relatively simple society. Civilization had brought inestimable benefits, such as law, but it had also exaggerated natural physical inequalities and created other, artificial inequalities.

As Rousseau's thought matured, the outlines of his philosophy of culture began to emerge. In three masterpieces, he explored the relation of reason and passion—in personal relations with his *Nouvelle Héloïse* (1760), in education with *Emile* (1762), in politics with his *Social Contract.* These, and

One of the most emotionally admired reformers of the latter half of the eighteenth century was Jean Jacques Rousseau. Here, Rousseau on a pedestal, observes Philosophy, holding the torch, as she discovers the "Truth." Apparently the artist thought that Rousseau's *Social Contract* was the greatest source of Truth and that his *Emile*, at the lower right hand corner, was in second place. (Bibliothèque Nationale, Paris.)

other important works (including the celebrated *Confessions*), show that Rousseau was not a primitivist: human nature cannot go back to some state of innocence, but must go forward to create both a better man and a better society. Hence his book on education and his book on politics were not only published close together, but should be read together. The possibilities for human and social renovation exist; because man is good by nature; it is evil social institutions, not man's disobedience to God, that have ruined him—a doctrine that set Rousseau into irreconcilable conflict with Christianity. One grave social ill is the atrophy of emotions: family feeling, the warmth of friendship, the glow of honesty. The emotions come first, both in time and in importance, and when they are starved, a cold calculation that is a poor substitute for reason takes over. But while feeling—the effusion of sentiment, the love of the outdoors, and the admiration of simplicity—must be liberated from stifling social conventions and the lies of politeness, reason too must not be neglected. In his epoch-making *Emile,* Rousseau argued that the pupil must not be made to learn abstract concepts, or even reading, until he is ready for it. This is not how his contemporaries and his admiring followers read him: for the German *Sturm und Drang,* Rousseau was the prophet of anarchy, the enemy of all rules, the destroyer of law and self-restraint. But Rousseau himself did not hold such views. He did not reject reason, but wanted reason to be securely grounded in feeling—only then would the reasonable man flourish.

The Dignity of Man The Enlightenment, then, was an age of reason in the sense that the *philosophes* preached the elimination of supernatural explanations of the world and wanted to substitute scientific methods of observation, experimentation, and the application of science to society. That this desire for social engineering was a matter of reason *and* feeling is obvious from the *philosophes'* humanitarianism. Whether atheists or Deists, the *philosophes* preached the dignity of man, and had a high esteem for human life. As late as the seventeenth century, kindly and cultivated men and women had visited executions or insane asylums for entertainment. The *philosophes* strenuously objected to all this. Insanity they conceived simply as a disease; the torture of prisoners or cruel executions they fought with increasing fury as the eighteenth century went on.

Voltaire, once again, took the lead. He had achieved fame as a poet and notoriety as an irreligious wit; in the 1760's he became the most famous man in Europe with his campaigns in behalf of the victims of the French judicial system. These began in 1762 with the notorious Calas case. Late in 1761, a young Huguenot in Toulouse had been found hanged in his father's shop, and his father was convicted of murder, tortured, and executed, even though the probabilities were that the moody young man had committed suicide. Voltaire took up this obscure case, wrote letters and pamphlets, and spread word of it all over Europe. As a result, the memory of the elder Calas was vindicated and Voltaire—his anger fanned further by similar cases—launched into a wholesale indictment of the French legal system. He was much buoyed by the appearance of *On Crimes and Punishment,* a humanitarian legal treatise by the Milanese jurist Cesare Beccaria (1738–1794). Beccaria was a utilitarian: he argued that the supreme object of the state is the greatest happiness of the greatest number. This principle applied to crime: the first task of the state is to find ways of preventing crime; its second task is to punish criminals as leniently as it could do rationally and safely. Laws must be clear and public; punishment must be proportionate to the crime; torture is barbaric and irrational; great care must be taken in the definition of crime. In Voltaire's campaigns and Beccaria's book, the humaneness of the Enlightenment found moving expression.

The Freedom of Man There remains a final, political plank to the platform of the Enlightment: freedom. The *philosophes,* seeing man as at least potentially autonomous, agreed that political institutions should give man scope for the exercise of his rationality. They did not agree on how much scope was practicable and what institutions were best calculated to insure freedom. In addition, they found themselves in disagreement because they were involved in the controversies of their own time. The political thought of the *philosophes,* therefore, must be seen as a judicious mixture of theoretical considerations and practical involvement.

A striking example of this mixture is Montesquieu's treatise *On the Spirit of the Laws* (1748). This great work shows Montesquieu to be a pioneer in sociology, a humanitarian, and a libertarian. As a sociologist, Montesquieu developed a correlation between forms of government and their "principle," that is, the kind of social quality best calculated to maintain a state. In addition, he worked out a theory of the relation of climate, and physical environment in general, to forms of government. This kind of thinking permitted political theorists to move from formal considerations of institutions to their social, economic, and geographical underpinnings. As a humanitarian, Montesquieu denounced harsh punishment and loose application of such terms as "treason," objected to the persecution of religious minorities, and sought to introduce legal rationality into court procedure. As a libertarian, Montesquieu extolled what he claimed was the English constitutional system of the separation of powers, by which the English preserved their freedom. This interpretation of English institutions was a misreading, but its aim was the fragmentation of power for the sake of liberty. It was here that general theory encountered concrete politics: Montesquieu's praise of England, and of "intermediary institutions" between king and people, were taken in France as support of the aristocratic position against the king.

Many *philosophes,* who honored Montesquieu's genius, therefore disagreed with his politics. Voltaire supported the royal claims to power in France, on the grounds that the French aristocracy—a neat alliance between the old nobility of the sword and the newer legal nobility of the robe—was reactionary, intent only upon preserving its freedom from burdensome taxation. This position has given Voltaire (and other *philosophes*) the reputation of being a supporter of "enlightened despotism." This notion—of an all-powerful prince legislating for the good of his people in accord with enlightened principles and upon the advice of a *philosophe*—struck many of the *philosophes* as plausible. In fact, many leading *philosophes* were closely associated with rulers. Voltaire corresponded with Catherine the Great and Frederick the Great, and spent more than two years at Frederick's court. Diderot visited Catherine the Great and wrote memoranda for her on a variety of political and educational subjects. Yet, "enlightened despotism" is too porous a sieve to contain the political ideas of the *philosophes.* Most of the *philosophes* were relativists: they defended absolutism against powerful aristocracies not because they were against freedom but because they distrusted the aristocracies; they thought that relatively uncivilized nations, like the Russians or Prussians, needed firm guidance. But Voltaire, who supported both Catherine's and Frederick's reigns, also believed in parliamentary government for England and the Netherlands, and could even glimpse the virtues of democratic institutions for such literate countries as Switzerland.

Rousseau's Politics The great philosopher of political democracy, one of the few to develop a consistent system in the Enlightenment, was Rousseau. His underlying principle is the compatibility of liberty and equality. In grossly inegalitarian systems, liberty is purely formal, and the poor cannot be said to be free if they must sell themselves to the rich. Equality, therefore, far from being the enemy of liberty, is its precondition. Rousseau's second principle was the conviction that free political institutions can work only if the members of the community have a certain moral character: honesty, devotion to public affairs, coupled with a desire for the general welfare. A society of men, we might say, educated in the manner of Rousseau's *Emile,* could make freedom work. Others could not. Rousseau distinguished between the "will of all," the desires of a community of self-centered men added together, and the "general will," the true interest of the community, which found expression only if citizens made public decisions with the welfare of the community in their minds. Finally, Rousseau argued that man's freedom can be compatible with his submission to authority only if man is at once ruler and subject, obeying laws which he himself has made.

Rousseau never forgot that he was a citizen of Geneva, and hence praised small and disparaged large states. He admired ancient Sparta as described by Plutarch, and advocated personal discipline and the concentration of loyalties on the community. It is not that his work was contradictory: it was held together by the conviction that man is good, has been corrupted by institutions, and can be rescued by a total renovation. But his work influenced many incompatible movements, and his name was invoked by many disciples, including some who made the revolution in France, even though Rousseau had always, and rightly, described himself as the most conservative of men.

CONCLUSION

By the early 1780's, most of the great *philosophes* were dead. David Hume had died in 1776, Voltaire and Rousseau in 1778, d'Alembert in 1783, and Diderot in 1784. A group of younger men carried on their work: the brilliant mathematician and propagandist Condorcet (1743–1794), the friend and biographer of Voltaire who paradoxically died in the Terror; and the public servant Turgot (1727–1781), who was the *philosophes'* ideal, trying in vain to reform the state as chief minister to Louis XVI during two fateful years. By the time the great generation had passed from the scene, many of their ideas were, if not commonplace, widely accepted. They gave voice to inchoate grievances, and offered practical men alternatives in the sphere of law and government. In countries other than France, they were a great force for modernization. But in addition to being a powerful machine for bringing educated Europeans into the modern world, they were also a reflection of forces, of the beginnings of industrialism, of the new science, and of urbanization. It is this double aspect—this adaptation of ideas that were becoming dominant, and the formulation of humanitarian and libertarian principles—that made the men of the Enlightenment more influential than any other group of intellectuals ever has been.

FURTHER READING

The most impressive study of this subject is Ernst Cassirer, * *The Philosophy of the Enlightenment* (tr. 1951), complex, centered on the Germans, and highly rewarding. A very different picture of the Enlightenment emerges in parts II and III of Alfred Cobban's lucid and rather more popular *In Search of Humanity* (1960). For a series of essays on the French Enlightenment criticizing widely held notions and close to Cobban, see Peter Gay, *The Party of Humanity* (1964). Gay's * *The Enlightenment: An Interpretation,* Vol. I, *The Rise of Modern Paganism* (1966), and Vol. II, *The Science of Freedom* (1969) offer a comprehensive interpretation of the Enlightenment in Europe and America. A lucid sketch of the French *philosophes'* political environment and program is Kingsley Martin, * *French Liberal Thought in the Eighteenth Century* (1929). R. V. Sampson, *Progress in the Age of Reason* (1956), is a nuanced discussion on a subject handled more naively, but still usefully, in J. B. Bury's * *Idea of Progress* (1920). The last should be read in conjunction with Henry Vyverberg's persuasive *Historical Pessimism in the French Enlightenment* (1958).

On a few leading figures, see Robert Shackleton, *Montesquieu* (1961); F. N. Brailsford, * *Voltaire* (1935); to be supplemented by Peter Gay, * *Voltaire's Politics* (1959). The best, but far from satisfactory biography of Rousseau is by F. C. Green (1955). Arthur M. Wilson's *Diderot* (1972), supersedes all earlier efforts. Douglas Dakin's *Turgot and the "Ancien Régime" in France* (1939) is comprehensive. Ernest C. Mossner's *Life of David Hume* (1954) is full and reliable, but needs to be filled out on his ideas by Norman Kemp Smith, *The Philosophy of David Hume* (1941), and J. A. Passmore's *Hume's Intentions* (1952). A. D. Lindsay's *Kant* (1934) is a clear introduction to a seminal thinker.

*Books available in paperback are marked with an asterisk.

3 The Emergence of Two New Powers: Prussia and Russia

Until the eighteenth century, Prussia and Russia were too weak or too remote to play an influential role in European affairs; but in this century, these eastern countries came to wield an influence that was to persist and grow. What happened in the previous centuries to make it possible for Prussia to serve in the nineteenth as the nucleus of the German Empire and, in the twentieth, as the heart of the Weimar Republic and of the Nazi Third Reich? How could Russia, once a weak and insignificant territory on the Moscow plain, come to straddle two continents in the twentieth century?

It is not only to try to understand our present-day world that we need to explain the rise of Prussia and Russia in early modern times. Such an understanding is also necessary in order to comprehend the eighteenth-century changes in the European state-system, as reflected by the "Diplomatic Revolution" of the 1750's. This shift in historic alliances was more than a cessation of hostilities between the French Bourbon kings and the Austrian Habsburgs. It was a response to fundamental changes in the power structure of Europe, most notably of eastern Europe. Let us turn in this chapter, then, to the old kingdoms and empires of the East—to Habsburg Austria, the Ottoman Empire, Sweden and Poland—and to two rising powers, Brandenburg-Prussia and Russia.

THE HABSBURG MONARCHY

In 1683, the Muslim ruler of the Ottoman Turkish empire gathered his polyglot forces for an assault on the greatest bastion of eastern Europe: the glittering city of Vienna, gateway to Christendom and home of the Austrian Habsburg emperors. After several months of bombardment and siege, during which it appeared that the city would fall, imperial armies led by a Polish king, Jan Sobieski (ruled 1674–1697), succeeded in routing the numerically superior Turkish forces. The last Crusade had been launched and won. The victory was trumpeted throughout Europe.

In 1715, the Austrian Habsburgs ruled a mighty realm. In the West, they had been cut off by the treaties of Utrecht, Rastatt, and Baden from the crown of Spain, but they still held substantial parts of Italy and the Netherlands. In central Europe, their lands ran from Silesia in the north through Bohemia and Moravia down to the heartlands of the Habsburg heritage in Austria, Styria, Carinthia, Carniola and the Tyrol—all the way south to the head of the Adriatic Sea. The rebellious Hungarians had been pacified. The Turks were at bay. For the moment, at least, Charles VI (1711–1740) was secure enough on his several thrones. The emperor's main concern was that his wife seemed unable to produce male children and thus the line of succession was in doubt. He accordingly persuaded the Habsburg family to agree to a document known as the Pragmatic Sanction. This proclaimed, first, the indivisibility of all Habsburg lands and, second, that, failing a direct male heir, the realms should pass to his daughter Maria Theresa. He went on to try to ensure the viability of this agreement by obtaining the formal endorsements of his several realms, as expressed in their Estates, and of the other European courts. The last twenty years of his reign were largely devoted to these efforts, which were partially successful. After his death in 1740, some of the foreign powers failed to honor their promises, but Maria Theresa did inherit his throne without serious internal opposition.

Emperor Charles VI of Austria (1685–1740), once a chief contender for the Spanish throne and the father of Maria Theresa, inherited the eastern Habsburg empire in 1711 at age 26. His elaborate costume seems as anachronistic as was his dynastic empire in the eighteenth century. (Kunsthistorisches Museum, Vienna.)

During his lifetime, Charles was not able to contribute substantially to the unification of his realms, partly, perhaps, because he was unable to find a team of capable administrators like that developed by some of his contemporaries: in England under Walpole, in France under Fleury, and in Brandenburg-Prussia under Frederick William. The next attempts to assemble a state out of the component Habsburg realms were left to Maria Theresa and her ministers.

POLAND AND SCANDINAVIA

Once a formidable eastern power, Poland very nearly lacked political form at this time. The kings of Poland were elected by the principal nobles who, jealous of their own power, tended to select rulers who could not, in fact, rule. The local landlords met in regional diets. Each of these sent a representative to the Central Diet which stood to Poland as the Diet of the Holy Roman Empire stood to Germany. Because any member of the Diet could cause it to be dissolved simply by using his right of free and absolute veto (*liberum veto*) and because the members of the Diet seldom agreed on anything save the necessity for maintaining their noble privileges, the Diet could not serve to unify or organize Polish political life. The result was anarchy. The king had no army, virtually no revenues, and no bureaucracy. Yet, geographically, Poland was situated so that its frontiers touched those of three of the major powers of eighteenth-century Europe: Russia, Prussia, and Austria-Hungary. At least two of these powers were highly expansive. As a result, Poland as a state was on the road to extinction.

Even before the death of Charles XII in 1718, the once great seventeenth-century Swedish empire in the Baltic region was being diminished. The conclusion of the Great Northern War (1700–1721)—the Baltic phase of the War of Spanish Succession—drove the Swedes off the south coast of the Baltic Sea and confined them to Sweden proper and to present-day Finland. Having lost so much during the wars they now felt that an oligarchy of nobles as rulers would be more pacific than the previous more-or-less absolute monarchs. Accordingly, in a quiet revolution, Swedish administration was put into the hands of a council of nobles in which the monarch could be outvoted. The affairs of the *Riksdag* (Estates General) were given over to a secret committee dominated by aristocrats. For a time, the aristocracy enjoyed what the Swedes call their "Era of Freedom." In Denmark-Norway, on the contrary, King Frederick IV (1699–1730) managed to maintain the apparatus of monarchical centralization.

THE OTTOMAN EMPIRE

Despite the fact that the Turks still held Bessarabia, Wallachia, Bulgaria, Macedon, Serbia, Bosnia, and peninsular and insular Greece in Europe, as well as North Africa and the entire Near East, and despite the fact that they were to continue to hold a substantial part of the Balkan area until well into the twentieth century, the Ottoman Empire in the eighteenth century was already an anachronism. In theory an absolute despot, the sultan was a prisoner in his gilded palace. The administration was in the hands of officials who sought to keep themselves in power through systematic corruption and intrigue. The Janissary troops, once the best disciplined and most effective soldiers in the world, had become virtually an independent corporation, not really under the sultan's control. High finance and commerce were carried on by Greeks and Jews. The Empire chose its administrators for the European provinces from a number of influential Greek families. In sum, the Ottoman Empire was losing the capacity to manage its own affairs. Its continued existence in Europe depended upon the inability of powers like Venice, Austria-Hungary, and Russia to agree upon a partition of its territory and upon the fact that France, Holland, and England were not ready to see the status quo in southeastern Europe upset.

BRANDENBURG-PRUSSIA

Unlike the Turks, the Poles, and the Swedes, the German-speaking people of Brandenburg-Prussia in north central Germany were on the rise. They were led, in the seventeenth century, by an especially able series of rulers. Fathers and sons, they were members of the Hohenzollern family, a dynasty that seems to have originated in one of a thousand hilltop castles in the Swabian hills of southwestern Germany. In the early years of the fifteenth century, the Hohenzollerns acquired the duchy of Brandenburg, consisting of four "marks": the Middle Mark, which included Berlin and the town of Brandenburg; the Old Mark, on the west bank of the Elbe; the New Mark, east of the Oder; and the Uckermark, comprising the territory on both sides of the Ucker and Priegnitz Rivers to the north of the Middle Mark. None of these territories was anything to boast about, consisting for the most part of sandy plains. Although abounding in lakes, forests, and waterways, these lands were not fertile or productive of great revenues. As for the capital city of Berlin, the common saying was that by nature it was the best of burying grounds.

In the second decade of the seventeenth century, the Hohenzollerns continued to add territories to their scattered possessions. Thanks to the extinction of the Cleves-Jülich line, the claims of the elector[1] of Brandenburg to that family's territories were honored and they were eventually incorporated into the Hohenzollern holdings. In 1618, yet another branch of the Hohenzollerns died out, leaving the electors of Brandenburg heirs to the Polish fief of Prussia and giving them another capital at Königsberg. Finally, in 1637, they came into possession of the province of Pomerania. This opened up new vistas of power along the Baltic and eventually brought them into direct conflict with Sweden over the possession of the coastline from west of Stralsund to east of Königsberg.

The acquisition of the Cleves inheritance brought the Hohenzollerns into active conflict during the Thirty Years' War with France, the Netherlands, Austria, and Spain, all of whom desired the strategic territory. The war itself was potentially destructive to the Hohenzollern position. Brandenburg was one of those parts of Germany that suffered most severely from

[1]The margrave was also an electoral prince (*Kurfürst*) in that he was one of those who participated in the election of the Holy Roman Emperor.

the devastation. Large numbers of villages were destroyed and a substantial percentage of the population wandered or was recruited away. As a result, the countryside, not very fertile in normal times, could barely support the electoral army of 5,000 men. Only distant Prussia was spared major devastation.

The Great Elector It was during this unpropitious period that one of the very able Hohenzollerns, Frederick William, the "Great Elector" (1640–1688), became ruler of Brandenburg and of the other Hohenzollern possessions. He saw the necessity of ridding his territory of foreign troops and reasserting his authority over the recalcitrant Estates of his various domains. In 1653, the Great Elector induced the most docile of his Estates, that of Brandenburg, to grant him the right to levy a direct tax (the *Contribution*) under the condition that the nobility should be exempt from it. Having thus established both an income and a precedent, the Great Elector proceeded to break the power of the outlying Estates (for instance, those of the Rhenish provinces) by force, quartering troops, and arresting recalcitrant noblemen where necessary.[2] The pressure proved successful: while none of the local assemblies had to be permanently dissolved, the right of the ruler to levy a general, permanent tax was recognized throughout his domain. He could now be virtually independent.

Frederick William also devoted himself to improving his position on the international scene. When the Swedes invaded Brandenburg during the Swedish-Polish war, the Great Elector led his forces against them, and, in 1675, to the surprise of all Europe, defeated the supposedly invincible Swedish army.

His successor, Elector Frederick III (1688–1713), drew permanent gains from his political and military maneuvers. As a reward for aid in his quarrels with Louis XIV, the Habsburg emperor bestowed upon Frederick the right to assume the title of king in his Prussian possession (outside the Holy Roman Empire), and Frederick III, Elector of Brandenburg, became Frederick I, King *in* Prussia. (The word "in" instead of "of" recognized Frederick's continued subservience to the emperor in his German possessions.)

Frederick William I In 1713, Frederick I was succeeded by Frederick William I (1713–1740), whose reforms in Brandenburg-Prussia ultimately brought that country to the front rank in Europe. These reforms were primarily administrative and economic in nature—in fact, the work of this ruler can best be discussed and understood as a case study in the successful application of mercantilist doctrines in government. It will be remembered that mercantilism was the attempt to enhance the power of the state through careful management of the internal and external economic affairs of its populace.

Ever since the time of Frederick William, the Great Elector, the rulers of Brandenburg had been familiar with the doctrines of mercantilism and

[2]For an interesting parallel see Louis XIV's use of the *dragonnades* (Part X, Chapter 3).

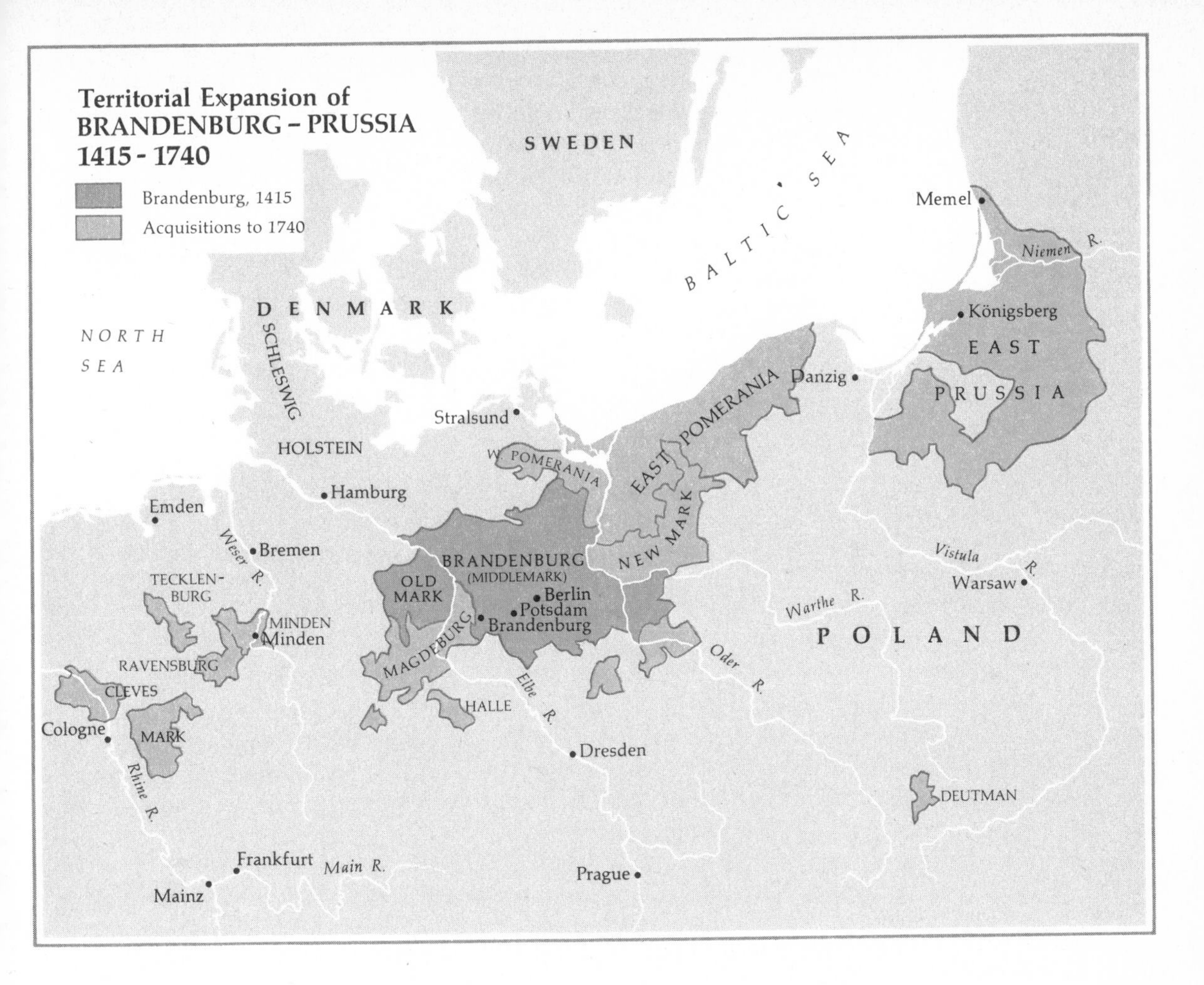

had attempted to put them into effect chiefly by trying to eliminate economic frontiers between their various territories and to create a unified tariff barrier against foreign states. But Frederick William I was the first to put the doctrines of mercantilism successfully into effect on a large scale. The power of the state was the center of his concern. The army he saw as the major tool of state power; finances were the "sinews of war"; a large and contented populace was the foundation of efficient government; and a well-organized administrative system was necessary to assure the close link between a prosperous population and a well-filled royal treasury. At his death, he managed to leave to his successor a state much more highly organized than that he had inherited, an army twice the size of his predecessor's, a huge war treasury, and a population that had not only greatly increased but was, on the whole, content. Gradually this king *in* Prussia came to be known as the king *of* Prussia.

Encouragement of Immigration In a country as small and as sparsely populated as the Hohenzollern possession, it had long been a tradition to welcome strangers as settlers. The most notable instance of this policy was the influx of large numbers of skilled Huguenot refugees from France after the revocation of the Edict of Nantes in France in 1685. Under Frederick William I, immigrants were not only welcomed but actively recruited. The king maintained regular agents whose duty it was to encourage the immigration of respectable citizens from all over Europe. In 1732, for example, he succeeded in attracting most of the Protestants evicted by the Bishop of Salzburg. But even in years when no such wholesale migration took place, a steady stream of immigrants was maintained by his agents, who made a point of visiting towns that had been recently afflicted by war, religious conflict, floods, fires, or any other form of disaster that would make migration attractive to its citizens. Because these agents were empowered to advance certain sums for travel and to promise land to peasants, loans to merchants, and freedom from guild restrictions to artisans, their efforts were generally successful. As we shall see later, this policy was continued by Frederick II, and it is estimated that in the 1780's roughly one-fifth of the population resulted from migrations since the 1640's. In more advanced parts of the Hohenzollern lands such as Brandenburg, the population trebled.

In order not to reduce productivity, recruits for the army were systematically found abroad or in the less economically vital segments of the local population. It was usual for noble families to send at least one of its sons into the army. Master craftsmen of skilled trades, on the other hand, were exempt from all army service as were those peasants who were the sole support of their families.

Industrial Reform To make sure that his flock of subjects prospered sufficiently to be able to pay taxes in hard cash, Frederick William attempted, first of all, to curb the nobility's tendency to squander money abroad on foreign luxuries. He increased the taxes on all luxuries imported into Brandenburg-Prussia while at the same time he encouraged the local output of such goods. He was particularly interested in increasing cloth manufacture, partly because of the necessity to clothe his army in uniform blue and partly because it seemed for a while as if Brandenburg-Prussia would be able to replace England as supplier of cloth to Russia. Although he was unsuccessful in this endeavor, the growing demands of his army and the establishment of a central warehouse in Berlin, where cloth and uniforms were assembled, contributed significantly to the development of internal manufacture. The army also stimulated the economy by helping to keep money in circulation, since soldiers were billeted among the local population and usually paid for what they consumed.

Among the greatest obstacles to mercantilist economic reform were old-fashioned guild restrictions. Frederick William objected to the guilds not only because they tended to discriminate against the foreign skilled labor that he worked so hard to import and because they impeded even the employment of workers from other parts of his realms, but also because they encouraged the existence of wandering journeymen—an unsupervised, foot-loose element which seemed to represent a menace to a well-organized state. Between 1732 and 1735 an industrial code was drawn up which subjected the journeymen to strict state discipline and, though it recognized the existence of the guilds, in fact made them part of the state administration.

Administrative Reforms The income of the kings of Prussia was derived from their extensive private domains and from the *Contribution* or permanent direct tax which the Great Elector had wrested from the Estates. This division of the royal income into two parts had led to a dual form of administration. The private domains of the king had always been managed by *Beamte,* civil officials who formed a direct administrative body under the king and delivered the domain income to the royal treasury. Like the French *intendants,* these *Beamte* were employees of the crown and professional civil servants. The *Contribution* (direct tax) was levied by a different set of officials—*Landräte* in rural districts and *Steuerräte* in the cities. Previously representatives of the local Estates, these officials had been taken into the royal administration when the Estates yielded their major tax powers to the crown. They represented the local gentry and were in most cases elected by them—except where the king objected and nullified a particular election. In addition to being tax collectors, they fulfilled the general functions of local justices of the peace; controlling weights and measures; sampling foods; inspecting merchandise; granting liquor licenses; finding hospitals for the indigent and sick and employment for "sturdy beggars"; and in general keeping down idleness, drunkenness, and disaffection.

The advantages to the squirearchy (*Landräte*) of entering the king's administration were obvious. The nobility of Brandenburg-Prussia was notoriously poor; and, although the service of the king brought little recompense (*travailler pour le roi de Prusse*—to work for the king of Prussia—was synonymous with hard work and bad pay in eighteenth-century Europe), it did lend prestige and real, if petty, power.

The dual tax system did result in the overlapping of functions of the two central offices: the General Finance Directory, in charge of the revenue from the royal domains, and the General War Commissariat, in charge of the collection and spending of the *Contribution.* In 1723, Frederick William attempted to put an end to the wrangling this produced by combining the two bodies into the General Finance and Domains Directory, thus merging at the top two kinds of administration. Because the sale of offices was frowned upon and because officials were organized by chambers or committees, it was difficult to bribe the administrators, and Prussia enjoyed a less corrupt administration than did most other European countries of the time.

The Growth of the Army With the aid of a growing population, an improving economy, and a more efficient administration, Frederick William was able to pursue his two major aims: the accumulation of a war chest and the organization of a first-rate army. Being by nature something between a drill sergeant and a clerk, he could spend hours at his desk, adding up figures (he wore linen sleeves to protect his uniform). To revive his spirits he drilled his special regiment of giant soldiers in the newest drill devised by Leopold of Dessau. He felt no inclination to spend money on himself, his family, or his court. The Muses did not tempt him. He viewed learning from a purely utilitarian point of view and left elementary education to the church, local craftsmen, or retired soldiers. At the universities he supported only faculties of medicine, useful in producing army surgeons, and economics, useful for training administrators. He measured his success by the service he felt he had rendered the state, and the strength of his army was his principal yardstick. "Fifty thousand soldiers," he said, "are worth a million ministers."

He succeeded in increasing the army to a peacetime strength of 72,000 men or about 3.6 percent of a total population of a little over 2 million. Though he encouraged recruitment of soldiers abroad, he worked steadily at eliminating foreign officers, replacing them with the sons of the local nobility. "Junker," originally *jung Herr* meaning "young lord," became the accepted name for the noble class, which achieved in Brandenburg-Prussia a status that it had lost or was losing in other countries. The career of an officer was given added prestige by the king, who appeared regularly in uniform and who established special royal military schools for young men of noble blood.

Frederick the Great Frederick William's prudence and moderation in public affairs was in contrast to the extreme violence of his dealings with his own family. His treatment of his son Frederick was so severe that the young man tried to escape to England. He was caught, imprisoned, and forced to witness the execution of one of his friends and accomplices, a young army officer. For a while the king thought of executing the young prince as well. One of the greatest of German historians, Leopold von Ranke, believed that the state would have collapsed if young Frederick had been executed, since several generations' work of organization would thus have been destroyed.

Fortunately for the continued rise of Prussia, the rebellious prince promised to submit to his father's wishes and was permitted to survive. The result was that Brandenburg-Prussia enjoyed in the eighteenth century the services of two very able rulers of different but complementary abilities. Where Frederick William I was slow, methodical and unimaginative, a cautious builder of the machinery of state, his son, Frederick II, the Great (1740–1786), as we shall see in the next chapter, put the apparatus he inherited boldly and imaginatively to work.

ORIGINS OF THE RUSSIAN STATE

During most of modern historical times, "Mother" Russia has been in the process of becoming a mother to the varied peoples that live in the great forests and plains of eastern Europe between the Urals on the east and the

King Frederick William I of Prussia took pride in a special corps of giant grenadiers like the one shown here. Their brimless helmets were designed not only to add to their height but to make it easier to throw grenades. (Royal Library, Windsor.)

Dvina and Dniester rivers on the west. Throughout most of the Middle Ages, there had been, strictly speaking, no Russian state. The Mongols had ruled the grasslands in the south of what we today call the Soviet Union; while in the forested north, small vassal states had continued to exist by paying tribute to the Mongols or Tatars. One of these states, but by no means the largest, was the principality of Moscow or Muscovy. During most of the fifteenth and sixteenth centuries, Muscovy was an inland state cut off from the West by the great Polish-Lithuanian power which controlled the territory north and south from the eastern Baltic to the western parts of present-day Russia, including the Ukraine. Muscovy was kept from the Black and Caspian seas in the south by the Tatars, and represented only the east-central part of what is now European Russia. It was ruled by one of the princely families supposed to have descended from the Viking (*Rus*) Rurik the Red, and therefore was called "Russia." Although the Muscovite (or Russian) alphabet and religion came from the eastern part of the western world, and although there was some contact between Muscovy and the West, in many important respects Muscovy faced east. Many Muscovite notions about government and administration had been learned from the Mongols.

Then, in the second half of the fifteenth century, under one of its princes, Ivan III, "The Great" (1462–1505), Muscovy commenced to expand at the expense of other Russian principalities and Lithuania and the Tatars. Ivan managed to throw off Tatar overlordship. He married Zoë, the niece of the last Roman (Greek) emperor and began to style himself Caesar or Tsar. Territorial expansion continued during the reign of his successor, Basil III. The next ruler of Muscovy, Ivan IV, "The Terrible" (1533–1584), was officially crowned as tsar or emperor in 1547; and Muscovy (now Russia) expanded under his vigorous and often brutal leadership farther toward the Black Sea and the Caspian in the south and toward the Baltic in the north-west. Cossack warriors started the exploration and conquest of Siberia beyond the Urals, beginning a long and fruitful if sometimes interrupted Cossack collaboration with the tsarist government.[3] Ivan the Terrible engaged in a fierce and generally successful struggle with the old Russian nobility; and he created a new nobility—the "serving nobility" or *dvoryani*—of men who helped him in his wars against the Tatars.[4] Toward the end of his reign, Ivan IV lost territory to Poland and Sweden, both of which were still stronger than Russia.

[3]Some of the Cossacks or kazaks of the south central steppes were spirited refugees from the Tatars; others from Russian and Polish landlords. Their valor in battle and expert horsemanship made them highly prized as soldiers.

[4]There was a hereditary nobility dating from the thirteenth century or earlier, consisting of (a) Muscovite noble families, (b) descendants of the rulers of other principalities that had been merged with or annexed by Muscovy in the formation of Russia, and (c) nobles of these other principalities. The more important members of these groups, especially those who had court connections, were known as *boyars*. These nobles had suffered at the hands of Ivan the Terrible.

St. Basil's Cathedral (right) was rebuilt outside the stone walls of the Kremlin (fortress) of Moscow by Ivan the Terrible (above) to celebrate his victories over the Tatars in the sixteenth century. Russian Christianity stemmed from the eastern church of Byzantium in Constantinople. (Tass from Sovfoto.)

The Time of Troubles and the Early Romanovs Under Theodore I (1584–1598) and Boris Godunov (1598–1605), the great nobles (*boyars*) asserted themselves. When the direct line of succession to the throne died out with the demise of Boris' son Theodore II, there began a bitter dynastic struggle, complicated by attempts at social revolution and foreign invasion, rather like similar disturbances that had been plaguing parts of the West since the fifteenth century. A "Time of Troubles" in Russian history (1604–1613)

Procession of Boyars. Ivan the Terrible's passionate (he killed his own son and heir in a fit of rage) but intelligent actions had the effect of bullying the Russian *boyars* into something like subservience to a central state power. Shown here in a procession in Vienna, the ornately-dressed nobles carry gifts, including dangling objects which are the pelts of small furry animals such as mink and ermine. (Victoria and Albert Museum, Photo John Freeman.)

bloodied the land for years and ended with the elevation of Michael Romanov, a member of one of the princely Russian families (he was a distant relative of Ivan III), to the imperial office. Michael was chosen partly because of his links with the old dynasty, partly because his father was an important churchman, and partly because Michael himself seemed so insignificant that he did not represent a threat to the members of the *zemskii sobor* (consultative assembly) that elected him.

The work of the two Ivans in the fifteenth and sixteenth centuries had been important: Muscovy had become Russia and had expanded significantly, and one tsar had shown that it was possible to tame the nobility if one had few scruples. But the tsar's authority was by no means firmly established, and Russia still had no access to ice-free ports and little contact with the outside world. The beginning of the rise of Russia as a European power must, therefore, be dated from the end of the Time of Troubles.

The Romanovs, who ruled Russia throughout the seventeenth century, found that their major task was to organize the Russian state so that it could recoup the losses suffered during a long series of wars with Poland, Sweden, and Lithuania (the Livonian War, 1557–1582) and during the Time of Troubles. The greatest organizer of Russian strength was Peter the Great, but it would be a mistake to ignore the advances made during the reigns of his three Romanov predecessors: Michael (1613–1645), Alexis (1645–1676), and Theodore III (1676–1682).

When the first Romanov was elected tsar in 1613, his position was anything but strong. In spite of the fact that foreign forces had been driven from the greater part of Russian territory, the military position of Russia was extremely weak and Michael was forced into making further territorial

Mikhail Romanov. The first of the Romanovs, Mikhail or Michael (1613–1645) was not so terrible as his great-uncle, Ivan IV, but he had the support of his father, the patriarch (head of the church) of Moscow. As in the west, attempts at religious reforms produced great upheavals in Russia in the seventeenth century. Thirty thousand "Old Believers" are said to have immolated themselves rather than accept certain changes in the Christian ritual. (State Historical Museum, Moscow.)

cessions in order to secure recognition as rightful ruler. The tsar's treasury was empty and a regular income was almost nonexistent. In the first few months after his election, Michael had to borrow sufficient cash, fish, salt, and grain to pay his officials and soldiers. Moreover, the task of controlling the nobility was still far from finished despite the fact that the position of the great old *boyar* families of Muscovy had been all but destroyed in the Time of Troubles. Now it was a matter of dealing with the new or serving nobility that the crown had created.

The Status of Peasant and Merchant In a country as vast as Russia, land was easy to obtain. On the other hand, the relative paucity of population put a considerable premium on labor, and Russian landowners counted their wealth in terms of the number of "souls" that they owned and not in terms of the acres they controlled. The serving nobles were allowed the greatest latitude in exploiting their wealth, the state reserving to itself only the right of levying direct taxes on the serfs. The position of the Russian peasant thus steadily deteriorated throughout the seventeenth century. The general census of 1626–1628 attempted to fix the habitation of each peasant family and henceforward no peasant was allowed to leave the domain of the landlord on whose property he was found. The status of the serf thus became virtually unalterable. At the same time, slavery was officially abolished, not for humanitarian reasons, but because many peasants and even merchants had taken to binding themselves out as slaves in order to escape taxation. In the course of time, the difference between slave and serf became blurred and the Russian serf lost even the elementary right that European feudalism had bestowed upon its serfs: the right *not* to be sold away from the land he farmed. In increasing and fixing the powers of the nobility over the peasants, the crown managed to exact a primitive sort of loyalty from the Russian nobility.

Merchants as well as peasants suffered at the hands of the state in the seventeenth century. In order to help establish a sedentary population of fixed and organized groups, or estates, and also to strengthen the position of the serving nobility even further, the government attached merchants to certain cities by law and forbade them to move without express permission or to sell their businesses to anyone not of their estate or class. Russian nobles, on the other hand, were permitted to and did engage in trade when they so desired and used serf labor for manufacturing enterprises. Russia was well on the way toward becoming a heaven for the *dvoryani* and hell for everyone else.

The Split in the Russian Church Religious questions in Russia hinged on matters of ritual rather than dogma, because most Russians only dimly understood the larger implications of Christianity. (Church Slavonic, the language of the Russian Orthodox Church, was probably understood by a smaller percentage of Russians than was Church Latin by western Christians.) It was an attempt to change the ritual that brought about the split in the Russian Church. Influenced by the Ukrainian Church, the Russian patriarchs, particularly the patriarch Nikon, attempted from 1652–1658 to reform Church practices in such details as crossing oneself with two rather than three fingers and reciting two rather than three Hallelujah's. Nikon's innovations were officially accepted by the crown and imposed upon the people. Many Russians, henceforth known as "Old Believers," refused to accept the changes, believing that any change from the established ritual would deprive them of salvation. The Old Believers were condemned by a Church council and persecuted for a time, but in the long run they were merely deprived of official position and subjected to double taxation. Unlike the Reformation in the West, the schism in the Russian Church produced neither theological reappraisal nor political ferment. It did not undermine the power of the state church, nor did it add to the independence of the subjects. It added an element of instability to the Russian scene in the continuing opposition of the Old Believers to established authority, but this opposition was never focused clearly enough to form a serious threat to either church or state.

Peasant and Merchant Revolts More serious was the threat from peasant and merchant revolts. The restrictions imposed by the early Romanovs on the peasants and merchants led to a series of insurrections: a tax on salt led to a revolt in Moscow in 1647; in 1650, the merchants of Pskov and Novgorod revolted against new restrictions on merchant activity; and in 1656, the tsar's sudden debasement of the coinage provoked a still larger merchant and peasant revolt which ended in mass deportations and executions. These revolts, however, whether merchant or peasant, were doomed to failure without some support from a force not directly subject to the power of the state. The Cossack colonies and the non-Russian tribes on the borders of Russia provided such a force. In 1670, the Don Cossacks started a revolt led by one of their *hetmen,* Stenka Razin. Originally, the Cossacks protested

Stenka Razin and the Persian Maiden. Razin was a Don Cossack who terrorized the Volga during the seventeenth century with his army of runaway serfs, Cossacks, and adventurers. For a time, the tsarist government supported him because he drove off a Persian fleet which had been sent against him. In this illustration from a book published after his execution in 1671 he is shown throwing a captured maiden into the river, while Persian prisoners are towed along behind his ship. (LCRB.)

not so much against the central government as against the encroachments of the Russian nobility on what the Cossacks considered their territory; but, as the revolt spread northward from the region of the lower Volga, the Cossacks were joined by other tribes who resented their subjugation by Moscow. As the revolt spread still farther north, accompanied by vast slaughter and destruction, a regular peasant uprising took place and Razin was hailed as the liberator of the peasants from the yoke of serfdom. Having terrorized the whole Volga region as far north as the Oka for almost two years, Razin was finally defeated by regular troops and taken to Moscow where he was tortured and then quartered alive.

The border Cossack communities continued to play a disruptive role in Russian external as well as internal affairs until finally the government linked them to the state by giving them land, self-government, and something like noble status in return for the service by every Cossack male of twenty years in the imperial army.

Peter the Great During the last five years of Alexis' reign (1671–1676), the Russian state recovered from the effects of the Cossack and peasant revolts. In the next thirteen years, despite noble turbulence, Russia expanded in the Ukraine at the expense of the Ottoman Empire. Then ensued the all-encompassing reforms of Peter the Great (1682–1725). By all odds, one of the most interesting men of his time—a sort of Russian Paul Bunyan—Peter came at age ten to the throne as co-tsar with his half brother. He became sole ruler at age seventeen in 1689, the year of the Glorious Revolution in England. Peter was a heroic figure—nearly seven feet tall—who could drink staggering quantities of alcohol, build ships with his own hands, casually torture and kill persons who offended him, engage in monstrous orgies, and at the same time demonstrate a high level of sensitivity and intelligence. He was particularly interested in technology and military and naval service. When he sent a delegation of some 250 men to the western powers (1697–1698) to seek help against the Turks, Peter joined the group, incognito, to study gunnery, shipbuilding, printing, anatomy, and navigation. The mission did not achieve its prime objective, but Peter learned a great deal and the West enjoyed the opportunity of seeing what the Russians were like. Peter stayed in England at the house of John Evelyn near London. When his guests had left, Evelyn presented a bill to the English government for £250 in damages—item: ruined lawns, destroyed furniture, pictures used for target practice, scratched walls, and smeared floors.

Peter's Western Reforms During these travels, Peter's already developing convictions regarding the superiority of everything western and the inferiority of traditional Russian culture were reinforced. He came to see his life's mission as the task of making Russia into a powerful state on the western model. This sense of mission led him to become an eclectic collector of western ideas and modes which he transplanted into Russia, often without thoroughly considering their suitability to that country. He relied on his powers as an autocrat to carry through whatever reforms he deemed necessary. Thus he transplanted the Swedish system of central administration, German ideas on town government, the French system of direct taxation, and French court dress and manners, as well as Dutch ideas on local government and naval organization.

It is a measure of Peter's personal power as well as of his personal ability and energy that he introduced large numbers of these reforms and squelched all effective opposition during his lifetime, so that even after his death many of the reforms persisted. His major failure stemmed from the fact that he never managed to create a single class with a vested interest in his reforms powerful or large enough to carry them out on a systematic basis. Sixteen years after Peter's death, an English observer in St. Petersburg wrote: "After all the pains which had been taken to bring this country into its present shape I must confess that I can yet see it in no other light than as a rough model of something to be perfected hereafter, in which the several parts do neither fit nor join, nor are well glued together." Peter neglected to provide either an able heir or an able class of citizens to "glue" his works together.

Peter and the Nobility Like Frederick William of Prussia, Peter the Great attempted to tie all classes securely to the state, to bring the whole economy under state supervision and thus to assure a steady revenue for his growing army and a new navy. Unlike Frederick William, however, he failed to understand and accommodate himself to the existing power structure of the country. The kings of Prussia had succeeded in making the aristocrats the willing servants of the state by carefully building up their privileges and their positions of power in the state service and in the army. Peter, on the contrary, attempted to bully and regiment the aristocracy, insisting that they exist only for the good of the state, and that nobility be conferred solely as a reward for service to the state. Where the Prussian king made officer status in the army and jobs in the civil service a privilege of the existing nobility, Peter attempted to create a nobility open to talent and service. Everyone, whether of noble descent or not, had to start at the bottom of the fourteen grades Peter established in the army and civil service. Although a young nobleman maintained his rank when he started in the service, anyone reaching the eighth grade of service was automatically ennobled. This scheme opened up the ranks of the aristocracy to the lower classes, antagonizing the hereditary nobility and others who had earned their status by service to the state under former rulers. The resentment of the aristocracy was increased by Peter's "Law of Entail," which, like European primogeniture, decreed that only one son could inherit a noble landed estate, leaving the others presumably landless and dependent for favors on the state.

Peter and the Army A major purpose of Peter's reforms, like those of Frederick William in Prussia, was to create a strong and well-supplied army—with the difference that Peter was interested in a navy as well. Like Frederick William, he attempted to recruit from the economically non-productive elements of society. Where this proved impossible, a certain percentage of serfs was recruited from each peasant district—leaving behind a number sufficient to cultivate the land. He, too, attempted, though with less success, to replace foreign officers with a dedicated Russian corps.

Although the troops were supposed to be paid by the state, they remained chiefly dependent upon what their officers could requisition from local populations, both at home and abroad. Instead of increasing prosperity in their garrison towns they despoiled the populace.

Service in the army was for life. The local nobility and the communities were given some choice in the selection of candidates, and it was only natural that they tended to send the least able prospects. It is a tribute to the abilities of Peter and his generals that an army so selected was made into an effective fighting force. Apart from the regular conscripts, Peter relied heavily also on some 100,000 Cossacks. In 1724, his army numbered about 300,000 men—an enormous force for that day, four times as large, for example, as that of Frederick William I of Prussia.

Bearding the Nobles. This contemporary woodcut cartoon shows Peter "bearding" a Russian noble after his return from his European tour. (Note "Peter's" western hat and dress.) The cutting of beards was only the most obvious of Peter's attempts to make the Russian bear dance to western tunes. His most serious efforts were aimed at seizing territories, especially ports, from the Swedes and Turks.

Opposition to Peter's Reforms Peter shared Frederick William's basic conception of education as a tool for practical service to the state. He established admiralty schools in order to provide training in mathematics and sciences which could not be obtained in the Church schools; he set up printing presses for producing scientific works, hoping for their widespread circulation in Russia. The nobility, however, resented the state schools, where their sons were forced to rub shoulders with ordinary people; and, when they finally achieved some degree of literacy, they much preferred to read the latest romance or the old lives of the saints to Peter's scientific works.

Peter's reforms left virtually no area of Russian life untouched and each of them incurred the opposition of some group. His mercantilist measures were resented by the conservative merchants; noble service reforms were galling to the aristocracy; Old Russians of all sorts objected to his decrees forbidding beards and requiring western as opposed to Russian-oriental dress. Foreigners were continually amused and astonished by the behavior of the "new Russians." The English ambassador in Turkey wrote home in 1701:

The Muscovite Ambassador and his retinue have appeared here so different from what they always formerly wore that ye Turks cannot tell what to make of them. They are all coutred in French habit, with an abundance of gold and silver lace, long perruques and, which the Turks most wonder at, without beards. Last Sunday, being Mass in Adrianople, ye Ambassador and all his company did not only keep their hats off during ye service but at ye elevation, himself and all of them pulled off their wigs. It was much taken notice of and thought an unusual act of devotion.

There was, however, nothing ridiculous about Peter's successful foreign policy, and it is here that the true measure of his regime should be taken.

Peter's Foreign Policy Peter pursued the traditional Russian goals of expansion toward the Caspian, the Black, and the Baltic seas. Between 1696 and 1700, a number of minor campaigns temporarily secured for Russia the long-desired southern fortress of Azov, at the mouth of the Don and within reach of salt water. The major campaigns of Peter's reign, however, took place in the west, where Russian expansionism brought Peter into conflict with the still mighty power of Sweden, ruled (1697–1718) by Charles XII, one of the ablest and certainly one of the most impetuous military leaders of his day.

Russia's entry into the Northern War (1700) was followed by the resounding Swedish victory at Narva, where 40,000 Russian troops fled in disarray before the onslaught of 8,000 men led by the eighteen-year-old Charles. Much of the urgency of Peter's internal reformism must be attributed to the necessity to rebuild, retrain, and reequip the army after the defeat at Narva. Luckily for Peter, Charles spent the next six years campaigning in Poland and Central Europe in favor of his own candidate for the Polish throne. Peter used the breathing space to import foreign military advisors, to buy muskets and bayonets, to recruit and reorganize his army. He also retook some of the territory along the Baltic: Narva, Dorpat, and the swampy territory on the Neva where he founded his new capital city of St. Petersburg (now Leningrad) and constructed the fortress of Kronstadt. In 1705, Peter had to face a series of internal revolts stemming from his reforms; and three years later Charles of Sweden, his objectives achieved in Poland, started to march toward Moscow. Peter was ready with his new army. The future of Russia hinged on what would happen in the encounter.

After advancing some distance toward Moscow, and suffering from a "scorched earth" retreat on the part of the Russian army, the Swedish king decided to move south into the Ukraine. Charles thought that in the Ukraine he would find plentiful supplies for his troops, and he had been promised the support of the Cossack *hetman,* Mazeppa. This move proved fatal to the Swedish campaign. The winter was unspeakably cold, even in the south; Mazeppa failed to carry the majority of the Cossacks with him; and Charles was cut off from his supply train. Peter was able to fight the Swedish army and defeat it in two separate battles: one at Lesnaya where he destroyed the Swedish supplies and reinforcements, and the other at Poltava, in 1709. The Russian army, which had seemed to Charles only nine years before at Narva an imbecile array, was now not only far larger than the Swedish force but was also equipped with more modern weapons. Charles escaped to Turkey and did not return to Sweden until five years later. By this time, beleaguered by Denmark, Saxony, Poland, Prussia, and Hanover, as well as Russia, Sweden was rushing headlong into what was to be permanent decline.

Peter had to leave to his successors the task of conquering access to the southern seas. Charles' agitations in Turkey after his defeat led the Russians to a war with Turkey two years after Poltava, and Peter was forced to yield the fortress of Azov acquired in 1700. Nonetheless, at his death Peter left a Russian state vastly more powerful than it had been at his

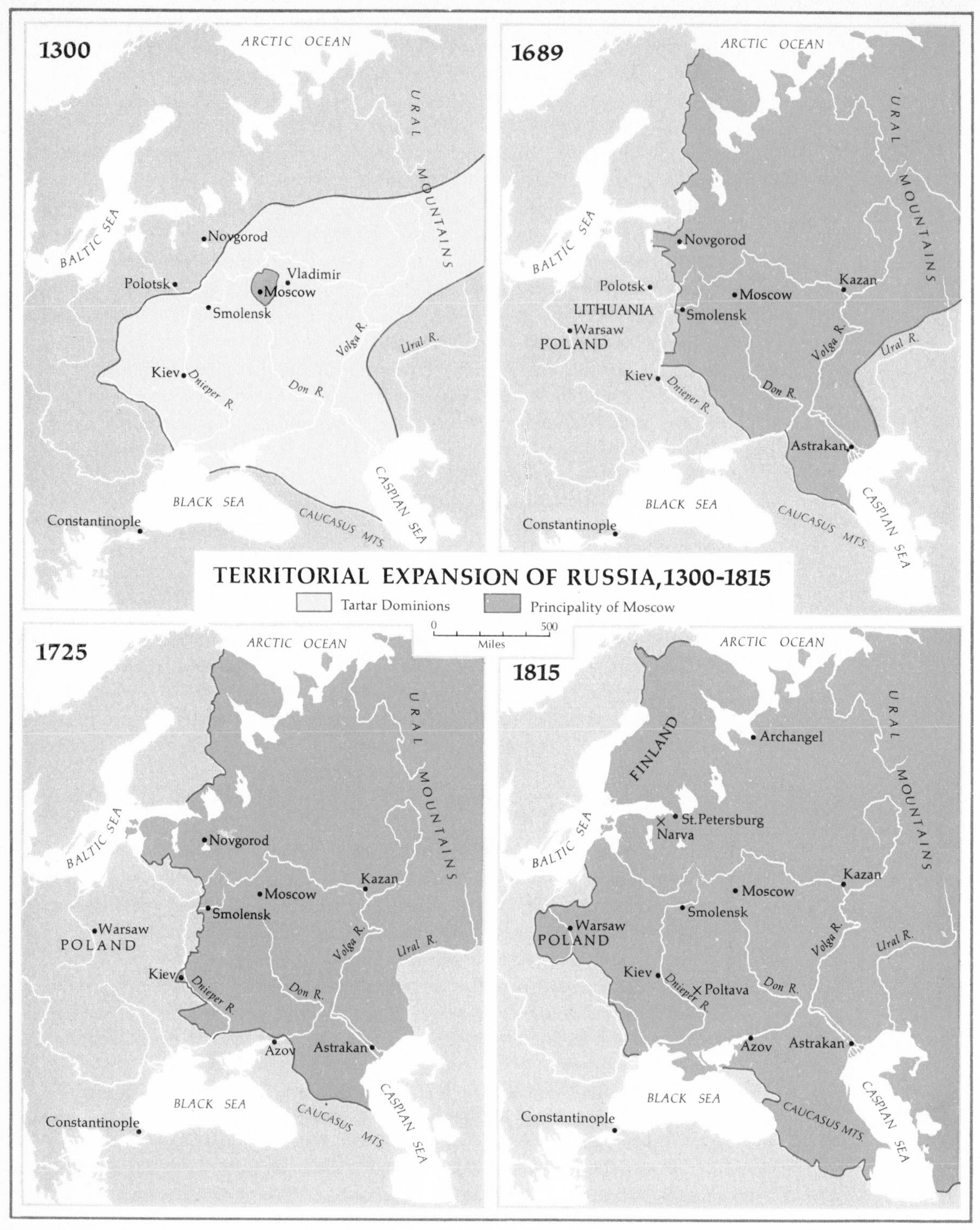
TERRITORIAL EXPANSION OF RUSSIA, 1300-1815
Tartar Dominions
Principality of Moscow
0
500
Miles
1300
ARCTIC OCEAN
URAL MOUNTAINS
BALTIC SEA
Novgorod
Polotsk
Vladimir
Moscow
Smolensk
Volga R.
Ural R.
Kiev
Dnieper R.
Don R.
BLACK SEA
CAUCASUS MTS.
CASPIAN SEA
Constantinople
1689
ARCTIC OCEAN
URAL MOUNTAINS
BALTIC SEA
Novgorod
Polotsk
LITHUANIA
Warsaw
POLAND
Moscow
Kazan
Smolensk
Volga R.
Ural R.
Kiev
Dnieper R.
Don R.
Astrakan
BLACK SEA
CAUCASUS MTS.
CASPIAN SEA
Constantinople
1725
ARCTIC OCEAN
URAL MOUNTAINS
BALTIC SEA
Novgorod
Moscow
Kazan
Smolensk
Warsaw
POLAND
Volga R.
Ural R.
Kiev
Dnieper R.
Don R.
Azov
Astrakan
BLACK SEA
CAUCASUS MTS.
CASPIAN SEA
Constantinople
1815
ARCTIC OCEAN
URAL MOUNTAINS
FINLAND
Archangel
St. Petersburg
Narva
BALTIC SEA
Kazan
Moscow
Smolensk
Warsaw
POLAND
Volga R.
Ural R.
Kiev
Dnieper R.
Poltava
Don R.
Azov
Astrakan
BLACK SEA
CAUCASUS MTS.
CASPIAN SEA
Constantinople

accession thirty years before. He had laid the cornerstone of Russia's future power.

Peter's Successors Despite his military successes, Peter did not leave his internal house in order when he died in 1725. The majority of the Russian people continued to resist his reforms, and he had not succeeded in converting even his own family to his point of view. His only son, Alexis, became the rallying point of Old Russian dissidents even before Peter's death. Relations between the Russian tsar and his son made Frederick William's treatment of young Frederick of Prussia seem like an excess of paternal love. Whereas Frederick survived, Alexis died in prison under torture, inflicted under orders of and witnessed by his father. Thus, Peter once again introduced the problem of succession into Russian politics.

Between 1725 and 1762, the Russian throne had five occupants, each reaching the throne not by hereditary right, but through military plots and the machinations of the aristocracy. Therefore, over a thirty-seven year period, the prerogatives of power that Peter had attempted to secure for the state were somewhat diminished. In 1762, however, there came to the throne an extraordinary ruler in the person of Catherine II, "The Great." Widow of Tzar Peter III—she possibly had a hand in Peter's deposition and assassination—this German woman applied her immense energy to rationalizing Russian administration, consorting with western intellectuals, and a long succession of lovers, meanwhile permitting the nobility to secure absolute power over their peasant-serfs. Catherine also used a huge and improved army to expand Russian territory at the expense of Poland and the Turks.

RUSSIA AND PRUSSIA COMPARED

Despite the numerous differences between Russia and Prussia in political structure, geography, and culture, the two countries shared certain historical patterns. The rise of both states from positions of weakness and insignificance to the front rank in Europe was accomplished by both very rapidly—in less than one hundred years. In both cases, advances in organization of the state were achieved at the expense of the peasantry and through the instrumentality of the army.

But within and outside of this pattern of similarity there were important differences. Russia was a very large country and derived certain advantages from the fact that its huge territory was contiguous and that its population, though sparse over large areas, was by no means small. The major obstacles to Russia's achieving great power status were its remoteness from the centers of European culture and the lack of communications over vast distances of territory, both of which combined to keep Russians out of touch with European progress. Notwithstanding the heroic efforts of the tsars, especially Peter the Great, the country continued to lag behind the rest of Europe in its cultural development. Unlike the rest of Europe, Russia was only superficially—and much later—subjected to the bracing economic, intellectual, and religious currents of "the Enlightenment," discussed in Chapter 2.

Those forces that in the rest of Europe helped to form the spirit of new and independent methods of inquiry, shaking the authority of the Roman Catholic Church and the feudal nobility and aiding the rise to power of centralizing secular rulers, were notably weak in remote Russia. The Russian Orthodox Church remained a powerful conservative force. The disorders of the "Time of Troubles" served to reestablish the conservative aristocracy both politically and economically. Peasants were more completely at the mercy of their landlords in Russia than anywhere else in Europe, and serfdom became entrenched in Russia just when it was disappearing elsewhere. Because of the problem of succession after Peter the Great's death in 1725, conservative forces were able to halt the progress made toward centralization of power and disciplining the nobility during his reign.

Prussia, on the other hand, enjoyed the advantages of a steady succession of able rulers whose right to the throne could be neither questioned nor controlled by hostile forces within the state. The rulers of Prussia held territories in which the aristocracy was either so poor that an alliance with the central power seemed advantageous or in which the power of the aristocracy had been steadily declining over a period of a hundred years. Furthermore, the Reformation and the Thirty Years' War had taught both the rulers and the aristocratic estates the advantages of religious tolerance. The Prussian kings—the Hohenzollerns—were able to make allies of the aristocrats, as the chief servants of unification and centralization. The objective obstacles to the rise of the Hohenzollerns—the natural poverty and insignificance of the territories they held, the small number of subjects under their rule, and the lack of a common frontier for their widely scattered holdings—were all overcome by the success of the alliance between able and tireless kings and an aristocracy both willing and able to lend support.

The manner in which Russia developed internally does not seem to partake of "Enlightenment," despite Peter's attempt to open Russia to what he considered more enlightened ways of doing things and despite Catherine's flirtations with the *philosophes.* What resulted from Russian dynamism did not contribute to the welfare of the overwhelming majority of the Russian people. Quite to the contrary, the lot of the Russian peasant was substantially worsened; and a highly unsatisfactory social organization was fixed on Russia, to survive virtually intact until the Russian revolution of 1917. In Brandenburg-Prussia, Frederick William I did not read the books of the Enlightenment and would not have liked them. His son, Frederick II, became fully aware of what the intellectuals were up to; but, as we shall see later, Frederick was highly selective in his use of Enlightenment ideas.

In the next chapter, we shall see that in the eighteenth century little Prussia continued to expand its territory and consolidate its power, to the astonishment of Europe. Russia also continued to grow; but it was not until Napoleon's Grand Army would freeze on the banks of the Niemen that the Great Russian Bear would demonstrate its particular strength.

FURTHER READING

For the general European background, 1610 to 1715, and some incisive comments on Prussia and Russia, see the volumes by C. Friedrich, F. Nussbaum, and J. Wolf in the *Rise of Modern Europe* series (1951–1953). The next two volumes in the same series carry on the story and provide bibliographical orientation: P. Roberts, * *The Quest for Security, 1715–1740* (1947, 1963), not the strongest volume in the series; and W. Dorn, * *Competition for Empire, 1740–1763* (1940, 1963), a fine book, especially on institutions.

S. Fay, *The Rise of Brandenburg-Prussia to 1786* (1970), is an excellent brief treatment of the title subject. Fay rightly emphasizes the part played by the Hohenzollerns. See also F. L. Carsten, * *The Origins of Prussia* (1954). Individual members of the family and their policies may be studied in F. Schevill, *The Great Elector* (1965); R. Ergang, *The Potsdam Führer: Frederick William I, Father of Prussian Militarism* (1973), which, while interesting, suffers from the author's tendency to cast Frederick William in Hitler's mold. G. Ritter, *Frederick the Great: A Historical Profile* (1968), is an important work by a great German historian, recently translated by P. Paret. For an argument to the effect that the Prussian state was essentially an army, see G. Craig, * *The Politics of the Prussian Army, 1640–1945* (1964). Other aspects of Prussian development are treated by R. Dorwart, *The Prussian Welfare State before 1740* (1971); and H. Rosenberg, * *Bureaucracy, Aristocracy, and Autocracy: The Prussian Experience, 1660–1815* (1966).

A fine older one-volume work in English on the broad sweep of Russian history is B. Pares, *A History of Russia* (1955). New and useful overall treatments are J. Clarkson, *A History of Russia* (1969); and M. Florinsky, *Russia: A History and an Interpretation,* 2 vols. (1954), and the same author's *Russia: A Short History* (1969). For the intertwining of Russia with Poland-Lithuania, see O. Halecki, *Borderlands of Western Civilization: a History of East Central Europe* (1952). A convenient treatment of the most troublesome problem in Russian internal history is G. Robinson, *Rural Russia under the Old Regime* (1967). J. Blum, * *Lord and Peasant in Russia from the Ninth to the Nineteenth Century* (1961), is a brave attempt at an immense topic. For the rise of Russia, F. Nowak, *Medieval Slavdom and the Rise of Russia* (1970); and R. Kerner, *Urge to the Sea: The Course of Russian History, the Role of Rivers, Portages, Ostrogs, Monasteries and Furs* (1942 and 1971), are most interesting.

In soft cover, there is G. Vernadsky, * *History of Russia* (5th ed., 1961), a solid account; B. H. Sumner, * *Peter the Great and the Emergence of Russia* (1972), an important book; and the volume in the Heath "Problems in European Civilization" series, Marc Raeff, ed., * *Peter the Great Changes Russia* (1972).

Finally, M. Raeff, *Imperial Russia, 1682–1825: The Coming of Age of Modern Russia* (1970), is in large part pertinent to what is discussed in this chapter.

*Books available in paperback are marked with an asterisk.

4 Competition and Reform: The Enlightened Despots at Work

In the eighteenth century, most European statesmen—even the most "enlightened"—continued to compete for the usual political objectives in the same old ways. Power and prestige, they continued to believe, were to be gained by the acquisition of a seaport here, a province there; bits of Italy, Silesia, parts of Poland were the rewards of successful diplomacy or war. Whether or not the young king of France married his cousin the Infanta of Spain or the daughter of a deposed king of Poland was a matter of much greater concern to European leaders than the price of bread at home or the shifts in allegiance of Indian tribes in North America.

Yet under this appearance of sameness ran some important changes. First, the old patterns of alliance on the continent of Europe were drastically altered, primarily because of Russia's and Prussia's assumption of great power status. Second, British fortunes, especially overseas, rose dramatically—chiefly at the expense of France. Third, many of the rulers of Europe became infected with the ideas of the Enlightenment. Before dipping into the complex diplomatic and military history of the eighteenth century and the reforms attempted by some of the "enlightened" monarchs within their own countries, let us turn back to France, the cradle of the Enlightenment, and England, whose political institutions were the envy of the French intellectuals of the eighteenth century.

We have noted that the funeral of Louis XIV not long after the signing of the treaties of Utrecht, Rastatt, and Baden in 1713–1714 was an occasion for popular celebration. The new French king, Louis XV, the great-grandson of the king he succeeded, was only five years of age. The death of Louis XV fifty-nine years later was to call forth similar demonstrations, but for the time being he was a child, and the government was in the hands of a regent, the Duke of Orléans. A profligate and cynical man, busy with his pleasures and his vices, Orléans was, withal, intelligent and able. Many expected that he would poison the sickly boy-king to secure the French throne for himself (he was Louis XIV's nephew). The regent's chief antagonist was Philip V of Spain (Louis XIV's grandson and Louis XV's uncle) who, in anticipation of young Louis XV's death, made plans to hand Spain over to *his* son so that he, Philip, could become king of France.

Although more discreet, French ruling circles reacted very much as had the people in the streets to the death of the old king. Nearly everyone wished to see the end of strong royal control. In an effort to decentralize the administration, Orléans created a series of councils staffed by great nobles of the sword as well as by members of the nobility of the robe and by bureaucrats. At the top, presided over by himself, was a Council of Regency. This consisted of eleven men, most of whom were princes of royal blood or great aristocrats. There were seven other noble-dominated councils: for ecclesiastical matters, foreign affairs, war, finances, navy, interior, and commerce.

Orléans' new councils did not work. The nobles tended to spend their time arguing about who should enter the room first and who should take off his hat when addressing whom; and it soon became eminently apparent that the Sun King had done his work of emasculating the nobles only too well. They were now not only incapable of rebellion, they had forgotten how to govern. One of their own number characterized them as "good only to be killed off in war."[1] In 1718, after three years' trial, the council system was abandoned and control of the various departments was handed back to ministers, one of whom was the Abbé Dubois. Dubois had been the regent's tutor and companion in debauchery. Though a bad priest, Dubois was an able statesman. In time, he became Chief Minister and a cardinal of the Roman Catholic Church. His foreign policy sought to ensure European peace by resisting the Spanish Bourbon's attempts to gain the French throne and otherwise undo the Treaty of Utrecht. France now became allied with England and Holland against Spain—a complete reversal of the alliances of Louis XIV.

A peace policy was sorely needed by France at this time. That the country and the people had suffered during Louis XIV's last two wars is attested to by contemporary reports filled with descriptions of deserted villages and famine. The population had undoubtedly decreased. The regent found in 1715 that he could not meet the most urgent expenses of government, much less pay the interest on the tremendous inflated royal debt. At first, Orléans permitted the noble-dominated Council of Finance to try to deal with the problem by the simple means of repudiating certain royal obligations. When this device did not produce the needed improvement in royal finances, the regent turned to a radical scheme proposed by a Scottish gambler and financial "wizard," John Law.

Law's proposal was to found a central bank of issue or Royal Bank—modelled more or less after the Bank of England—and a Company of the

[1]Quoted in P. Roberts, *The Quest for Security, 1715–1740* (New York: Harper & Row, 1947), p. 44.

West. The latter would take over the royal debt and issue its own shares or securities in exchange for outstanding government obligations. To finance its operations, the company was given monopoly over all colonial trade, the tobacco industry, the French share of the world's slave trade, as well as the right to collect indirect taxes (such as the *gabelle* or salt tax) in France. Law's overall project also called for drastic reform of the French tax system so as to make it more equitable and more productive of revenue. The Company of the West—which came to be known as the Mississippi Company—was to pay dividends on its shares from profits growing out of its trading and other monopolistic ventures.

Law's advanced schemes, had they succeeded, would have modernized French finances and greatly stimulated economic activity. As it turned out,

John Law's French bank issued notes like the one shown here (right) for ten *livres tournois,* dated 1719. Speculation in shares of the "Mississippi Company" or "Company of the West" made millionaires—for a while—of beggars and priests as well as the traditional moneyed classes. The animated scene above is the Hotel de Soissons, site of the present-day Paris *bourse,* where business was transacted. (Bibliothèque Nationale, Paris.)

N.° 65292 Dix Livres Tournois.
La Banque promet payer au porteur à Vüe, Dix Livres Tournois en Espéces d'Argent, Valeur receüe à Paris le
Signé p.r le S.r Bourgeois.
Vû pour le S.r Fenellon.
Contrôlé p.r le S.r Durevest.

however, there was great resistance on the part of tax-farmers and office-holders whose incomes and places were threatened by Law's reforms. Further, the new Bank overissued paper money—to which the French were not at this time accustomed—in order to encourage purchase of shares in the Mississippi Company. Finally, Law's promotional techniques led to a feverish speculative boom: the shares rose in price beyond all expectations of return as French "investors" were carried away by the seeming magic of this vast scheme. In 1720, after two years, the bubble burst, and the shares plummeted in value. Although the crash did not significantly damage the French economy, which was slowly recovering under peacetime conditions, it did produce a certain amount of wreckage amongst the greedy and the gullible. Law fled the country.

The young king was declared of age in 1723; the regent and Dubois died in the same year. In 1725, young Louis was married to Marie, the daughter of Stanislaus Lesczynski, a deposed king of Poland; and in the next year the management of French affairs was taken in hand by the king's tutor, the Cardinal Fleury, an old man of 73 who stayed in power for seventeen more years. Under Fleury's guidance the economy recovered; the budget was nearly balanced; and the value of French trade more than doubled.

ENGLAND

In 1715, the crown of England was worn by a German prince, George of Hanover, great-grandson of James I. The decision to reach so far afield for an English monarch (there were other persons with better genealogical claims) had been made fourteen years before in the Act of Settlement (1701), by a Parliament anxious to secure a Protestant succession at the expense of the claims of James II and his son, both of whom were Roman Catholics. George's predecessor, Anne Stuart, had died without issue. The twelve years of her reign had been filled with the glory of Marlborough's campaigns against Louis XIV on the continent and embellished by something like an artistic and intellectual renaissance at home. Also during Anne's reign, England and Scotland had joined in a parliamentary union (1707) as the kingdom of Great Britain.

George I of Hanover spoke no English and didn't care to learn. He brought with him some German advisors and two blowsy, middle-aged mistresses (his disgraced and divorced wife he left in Hanover). Because he understood that he owed his kingdom to the Whigs, he tended to favor the Whig interest. Shortly after his arrival, some of the Scots Highlanders and a few north-of-England squires rose in revolt. The Pretender "James III" arrived on the scene from France to rally his supporters, but nothing went well for the Jacobite rebels in this rising (known as "the Fifteen" after the year, 1715, in which it took place) and it soon evaporated.[2] Thereafter

[2]"Jacobite" is derived from Jacobus or "James" in Latin. The word designates the supporters of James II, of his son James Francis (the Old Pretender) and of his grandson Bonnie Prince Charlie (the Young Pretender), in the years after 1688. Thirty years after "the Fifteen," there was another rising (1745) participated in by the Young Pretender with much derring-do. This rising is known as "the Forty-Five."

The first of Britain's "prime ministers," Robert Walpole, came to power as a direct result of the failure of the British South Sea Company in 1720. Sir Robert's sixth child, Horace (1717–1797), was a famous man of letters and art collector. (National Portrait Gallery, London.)

George I sparred (in French and Latin) with his Whig ministers and with Parliament, trying to see how many of the limitations that had been imposed upon the crown actually applied to him. In this sparring the king was overmatched; and in 1721 he finally reconciled himself to putting up with Robert Walpole, who came to preside over the meetings of the king's ministers and gradually assumed many of the functions of prime minister. Thus began to evolve English "cabinet government"—that is, government by an executive committee chosen in the king's name by a prime minister who is the leader of the dominant party in the House of Commons and responsible to that body.

One of the great events of the early part of George I's reign was the development of a financial-commercial scheme, called the South Sea Company, similar to John Law's enterprise in France. After a fever of speculation, the South Sea Bubble broke in 1720, disgracing many politicians who had become involved in the speculation and who had profited thanks to their political influence. Because he had not been involved and because he had made public statements questioning the wisdom of the scheme, Robert Walpole was now appointed Chancellor of the Exchequer and First Lord of the Treasury.[3] After the Bubble, Walpole, the Whig oligarchy, and the king presided over an economically advancing and generally pacific and united country. George I died in 1727, but Walpole's influence continued until 1742 under George II (1727–1760).

THE PEACE IS BROKEN: POLISH AND AUSTRIAN SUCCESSION

A close analysis of the situation of the continental powers as they approached the middle of the eighteenth century will show that the peace of Europe was faced with four serious threats: first, the desire of the Spanish Bourbon to regain territories in Italy that had been taken from Spain in 1713; second, a power vacuum in Poland; third, the decline of the Ottoman Empire; and, fourth, the question of the Austrian succession. We have already seen how, shortly after 1713, the Spanish King Philip V's attempt to revise the Treaty of Utrecht was frustrated by a coalition of England, France, Holland, and Austria. A treaty in 1720 did give Philip some Italian duchies for his eldest son; but he had to await disunity among the peace-keeping powers before he could pursue his larger aims.

The opportunity arose in 1733 when the death of Augustus II, King of Poland and Elector of Saxony, opened the question of Polish succession. The Polish Diet elected Stanislaus Lesczynski, now father-in-law of the French king. The Russians favored a new Saxon elector, Augustus III. France determined to assist Stanislaus and to that end formed an alliance with Spain and Savoy—both remote from and uninterested in Polish affairs. France declared war on the Empire and invaded Germany.

[3]The title "prime minister" was not legally recognized until 1905. Even the concept of a royal minister superior to others did not achieve full development in Walpole's time, though he did much to further it. The older title usually held by a British prime minister is "First Lord of the Treasury"; and a placque by the door of number 10 Downing Street proclaims the occupant as such.

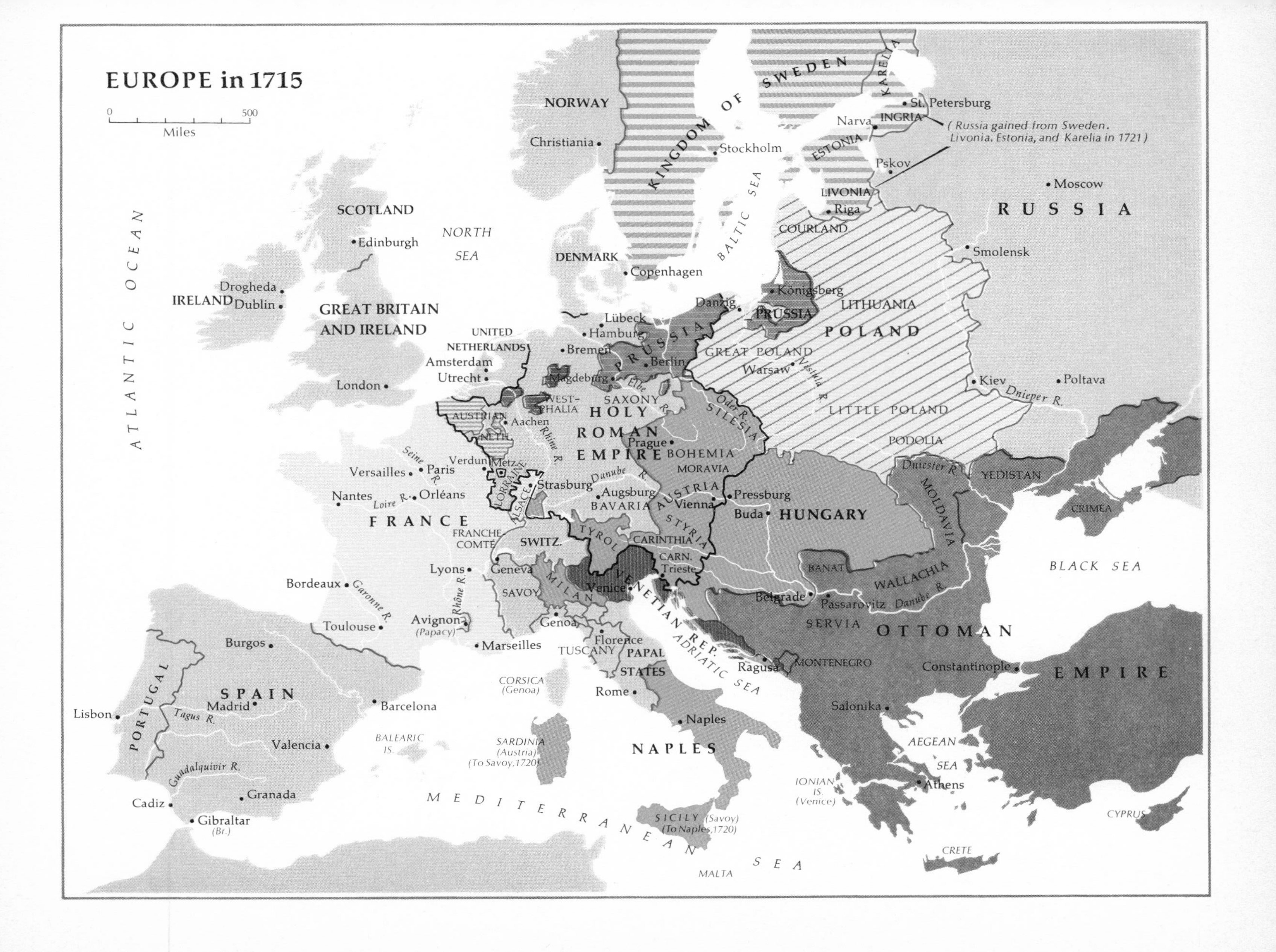
EUROPE in 1715
0
500
Miles
ATLANTIC OCEAN
NORTH SEA
NORWAY
Christiania
KINGDOM OF SWEDEN
KARELIA
St. Petersburg
INGRIA
Narva
(Russia gained from Sweden. Livonia, Estonia, and Karelia in 1721)
ESTONIA
Stockholm
Pskov
Moscow
LIVONIA
Riga
RUSSIA
SCOTLAND
Edinburgh
COURLAND
BALTIC SEA
DENMARK
Copenhagen
Smolensk
Drogheda
IRELAND
Dublin
GREAT BRITAIN AND IRELAND
Königsberg
LITHUANIA
Danzig
PRUSSIA
Lübeck
Hamburg
UNITED NETHERLANDS
Bremen
POLAND
GREAT POLAND
Berlin
Amsterdam
Utrecht
Warsaw
Vistula R.
Magdeburg
Elbe R.
London
Kiev
Poltava
Dnieper R.
WEST-PHALIA
SAXONY
HOLY ROMAN EMPIRE
AUSTRIAN NETH.
Aachen
Rhine R.
Oder R.
SILESIA
LITTLE POLAND
PODOLIA
Prague
BOHEMIA
MORAVIA
Seine R.
Paris
Versailles
Verdun
Metz
LORRAINE
ALSACE
Strasburg
Danube R.
Dniester R.
YEDISTAN
MOLDAVIA
Nantes
Loire R.
Orléans
Augsburg
BAVARIA
AUSTRIA
Vienna
Pressburg
Buda
HUNGARY
CRIMEA
FRANCE
FRANCHE-COMTÉ
SWITZ.
TYROL
STYRIA
CARINTHIA
CARN.
Trieste
BANAT
WALLACHIA
BLACK SEA
Lyons
Geneva
Bordeaux
Garonne R.
Rhône R.
SAVOY
MILAN
Venice
VENETIAN REP.
Belgrade
Passarovitz
Danube R.
SERVIA
OTTOMAN EMPIRE
Toulouse
Avignon
(Papacy)
Genoa
Florence
TUSCANY
PAPAL STATES
ADRIATIC SEA
Ragusa
MONTENEGRO
Constantinople
Burgos
Marseilles
CORSICA
(Genoa)
Rome
PORTUGAL
SPAIN
Madrid
Barcelona
Lisbon
Tagus R.
Salonika
Naples
Valencia
BALEARIC IS.
SARDINIA
(Austria)
(To Savoy, 1720)
NAPLES
AEGEAN SEA
Guadalquivir R.
IONIAN IS.
(Venice)
Athens
Cadiz
Granada
MEDITERRANEAN SEA
Gibraltar
(Br.)
SICILY (Savoy)
(To Naples, 1720)
CYPRUS
CRETE
MALTA

The Russians sent an army into Poland to help their candidate and were able to settle the Polish aspect of the war quite quickly in their favor. The major military campaigns did not take place in Poland at all, however, but in Italy where the Spanish were active and in the Rhineland where the French fought imperial troops.

Within a short time, the War of Polish Succession (1733–1735) was over, peace being concluded in a Treaty of Vienna. Everyone except the Poles got something. Stanislaus Lesczynski renounced his claim to the Polish throne, but in return was given Lorraine, with the understanding that on

his death this province would pass by way of his daughter to the French crown. Duke Francis of Lorraine, husband of Maria Theresa, was given Tuscany in Italy to compensate him for the loss of Lorraine. The Spanish Bourbons and the Habsburgs shuffled other Italian provinces. The result of it all was that everyone—excepting, of course, the Poles—was content for the time being. The occupation of Lorraine by the French represented a fine political coup by Fleury, who probably had had no serious intention of putting Louis XV's father-in-law on the Polish throne. He had used the whole affair as an opportunity to secure this important province for France.

The war of Austrian Succession (1740–1748) was raging when Maria Theresa (left) was crowned queen of Bohemia in the Cathedral in Prague in 1743 (right). Ill prepared to rule, she nevertheless succeeded in commanding the loyalty of her subjects. Her ministers brought France to the aid of Austria against Frederick the Great of Prussia. (LCPP Bildarchiv d. Ost. Nationalbibliothek, Vienna.)

The next important disturbance of the European peace came in 1740. With the signatures of nearly every other European ruler affixed to the Pragmatic Sanction guaranteeing the succession of his daughter to his throne (see Chapter 3), Charles VI (Habsburg) died. Immediately, the value of this agreement was in doubt: Charles Albert of Bavaria claimed the Austrian inheritance; so did that prime troublemaker, Philip V of Spain, as did Augustus III, presently King of Poland and Elector of Saxony. The beautiful young Maria Theresa was also threatened by young Frederick of Prussia, who claimed that the rich province of Silesia legally belonged to his family, the Hohenzollerns. Frederick invaded Silesia and the War of Austrian Succession (1740–1748), known in its German aspects as the Silesian War, was on.

Actually, fighting had started on the high seas the year before, when England and Spain had come to blows in what is known as the War of Jenkins' Ear over the question of English trading rights in the Caribbean. Walpole had tried to resist war-mongering elements in England, but had been forced to accede to the war. Fleury likewise tried to calm France, but he, too, failed; and before long Europe was once again engaged in a general and very complex war or set of wars. The French now moved into the Austrian Netherlands. Maria Theresa and her generals tried repeatedly and unsuccessfully to drive Frederick out of Silesia. The English fought the French on the European continent and in America and India; the French fought the Spanish in America. When the fighting was over and peace declared with the treaty of Aix-la-Chapelle (1748), everyone gave back what he had taken during the war—everyone, that is, except Frederick II of Prussia, who kept Silesia.

THE DIPLOMATIC REVOLUTION AND THE SEVEN YEARS' WAR, 1756–1763

We have suggested that despite the failure of either the Bourbons or the Habsburgs to win hegemony over Europe in the seventeenth and early eighteenth centuries, the historic balance and pattern of alignments within Europe was being disturbed nevertheless. Among the disturbing factors we have summarized were the decline of Sweden in the north and the Ottoman Empire in the south, and the increasing vacuum of power in centrally located Poland. Another disturbing factor was the rise of Russia to the east. Most disturbing of all, and especially to the Austrian empress Maria Theresa and her foreign minister, Count Kaunitz, was the rise of Prussia.

Kaunitz understood the changes that had taken place, and he knew what was needed. He knew that Prussia, which had humiliated Austrian arms and seized valuable Austrian territory in the latest war, was now the real threat to the imperial power—no longer France, Austria's historic enemy. Accordingly, Kaunitz plotted a "diplomatic revolution": he would try to align France *with* Austria against Prussia, and bring in Russia to boot. Patiently he cultivated relations with Versailles (getting some help from Madame Pompadour, the king's mistress, who disliked Frederick of Prussia), while he also kept communications open with St. Petersburg. By the time war broke out again, he had succeeded; and France and Russia joined Austria against Frederick of Prussia.

Vienna near mid-century as seen by the Venetian artist, Canaletto (1697–1768). Vienna looked both to Italy (Rome) and to France (Versailles) for inspiration. It was during the first half of the eighteenth century that German baroque art forms, especially in architecture and music, flourished in southern, Catholic Germany. (Kunsthistorische Museum.)

In the last war (Austrian Succession, 1740–1748), the English had been on the side of Austria. They were not slow to appreciate the new realities. Britain had come to fear any combination of powers that might dominate the continent. Furthermore, because the Electorate of Hanover, home of the British kings, was located uncomfortably close to Prussia, and because the sovereigns of Britain and Prussia were related, it seemed the better part of valor to assist, rather than to antagonize, Prussia. Finally, the French were beginning to cramp the expanding English colonies in America. Accordingly, Britain threw in her lot with Frederick of Prussia against France, Austria, and Russia. As it had in the previous war, the fighting began overseas in what became known as the French and Indian War (1754–1763).

Sensing what was coming and well aware of the coalition that had been formed against him, Frederick of Prussia, without declaring war, invaded Saxony. The fighting soon became general. At first it seemed as though Prussia would perish in the contest against the combined armies of France, Austria, and Prussia that encircled him. Frederick nearly gave up hope; but at a crucial moment the death of Elizabeth of Russia brought about Russia's withdrawal from the war. This fact, along with English infusions of money, kept Frederick going. His armies recovered to inflict two more defeats upon the Austrians. The exhausted French prepared to withdraw from the war, with the result that the Treaty of Hubertusburg confirmed Frederick in his possession of Silesia. Proud France and Austria had both been humbled. Frederick's military virtuosity had astounded all Europe.

COMPETITION OVERSEAS: FRANCE AND BRITAIN

We have seen that the "Diplomatic Revolution" (1756), engineered by an Austrian minister prior to the Seven Years' War, had brought about a realignment of the powers on the continent of Europe. Further, France and England, allies since 1717, resumed hostilities in 1740 with the war of Austrian Succession. Then, during the Seven Years' War, although the British avoided sending men across the Channel to attack France, they did not hesitate to supply the Prussian armies in central Europe nor to take advantage of France's resulting distractions by gobbling up her trading posts and colonies overseas.

It will be remembered that in the course of the seventeenth century the English and French had gradually superseded the Spanish, Portuguese, and Dutch as the most aggressive competitors for overseas empire. Collision between these two was perhaps inevitable, the more so because both France and England sent explorers, traders, and eventually settlers to roughly the same geographical areas. For example, at almost exactly the same time, the English and the French established colonies in North America, in Virginia (1607) and Quebec (1608) respectively. The English East India Company arrived in India first (1603), but in 1664 the French East India Company was founded and shortly thereafter began staking out trading posts.

By mid-eighteenth century the greatest imperial progress in India was being made by the French. Joseph Dupleix developed the technique for European penetration of this vast and populous subcontinent: offering military assistance to native princes in their wars with each other in return for territorial and trading concessions. In this way Dupleix was able to make substantial gains for the French East India Company, especially along the Carnatic coast and in the Deccan. The British East India Company, which came to be served in India by Robert Clive, adopted the same system; and in the interval between the War of Austrian Succession and the Seven Years' War the two companies continued to fight one another although their countries were not at war. In this struggle, Dupleix suffered from insufficient support from home. He was, in fact, recalled in disgrace in 1754; and before the Seven Years' War started in Europe, Clive began the ascendancy of the British in Indian affairs. During the war, Clive with his Indian allies defeated the French and their native supporters at Plassey (1757); the English took the French post at Pondichéry; and the Company gained more than 800 square miles at the mouths of the Ganges. By 1764, the British ruled all of Bengal; and five years later the French acknowledged the state of affairs by dissolving their East India Company.

In America, the conflict between the French and the English had begun early, as during the sixteenth and seventeenth centuries French and English freebooters attacked one another, as well as Dutch and Spanish colonies in the New World, especially in the West Indian islands. Then, during the War of Spanish Succession (1701–1714), known in America as Queen Anne's

THE SECOND HUNDRED YEARS' WAR

European Name	Date	American Name
War of the League of Augsburg	1689–1697	King William's War
War of the Spanish Succession	1701–1714	Queen Anne's War
War of Austrian Succession	1740–1748	King George's War
Seven Years' War	1756–1763	French and Indian War
War of the American Revolution	1775–1783	War for Independence
Wars of the French Revolution	1792–1801	
Napoleonic Wars	1801–1815	War of 1812

War (see chart), the English wrested present-day Nova Scotia—important to fishing fleets—from the French and replaced the French as holders of what was considered a desirable commercial privilege, the *Asiento,* from Spain.[4] French and British forces continued to fight sporadically in the New World, resorting to any and all means to win allies from among the native Indian tribes. The French and Indian War of 1754–1763 coincided with the Seven Years' War on the continent and was a war not, of course, between the French and the Indians but between the English and the French for control of the waterways of the Ohio country. Recovering from initial defeat at Fort Necessity, (near present-day Pittsburgh, Pennsylvania), the English formally declared war and went on to conquer all of French Canada. Quebec surrendered in 1759; Montreal in 1760; and in 1762 the English took Martinique, Grenada, and the other French islands in the Caribbean. Although France recovered the islands in the Treaty of Paris that ended the war that country had to all intents and purposes been driven from the continent of North America. The way had been prepared for Britain's nearly total mastery of the seas at the end of the Napoleonic era (1815).[5]

ENLIGHTENED DESPOTISM

The wars of the first half and middle of the eighteenth century which terminated in the treaties of Paris and Hubertusburg (1763) absorbed much but not all of the energy of the peoples of Europe and their rulers. By some strange coincidence of history or fate, a surprising number of the ruling

[4] The *Asiento* gave its holder the right to send a shipload of African slaves and one trading ship every year for a period of thirty years to the Spanish-American colonies. The profits from this trade proved more illusory than real, and England eventually relinquished the contract.

[5] An English historian of the late nineteenth century, J. R. Seeley, wrote an influential essay called *The Expansion of England* (1873), in which he noted that in every war from the beginning of the War of the League of Augsburg (1689) to the conclusion of the Napoleonic Wars (1815) England and France had been on opposite sides. He noted, moreover, that all of these Anglo-French conflicts were primarily struggles for overseas territories. Seeley seems to have forgotten that for many years during the ministries of Fleury in France and Walpole in England, the two kingdoms were allied; but, nevertheless, his concept of a "Second Hundred Years' War" (actually the total time-span was 125 years) of competition for empire does serve to make some sense out of the confusion of eighteenth-century warfare, especially in its overseas aspects.

monarchs of this period and the generation which followed were not only aggressive but sensitive, alert, active human beings who were interested in using their more-or-less despotic powers to improve the lot of their subjects at home. Frederick II of Prussia came to the throne of Prussia in 1740 already indoctrinated with the message of the Enlightenment. Within a period of less than ten years, no less than eight new rulers came to power, most of whom believed that they were the servants of the states they ruled, that reform of institutions was both desirable and possible, and that they were the instruments of progress.

NEW MONARCHS NEAR THE END OF THE SEVEN YEARS' WAR

		Date of Accession	Age at Accession
Naples	Ferdinand I (Bourbon)	1759	9
† Spain	‡ Charles III (Bourbon)	1759	43
† England	George III (Hanover)	1760	22
† Russia	‡ Catherine II (Anhalt-Zerbst)	1762	33
† Austria, etc.*	‡ Joseph (Habsburg) as co-regent	1765	24
Holy Roman Empire	Joseph as Joseph II		
Denmark	Christian VII (Oldenburg)	1766	16
United Provinces	William V (Orange-Nassau)	1766	

OLD RULERS CARRYING OVER THE 1760's

Sweden	Adolphus Frederick	1751 (to 1771)
† France	Louis XV (Bourbon)§	1723 (to 1774)
† Austria, etc.*	Maria Theresa, as co-regent with her son	1740 (to 1780)
† Prussia	‡ Frederick II (Hohenzollern)	1740 (to 1786)

*The Habsburg heritage was made up of many different provinces. Maria Theresa was Archduchess of Austria, Queen of Hungary and Bohemia. Austria was a small part of her realm, which included also, in addition to Hungary and Bohemia, Styria, Carinthia, Carniola, the Tyrol, Transylvania, as well as the South Netherlands (roughly present-day Belgium) plus Luxemburg, the Duchy of Milan (Lombardy) and Tuscany.

†Major Power

‡Enlightened Despot

§During Louis XV's minority, 1715–1723, France was ruled by a regent, Philip, Duke of Orléans.

Six new men, a boy, and one woman, came to power in Europe between 1759 and 1766 (see chart). Some of them had, of course, little influence on events—notably the kings of Naples, Poland, and Denmark. But four of the new rulers inherited or acquired major states. They were young adults who tended more to resemble the vigorous king of Prussia than the "aging voluptuary," Louis XV of France. Three of these four—Charles of Spain, Catherine of Russia, and Joseph of Austria—are usually identified as "enlightened despots," along with Frederick of Prussia.

In addition to these major figures, some minor rulers and several powerful ministers caught the disease of Enlightenment. For instance, the Marquis of Pombal was a highly despotic and effective reforming minister in Portugal (1750–1777); Johann Struensee created a brief whirlwind of "rational" but arbitrary change for one year in Denmark (1770–1771); and Sweden had its day of Enlightenment under Gustavus III (1771–1792). We shall not be able to examine each of these regimes or even consider all the major ones, but rather focus on a few: one north German Protestant state (Prussia), one southern Latin Roman Catholic country (peninsular Spain), and one cosmopolitan European state (the continental Habsburg monarchy), to see in some detail how the idea of enlightened despotism fared in these representative areas.

PRUSSIA

Frederick the Great Since the time when they had acquired control over the old Mark Brandenburg back in the fifteenth century, the Hohenzollerns as individual rulers had maintained a high level of competence. Of this remarkable family, Frederick II, the Great (ruled 1740–1786), was by all odds the most capable and interesting member.

After an upbringing that would have driven most sensitive children to bedlam, young Frederick almost miraculously made his accommodation to the world. Having undergone an intensive, enforced apprenticeship in the arts of war and administration, and a good deal of covert study of French enlightened books, of music and economics, Frederick came to the throne in 1740 at the age of 28. The territories that he inherited, though small and sparsely populated, were spread noncontiguously over 18 degrees of longitude from the river Rhine on the west to the Niemen on the east. These realms possessed no internal unity or logic. They were held together only by the determination of Frederick's ancestors who had acquired them.

Why, shortly after he came to power, did Frederick risk throwing the magnificent army created by his father into 23-year-old Maria Theresa's Austrian province, Silesia, in the valley of the upper Oder? "It was," he said later, "a means of acquiring reputation and of increasing the power of the state." The enterprise took 23 years and nearly cost Frederick his life. At one point, while he was contending against the combined powers of France, Austria, and Russia, Frederick wrote to one of his ministers: "All is lost . . . I shall not survive the ruin of the Fatherland. Adieu forever!" After it was over, Frederick mourned the cost of taking and keeping Silesia with its million and a half population: whole provinces devastated, deserted farms, ruined cities, food in scarce supply, commerce, industry and finance at a standstill. Even more serious, Frederick thought, was the moral collapse resulting from the war. Discipline and the habit of work had fled the land. What is more, although the Prussian state had gained territory from the war, East Prussia was still not connected with the Mark Brandenburg, the

This intriguing picture from an eighteenth-century treatise on the art of warfare shows a solution to the problem of how to sleep nine soldiers in one tent. Note that most of the soldiers have taken off their boots and covered themselves with their coats; the commanding officer (upper left, with sword sleeps fully dressed. (LCRB.)

heart of the Hohenzollern lands. The frontiers still lacked natural boundaries and lay open to invasion on every side. Frederick could feel no more secure in 1763 than he had in 1740. But his prestige was high.

Reconstruction of the Army Although his kingdom seemed nearly ruined, Frederick's royal treasury was still ample, his magazines were full, remounts and draft animals for the army were in good supply. The army, on the other hand, desperately needed rehabilitation, having lost 180,000 soldiers and 1,500 officers in sixteen pitched battles during the Seven Years' War alone. The dead make poor soldiers. With money he could lure some soldiers from abroad—especially from western and southern Germany. Others his officers kidnapped—fine tall men, preferably—surprised by Prussian "recruiting" parties as they emerged from church in Mecklenburg or Saxony. By whatever method, the recruits came in at the rate of seven to eight thousand per year. To supplement his precious *Junker* nobles, generations of whom had been sacrificed to Silesia, Frederick found officers where he could, so long as they were noble. Only desperation would lead him to use non-noble officers, who, Frederick believed, lacked the necessary bravado and habit of command. Prussian noble boys were trained in *Cadettenhäuser* (military schools). Spring and autumn the regiments maneuvered under the king's watchful eye; and what had been in 1763 a wreck of 151,000 dispirited men became by 1771 a polished weapon 186,000 strong.

Economic Reconstruction Economic reconstruction was as essential as the recruitment of soldiers. To replace the 500,000 farmers and workers lost

Frederick the Great's disciplined troops were the envy of other European rulers, but thousands of Germans emigrated rather than submit to the harsh military regimen. Some of the "draft-dodgers" came to Pennsylvania, where they were known as "Dutch" for "deutsch" or German. Death came to Frederick the Great at the age of 74, as the result of exposure to a storm during a military review like the one shown here. (LCPP.)

during the war, Frederick followed his father's example and encouraged immigration of foreign colonists to such effect that ten years after the end of the war the devastated provinces had greater populations than in 1756. Soldiers were granted furloughs at harvest time to work in the fields. The government made available horses, seed, and cattle and established banks to supply credit for rural improvements. The upshot of this carefully administered and supervised program was quick rebuilding of the villages and an increase in agricultural production to the point where Prussia became a substantial exporter of grain.

Industry, too, profited from this energetic zeal. High protective tariffs on imported goods and subsidies for what the king considered desirable new industries, along with exemption from excise taxes for the products of these enterprises, were the main features of this support. To make credit available to entrepreneurs, Frederick created more banks which could reduce interest rates to reasonable levels. The king carefully watched the new industries grow: when they seemed to be able to stand on their own feet their subsidies and tax exemptions were removed.

Within ten years after the conclusion of the Seven Years' War, Frederick's industrial and agricultural policies, along with a program of internal improvements, had produced an economically rebuilt country which enjoyed a highly favorable balance of trade. In 1740 there had been a trade deficit of half a million *thalers;* in 1775 this had changed to a *credit* of 4,400,000 *thalers.* The incoming payments helped to provide grist for the tax-collector's mill.

To relieve his subjects of their cash, Frederick imported the most skillful and experienced tax collectors he could find: Frenchmen. One of these—de

Launay—was paid three times as much as any other Prussian civil servant. Experts in the creation and imposition of indirect taxes, these French collectors managed to increase the annual royal revenues enormously. No other major European government could boast anything like Prussia's financial solvency despite the fact that their territories were far larger and their populations were greater and richer.

All this was very efficient, but not particularly enlightened; and many of Frederick's contemporaries thought of his kingdom as little more than a garrison. For example, on a visit to Berlin, Goethe, a non-Prussian German, compared Prussia to a military anthill or an immense clockwork machine and took the first opportunity to flee home to Weimar in south Germany. Frederick himself was not content with his reputation as a first-rate accountant and soldier; he also wished to be thought of as a philosopher-king, his kingdom a land not only of discipline but of culture.

Discipline and Education But discipline came first of all. Among the peasants a proper subserviency and stability was to be achieved primarily by maintaining the accustomed relationships between peasant and landlord. Although he wrote in 1772 that serfdom was a barbarous custom, Frederick did nothing to eliminate it on those private estates where it existed and where it served to support the nobility upon which he depended absolutely for his army officers and civil servants. Thus, most east Elbian Prussian peasants not only paid about 40 percent of their income to the state; they also continued to owe virtually unlimited service to their landlords.

For the population at large, discipline was to be sought through education. In 1763, the Prussian government promulgated the *Landschulreglement* (Rural School Law) which stipulated that elementary education was obligatory for all children. Schoolmasters, Frederick wrote, should "teach youngsters religion and morality. . . . It is enough for the people in the country to learn only a little reading and writing." They should also be instructed in practical matters like the cultivation of mulberry trees (the king was anxious to see silk produced in Prussia as it was in France); but, above all, they should be imbued (said this deist disciple of Voltaire) with a true fear of God.

Secondary education, limited to the middle and upper classes, had the same general objectives, though the curriculum was somewhat broader: ancient languages, French, and logic, in addition to religion in the *Gymnasium* (Classical High School); living languages, mathematics, economics, commerce, and technical studies in the *Realschule* (Technical High School). To prepare upper middle-class and noble youth for the civil service, and second sons and other impoverished young men for the clergy there were universities at Halle and Königsberg. Here, too, the emphasis was on useful subjects.

This tendency to emphasize the practical in education was not only a holdover from his father's reign but was prescribed by the French *philosophes,* with whose work we know Frederick was entirely familiar. On paper, the

Prussian educational system, from the compulsory rural schools to the universities, was an admirable and forward-looking structure that could have freed the people from ignorance and superstition. But the massive sums of money necessary for effective universal education were simply not available. The Prussian school and university system became, therefore, a sort of adjunct to the *Cadettenhäuser,* with order, piety, and cleanliness taking precedence over enlightenment.

Enlightened Despotism in Prussia Frederick knew relatively little about German culture. He tended to speak, write, and think in French; he was thoroughly familiar with French writers, but he was barely aware of the writings of his great German literary contemporaries: Lessing, Goethe, and Schiller, for instance. He rejuvenated the Royal Academy at Berlin, which had been neglected by his father, by drawing to it illustrious foreigners as academicians. French drama and French paintings were brought to Berlin and to Frederick's little French palace at Potsdam, from which the flute-playing king carried on a lively correspondence and even friendship with French intellectuals such as Voltaire.

In 1777, Frederick made his own contribution to the literature of the Enlightenment. His *Essay on Forms of Government* (1777) outlined the obligations of the "true" monarch as follows:

The prince is to the nation he governs what the head is to the man; it is his duty to see, think, and act for the whole community. . . . He must be active, possess integrity, and collect his whole powers, that he may be able to run the career he has commenced.

The "true" monarch, according to Frederick, must have a perfect knowledge of the genius of his nation; he must be indefatigably energetic and totally disinterested. He should move in the realization that he is a man "like the least of his subjects."

Frederick never saw fit to make this essay public. That he did not attests to a significant corollary of his credo, that the enlightened despot may trust no one but himself, and that he alone must supervise the management of his subjects and his realms. And he knew that there was a difference between the ideal and the practical problems of statecraft. For example, as philosopher-king, Frederick believed—in principle—in freedom of conscience. The sovereign must not, he wrote, interfere in the religious beliefs of his subjects:

Nay, Toleration is itself so advantageous to the people . . . that it constitutes the happiness of the state. As soon as there is that perfect freedom of opinion, the people are all at peace; whereas persecution has given birth to the most bloody civil wars, and such as have been the most inveterate and the most destructive.

But although he would not persecute a man for his religious convictions, Frederick would not permit the expression of ideas that might contribute to the subversion of the state. A distinction was also made between the expression of unorthodox ideas by university-educated elites (permitted, at the proper place and time) and by ordinary folk (forbidden). In practice, true freedom of expression was limited to the royal dinner table and there to the king alone.

While Frederick felt and declared that he had the interests of all his subjects at heart, his efficient tax collectors saw to it that none of these subjects—peasants and nobles alike—became any richer than they had been before he began his reforms. There was no land reform under his administration. In fact, during his reign the Junkers reduced the condition of their serfs to something very near slavery, especially in the east. His attitude toward the rights of other peoples to self-determination was clearly demonstrated in 1772, if it had not been clear enough before: the supposed or pretended danger of renewed Turkish penetration gave him the excuse to

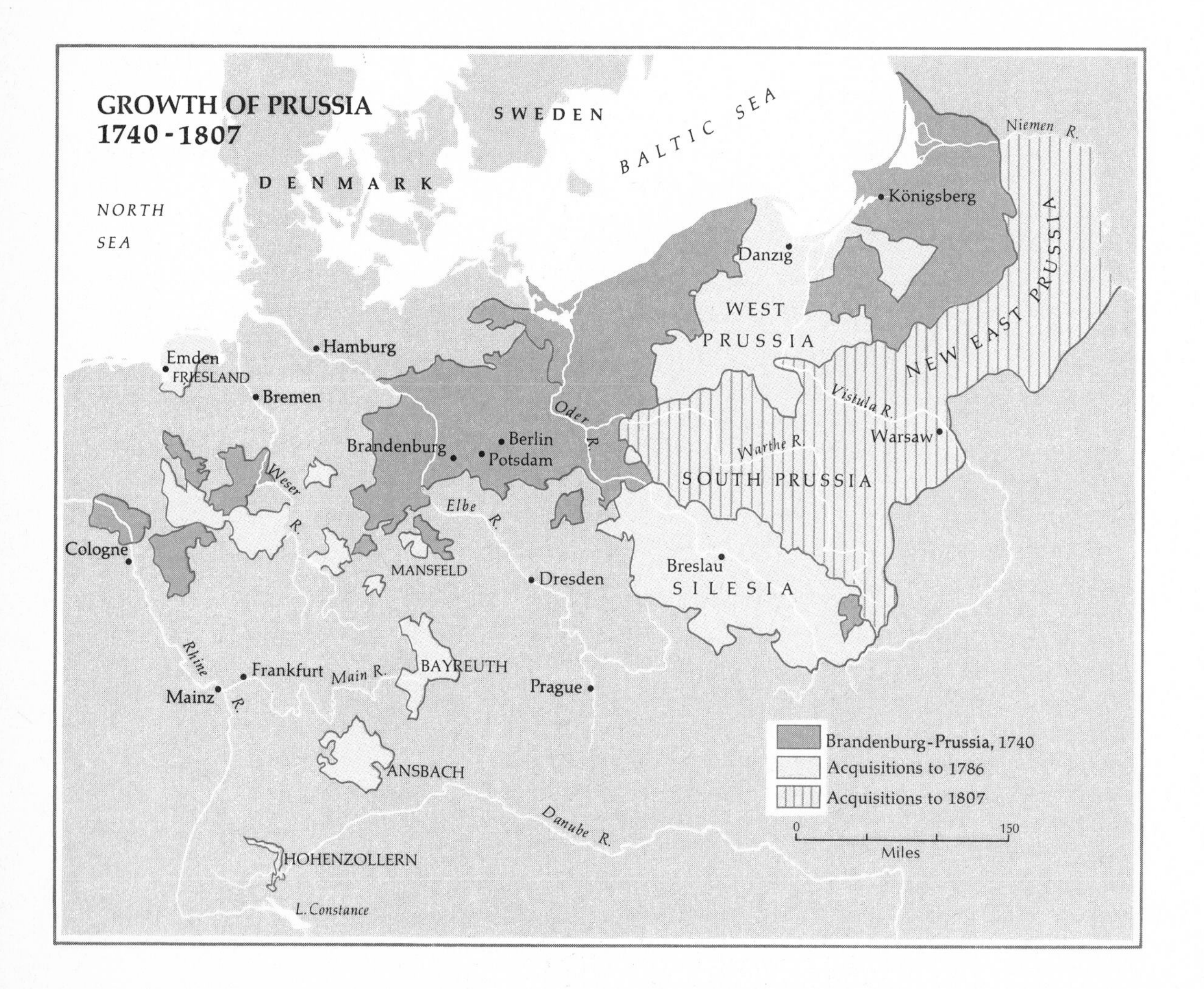

engineer one of the starkest land-grabs in all history, the First Partition of Poland.[6] Ridiculing Maria Theresa's qualms ("She cries, but she always takes," was Frederick's comment), he calmly annexed the Polish lands west and south of East Prussia so as to provide what he saw as the necessary territorial connection between his realms.

Enlightened despotism, Prussian model, then, was clearly a despotism. If it shared some of the ideals of the Enlightenment, it did not let these interfere with the practical requirements of preserving absolute political power. Dependent upon the tireless personal attention of one severe yet strangely sensitive leader, its guiding principle was, in the final analysis, the consolidation and expansion of the Hohenzollern realms.

CHARLES III OF SPAIN

Far to the south and west, one of the new generation of monarchs faced very different problems in a somewhat similar manner but without making such a great splash on the European scene. Charles III (Bourbon) of Spain (ruled 1759–1788) was a man with training in statecraft, having served his apprenticeship as Duke of Parma and King of the Two Sicilies before his elevation to the throne of Spain. While in Italy, this methodical if unimaginative Bourbon had read the script of progressive Enlightenment, which he endeavored with no small success to enact on the larger Spanish stage.

Charles selected able ministers (Aranda, Campomanes, and Floridablanca) through whom he endeavored to reform the manners (one of his edicts forbade dumping slops out of the windows in Madrid), as well as the economic life of his subjects. He abolished laws that restricted Spanish internal trade and reduced tariffs. He pushed the construction of roads, bridges, and harbors, and worked to distribute land among the peasants. These reforms and public works were made at great cost, but the results were measurable. Private enterprise thrived in Spain, and at the end of Charles' reign, foreign trade had increased to many times its previous volume.

Charles III and the Jesuits The most characteristic aspect of Charles' enlightened policy was his attitude toward the Roman Catholic Church. Personally devout, he was opposed to Church influence in temporal affairs and suspicious of the Society of Jesus, the most vigorous and militant arm of the Church. The Jesuits were a favorite target of the intellectuals of the Enlightenment, who delighted in revealing Jesuit "scandals" and in attacking Jesuit obscurantism (see, for instance, Voltaire's description of the activities of the Jesuits in Paraguay in *Candide*). Organized as a semi-autonomous body ruled by a general whom the monarchs could not dominate, the order had acquired (whether rightly or wrongly) a reputation for mysterious and often

[6] The First Partition of Poland was arranged through bilateral treaties between Prussia, Austria, and Russia (1772) and confirmed by separate treaties of each nation with Poland (1775). Each neighbor took Polish territories on its borders considered important to its own security. The Second Partition, in 1793, enormously expanded these annexations, and in 1795 Poland literally ceased to exist when the Third Partition occurred under cover of the French Revolution.

subversive intervention in political affairs. Moreover, in the eighteenth century the Society was violating its own charter by branching out into large-scale commercial enterprises. It accumulated great wealth from these activities as well as from the contributions of the faithful.

The first attack on the Jesuits was begun in 1741 by Pope Benedict XIV, who denounced the trading activities of the order. Then Pombal, the enlightened minister in Portugal, who had long been at odds with the Society, accused the whole Order of conspiring with certain nobles in an attempt to assassinate the king of Portugal as that worthy returned from a visit to his mistress. Pombal made his charge stick and in 1759 ejected every Jesuit from Portugal and its colonies. A few years later, a French court (the *parlement* of Paris) ruled that the constitution of the Society of Jesus was subversive of the fundamental laws of France. As a result, in 1764 all Jesuit foundations and schools in France were closed and the Society's members exiled from the kingdom.

Charles III of Spain (1716–1788) in hunting garb, by Francisco José de Goya y Lucientes (1746–1828), one of Goya's first court portraits. Already over seventy when it was painted, Charles died in 1688, a few months before the outbreak of the French Revolution. This "enlightened despot" was passionately devoted to hunting. (Prado, Spain)

In Spain, Charles III was galvanized to action in 1766 by his suspicion that the Jesuits participated in or organized a riot against his royal authority in Madrid, and the next year he expelled the Jesuits from all his realms. He followed this up by bringing pressure on the pope to suppress the order entirely. The campaign reached its climax in 1773, when Pope Clement XIV, under threat of war from France, Spain, and the Two Sicilies, did in fact abolish the Society. Its 23,000 members took refuge where they could. (Their principal havens were the realms of two non-Roman Catholic enlightened despots: Prussia and Russia.) This victory achieved, Charles moved successfully further to restrict the power of the Church in his Roman Catholic country by reducing the numbers of the clergy and monasteries.

Like Frederick of Prussia, Charles III of Spain was an enlightened despot who can be described as a success. His objectives were limited, but he brought his anticlerical policy to the conclusion he intended; and, although he did not sweep away all of the cobwebs, he did infuse new life temporarily into Spanish administration, agriculture, and commerce.

THE HABSBURG MONARCHY

The Austrian experiment in enlightened despotism was, on two counts, quite a different affair. First, Joseph II, unlike Frederick, was not willing to compromise his principles and was determined to do a thorough job. Second, his work did not take place in a compact and more-or-less isolated country like peninsular Spain, nor in a small and, therefore, easily supervised state like Prussia.

Joseph II had one great asset: his charming and capable mother. Like Frederick II in Prussia, who was able to superimpose his "Enlightenment" on top of the police state established by his father, Joseph profited from the work of his royal predecessor and then co-regent, Maria Theresa. This "empress,"[7] who reigned for forty years (1740–1780), had, with the help

[7] Maria Theresa was not really an empress. First her husband and then her son was Holy Roman Emperor. But her subjects tended to call her Empress simply because this title was simpler than "Queen of Bohemia and Hungary, Archduchess of Austria," etc.

of her great ministers, Counts Haugwitz and Kaunitz, accomplished in the years between 1749 and 1763 a considerable administrative reform. Before Joseph came of age, a collection of principalities had very nearly been molded into a unified state. The new Austrian administration, modelled after the Prussian, was highly centralized in Vienna; and meetings of estates and diets in most parts of the empire had been quietly suspended.

This high-minded and pious woman was anxious to promote the well-being of her people. In this endeavor her government substantially reduced the labor services that landlords were permitted to exact from peasant-serfs, and managed to subject nobles to taxation so that they would bear at least part of the burden of government. However, Maria Theresa was afraid of the ideas of the *philosophes* which, she believed, represented a threat to her imperial power. While her son and young men in the University of Vienna eagerly read and talked about "natural law," she tried through censorship to prevent these dangerous ideas from circulating in her realm.

As devoted to her family as she was to her empire, Maria Theresa of Austria produced sixteen children. Among these were the future Emperor Joseph II (standing, to the right of the "Empress") and Marie Antoinette, future queen of France. Only eleven of her brood are shown in this family portrait. (Kunsthistorisches Museum, Vienna.)

When, in 1765, the Emperor Francis, Maria Theresa's husband, died, the sorrowing widow admitted her son Joseph to a co-regency with her. The young man became Holy Roman Emperor as well. During the remaining fifteen years of her life she entrusted her old servant Kaunitz with the task of keeping Joseph and his dangerous ideas within the bounds of prudence. Partially effective so long as she lived, this control terminated with her death in 1780.

Joseph II Joseph was also high-minded and pious, but, unlike his mother, he was a doctrinaire child of the Enlightenment. He believed passionately in the necessity for and the possibility of organizing life on earth according to a rational system. He thought that he spoke for the state and was possessed both of the "right reason" to decide what should be accomplished and the power to get it done. His "reason" was humanitarian and egalitarian. He was deeply revolted by injustice; he abhorred the exploitation of the many weak by the few strong. Injustice and exploitation resulted, he thought, from the workings of unnatural and outmoded institutions carried over from the past. All these should be destroyed and replaced by the beneficent and watchful state. Negatively, he would eliminate serfdom, destroy the guilds, and terminate the privileged corporativeness of the church, of the aristocracy, and of all other constituted bodies—except the state. Positively, he would establish equality of taxation as well as religious, civil, economic, and intellectual liberty—complete freedom, that is, from everything except the police. This was a big program, far too ambitious for the time and place and certainly more than he could have achieved during the ten short years (1780–1790) that remained to him after his mother's death.

That decade was full of activity as Joseph attempted to realize his vision through his own arduous toil and that of his increasingly intimidated bureaucracy. No usage, no institution, and no rights (except what he decided were "natural rights") were sacred in his view. His methods were drastic and arbitrary. His intentions were socially revolutionary.

As the thousands of edicts that issued from his office in Vienna after 1780 changed time-honored usages and eliminated ancient privileges, Joseph's enemies multiplied. Many Roman Catholics were appalled when he decreed religious toleration for Protestant and Eastern Christians, as well as for Jews, and when he closed monasteries and put the Roman Catholic clergy under government control. When he moved not only to liberate the serfs but also to free the peasantry from all forced labor, landlords joined the resistance. Hungarians, Bohemians, Belgians, and Italians resented the loss of their autonomy and the upsetting of their local customs. They protested a policy designed to make German the official language of the entire empire. Even the peasants, who were the primary objects of Joseph's benevolence, became confused by agrarian reforms that they did not fully understand, and rose in revolt. As resistance increased so did Joseph's determination to have his way, and the prisons of this liberally enlightened monarchy were soon stuffed with political prisoners.

Like "Farmer George" in England and Louis XVI in France, Joseph II of Austria espoused the new agriculture and pretended great personal interest in its techniques. Here the zealot king is shown holding a plow pulled by two horses. The moldboard plow was relatively new to eastern European agriculture. (Bildarchiv d. Ost. Nationalbibliothek, Vienna.)

The upshot of Joseph's revolution from above was failure and revolt. While he wore himself out with work, rebellion broke out in the Austrian Netherlands and in Hungary. Rioting Bohemian peasants were slaughtered by Joseph's army. Landlords, ecclesiastics, and intellectuals all opposed him. His mother's old minister, Kaunitz, refused to see him, even on his deathbed.

The ambitious foreign policy he had directed toward aggrandizing Habsburg prestige and power also ended in failure. Returning from an unsuccessful military campaign in the Balkans late in 1788, Joseph took to his bed, broken in health at age forty-eight. He died a year later, fully aware that his vast rational-humanitarian storm had failed to destroy the old edifices. It remained for his much more conservative brother and successor, Leopold, to salvage some small parts of Joseph's program and to try to regroup the Habsburg empire to withstand the new revolutionary winds that were already blowing from France.

Joseph was a tragic figure. No other ruler, enlightened, benevolent, or otherwise, seems to have sympathized more with the desires of the late eighteenth-century visionaries. He shared their ideal of a society where power and rank should be open to talent, where economic activity could prosper free from artificial restraints. He worked harder than any other monarch to make this vision a reality, and yet he was rejected by his own subjects.

THE FAILURE OF ENLIGHTENED DESPOTISM

So fared three rulers during the era of enlightened despotism. As regards the achievements of others, like Catherine of Russia, there were differences in detail; but, by and large, in no place did the enlightened scheme of reform or revolution from above serve to provide a system of government or an arrangement of society in harmony with the demographic, economic, and social changes that were going on at the time. By 1790, it could have been justly said that in terms of the programs of the Enlightenment the benevolent despots had tried and been found wanting.

Taking its ideas of statecraft from French and English intellectuals, enlightened despotism was intended to alter the *ancien régime* and to create the open society desired by the growing middle classes. Translated into action, as we have seen, these ideas were diluted or subverted, ending usually in discouragement and failure. Frederick of Prussia and Catherine of Russia tamed the aristocracy but vastly increased their own autocratic power, and gave landlords even more power over the peasants on their estates than they had previously enjoyed. Despite the considerable achievements of Charles III and his ministers, the Spanish grandees prospered at the expense of the peasants and the crown. The aristocracies of the Habsburg realms weathered Joseph's storm, their peasants' hopes deceived, and the relatively insignificant Austrian middle class did not measurably increase its power. Everywhere, the advantages accruing to the middle classes as a result of enlightened despotism were slight.

Were these rulers' efforts, then, in vain? Were they ahead of their times? Were the changes they attempted to make beyond the power of ordinary mortals? As we shall see, the governmental structures they left behind proved too fragile to stand successfully against the forces unleashed by the French Revolution in the next decades.

FURTHER READING

Again the student should refer to the *Rise of Modern Europe* volumes, mentioned previously, by Roberts and Dorn, as well as to the one by L. Gershoy, * *From Despotism to Revolution, 1763–1789* (1944); and to M. Anderson * *Europe in the Eighteenth Century, 1713–1783* (1970). Also useful is C. Behrens, * *The Ancien Régime* (1967). Ms. Behrens' illustrated work considers the *ancien régime* in France between 1748 and 1789 in the setting of European political events and struggles for trade and colonies.

On the international balance, A. Sorel, * *Europe under the Old Regime* (1968), a translation of the first volume of Sorel's great study of Europe and the French Revolution, is still best. This may be supplemented with the recently reprinted, R. Lodge, *Studies in Eighteenth-Century Diplomacy, 1740–1748* (1973). Most useful for France in this period is A. Cobban, * *History of Modern France, 1715–1799* (1965), the first volume of a Penguin series. For England, see J. H. Plumb, * *England in the Eighteenth Century* (1950); and for Spain, R. Trevor Davies, *Spain in Decline* (1957). For Italy, which is not covered in the excellent volume by Dorn, Janet P. Trevelyan, *A Short History of the Italian*

*Books available in paperback edition are marked with an asterisk.

People (1956), will provide a sympathetic introduction. Polish problems and related diplomacy are thoroughly handled by H. H. Kaplan in *The First Partition of Poland* (1962).

The historian who invented the concept of the "Second Hundred Years' War" was J. R. Seeley, Regius Professor at Cambridge in the late nineteenth century. His series of lectures, intended to point out that England's history is essentially the history of English expansion, is a classic dating from 1883, recently edited by J. Gross, that should be read: J. R. Seeley, * *The Expansion of England* (1973). C. E. Carrington, *The British Overseas* (1968), and H. I. Priestly, *France Overseas through the Old Regime* (1939), provide more details. A. M. Davies, *Clive of Plassey* (1973); P. Moon, *Warren Hastings and British India* (1947); and H. Dodwell, *Dupleix and Clive, the Beginnings of Empire* (1967), all deal with persons and places of the struggle. The most convenient treatment is A. H. Buffington, *The Second Hundred Years' War, 1689–1815* (1929). The great work on the naval contest and its wider implications is by Rear Admiral A. T. Mahan, * *The Influence of Sea Power on History* (1957).

For enlightened despotism, the "Berkshire" study by G. Bruun, *The Enlightened Despots* (1973), has the advantage of being brief. Biographical studies of some of the despots include G. P. Gooch, *Frederick the Great* (1947), which sees "Old Fritz" through English eyes. S. K. Padover, *The Revolutionary Emperor: Joseph the Second* (1967), is readable and sound. R. Herr, * *The Eighteenth-Century Revolution in Spain* (1969), is the best volume in English on Charles III and his works. For Catherine of Russia, see G. P. Gooch, *Catherine the Great and Other Studies* (1954 and 1973). J. G. Gagliardo in * *Enlightened Despotism* (1967), maintains that "enlightened despotism" was mere expediency. This little book has an excellent bibliography.

PART XII

We have seen that the eighteenth century was a period of contrast and change—change that became progressively faster at mid-century and beyond. New technologies were willy nilly beginning to force new patterns of economic and social organization in Europe. Shifts in population and wealth began to affect the lives of ordinary men, especially in the western and more advanced areas. The ideas that many people held about themselves and their roles in society were subversive of the seemingly stable ancien régime. *In the next century, Alexis de Tocqueville could write of the eighteenth: "Everything that was alive and most active in the life [of the period] was of a new order; indeed not merely new but outspokenly hostile to the past."*

In the course of the eighteenth century the horizons and boundaries of Europe continued to expand to a wider world. Conflicts between Europeans were now fought with as much intensity (and with even more fateful consequences) in India and America as on the Rhine and the Elbe. As we have seen, new powers, Prussia and Russia, pulled the European center of gravity to the East. Thus Europe lost its geographical cohesiveness at the very time that the philosophes *and others loosened the mortar in its social and ideological foundations. The so-called Enlightened Despots endeavored to adjust their governments and the societies over which they ruled to the changing conditions—but tried to retain absolute power for themselves. Was it too much to expect to reap the benefits of revolution without permitting a Revolution to take place?*

The word "revolution" is, of course, too freely bandied about by most of us. Purists would have us use the term to refer only to relatively short periods of violent political and social change that decisively and not very gently oust one ruling group and replace it by another.[1] *Under this definition, the British events of the 1640's were a true Revolution, while the "Glorious Revolution" of 1688 was not (since there was no bloodshed and King James II was allowed to escape unharmed). The British referred to the "American Revolution" as a "rebellion" and many historians have argued that the lack of basic social change which characterized the American crisis hardly made it a "Revolution" in the true sense.*

At times in the histories of nations and civilizations, events overtake one another so rapidly, changes are so momentous, the dislocation of men and institutions so convulsive that there is no question, in anyone's mind that a Revolution—with a capital "R"—has occurred. Such an event was the great French Revolution. To those who lost their heads, as well as to those who survived, there was no question but that a Revolution was going on; and it is safe to say that every Revolution or revolution since has been weighed in the light of the French version.

"Revolutions are not made; they come," said Wendell Phillips, the nineteenth-century American orator. And in the years from 1763 to 1815, they came: first in America and then in France, the Netherlands, Ireland, Switzerland, Italy, Germany, Poland, and Hungary. Was this an "Age of Democratic Revolution," as one contemporary historian terms it?[2] *Or was it merely a time for substitution of the power of the aristocrats by that of the* bourgeoisie *(middle class), as the French historian Georges Lefebvre*[3] *and the German social scientist Karl Marx thought it?*

[1]See Clarence Crane Brinton, *The Anatomy of Revolution.* (N.Y., Vintage, 1965). Recently some Americans have discerned—or hoped for—a new phenomenon, a "long Revolution" which effects radical social change but omits bloodshed.

[2]R. R. Palmer, *The Age of the Democratic Revolution,* 2 vols. (Princeton, N.J., 1959–64).

[3]G. Lefebvre, *The Coming of the French Revolution* (Princeton, N.J., 1947).

FRENCH BOX SHOWING PORTRAITS OF VOLTAIRE, ROUSSEAU, AND BEN FRANKLIN. (The Metropolitan Museum of Art, Gift of William H. Huntington, 1883.)

THE AGE OF REVOLUTION, 1763-1815

LEGACY OF THE PAST

Delacroix' romantic canvas, "Liberty Leading the People," was painted in 1830, long after the end of the French Revolution. But his heroic female figure of "Liberty" carrying the tricolor and leading the French "people" over the barricades had already become the symbol of revolutionary aspirations the world over. (Louvre, Paris.)

The two main legacies of this period were the foundation of the United States in America and the French Revolution in Europe. The United States became the first modern "new nation" to free itself from imperial domination. Its Declaration of Independence, asserting that all men are created equal, and its successful establishment of a constitutional federation based on representative government and a Bill of Rights have had a major impact on the civic ideals of the modern world.

The French Revolution was the greatest of modern revolutions. It had both immediate and long-term effect on the development of modern society. Its influence was long felt in many different areas: for continental Europe it asserted the principle of representative constitutional government; in its radical phase it introduced the concept of modern revolutionary dictatorship based on mass terror; and it created the first complete example of popular mass nationalism and a national army. Finally, in its imperialistic Napoleonic phase, the French Revolution was exported to much of western and central Europe. It not only changed many of the prevailing political attitudes, but introduced new standards of social equality and reorganized legal structures on the basis of uniform, rationalized law codes. The consequence was to prepare the world for nineteenth-century middle-class liberalism on the one hand, and encourage the growth of doctrines of authoritarian revolution on the other.

MAJOR EVENTS, 1763-1815*

	France	General Politics	Economics, Technology and Culture
1760		Accession George III (1760)	Voltaire: *Candide* (1759)
		Treaties of Paris and Hubertusberg (1763)	Winckelmann: *History of Ancient Art* (1764)
	Suppression of Jesuits in France (1764)		
1765		Emperor Francis dies (1765)	
	Birth of Napoleon Bonaparte (1769) Fall of Choiseul (1769). Dauphin and Marie Antoinette married		Arkwright's water frame (1769)
1770		Struensee's reforms in Denmark (1770)	
	Maupeou suppresses the *parlements* (1771)	First Partition of Poland (1772)	Arkwright's spinning mill (1771)
	Louis XV dies; accession Louis XVI; recall of the *parlements* (1774)	Abolition of Society of Jesus (1773)	Goethe: *Sorrows of Werther* (1774)
1775	Fall of Turgot; enter Necker (1776)	Declaration of Independence, U.S. (1776)	E. Gibbon: *Decline and Fall of the Roman Empire* (1776–1788) Adam Smith's *Wealth of Nations* (1776)
	Voltaire dies (1778)	Franco-American Treaty (1778)	
1780	Necker dismissed after publishing his *Compte-rendu* (1781)	Maria Theresa dies; Joseph II on his own (1780)	
		Treaty of Paris—end of War of the American Revolution (1783)	Watt's double-acting steam engine (1782)
1785			Mozart composes the "Marriage of Figaro" (1785) Cartwright's power loom (1785)

American Revolution

*For 1763–1770 see also Major Events, Part XI.

French Revolution and Republic — Napoleon

Year	France	Europe	Culture and Society
		Frederick the Great of Prussia dies (1786)	Eden Treaty (1786)
	First Assembly of Notables (1787)		Mozart composes "Don Giovanni" (1787)
			Kant: *Critique of Pure Reason* (1788)
	Meeting of Estates General (May 1789)		Lavoisier's treatise on chemistry (1789)
	Bastille Day (July)		
1790		Joseph II of Austria, etc. dies (1790)	Edmund Burke: *Reflections on the Revolution in France* (1790)
	Flight to Varennes (1791)		Thomas Paine: *Rights of Man* (1791)
	Storming of the Tuileries and fall of the monarchy (August 1792)	French Revolutionary Wars begin (1792)	
		Second Partition of Poland (1793)	
	Fall of Robespierre (July 1794)		Abolition of slavery in French colonies (1794)
1795	Constitution of the Year III (1795)	Third Partition of Poland—end of Poland (1795)	
			Malthus on population (1798)
		Bonaparte to Egypt; Battle of the Nile (1798)	Wordsworth and Coleridge travel to Germany (1798)
	Coup d'état of Brumaire (1799)		
1800			Beethoven composes his "First Symphony" (1800)
	Napoleon Consul for life (1802)		
	Napoleon crowned Emperor (1804)		
1805		Battles of Trafalgar and Austerlitz (1805)	
		End of Holy Roman Empire (1806)	Berlin decree: Continental System (1806)
			Fulton's steamboat (1807)
		Spanish rising against France (1808)	
1810	Napoleon marries Marie Louise (1810)	Napoleon to Russia; U.S.A. declares war on England (1812)	Founding of Baptist Union of Great Britain (1812)
		Battle of Leipzig (1813)	
	Napoleon to Elba (1814)	First Peace of Paris; Congress of Vienna opens (1814)	Stephenson's locomotive (1814)
1815	The Hundred Days; Napoleon to St. Helena (1815)		

1 Crisis in the British Empire

Turgot, the French liberal economic thinker, said that colonies, in general, are like fruit: when they ripen, they fall from the tree. Were the American colonies "ripe" in 1763 at the end of the Seven Years' War (which Americans called the French and Indian War)? Or was it that the mother country was so "rotten" that she could no longer support this fruit? How much influence did the ideas of the contemporary European Enlightenment have on George III of England or the hotheads overseas? And, finally, was the American Revolution, which came first, the precursor of the French Revolution which followed—or was it merely a "crisis in the British Empire" which in the end changed little either in the former colonies or in the configuration of European and world power? We shall attempt to provide clues to the answers to these and other questions in this chapter.

GEORGE III

The End of the Seven Years' War The year before George III, filled with self-doubts but determined to be a "patriot king," came to the throne, is known in English history as the "miraculous year." It was 1759, the "year of victories," during which "every wind brought some messenger charged with joyful tidings and hostile standards."[1] In September 1759, Quebec fell to young General Wolfe, who was covered with posthumous glory and mourned by a grateful nation. General Amherst took Ticonderoga; Johnson secured Niagara. And as news of these strategic British victories was received it appeared that the French might lose all foothold in North America. They did so in the next year when the fort at Montreal surrendered.

In India, British victories multiplied. Closer to home, English naval squadrons broke up a desperate French plan to invade England from Ireland and swept the seas clear of French warships for the remainder of the War. Even on the continent, where for the most part the English had been content to provide subsidies and leave the fighting to others, British arms triumphed when the English infantry helped to rout a French army in Westphalia at

[1]T. B. Macaulay, Article, "William Pitt," *Encyclopaedia Britannica,* 11th Edition.

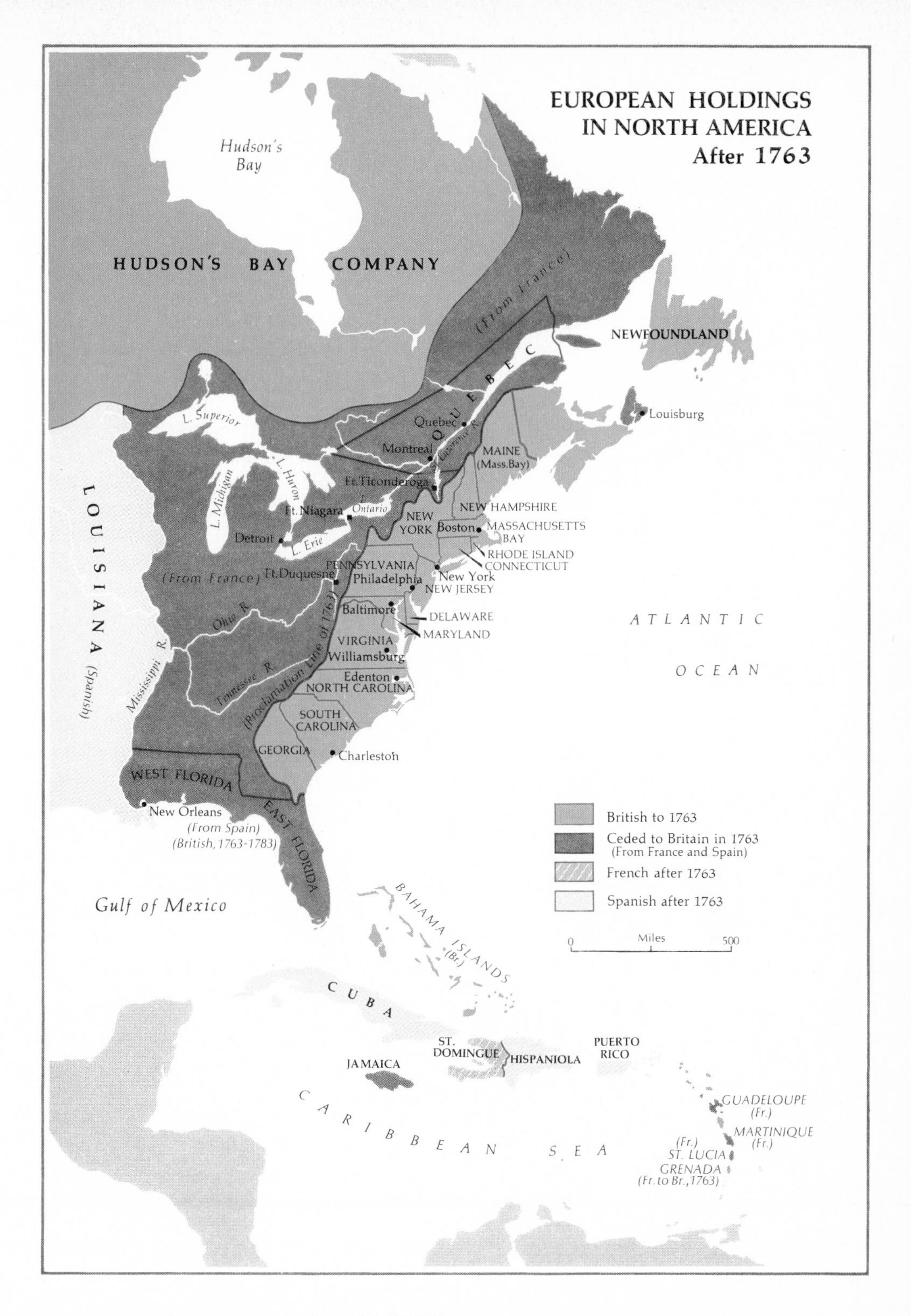
EUROPEAN HOLDINGS
IN NORTH AMERICA
After 1763
Hudson's Bay
HUDSON'S BAY COMPANY
(From France)
NEWFOUNDLAND
QUEBEC
Louisburg
L. Superior
Quebec
Montreal
St. Lawrence R.
MAINE
(Mass.Bay)
L. Michigan
L. Huron
Ft.Ticonderoga
Ft. Niagara
Ontario
NEW YORK
NEW HAMPSHIRE
Boston
MASSACHUSETTS BAY
LOUISIANA (Spanish)
Detroit
L. Erie
RHODE ISLAND
CONNECTICUT
(From France)
Ft.Duquesne
PENNSYLVANIA
Philadelphia
New York
NEW JERSEY
Ohio R.
Baltimore
DELAWARE
MARYLAND
ATLANTIC
OCEAN
Mississippi R.
VIRGINIA
Williamsburg
(Proclamation Line of 1763)
Tennessee R.
Edenton
NORTH CAROLINA
SOUTH CAROLINA
GEORGIA
Charleston
WEST FLORIDA
EAST FLORIDA
New Orleans
(From Spain)
(British, 1763-1783)
British to 1763
Ceded to Britain in 1763
(From France and Spain)
French after 1763
Spanish after 1763
Gulf of Mexico
BAHAMA ISLANDS
(Br.)
0 Miles 500
CUBA
ST. DOMINGUE
HISPANIOLA
PUERTO RICO
JAMAICA
GUADELOUPE
(Fr.)
MARTINIQUE
(Fr.)
(Fr.)
ST. LUCIA
GRENADA
(Fr. to Br., 1763)
CARIBBEAN SEA

George III was king of England for sixty difficult and eventful years (1760–1820). Winning and then losing empire in North America, his ministers and generals eventually succeeded in bringing Napoleon to his knees. (The Royal Collection, by Gracious Permission of Her Majesty the Queen.)

Minden (August 1759). Tiny England stood in a new summit of power and prestige, an object of envy and fear.

When the peace treaties were concluded a few years later, these victories had succeeded in more than doubling the territory under the British flag. England gained all the land between the Appalachians and the Mississippi as well as French Canada and Spanish Florida, Cape Breton Island in the north, and Grenada in the West Indies. What had been a fairly compact string of colonies along the eastern seaboard of North America became a vast semicontinental empire with the valuable West Indian sugar islands as satellites. In India, the gift of war was control of most of the east coast of the Indian peninsula and the mouth of the Ganges. The organization and government of this huge empire now fell to the British crown and Parliament.

England—unlike France, Prussia, Russia, and most other continental states—was no longer ruled by a king working in consultation with advisors of his selection, but by King, Parliament, and Cabinet, the last being a committee of leaders drawn from Parliament.[2] Throughout the long reign of the new king's grandfather, George II (ruled 1727–1760), this body had been dominated by about seventy-five aristocratic families known as "Big Whigs" who, through careful manipulation of voting districts and equally careful outlays of cash and favors, controlled the membership of the House of Commons and the ministries of the government. The second German Hanover king was not powerless, of course; through pensions, honors, jobs, and sinecures, he had considerable patronage resources at his disposal. However, he tended not to use even the power that he had. His English-raised grandson chose a different course.

George III, who was plagued throughout his life with a disease (porphyria) which brought on temporary symptoms of madness, was a well-meaning man of limited intelligence. Accused during his lifetime of attempting to undo the "Glorious Revolution" and set up a new tyranny, the king appears merely to have wished to see to it that people friendly to him were brought into the government so that he could improve its administration—the fashionable thing for monarchs to do in this Age of Enlightened Despotism. Far from seizing power, he used all the customary "Big Whig" methods of rigging elections and bribing members of Parliament to effect a sort of "housecleaning" in his favor. His efforts ushered in a period of confusion and disorder—just at the time when England needed to gather all her political energies and talents to cope with the problems left by the conclusion of a great war.

[2]The first definition of "cabinet" is small room. The second is a piece of furniture designed to contain papers or other materials. Hence, when continental Europeans spoke of "cabinet government" they meant government from the rulers' office and desk, as in the case of Frederick the Great of Prussia. In England, on the other hand, and quite improperly from the etymological point of view, cabinet came in the eighteenth century to denote a group of people, a standing committee of both Houses of Parliament. By the time of George III's accession, the king never attended meetings of the cabinet.

The Elder Pitt and Lord Bute At the time of George's accession on a wave of patriotic euphoria in 1760, the magnificant William Pitt the Elder (who, more than any other man, was given credit for the victories of the previous year) was playing the role of patriot-leader aspired to by the king himself. Pitt's very magnificence was a liability, in the king's estimation. Moreover, policy differences developed between the two: Pitt was anxious to continue the war whereas the king wanted to sue for peace as soon as possible. In his effort to get rid of the Elder Pitt, George was encouraged by the minister's own colleagues, who, like the king, were anxious for peace. Eventually, Pitt was maneuvered into a position where he had no choice except to resign, which he did in 1761. Thereafter the direction of English affairs fell into much less competent hands. Newcastle, the old Whig manipulator, continued for a few months as prime minister with the king's friend, James Stuart Bute, as the king's confidant and advisor. Then in 1762 Bute was made prime minister in his own right. He moved with more than dignified haste to negotiate a treaty with France. The treaty (Treaty of Paris, February 10, 1763) concluded, George and Bute could proceed with their self-imposed tasks, the first of these being to wrest control of Parliament from the "Big Whigs." The second was to cope with new and enlarged responsibilities engendered by the losses of war and the gains of victory.

The internal political project did not at first go well, and for many years George was unable to dictate the composition of the ministry. After a few months, Lord Bute, deciding that his long experience as a Scottish gentleman and sportsman had not fitted him for statecraft, resigned. Two unstable ministries (Grenville, 1763–1765, and Rockingham, 1765–1766) followed in rapid succession; and in 1766 the young king, through want of an alternative, turned once again to the terrible figure of the Elder Pitt (now Earl of Chatham) as the nucleus of what he hoped would be a viable cabinet. Unfortunately, this giant among English statesmen was already, at age fifty-eight, broken in health and lapsing in mind. During his short ministry the developing crisis in the colonies was allowed to drift, and the ministry of many interests that he put together was unable to control Parliament. In 1767, Lord Chatham tendered his resignation on grounds of ill health.

Not only in Parliament and in the cabinet did the king encounter difficulties, but also in the country at large, especially in and about London. Popular dissatisfaction with the crown was aroused especially by the Treaty of Paris, which many patriots considered a blot on the national honor and unworthy of the victories of heroic commanders like Wolfe and of the hearts of oak at Minden. This discontent was freely expressed in the clubs and coffee houses of London and somewhat more guardedly (because of libel laws) in England's precocious periodical press.[3]

Wilkes and Liberty One journal, the *North Briton*, was founded in 1762 expressly to attack Lord Bute and the king. The founder was a member of

[3]England was the first country to develop daily newspapers as well as weeklies and monthlies.

Parliament of questionable morals and scandalous habits, but some gaiety and wit, named John Wilkes. He compared the Treaty of Paris to the Peace of God, "for it passeth all understanding." In the famous issue Number 45 of his journal he attacked the king personally in the most violent terms, using the word "odious" and implying that the king had lied to Parliament. The king was understandably annoyed; one of his secretaries of state issued a general warrant for the arrest of all "authors, printers, and publishers" of the objectionable piece. Forty-eight persons were arrested. Wilkes pleaded privilege from arrest as a member of Parliament; the courts upheld his plea and then went on to slap the king by pronouncing that general arrest warrants were illegal and awarding damages to Wilkes.

The matter might well have rested there as a triumph for traditional English liberties had not Wilkes (who had a taste for pornography as well as for political strife) republished his offensive Number 45 of the *North Briton* along with an obscene *Essay on Woman,* in which one of the characters was a libidinous and very much alive bishop of the Anglican Church. This breach of the rules of good taste was sufficient to re-open the whole matter and led to a storm. Wilkes was attacked in the House of Lords (of which the offended bishop was a member) and in the Commons (of which Wilkes was a member) and by the king. His paper was publicly burnt; he was expelled from the Commons; his immunity was lifted; and he was ordered to be prosecuted. After being wounded in a duel, he fled to France to recover. But the crowd was with him and the king's Whig opponents saw in Wilkes a popular rallying point for their side.

The bookburners were surrounded by a crowd shouting, "Hurrah for Wilkes and Liberty!" Some years later, in 1768, the voters of Middlesex (a county adjoining London on the north and west) elected Wilkes, though he had been declared an outlaw and was lodged in jail, to Parliament. The House of Commons once more threw him out; Middlesex elected him again. Parliament rejected him once more; and before this nearly incredible affair was over Middlesex had voted four times for Wilkes, thereby expressing the County's rejection of the wishes of both king and Parliament. In 1769, Wilkes was elected alderman of the City of London. Artisans, businessmen, and Whig aristocrats rallied around him as a symbol of resistance to arbitrary authority, nakedly displayed, according to English standards. The culmination of this fantastic story was reached when Wilkes was elected Lord Mayor of London in 1774 and resumed his seat in Parliament.

At least as far as London, the Home Counties, and eastern and southern England were concerned, the contest between Wilkes and his supporters versus crown and Parliament was serious. While Wilkes was in prison awaiting trial, a crowd of his humble followers demonstrated outside London and were shot down by soldiers in what was known as the "Massacre of St. George's Fields." Workers went out on strike in support of Wilkes. Mobs patrolled the streets of London "knocking down all that will not roar for Wilkes and liberty." Wilkite agitators travelled over the whole country organizing public meetings; and the movement eventually developed a program calling for significant democratic reforms: (1) shorter terms for Parliament (i.e., more frequent elections), (2) exclusion of public job holders and pensioners from Parliament, (3) "fair and equal representation of the people in Parliament."

By attacking both Parliamant *and* king, the Wilkites caused these two to make common cause against what seemed to them an increasingly dangerous democratic movement. One observer on the scene, Ben Franklin, remarked at the height of the disturbance that the only thing that prevented George III from losing his throne was the fact that Wilkes possessed a bad personal character while George had a good one.

The movement reached a climax in 1773, and began to disappear after Wilkes returned to Parliament. He introduced a bill to reform that body which was treated as a joke by members who had no desire to reform themselves. Wilkes' willingness to climb on whatever bandwagon happened to be passing by got him into trouble with the earnest reformers; and eventually the popular aspect of the movement was destroyed when, in 1780, Wilkes, as chamberlain of the City of London, himself led troops to suppress and slaughter some of his humble followers during the anti-Catholic Gordon Riots.

There is no doubt whatever that, despite the fact that he was for a number of years the symbol of opposition to royal and parliamentary corruption, Wilkes was a kind of a scoundrel. There is also no doubt that he was beaten by the king in every contest except the one having to do with general arrest warrants. Opposed to Wilkes' somewhat pyrotechnical gambits was the king's patient political fence building. After ten years of this work, George got rid of the Big Whigs and managed to elevate his servant, Lord North, to the head of his government.

Lord North and the Younger Pitt North was unpopular; he was frequently attacked in the press and in Parliament; but he survived as prime minister for twelve long years, supported by a hard core of about two hundred Parliamentarians who were on the royal payroll. Thanks to this support, he weathered the final flurries of the Wilkes and Liberty agitation and led the government in its disastrous handling of the American problem.

When the American problem turned into a revolt and then ended as a successful Revolution, opposition to Lord North became stronger and more telling politically. In 1780, as the English military situation in America was obviously deteriorating, a resolution was carried in the Commons to the effect that "the influence of the crown has increased, is increasing and ought to be diminished." Two years later, after it was eminently clear that the thirteen colonies were lost, the first English parliamentary motion of "no confidence" was put to the vote and nearly carried. North resigned.

For a few months, George had to put up with Whig ministries, but once again the machinery of royal influence was put into operation. A young man with a great name, the 25-year-old Younger Pitt, was brought safely home with a pliant majority in the parliamentary election of 1784. After

THE ANGLO-AMERICAN REVOLUTION

The material in this chart has been arranged so as to emphasize the fact that disorders and difficulties in England and in America were an historical unity until 1775 when organized armed conflict began and the histories of the two countries began to diverge in blood.

Political events that affected both England and America are printed in italics across the two columns.

Date	America	England
1756–1763	*Seven Years' War*	
1757	*William Pitt Secretary of State for War Policy*	
1757	*Clive's victory at Plassey*	
1759	*Year of Victories: Quebec, Quiberon Bay, Minden, etc.*	
1760	*Accession of George III*	
1761	*Pitt resigns*	
1761	Writs of Assistance in Massachusetts (James Otis)	Bute as Prime Minister (1762–1763)
1763 (Feb.)	*Treaty of Paris ending Seven Years' War*	
1763	Conspiracy of Pontiac	Number 45 of the *North Briton:* beginning of the Wilkes affair
1763 (Oct.)	Royal Proclamation: Line of Demarcation	
1764	Sugar Act	Wilkes affair continues: general warrants declared illegal
1765	Stamp Act Stamp Act Riots Quartering Act Stamp Act Congress	Wilkes outlawed, flees to France
1766	Repeal of Stamp Act Declaratory Act	Ministry of Elder Pitt (Lord Chatham) Ben Franklin before Parliament
1767	Townsend Acts	
1768	Seizure of Hancock's sloop, *Liberty*	Wilkes returns to England, elected to Parliament, arrested Massacre of St. George's Fields
1769	Virginia Resolves	Wilkes expelled from Parliament; Wilkes re-elected to Parliament Formation of the Society of Supporters of the Bill of Rights
1770	Boston Massacre	Formation of Constitutional Society Ministry of Lord North begins
1772	Local Committees of Correspondence	Wilkite democratic movement controls government of City of London
1773	Intercolonial Committees of Correspondence	Wilkes and Liberty movement approaches climax
1773 (Dec.)	Boston "Tea Party"	

THE ANGLO-AMERICAN REVOLUTION (Continued)

1774	Quebec Act Coercive Acts First Continental Congress	Wilkes Lord Mayor of London
1775	Lexington and Concord; Bunker Hill (war)	
1776	Declaration of Independence	Wilkites lose control of London; collapse of Wilkite movement (rapid decline of the English aspect of the revolution)
1777	Battle of Saratoga	
1778	Treaty with France	
1781	Articles of Confederation ratified	Motion of "no confidence" passes in Commons
1782	Surrender at Yorktown	Lord North resigns; William Pitt, the Younger, Chancellor of the Exchequer
1783	*Treaty of Paris between the U.S. and England*	
1787	Constitutional Convention	First Ministry of William Pitt, the Younger (Dec., 1783)
1788	Ratification	(Calm and prosperity with some gestures at political reform until 1793)
1789 (April)	George Washington inaugurated	Gradual decline of king's influence

William Pitt the Younger. This engraving from a portrait by Copley shows Pitt as he looked about 1782 when he became Chancellor of the Exchequer under George III. (LCPP.)

this, Pitt ruled as the more-or-less enlightened minister while the king affected great interest in agriculture.

In the years between the early 1780's and the French Revolution, Pitt the Younger managed to achieve a certain reputation for reform based on a very few accomplishments. An "Economic Reform Bill," the effect of which was to abolish a number of sinecures and to save the government a few thousand pounds annually, was introduced into Parliament by Edmund Burke and passed with Pitt's fledgling (he was twenty-three years old) oratorical assistance. However, Pitt's own bill of 1782, intended to reform representation in Parliament through reapportionment and the elimination of rotten boroughs (and thus to strike at one of the bases of aristocratic and royal corruption and power), was defeated by twenty votes. Although the proposal for electoral reform had been seriously considered (unlike Wilkes' proposal which had been laughed out of the House), fifty years were to go by before a similar measure would pass.

Pitt encouraged Wilberforce, the leader of the anti-slave-trade movement; he endeavored to put the economic doctrines of Adam Smith into practice by reducing tariffs[4] at a time when English farmers and manufac-

[4] Especially through the Eden Treaty of 1786.

turers had little or nothing to fear from foreign competition; and he generally sided with virtue and was in favor of peace. Later, after 1792, the pressures of French revolutionary ideas in England and the exigencies of national defense led Pitt to the position where he presided over one of the most retrograde and repressive governments in English history.

The English and American aspects of the late eighteenth-century revolution were born at the same time, at the end of the Seven Years' War. The English aspect achieved its height at the climax of the Wilkes and Liberty movement in the early 1770's. It sickened and died as a result of American resistance to the George III–Lord North reform scheme for the colonies and English reaction to that resistance. It was buried by the younger Pitt in a time when revolution—and even reform—seemed unnecessary.

The turning point in the English revolt came when the king found that, with very few exceptions, English parliamentarians, merchants, manufacturers, landed taxpayers, and common people would follow him in a vigorous policy toward the colonies. It did not seem strange to them that the sovereign "crown in Parliament" should regulate and tax the colonies just as it did the metropolis. After all, England was the most mildly and decently governed country of the Old World. If the colonists were Englishmen, as they tiresomely claimed, should they not share English obligations as well as English rights? For the English, at the time of Bunker Hill, it was a case of "rally 'round."

ENGLISH COLONIAL POLICY IN THE 1760'S

It is often said that England acquired its empire "in a fit of absence of mind," and it is true that the thirteen English colonies had, since the late sixteenth century, come into being rather by mistake. The English government had taken the initiative in North America only on rare occasions, the work of settlement having been done mainly by English individuals, trading corporations, and groups of religious dissidents. Of the thirteen colonies, only four (New York, New Jersey, Delaware, and Georgia) were established under English rule as the result of direct intervention by the English crown and government; and, of those four, three had been secured at a single stroke in 1664. In the foundation of the other nine, the role of the crown had been merely permissive. Even after the thirteen colonies had developed a considerable population as well as some important exports (tobacco, lumber, naval stores, rice, indigo) and after it became apparent that the French valued North America sufficiently to fight for it, it was still possible for the English negotiators at the end of the Seven Years' War to consider giving up all of Canada for one West Indian sugar island.

The Regulation of Colonial Trade After establishment, these colonies had been attended to by the home government only sporadically. Royal governors presided in each colony, but the leading colonists had acquired the habit of legislating for themselves through the several colonial assemblies. Legally, the colonies were subject to crown and Parliament: the royal governors had veto power over actions of the colonial assemblies, and Parliament possessed the power to regulate and tax colonial external trade, as well as to tax the colonists. The high degree of self-rule that had grown up as a result of English "salutary neglect" was, therefore, not constitutionally grounded.

Traditionally, Parliament had tended not to interfere with American internal taxation. The power to regulate colonial trade was exercised, however, if only sporadically and ineffectually. During the course of the later seventeenth century, the English Parliament had moved to include the colonies within the English mercantilist system.[5] The Navigation Acts of 1651 and 1660 provided that all goods exported from or imported to the colonies should be carried by English or colonial ships and that certain enumerated colonial products (sugar, tobacco, indigo, ginger, dye-woods) would be exported directly to England. Further legislation in 1663 and 1676 provided that European goods could be imported into the colonies only if

Making Sugar from Cane. Sugar, molasses, and rum—all made from sugar cane—were extremely important commodities in Europe before beet sugar came into use. Literally millions of blacks were brought forcibly from tropical Africa to the Americas to chop and process the cane grown in the West Indies. See chart on page 962. (LCPP.)

these goods had been put on board ship in an English port and that the specified articles could not be shipped duty free from one colony to another. In other words, Parliament was trying to see to it that all trade of each colony should be with or through England. If enforced, these laws would have drastically limited colonial commerce. The colonists responded by systematically evading them. Smuggling became a profitable and even respectable colonial occupation.

As the colonial merchants developed their profitable and illegal triangular trade in rum, slaves, molasses, fish, lumber, and grain with Africa and the French West Indies and an equally profitable and illegal direct trade

[5] See Part IX, Chapter 2 for a discussion of English mercantilism.

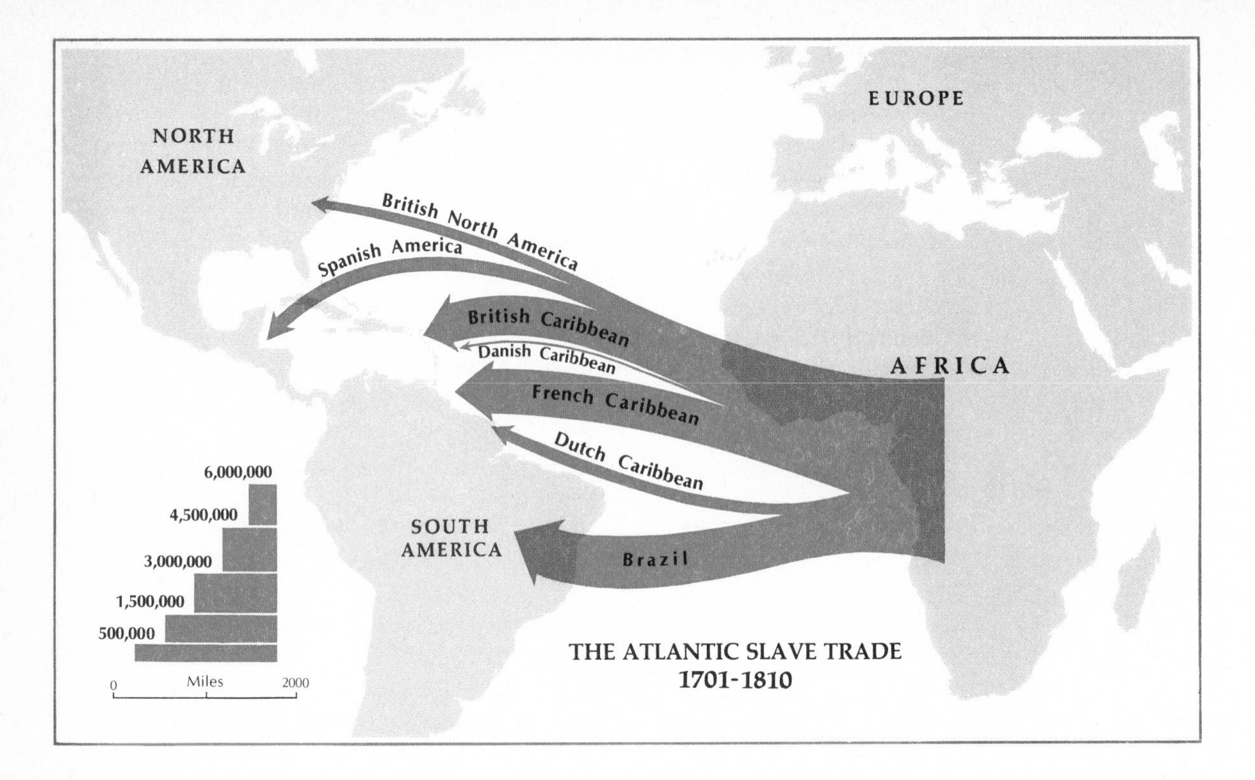

THE ATLANTIC SLAVE TRADE
1701-1810

with the same French West Indies, the British West Indian planters pressured Parliament to pass the Molasses Act of 1733. This act put a heavy duty on foreign molasses (French West Indian molasses was "foreign") imported into the colonies. It was, in fact, mainly honored in the breach.

Prior to 1761, the mercantilist colonial system was intended to regulate colonial trade, not to produce revenue. The system was meant to direct the colonial economies so as to contribute to the general economic welfare of the mother country rather than to the expenses of government. English sea power was used to render England independent of imports from potential or actual enemies. Because it was not designed to produce governmental revenue, the arrangement did not involve "taxation" as such. Regulation had been tolerable over the years because the mercantilist principles upon which it was based were generally accepted and because the regulations themselves had not been seriously enforced.

Toward the end of the Seven Years' War, however, a more determined spirit developed in England. The cost of the war, which had been fought in large part to defend and enlarge the colonies, was a pressing reality. While the English taxpayer was spending his substance and mortgaging his future to defend the colonies, the colonists responded by continuing their trade with the French in Canada and the West Indies, thereby giving succor to the enemy, prolonging the war, and increasing the burden on the English taxpayer. The time for "muddling through" and for good-natured half measures was over.

The new spirit injected into English colonial administration toward the end of the Seven Years' War made for changes that worked on colonial interests and sensibilities in three unfavorable ways. First, the new administration tried seriously to enforce the existing regulations. Second, it went beyond mere regulation of colonial trade, to which the colonists were reconciled in principle, and demanded that the English commercial monopoly should be made to produce revenue. Third, the home government moved to limit the expansion of the colonies and thereby to interfere with what most colonists believed to be a strictly internal matter, quite beyond the prerogatives of the English government.

Enforcement of Colonial Trade Regulations The drive for efficiency began when British officials in the colonies made a concerted move to cut down on what they considered treasonable trade with the enemy. Royal governors and customs officials stopped taking bribes and looking the other way when illegal goods were landed and started seizing illicit cargoes. Armed in 1761 with general search warrants—"writs of assistance"—they entered and searched ships, warehouses, and any premises where they thought contraband might be hidden. The colonial merchants howled in protest at what they saw as an unconstitutional invasion of privacy. Sixty-three of them petitioned the Massachusetts Superior Court against these writs which violated "one of the most essential branches of English liberty [which] is the freedom of one's house." Breaking and entering by the authorities, they said, could be done only under a special, not general, warrant. James Otis brilliantly argued the merchants' cause, but the court, presided over by a chief justice (Thomas Hutchinson) newly appointed by the royal governor, found the writs legal. We have already seen that, two years later, in the Wilkes case, an English court was to declare that in England general warrants were illegal. The conclusion that irate colonists could reach was that a double standard existed, that English liberties at home took precedence over English liberties in the colonies. Recalling James Otis' arguments, John Adams wrote later: "Then and there, the child Independence was born."

Revenue Acts The second change in English colonial policy was the move from simple regulation to regulation *and* production of revenue. The first clear sign of this change was the Sugar Act (sometimes called the Revenue Act) of 1764. This measure (which was proposed by the same ministry that got involved in the Wilkes affair) read in part as follows: "That a revenue be raised in your Majesty's dominions in America for defraying the expenses of defending, protecting and securing the same." Improving upon the often-violated Molasses Act of 1733, the Sugar Act provided that the then unreasonably high duty (placed at an unrealistic level because it was intended to discourage trade, not to tax it) on foreign molasses should be reduced by one half. The idea was that since it now would be economically feasible to pay the duty, it should actually be collected.

But it was too late. The protests in Boston, New York, and other colonial ports were as loud as they had been about the writs of assistance. Merchants and lawyers freely used the word "unconstitutional" to describe the measure, and before long an English friend of the colonies, Edmund Burke, took their side:

Whether you were right or wrong in establishing the colonies on the principles of commercial monopoly, rather than on that of revenue, is at this day a problem of mere speculation. You cannot have both by the same authority. To join together the restraints of an universal internal monopoly with an universal external taxation is an unnatural union—perfect, uncompensated slavery.

The old Acts of Navigation the colonies could accept because they were used to them and knew how to evade them. Taxation piled on top, and with efficient collection, at one stroke emptied the purse and oppressed the spirit.

Western Lands The third change in English colonial policy (the second chronologically), unlike the first two, affected men and women who lived on the frontier. The frontier farmer, who has become famous in song and story for his independent spirit, his restlessness, and his disregard of authority, had by the 1760's made his way into the western Carolinas, the valley of Virginia, western (now central) Pennsylvania, and along the Mohawk Valley in New York, and was ready to go farther west. During the Seven Years' War these frontier settlers had borne the brunt of the French and Indian raids from the northwest and west. At the end of the war, an Indian statesman, Pontiac, managed to organize the tribes of the Old Northwest for an all-out attack on the English. It took British regular troops to defeat the Indians—who devastated many settlements, especially in Pennsylvania, before the rising was over. The episode served to convince English statesmen that the colonies were either unwilling or unable to defend themselves from the Indians at the same time that colonial expansionism tended to aggravate Indian hostilities.

By driving the French out of the trans-Appalachian west, the English and the colonists created a problem greater than the one that had faced the French when they had controlled the area. The French North American empire had been essentially a trading empire wherein the French had dealt with the Indians in the fur trade. In the English colonies, on the other hand, most colonists were settlers on the land who wanted to drive out or otherwise eliminate the Indians, whose presence they felt was intolerable.

Ideally, the problem of how to deal with the new western lands should have been approached through consultation among the Indians, colonists, and Englishmen. Actually, it was handled unilaterally in London and Westminster. As the short-lived and unstable ministries of the period 1760 to

1770 came to grips with the matter, they had to consider whether the territory should be kept as a wilderness and hunting ground for the Indians so as to ensure a continuing supply of furs (thereby favoring the Hudson's Bay Company already engaged in the fur trade) or whether the white settlers should be allowed to continue to move in on the Indians (thereby provoking more Indian wars and greater imperial expenditures for defense) or whether some combination of these alternatives could be worked out.

The home government did not come to a definitive conclusion. It was obvious that the matter needed further study, but it was equally obvious that something had to be done immediately to maintain order and to hold the line. There was a feeling that, if the colonists were to be allowed to move west of the Appalachians, they must not be permitted to do so until the land had been duly purchased from the Indians. Then, surveys would have to be made and terms of settlement worked out so that the government should be reimbursed for the expenses of conquest that had been paid by the English taxpayer.

The Line of Demarcation The reaction of the Grenville ministry to the problems of the West took the form of a document signed by the king in October 1763. This Royal Proclamation established four new governments (Quebec, East Florida, West Florida, and Grenada) so that the king's new subjects there might be governed by English laws. Second, and more important in the eyes of the colonists, the Proclamation stated that "it is just and reasonable . . . that the several . . . tribes of Indians should not be molested," and that, therefore, for the present, no officials should "grant warrants of survey or pass patents for any lands beyond the heads or sources of any of the rivers which fall into the Atlantic Ocean from the west or northwest. . . ." The decree went on to say that for the present it was the royal pleasure to reserve for the use of the Indians all land lying westward of the Allegheny divide and forbade all of his royal majesty's "loving subjects from making and purchases or settlement whatever, or taking possession of any of the lands above reserved. . . ."

Commendable as the sentiments expressed in this document might have been, many colonists saw the matter differently. The original charters given by the crown to the several colonies had set no western boundary; except for one grant in 1606, the royal grants had been "from sea to sea." The colonial assemblies tended to think, therefore, that when the war was over and the French driven out they could proceed forthwith to fulfill the terms of their charters, at least as far west as the Mississippi, and that the crown had no right to take away what it had already given. The frontiersman felt that he should be protected from the Indians, not vice versa. They were not willing or able to see the wisdom of calling a halt, of taking stock and making orderly plans and preparations. They passed over the reiterated phrase, "for the present." In their view, the English government was bent on aiding the interests of the established British fur-traders just as it had traditionally favored the British West Indian sugar planters.

Growing Colonial Opposition to England The result of these three imperial innovations was a marked worsening in English-colonial relations leading to fairly unanimous colonial opposition on the part of merchants and their dependents as well as by planters, lawyers, manufacturers, and frontiersmen. Most Americans, to be sure, did not think seriously in the 1760's about breaking away from the mother country, but many of them were convinced that the new imperial relationship was intolerable. They were prepared to use violence to thwart the reforms. When they did so, the revolution began.

Ships containing tea taxed by order of the English parliament landed in Boston Harbor in the winter of 1773. The "Boston Tea Party," in which colonists dressed as Indians dumped the tea in the harbor, protested the collection of such revenue. This British cartoon shows the fate of a tax-collector. (LCPP.)

From the base of the disagreements inspired by the three innovations just discussed developed the familiar story of colonial intransigence and royal or ministerial retaliation. Efforts of middle-of-the-roaders like the American Ben Franklin and the Englishman Edmund Burke to make order out of the muddle and to save the empire foundered on mutual recriminations and were eventually washed away in blood. There followed twenty years of Stamp Acts, Quartering Acts, Stamp Act Congresses, Declaratory Acts, Townshend Acts, riots, nonimportation agreements, "massacres," tea parties, intercolonial organizations, Continental Congresses, war, foreign intervention, independence and, finally, experiments in republican, federal government.

THE AMERICAN REVOLUTION

The American Revolution began as the Seven Years' War was ending. The first phase of the revolution (1760–1770) was the work of colonial merchants and their lawyer spokesmen. By 1770, resistance on the part of these merchants had forced the English government to retreat from its extreme position and to accede to the most important demands of colonial businessmen. The years between 1771 and 1773 were marked by relative calm. The original merchant leaders were more-or-less satisfied with the repeal of the Stamp Act (1766) and of the Townshend Acts (1770). That is to say, the merchants were interested primarily in working out a relationship with the mother country that would enable them to do business profitably and only secondarily in the question of whether crown and Parliament had the right to regulate and tax the colonies. Inasmuch as the merchants were the natural leaders of the New England and Middle Colonies, these years represented a propitious moment for reconciliation.

Surrender at Yorktown. Cornwallis' surrender following seige at Yorktown on October 19, 1781, assured American independence. The victorious forces were commanded by General Washington and a host of French officers including Rochambeau, Grasse, and Lafayette. In this contemporary French engraving, the British general is shown handing his sword to General Washington while a French officer looks on. (LCRB.)

Unfortunately for the continuation of the old empire, extremism on both sides caused this opportunity to be missed. Lord North came into power in 1770. Subservient to the king and his determination to assert royal authority by disciplining the colonies, this government soon played into the hands of a group of colonial popular agitators like Sam Adams who kept resistance alive through the skillful use of propaganda and by organizing incidents like the Boston Tea Party (December 1773). In the next period of the revolution (late 1773 to 1776), events moved rapidly in the radical direction, culminating in the decision to separate from the mother country. This step was more radical than any intended by the original revolutionaries. It was in this period that armed conflict (Lexington, Concord, and Bunker Hill were fought in April and June 1775) began. From 1775 to 1783 the matter was put to the test of war and brought to a clean conclusion with the military and naval assistance of the French government (1778–1783). From 1783 on, the victoriously independent United States faced the same problems of regulation, taxation, and organization of their territory and population that had plagued the British Empire at the conclusion of the Seven Years' War. The story of how the new republic met these challenges is not within the compass of this survey.

The European Reaction For decades, Europeans had been talking and writing about natural rights. Theorists like Montesquieu and Rousseau, and propagandists like Voltaire and Diderot had propounded a political program for enlightened man. Ideas like Montesquieu's notion of the separation of powers, Locke's explanation of the origin and justification of government, and Rousseau's concept of general will had been bandied about for decades. Almost everyone agreed that government ought to be by consent of the governed, that the people should be sovereign, that they should be represented in government. Even the despot, Frederick II of Prussia, seems to have believed that men are born equal in their natural rights. However, with so much agreement among the most brilliant and powerful Europeans of the day, very little tangible progress had been made toward implementing these ideas.

Yet, in America, people who had been described by Samuel Johnson as "a race of convicts" and by a Dutch writer as physically degenerate, had managed to carry off the great enterprise and to write their ideas into law. Europeans were enchanted. Americans and American problems they may have understood only vaguely; but the language that the Americans used in their constitutional charters was entirely familiar. When they read the second paragraph of the Declaration of Independence; it was a case of *déjà vu.* But the great question was not whether these "truths" of the Declaration of Independence were self-evident; it was whether the colonists would be able to apply these widely accepted truths to their own affairs.

It had long been understood that the blessings of liberty ought to be secured. Until the American Revolution succeeded, there had been confusion about how to proceed with the endeavor, and, as we have seen, many of the *philosophes* had looked to the despot as the agency through which enlightened government would be achieved. After the American Revolution, the role of the sovereign people seemed more nearly clear.

The Horse America. Many Englishmen sympathized with the colonists, among them the orator Edmund Burke (1729–1797), who later opposed the French Revolution. "The Horse America, throwing his Master," is the title of this contemporary British cartoon. Note the French officer (right) carrying a standard filled with *fleurs de lys.* (LCPP.)

Significance of the American Revolution Essentially a political and territorial-national movement, the American Revolution did not make for momentous social changes within the erstwhile colonies. The American Revolution was not, of course, simply a war of independence against England. In a way it was a savage civil war among Americans. Many colonists sympathized with the imperial cause and some of them fought effectively on the British side. When they had the upper hand, the Loyalists terrorized the Patriots just as the Liberty Boys persecuted Tories when they had the opportunity. During the revolution, some sixty thousand Empire Loyalists (about 2.4 percent of the total population) fled to Canada or to England. The overwhelming majority of these people lost valuable property and were unable or unwilling to return to their American homes. These Loyalists looked, thought, talked, and lived very much like those who took over their places and properties.

The fact was that American society had been comparatively democratic and egalitarian before the Revolution and continued so afterwards. In 1765, a French settler in Pennsylvania, J. Hector St. John de Crèvecoeur, could write that America

> *. . . is not composed as in Europe of great lords who possess everything, and of a herd of people who have nothing. Here are no aristocratical families, no courts, no kings, no bishops, no ecclesiastical dominion, no invisible power giving to the few a very visible one; no great manufacturers employing thousands, no great refinement of luxury. The rich and the poor are not so far removed as they are in Europe.*

This situation was little changed after the events of 1776–1783.

There were slaves in America before and there were still slaves after the Revolution. The suffrage was fairly wide (but not universal, even among free, adult males) before the Revolution and did not change significantly because of the Revolution. As regards the disposition of the western lands, the decisions of the new government did not vary widely in their social impact from those the British imperial government would have come to. Although the Northwest Ordinances of 1785 and 1787 provided that the territory north of the Ohio River should *not* be preserved as a wilderness for the Indians and that the land should be open to settlement by individuals, these laws and later land legislation were also intended to carry out the intentions of the English policy of the 1760's by providing for orderly development in the West. Surveys were made and then land purchased by individuals who could pay fairly high prices for large tracts of land. The American frontiersman who wanted the West thrown open to free and uncontrolled settlement found that the New Nation was nearly as restrictive as the Old Empire. In general, then, social or even political democracy did not come to the United States with a rush during the Revolution. Most of the democratic forms that existed in the 1790's had been there before; and most of the limitations upon democratic growth that had resulted from English rule continued to be effective after independence.

The American Revolution may not have been a great and complicated social and economic revolution, but it was an immensely significant and pregnant political step in the history of western civilization. In the first place, the American Revolution was a success as a territorial-national revolution; and this fact would give hope in the future to other subject peoples and to influence their behavior until our own day. Second, the Revolution was a success as a political revolution. This fact was widely noted at the time and had an almost immediate bearing on events in France, as we shall see in the next chapter.

FURTHER READING

For the English background, see B. Williams, *The Whig Supremacy, 1714–1760* (1962); and the recent study by J. Henretta, *"Salutory Neglect": Colonial Administration under the Duke of Newcastle* (1972), an excellent account. On Pitt the Elder, O. A. Sherrard, *Lord Chatham,* 2 vols. (1952–1955), is good, the second volume being particularly pertinent; but J. H. Plumb, *Chatham* (1965), is briefer. The important study by the late Sir Lewis Namier, **England in the Age of the American Revolution* (1961), helps the reader to relate the American Revolution to the mother country. Namier revises the traditional interpretation of English late eighteenth-century politics in his magistral **The Structure of Politics at the Accession of George III,* 2 vols. (1929). G. Rudé, **Wilkes and Liberty: A Social Study of 1763 to 1774* (1962), is a sociological approach

*Books available in paperback edition are marked with an asterisk.

to political adveturism. A useful historiographical essay is H. Butterfield, *George III and the Historians* (1959).

On the American side, L. H. Gipson, **The Coming of the Revolution, 1763–1775* (1954); and J. R. Alden, **The American Revolution, 1775–1783* (1954), give fairly thorough accounts and up-to-date interpretations. C. M. Andrews, **Colonial Backgrounds of the American Revolution* (1961); and C. Rossiter, **The First American Revolution: The American Colonies on the Eve of Independence* (1973), are important studies that have appeared in soft cover. E. S. and H. M. Morgan present a revisionistic approach to the question of colonial taxation as a cause of the revolution in *The Stamp Act Crisis* (1953). K. Knollenburg, in **Origins of the American Revolution, 1759–1766* (1965), argues a case for English bad judgment. P. Maier, *From Resistance to Revolution: Colonial Radicals and the Development of American Opposition to Britain, 1765–1776* (1972), is a recent contribution, well written.

The first important historian to suggest seriously that the American Revolution was a social as well as a territorial-political revolution was J. F. Jameson in **The American Revolution Considered as a Social Movement* (1940). The present writer does not agree with Jameson's thesis, but the book is valuable nonetheless. J. T. Main, **The Social Structure of Revolutionary America* (1965), is a necessary and important supplement to the work of Jameson.

For the essential documents see H. S. Commager, ed., **Documents of American History* (1968); and R. B. Morris, ed., **The American Revolution 1763–1783* (1971), which has a sampling of documents and a brief text. C. Becker, **The Declaration of Independence* (1942), analyzes the roots of the ideas contained in our most famous charter.

The idea that toward the end of the Seven Years' War the western world as a whole entered a period of revolution is most explicitly developed by R. Palmer in **The Age of the Democratic Revolution: A Political History of Europe and America, 1760–1800,* 2 vols. (1959 and 1964, reprinted). One of the Heath pamphlets, P. Amann, ed., **The Eighteenth Century Revolution—French or Western?* (1963), deals with the controversy raised by Palmer and by J. Godechot, the French advocate of the same idea.

2 Background of the French Revolution

On March 4, 1789, while the first Congress elected under the new Constitution of the U.S.A. met in New York, elections were being held in France for the Estates General. Within a week after General Washington's inauguration as President (April 30, 1789), the opening ceremonies of the first meeting since 1614 of a French nationally representative assembly were conducted at Versailles in an atmosphere of almost universal enthusiasm. This chronological sequence, the overt beginning of the French Revolution at the very moment that the American Revolution was accomplished and consolidated, might make it seem that the French Revolution was the historical child of the American Revolution. But was there a real and effective relationship between these two revolutions?

THE AMERICAN REVOLUTION, THE FRENCH REVOLUTION

The French Image of England As we have seen earlier, many late eighteenth-century Frenchmen, particularly the unprivileged elites, the middle classes, the intellectuals, and even some of the aristocracy, were dissatisfied with their own government, their legal system, their religious institutions, their economic life, and their social structure. Moreover, the relative power position of France seemed to be shrinking as that of England grew. In general, it is correct to say that a people who are not pleased with life at home usually look somewhere else for a representation of their aspirations, somewhere on the other side of the fence where the grass is proverbially greener. During the first two-thirds of the eighteenth century, the western country most admired by dissatisfied and increasingly alienated French utopia seekers had been England. They envied the English who with monotonous regularity beat the French in war after war while at the same time enjoying a high degree of personal liberty and what seemed to be an admirably decent legal system. English commerce, manufacturing, and agriculture seemed healthier than their French counterparts; English letters, science, and technology seemed more advanced. The French aristocracy admired England because their understanding of the English constitution and of English society indicated that English peers were both rich and politically powerful. The French bourgeoisie admired the apparent ease with which English businessmen joined the aristocracy. French *philosophes* admired English legal institutions, civil liberties, and intellectual life. Although no right-thinking Frenchman could admire English eating and drinking habits and although the gloomy English sabbath was supremely wearisome to visiting Frenchmen, they tended to ignore these details as they projected onto the island neighbor an image of their hopes.

With the advent of George III and the crushing defeat of France by what was soon to be called "perifidious Albion" and with the antigovernment agitation centering about Wilkes in the 1760's, many would-be French reformers began to lose some of their enthusiasm for things English. The previously admired (if misunderstood) government was caught operating in arbitrary ways and many Frenchmen applauded when an English court proclaimed general arrest warrants (rather like the infamous French *lettres de cachet*) illegal. They bought and displayed "Wilkes and Liberty" handkerchiefs; and when the effective center of English opposition moved from England to America they shifted their enthusiasm accordingly.

The French Image of America This shift in focus of French intellectuals from England to America seems to have begun between 1767 and 1770, and it was marked by increasing attention to what was going on in the English colonies. Within a decade, America was transformed in the mind of the French reading public from a series of colonies inhabited by "a race of convicts" to the "hope of the human race." Between 1767 and 1791, at least twenty-four books on America were published in French, not to speak of possibly hundreds of pamphlets. Some of these works on America (which became increasingly laudatory as time went on) were widely read. Raynal's *Histoire philosophique et politique des éstablissements et du commerce des Européens dans les deux Indes*—to which Diderot contributed—was sufficiently in demand to require thirty-seven editions between 1770 and 1820.

The French image of America was tremendously improved through the very deliberate work of that most effective of ambassadors, Benjamin Franklin. When he visited France in 1767 and 1769, Franklin was the most admired experimental scientist of his day, and he had recently magnified his already formidable reputation by his supple yet defiant defense in 1766 of the colonial cause before the English Parliament. During these two short visits to France, he made friends with and charmed many of the important French intellectuals who were also the molders of French opinion. Talking with Franklin and some other American intellectuals like Dr. Benjamin Rush and looking at some very tall Americans whom Franklin showed off at a meeting of the *Académie des Sciences* (of which Franklin was made a member in 1772), Frenchmen found it difficult to believe in the theory of American degeneration and easy to develop a picture of Americans as a sturdy race of simple, but noble philosophers. In December 1776, Franklin returned to France for a nine-year stay wearing a fur hat. Within a month fur hats were the rage and Franklin's picture was hung over thousands of French mantels. In his simplicity he appealed to the masses; with his gallantry he charmed the ladies; by his wit he seduced the court; through his scientific and literary works he won the intellectuals; and through his careful diplomacy he gradually but surely brought the French government to the point of open support of the colonies.

France and American Independence This last achievement was, of course, the object the American Continental Congress had in mind when it sent Franklin to France. It was an effort that called for the most sagacious of ambassadors: to persuade a government ruled over by an absolute, divine-right monarch with his own widespread and closely regulated colonies to

Departure of the Dragoon by Michel Garnier. A young French nobleman is about to follow Lafayette's route to America to fight for liberty in this painting of 1789. A woman (possibly his mother) hands him his sword with a histrionic gesture. The privileged French aristocrats saw nothing inconsistent about fighting for the rights of English colonists in revolt against their king. (Musée Carnavalet.)

take the side of a colonial people in revolt against their king. Somehow Franklin managed to allay official French fears that the American Revolution might precipitate further revolution in France. Through his own writings (and those of a stable of French writers he gathered about him and whose works he printed on his own press in Passy) he carefully nurtured the French people's intellectual alienation from England and their admiration for America. Sinously he encouraged the French government to believe that it could do well by doing good in the American cause: assistance given to the colonies would double as a blow at England and would serve to redress the balance of power that was tipped far on the English side. The result of Franklin's masterful execution of his mission (he was aided by news of the American victory at Saratoga) was a Treaty of Commerce and Alliance between the United States of America and France (February 6, 1778). The direct result of that treaty was the independence of the United States. An indirect result was the beginning of the French Revolution.

The statement that American independence resulted from this treaty may be justified as follows: As the war between the colonies and England developed, it became clear that the Americans by themselves would never

Marie Antoinette on Horseback. The ninth child of Maria Theresa of Austria, Marie Antoinette was married to the French *dauphin* in 1770 at age fifteen. A beautiful child, she was, at first, enthusiastically received. Later, she alienated court and public opinion through her extravagant and licentious behavior. (Bibliothèque Nationale, Paris.)

be able to drive the English out into the sea. On the other hand, the English were not able to put enough men and supplies ashore in America to subjugate the colonists. Without outside intervention the war would have gone on until both sides had become exhausted, whereupon a negotiated settlement would have been achieved in which the colonies would have received most of what they had demanded in the early stages of the revolution, while the English crown would have retained sovereignty. French intervention tipped the balance.

That French participation in the War of the American Revolution was an indirect cause of the French Revolution is equally clear and was foreseen by some contemporaries. The more cautious French statesmen of the day (Turgot is the best example) believed that France could not afford to let its enthusiasm for the American cause lead the French government into a war with England at that time. The state of French governmental finances was so weak, they argued, that a war would do irreparable damage to the state. These advocates of nonintervention proved to be right; but, in the face of anti-English and pro-American enthusiasm and pitted against the masterful diplomacy of Franklin, they lost the argument. The French government fitted out a fine army and an excellent fleet, declared war against England, and struck the crucial blows in the Battle of the Capes and at Yorktown. Frenchmen fought in America and many of them, like Lafayette, went home to France exalted by victory and enthusiastic for liberty. French participation in the war brought with it no measurable advantage for the French government; and in 1787, as the Constitutional Convention was doing its work in Philadelphia, it became obvious in Versailles that the French government had reached the end of its fiscal rope.

Louis XVI by Duplessis. This official portrait shows the ill-starred Louis XVI at his best. Born in 1754, the king was continually threatened with overweight. He indulged in strenous physical exercise, such as riding and hunting, in order to combat it. (Versailles Museum.)

The Financial Crisis of the French Government The returning heroes from America found their pious and simple young king, Louis XVI, still on the throne—or, rather, in his workshop puttering with locks or out hunting. His beautiful and giddy young queen, a daughter of Maria Theresa of Austria and sister of the Emperor Joseph II, had regained some of the reputation she had previously lost through indiscreet behavior and espousal of Austrian causes by managing to be delivered of a male child in 1782. A mother as handsome as Marie Antoinette was irresistible. Things were looking up: in helping the American colonies to independence, France had successfully struck a blow at England; and, now that an heir had been produced, the dynasty seemed secure.

On the other hand, the dour prophecies of Turgot, who had been dismissed in 1776 from the management of French finances, were being fulfilled: the cost to the French government of the American war was the immense sum of two billion *livres,* and the public debt was rising rapidly to the figure of four and one-half billion *livres* it attained in 1789.[1]

Almost half of the French debt of 1789 resulted from borrowings during the American War. At the then usual rate of 5 percent, the interest on this part of the debt was 100 million *livres* annually. In 1788, when the first and last budget of the *ancien régime* monarchy was made public, it was revealed that anticipated expenses were 629 million *livres* and revenues 503 million *livres,* a deficit of 126 million. Thus, about four-fifths of the budgetary deficit

[1]The French *livre* (which became the *franc* during the Revolution) was not a coin; it was a standard of value like, for instance, the English "guinea" for which there is no corresponding coin or note. The *livre* just before the Revolution was worth ten and a half English pence (twelve pence equalled one shilling) and about twenty American cents at the time. A day's labor in France could be hired for less than one *livre.*

The French *livre* of 1789 can be equated with something considerably over $1.00 in terms of purchasing power. A person like Lafayette, who in the 1770's had an annual income of 140,000 *livres,* was in something like the position of an American today who has more than $150,000 annually after taxes.

expected (the actual deficit was probably considerably greater) in 1789 was the price the French government paid for American independence. Debt service was anticipated to account for at least 50 percent of French governmental expenditures. Hard on the heels of this fiscal crisis followed the Revolution.

Great as it was, this debt could probably have been supported had the government been able to get its fiscal house in sufficient order so that it could meet the interest payments. As it turned out—and as it was revealed in the budget of 1788—the deficit of 126 million *livres* was so large that undertaking a governmental economy program (eliminating surplus army officers, reducing pensions based on favoritism, and lowering the expenses of the royal court) would not suffice. The estimated figure for the expenses of the court was only 6 percent of the total budget; the entire civil administration accounted for 19 percent; war, navy, and diplomacy, 26 percent; and substantial economies had already been effected. Cutting 126 million more out of the 318 million budgeted for court, administration, and defense would have seriously jeopardized the security of the kingdom. There remained, then, only three courses for the government to follow: (1) it would have to repudiate at least part of the debt; (2) it would have to raise the existing taxes, which were paid mainly by the lower classes; (3) it would have to revise the tax structure so that those parts of the realm where the tax rates were lower and those classes that were exempted from taxes should bear their share of the burden.

It is at the same time a sign of governmental restraint and of the influence of the French financial class and investing bourgeoisie that the easy but dangerous course of open repudiation was not seriously considered. Disguised repudiation through inflation was limited to putting only 100 million paper *livres* into circulation in 1788. Existing taxes were already so heavy that any increase—especially of indirect levies like the salt tax—would result in increased evasion and would yield no more return. There remained only the third possibility, that of tax reform.

Even before the War of the American Revolution, the French government had taken steps under the direction of Turgot (Controller General of Finances from 1774 to 1776) toward tax reform. Now in the 1780's under Calonne, who was Controller General from 1783 to 1787, with the need for reform obviously greater, further moves were proposed. But, as Turgot had discovered earlier, the tax reformer's stirrings not only raised a cloud of hornets determined to resist him but also awakened all manner of other creatures anxious to contribute to the process of change he had initiated. Without half trying, Frenchmen could think of dozens of elements in French life that needed reform—now that the opportunity had arrived. The violent implementation of these projected changes, along with a number of others that had not even been thought of beforehand, became the French Revolution.

Tax reform by itself, which, if successfully carried through, would have saved the old regime, at least for the time being, did not require a revolution.

The government's financial crisis was, then, not so much the cause of the French Revolution as it was the opening of a door which permitted the on-going Revolution of the West to enter and to find its principal seat in France.

SOURCES OF DISCONTENT IN FRANCE

When, in 1774, the twenty-year-old Louis XVI was told that his grandfather had died horribly of smallpox and that he was king, the young man exclaimed, "O my God, what misfortune! O my God, help me!" The unfortunate young man was probably as much depressed by the troubles that beset his kingdom as he was by his nagging and entirely justified feeling of personal inadequacy.

The Position of France in the World However inadequate the new king may have been, his realm was one of the biggest countries in Europe, surpassed significantly in area only by Russia. The pleasant land of France was endowed with remarkable natural riches of the sort that were most important in the pre-industrial era: varied climate permitting the cultivation of a wide range of crops, an extraordinarily large area of good-to-excellent soil, ports on both the Atlantic and the Mediterranean, as well as on the Rhine. The industrious French population was nearly three times greater than that of Britain, two and one-half times larger than that of Spain, five times larger than that of Prussia, and about the same as the population of the widespread Habsburg monarchy. France had for over a century been the focus of European envy and emulation; and Frenchmen were accustomed to greatness and power. French was the civilized language for all Europe; French art, letters, thought, food, and fashion were still the style of the West.

It was thus especially painful for the French to witness the sensational English military and naval successes up to the War of the American Revolution and the rapid growth in prestige of "the Carthage of the West." As English power and influence waxed, informed Frenchmen were troubled by feelings of insecurity; and, as is often the case, they blamed their government for the situation that prompted their uneasiness. This feeling of insecurity was not without foundation. To illustrate: after the loss of French Canada and because of the English diplomatic control of timber supplies from the Baltic, French naval officials were hard put to it to obtain enough mast timbers and other naval stores to keep the fleet in being.

In addition to the apparent threat from the English, there were internal problems that troubled almost all Frenchmen. Many of these resulted from the rapid and general western European demographic, economic, social, and technological changes, while others derived from the peculiar nature of late eighteenth-century France.

French Population and Social Classes France, a bit smaller than present-day Texas, was populated by twenty-three to twenty-five million people in the late 1780's. For purposes of analysis we may break this population down into seven groups:

1. Great privileged aristocrats, both clerical and lay, including the nobility of the robe or judicial nobles.

2. Landed nobles, also privileged but without significant power and often without wealth.

3. The upper or true bourgeoisie, including non-nobles living "nobly off their possessions," the more important non-noble civil servants, wholesale merchants, financiers to the court, military and naval contractors, and the Farmers General who collected the royal indirect taxes—great personages all, many of whom married or bought their way into the privileged aristocracy and none of whom worked with his hands.

4. The lesser or petty bourgeoisie (the true "middle class"), storekeepers, doctors, lawyers (except for those lawyers who as hereditary judges were members of the nobility of the robe), lesser *rentiers* (people living modestly on the return from investments), and craftsmen who maintained their own shops.

5. A small group of urban workers (proletarians) concentrated in Paris and a few other cities.

6. A very large mass of peasants, some of whom were substantial agricultural entrepreneurs while others were impoverished rural laborers, with a very large middling group, many of whom engaged in manufacturing as organized by the putting-out system. A few peasants were quasi-serfs (*mainmortables*).

7. A special category of people who lived apart from and at the same time permeated the hierarchy described above: professors, writers, students, musicians, journalists, artists, law clerks, actors, and dancers—an unstable and yeasty group of human beings, some of whom (e.g., actors) were considered outside the law.

Legally, the structure of French society was quite different. Instead of these seven classes, French law recognized only three groups or orders: the First Estate (Clergy), the Second Estate (Nobility) and the Third Estate (everybody else). The first two orders were privileged; the third was not. The principal sign of privilege was exemption from the main direct tax—the *taille.* This official and legal classification was seriously out of date in the eighteenth century and bore little relationship to the actual groupings of society.

Because of the great social gulf that existed between the aristocratic archbishops, bishops, abbots, and canons on the one hand and the workaday priests on the other, the clergy lacked social unity and was more nearly an occupational grouping than a social order. Neither was the nobility a cohesive unit, since most provincial nobles lived in quite a different world from that inhabited by the Court nobility and by the powerful judicial aristocracy. The Third Estate was, of course, a massive conglomeration of unlike parts; and nowhere does this threefold legal classification of French society seem more unreal than it does in putting great industrialists in the same category with a village blacksmith or an army contractor with an ignorant and impoverished rural day-laborer.

The one tie that bound the Third Estate together was the fact that theoretically all members were subject to the *taille* (income or property tax). In fact, most of the upper bourgeoisie and the middle class avoided this tax, which was paid almost exclusively by the peasants; but it was still galling for a bourgeois who lived like a noble to be classified with rude and ignorant peasants. And as the bourgeoisie and middle classes resented being lumped with what they considered their inferiors, they also resented being looked down on by the aristocrats whose ranks the more enterprising and ambitious members of the bourgeoisie often strove, with less and less success, to join. One young man who was to become a prominent revolutionary wrote, "The road is blocked in every direction." As the doors closed, the bourgeoisie became increasingly inclined to break them down.

Nor was the aristocracy entirely satisfied. With the threefold classification of Estates they had no argument; but they were determined not to lose any of their privileges, among them the exemption from the *taille,* the right to wear a sword, and what they thought were their prerogatives: the better positions in the state, both civil and military, as well as in the Church. They were alarmed at the pretensions of the upper bourgeoisie and at the demonstrated power generated by money in modern society. While coveting moneyed as well as landed wealth, they deplored the plutocracy and bemoaned the fact that sons of rich bourgeois could buy army commissions while poor nobles, born to the sword, were left out. When angered by a waspish intellectual like Voltaire they sent their lackeys to beat him up with sticks. Although since 1718, all but three of the Royal ministers (seventy-two of seventy-five) had been noble and although after 1783, all of the 135 French bishops were noble, the hereditary aristocracy was still not satisfied with its share of French power.

FRENCH POPULATION IN 1789

Total: from 22,000,000 to 25,000,000

Estate	Group	Population
First Estate	Clergy	100,000 to 130,000
Second Estate	Nobility	400,000 or fewer
Third Estate	* Upper Bourgeoisie	5,250,000, more or less*
	* Bourgeoisie	
	Urban Proletariat	
	Peasantry	16,250,000 to 21,500,000

* All bourgeois did not live in cities and towns. Many—especially doctors, lawyers and *rentiers* (those living on income from investments)—lived in the country or in small villages. Total *urban* population was surely less than 4,000,000 and perhaps as low as 2,000,000.

Thus the aristocracy—consisting of the nobility of the sword plus the nobility of the robe and their relatives in the important Church offices—were in the last decade of the *ancien régime* engaged in a concerted effort to capture the state.

Religion France was an overwhelmingly Roman Catholic country, but there were a number of Protestants—especially in the south and east and in towns remote from Paris—and a fairly large group of freethinkers. There were two groups of French Jews: the first living in and around Bordeaux, to which area they had come from Spain and Portugal in the sixteenth century, and the second in Alsace. Having lived in France for over 200 years, the Bordeaux Jews were as well assimilated as they could be in a society that excluded them from most social relationships; the Alsatian Jews, on the other hand, dwelling in a region that had been recently annexed to France, were considered outlandish. No Jews enjoyed civil rights in France before the Revolution. Protestants were granted civil rights in 1787.

During the eighteenth century, the French government embarked on a vast highway program. Here we see *corvée* (forced) labor at work laying cobblestones. The mounted supervisors could be the local Intendant and/or engineers from the royal Department of Bridges and Highways. Note the sophisticated stone bridge being built in the background. The painting is by Joseph Vernet. (Louvre.)

The established Gallican (French Roman Catholic) church was not supported by voluntary contributions of the faithful or by the state but by the *dîme* (tithe—theoretically a tenth but usually less) that it collected on all crops. In addition, it received a large return from its landed property, which consisted of no less than one-tenth of all French real estate. The French church's income ranged from 203 to 243 million *livres* annually (it will be remembered that the anticipated deficit of the royal government for 1789 was 126 million *livres*). Church property and income were not taxed, but every five years the French church voted a "free gift" (*don gratuit*) as its contribution toward meeting the expenses of government. A very large share of the remainder went, as was well known at the time, not to carry on the spiritual, educational, and charitable functions of the church, but to support, often in the grandest imaginable style, the great ecclesiastical officials. These men were usually aristocrats by birth and some of them did not even pretend to believe in God. The lower secular clergy, by and large conscientious and impoverished servants of the Lord, from whom most of the "free gift" was extracted, complained that this was a diversion of church revenue from its proper destination.

Obstacles to Economic Progress Economically, France was growing—not as fast as England was at the same time—but still measurably. As population grew, production of food increased. French entrepreneurs—often bringing into partnership a great noble like the duke of Orléans so as to have a friend at court—were gradually introducing the new English machine methods into the French textile industry. The government was constructing a great set of royal highways that served to stimulate inland commerce.

French economic progress was not, however, as rapid as it might have been. Many obstacles to economic growth existed, and these served partially to negate the effect of any improvements in the production and distribution of goods and services that were taking place. The secondary roads were very bad. Even on the highroads, the cost of land transport was so high as to double the price of grain for every 300 miles it was transported; and, because of the insufficient natural navigability of French rivers and the limited development of canals, water transport was not nearly so available as it was in England.

In addition to these more-or-less natural obstacles to commerce and to economic growth, there was a regular minefield of man-made restrictions on trade: an intricate system of internal tolls, tariffs, and levies. France was divided into three major customs areas: the central area, known as the Five Big Farms, had one tariff; the "Provinces termed foreign" (Southern France, Brittany, Franche Comté, Artois, and Flanders) had each its own; the "Provinces effectively foreign" (Lábourd, Gex, Lorraine, Alsace and the bishoprics of Metz, Toul, and Verdun) as well as the free ports of Marseille, Saint-Jean-de-Luz, Lorient, and Dunkirk, had the right to trade freely with the outside world but with the rest of France only upon the payment of duties. Despite the fact that this system of internal tariffs came under fierce and concentrated attack in mid-century by the Physiocrats and despite the fact that important neo-Physiocrats like Turgot gave political assistance to the move to abolish internal tariffs, the system remained essentially unimpaired up to the Revolution.

Besides the tariffs, there were the local tolls and imposts which were so numerous that a wagonload of wine coming from the upper Loire to Paris was subjected to eleven customs duties and twelve tolls. The rights to collect these tolls were most often the inherited privilege of aristocrats. The royal government added to the confusion by imposing a series of prohibitions designed to prevent the exportation of grain, not only from France but also from the community in which it was grown. These restrictions were in fact an attempt by the government to protect the peasantry from speculators who would buy surplus grain to export in times of plenty, thus forcing the peasants to pay high prices in time of crop failures in order to have bread. Most peasants as well as many administrators believed that to prevent famine the grain trade should be restricted. But large-scale producers and traders called for an end to restriction.

The restrictions on the grain trade represented but one facet of traditional mercantilistic policy, which was designed to enhance the power of the state through careful regulation of economic activity. In this effort, the

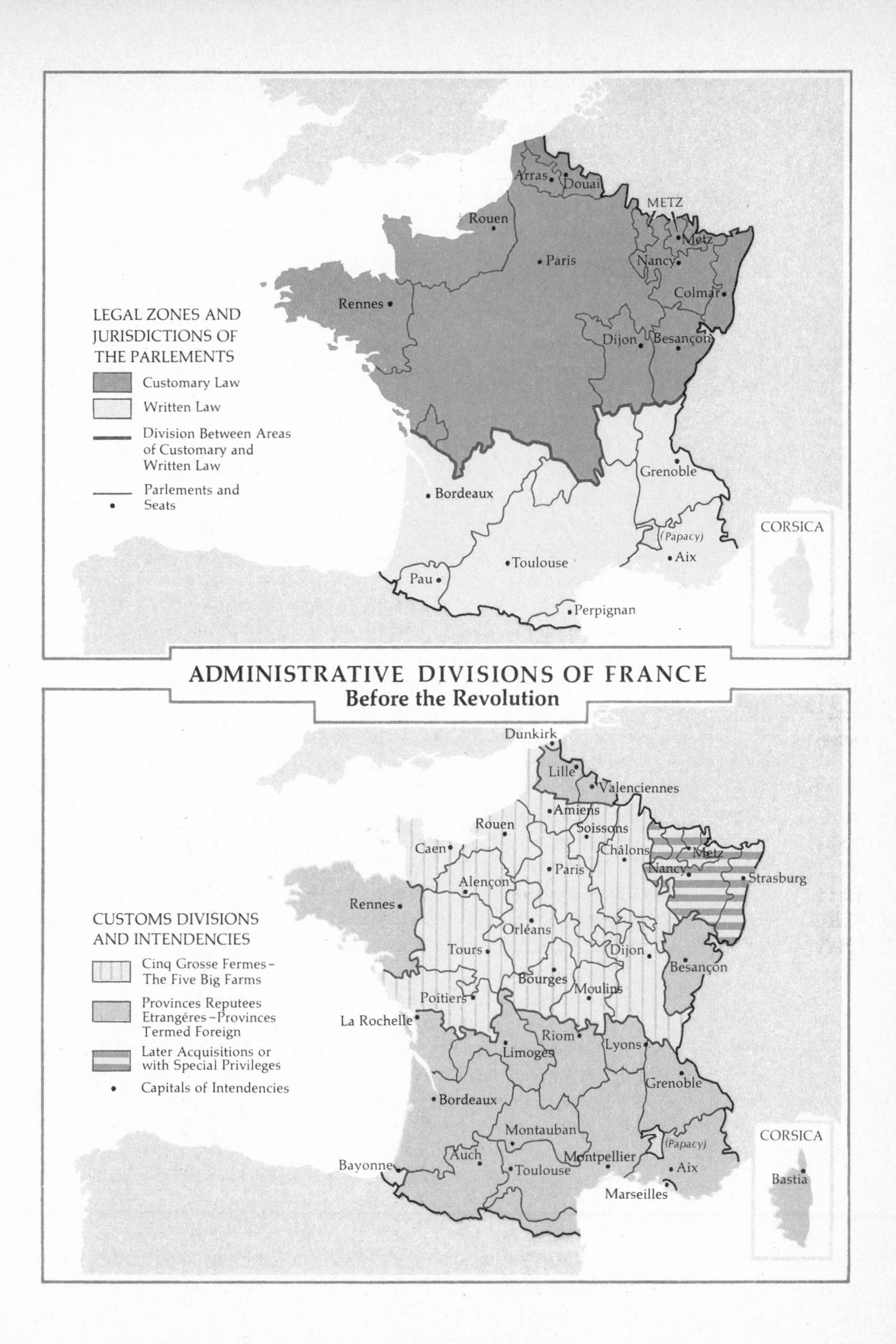
LEGAL ZONES AND JURISDICTIONS OF THE PARLEMENTS
Customary Law
Written Law
Division Between Areas of Customary and Written Law
Parlements and Seats
Arras
Douai
METZ
Metz
Rouen
Paris
Nancy
Colmar
Rennes
Dijon
Besançon
Grenoble
Bordeaux
(Papacy)
Aix
Toulouse
Pau
Perpignan
CORSICA
ADMINISTRATIVE DIVISIONS OF FRANCE
Before the Revolution
CUSTOMS DIVISIONS AND INTENDENCIES
Cinq Grosse Fermes – The Five Big Farms
Provinces Reputees Etrangéres – Provinces Termed Foreign
Later Acquisitions or with Special Privileges
Capitals of Intendencies
Dunkirk
Lille
Valenciennes
Amiens
Rouen
Soissons
Caen
Châlons
Metz
Paris
Nancy
Strasburg
Alençon
Rennes
Orléans
Tours
Dijon
Besançon
Bourges
Moulins
Poitiers
La Rochelle
Riom
Lyons
Limoges
Grenoble
Bordeaux
Montauban
(Papacy)
Auch
Montpellier
Aix
Bayonne
Toulouse
Marseilles
CORSICA
Bastia

mercantilist French government also established monopolistic royal factories (the Gobelins tapestry works, for instance) and gave monopolistic privileges to certain private companies. Because a small number of known producers were more easily inspected and regulated than a large number of scattered firms, the government supported the exclusive guilds of the towns with the understanding that the guilds would help the government in the task of regulation.

Would-be entrepreneurs were not, therefore, free to establish new businesses—as they were inclined to do in this period of rising prices and population growth—when and where they desired. In the towns they ran up against guild exclusiveness (guild membership tended to be hereditary), and when they sought to escape guild control by setting up manufactories in the country they usually had to apply to the central government for authorization which might or might not be granted.

As France lacked customs unity and as some merchants and manufacturers were vexed by a complex system of regulations and restrictions, so France also lacked that which is most important to the rational carrying on of any business: a uniform and understood system of weights and measures. There were two national measures of land, the *arpent de Paris* and the *arpent de France,* which were often confused; and there were many local variations. In some regions, peasants used such functional measures as the "plow of land," meaning the amount of land that could be tilled by one man with one plow, a measure that could hardly be made uniform. There were no uniform measures of volume, dimensions, or weight. Arthur Young, an English traveller in France in the 1780's, found it difficult to understand how the French could do business at all in the face of this confusion:" . . . the infinite perplexity of measures exceeds all comprehension. They differ not only in every province, but in every district and every town; and these tormenting variations are found equally in the denominations and contents of the measures of land and corn."

Foreign Trade Restrictions As was the case in most mercantilist economies, foreign trade was subject to high tariffs. Commercial relations between France and England had become particularly difficult over the course of the eighteenth century as each government prohibited, in a series of trade-war reprisals, the importation of those goods that the other country was most anxious to export. Thus the French prohibited importation of many English textiles and hardware while the English placed high tariffs on French wines and brandies. The walls of tariffs and prohibitions reached such proportions that even in peacetime a large percentage of the considerable trade between the two countries was being carried on by smugglers. By 1783 it was plain to English and French statesmen that the situation was unsatisfactory, and in the treaty of peace between England and France after the War of the American Revolution it was proposed that the two countries should negotiate an end of their commercial difficulties.

A long series of negotiations culminated in the Eden Treaty of 1786. This agreement provided that each country should substantially reduce its tariffs on certain of the other's manufactured products (cottons, hardware, china, pottery, and glassware). This was a tremendous concession on the part of the French, because England, as we know, had a much more highly developed and mechanized industry in all these lines than had France. In return, the English agreed to reduce their tariffs on French wines, vinegar, brandy, and olive oil. English negotiators refused, however, to allow the importation into England of French silks. The silk industry was one of the few in which France had a clear superiority over England.

When this treaty was made public, it was greeted with dismay by French manufacturers. During his travels in 1787–1789, Arthur Young found widespread opposition to it in all French manufacturing centers. Indeed, at Lille he heard the manufacturers calling for war with England "as the only means of escaping that ideal ruin which they are all sure must flow from the influx of English fabrics to rival their own." Only in Bordeaux, the most important port in the French wine trade, did he hear merchants describe the treaty as "a wise measure." Evidently, the Eden Treaty did not, as some of the chambers of commerce anticipated that it would, destroy French industry; but French manufacturers and artisans felt the new English competition and were hurt by it. A result of this experience was the fact that although most French businessmen were calling for free internal trade, they did not join the Physiocrats and other liberal economists in seeking an international division of labor. The customs barriers should, they believed, be pushed back to the national frontiers; but they should not be eliminated.

This etching dating from about 1774 shows a French peasant dwelling in its most charming aspect. Actually, such houses were little more than hovels, serving as barns as well as homes. (LCPP.)

Agriculture and the Peasants The French economy was still essentially agricultural and the overwhelming majority of Frenchmen were peasants. Thus the agricultural aspects of the economy and the agrarian aspects of the society were probably of greater import than the commercial and industrial features just described.

Farming was carried on in France not much better and not much worse than it was elsewhere in Europe. Most French peasants farmed according to the fallow rotation system. In the late eighteenth century, it was obviously the peasantry of France that did all the farm work. Moreover, the French peasantry held or owned no less than 30 percent of the French rural landscape, and perhaps more. As for the rest, a good guess is that the clergy had from 10 to 20 percent, the nobility about 20 percent or a bit more, and the bourgeoisie about 20 percent in the years just before the Revolution.

Nearly all the peasants, as we have seen, were free men. Among the peasants who held land, the most substantial were the *laboureurs,* who had hereditary title of one sort or another to the use of a piece of land (or pieces of land) big enough to support themselves and their families. The *laboureur* was the aristocrat of the late eighteenth-century French peasantry. His numbers were increasing on the eve of the Revolution and he was increasing his landholdings. Other peasants who had hereditary titles to land held it in smaller portions and derived part or all of their incomes as day agricultural workers or from cottage industry or as sharecroppers. The number of these peasant-farmers whose land did not support them was increasing during the last years of the *ancien régime,* as was the number of peasants who held no land at all, the rural proletariat.

A special group among the peasants who held no land but who were hardly rural proletarians were the *fermiers,* tenants with money leases, often large-scale farmers with considerable capital. *Fermage* was a fairly special kind of land tenure at the time and was localized in the north and a few other regions. A growing group, the *fermiers* were the plutocrats of the French peasantry.

Causes of Peasant Discontent The main burden of supporting the French government, clergy, and nobility fell upon the peasantry. It was the peasants who paid the most important direct government taxes like the *taille* and the lucrative indirect taxes like the *gabelle* (a tax on salt). The tithe (*dîme*) that the Church took of their crops along with the rents that many peasants paid to ecclesiastical landlords provided nearly the entire support of the Church. To the nobles, the peasants paid quitrents and various other dues. They maintained the royal highways without pay and unwillingly staffed the militia. They were forced to stand by while wild game and noble hunters devastated their crops.

Under the weight of what seems to have been a monumental heap of burdens, the peasants resorted to fraud, evasion, and disguise. To avoid the *taille réele,* they took advantage of legislation exempting newly cultivated lands from this tax by abandoning their old and more productive fields for new ones which they carved out of barren wastes. Prosperous peasants went about in rags and refrained from making capital improvements in order to avoid the *taille personelle.* All systematically disguised income in order to escape the *vingtième* and the *capitation.* To avoid military service, young peasants who could ill support wife and children got married; others evaded the draft by taking to the hills and highways where they became brigands.

Meanwhile, the more prosperous peasants in the villages chafed under what remained of communal controls on their own enterprise. They joined some of the more aggressive landlords in attempting an agrarian revolution—in favor of themselves. They tried with some success to "enclose" common pasture; they bought out the poorer peasants who found they could not make a living without access to the commons; they participated in the

A LITTLE LIST OF TAXES AND OTHER PEASANT BURDENS

I. Taxes and Obligations Owed to the Crown

A. Direct taxes paid to the Crown

taille réele	A direct real-estate tax
taille personelle	A direct tax on "outward signs of wealth"
vingtième	(twentieth) an income tax
capitation	(head tax) really another income tax

B. Indirect taxes paid to the Crown through agency of the Farmers General

gabelle	(salt tax) the principal indirect tax and the most infamous; very harshly enforced; tax amounted to as much as 13 *sous* per pound of salt

C. Labor services rendered to the Crown

corvées	*transports militaires*	obligatory loan of carts and draft animals to transport royal troops and military supplies
	corvée des routes	required work building and repairing royal highways; 6 to 30 days labor per peasant per year; required of peasants living near royal highways

D. Military service rendered to the Crown

The French Army was recruited through more-or-less voluntary enlistment; but the regular army was supplemented by a militia drawn by lot in what was really an early form of conscription. The peasantry supplied the entirety of the enlisted personnel of the militia, which consisted of about 60,000 men in 1789.

II. Obligations to the Church

dîme	tithe (usually about 1/13th or less) of the crops taken from the field for support of the Church

III. Obligations, Burdens, and Annoyances Deriving from Landlords

cens	quitrents paid by peasants to landlord in money or in kind
lods et vents	large payments to landlord on occasion of peasant's sale or transfer of landed property
rachat	dues of succession (like the Medieval English "heriot") paid to landlord on peasant inheritance of land—sometimes as high as 50 percent of the value of the land in question
banalités	a variety of requirements put on peasants, according to local usages; these involved such matters as obligatory use of the seigneur's mill, of his wine-press, baking-oven, or ferry—all for a fee

A LITTLE LIST OF TAXES AND OTHER PEASANT BURDENS (Continued)

capitaineries	hunting privileges granted by the Crown to Princes of the Blood, who had exclusive hunting rights over tracts of land as large as 800 square miles where the game was protected, greatly to the detriment of the resident peasants, who were forbidden to disturb the wildlife and who were required to adapt their farming procedures to the desires of the princely hunters
other hunting customs	in general, even outside the *capitaineries,* peasants were not allowed to hunt or shoot or to disturb wild animal life which was reserved for the sport of the nobility. Rabbits, in particular, seem to have been a dreadful scourge
colombiers	(pigeon houses) the noble right to maintain a pigeon loft was a sign of status. Peasants were forbidden to bother the birds which ate seed and harvest at will.

As regards all payments to the seigneur, it should be noted that if the payment was in money it was likely to be relatively painless to the peasant because generally the contracts and the terms thereof were so old that the price rise of the eighteenth century minimized their real value. If in kind, the payment was likely to have considerably higher real value.

attack upon common usages like that of pasturing livestock in open fields after harvest (*vaine pâture*). Faced with the loss of these important common rights, increasing numbers of peasants were unable to make a go of things and left the villages to joint the draft evaders in the hills or to migrate to towns and cities. Vagrancy and brigandage were serious problems in France during the 1780's.

Although the peasants who remained on the land tended to profit from the misfortunes of those who were displaced, they had reason to be disturbed by what seemed to them to be a concerted attempt on the part of landlords to extract even larger dues and more services from them.

The "Feudal Reaction" Pressed, as members of a group living on more-or-less fixed incomes must necessarily have been, by the rising prices of the period, many nobles were attempting in the late eighteenth century to improve their financial position by hiring lawyers to seek out ways and means to relieve the peasantry of any new wealth they may have been acquiring from rising prices for agricultural products. These lawyers—specialists, as they put it, in "renovating" manorial records—inspected the

It Won't Last Forever! Harassed by dogs and a monkey, the peasant of this cartoon carries the entire burden of society. He is observed by representatives of the privileged clergy (left) and nobility (right), both of whom lean on royal authority, as symbolized by the fleur-de-lis. (Bibliothèque Nationale, Paris.)

seigneurial archives to determine whether or not the landlords were overlooking any charges that they might legally make on the peasants. In the course of this research, they often found obscure seigneurial rights dating from, perhaps, the Middle Ages, usages that had been overlooked for generations or had been allowed to lapse sometime in the past by oral agreement between lord and peasant, without any documentation. When confronted with the lawyer's statement that he had to pay such and such a forgotten due or render such and such a lapsed service, the peasant's only recourse, in most instances, was to the seigneurial court presided over by the landlord or his representative. Inasmuch as the peasant probably could not read and because his opponent controlled the court, he was usually forced to accept the lawyer's anachronistic finding. An important aspect of the late eighteenth-century "feudal reaction," this renovation of the manorial records (*terriers*) was a source of a festering peasant sense of injustice and led, as we shall see, to peasant violence in 1789.

Moreover, the peasants were often upset when the seigneurial rights to their lands were acquired by new landlords. When a prosperous merchant, for example, purchased an estate from an impecunious noble, he was very likely to try to carry over his business-like habits to the management of his new lands. His lawyers were sometimes more efficient than those hired by the nobles; and because he did not have long, inherited experience in dealing with peasants he was often liable to move in what seemed arbitrary ways. Because he had recently elevated himself to the dignity of a landed proprietor, he was likely to be even more jealous of his seigneurial rights than were those born to the station. Bitterly the peasants complained about the upsetting of old ways by these new landlords. But they also complained about the "renovations" attempted by the old seigneurs, about rabbits and pigeons, about taxes, *corvées, banalités,* and all the rest. Their list of complaints was formidable; but because they were only peasants, no one paid any attention to them until they took matters violently into their own hands during the summer of 1789.

Grain Warehouse in Paris. In order to assure sufficient food supply for Paris in time of crop failures, the city authorities built this circular warehouse for wheat and flour. Such measures may have permitted population growth in the eighteenth century. (Bibliothèque Nationale, Paris.)

Economic Crisis and the Workers A growing and strategically located part of the prerevolutionary working population was composed of urban proletarians and journeymen employed in commerce, building trades, and manufacturing. Paris was at that time a city of some 600,000 inhabitants, of whom about half were wage-workers and their families. In Sedan, there were 15,000 workers in the textile industry. Troyes, Lyons, Bourges, Rouen, and a few other large towns had substantial numbers of workers.

There is no doubt that the lot of these people was worsening in the decades before the Revolution. Between 1730 and 1789, wages increased only 22 percent while grain prices (which helped to determine the price of bread) rose 60 percent. The result was that urban workers, like rural proletarians, were being painfully stretched between the opening blades of the wage-price scissors. Probably one-fifth of the town workers and their families were indigent.

The urban workers, like their employers, were very sensitive to fluctuations in business activity. Any important reduction in market forced the manufacturers to close down their shops or suspend putting-out enterprises. During the course of the eighteenth century there had been a number of such economic crises, all caused—as to be expected in an economy that was primarily agricultural—by bad weather and resultant crop failures. Because the peasants made up the overwhelming majority of the population, they also formed a considerable part of the French market for goods. During years of bad crops the peasants suffered, despite the fact that scarcity drove up the prices of the commodities they produced, because they had little surplus to sell. Accordingly, the peasants were driven out of the market by crop failure; and landlords—to the extent that they received payments in kind—had less to put on the market and thus had less to spend. Consequently, consumption of goods declined and manufacturers had to close their establishments; and middlemen and storekeepers also suffered. The upshot was a real business depression in a time of high prices for food.[2]

France experienced the worst of its late eighteenth-century economic crises during the years 1788–1789. Earlier in the 1780's, grape production had fluctuated: large harvests had produced a glut and falling prices; later the vintage was so small that the large number of peasants who depended

[2]This interpretation of late eighteenth-century agriculturally generated business depressions is derived from the work of C. E. Labrousse. This interpretation, as well as the data upon which it is based, has been sharply challenged by an American, David S. Landes. For convenient summaries, see Stanley Idzerda, *The Background of the French Revolution* (1959), pp. 15–16 and R. W. Greenlaw, ed., *The Economic Origins of the French Revolution: Poverty or Prosperity?* (1958).

upon the sale of wine for cash could not profit from the rising prices. In 1785, drought and disease carried off a significant percentage of the French peasants' livestock. The impact of the Eden Treaty on some sectors of French manufacturing was sufficiently severe as to result in the laying-off of many workers. Even before 1788, unemployment was growing.

Then catastrophe was added to misfortune. Abominable weather caused the spring and winter grain crops of 1788 to fail. The peasants not only had little grain to sell; they had little to eat. Rural proletarians out of work migrated to the towns where bread was already dear. Unemployment—already high—soared. In Paris, early in 1789, a pound of bread cost four *sous.* The going daily wage for those fortunate enough to be employed was 19 *sous.* An adult manual worker consumed two or three pounds of bread per day; it was the staple of his diet, for which he spent 50 percent of his earnings in good times, more in bad.

With a shortage of grain, all the little people were hurt: workers, storekeepers, artisans, owners of small manufacturing enterprises, as well as peasants. The population of Paris was swollen by a crowd of half-starving vagrants. The omens were not auspicious as the representatives of the French nation were elected during the winter and spring of 1789.

FURTHER READING

First, there is a useful survey of the literature on **The Background of the French Revolution* by S. Idzerda, published in 1959 by the American Historical Association (Service Center Pamphlet). Again, see L. Gershoy, **From Despotism to Revolution* (1944), for general background.

The relations between the American and French revolutions can be studied in L. Gottschalk, "The Place of the American Revolution in the Causal Pattern of the French Revolution," published in the first volume of H. Ausubel, ed., *The Making of Modern Europe* (1951); in B. Fay, *The Revolutionary Spirit in France and America* (1927); and most satisfactorily in D. Echeverria, *Mirage in the West: a History of the French Image of American Society* (1957), which is especially strong on Franklin's role as an image maker. Also pertinent is L. Gottschalk's still unfinished biography of Lafayette, full and interesting.

The great classic is A. de Tocqueville, **The Old Regime and the French Revolution* (1955), first published in 1856. By far the best book for the beginning student or anyone else interested in a brief treatment is G. Lefebvre, **The Coming of the French Revolution,* tr. R. R. Palmer (1947). Lefebvre has been attacked posthumously by E. Eisenstein in an article entitled, "Who Intervened in 1788? A Commetary on the Coming of the French Revolution," excerpted in F. Kafker and J. Laux, eds., **The French Revolution: Conflicting*

*Books available in paperback edition are marked with an asterisk.

Interpretations (1968). The first four chapters of L. Gershoy, *The French Revolution and Napoleon* (1964), and the opening sections of L. Gottschalk, *The Era of the French Revolution, 1715–1815* (1929), are useful. A. Cobban, *The Social Interpretation of the French Revolution* (1964), is controversial. A specialized study that challenges the idea of an aristocratic reaction in the late eighteenth century is V. Gruder, *The Royal Provincial Intendants: A Governing Elite in Eighteenth-Century France* (1968).

Among the pertinent biographies, D. Dakin, *Turgot and the Ancien Régime in France* (1965), stands out. H. Sée, *Economic and Social Conditions in France during the Eighteenth Century* (1928), is still indispensable for the economic background. I. O. Wade, *The Clandestine Organization and Diffusion of Philosophic Ideas in France from 1700 to 1750* (1938), gives a glimpse of the intellectual ferment. The debate aroused by C. E. Labrousse over the possible effect of the business cycle on the coming of the Revolution is surveyed in the volume in the Heath series, "Problems in European Civilization," R. W. Greenlaw, ed., **The Economic Origins of the French Revolution—Poverty or Prosperity?* (1958). Two important articles by G. Taylor shed light on possible economic causes of the Revolution: "Types of Capitalism in Eighteenth Century France," in the *English Historical Review* (1964), and "Non-Capitalist Wealth and the Origins of the French Revolution," in the *American Historical Review* (January 1967). The best primary source is a travel diary written by an Englishman who visited France three times during the years 1787, 1788, and 1799; Arthur Young, *Travels in France,* edited by C. Maxwell (1929). There is also a somewhat unsatisfactory but recent abridgement by J. Kaplow.

To understand how historians have presented the causes, see A. Cobban, *Historians and the Causes of the French Revolution* (1958). J. Kaplow, ed., **New Perspectives on the French Revolution: Readings in Historical Sociology* (1965), contains translated articles by French (and some English) scholars, most of which deal with the social background of the French Revolution.

3 The French Revolution (I)

During the summer of 1788, the French crown agreed to call together the old Estates General, a national representative body with partial legislative powers, that had last met in 1614. Amidst crackling excitement and tempestuous debate, the French people selected representatives to confer with their king about the difficulties in which France found itself. Some of these difficulties, financial, religious, economic, and social, have already been described. Of these, only the financial problem touched the government directly; and it was not in itself so complicated as to be impossible of solution.

Obviously the government had not done what was necessary. That it had not done so constituted a political failure, the outward and visible sign of which was the calling of the Estates General. Let us turn to the political aspect of the decades before the Revolution in order to understand precisely why this failure occurred.

POLITICAL BEGINNINGS OF THE FRENCH REVOLUTION

The political failure of the *ancien régime* monarchy was partly the result of well-known personal shortcomings on the part of the last two kings. Although moderately intelligent and sometimes forceful, Louis XV was indolent, intensely preoccupied with his amusements, and mistress-ridden; Louis XVI was timid, unintelligent, indecisive, and wife-ridden. But despite royal unwillingness or incapacity, the government tried with considerable vigor in the last decades of the *ancien régime* to bring about the much-needed financial and tax reforms. This attempt was frustrated by effective aristocratic resistance, a resistance organized and led by the hereditary members of the *parlements*, the French law-courts.

The Parlement The *parlement* of Paris was rather like a supreme court for central France. There were twelve other provincial *parlements* located along the periphery of the kingdom and having jurisdiction in their areas. In addition to their judicial functions, the *parlements* acted as the registrars of law. On occasion, a *parlement* would refuse to enregister a royal edict or order-in-council; whereupon the king, if he was determined to have the law enacted, would appear in the *parlement* chamber, recline upon a pile of pillows and order the enregistering of the law in question. The significance of this ceremony (*lit de justice*) was that it served to remind the judges of the royal view that the *parlement* was not an independent agency, that it was a creation of the crown, subject to royal will. In the late eighteenth century, the judges did not necessarily agree with this interpretation of their constitutional position.

As the personal authority of the monarchs waned after 1715, the *parlements* became more than ever convinced that they limited the crown, that theirs was the right to interpret the constitution, to determine the constitutionality of law, and to refuse to enregister those royal edicts that they considered unconstitutional. Because the judges in the *parlements* were privileged aristocrats, they were particularly sensitive and aggressive about any projected changes in French tax structure that might increase the tax burden of the aristocracy. They maintained that the right to levy existing rates had been granted to the crown by the Estates General in the fifteenth century and that, although there might be a need for tax reform, it could not be done legally by royal fiat. By holding to this argument, the *parlements* hoped to guarantee that the aristocracy would be able to control the reforms when and if they should come about. Moreover, their argument obviously pointed to a re-assembly of the old Estates General to reconsider the work of the fifteenth century. Backing up their self-confidence was the considerable popularity that the *parlements* enjoyed by virtue of their position as opponents of an ineffectual government that moved in arbitrary and capricious ways.

Lettres de Cachet The tendency of the crown to legislate more or less at will and sometimes without reference to previous law or existing custom did make French government seem capricious, especially when there was considerable legislative activity, as was the case in the period from the 1760's onward. Arbitrariness was illustrated for many Frenchmen by the *lettre de cachet*—which many believed was so widely employed that every royal fortress in the kingdom was stuffed with miserable prisoners, arbitrarily denied their freedom.[1]

Most infamous of all the fortress-prisons was the grim Bastille towering over the *faubourg* (suburb) St. Antoine and dominating the east end of Paris. Today, we know that in June of 1789 the Bastille was garrisoned by a hundred old and disabled soldiers who guarded seven prisoners, including

[1] *Lettres de cachet* were administrative arrest warrants issued in the name of the king and valid if sealed and countersigned by a secretary of state. *Lettres de cachet* were used by the government as a means quietly to lock up political opponents, seditious writers, and prominent people who needed to be removed from activity. Actually, it was fairly easy for anyone with any influence at all to get his hands on a signed *lettre de cachet* in blank—that is, without the name of the person to be arrested. Thus, a private person who could command such a *lettre* could have another person imprisoned without trial or hearing indefinitely.

Lettres de cachet were sometimes used by fathers, wives, and husbands who had reason to desire their children, husbands, or wives put away for more-or-less delicate reasons.

two lunatics, a sexual deviate, and four forgers, and that plans to tear the old fort down had been discussed. But in the excitement of 1788–1789 most Frenchmen would not have believed these facts.

The Crown versus Parlement Why were they so worked up over a kind of arbitrary tyranny which they had known for centuries and which was milder under Louis XVI than it had been under his predecessors? The answer lies partly in the fact that the government was not only absolute and arbitrary (at least in theory), but it was also highly inefficient. It did not work well; moreover, it worked less well than it had in its fairly recent past.

The military and naval inefficiency of the French government had been amply demonstrated during all the wars of the eighteenth century save one. And in the one victory—the War of the American Revolution—the cost of triumph was far greater than any real advantages derived from the effort, as we have seen. Administratively as well, the Bourbon regime found it increasingly difficult to get anything done, despite, or, perhaps, because of, frenetic attempts at reform. If the king and his ministers did not know how to proceed through the haphazard maze of law and administration, the French people were even more at a loss. The people blamed the crown for their predicament; the crown blamed *its* troubles on the *parlements* which acted as conservative forces resisting the rational changes that seemed necessary.

When, therefore, despite the preoccupation or timidity of Louis XV and Louis XVI, the royal government endeavored to effect some changes, these attempts tended to take on the aspect of an anti-*parlement* crusade. With hindsight, we can now understand that in order to move in the direction desired by the most vital segments of the population—the unprivileged *élites*—the royal government would have had to break the power of the *parlements,* which were the legal bastions of constituted, hereditary aristocracy. What is clear to us now, however, was not immediately apparent to the majority of the French people, who persuaded themselves, for the time being, that the *parlements* stood for liberty and law as opposed to despotism and whim.

ROYAL ATTEMPTS AT REFORM

Before the death of Louis XV, the royal government was presided over during the decade of the 1760's by the Duke of Choiseul, who had come into power through the favor of Madame de Pompadour. Then for four years, 1770–1774, it was supervised by René de Maupeou (1714–1792) who had been made Chancellor of France through Choiseul's influence and who reciprocated by joining a cabal centered around Madame du Barry that brought about Choiseul's disgrace in 1770. Both of these statesmen had some of the qualities of reforming, enlightened-despotic ministers, like, for instance, Pombal in Portugal. Choiseul teamed with the *parlement* of Paris to banish the Jesuits from France; but when that *parlement* dared to demand that it should examine the royal budget and then went on to form a confederation of all the *parlements* and to call a general judicial strike and generally obstruct the royal government in its attempts to achieve fiscal and administrative reforms, Choiseul retaliated by exiling the judges. After Choiseul's fall, Maupeou, likewise, ran afoul of the *parlements*, and he moved vigorously to the attack. The *parlements* were abolished; councils of magistrates appointed by the king were created in their place. This move was forward-looking in that it removed the hereditary principle from the magistracy and tended to separate judicial from political functions. Some intellectuals of the day, notably Voltaire, praised this little revolution. Majority sentiment, however, was still on the side of the *parlements.*

Some historians have suggested that, given ten more years for the royal reforms to take hold and ten more years of firmness on the part of the old king (Louis XV, that is), who late in his reign seemed to show more vigor than he had for decades, the monarchy could have rearranged itself to meet contemporary forces of change so that it could have survived for generations. Unfortunately, Louis XV did not manage to survive. His grandson, a vague and well-intentioned young man of 20 years, came to the throne in 1774, as we have seen, full of doubts about his competence. Above all things, Louis XVI wanted "to be loved." His first move to cultivate popularity was to nullify the achievement of Maupeou and to recall the *parlements.* They returned to their duties as determined as ever to obstruct royal reforms.

But while with one hand Louis XVI called back the forces of aristocratic reaction, with the other he tried tentatively to continue the work of reform by appointing some of the ablest Frenchmen alive to important government posts: A. R. J. Turgot (1727–1781) as controller general,[2] the Count of Saint-Germain as minister of war, the Count of Vergennes as minister of foreign affairs, and Lamoignon de Malesherbes as minister in charge of police.

Bust of Turgot by Houdon. Turgot, a liberal administrator and economist, might have saved the French monarchy if Louis XVI had had the wit and strength to support him against his many enemies. He was disgraced in 1776 after only two years in office. With Adam Smith, Turgot was one of the fathers of liberal economic theory. (Courtesy, Museum of Fine Arts, Boston.)

Turgot These were all vigorous and often unpopular men, but Turgot was outstanding. A brilliant economist who had been associated with the Physiocrats and one of the principal *philosophes* of his generation, he came to his important post with a background of long and distinguished experience in public service. He was one of those late eighteenth-century statesmen dedicated to the propositions of enlightened despotism.

One of Turgot's first official acts was to submit to his master a statement of principles including, "No bankruptcy, no increase of taxation, no borrowing." Respect for these prohibitions left him with only one recourse: revision of the tax structure so that the burden of taxes should fall equally on all classes of French society. Turgot's platform also included such physiocratic planks as elimination of the guilds and all other artificial restrictions on internal trade and manufacturing, reduction of pensions and sinecures, and careful accounting and controllership in all branches of government.

[2]The controller general (finance minister) in the *ancien régime* government was a very important official. Under his department came all such matters as finance, taxation, roads, agriculture, industry, and commerce—nearly everything except foreign affairs, the army, and the navy.

These reforms were clearly in line with the needs of the times and long overdue, but they were not well received.

For many months the king defended Turgot against the hornets that attacked him and his program. Turgot's problems resulted partly from the king's error in recalling the *parlements*, partly from his own personality, but mainly from the nature of his program, which threatened to pierce the vitals of the aristocratic establishment. As time went on, his opponents came to include most of the people who had a stake in the status quo: holders of pensions and sinecures, the privileged aristocracy, large segments of the clergy. Some of the king's ministers—even those who shared his desire for reform—came to resent the way the schoolmasterish Turgot would read them lectures on natural law; and the queen was embittered by his opposition to pensions for some of her friends. The upshot was such concerted pressure on Louis as to break what little will he had: Turgot was ordered (1776) to hand in his resignation. Into the political scrap-heap with Turgot went Malesherbes, who had done much to reduce the abuse of the *lettre de cachet*. In the next year, Saint-Germain, who had made the tactical mistake of reducing the number of idle officers on the army payroll, joined the ranks of unemployed reforming ministers. At the end of 1777, the only great minister left on his perch was Vergennes, who served to hasten the collapse of the monarchy by leading France into the War of the American Revolution. The aristocratic counteroffensive had won this round.

Jacques Necker served three times as finance minister. He succeeded Turgot in 1776; was fired in 1781; returned in 1788; was dismissed again in early July, 1789; and was recalled after the fall of the Bastille. (LCPP.)

Necker The controller general of finances who succeeded Turgot was a Swiss banker, Jacques Necker, father of the energetic girl who became Madame de Stäel. For some years he enjoyed a profound respect on the part of the French business community because he was a businessman and, obviously, the government needed businesslike treatment. Necker talked learnedly about the need for reform but did little until 1781 when the expenses of the American War made themselves felt in the treasury. At this point, Necker published a remarkably disingenuous accounting of the royal finances; and, despite the fact that he had juggled the figures to make it seem as though income exceeded expenditure, there was such an uproar as a result of this publication that the privileged, who enjoyed tax immunity and who feared that Necker's revelations might lead to tax reform and to the abolition of sinecures and pensions, brought about his enforced retirement.

Calonne After two years of drift, another reforming finance minister, the Abbé de Calonne (1783–1787), returned to the struggle. His first effort was to try to increase public confidence in the government by spending freely, which course he hoped would improve the royal credit. Second, realizing quite clearly that tax reforms were essential to fiscal soundness, he proposed a sweeping set of changes designed to modernize and strengthen the royal power and to subject the privileged orders to taxation. Because Calonne feared that the king would not back him up in an open power fight with

Calonne, who called the Assembly of Notables in an effort to win aristocratic support for fiscal reform, is portrayed in this contemporary cartoon as the monkey-cook in a poultry yard. He asks the assembled fowl, the Notables, with what sauce they wish to be eaten. They reply that they do not at all wish to be eaten; in short, they will not give up their tax exemptions and other privileges. Calonne replies that they are avoiding the question. (Musée Carnavalet.)

the *parlements,* he decided to present his proposals to a hand-picked assembly of 133 notables of the realm. In this way, he hoped to get impressive backing for his scheme—backing that would strengthen his hand against the resistance he knew the *parlements* would offer.

Somewhat strangely, however, Calonne picked his Assembly of Notables entirely from the aristocracy: fourteen ecclesiastical prelates, thirty-six great nobles, thirty-three members of *parlements,* thirteen intendants and thirty-seven members of provincial estates—no bankers, merchants, or industrialists. In view of this fact, it is not surprising, then, that this first Assembly of Notables (February to May 1787) reacted unfavorably and even violently to Calonne's propositions—so violently, in fact, that the king dismissed Calonne. A few days later, the Assembly of Notables was dissolved.

Brienne Calonne's successor, Lomenie de Brienne (a personally ambitious man and would-be reformer as well as an aristocratic archbishop) tried to carry his predecessor's program through the hostile *parlements* and ran, again, into effective opposition. Meanwhile, as the financial crisis became more and more critical, Brienne proposed to raise money by floating in France a loan of 120,000,000 *livres.* Brienne had to have the consent of the *parlements* before the attempt could be made. The judges stipulated their condition: The Estates General must be called to consider the matter. Brienne countered by offering that the loan should be floated first and that the Estates General would be convoked after the crown had the money. When the *parlement* refused to agree to this, the battle-lines were clearly drawn.

Less wise and no more successful than Calonne, Brienne tried to bull through. The timid king was pushed into the *parlement* of Paris for a *lit de justice,* to command that the judges enregister the edicts enabling the loan. The king's own cousin, the Duke of Orléans, rose to speak in opposition saying, "Sire, this is illegal!" At that point Louis XVI showed that, if he did not have the will of his great-great-great-grandfather, at least he had inherited Louis XIV's instincts. "It is legal," he cried as he stormed from the room, "because I wish it!"

The result was an insurrection of nearly the entire aristocracy, with the *parlements* in the lead. Once again, the royal government banished the *parlements* and put other judicial bodies in their places. Once again the *parlements* appealed to the people in the name of Law and Liberty. All over France there were riots. The aristocrats formed revolutionary committees, propagandized the army and royal officials to such effect that the king's own forces refused in some localities to move against the rebellious elements. They even managed, for the time being, to appeal successfully to the bourgeoisie for support. It became obvious, even to Brienne and his royal master, that a large loan could not be floated in this revolutionary atmosphere.

While they were drawing this conclusion, the treasury approached emptiness. On July 5, 1788, Brienne capitulated and promised to call the Estates General for assembly in the spring of 1789. By July 24, the treasury was completely empty; Brienne resigned. Reluctantly, the king recalled Jacques Necker who completed the retreat of the government by reinstating the *parlement* of Paris (September 23, 1788). As the victorious and still-applauded judges returned from banishment, it was clear that the aristocratic revolutionaries had won another round in their fight to prevent the crown from reforming the tax structure of France and to gain more political power for themselves. In this struggle, they had been assisted, of course, by the failure of the royal government to disassociate itself from the aristocracy and rely for support on the bourgeoisie and other members of the unprivileged elites. This failure was clearly demonstrated by Calonne's choice of the membership of the obstructionist Assembly of Notables of 1787 and by Necker's decision to reinstate the *parlement* in September 1788.

Calling the Estates General of 1789 When on July 5, 1788, Brienne capitulated to the aristocracy by promising to call the Estates General, very little could precisely be remembered about what that body was or how it was convoked—the last one had met in 1614. The first official step—or promise—took the form of an order-in-council by means of which the king called for historical research: royal officials, provincial estates, universities, and learned societies were requested to look into whatever records they could find bearing on the convocation of Estates Generals and to send this information to the Royal Keeper of the Seals. Thousands of Frenchmen responded enthusiastically to this request and the upshot was a flood of memoranda and a lake of documents, enough nearly to drown the bemused Keeper of the Seals in paper. Moreover, hundreds of Frenchmen decided to spread their views in print. At least 500 pamphlets were published in the five months between July 5 and the end of 1788. All sorts of constitutional and economic reforms were proposed; these proposals were avidly discussed in clubs and lodges; crowds were harangued in the garden of the *Palais Royal* and on street corners; cafés buzzed with controversy.

During the late summer of 1788, the *parlements,* up to this point the leaders of revolutionary activity, began to show themselves to the public in their true colors as aristocratic reactionaries. Some of the pamphlets seemed excessively radical to the judges, who thereupon set themselves up as censors and began to condemn specific pamphlets and their authors. On September 23, 1788, the *parlement* of Paris showed even more clearly where it stood when it proclaimed on its own authority that the Estates General of 1789 should be constituted exactly as it had been at the last meeting in 1614: that is to say, in three orders or bodies (First Estate, Second Estate, and Third Estate), with equal membership and one vote for each order. Such an arrangement, of course, would give the aristocracy, which dominated both the First and Second Estates, a majority over the Third Estate.

Immediately, the whole complexion of the Revolution changed. The bourgeoisie and other unprivileged elites began to denounce the *parlements* as aristocratic strongholds. They changed their mind about attacking the monarchy and Louis XVI, both of which they now hailed as the reforming instruments that should lead in the rejuvenation of France. Later on, of course, the Revolution was to shift its allegiance several more times.

During the autumn of 1788, Jacques Necker, once again the presiding officer over the Revolution, called another Assembly of Notables to discuss the manner of convocation of the Estates General. Majority sentiment among the notables was in favor of convocation in three orders of equal membership; but Necker, perhaps sensing that the Revolution had already passed the aristocracy by, persuaded his royal master to accept the principle that the Third Estate should have as many deputies as the sum of the First and Second Estates. Accordingly, in the last days of the year (December 27) an order-in-council proclaimed the "doubling of the Third."[3] But this order said nothing about how the deputies should vote after they had been convened.

The General Regulation for the Elections As excitement all over France and in the colonies mounted at the prospect of a revival of the Estates General, the crown, after due thought and hesitation, issued, January 24, 1789, a General Regulation which set the ground rules of the election. It was to be a complicated affair: direct elections for all of the nobility and most of the clergy in 234 electoral districts; and indirect elections in two, three, or four stages for the Third Estate in the same electoral districts. Thus the nobles and clergy went directly to their assemblies, aired their views and then elected one or more of their number as deputies. The elections for the Third Estate, on the other hand, started in primary assemblies of various kinds in the towns, villages, and parishes where electors were selected. The overwhelming majority of these primary assemblies took place

[3]In theory, the Estates General was to have 300 clergy, 300 nobles, and 600 commoners.

in rural parishes where the peasants, more often than not, chose as electors local notables who could read and write. These electors then went to the principal towns of their electoral districts where they participated in the secondary elections. The men from the parishes were politely enough received by the townsfolk; but from then on their role tended to be passive. One result of the workings of this system was the fact that although the election was conducted according to something very like universal manhood suffrage and although about 90 percent of the French people were peasants or workers, all but perhaps one of the 648 deputies for the Third Estate were middle-class people or liberal nobles and clergymen. Over half of them were lawyers; eighty-five were businessmen; sixty-seven were *rentiers* living on return from investments; and thirty-one were professional men, mainly physicians.

The Cahiers The General Regulation also provided that at each electoral assembly the views of the electorate should be inscribed in a *Cahier des doléances* (list of grievances). Perhaps something approaching 40,000 *cahiers* were drafted; about 20,000 of them still exist. Six hundred fifteen of the *cahiers* were general *cahiers*—that is, they were prepared at the final stage in the electoral process; the others were made at the primary level in the towns, villages, and parishes. At the time, the general *cahiers* were politically important because they represented instructions for the deputies and at least in part governed their behavior after they assembled at Versailles. The thousands of primary *cahiers* filled with peasant complaints and hopes were at first virtually ignored by those who participated in the Revolutionary assemblies; but the peasants later found more brutal and effective ways to make their desires known.

Unlike the primary *cahiers,* the general *cahiers,* especially those of the Third Estate, were cerebral; and many of them were composed according to one of a number of model *cahiers* that were circulated from town to town by literary clubs and masonic lodges and other "committees of correspondence." These *cahiers* tended to contain ideas that Third Estate leaders believed ought to be expressed for strategic or tactical reasons; they were not, therefore, true measures of contemporary French public opinion. The same may be said of the *cahiers* of the First and Second Estates. However, by placing the ideas presented in the general *cahiers* in juxtaposition with the views of the royal government as expressed in the official documents issued in connection with convoking the Estates General, we are able to ascertain what sort of consensus was reached by the French educated classes and their government. First, the crown repeatedly stated that, while the primary reason for assembling the Estates was "the difficulty in which we find ourselves relative to our finances," an important subsidiary motive was the king's desire "to establish . . . a constant and invariable order in all parts of the government . . ." This thought appeared three times in two pages in a royal letter of March 28, 1789. Possibly out of gratitude for what seemed clearly to be a governmental promise of a constitution, all three Orders expressed a genuine devotion to the monarchy. Republican sentiments do not appear in the *cahiers.* But all three orders, from the clergy to the Third Estate, expressed the desire to eliminate absolutism. In various ways they joined the king in calling for a rule of law, in short, for an agreed-upon and written constitution and for guaranteed civil liberties. Nearly all of them had something to say about the need for administrative and judicial reform, about creating a uniform set of weights and measures, and about making all of France a customs union. Even as regards the principle that everyone should be subject to taxation all three orders seemed in substantial agreement.

The area of serious disagreement was found in clauses touching on privileges other than tax privilege. The Third Estate *cahiers* called for full equality, for the end of all honorific distinctions save those based on personal merit. An immediate sign of progress in this direction, they suggested, would be vote by head in the Estates General. The *cahiers* of the privileged orders, on the other hand, often insisted on vote by Estate and on the maintenance of the three legal and traditional orders of French society.

PARLIAMENTARY BEGINNINGS OF THE REVOLUTION

The greatest hero of the Third Estate during the period of the elections was the "American" and highly privileged Marquis de Lafayette. The principal spokesmen of the Third also belonged to the privileged orders: the Count of Mirabeau and the Abbé Siéyès. The last, son of a Provençal notary, had

Opening of the Estates General. The site for the opening session was the "Hall of Small Pleasures," built at Versailles for theatrical and musical performances. The Third Estate deputies were said to be displeased by the fact that they were placed behind pillars or in the back while First and Second Estate deputies had the best seats. (Bibliothèque Nationale, Paris.)

made good in the Church but was elected Deputy for the Third Estate of Paris. In January 1789, he published a pamphlet entitled *What Is the Third Estate?* that quickly captured wide readership: sales alone mounted to tens of thousands of copies in three weeks. In the opening phrases of this essay Siéyès asked three rhetorical questions and supplied the answers:

1. *What is the Third Estate? Everything.*

2. *What has it been in the political order up to the present? Nothing.*
3. *What does it demand? To become something.*

The Humiliation of the Third Estate The doubling of the numbers of deputies from the Third Estate had seemed like a step toward "something" for the Commons, but as the opening ceremonies unrolled at Versailles it became apparent to the increasingly humiliated deputies of the Third Estate that the whole procedure was organized along aristocratic lines, from the reception that the king held for the deputies, Saturday, May 2, through the religious ceremonies on Monday (during which the king slept through a sermon two hours long) and including the opening meeting of the three orders in the Hall of Small Pleasures, a converted warehouse, in the presence of the king and his ministers. In each of these ceremonies, the deputies of the Third were segregated. They marched in dingy black at the head of the processions, followed by the nobles in brilliant robes and plumed hats.

In the May 5 opening session, after the deputies for the Third had waited for five hours while seats behind pillars were assigned to them, the king made a nice enough little speech. Applause followed the king's remarks; but confusion ensued when the king sat down and put his hat on. When the nobility—described in the official account as "gentlemen"—also covered, some of the bolder members of the Third Estate began, likewise, to put on their hats. "At that point," the official account records "a buzzing arose during which one could hear only the words 'Put it on!' and 'Take it off!'" Eventually, the king solved the problem by taking off his hat and everyone followed suit. Again, the Third had been humiliated.

Then, Barentin, the Keeper of the Seals, took over for a very long speech which few could hear. Next, Necker, the controller-general of finances rose, fat manuscript in hand, and began a speech that consumed three hours. The deputies for the Third were annoyed: limiting his remarks to the financial crisis and possible ways of solving it, Necker had nothing to say about a constitution or the end of privilege. He announced that the voting in the Estates General would be by order, the three Estates sitting and deliberating separately.

As the opening session broke up and the deputies of the Third repaired to their lodgings in Versailles, the Revolution began to take a turn. For weeks they had been talking, reading, and writing about a constitution and the end of privilege. They had attended the opening session full of enthusiasm and gratitude for the fact that the king seemed ready to lead the way. The "doubling of the Third" had inspired the hope that the king intended to second the Commons in its struggle for equality. Now this hope seemed deceived. It appeared quite clear that the crown had not managed to separate itself from the aristocracy and that the Third Estate had to depend upon its own resources.

The Third Estate Takes Command The next morning what has been called "the bourgeois revolution" began in earnest. The deputies for the Third met in the great hall (the only one in Versailles big enough for them) that had been intended for the plenary sessions of the three orders. Under the vigorous and eloquent leadership of Mirabeau they refused to organize themselves or to conduct any business until such time as the three orders should be united in one body voting by head. For six weeks, the Third Estate held up proceedings by its refusal to consider itself as a separate order. Early in June, the Third passed a resolution inviting members from the other orders to join it. A few clergy responded. Then on the 17th of June, the Third had the effrontery unilaterally to proclaim itself, along with the clergy who had "gone over," as the National Assembly and to announce that it had the power to approve taxation.

The king viewed this move on the part of the Third with alarm; it was decided that a policy of firmness was in order. The crown would announce its program at a Royal Session with the three Estates; and in the interim the unruly deputies of the Third were to be made aware of the king's displeasure and of his power. Accordingly, in the morning of June 20, without prior notice, the self-styled members of the National Assembly were

Formation of Paris Militia. During the troubled nights of July 12 and 13, 1789, Parisians organized themselves to protect their property from marauding bands and looters. Organized rather loosely by districts and armed with whatever weapons they could find, they tried to keep the nocturnal peace. Meanwhile, others prepared to confront the king's troops. (LCRB.)

forcibly denied admission to their meeting place. Aroused and indignant, the deputies adjourned *en masse* to a nearby indoor tennis court where, in a moment charged with intense excitement, they took a collective oath "never to separate from the National Assembly . . . until the constitution of the kingdom shall be established. . . ."

Once again the king was shocked at the temerity of his Commons; and when the day (June 23) came for the royal session there was an impressive display of royal soldiery about the hall. Through the mouth of his Keeper of the Seals, the king announced—six weeks too late—a program for constitutional reform, one that might very well have been greeted by nearly universal approval had it been stated on the fifth of May. But now, inasmuch as this program insisted that the three orders should deliberate separately on all matters touching on equality of taxation, manorial privileges, and honorific distinctions, the Commons received his address in sullen silence and then pointedly refused to obey a royal order to disperse, delivered as the king left the hall followed by all of the nobility and a good share of the clergy. Mirabeau took the occasion to make a speech. Then, when the Royal Master of Ceremonies returned to remind the deputies that the king had expressly ordered them to leave the hall, he was told by the scientist-deputy Bailly that "The assembled nation cannot receive orders." Later, Mirabeau wrote (wishing, no doubt, that he had said it at the time) "Go and tell those who sent you that we shall not stir from our seats unless forced by bayonets."

Confused by conflicting advice from his minister Necker on the one hand and from his queen and his reactionary brothers on the other, the king could not immediately decide how to respond to this defiance. Then, after a majority of the clergy and about one quarter of the noble deputies announced that they were casting their lot with the Third Estate, the king retreated by ordering (June 26) all of the members for the First and Second Estates to do likewise. At this point, the Revolution finished the turning that had started during the opening session on the fifth of May. What had begun as a revolt of the aristocracy was now clearly in the hands of the bourgeoisie who, with their liberal clerical and noble allies, commanded a clear majority in what they renamed the National Constituent Assembly.

For the time being, it did not seem possible for the Court to take up the challenge embodied in Mirabeau's postscript to the royal session. That is to say, the troops available to the king around Paris and Versailles could not be depended upon to force the deputies from their seats with bayonets. It now seems apparent that the king's concession of June 26 was only partly an outward show of his vacillating character; mainly it was a move intended by the aristocratically-oriented queen and the king's brothers to gain time during which they could call in from the frontiers enough reliable regiments to dislodge the Estates General, arrest its leaders, and drive the rest home. Everyone realized that the royal fist would strike in due time; and, despite the apparent calm in the Assembly, it seemed that the bourgeoisie had gained control of a Revolution that, barring providential intervention, was about to die a violent death. Providence responded in the form of the little people who had complaints of their own and who rose up to save the day for the Third Estate.

THE PEOPLE TAKE A HAND

We have already seen that actual representation in the Estates General was limited to only a small part of the Third Estate and that there were probably no peasants or workers in the body that assembled at Versailles. Yet the Revolution that was going on belonged to all Frenchmen and not to the privileged orders and the upper bourgeoisie alone. There was no way of denying to the little people what had been given to them in the thousands of electoral assemblies that had taken place all over France during which virtually every Frenchman had listened to speeches and had aired his grievances.

Until quite recently, these little people have been all too much ignored by western historians who have had a way of generalizing them as a many-backed beast fitted with a definite article: "The Mob" or "The Rabble." Actually these men and women were humble but they were not a rabble. They were peasants, workmen, shop-keepers, artisans, master craftsmen, petty industrialists, even artists, actors, and musicians. Many of them were respectable and solid members of their communities, conscious of their dissatisfactions with the present and their hopes for the future. They looked to the Estates General, as transformed into the National Assembly, as the agency that would meet their grievances. Any move threatening that assembly they were quite prepared to interpret as a threat against them. Although many of them could not read, they could and did follow with intense interest the news that was read to them from the Paris newspapers and that was recited in every town and village whenever the post came from Versailles or Paris. Almost as rapidly, therefore, as the deputies for the Third at Versailles realized that the "Queen's party" had gotten the upper hand at Court and had persuaded the king to use force against the National Assembly, the little people in the country at large came to the same conclusion.

The masses were suffering from real scarcities of food. As bread and grain became more and more scarce, the rumor started, persisted, and grew in the streets and alleys of Paris and other towns that it wasn't simply bad weather and crop failure that caused the shortage, but that it was the result of a plot, of deliberate hoarding on the part of speculators, and that the aristocracy was involved in this conspiracy, through which it hoped to starve the Third Estate into submission.

At this time, perhaps ten million French people were unemployed and about two million were paupers. Gangs of desperate people roamed the countryside begging and robbing. Here and there they invaded the fields and cut the standing grain before it was ripe. Peasants came widely to believe that "brigands," paid by the aristocracy, would systematically pillage the harvest; townspeople feared that gangs were being organized to raid their markets. The result of these fears was panic and violence in both Paris and in the provinces.

Paris and the Bastille As early as the latter part of April 1789, rioters in Paris had put some suspected grain speculators "to the lantern" (hanged them from the street lights), and had raided shops and businesses. During May and June, Parisian disorder multiplied. The French Guards, supposedly the most reliable of royal troops, began to side with the rioters. The court's reaction to this violence and military insecurity in Paris was the decision (already described) to try to mollify the people for the time being by ordering the three orders to sit and vote together (June 26) and to call in reliable troops. The reaction of respectable Parisians was to try to develop some sort of urban organization to maintain order and protect property in a city where the influence of the traditional police had disappeared. Up to this point, there had been tension, near panic, and occasional violence. The court's next step in its attack upon the Revolution precipitated matters and led to city-wide insurrection. By early July, foreign mercenary troops (Swiss and Germans) had arrived. They were encamped around the palace at Versailles, along the road between Paris and Versailles and on the *Champ de Mars* (today a park stretching from the Eiffel Tower to the *Ecole militaire*) at the west end of the city on the left or south bank of the Seine. The presence of these troops far from their usual stations on the frontier reinforced the already commonly accepted idea that the king was hostile to the city and the Assembly.

On July 12, the news reached Paris that Necker, the only person at court or in the government who had enjoyed any confidence among the Third Estate, and especially within the business community, had been dismissed and ordered to leave the country. Panic took a firm hold. The Parisian populace had already been alarmed by the presence of foreign mercenaries; now the more substantial people—those who held government securities—saw in the dismissal of Necker a step toward repudiation of the

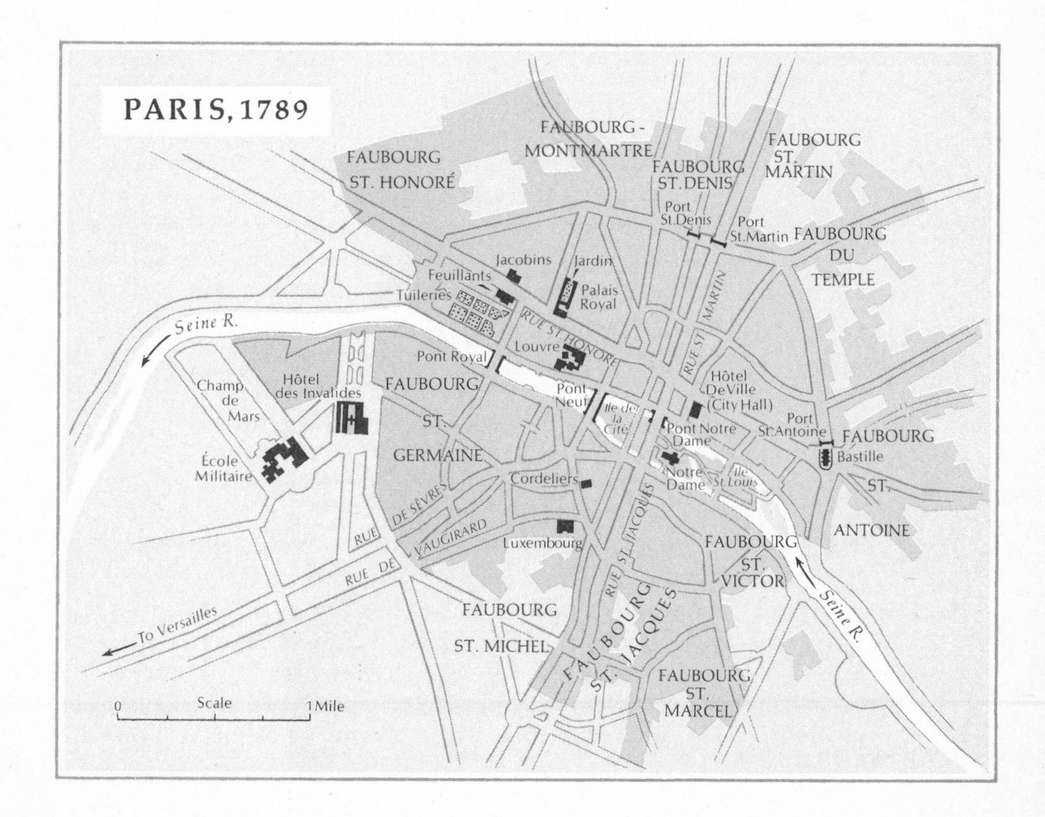

royal debt. Orators harangued turbulent listeners about the necessity for self-defense, and the cry "To arms!" sent a crowd off demonstrating its sympathy for the deposed Necker and at the same time looking for weapons. The rioters fought with a unit of German cavalry in front of the Tuileries palace. Shops and homes were looted for arms and for anything else portable.

In the midst of this disorder with its threat to property, the electors of Paris (the men who had prepared the city's *cahiers* and who had selected the Parisian deputies to the Estates General) met in haste to create a civic force to protect their homes and shops from the people and to organize the defense of their city against crown, aristocracy, and foreign troops. Each of the sixty electoral districts was requested to contribute men to civic militia. The surprising fact is that the districts responded to this request; and immediately the new police force began to patrol the streets and to maintain order.

On the morning of Tuesday the 14th of July, events began to move on two levels at once: the more-or-less directed activity of the new and still extra-legal Paris government (the Permanent Committee of Electors) which was trying to maintain order on the one hand, and the disorderly work of roaming groups on the other. In the morning, a deputation from the new municipality called on the commandant of the *Invalides,* the huge military hospital near the *Champ de Mars,* respectfully to request that whatever arms were stored there be turned over to them so that they could use them to equip the civic guard. When the Commandant replied that his orders did not permit him to make such a disposition of the arms entrusted to his care, the deputation retired to the City Hall (*Hôtel de Ville*) to report. Thereupon, within sight of several thousand mercenary troops lined up on the *Champ de Mars,* a crowd stormed the *Invalides,* ransacked the cellars and triumphantly emerged waving thousands of muskets, some of which were carried back to the City Hall. The next requirement was ammunition; and someone conceived the notion that the Bastille was a likely place to look for gunpowder.

There was another reason for attention to the Bastille that day. Located at the east end of Paris proper, the towering fortress with its cannon newly mounted on the battlements appeared to be and was a serious threat to the security of Paris—as one arm of a pincer (the other was the soldiery on the *Champ de Mars*) by which the king could crush the resistance of the city and turn it over to pillage.

Again and on the same day action took place on two levels. The Permanent Committee of the new municipality sent a deputation to de Launay, the governor of the Bastille, to ask that in order to eliminate a probable cause of civil disorder he remove his cannon from the battlements. De Launay asked the deputation in for lunch and withdrew the guns. Meanwhile, an immense crowd gathered outside. Later in the day, another deputation was sent to the Bastille by the Permanent Committee to ask that the fortress surrender in the name of the Nation. De Launay politely refused but said that he would not fire unless attacked. As the second deputation was bringing this news back to the City Hall, gunfire was heard from the direction of the Bastille. The little people had taken over.

After a fierce and messy battle, the old fort fell. Not that it was overwhelmed—the sad facts are that de Launay lost control both of himself and of his troops and that eventually the drawbridge was lowered to admit the attackers. De Launay and 6 of his 110 men were slaughtered. At the City Hall, shortly afterwards, someone shot down Flesselles, the Provost of Merchants, who had been head of the recently formed municipal government. His head and that of de Launay were displayed on pike-staffs about the streets of Paris.

Attack on the Bastille. A towering fortress on the east side of Paris, the Bastille had served in the eighteenth century as an abode for a few old soldiers and jail for a small number of prisoners, including some famous ones like Voltaire and the Marquis de Sade. Its symbolic "fall" on July 14, 1789 is still celebrated in France as a national holiday. (Versailles.)

July 14–17 When the commander of the royal troops in Paris heard the news, he ordered his troops out of the city. The next day, the electors of Paris appointed Bailly—a noted astronomer turned revolutionary politician and deputy to the Third Estate—as Mayor of Paris and Lafayette as commander of the National (i.e., Parisian) Guard. The king responded to the events of July 14, which made clear the fact that the court could not subjugate Paris, by appearing the next day in the National Assembly to announce that he was sending away his troops. Then he sent horsemen to recall Necker to his Ministry; and on the 17th he completed this stage of his humiliation by coming to Paris, recognizing Bailly as Mayor and donning the newly devised tricolor cockade: red and blue were the colors of the city of Paris, white of the crown. Later, these colors came to represent "Liberty, Equality, and Fraternity."

The events of July 14–17 saved the city of Paris and the National Assembly from a real threat; they did not, however, eliminate panic in Paris or in the country at large. In the city, where shortages and hunger had been increased by the stoppage of economic activity attendant upon the disorders of mid-July, this fear led to some rather basic reactions in the weeks after Bastille Day. Riots broke out again in the suburbs. Rumors persisted that "the brigands" were coming, and this notion fed on the fact that large numbers of hungry and desperate vagrants from the countryside were converging on the Paris region looking for food and/or excitement. Within the week after the fall of the Bastille, there occurred further atrocities: Joseph-François Foullon, who had been the court's replacement for Necker as minister of finance, was ferreted out of his cellar by an angry crowd, taken to the square in front of the City Hall and hanged from a "lantern." Shortly thereafter, he was joined in the same place and posture by Bertier de Sauvigny, Royal Intendant of Paris, whose crime consisted of the fact that he was Foullon's son-in-law and that he was suspected (probably erroneously) of having conspired to aggravate the food shortage.

Grand Peur. Convinced that "brigands" inspired by an "aristocratic conspiracy" planned to damage their ripening grain or otherwise harm them, peasants in many parts of France rioted in late July and August, 1789. This representation of the "Grand Peur" or "Great Fear" shows a number of actions that probably did not take place at one time: at left, rioting peasants; center, the landlord fleeing in his carriage; at right, peasants breaking into a château that is already in flames. (Bibliothèque Nationale, Paris.)

When voices were raised in the National Constituent Assembly protesting these deeds, one of the outstanding deputies, Barnave, hardly a member of the "mob" or "rabble," rose to defend the murderers by asking "Is this blood then, so pure?" Other deputies, including one member of the prestigious French Academy (Target) and a nobleman (Gouy d'Arsy) suggested that this sort of violence was justified by the situation. Madame Roland, wife of a respectable inspector of manufactures who subsequently became Minister of Interior, wrote in panic from Lyons to say that there could be no security in France until the king and queen were executed or murdered.

These events and the fact that a good cross-section of the French people seem to have been convinced that a great aristocratic conspiracy existed and that it could only be washed away in blood, tend to lead to the conclusion that the Count of Artois and some other members of the reactionary party at Court were wise to have left the country when they did, on the 15th of July. Had they not done so, their continued presence at Versailles probably would have led to much more unpleasant violence than that which actually took place. The royal couple, though urged to emigrate while there was still time, considered it beneath their dignity to run. Later on, after the maneuvers of the Count of Artois and others who took part in the "first emigration" had indeed developed a real conspiracy against the Revolution, Louis and his queen found escape routes closed.

The Countryside and the Great Fear Little people in the villages had likewise responded to the hopes that the calling of the Estates General seemed to hold for the future. The peasants were firmly convinced that their "good king" meant to abolish the heavy burden of manorial dues under which they struggled; but even before the opening of the Estates they began to be troubled by the suspicion that in some way the aristocracy would prevent the king from realizing the projected reforms. Many peasants got the idea at their electoral assemblies that they were then and there relieved of the manorial dues, and they stopped paying them. They also stopped paying taxes. Unsettled by the crop failures and the resulting agricultural crisis, which tended to increase the number and size of bands of vagrants roaming the countryside, the settled peasants became convinced, as we have noted, that their homes and crops were about to be pillaged by "brigands."

As early as March 1789, serious peasant riots spread all over upper Provence (near the Mediterranean coast), and again in April. During the first week of May, more peasant uprisings broke out in the far northern provinces, and here and there all over the country. Then, as the news of July 14 travelled outward from Paris, mass panic broke out in six specific communities where local incidents happened fortuitously to lend credence to the idea that the "brigands" were coming. Four of the six "trigger" panics occurred on the edges of great forests which, with their half-savage woodcutter populations, were traditionally held in dread by the farming peasants. Within days the fear was spread from these six localities to almost all of rural France. From July 20 to August 6, hundreds of thousands of peasants went wild: they burned and looted *châteaux;* they occupied noble (and sometimes bourgeois) land; they shot game; and in more than a few instances they murdered their landlords. Particular objects of peasant attention during the Great Fear were the manorial archives, which they took great pains to destroy even in cases where they did not seriously damage other property. Even though the immediate cause of their uprising was a vague panic, the peasants did not forget that some of their landlords and their lawyers had been using these mysterious records to multiply manorial charges.

Return of the King to Paris. Two days after the fall of the Bastille and his failure to end the life of the Estates General by military force, Louis XVI was escorted from Versailles to triumphant Paris. He was welcomed by the new mayor of the city, Jean Sylvain Bailly, a noted astronomer. "I give your Majesty the keys of the good city of Paris," said Bailly. "These are the same keys that were given to Henry IV. He reconquered his people; in this case it is the people who have reconquered their king." (Bibliothèque Nationale, Paris.)

When the Great Fear subsided—the "brigands" never materialized—it was clear that the peasants had struck a mighty blow not only for themselves but also for the lawyers of the Third Estate by brutally destroying the remnants of the manorial system in France. Acting on their own and for their own homely reasons, the peasants guaranteed that the French Revolution should become a great social revolution.

END OF "FEUDALISM"

The news that the peasants of most of France were violently and effectively revising agrarian relationships poured into Versailles where it shocked the National Assembly out of debates over parliamentary procedure and into action. It was obvious that it would be unwise to ask the king to use military force to put down the uprisings: the king might then use the same force to suppress the Assembly. Though somewhat less obvious, the idea came to some of the more radical members that the news of the Great Fear could be used on the Assembly as "a kind of magic" that would lead it to abolish privilege. These radicals laid their plans and came to an agreement with a number of liberal nobles who were persuaded to make a magnanimous gesture by proposing in the Assembly the abolition of the "feudal" (that is, manorial) system that was already in the process of being destroyed.

Accordingly, shortly after a special evening session opened on the 4th of August, 1789, the Viscount of Noailles (Lafayette's brother-in-law) rose to make a proposal:

The National Assembly entirely destroys the feudal system. The Assembly decrees that among [manorial] rights and duties those which have the nature of personal . . . servitude . . . are abolished without indemnity; all others are declared redeemable. . . .

Noailles was followed on the rostrum and, in a way, seconded by the Duke of Aiguillon, one of the greatest landowners in France who had much to lose if the proposal should be adopted. Applause greeted his altruistic and sacrificial gesture; and soon enthusiasm for giving up privileges approached frenzy. At one point a conservative member sent a note to the President suggesting that the deputies had lost their minds and that the meeting be adjourned; but the proceedings went on until dawn.

In all, it was a great piece of work. Definitively abolished without recompense were hunting privileges, all personal rights and duties such as *mainmorte,* personal *corvée* along with the rights of the hunt, *banalités,* and whatever advantages landlords had derived in recent years from the partition of the commons as well as the right of the *seigneur* to dispense justice. Abolished subject to recompense for loss of the privileges were hereditary offices (judicial and municipal) and all "real" as opposed to "personal" dues or rents owed to landlords. Established as positive principles of the Revolution were equality of taxation, that "all citizens, regardless of birth, can be admitted to all ecclesiastic, civil and military dignities . . .", and that justice should be free and equal for all. In short, by morning the Assembly had destroyed the *ancien régime.*

This is to say, they had destroyed the *ancien régime* if the work of the intoxicating night could be made to stand. At the time it was not at all clear that it could. The National Constituent Assembly was, after all, a sovereign body only because it said it was; and constitutionally the king was the source of law. Thus it was embarrassing to the Assembly when, despite the fact that in the cold light of day (from August 5th to 11th) the Assembly cautiously revised a number of the provisions that had been carried during the intoxication of the night and despite the fact that Louis XVI was described in Article 17 as the "restorer of French liberty," the king refused to sanction the decrees. Royal opposition was, of course, seconded by those nobles and clergy who could not think of themselves as members of a nation rather than as members of privileged orders. And the peasants, however enthusiastic they might have been at the first reception of the news from Versailles, were later depressed by the legalistic notion that only part of their dues were suppressed, that those of a "real" nature (and these included the greater part of the payments they had actually been making to their landlords) had to be bought off or redeemed on the basis of twenty to twenty-five times the annual payment, such payments to be continued until the redemption had been made. Unprepared to understand the difference between personal dues and real dues or to cooperate if they did understand, they refused to pay anything at all. The upshot was continued rural violence until the revolutionary government, in 1793, abolished *all* seigneurial charges without indemnity.

It would be a mistake, therefore, to conclude, as has been done, that overnight the Assembly transformed France from an assemblage of corporations into a nation; but a substantial step had been made in that direction.

FURTHER READING

G. Lefebvre, * *The Coming of the French Revolution*, translated by R. R. Palmer (1947), is a fine, concise treatment of the early stages up through the "October Days," 1789. By far the best larger study of the Revolution in France, with attention to the rest of Europe, is the same author's *La Révolution française* (2nd ed., 1957). The first half of this work has been translated by E. M. Evans as * *The French Revolution from Its Origins to 1793* (1962), and the second, * *From 1793 to 1799* (1964), by J. Stewart and J. Friguglietti.

The late C. Brinton's witty and somewhat sardonic volume in the *Rise of Modern Europe* series, * *A Decade of Revolution, 1789–1799* (1935), which covers all of Europe, remains a stand-by; the paper edition is equipped with a bibliography revised as of 1959. One of the best-written one-volume works in English is J. M. Thompson, * *The French Revolution* (2nd ed., 1944), strong on narrative and rich in detail for France.

*Books available in paperback edition are marked with an asterisk.

A recent and well-illustrated paperback by a British historian is N. Hampson, * *The First European Revolution, 1776–1815* (1969), with a useful bibliography.

Another recent paperback by a good scholar is G. Rudé, * *Revolutionary Europe, 1783–1815* (1966). A fairly recent study based on the scholarly work of some of the younger historians is M. J. Sydenham, * *The French Revolution* (1966). On the "little people," most of whose revolutionary aspirations were not realized, see A. Soboul, * *The Sans Culottes* (1972), a translated abridgement of Professor Soboul's *Les sansculottes parisiens en l'an II* (1958). See also R. Cobb, * *The Police and the People: French Popular Protest, 1789–1820* (1970), and the same author's *Reactions to the French Revolution* (1972). For opposition to the Revolution, see J. Godechot, * *The Counter-Revolution: Doctrine and Action, 1789–1804,* translated by S. Attarasio (1971).

Two collections of sources recommend themselves immediately: J. H. Stewart, *A Documentary Survey of the French Revolution* (1951); and E. L. Higgins, *The French Revolution as Told by Contemporaries* (1938). For those who read French and like their documents in the original language, J. M. Thompson, *French Revolutionary Documents, 1789–94* (1948) is fine. The *cahiers* of 1789 are among the most fascinating documents available to historians of this period. A convenient introduction to the *cahiers* is by the late B. Hyslop, *A Guide to the General Cahiers of 1789, with the Texts of Unedited Cahiers* (1936). Needless to say, many of the books cited for the previous chapter are useful for this one.

4 The French Revolution (II)

Once the matters of seating and voting had been settled and the question of "feudalism" had been more or less disposed of, the National Assembly could begin to become what almost everyone had thought it should be from the beginning: a constitutional convention or constituent body. A committee on the constitution had already been appointed, and after August 14, 1789, there began to be discussed the strategy for development of a constitution for France. One group of deputies held that the first step was to draft a general declaration or preamble setting out the rights of the citizen so that the rest of the constitution could be formulated in terms of general principles stated at the beginning. Others, notably Mirabeau, who were impressed with the way the English constitution had evolved over the centuries without any general statements of rights or principles, cautioned against such a procedure. They felt that a general declaration would unduly bind the hands of the Constituent Assembly (as the National Assembly began to be called about this time) during the rest of its work. They were opposed in debate by men like Lafayette and Alexandre de Lameth, both liberal nobles who had served in the American war, and who wished to emulate the American constitutional experience with its Declaration of Independence and its Bill of Rights. The latter point of view prevailed; and, after seven days of continuous debate about the proper contents of such a declaration for France, there was passed, August 27, 1789, the *Declaration of the Rights of Man and Citizen.*

THE "DECLARATION OF THE RIGHTS OF MAN AND CITIZEN"

The Declaration opened with a general statement in which the Assembly declared that it was about to make a statement about the rights of man. The second paragraph ran as follows:

In consequence, the National Assembly recognizes and declares, in the presence and under the auspices of the Supreme Being, the following rights of man and Citizen.

The reference to the "Supreme Being" does not indicate, it appears, that the bourgeois deputies were especially religious, but rather that they felt that reference to some kind of deity was socially useful and that they depended on their friends among the liberal clergy for their majority in the Assembly.

There followed seventeen articles, of which the first did not deal with rights but, rather, with the notion dearest to the hearts of the Third Estate, the principle of equality: "Men are born free and equal in rights. Social distinctions can be based only upon public utility." Then, in Article II, came the listing of the rights that free and equal men should enjoy: "Liberty, property, security, and resistance to oppression." Most of the remaining fifteen articles were devoted to refinements and amplification of Articles I and II. For instance, seven articles dealt with liberty, which was defined as "the power to do anything that does not injure others. . . ." Security was alluded to in two articles as resulting from the simple maintenance of public order which would provide security of person and property; but nothing was said about the implications of the word "resistance" in the phrase "resistance to oppression," though several articles treated of specific ways (arbitrary arrest, for instance) in which the government should not oppress the citizen. Property received very explicit attention in the last article: "Property being a sacred and inviolable right, no one can be deprived of it, unless a legally established public necessity evidently demands it, under the condition of a just and prior indemnity." This clause was intended, among other things, to guarantee that landlords would be compensated for the manorial dues that they gave up on the night of August fourth. The great, over-riding principle of "equality" was touched on again in Article VI where it was stated that all citizens are equally admissible to public employments. Article XIII further refined the notion by stating that taxation "ought to be equally apportioned among all the citizens according to their means." In several articles the nature of the forthcoming constitution was touched on or hinted at: sovereignty resides in the nation; all citizens should take part in the formulation of law, either in person or through their representatives; public forces are for the advantage of all and not for the personal benefit of those to whom they are entrusted; public officials should be held accountable to society; and, finally, unless there is separation of governmental powers there is no constitution.[1]

The *Declaration of the Rights of Man and Citizen* was a liberal, and not a democratic or levelling document. Equality was defined in its most limited and legalistic form. The sanctity of private property was taken for granted. Rights of assembly and association—means by which the propertyless can organize to defend themselves against property owners—were not even mentioned as natural rights of man. In other words, under this document all men were proclaimed equal in rights, but the rich would remain more equal than others, as it were, because they had property rights to enjoy.

This last omission is evidence of the fact that the framers of the Declaration of 1789 were not the radical, impractical idealists they are often accused of having been. Like the English Declaration of Rights of a century before and like the Declaration of Independence in America, the French

[1]The reader should examine the *Declaration* which can be found in E. Weber, *The Western Tradition* (Boston, 1959), pp. 507–508. It is interesting to compare it with the Virginia Bill of Rights (1776) and the Massachusetts Bill of Rights (1780).

document was a combination of the generally accepted liberal notions of the day with a listing of specific, *negative* principles intended to stop the government from doing what it had been doing in the recent past: legislating arbitrarily, imprisoning people administratively, torturing suspects, taxing capriciously, wasting the taxpayers' money, and maintaining outmoded and galling privileges. For these reasons—the familiarity of the general frame of reference and the immediacy of the problems dealt with—the Declaration found an enthusiastic response both within and outside France; and for the time being nearly everyone approved of what was going on at Versailles.

THE FINANCIAL CRISIS AND THE CIVIL CONSTITUTION OF THE CLERGY

The main reason, of course, for the existence of the National Constituent Assembly was the financial crisis that faced the French government. During the period of transition from Estates General to National Assembly (May–June 1789) and through the turmoil of July and August, the crisis became more acute. Eventually, after August, the Assembly tried to solve the problem by wiping out the old tax system and establishing a new one as demanded by the *cahiers;* but, because neither the Assembly nor the king could really control the country, the new taxes were only sporadically collected. Necker, still the financial minister, used his Swiss-banker methods of borrowing. The nation was called upon to make a "patriotic gift"; but no improvement of the state finances was made until October 1789, when one of the deputies, Charles Maurice de Talleyrand-Périgord (1754–1838), a bishop of the Roman Catholic Church and a financial wizard in his own right, proposed that the nation take over the assets of the Church in France, which property could be sold by the state to cover its debt. After furious debate, Talleyrand's argument that, by taking over the functions of the church, the state had a right to take over its lands, prevailed. On November 2, 1789, the Church property was seized by the nation.

Some weeks later (December 14), the Assembly decided that it would use the church (now national) property as the base against which to issue government bonds called *assignats* which the receiver could use to purchase the former church lands from the government. At first, the *assignats* were issued in large denomination and in limited quantity; but early in 1790, it was decided to issue them in smaller denominations, to give them force of legal tender, and to issue the notes in ever-increasing quantities. The result was inflation as the new paper drove gold and silver money out of circulation and as the *assignats* rapidly lost value. By the end of 1791, the *assignats* were worth only 75 percent of their face value. Five years later they had fallen to zero and were repudiated as worthless. Unintentionally and in a roundabout way, therefore, the National Constituent Assembly and its successor assemblies did, in fact, achieve a solution of the government's financial problems by what was in fact a repudiation of its debts.

State Administration of Religion The decisions described above got the state into a new enterprise: the administration of religion in France. There was substantial agreement among the deputies that a state church was a necessity for social control; and, therefore, they were anxious that the state should honor the commitment they had made when they acted on Talleyrand's proposal. But now that the lands of the church had been confiscated and the church tax (tithe) abolished, the state had to step in to budget for and take over the functions of the church: maintaining worship, carrying on education, and dispensing poor relief. To regularize these matters, the Constituent Assembly prepared the Civil Constitution of the Clergy (completed July 12, 1790). Supplementary to the Constitution of 1791, this document proved an explosive measure, to the surprise of the deputies who had up until this time enjoyed the cooperation of the lesser clergy. It served to create serious and fundamental divisions within revolutionary France.

The Civil Constitution of the Clergy turned the clergy into civil servants. For each of the eighty-three *départements* there was to be a bishop, selected by the electors of the *département.* (Previously, there had been 139 bishops.) The bishop's primary loyalty was to be to the state: he was permitted only to inform the pope of his election. All clergy were to be paid by the state, the income of parish priests being increased somewhat and that of bishops reduced. Monasteries and nunneries were abolished, and the number of church jobs was greatly decreased. After this action, the Assembly and individual Frenchmen began to explore ways and means to fill the educational and charitable gaps they had thus created.

State Church and Roman Church The reaction of Pope Pius VI to this move was understandable. To him the Civil Constitution of the Clergy represented a unilateral abrogation of the Concordat of Bologna (1516) between the French state and the Roman church. He rejected the decree. The majority of French bishops refused to conform or to take the required oath to the Civil Constitution—in fact, only seven bishops, including Talleyrand did conform. More than 50 percent of the parish clergy likewise refused to take the oath (*jurer*). The king, a devout man, felt that it was sacrilege to hear Mass from or to confess to one of the official, "juring" clergy and insisted on carrying out his religious devotions before refractory or "nonjuring" priests. Millions of Frenchmen followed their king's example and the result was that France reverted to something like the condition it had suffered under in the late sixteenth century, before the Edict of Nantes (see Part X, 3), with an official state church existing beside a very active illegal church enjoying the support of large numbers of the faithful. It was principally because of this religious split that a viable counter-revolutionary movement developed. The likelihood of violence was increased by the fact that, at the same time that large numbers of Frenchmen were becoming disenchanted with the religious "settlement," the Revolution was turning further to the left, thereby creating new enemies at home and abroad.

PARIS CAPTURES THE REVOLUTION

At the beginning, during the elections for the Estates General and during the early days of the National Constituent Assembly, there had been substantial agreement among the overwhelming majority of Frenchmen about what general course the Revolution should take. In July 1789, this consensus began to deteriorate. First, the king's brother and a few court reactionaries plus a number of right-wing deputies left the country to stir up trouble for the Revolution abroad. Later, as violence continued and as the Constituent Assembly showed that it intended to destroy the institutions and privileges of the *ancien régime,* more nobles and other reactionaries emigrated—according to rumor, as many as 200,000 between July 14 and September 10, 1789—while others remained to keep up opposition at home and in the Assembly. During the autumn, winter, and spring of 1789–1790 tension began to build up in the Constituent Assembly and several duels were fought between right- and left-wing members.

The Patriot Party Further, the left majority in the Assembly, the Patriot Party as they styled themselves, found that as the Revolution moved onward they lost their unanimity. One group of moderately conservative Patriots led by Mounier disapproved of the abolition of the "feudal" system and decried the Declaration of Rights. They believed that France should copy the English constitution as closely as possible, that there should be a hereditary upper house in the legislature, and that the king should have an absolute veto over legislation. Another group, led at this point by Barnave, was committed to the agrarian reform of August 4th; to the idea of a unicameral legislature; and, at most, to only a suspensive veto for the king. In the city of Paris, there was violent opposition to the idea of an absolute royal veto. Stirred up by popular orators (some of them paid by the Duke of Orléans), the Parisians showed their readiness to defend the left-wing Patriots by force if need be. Excitement was further stimulated in late August and early September when the king declined to give his assent to the Assembly's decrees of August 4th or to the *Declaration of the Rights of Man and Citizen.* It was suspected that the king was up to some trickiness; and he was.

Listening to his usual bad counselors, Louis XVI decided on the 15th of September to try to use force again. He ordered the Flanders Regiment to march from the frontier to Versailles in order to back up his rejection of the Assembly's decrees and ostensibly to help maintain order in the face of increasing turmoil in Paris. Many citizens read Louis' intentions correctly, however, and the arrival of the troops served to increase rather than to diminish disorder in Paris. Soon after the arrival of the Flanders Regiment, news spread to the city that during a dinner party, given October 1 at Versailles for the officers of the new regiment, toasts had been drunk to the royal family but not to the nation, that the tricolor cockade had been trampled underfoot, and that the black cockade of Austria had been worn instead.

March of the Women Swollen by an influx of unemployed vagrants, suffering from a serious shortage of food, stimulated by agents of the ambitious Duke of Orléans, the population of Paris reacted violently to this

The "Women of Paris" on Their Way to Versailles on October 5, 1789. Obviously an aggressive lot, the women were backed up by a number of armed men. This less-than-spontaneous intervention led to an important turning-point in the French Revolution, the bringing of the king to Paris. (Bibliothèque Nationale.)

news. Orators redoubled their efforts. A mob of women went to the City Hall on the 5th of October to demand bread. They ransacked the building. Then, as they set off in search of further mischief, the women found a leader in Stanislas Maillard, one of the heroes of Bastille Day, who put himself at their head and marched them off in the rain to Versailles. A few hours later, Lafayette, commander of the Parisian National Guard, who had done nothing to prevent this "March of the Women," mounted his horse and led his troops along the same road.

When the women arrived at Versailles they forced the king to agree to sanction the Assembly's decrees. They also made the king promise to see to the provisioning of Paris. Finally, after some of the more determined and violent women had penetrated the palace, had killed several of the king's bodyguard, and had very nearly caught Marie Antoinette, the bedevilled king agreed that he and his family would return to Paris with the women. Lafayette's presence with the Parisian National Guard had been enough to prevent major disorder and to save the king and queen from bodily harm; but it was not enough to prevent what the women called "the baker, the baker's wife, and the baker's boy" (the king, queen, and dauphin) from being ignominiously removed from the grandest of palaces, taken to Paris in a procession adorned by the heads of some of the king's bodyguard, and installed in the old Tuileries palace near the Seine where, as it happened, there were several hundred tenants who had to be turned out to make way for the royal family.

Paris Captures the King This was a great day for the Parisians. For the second time they had undertaken direct action, and for the second time they had frustrated the counter-revolutionary plans of the king. And now they had captured the king. Ten days later, the Assembly also moved to Paris to take up its meetings in an indoor riding academy near the Tuileries. The Revolution now seemed secure; and the little people of Paris could take the credit for this security. They were also responsible for the fact that the pace of emigration increased and for an increasing air of violence.

The atmosphere, in fact, was becoming ominous. Conservative and moderate deputies fell away from the Constituent Assembly, some of them, like Mounier, to take up opposition to the Revolution in their home communities. When meetings of the Assembly began in Paris in October 1789, there were 300 fewer members. (More than 1200 had met at Versailles in May of 1789.) The Revolution was purging itself.

Revolutionary Organizations When the deputies assembled in Versailles in May of 1789, it was natural for them to seek out like-minded men with whom they might carry on conversations; and eventually, political clubs were formed. One of the first of these was the *Club Breton,* composed of deputies, fairly far to the left, from Brittany. Originally a dining club, the *Club Breton* expanded to become the Society of the Friends of the Constitution and, after the move to Paris in October 1789, the group took as its meeting place the abandoned library of an order of Jacobin monks, and became the Jacobin Club. This proved to be the most important of the revolutionary clubs. Dues for membership were steep and the membership predominately bourgeois, but the Jacobins' political orientation was consistently to the left of center. The Jacobins were among the first to become antimonarchical and pro-republican. At one time or another, most of the leftist revolutionary leaders belonged to the Jacobins; but, as situations and, therefore, opinions changed, groups of Jacobins tended to splinter off to form their own clubs. The Jacobins colonized branch clubs all over France, and corresponding secretaries kept the provincial branches aware of what was going on in Paris and *vice versa.* At one time—from September 1792 to July 1794—the Jacobin Club was virtually the executive committee of the formally constituted legislature. The most important Jacobin leaders were Robespierre, St. Just, and Couthon. Many Jacobins belonged to other clubs as well.

An Early Casualty of the French Revolution, the Count of Mirabeau (1749–1791). A nobleman who disowned the nobility, Mirabeau tried to straddle the forces of the Revolution while supporting the king. (LCRB.)

A more radical club was the *Cordeliers,* officially The Society of the Friends of the Rights of Man. The *Cordeliers'* symbol was the open eye, suggesting the role of the watchdog in public affairs. The *Cordeliers* were petty bourgeois but included some workers. This club was more Paris oriented than the Jacobins, more radical and more disposed to direct action in the streets. Important *Cordeliers* leaders (some of whom were also Jacobins) were Marat, Danton, and Hébert.

One of the first splinters from the Jacobins was the Society of 1789, composed of moderate, constitutional monarchists like Condorcet, Siéyès,

Mirabeau, Talleyrand, and some of the other more distinguished members of the Estates General and National Assembly. Hampered by its position in the embarassed political middle, the Society of 1789 did not exercise great influence. A more important fraction of the Jacobin Club was known sometimes as the Brissotins (after one of the prominent members, a journalist named Brissot) and sometimes as the Girondins (after the region around Bordeaux where many prominent Girondins originated). Like the Jacobins, the Girondins were republicans, but they represented upper middle class interest and the idea of governmental decentralization and physiocratic or liberal economic policy, as opposed to the Jacobin tendency to support the interests of the petty and middle bourgeoisie, to advocate extreme centralization, and to favor mild governmental intervention in economic affairs. The Girondins met in Paris at the homes of prominent and ambitious women like Madame Roland, wife of the minister of interior under the Constitutional monarchy. More than any other group, the Girondins were responsible for preparing the fall of the monarchy in 1792. They continued to exercise great influence until they were beaten in a power fight with the Jacobins in the summer of 1793, at which time many important Girondins were killed.

In 1791, when it became apparent that the Jacobins were moving toward republicanism, some of the more conservative members, including a number who belonged to the Society of 1789, broke away to form a new society, the *Feuillants,* intended to bolster the idea of constitutional monarchy. Including such men as Lafayette, Talleyrand, Siéyès, Duport, and Lameth, the *Feuillants* passed from the scene after August 1792. There were many other clubs, perhaps 200 by the end of 1790. After 1791, the number of clubs decreased; and the Jacobin Club was very nearly *the* political club in France by the summer of 1794. Later, under Napoleon, all political clubs were outlawed.

The Commune of Paris In addition to the clubs, there were other instruments of revolutionary organization. Of these, none was more important than the Commune of Paris. Growing out of the municipality formed in July of 1789, the Commune of Paris was a federation of forty-eight urban districts or sections. Each section of Paris had its own council and sent representatives to a city-wide council. All males, whether "active" or "passive," could vote. The sections were armed and could be called upon to go into the streets to back the hand of their leaders, among them Hébert. They could thus intimidate the central government or the legislature, as was done in 1793 when the Commune was responsible for purging the Girondins from the Convention. The overthrow of the monarchy in August 1792, was primarily the result of the Commune's action.

Thus, we see that in addition to the action and interaction of crown, assemblies, conventions, ministers, constitutions, and laws, there were many other lines of force bearing upon the revolutionary developments.

THE CONSTITUTION OF 1791

Beginning with the *Declaration of the Rights of Man and Citizen,* the work of making a constitution was completed two years later in September 1791, when the king reluctantly accepted the finished document. By that time some of the statements in the *Declaration* seemed out of place because the full constitution failed to live up to some of the ideas that had seemed so compelling in August 1789.

One reason that the first written French constitution deviated from the principles of 1789 was the fact that the National Assembly had to serve as legislature for France at the same time that it wrote the constitution. Thus, practical, day-to-day experience came to bear upon the long-range decisions of the deputies. For instance, the behavior of the masses both in Paris and in the country at large did not inspire confidence in the responsibility and stability of the poorer elements of society which, it became apparent, were quite as willing to destroy or to take private property as they were to fight in the name of liberty or equality.

Actually, the Constitution of 1791 did contain provisions directed toward exclusion of the propertyless from political activity. The French people were divided into two groups: active citizens and passive citizens. Active citizens were those males who paid taxes equivalent to something like fifty cents per year. These active citizens could vote for members of electoral colleges. To be an elector one had to pay direct taxes equivalent to as much as two dollars per year. The electoral colleges selected the deputies who in some parts of France had to pay eleven dollars in taxes. Thus, if there were (as there might have been) about 7,280,000 men in France over the age of twenty-one and if there were, as was estimated at the time, 4,298,360 "active citizens" in 1791, then about 3 million men (there was no question of enfranchising women) over the age of twenty-one were disenfranchised by the terms of the Constitution. But probably the age limitation, which was, in fact, twenty-five and not twenty-one, disenfranchised more males than did the property qualifications for voting. All in all, the Constitution of 1791 was one of the most "democratic" that the European world had seen up to that time. Certainly, it provided for a more nearly democratic political situation than prevailed in England and Massachusetts at that time.

All in all, a great work was constructed by the National Constituent Assembly between August 1789 and September 1791. Negatively, it destroyed the institutions of the *ancien régime;* and, positively, it laid the basis for modern France. It swept away the old royal administration and legal system, the old administrative units and provinces, the institution of nobility and even the organization of the Church, as well as the hodge-podge of customs barriers and restrictions upon entrepreneurial economic activity. Although the National Constituent Assembly did not, in the two years of its activity, complete the reconstruction of France on the ruins of its demolition, it made positive beginnings by producing what the overwhelming

FRENCH REVOLUTIONARY CONSTITUTIONS AND GOVERNMENTS

Dates and Duration	Constitution	Assembly or Legislative Body	Executive
(1) to May 1789	Unwritten constitution of absolute monarchy	None (since 1614) except for two Assemblies of Notables in 1787 and 1788	The King and his Council—ministers appointed by the Crown
(2) May 1789, to June 1789 (seven weeks)	as above	Estates General, meeting as three separate orders (tricameral)	as above
(3) June 1789, to September 1791 (two years and three months)	A new constitution in process of formation	The National Constituent Assembly with same membership as the Estates General (above) but organized unicamerally	as above
(4) October 1791, to August 1792 (ten months)	Constitution of 1791; a limited parliamentary monarchy	Legislative Assembly (unicameral); entirely new membership	The King and his Council; ministers appointed by the Crown, which had only a suspensive veto over legislation
(5) September 1792, to October 1795 (three years and one month)	Constitution of the Year I (never fully implemented); first constitution of the First French Republic; a democratic constitution	The National Convention (unicameral); called first as a constitutional convention; remained as "legislature" after completion of the constitution in 1793	*Theory:* Executive was to be a board of 24 members *Practice:* Executive power in the great Committees as supervised by the Jacobin Club
(6) October 1795, to November 1799 (four years and one month)	Constitution of the Year III; a conservative republic; second constitution of the First French Republic	The *Corps legislatif* (Legislative Body) composed of two houses: the Council of Ancients and the Council of Five Hundred (bicameral)	A Directory of Five members

majority of the French people had been calling for most loudly, a written constitution for France.

The essential provisions of the Constitution of 1791 provided for the separation of powers that had been called for in the *Declaration.* The legislative power was delegated to a unicameral Legislative Assembly whose members were to be elected, according to the manner described above, for two-year terms. The Assembly could not be dissolved by the king. Only the Assembly could initiate legislation. The executive power remained with the king and his appointed ministers. The king could exercise a suspensive veto which could be overridden by three successive Assemblies. The judicial power was put in the hands of elected judges. Local administration was given to locally elected officials. Later revolutionary regimes and constitutions were, however, to reassert the primacy of the central government in local administration.

One of the last acts of the National Constituent Assembly, September 30, 1791, was to pass, on the motion of Maximilien Robespierre, a self-denying ordinance providing that no member of the old assembly could serve in the new. Then elections were held under the terms of the new constitution; but by that time, partly because of decisions made by the Constituent Assembly and partly because of forces and antagonisms outside of their control, it was highly unlikely that the new constitutional monarchy would last for long.

Other works undertaken by the Constituent Assembly were the division of France into eighty-three Departments (almost as they are today) instead of the old *provinces, baillages, sénechaussés,* etc. The Constituent also set afoot the process of developing a uniform system of weights and measures which reached completion with the report of the commission on the metric system in 1799 and the adoption of that system in 1801. Further, the Assembly did not fail to face up to the financial crisis, which it solved for the time being, as we have seen, by seizing church property. But in so doing it plunged the Revolution into the stormy waters of religious controversy, with violent results.

The Flight to Varennes The new legislative assembly provided for by the Constitution of 1791 was elected during the summer of 1791 and met in October. The Assembly consisted of 745 members of which 264 were moderate men of the center. They sat on chairs in the middle of the meeting hall in Paris. On the right sat about 260 constitutional monarchists, including the *Feuillants.* On the left the Jacobins and Girondins took their seats, while on the extreme left, on a high tier, sat the extreme radicals who became known as the *Montagnards* (Mountaineers) because of their seating, or as *"Enragés,"* a term used to describe the more unruly horses that had once been trained in the riding academy where the Assembly met. The men on the right were determined to make constitutional monarchy work; those on the left were equally determined to push the Revolution further along the road toward republicanism. Because the left had the City of Paris to call upon for aid, its position was stronger than the number of its representatives in the Assembly would indicate.

Moreover, the republican left had a useful, if unwitting, ally in the king himself and in his *émigré* friends and relatives. The previous summer (June 21) the misguided or, rather, queen-guided king had tried to flee the country, slipping out of the Tuileries by night with his family and heading for the northeast frontier. To complete his folly, he left behind him a long, petulant letter complaining of the manner in which he had been treated and stated his dissatisfaction with the constitution and with virtually every aspect of the Revolution. The king was caught at Varennes before he reached the frontier and was brought back to Paris in disgrace. His supporters like Lafayette were as embarrassed as was the king. It is difficult to bolster a monarchy whose king tries to flee the country. About two months after the king's return (August 27, 1791), the *émigré* princes, who had been pressing the king of Prussia and Marie Antoinette's brother, Leopold II of Austria, to do something to restore royal authority in France, achieved a limited success that further jeopardized Louis XVI's position as king of France. In a joint Declaration at Pillnitz, Frederick William II and Leopold stated that if all other powers agreed and would cooperate, then they would intervene in French affairs. This was safe enough: there wasn't a chance that the other powers, especially England, would agree. But the Jacobins and the *Cordeliers* and the French republican press played up this Declaration as evidence that the king was engaged in treasonable correspondence with foreign powers in order to suppress the Revolution.

FOREIGN POWERS AND THE FRENCH REVOLUTION

At first, foreign reaction to the revolutionary developments in France was favorable, particularly among the enlightened who interpreted the opening stages as the beginning of a long overdue rationalization of French government and society. Further, the foreign powers were, for several reasons, disinclined to take the opportunity offered by French internal disorder to try to intervene in French affairs or to attempt a partition. In the case of England, the Tory prime minister, William Pitt the Younger (see pp. 959–960), was dedicated to a peace policy. In his view, French internal affairs were no concern of England's as long as the French did not threaten English security. Moreover, the opposition Whigs in Parliament were led by several ardent admirers of French revolutionary developments. A strong current of approval continued to flow in the country at large until Englishmen came around to understanding that the French were not simply trying to follow the English example and that the Revolution would go much farther than English instincts could support. The first important English verbal attack on the French Revolution was Edmund Burke's *Reflections on the Revolution in France,* published in November 1790. Burke did not object to the attempt of the French to produce a constitution or to develop freedom in France; what he did object to was the lack of respect that the National Constituent Assembly demonstrated for the institutions of the *ancien régime.* The demolition work of the Constituent Assembly violated Burke's historical sense:

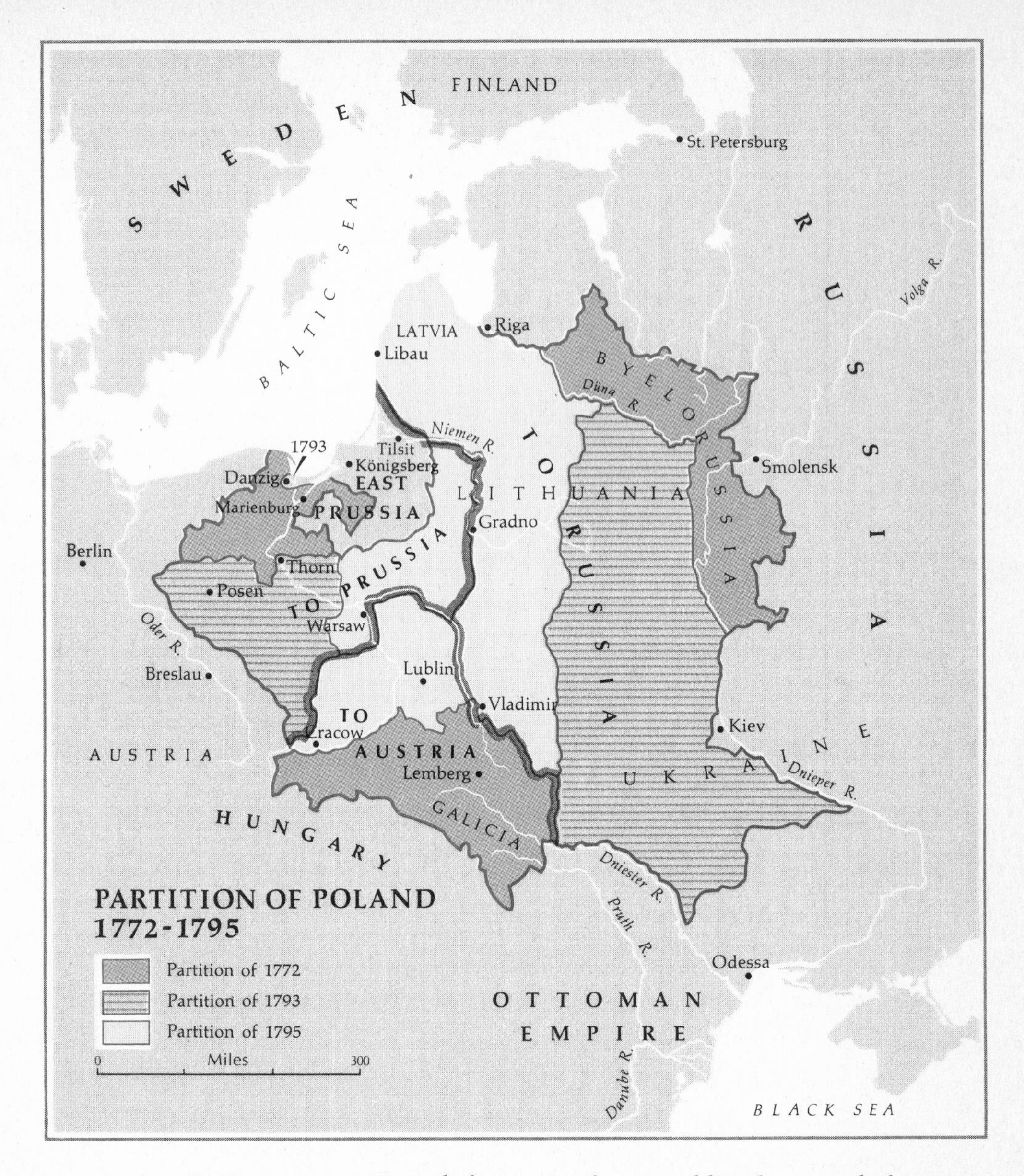

institutions are not made by men or by assemblies, he argued; they grow organically. Burke's famous essay was intended to demonstrate that French developments represented a potential danger to England and to its sacred constitution. But until the time when Thomas Paine muddied the waters by publishing his *Rights of Man* (1791)—an outright antimonarchical diatribe—and until sizeable numbers of French *émigrés* in England, as well as violence in Paris, convinced the majority of Englishmen that the French Revolution was a danger to England, Pitt had little trouble in pursuing his peace policy.

Prussian and Austrian ruling circles had no reason to applaud French revolutionary developments, but neither did Prussia and Austria feel at first any compelling motive to intervene. Before his death in 1790, Joseph II of Austria counselled his sister, Marie Antoinette, to be moderate and to accept the Revolution. His brother and successor Leopold II (1790–1792) was quite able to turn a deaf ear to the pleas of the *émigré* French princes. Even had the Prussians and the Austrians been inclined to intervene in France, they were both preoccupied with the question of Poland.

Back in 1772, the Polish state, which last we saw on its way to extinction, had been helped in that direction when Frederick the Great of Prussia had engineered what is known as the First Partition of Poland. Russia, Prussia, and Austria had each taken a substantial bite, and Poland lost a third of its territory and half of its population. Now, in the early 1790's, the auguries seemed favorable for a second bite; and the Austrians, Prussians, and Russians were warily watching each other to see to it that no one got more than his share. As it turned out, in the Second Partition (January 1793) Russia and Prussia took sizeable territories while Austria got nothing. Two years later (1795), the three powers moved in to take all the rest of Poland; and the national death wish of the Polish nobility was fulfilled. Meanwhile, *émigrés* continued to leave France and to take their pleas for foreign intervention to Vienna and Berlin. Then, in 1792, an accident of history—the death of the statesmanlike Leopold II and the accession of Francis II to the imperial and Habsburg thrones—led to a change. Quite soon Francis came under the influence of the *émigrés* and of a growing war party in vienna. Thereafter the Austrian government played a strong role in encouraging a warlike situation.

THE REVOLUTION GOES TO WAR

The onset of hostilities in April 1792, cannot be blamed entirely on the Austrians and the Prussians, for, in fact, the French themselves did much to precipitate war. In the first place, some of the actions of the National Constituent Assembly injured foreigners: in particular the decrees of August 1789, eliminating "feudal" privileges, touched those German imperial princes who held lands in Alsace, once part of the Holy Roman Empire. Unwilling to accept the resultant reduction in their income, these princes appealed to the German Imperial Diet for redress. Eventually (July 1791), the Diet issued a decree condemning the action of the Assembly in unilaterally suppressing the German princes' feudal and manorial rights. Thus, the French Revolution came into conflict not only with the monarchical principle and with the Habsburg family of Marie Antoinette but also with a significant portion of the German nobility.

Quarrel with the Papacy The second revolutionary move that showed France as a danger to established interests outside of France grew out of the Civil Constitution of the Clergy. We have seen that the pope refused to sanction this arrangement, thus providing the counterrevolution in France with popular support. In May of 1791, the pope took the further step of recalling his nuncio (ambassador) from France, thus breaking off diplomatic relations. Then, in September 1791, shortly before its dissolution, the Constituent Assembly voted to retaliate against the papacy by annexing two papal territories enclaved by France: the city of Avignon and the Comtat-Venaissin. Again, the Constituent Assembly had seemed deliberately to challenge the European establishment. These moves were part of the troublesome heritage taken over by the new Legislative Assembly when it met in October.

These illustrations are taken from a volume of "Memoirs" by an unknown author published in the United States after the queen's execution in 1794. They accuse Marie Antoinette of illicit relations with such notables as Lafayette and the Cardinal Rohan. (LCRB.)

The Desire for War Theoretically, the Revolution was over at this time. The *ancien régime* had been destroyed; France had its new constitution; the ship of state was supposed to sail calmly on the new course charted by the Constituent Assembly. Unfortunately, this course ran close to dangerous shoals. Moreover, between the idea that the Revolution had arrived at its conclusion and the aspirations of many Frenchmen there remained a wide gap. The king and his queen found the new arrangement intolerable in both its political and its religious aspects. Hoping for at least a political restoration of royal authority, Louis and Marie Antoinette came to believe that only through a war—won or lost—could they achieve their objectives. If, as commander of French forces, Louis should lead France to victory, then he might be in a position to effect a revision of the constitution. If, on the other hand, France should lose, then the foreign victors would certainly re-establish him on his throne in something like his old posture. The Feuillant supporters of the new regime, men like Lafayette, also found their sword-hands twitching. What, they asked, could provide a more propitious beginning for the new regime than a glorious victory in war—a victory they were sure they would have? On the left, the Girondins were also for war, although their analysis of the situation and their motives were different. If France goes to war, they reasoned, the king will be unable to resist the temptation to collaborate with the enemy. His treason will serve as excuse to overturn the monarchy and to establish a republic. Only the extreme leftists opposed war; and they did so on the ground that war would militarize the Revolution and lead to military dictatorship. As things turned out, both the Girondins and the Montagnards on the far left were proved correct.

War with Austria During the early spring of 1792, Franco-Austrian diplomatic relations deteriorated to the point of rupture. On the twentieth of April, the French Legislative Assembly voted nearly unanimously to declare war on the "King of Hungary and Bohemia." By declaring war in this fashion on the Habsburg Francis II, they hoped to avoid war with the Empire at large and with German states like Prussia; but previous French affronts to German opinion served to bring Prussia into the Austrian camp nonetheless. At first, the war did not go well for the French, and this despite the fact that, because of involvement in the developing Second Partition of Poland, the Prussians were unable to concentrate all of their forces on the French war. The French army was woefully unprepared. Half of its officers had emigrated, and the new men who were to make the French revolutionary army one of the most remarkable of all time had not yet risen to fill the gaps. In total numbers the French army was less than half what Louis XIV would have considered necessary to fight a major war. Discipline had been undermined by the revolutionary disorders. (It was said that on one occasion when a general ordered a bayonet charge, the soldiers decided to have a vote on the matter.) And some of the officers carried over from the *ancien régime* were less than determined to do their utmost. Two of the French armies were defeated in the field; and news of this caused great concern in Paris and played into the hands of the Girondins who began organizing the sections of Paris for the overthrow of the monarchy.

In July, representatives from all France converged on Paris for the third anniversary of Bastille Day. They stayed on after the fourteenth of July, and some of them demanded the removal of Louis XVI. Or, at least, they submitted a petition to that effect. The author of this petition was a rising member of the Jacobin Club and ex-constituent: Maximilien Robespierre. The Cordelier club called for a new constitutional convention. The armed sections of Paris with their reinforcements from the provinces could barely be held in check.

The Brunswick Manifesto Into this charged atmosphere, the Duke of Brunswick, commander of the Austrian and Prussian forces, dropped a bombshell (August 1, 1792) in the form of a manifesto drawn up for him by French *émigrés*. The Brunswick Manifesto, as it is called, announced that the Austrians and the Prussian armies were invading France in order to restore Louis XVI to his rightful position. The Manifesto went on to say that Frenchmen who resisted the allied invasion could expect to be punished and to have their houses burned and that if the people of Paris should invade the Tuileries (as they had done in a minor riot on the twentieth of June) or otherwise perpetrate the least affront to the royal family, then Paris would call upon itself an exemplary military vengeance. The implication was that the Duke of Brunswick would permit his troops to sack the city. It was at this point that a delegation of volunteers reached Paris from Marseille singing the newest and certainly the most stirring of revolutionary and patriotic songs—the *Marseillaise.* The Parisian leftist press welcomed the newcomers and responded to the Duke of Brunswick's challenge by openly accusing the king of complicity with the enemy. Why, it was asked with heavy sarcasm, should the invading foreign enemy be so solicitous of the welfare of the French head of state? The royal treason that the Girondins had predicted seemed established. From this point, the overthrow of the monarchy was a foregone conclusion.

The Sans-Culottes The energy behind the August 10, 1792 attack on the Tuileries was supplied by the fears of Parisians and of the visiting revolutionaries (the *fédérés*) concerning foreign invasion and counter-revolution. The organization was supplied at first by the Girondins and later by the

The *Sans-Culotte.* Before the Revolution, gentlemen wore knee-britches (*culottes*) and silk stockings. The proper revolutionary showed his colors by wearing long trousers or *sans-culottes* (without knee-britches). (Musée Carnavalet.)

forty-eight sections of Paris which moved on the 9th of August to displace the legal Parisian government and to replace it with the Revolutionary Commune. Not exactly rabble, the leaders of the sections were, however, convinced revolutionaries and republicans. They distrusted the Assembly nearly as much as they did the king. They affected republican simplicity in their dress and were known as *sans-culottes* because of their ostentatious rejection of the knee-breeches (*culottes*) customarily worn by aristocrats and gentlemen. Because they represented the unwashed sector of humanity, these leaders were distrusted by the Girondins, who wanted to see only political—and not social—revolution in France. Between the 20th of June and the 1st of August 1792, the Girondins drew back from the prospect of inciting popular insurrection; and, as a result of their recoil, revolutionary leadership passed from their hands into those of more violent men, exactly whose it is difficult to ascertain. Danton may have played an important part in organizing the affair of the 10th of August, as he later claimed, or he may not. At any rate, on the 10th of August a crowd stormed the Tuileries, massacred many of the Swiss Guardsmen, and forced the king to flee to the nearby meeting hall of the Assembly. The government passed into the hands of the Commune and of a provisional governmental committee. The call was sent out for the election of a Convention to prepare a new constitution for a France that had already outworn the brave attempt of 1791. Thus, the "Second French Revolution," more republican and somewhat more nearly egalitarian than its predecessor, ushered in a new regime.

THE REIGN OF TERROR

The new revolutionary authorities were faced with the same problems that had bedevilled the constitutional monarchy, with some new ones added. Foreign troops were invading the country; counter-revolutionary insurrections were afoot in France; *émigrés* abroad and non-juring clergy at home represented serious threats to revolutionary security. Whether one approves of it or not, therefore, one can at least begin to understand what happened in September 1792, and carried on until late 1794: the so-called Reign of Terror.

The first step toward Terror, which seems to have been intended to secure the home front so as to enable the revolutionary regime to concentrate on repelling the foreign enemy, took the form of what is known as the September Massacres—a sickening business in the course of which the prisons of Paris and a number of other localities were ransacked for prisoners, including large numbers of non-juring clergy, who were killed almost out of hand. Later, after the new Convention was elected, the revolutionary Terror was better organized as an instrument for securing the Revolution.[2]

[2]Some historians insist that the Terror was basically an irrational manifestation, and that, indeed, the Terror became most fully developed after the danger from foreign invasion had passed. The present writer holds to the more old-fashioned interpretation that, though unpleasant, probably unnecessary, and certainly not effective in terms of its announced goals, the Terror can be explained as an attempt on the part of the revolutionaries to see to it that the Revolution should not be undermined from within.

Robespierre. A small-town lawyer before the Revolution, Robespierre became a doctrinaire revolutionary leader determined that the Revolution should be purified, if necessary, with blood. He always dressed in the costume of the *ancien régime* gentleman. (Bibliothèque de Versailles.)

Generally speaking, it has been taken as axiomatic by revolutionaries ever since the French Revolution that if a revolution is to succeed it must eliminate the personnel of the old regime. That seems to have been what the revolutionary tribunals and the guillotine were intended to do during the two years from the autumn of 1792 to the summer of 1794. Substantial numbers of people were killed during the Terror (but fewer than during the few days of the suppression of the Paris Commune some eighty years later, in 1871). Emigration reached new heights as those Frenchmen of all classes and occupations who found the new revolutionary regime intolerable left the country. The king was imprisoned, tried by the Convention sitting as tribunal, and executed; the monarchy was abolished; and September 22, 1792, 9:18½ A.M., the autumnal equinox, was proclaimed as the beginning of the New Regime. The First French Republic was born.

Then the new revolutionaries attempted once and for all to wipe clean the slate of the *ancien régime.* The old calendar—full of references to tyrants and to outmoded deities—was abandoned in favor of a modern one. Queen bees became "bees of fecundity." *Sans-culotte* austerity became the order of the day; and people gave up using ordinary titles of respect. A new, democratic constitution was prepared by the Convention; but the emergency situation prevented its implementation. From the autumn of 1792, therefore, until the summer of 1794, France was governed by extraordinary means—actually by the Jacobin Club and by the great revolutionary committees (the Committee of Public Safety and the Committee of General Security), as well as by the ever-watchful Commune of Paris.

Robespierre The extraordinary figure in this period of French revolutionary history was Robespierre, a relatively obscure, small-town lawyer before the Revolution. A fanatic revolutionary, convinced of the rightness of his position, determined that the Revolution should prove itself to the world through virtue and austerity, Robespierre came to make deadly enemies of the very human types who made up the cadre of revolutionary politicians. One by one Robespierre ran afoul of other revolutionary groups and individuals; and one by one this mild-appearing but single-minded man managed to overcome them and to send them off to the guillotine. First, the Girondins, who were purged (summer, 1793) from the Convention and their leaders executed; second, the *Enragés,* or extreme Parisian radicals, and the radical journalist Hébert, who disturbed Robespierre's highly developed sense of order and propriety and who represented a threat to a leftist leader by being farther to the left than he; and, finally, Danton, whom Robespierre suspected (and quite rightly) of corruption. In the spring of 1794, Robespierre stood alone for a few moments until the surviving politicians decided that as long as Robespierre the incorruptible lived their own very corrupt existences were in jeopardy. Accordingly, a simple plot was hatched which led to the arrest and execution of Robespierre and nearly a hundred of his followers in the month of July (Thermidor, according to the new revolutionary calendar) 1794. Thereafter, Frenchmen could, as an American president put it much later, "return to normalcy."

Me too free. The question of the status of Blacks in the rich French West Indian sugar islands troubled all revolutionary regimes. The Society of Friends of the Blacks, founded in 1788, advocated the abolition of slavery. However, when the Estates General met in 1789, the French sugar planters formed a powerful lobby which saw to it that the Constitution of 1791 did not free the slaves in French colonies. Later, the Convention abolished slavery; but, still later, Napoleon sent an army to Haiti to put down a rebellion led by the former slave, Toussaint L'Ouverture. (Bibliothèque Nationale.)

Achievements of the Convention Revolutionary achievements during the period of the Convention, of Robespierre, and the Terror were not nearly so great as those that came before under the National Constituent Assembly; nor were they so nearly permanent. The Convention's new calendar was soon abandoned; but the new system of weights and measures, the development of which was initiated by the Constituent Assembly, spread to all but the Anglo-Saxon world. The democratic constitution of the Year I was never implemented; but something more nearly like the Constitution of 1791, lacking some of its imperfections, came to prevail in France during much of the nineteenth century. All the bloodshed of the Terror did not solve the problem of counter-revolution in France. The religious problems of the country were only toyed with in a mechanical, irresponsible, and unsuccessful fashion. Certain egalitarian notions put forward by Robespierre's young colleague, St. Just (for instance, the idea that the land of those suspected of counter-revolutionary activity should be given to the poor—the Ventôse Decrees) were never implemented, though price controls—the Laws of the Maximum—were enacted and served in some measure to protect the poor against inflation. By and large, when the head of Robespierre dropped into the basket it was almost as though he and his regime had never been.

On the other hand, this violent phase of the Revolution did serve to carry on and to make effective a number of decisions and beginnings that had been made earlier. The first of these implementations was forced by the stress of war when the republican government came to realize that if the peasant four-fifths of the nation was to support the Revolution and to lend its sons to the revolutionary armies, then the promises of August 1789 would have to be fulfilled. Accordingly, in 1793 the peasants were given what the Constituent Assembly had tried to hold back: free and clear title to their land without redemption. This was without doubt one of the most important reforms of the French Revolution, but its origins lay in the period of the National Constituent Assembly, as we have seen. The second fulfillment was the reorganization of the French army, started as far back as the last decades of the *ancien régime* when the staff work had been done and the new tactical manuals had been written. To these achievements, the Legislative Assembly had added the idea that all Frenchmen should rise to defend the fatherland; and during the Convention the *levée en masse* became a reality. Finally, the revolutionary regime of the Terror continued the mammoth sale of real estate, beginning with the Church lands, that had been started by the National Constituent Assembly. The Convention added to the auction the lands of *émigrés*. In all, something over one-fifth and not much less than two-fifths of French land changed hands. In permitting this sale, the governments of the Revolution bound substantial numbers of Frenchmen to the Revolution not with hoops of corruptible steel but with the bonds of property. For he who had acquired land as a result of the Revolution could hardly forsake it. Thus, the regime of the Robespierrian period contributed to laying the base for French solidarity and French expansion under Napoleon Bonaparte.

FURTHER READING

All the books listed for the previous chapter are pertinent to this one. In addition, the reader should see a fine brief biography, J. M. Thompson, * *Robespierre and the French Revolution* (1953). G. Rudé has edited a useful book of readings: * *Robespierre* (1967), in which the Incorruptible One is revealed by his own words, by those of his contemporaries, as well as by the assessment of later historians. R. Palmer, * *Twelve Who Ruled: the Committee of Public Safety during the Terror* (1958); G. Bruun, *Saint-Just: Apostle of the Terror* (1932); C. Brinton, *The Jacobins* (1930), and * *The Lives of Talleyrand* (1936); L. R. Gottschalk, *Jean-Paul Marat: a Study in Radicalism* (1927); and L. Gershoy, *Bertrand Barère: a Reluctant Terrorist* (1962), all deal with the prominent figures of the Revolution. In this regard, the reader might do well to begin with J. M. Thompson, *Leaders of the French Revolution* (1932), for a series of brief biographical sketches.

Readers interested in a modern approach to Revolutionary studies should see G. Rudé, * *The Crowd in the French Revolution* (1959), a sociological approach to the "little people"; and M. J. Sydenham, *The Girondins* (1961), which maintains that there was no real Girondist party, that there was no basic difference between the socioeconomic policies of the Girondins and the Montagnards, and that the interpretation of the Girondins given in this chapter and the next is a "myth." A. Patrick, *The men of the First French Republic: Political Alignments in the National Convention of 1792* (1972), is revisionistic regarding the third (or fourth?) revolutionary assembly.

Illuminating works on the Terror and emigration are D. Greer, *The Incidence of the Terror during the French Revolution: a Statistical Interpretation* (1935), which attempts to demonstrate that the Terror did not operate entirely at the expense of the nobles and clergy, and that, in fact, the guillotine cut across all classes of French society. The same author's *The Incidence of Emigration during the French Revolution* (1951) would show that Frenchmen representing all classes fled Revolutionary France at one time or another. Greer has been attacked by Richard Louie in "The Incidence of the Terror: A Critique of a Statistical Interpretation (*French Historical Studies,* Spring 1964). Greer's exposition is easier to understand than is Louie's mathematical critique. A recent study in depth is C. Lucas, *The Structure of the Terror: The Example of Javogues and the Loire* (1973). For an idea of how the Terror worked outside Paris, see J. Sirich, *The Revolutionary Committees in the Departments of France, 1793–1794* (1943, reprint 1971).

*Books available in paperback edition are marked with an asterisk.

5 The Great Nation and Napoleonic Europe

The Thermidorians—those who arranged the conspiracy against Robespierre in July 1794 (men like Barras, Tallien, and Fréron)—had not intended initially to terminate the Reign of Terror after disposing of Robespierre; but they soon came to realize that French public opinion had turned so violently against the Terror that they would have to disassociate themselves from Robespierre and all his works if they were to remain in power.

THE THERMIDORIAN REACTION

The simple fact was that in late 1794 the overwhelming majority of the French people was surfeited with exaltation, revolutionary enthusiasm, austerity, virtue, and Terror; and the political leaders had to adjust accordingly. Thus, these men who had voted for Louis XVI's death and who had participated actively in the Terror moved to suppress the Jacobin Club and the Revolutionary Tribunal. They repealed the radical Ventôse decrees, the laws of suspects, and the revolutionary price control laws; and they participated in the flamboyant relaxation of manners and morals that was one of the outstanding social characteristics of what is known as the Thermidorian Reaction, a rightist swing of the political and social pendulum after a period of movement fairly far to the left. Thousands of suspects and prisoners of the Terror were released. Those Girondin deputies who had survived the executions of 1793 were readmitted to the Convention and became, once again, the dominant group. It was at Girondin insistence that the Laws of the Maximum (price controls) were abolished.

Economic and Political Disorganization The end of price controls combined with a period of bad weather and certain provisioning problems created by the wartime situation (France was still at war against the First Coalition—see chart, p. 1052) sent food prices soaring at the same time that the paper *assignats* became rapidly valueless. Further, the economic disorganization contributed to by the fall of the *assignats* created wide-spread unemployment. Thus, the little people of Paris suffered in the winter of 1794–1795 as acutely as they had in 1788–1789. These little people had been

The New Society. Taking the place of the old nobility and the great merchants and financiers of the *ancien régime* was a new society of speculators, military contractors, and venal politicians. Here we see some ladies of this new *bourgeoisie* enjoying an ice-cream parlor—something new in post-Thermidorian Paris. (The Metropolitan Museum of Art.)

the faithful support of the revolutionary Paris Commune, and it was with alarm that they saw their hero Robespierre and most of the leaders of the Commune put to death during Thermidor. They were further upset when the Convention showed signs of being prepared to revise the Constitution of 1793 which, though never fully implemented, had a great reputation as being a democratic document. Twice—in April and May 1795—the Parisians rose up in arms to demand bread, jobs, and the continuation of the Constitution of 1793. Both times they were put down by National Guards from the more prosperous sections of Paris and by regular troops. Hundreds of these humble insurgents were executed. All but three of the old Committee of Public Safety, men who had saved the Revolution from internal and external threats during the dark days of 1792 and 1793 and who had organized the victorious progress of French arms after the Battle of Valmy, were executed, imprisoned, or banished. Then, the Thermidorian reaction developed its own "White" Terror in the provinces, where Jacobins, and even those moderates who had not actively opposed the previous Terror (the "Red" Terror), were hunted and killed, sometimes by royalist groups that once again dared to show themselves and thereby bore witness to the failure of the Reign of Terror to purge enemies of the Revolution from France. At this time, it seemed for a while that the royalists, aided by English agents, would effect a restoration of the monarchy. But in June of 1795 an invasion by French royalist *émigrés,* supported by the English fleet and by French royalists of the Vendée region at the base of the Breton peninsula, was repulsed by the Republican army. Also, as we shall see, a royalist-inspired rising in Paris itself was suppressed by Republican troops. For the moment the Republic was saved.

The Constitution of the Year III Meanwhile, the Convention, now dominated by the Girondins, turned to writing its second constitution for France, and the result was the Constitution of the Year III (1795). This document was neither democratic nor royalist. France was to remain a republic so as to guarantee the land transfers started in 1790 and still going on, but it was to be an orderly republic dominated by people of upper-middle-class orientation. In some respects, this constitution resembled that of 1791, requiring property qualifications for voting and indirect elections. The main differences were, first, that now the executive was entrusted to a committee of five Directors (hence the application of the term "Directory" to the period from 1795 to 1799) and, second, that the legislative power was given to a bicameral (two-chamber) *Corps législatif,* rather like the Congress of the United States. The hope was that an upper house would tend to check levelling or democratic tendencies and make it more difficult for the Parisian populace to intimidate the legislature. The main shortcoming of this constitution proved to be that it provided a too nearly perfect balance of power between the executive and the two legislative councils (the Council of Elders and the Council of Five Hundred). Since there was no legal way for disputes between the executive and the legislature to be resolved, the result was recourse to force through a series of *coups d'état.*

In order to prevent victory at the polls by royalists and in order to ensure their own continuation in public office, the members of the Convention decreed that five hundred of them—about two thirds of the outgoing body—would automatically find seats in the new council of the *Corps législatif.* This was an unpopular decree: many members of the Convention had been in office for so long that they were well known as corrupt, bloody-handed men; and they were held responsible for the economic disruptions of the day. When the decree regarding the "Perpetuals," as they quickly were dubbed in the press, was made public, the city of Paris reacted characteristically. But this time the rising was inspired by a royalist insurrectionary committee in contact with English agents. On the 13th day of Vendémiaire (October 5, 1795) some 20,000 men from the more substantial sections of Paris marched against the Convention meeting at the Tuileries palace. As they debouched from the narrow streets into the broad expanses before the palace and along the Seine they were mowed down with grapeshot fired from cannon hastily assembled the night before by a young cavalry officer, Joachim Murat, and supervised by a young artilleryman, Napoleon Bonaparte, who had been recruited at the last moment to arrange for the defense of the Convention. Shortly, in the bloodiest of the Paris revolutionary *journées,* the attackers were killed or dispersed. On October 16th, Bonaparte was made general of a division and ten days later, at the age of twenty-six, he became general-in-chief of the Army of the Interior. Moreover, he met and fell in love with a charming lady, Joséphine Beauharnais, widow of an officer who had been guillotined during the Terror. In the spring of 1796, Napoleon, now a bridegroom, was given command of the French army in Italy, where he went on to achieve astonishing victories.

The Committee on Public Instruction Among the demolitions of the Revolution, none was more significant than the destruction of the educational system of the *ancien régime.* As early as 1790, Frenchmen began to think about providing a substitute worthy of the Revolution. The Constitution of 1791 stated the principle of free elementary education. The Legislative Assembly of the constitutional monarchy created a Committee on Public Instruction of which the mathematician and philosopher Condorcet was a member. Condorcet drew up a report of this committee's deliberations. One of the landmarks in the history of education, this report urged free, universal education as the basic means for enhancing national power and promoting social equality. Later, the Convention also appointed a Committee on Public Instruction which was composed of some of the most distinguished Frenchmen including a poet (Chénier), a chemist (Fourcroy), a professional educator (Lakanal), and a historian (Daunou). Finally, the day before the Convention was dissolved (October 25, 1795), the outgoing body voted on and passed a series of laws providing for public primary and secondary education. On the same day the Convention acted on the committee's recommendation that the old royal academies (the French Academy and the Academy of Science among others), which had been abolished earlier in the Revolution as aristocratic and privileged bodies, should be recreated in new republican guise under the Institute of France. Previously the Convention had created the Polytechnic School (*École Polytechnique*) for training scientists and engineers, which immediately attracted a fine faculty and soon started turning out a brilliant group of graduates. The new Academy of Science was also a star-studded body. In general, the Revolution was good to scientists, many of whom were ennobled by Bonaparte and heaped with honors and offices. The three important scientists who perished in the Revolution—Lavoisier, Bailly, and Condorcet—got into trouble for reasons that had nothing to do with science: Lavoisier because of his association with tax farming in the *ancien régime,* and Bailly and Condorcet because of their political activities.

The Committee on Public Instruction also prepared an elaborate revolutionary pageantry and mythology for the purpose of stimulating patriotism. This work was carried on by the Directory and by the Napoleonic regimes; and, together with the excitement of revolutionary events, the threat of foreign invasion, and spirited revolutionary songs, it helped develop the exaggerated form of patriotism typical of modern nationalism.

Thus inculcated with do-or-die ardor, and thanks to the Revolutionary army, the French people became a nation capable of playing, on a larger scale, the protagonist role in European affairs, as it had during the reign of Louis XIV.

THE DIRECTORY, 1795–1799

After the Constitution of 1795 was put into effect for the second time, the Revolution was supposed to be over; but many Frenchmen were unwilling to accept the idea of permanence. Royalists within France and *émigrés* without fought and conspired to work a restoration of the monarchy while leftists sought to push the conservative Republic in the direction of socialism. The government of the Directory was able for the time being to stamp out armed uprisings in the Vendée and in Brittany. The Directors were also able to deal with a conspiracy of radical malcontents led by a primitive socialist, "Gracchus" Babeuf.

Babeuf and his "Society of Equals" maintained that equality as expressed in the French Revolution was a fraud, that equality before the law was not true equality, that the people "demand henceforth to live and to die equal, as we have been born equal." Babeuf called for the end of all distinctions between human beings save those of age and sex. "Let disappear, once and for all," he wrote in a manifesto, "the revolting distinctions of rich and poor, of great and small, of masters and valets, of governors and governed." This frightening conspiracy was discovered by the Directors and thoroughly suppressed in 1797. Babeuf was guillotined.[1]

One who refused to accept the new turn of events was François Babeuf (1760–1797), who styled himself Gracchus Babeuf after the ancient Roman popular leader. Calling the Revolution a "war declared between the patricians and the plebians, between the rich and the poor. . .", Babeuf organized a "Society of Equals" which joined the Jacobins in calling for the fall of the Directory and a return to the Constitution of 1793. (Bibliothèque Nationale.)

With such threats to the Republic the government could deal, but not with the problems posed by the nature of the constitution. When the elections of 1797 went violently against the "Perpetuals" in the two legislative councils, the executive was controlled by ex-Jacobins and the councils by moderates and royalists. The latter group put afoot a conspiracy to overthrow the Directors; but, in what is known as the *coup d'état* of 18 Fructidor (September 1797), the republican Directors called in 30,000 troops to back them while they illegally purged nearly two hundred members of the legislative councils, condemning many of them to deportation. This was the first violation of the Constitution, and it was perpetrated by the republicans.

Less than a year later, new elections returned many republican extremists, farther to the left than the Directors, and these too were purged from the Councils by the executive. In 1799, the councils got their revenge when they managed to purge the Directory. Both sides had now violated the Constitution, which no longer commanded anyone's respect. One of the new directors after the *coup* in 1799 was Siéyès, who ever since 1789 had been itching to write what he was sure would be the definitive constitution for

[1]In the early years of the twentieth century, Marxist historians used to make their French revolutionary hero out of Robespierre whom they described as the leader of a premature dictatorship of the proletariat. More recently, these Marxists have decided that Robespierre was really a bourgeois counter-revolutionary and have taken up Babeuf as their hero.

France and who had, until this time, been frustrated in his desire. Now, he thought his opportunity had arrived—an opportunity that was improved when General Bonaparte returned triumphantly from Egypt in the autumn of 1799.

THE EXPANSION OF FRANCE, 1793–1799

Napoleon's "success" in Egypt was actually more of a defeat. He had made good a landing; he had won some battles; but Nelson's victory of the Nile (or Aboukir Bay) over the French fleet, in August 1798, bottled the French up without hope of escape. Bonaparte's army was in a hopeless situation when he decided to desert it in order to return to France, where his fine political sense detected an opportunity for an ambitious young soldier like himself. Napoleon was only one of a large number of remarkable young officers who had risen with the revolutionary army, and he was by no means the most skillful soldier among them. But his particular luck so combined with his ambition as to enable him to play a role out of all proportion to his intrinsic merits. He rose with the army, and always he was a man of the army, dependent upon it for his power. But before taking up the Napoleonic wars, we must backtrack to 1792 and the beginnings of the conflict.

The French Challenge and the First Coalition The French revolutionary army quickly reshaped itself after the initial reverses in 1792. At Valmy (September 1792), the troops gave evidence of their improvement by not running away during a cannonade. Then they went on the offensive, drove the Prussians across the Rhine and penetrated Germany, while another French army took Nice and Savoy in the southeast. Other troops conquered the Austrian Netherlands. At this point (November 19, 1792), the Convention, newly met in Paris and flushed with news of victory, proclaimed the willingness of the French people to assist all peoples who wished to overthrow their governments. The result of this cocky challenge to all of the powers of Europe was the creation of the First Coalition against France: England, Holland, Spain, Austria, Prussia, the Empire, Sardinia. The real power in this alliance was England which, despite the younger Pitt's inclination toward peace, was forced into war by French intransigency, by the French capture of the Belgian Netherlands, and by the opening of the Scheldt river. (It will be remembered that ever since the sixteenth century the English had been dedicated to the proposition that the Scheldt should be closed and that Antwerp should not be a port.) Moreover, reaction in England to the execution of Louis XVI and to the now obvious (because of the proclamation of November 19) threat of the French Revolution to English institutions tended to create a warlike spirit in England, which Pitt could not have thwarted even had he sincerely desired to do so. The result was that France and England entered a state of war February 1, 1793. England continued to fight France on the continent as well as overseas almost continuously for the next twenty-one years.

The allies of the First Coalition made good headway against the French on nearly all fronts and soon were again on French soil. Once again the

Revolution stood in deadly danger. In this crisis, Bertrand Barère rose in the Convention to propose a national rising against the foreign enemies, and, on the 23rd of August 1793, was passed the *levée en masse* which ordered:

> *From this moment, until that time when the enemies have been chased from the territory of the Republic, all the French people are in permanent requisition for the army.*
>
> *The young men will go to fight; married men will make arms and transport supplies; women will make tents and uniforms and serve in the hospitals; children will shred rags for bandages; old men will betake themselves to public places to excite the courage of the soldiers, the hatred of kings, and the unity of the Republic.*

The mass mobilization worked. Fourteen armies were raised according to a system of universal conscription; and by autumn 1793, the allies were being pushed back across the Rhine. In 1794–1795, the French recaptured Belgium and invaded Holland. Before Thermidor, therefore, the French citizen armies had gone vigorously on the offensive. Belgium and the Rhineland were absorbed, and in one year the French revolutionary government had made a far more substantial move toward achieving the "natural" frontiers of France than had Louis XIV during all his years of trying. Under the Thermidorian Convention and under the Directory, France continued to expand, creating buffer republics between France, as expanded, and its foreign enemies. Thus, Holland became the Batavian Republic in 1795; Switzerland was turned into the Helvetian Republic in 1798; and in Italy after Napoleon's victories in 1796–1797 a whole flock of republics was established. In each area the French found and developed a core of native revolutionary enthusiasts to head the new republics. These people suffered when the French conquests were rolled back during the opening phases of the War of the Second Coalition while Bonaparte was posturing among the pyramids in Egypt.

The Second Coalition In the Second Coalition France faced most of its old enemies and some new ones, including Russia. The Russian forces were commanded by an extremely able general, Suvarov, who in conjunction with the Austrians repeatedly defeated the French. In 1799, the French-sponsored republics in Italy were extinguished as the French found themselves hotly engaged in many quarters. But severe as these defeats were, they did not produce a real threat to French security like that of 1792 or 1793. The French policy of creating buffer states outside of expanded France meant that, during the period of military disaster in 1799, the new, greater France was never in danger of invasion. The fighting took place outside of the country at the expense of others. When the tide of battle began to turn, as it did in September 1799, when the Russian general Suvarov, far from home and supplies and badly supported by the Austrians, was no longer able to keep the pace, the French were still in a strong position. Thus, when Napoleon returned hastily from Egypt, announcing himself as the hero who would save France in her hour of danger, there was really no danger and no need to save her from anything except her problems at home.

THE BRUMAIRE COUP

The real problem facing France in October 1799, when Bonaparte landed at Fréjus on the Riviera and slowly made his way north to Paris, was not one of external threat; it was one of internal organization. The constitutional republic was unsatisfactory on many counts, and on none more so than its failure to maintain order within a framework of law that had the respect of the majority of the French people. Insurrection in Paris seemed the only way in which the government could proceed; and in the provinces, especially in the Vendée, armed uprisings broke out again. By 1799, a substantial portion of the French people, as well as of French politicians, had given up on the constitution of the Directory.

Brumaire Coup. A meeting of the Council of Five Hundred at St. Cloud, away from turbulent Paris, was engineered by Siéyès on November 9, 1799 (18 Brumaire). In this picture, Napoleon's entry followed by soldiers is provoking some confusion. The *coup* succeeded when the presiding officer (right), Napoleon's brother, ordered uncooperative deputies forcibly removed from the hall. (LCRB.)

Many politicians in the Directory and in the councils believed that the state as then organized did not provide a sufficiently stable bark to keep them in office. Accordingly, before Bonaparte's return from Egypt, several of them, led by Siéyès, entered into a conspiracy to establish a regime that would enjoy confidence from below while power was actually exercised from above. These conspirators realized that there was little in them or in their history that was likely to inspire confidence from below. They also realized that the only truly popular element in French government was the army with its attractive and valiant young generals who had won the love and admiration of the French people. The plotters decided, therefore, to draw one of these generals into their conspiracy so that he could act as their front man. Their first choice had the bad luck to be killed in battle; several others seemed unsatisfactory for one reason or another. Then, Napoleon came upon the scene with the palms of victory gracing his brow. Within a few days contact was made between Siéyès and Bonaparte; the latter agreed to participate in the plot.

The plan was simple. First, it was to be announced that the government had uncovered evidence of a projected Jacobin uprising. Napoleon would then be made commander of the military in the Paris region with instructions to defend the government. The two legislative councils would be moved out of Paris to nearby Saint-Cloud to remove them from the influence of unruly Jacobin crowds in paris. Next, the executive branch of the government would precipitate a constitutional crisis by disappearing, through the resignation of those Directors who were privy to the conspiracy, and the house arrest of those who were not. Then, Napoleon would harangue the two councils and impress them with the dangers that beset the state and with the need for a new, strong, and orderly regime. The scheme very nearly worked as planned; but at a crucial moment on the 18th of Brumaire (November 9, 1799), when Napoleon entered the Council of Five Hundred to make his speech, some of the Jacobin deputies smelled a rat (Napoleon was accompanied by soldiers with mounted bayonets) and actually put on the floor a motion to outlaw Napoleon. Fortunately for Napoleon the presiding officer of the council happened to be his brother Lucien Bonaparte. Lucien was able to prevent the motion of outlawry from coming to a vote; and then with a histrionic gesture he was able to persuade a reluctant detachment of soldiers to clear the hall of councillors. Later, a rump session of conspirators reassembled to give some semblance of legality to the proceedings by voting to form a new republic, the Consulate, with Napoleon as the first of three consuls.

In the next days, all France was placarded with bulletins proclaiming the change and Siéyès was permitted to dabble at writing a constitution. The constitution was submitted to the people for approval in December 1799 Over three million Frenchmen accepted it.

Unfinished Portrait of Napoleon by Jacques-Louis David (1748–1825). (The Louvre.)

The Consulate Of Italian ancestry, Napoleon came from the petty aristocracy of Corsica where he had been born (1769) in the year after that island was acquired by France. His father had made his peace with the French authorities and had entered their service. This relationship paved the way to a French military education for young Bonaparte, who was graduated from the *École Militaire* in Paris. In 1785, after having been given good marks in mathematics by no less a person than Laplace, he passed into the field artillery, becoming a junior lieutenant in 1786 at the age of seventeen. His prospects were not bright. Without influential family or powerful connections in France, he could look forward to no more than the rank of lieutenant colonel after long service as what was known in the French army as a "soldier of fortune." That he rose to far greater heights was due to the Revolution and the reorganization of the French army. Thus, in a sense, Napoleon was the child or the heir of the Revolution.

If Napoleon was a child of the Revolution, he was also a child of the army; and his main orientation seems to have been toward order, rationality, and authority. He could not understand the meaning of words like "liberty" and "fraternity," which he considered expressions of romantic notions. "Equality" he could understand in its limited sense: equality for all before the law and careers open to talent. At one point early after the *coup* of 1799 he is said to have said something like, "The romance of the Revolution is over; let us now begin its history!" This meant terminating the disorder of the revolutionary regimes and clearly establishing in law the least that the French people would settle for from their Revolution. As a French nationalist, despite his Italian background, he also determined to continue the work of nation making begun by the previous revolutionary regimes. Hence, his constant use of patriotic notions in his public utterances: glory, fatherland, freedom, honor, courage, and constancy.

The general problem of creating order in 1799 was composed of six subsidiary tasks: first, fulfilling the Oath of the Tennis Court and drafting a satisfactory constitution for France; second, ending the civil war in the Vendée; third, making order out of the governmental finances; fourth, codifying revolutionary legislation; fifth, concluding an honorable peace in Europe; sixth, settling religious discord. To its eternal credit and glory, the history of the first years of the Consulate in France was marked by the satisfactory performance of three of these tasks, along with serious attempts at three others. The only failure was the Constitution. The oligarchs, including Siéyès, who had helped Napoleon to power, thought that they would write the document; but they found an active participant in the thirty-year-old general. The latter saw to it that the constitution gave power to him and not to the oligarchs. The completed document rewarded the principal conspirators by allowing them to name the majority of the new Senate, thus giving them substantial patronage and permitting them to see to it that their old friends among the "Perpetuals" should not retire to private life. In addition to the Senate there was a tribunate and a legislative body, members of which were appointed. The executive belonged to Napoleon, assisted by two other consuls. The consuls appointed the ministers for the central government.

AUTHORITY, ORDER, AND PEACE IN FRANCE

In choosing his ministers, Bonaparte soothed the frayed nerves of France by selecting Frenchmen of all types and thereby suggesting that the time of terror and party strife was over. His brother he made minister of interior; for minister of police he chose Fouché, an ex-Terrorist; Talleyrand, a constitutional monarchist, was made minister for foreign affairs. For expert guidance in government, Napoleon created the Council of State composed of bright young men without any particular political past who served him as a sort of "brain-trust" in preparing legislation. Rights of citizenship were restored to *émigrés* as long as they clearly understood that they should not expect to retrieve any of their *ancien-régime* property that had been sold by the government. By the thousands, the *émigrés* returned, brushing the alien dust of America, England, Germany, and Austria off their coats and delighted to be home. In all, it seemed like an era of reconciliation for a people sorely in need of pacification.

In continuing the work of centralization of the French government—a work begun at least as far back as the time of Louis IX, continued under the Valois and Bourbon kings, and drastically furthered during the period of Robespierre—Napoleon and his advisors made their most characteristic contribution. His authoritarian ideal coincided with the deposed monarchy (and not with the liberal ideal of the National Constituent Assembly) and led him to eliminate the elected councils in French local government. For each *département* there was to be a prefect; for each *arrondissement* a sub-prefect; and for each *commune* a mayor. All of these officials were to hold their authority from the First Consul. The prefects were actually chosen from lists of names prepared by Lucien Bonaparte, who tried to select moderate men.

Moderation also marked the successful pacification of the Vendée, where rebels were told in an interview between the First Consul and a rebel leader that France now had a government that all Frenchmen could trust and that, therefore, there was no further excuse for resistance. Then Napoleon proclaimed an amnesty for all rebels who surrendered; and after a suitable waiting period the army moved in to wipe out those who did not accept the offer. The internal civil war was ended.

Fiscal reform had already been far advanced by the preceding regimes, which had in effect repudiated two-thirds of the public debt. The Consulate further improved the government's finances by using its new centralized power to tighten up tax collection in the provinces and by imposing strict economies in all branches of government. But the reforms were far from complete, and the Napoleonic regimes were always pinched for credit. In 1800, the French government had to pay 5 percent on its bonds while English bondholders were getting only 3 percent. If the truth be known, we know very little about the finances of a regime that was less than regular in its accounting and less than candid in its budgetary pronouncements. All we know surely is that Napoleon was able to find the immense sums necessary to finance his wars.

The Napoleonic Codes The codifying of revolutionary legislation was the outstanding success of the Consulate. This major effort by a group of able lawyers, who were often joined in their labors by the First Consul, produced the civil, criminal, and commercial codes of law known as the Napoleonic Codes. These codes fell far short of giving legal form to the more advanced libertarian ideas of some of the French revolutionaries, for they protected the interests of property owners and employers against those of the propertyless and employees, of husband against wife, and of father against children. However, the Codes represented a great advance over anything Frenchmen—or any other European group—had known in the way of law. They asserted and codified the equality of all citizens before the law; they provided for freedom of occupation and freedom of conscience. In a sense, they expressed the basic aspirations of the Revolution by putting all men (but not women or children) on a basis of equality at birth, by opening careers to talent, and by discouraging large landed estates. Wherever these Codes were introduced outside France during the conquests of the Consulate and Empire they were considered revolutionary.

The Concordat of 1801 Settlement of religious discord was another substantial success. Napoleon saw in the French Roman Catholic Church a dissident and potentially revolutionary group, capable of stirring up more insurrections like that in the Vendée where the clergy had provided the driving spirit. Like Henry IV before him, Napoleon determined to heal the schism begun in this case by the Civil Constitution of the Clergy. In order to make loyal citizens of the refractory clergy and their flocks, he had to approach the papacy, and as soon as French arms had won a notable victory in Italy at Marengo in June 1800, he did.

At first, Pope Pius VII was reluctant to negotiate with Napoleon. He and the curia wanted first to be sure that the new French regime would be more permanent than its predecessors. After a second great French victory at Hohenlinden (December 1800), the papal court proclaimed the Concordat of 1801. The Concordat re-established formal relations between the French state and the papacy and regulated religious life in France. It proclaimed Roman Catholicism as the religion of the Consuls (including Napoleon) and of the majority of the French people, though it did not commit the French government to seeing to it that the majority remain Roman Catholic. In return for this token, the pope permitted the refractory clergy to reconcile themselves with the French state. The state took on the duty, as established earlier in the Civil Constitution, of paying the salaries of clergymen, retaining the right to nominate bishops. Later, in order to mollify those anti-clerical soldiers and intellectuals who resented this agreement, the Consulate promulgated a law which gave minority churches in France the same support, with freedom of religion. By and large, these religious settlements contributed substantially to the development of internal concord in France. Napoleon was understandably proud of the achievement.

The Treaty of Amiens The task of concluding an honorable peace with the rest of Europe was accomplished by defeating or isolating the remaining

THE NAPOLEONIC REGIMES

1799	*Coup d'état*
1799–August 1802	The First Consulate—a "republic"
1802–1804	The Life Consulate—Napoleon Consul for life with power to appoint his successor
1804–1814	The Empire—Napoleon as Emperor of the French; development of a new nobility; succession set according to the hereditary principle

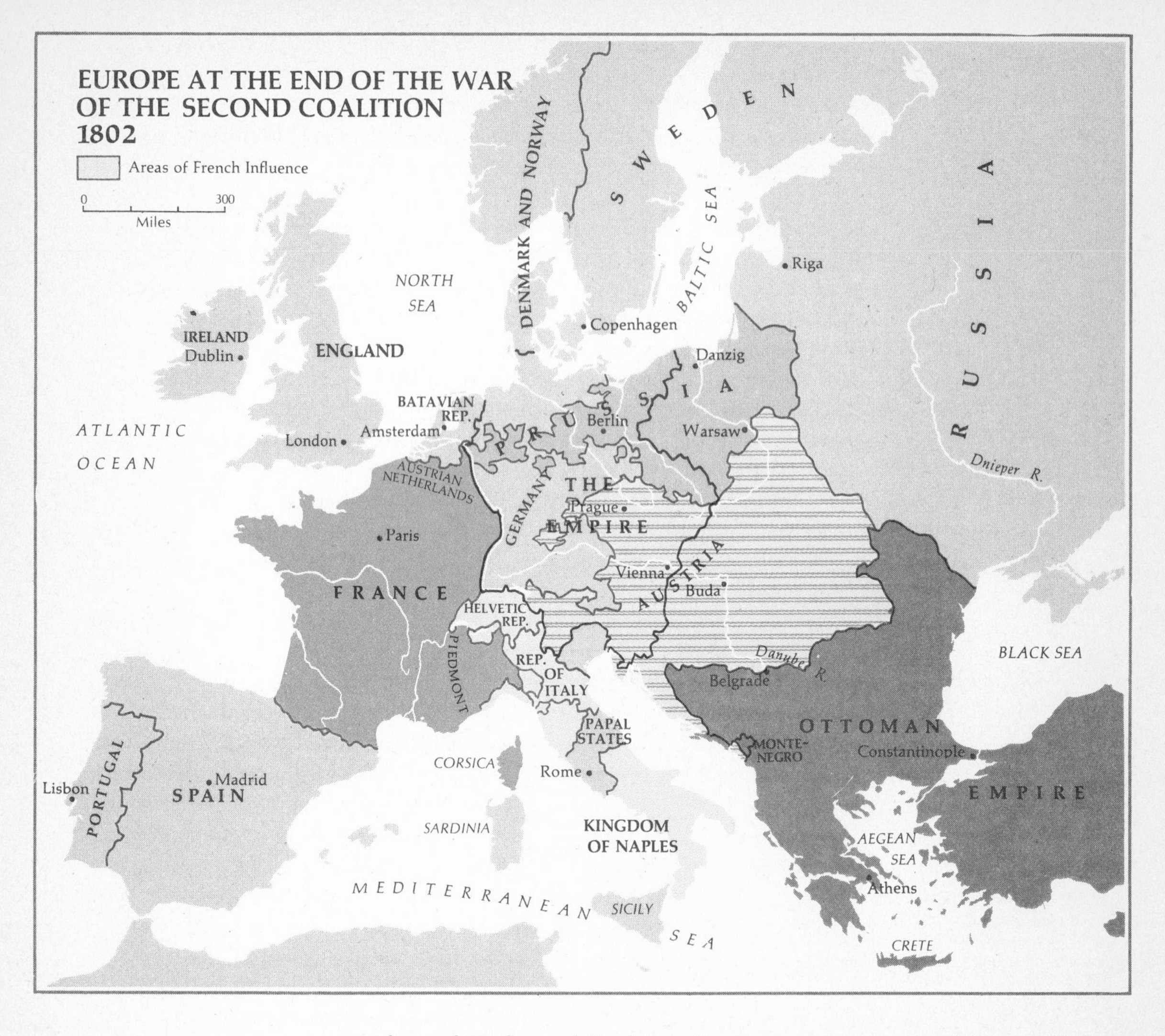

members of the Second Coalition. Russia was already out of the war. Prussia had never been in it. There remained England and Austria, and at first they were not open to peace overtures. Because England could not be reached, Napoleon mounted against Austria a vigorous campaign which came to a successful conclusion after the battles of Marengo and Hohenlinden (mentioned above). The Treaty of Lunéville (February 1801) put Austria out of the war, once again established the Rhine as the French frontier, and led to the re-creation of buffer states outside of expanded France. After this achievement and after the establishment of peace with the papacy, it was easier to approach England, now staggering under the burden of debt contracted during the last nine years of war and without allies.

The Treaty of Amiens (1802) concluded peace between the two countries on terms very favorable to France. The English made peace primarily in the hopes of recovering European markets for their goods, but the treaty did not guarantee that English goods could go to the French-dominated parts of the continent. Moreover, Belgium remained in French hands, and the English were required to surrender all the places in the Mediterranean that they had taken over during the war, including the strategic island of Malta. When it became obvious that the Consulate's economic policy was directed toward making France economically self-sufficient and Europe economically dependent upon France, English businessmen quickly decided that war with France was less expensive than peace, and hostilities were resumed (May 1803). Thus, the Consulate's attempt at peace making was hardly permanent.

Napoleon continued to consolidate his power while fighting England. In 1802, a new constitution was drawn up, one that increased the First Consul's power at the same time that he was made consul for life. In 1804, after the discovery of a conspiracy against him, Napoleon presided over the creation of another constitutional change. The new document stipulated that "The government of the French Republic is entrusted to an emperor. . . ." Three and one half million Frenchmen approved the change in the plebiscite that followed. Thus perished the republic.

Within a few years the "revolutionary" emperor was in process of creating a new imperial nobility, to such effect that by the end of his regime there were 31 dukes, about 1000 barons, and over 1500 imperial knights.

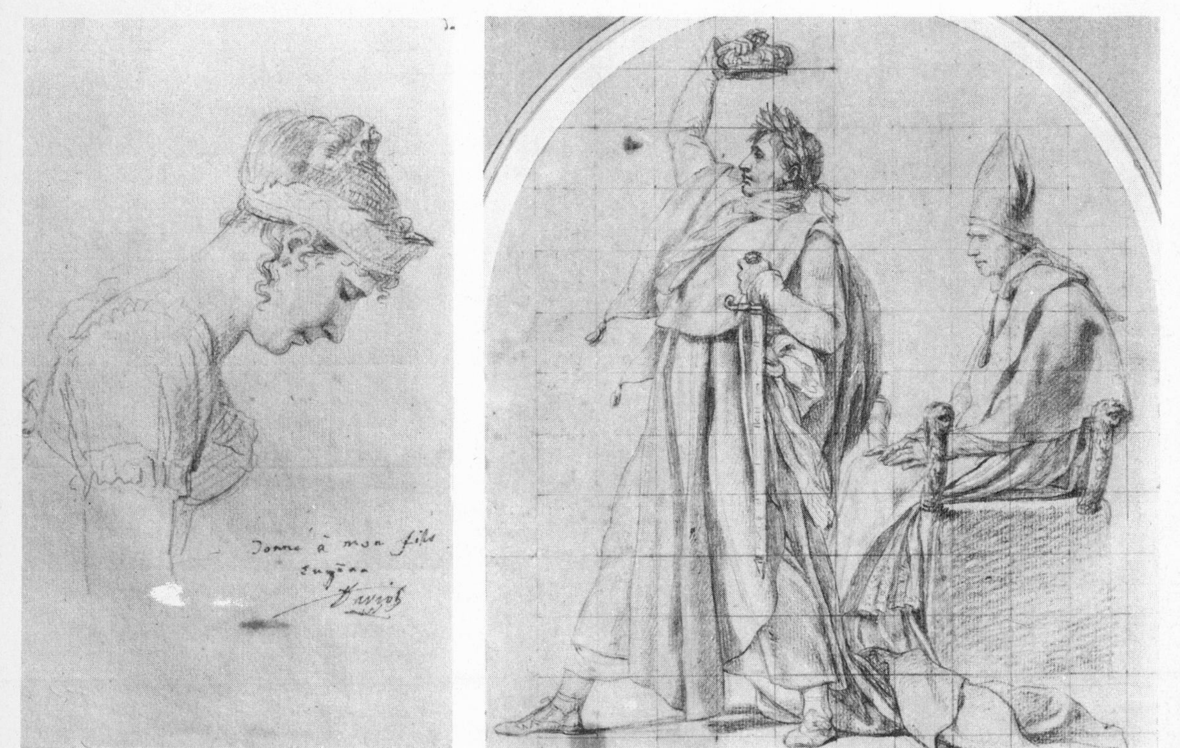

Coronation of Napoleon. Napoleon persuaded Pope Pius VII to come to Paris for his coronation as Emperor of the French. "Le Sacre" or sacred ceremony took place on December 4, 1804, in Notre Dame. At the climax, Napoleon took the crown from the Pope and set it on his own head. Below, the Empress Josephine is shown, bowing her head respectfully. These studies were made by David for his huge painting of the spectacle now in the Louvre, Paris. (The Louvre.)

Members of his family and other close associates became kings and princes. Further, Napoleon turned his attention to creating a court ritual vaguely reminiscent of that established by Louis XIV. Thus perished equality.

THE EMPIRE AND THE BALANCE OF POWER

The remaining story of France under Napoleon can be quickly told. The Revolution was now halted. The French people were organized under the Empire for ever-grander military efforts against coalition after coalition, in each of which England was the only undefeatable opponent. For a while Napoleon toyed with the notion of invading England, but gave up the idea and marched his troops east to crush the Austrians and Russians at Austerlitz even before news of the defeat of the French fleet in the battle of Trafalgar off Portugal (1805) ended all hopes of a successful trans-channel amphibious operation. Next, when Prussia was forced to war by Napoleon's creation of a great buffer state in western Germany (the Confederation of the Rhine, including territories that had belonged to the Hohenzollerns), Prussian armies were overwhelmingly defeated at Jena and Auerstadt (1806). The Russians were beaten in the next year. A grand set of treaties following these victories was signed at Tilsit (1807) between the Emperor of the French and the tsar of all the Russias and between France and Prussia. Both arrangements were intended in large part to help Napoleon wage economic war on England which was still in the field against him. Two years later, English diplomacy was able to persuade Austria to join yet another coalition against France. Once again the Austrians were beaten; but England continued the war.

Why did powers like Austria stand up time after time against the French and their allies? Why did Russia and Prussia join coalition after coalition, and why did England fight so nearly continuously against revolutionary and Napoleonic France? The reason was probably that the expansion of France, begun in 1792 and continued by the subsequent regimes, upset the European balance of power so seriously that the several states could not acquiesce in this French expansion any more than they had been willing to acquiesce in Louis XIV's plans for European hegemony. The European family of states

PARTICIPATION OF MAJOR POWERS IN COALITIONS AGAINST FRANCE

	1st	2nd	3rd	4th	5th	6th	7th	Total
Austria	*	*	*		*	*	*	6[1]
Prussia	*			*		*	*	4[1]
Russia		*	*	*		*	*	5
England	*	*	*	*	*	*	*	7[1]

[1] In addition, Austria and Prussia fought France in the opening war of 1792 before the formation of the First Coalition. Further, Russia fought France in 1812, between the end of the War of the Fifth Coalition and before the formation of the Sixth Coalition. Finally, England fought France continuously from 1793 to 1814, except for thirteen months of peace after the Treaty of Amiens (1802).

was still fighting for the continuation of the settlement of 1648, for the division of Europe into congeries of sovereignties. In the end, the principle of independent sovereignty, greatly strengthened by the modern nationalist emotion that was born of the French Revolution, prevailed over the Napoleonic principle of pan-European (but always France-centered) empire.

The Continental System Napoleon's failure, through either diplomacy or war, to knock out England, the main obstacle to French hegemony over Europe, led him to place his main reliance on economic warfare as waged in what came to be known as the Continental System. Like many of Napoleon's ventures, the Continental System was not originated entirely by him. Rather, it was an extension and intensification of traditional French mercantilism as refined by previous French revolutionary regimes.

As early as 1791, the National Constituent Assembly had broken with the theories of international division of labor and free trade as represented by the Eden Treaty (1786) between France and England (see p. 984), by imposing a protective tariff on many goods. Then, after the outbreak of war with England, the Convention went on to prohibit the existence on French republican soil of any merchandise manufactured in any country subject to the British government. In addition, the Convention passed a French version of the famous English Navigation Acts intended, on the one hand, to bolster the French merchant marine and, on the other, to attack one of the principal bases of English prosperity, to destroy "the island of shopkeepers." The Directory intensified this program of economic warfare and extended the restrictions on imports of English goods—or even of goods that might have been manufactured in England—to countries outside of France that came under French control. There is no doubt that these measures ate into English prosperity; but it is also true that they injured the French economy by driving neutral shipping from French ports and by decreasing the supply of needed goods, especially raw materials.

Napoleon's contribution to this system was to try to extend its application to the whole continent of Europe, and hence the name Continental System. The attempt was expressed in the Berlin Decree of November 1806, just after the defeat of the Prussians, and was supplemented by the Milan Decree of the next year. In brief, Napoleon intended to cut off (to "blockade") all English trade with the continent as far east as Russia and to make France the economic focus for Europe. As a result of these measures, the Dutch and the Portuguese, who were in large measure dependent on English trade, were faced with ruin. The Spanish sheep-owning aristocracy did not want to sell its wool only to France and at French prices. Russian aristocrats and merchants wanted to sell their timber and flax to England. All Europe, even the Empress Josephine, clamored for the coffee, tea, sugar, spices, and cotton textiles, china, and hardware that the English could supply. European businessmen in general came to realize that the Continental System was not, as was claimed, directed toward the welfare of the continent at large but was actually a French-centered program devoted to the economic well-being of France at the expense of the rest of Europe.

WARS AND COALITIONS OF THE FRENCH REVOLUTIONARY AND NAPOLEONIC PERIOD

April 20, 1792	France declares war on Austria; Prussia joins Austria Battle of Valmy (September, 1792)
February 1, 1793	France declares war on England
1793–1797	War of the First Coalition (England and all continental powers except Russia and Sweden) *versus* France. French successes in the Netherlands, in Germany and Italy Treaty of Basel (1795) between France and Prussia Treaty of Campo Formio (1797) between France and Austria
1798–1802	War of the Second Coalition (Russia, England, Austria, Naples, Portugal, and Turkey *versus* France) Battles of Marengo and Hohenlinden Treaty of Lunéville (1801) between France and Austria Treaty of Amiens between France and England
March 1802—May 1803	Brief interval of peace
May 1803	France and England at war again
1805	Third Coalition (England, Austria, Russia, and Sweden) *versus* France and Spain English naval victory at Trafalgar French military victory at Austerlitz Treaty of Pressburg (1805)—Austria humiliated
1806–1807	Fourth Coalition (England, Prussia, Russia, Sweden) *versus* France Battles of Jena and Auerstädt (1806)—*débâcle* of Prussian army Battle of Friedland (1807)—Russia defeated Treaties of Tilsit and Königsberg (1807)
1808	The French invade Spain—beginning of the Peninsular War
1809	Fifth Coalition (Austria and England) Battles of Aspern and Wagram—Austrians defeated again Treaty of Schönbrunn (1809)
1809–1812	Continuation of the Peninsular War—France *versus* England
1812	French invasion of Russia
1813–1814	Sixth Coalition (England, Prussia, Austria, Russia, and Sweden) and the War of Liberation Battle of Leipzig (October 1813) Invasion of France Abdication of Napoleon (April 1814) First Treaty of Paris (May 30, 1814)
1815—March 1 to June 22	Return of Napoleon and The Hundred Days—alliance of Austria, England, Prussia, and Russia (Seventh Coalition) Battle of Waterloo (June 18, 1815) Second and final abdication of Napoleon Second Treaty of Paris (November 20, 1815)

It is not surprising, therefore, that Napoleon encountered difficulties in enforcing his blockade of English goods. Smuggling took place on a grand scale. Even Josephine was found with clothes made out of English cloth in her wardrobe. Napoleon's brother, as king of Holland, could not bring himself rigorously to enforce the restrictions and thereby ruin his Dutch subjects. Nearly everywhere there were leaks; and this fact led Napoleon in 1810 to annex Holland to France, as well as the northern coast of Germany, including the ports of Bremen and Hamburg. Previously (1808) the exigencies of the System had inspired him to remove the king of Spain and to replace him with another Bonaparte brother so as to prevent English goods from entering Iberia.

The Spanish enterprise turned out to be Napoleon's first really serious misadventure. Aided by an English army, the Spaniards rebelled against the invaders and locked hundreds of thousands of French troops in the difficult Spanish terrain. Second-string French armies were unable to cope with Spanish guerrilla tactics; the English army was well manned and effectively led by Sir Arthur Wellesley (later Duke of Wellington). Even Napoleon himself, with first-rate troops, was not able to win a clear-cut victory in what came to be called the "cancer" of Spain.

The French entanglement in Iberia was the spur that stirred Austrian courage to the point of joining the Fifth Coalition with England. The failure of Russia to enforce the Continental System left Napoleon with the alternatives of giving up his economic war or forcing Russian compliance. He chose the latter course, invading Russia in 1812 with his *Grande armée* of 500,000 men, only 50,000 of whom returned alive. This second and crucial misadventure imperilled the prestige of French arms and, combined with the economic and political frustrations of millions of Europeans, led to the formation of the Sixth Coalition in 1813 and the subsequent "War of Liberation."

The Collapse of The First French Empire To meet the challenge of the new coalition, Napoleon assembled a new army. With it he was beaten in a shockingly fierce battle at Leipzig (October 1813). He retreated across the Rhine into France. Still reeling from the shock of Leipzig, the allies cautiously followed while the Duke of Wellington crossed the Pyrenees into southern France. Napoleon fought the invaders with his greatest virtuosity, but eventually was forced to agree to an unconditional surrender. This man, who had so recently dominated most of Europe, was now not even permitted to rule over the French people.

France quickly underwent a restoration of the Bourbons in the person of the Count of Provence as Louis XVIII. There was little enthusiasm in France for this fat and prosaic brother of Louis XVI who arrived with English baggage, but the restoration was the only arrangement that the allies could agree upon. The First Treaty of Paris (May 30, 1814) was a remarkably generous document: France was allowed to keep its boundaries as of 1792—that is, with some expansion as compared with 1789. There was no indemnity; and the French retained the loot in the form of art treasures that

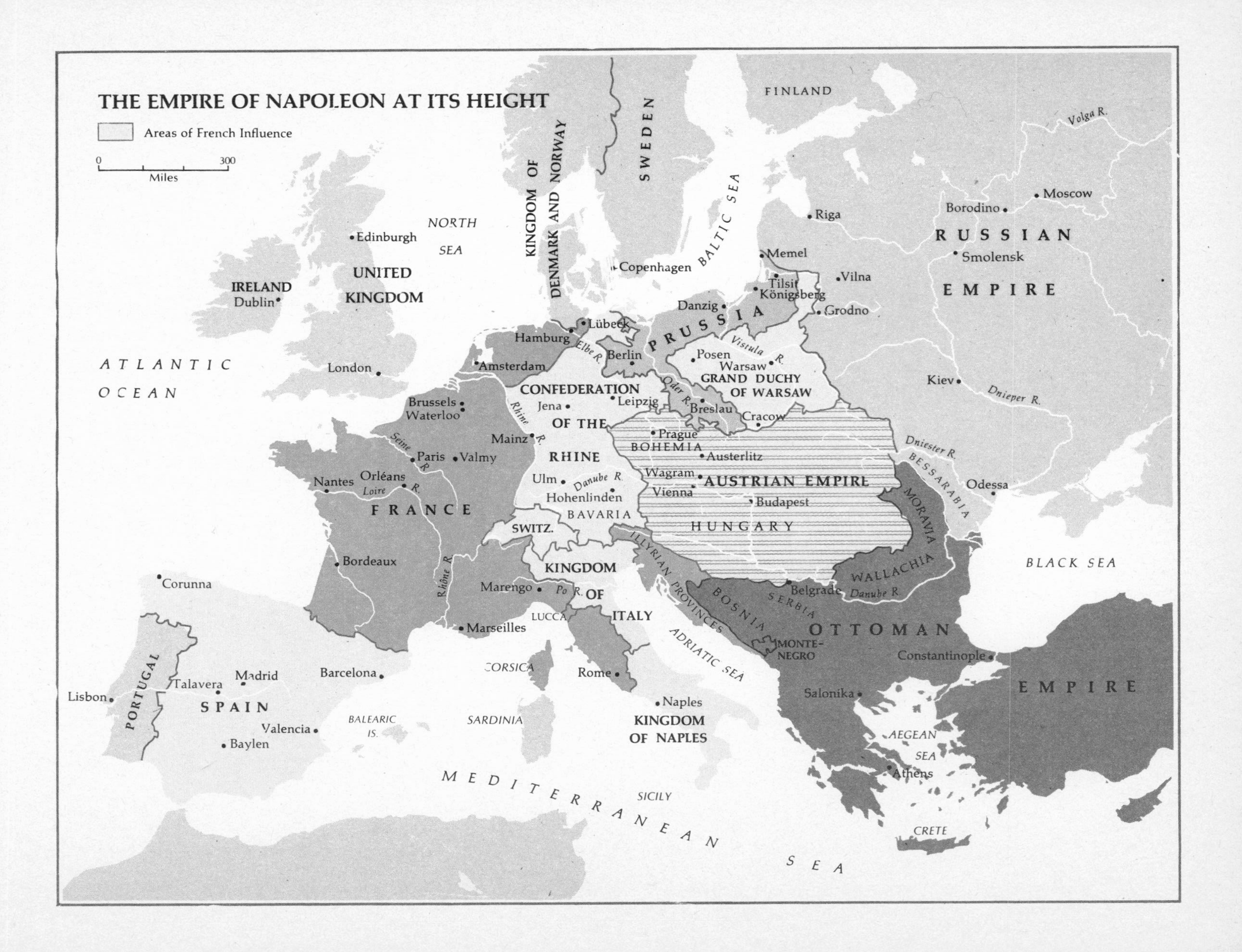
THE EMPIRE OF NAPOLEON AT ITS HEIGHT
Areas of French Influence
0
300
Miles
FINLAND
SWEDEN
KINGDOM OF DENMARK AND NORWAY
BALTIC SEA
NORTH SEA
ATLANTIC OCEAN
IRELAND
Dublin
UNITED KINGDOM
Edinburgh
London
Copenhagen
Riga
Memel
Tilsit
Königsberg
Vilna
Grodno
Danzig
PRUSSIA
Lübeck
Hamburg
Elbe R.
Berlin
Amsterdam
Posen
Warsaw
Vistula R.
GRAND DUCHY OF WARSAW
CONFEDERATION OF THE RHINE
Jena
Leipzig
Oder R.
Breslau
Cracow
Brussels
Waterloo
Rhine R.
Mainz
Prague
BOHEMIA
Austerlitz
Wagram
Vienna
AUSTRIAN EMPIRE
Budapest
HUNGARY
Seine R.
Paris
Valmy
Nantes
Orléans
Loire R.
FRANCE
Ulm
Danube R.
Hohenlinden
BAVARIA
SWITZ.
Bordeaux
Rhône R.
KINGDOM OF ITALY
Marengo
Po R.
LUCCA
Marseilles
Corunna
PORTUGAL
Lisbon
Talavera
Madrid
SPAIN
Valencia
Baylen
Barcelona
BALEARIC IS.
CORSICA
SARDINIA
Rome
Naples
KINGDOM OF NAPLES
SICILY
MEDITERRANEAN SEA
ILLYRIAN PROVINCES
ADRIATIC SEA
BOSNIA
SERBIA
Belgrade
MONTE-NEGRO
WALLACHIA
Danube R.
MORAVIA
OTTOMAN EMPIRE
Constantinople
Salonika
AEGEAN SEA
Athens
CRETE
BLACK SEA
BESSARABIA
Dniester R.
Odessa
Kiev
Dnieper R.
RUSSIAN EMPIRE
Borodino
Moscow
Smolensk
Volga R.

"Once again, let me tell you," wrote Bonaparte to one of his generals in 1809, "in war *morale* and opinion are more than half the reality." His failure to win the Spanish people to his side was the first breach of Napoleon's reputation for invincibility. The Spanish artist Goya recorded scenes of the brutality of French soldiers. (National Gallery, Washington, D. C. Rosenwald Collection.)

French generals had sent home from all over Europe. The generosity of this treaty, given by victorious powers to an entirely defeated enemy after twenty-two years of the most trying wars Europe had ever suffered is surprising. But the Nation of Shopkeepers had fought in Europe to see to it that the English would be able to do business in Europe, to sell hardware and cloth, to buy wine and brandy. They knew that their greatest potential customer was France. They also knew that a humiliated French nation would be a potential source of future conflict and damage to business. Represented by Castlereagh, therefore, the English wanted to give the French every encouragement to settle down as rapidly as possible to contentment, industry, and peace.

CONCLUSION

As he went to his island of Elba for a brief retirement, Napoleon left a revolution that he had halted for the time being in his own country. But the expansion of France over which he had presided had acquainted much of Europe with certain aspects of the Revolution: with its ideas of legal equality, with a rational system of laws, with the nationalist spirit, and with some of its driving, if unrealized, ideals. Many men and women in 1814 felt that the Revolution, which had brought so much turmoil and bloodshed, should be rejected and that western civilization should return to authority, to a firm union of throne and altar, and to stability. Many governments and ruling classes acted after 1814 on these premises. But the very fact that the Revolution of the West, starting with the work of the Enlightened Despots and continuing through the successful American Revolution to the drastic aspirations and events of the French Revolution, had taken place, seems to have made it inevitable that revolution should be endemic in the nineteenth century. And over all of Europe after 1814 hung the memory of Napoleonic glory, quite at odds with the practical ideals of victorious England.

FURTHER READING

G. Bruun, **Europe and the French Imperium, 1799–1814* (1938), is the most convenient starting point for a study of all of Europe in the age of Napoleon. Excellent bibliography, updated as of 1968.

On Thermidor and the Thermidorians see A. Mathiez, *After Robespierre: the Thermidorian Reaction* (1931), a by-no-means balanced interpretation by a Robespierrist, as well as Mathiez' *The Fall of Robespierre and Other Essays* (1927).

A fascinating study of the revolutionary symbolism is D. L. Dowd, *Pageant-Master of the Republic: Jacques-Louis David and the French Revolution* (1948), about the great French painter who became the revolutionary Le Brun. On the reorganization of science, see J. Fayet, *La Révolution française et la science, 1789–1795* (1960), which has received some knocks from historians of science but which is useful.

The army is treated in S. Wilkinson, *The French Army before Napoleon* (1915). R. W. Phipps, *The Armies of the First French Republic and the Rise of the Marshals of Napoleon I,* 5 vols. (1926–1939), is the extensive treatment in English. J. Clapham, *The Causes of the War of 1792* (1899), recently reprinted, is reliable on the causes of the war. A. T. Mahan, *Influence of Sea Power upon the French Revolution and Empire, 1793–1812* (1898), also reprinted, is a classic that goes far toward explaining why the French lost in the end. See also C. Oman, *Studies in Napoleonic Wars* (1929).

For the "constructive" Napoleon, see R. B. Holtman, **The Napoleonic Revolution* (1967). The best brief treatment of revolutionary and Napoleonic economic policies can be found in Chapters II and III of S. B. Clough, *France: a History of National Economics, 1789–1939* (1939). The impact of the Revolution on Europe is treated in J. Godechot, *La grande nation: l'expansion révolutionnaire de la France dans le monde, 1789–1799,* 2 vols. (1956), which stands by itself for the period covered. In English, there is G. P. Gooch, *Germany and the French Revolution* (1920); and A. W. Ward, et al., *England and the French Revolution* (1909). F. M. H. Markham, **Napoleon and the Awakening of Europe* (1954, paper ed., 1963), is partially a biography. O. Connelly, **Napoleon's Satellite Kingdoms* (1965), is an excellent book, highly readable.

There is too much biographical material on Napoleon. Perhaps one should begin with something like A. Guérard, *Napoleon I* (1956); or J. M. Thompson, *Napoleon Bonaparte: His Rise and Fall* (1952); and then proceed to C. Herold, **The Mind of Napoleon: a Selection of His Written and Spoken Words* (1955), a collection put together by the author of *Bonaparte in Egypt* (1962). A recent, well-written biography by an admirer of Napoleon is V. Cronin, *Napoleon Bonaparte: An Intimate Biography* (1972).

H. C. Deutsch, *The Genesis of Napoleonic Imperialism* (1938), is an important study. F. Pratt has done two books: *The Road to Empire* (1939) and *The Empire and the Glory: Napoleon Bonaparte, 1800–1806* (1949), for the general reader who may find them interesting. A historiographical treatment of Napoleon is P. Geyl, *Napoleon, For and Against* (1949).

*Books available in paperback edition are marked with an asterisk.

INDEX

1 2 3 4 5 6 7 8 9 0